# New Developments in Goal and Task Performance

This book concentrates on the last ten years of research in the area of goal setting and performance at work. The editors and contributors believe goals affect action, and this volume will have a lineup of international contributors who look at the recent theories and implications in this area for IO psychologists and human resource management academics and graduate students.

**Edwin A. Locke** is Dean's Professor of Leadership and Motivation (Emeritus) at the R.H. Smith School of Business at the University of Maryland, College Park. He received his BA from Harvard in 1960 and his Ph.D. in Industrial Psychology from Cornell University in 1964.

**Gary P. Latham** is the Secretary of State Professor of Organizational Effectiveness in the Rotman School of Management at the University of Toronto where he has cross appointments in Industrial Relations, School of Nursing and the Department of Psychology. His previous positions include staff psychologist at the American Pulpwood Association and the Weyerhaeuser Company and Ford Motor Professor in and Chair of the Management and Organization Department of the University of Washington.

# New Developments in Goal Setting and Task Performance

*Edited by*
Edwin A. Locke and Gary P. Latham

Routledge
Taylor & Francis Group

NEW YORK AND LONDON

First published 2013
by Routledge part of the Taylor and Francis Group
711 Third Avenue, New York, NY 10017

Simultaneously published in the UK
by Routledge
2 Park Square, Milton Park, Abingdon, Oxon OX14 4RN

First issued in paperback 2017

*Routledge is an imprint of the Taylor & Francis Group, an informa business*

*Library of Congress Cataloging in Publication Data*
A catalog record for this book has been requested

ISBN 13: 978-0-8153-9087-9 (pbk)
ISBN 13: 978-0-415-88548-5 (hbk)

Typeset in Minion
by Cenveo Publisher Services

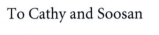

To Cathy and Soosan

# Contents

# Introduction

Goal setting theory was first presented in our 1990 book, *A Theory of Goal Setting and Task Performance*. The theory was based on close to 400 studies. Since 1990, over 600 additional studies have been done (Mitchell & Daniels, 2003), and the use of goal setting has expanded into many domains including education, leadership, psychotherapy, health promotion, creativity, bargaining, sports, and entrepreneurship, among others. Furthermore, new discoveries have been made about the core elements of goal setting; for example, mediators, moderators, learning goals, and subconsciously primed goals have been added to the theory. Long-term quantitative data have been reported. Qualitative data have been reported based on the use of goals in large organizations.

The avalanche of new data was too much for two people to handle in a reasonable time span. Thus, we asked authors who had expertise in goal setting to write chapters updating the literature in their area of expertise. Because the authors in turn asked co-authors to write with them, the present book has more than 70 authors and co-authors and 37 chapters (a few done by ourselves or with others). We don't claim to have reviewed all goal setting studies published since 1990; for example, there are many goal experiments in social psychology that are reviewed elsewhere. We focused mainly, though not exclusively, on studies in industrial organizational (I/O) psychology and organizational behavior (OB), although there is some overlap with other fields.

Each chapter was edited by both of us, and some went through as many as four revisions. We thank the authors for their hard work, patience, and cooperation.

We view this volume not as a replacement of our 1990 book, but as a companion piece. The original theory is still sound. But in line with our inductive approach to theory building, we view goal theory as an open theory, leaving it receptive to new discoveries. Science progresses not by going from nothing to omniscience, but by increments, some large and some small. We know more about goals than we once did. Each increment gives us more confidence in predicting, understanding, an influencing behavior through the setting of specific, difficult goals.

The success of goal setting theory in terms of validity and durability, we believe, is due not to genius but to method. In building goal theory, we rejected the hypothetico-deductive method because there was no theory to deduce from. We built the theory over a 25-year period by integrating the findings, as noted, of close to 400 studies—identifying core findings, causal mechanisms, and moderators, and showing generality across tasks, research designs, settings, participants, countries, and measures. We believe that induction is the basic method of science (Locke, 2007; Locke & Latham, 2005) and necessarily precedes deduction.

The reader will note that, at our insistence, none of the chapters contain formal hypotheses or elaborations of theory divorced from data. Our strong commitment to inductive theorizing continues in the present volume. These chapters not only further verify, but also expand, goal setting theory. Such a process could never have occurred had we followed the conventional insistence on the hypothetico-deductive method, which we believe greatly retards the development of sound theories. We hope this book, combined with our 1990 book, will stand as an object lesson in how to build an enduring theory.

We do not plan on another book like this, but we are confident that our knowledge of goal setting and its applications will continue to expand.

## How to Read This Book

Some may want to read this book from cover to cover, while others may not. We recommend reading Chapter 1 first for background and Chapter 37 for updates to goal theory. Other than that, readers may simply want to read the chapters that interest them. There are many interconnections between chapters (e.g., many deal with self-efficacy and/or commitment), so one chapter may lead to another. Further, there are many references that appear in more than one chapter due to relevance. We did not include a chapter on implications for research; there are endless possibilities. We leave those to the reader's imagination.

## References

Locke, E. A., & Latham, G. P. (2005) Goal setting theory: Theory building by induction. In K. G. Smith & M. A. Hitt (Eds.), *Great minds in management.* New York: Oxford.

Locke, E. A. (2007) The case for inductive theory building. *Journal of Management, 33,* 867–890.

Mitchell, T. R., & Daniels, D. (2003) Motivation. In W. C. Borman, D. R. Ilgen, & R. J. Klimoski (Eds.), *Comprehensive handbook of psychology: Industrial organizational psychology, 12,* 225–254. New York: Wiley.

# Acknowledgments

We owe a great debt of gratitude to the more than 70 authors and co-authors of the chapters in this book. We could never have covered such a plethora of studies on our own without taking many years to do so. All the chapters were edited by both of us, some as many as four times. We thank the authors for putting up with our insistence on clarity for the reader. We owe an extra debt of thanks to Peter Heslin, who stepped in at the last moment to mitigate an emergency due to an author who was unable to write a chapter. Peter graciously agreed to write a second chapter for this book.

We also thank Alana Arshoff for taking complete charge of storing and organizing the chapter files, writing the table of contents, and submitting everything to the publisher.

# About the Editors

**Edwin A. Locke** is Dean's Professor of Leadership and Motivation (Emeritus) at the R.H. Smith School of Business at the University of Maryland, College Park. He received his BA from Harvard in 1960 and his PhD in Industrial Psychology from Cornell University in 1964.

He has published over 300 chapters, notes, and articles in professional journals, on such subjects as work motivation, job satisfaction, incentives, and the philosophy of science. He is also the author or editor of 11 books, including *Study Methods and Study Motivation* (Second Renaissance Books, 1998), *Goal Setting: A Motivational Technique that Works* (Prentice Hall, 1984, with G. Latham), *A Theory of Goal Setting and Task Performance* (Prentice Hall, 1990, with G. Latham), *Handbook of Principles of Organizational Behavior* (Blackwell, 2000; 2nd edition Wiley, 2009), *The Prime Movers: Traits of the Great Wealth Creators* (AMACOM, 2000; 2nd edition Ayn Rand Bookstore, 2008), *Post Modernism and Management: Pos, Cons and the Alternative* (Elsevier Science, 2003), and *The Selfish Path to Romance: How to Love with Reason and Passion* (Platform Press, 2011, with E. Kenner). His goal setting theory (developed with Gary Latham) was rated as #1 in importance among 73 management theories.

Dr. Locke has been elected a Fellow of the American Psychological Association, the American Psychological Society, Academy of Management and the Society for Industrial Organizational Psychology (SIOP). He has won prestigious scholarly awards from the Association for Psychological Science, the Academy of Management, and SIOP. He is interested in the application of the philosophy of Objectivism to the behavioral sciences and the role of induction in scientific theory building.

**Gary P. Latham** is the Secretary of State Professor of Organizational Effectiveness in the Rotman School of Management at the University of Toronto, where he has cross-appointments in Industrial Relations, School of Nursing, and the Department of Psychology. His previous positions include staff psychologist at the American Pulpwood Association and the Weyerhaeuser Company, and Ford Motor Professor in and Chair of the Management and Organization Department of the University of Washington.

Gary is a past president of the Canadian Psychological Association and the Society for Industrial-Organizational Psychology (SIOP). He is president elect of Division 1, Work and Organizational Psychology of the International Association of Applied

Psychology (IAAP). He has served on the Board of Directors at the Center for Creative Leadership and currently serves on the boards of IAAP and the Society for Human Resource Management.

Among his awards is being elected to the status of Fellow of the Academy of Management (AOM), where he served as the Deputy Dean of Fellows, the American Psychological Association (APA), Association for Psychological Science, Academy of Human Resource Management, the Canadian Psychological Association, IAAP, the Royal Society of Canada, and SIOP.

He is the only individual to receive the awards for "Distinguished Contributions to Psychology as a Profession" and as a "Science" from SIOP. He received the Distinguished Scholar-Practitioner Award from the AOM, the Heneman Award for Career Achievement in HRM from the Human Resource Division of the AOM, life-time achievement award from the OB division of the AOM, the Thomas A. Mahoney Award for mentoring doctoral students from the HR division of the AOM, the "Harry and Miriam Levinson Award for Exceptional Contributions to Consulting Psychology" from APA, and the Michael R. Losey Human Resource Research Award from the Society for Human Resource Management (SHRM).

# About the Authors

**Alana S. Arshoff** is a doctoral student at the Centre for Industrial Relations and Human Resources at the University of Toronto. Her research interests include goal setting, priming goals in the subconscious, training, and leadership. She completed her undergraduate degree in business at the University of Western Ontario and her master's degree in IR and HR at the University of Toronto.

**Susan J. Ashford** is the Michael & Susan Jandernoa Professor of Management and Organizations at the University of Michigan. Sue's research and teaching focuses on personal effectiveness in organizations, individual proactivity, and leadership development. Her early research on individual feedback seeking has expanded to include such proactive behaviors as issue selling and self-leadership.

**J. Robert Baum** is Associate Professor of Entrepreneurship and Director of Entrepreneurship Research at the Smith School of Business, University of Maryland. His research interests include new venture creation and financing and quantitative methods. He has published in *Journal of Applied Psychology*, *Personnel Psychology*, *Academy of Management Journal*, *Organization Science*, *Strategic Management Journal*, and *Journal of Business Venturing*. Baum founded three businesses and serves on four corporate boards. He is chairman of a national health insurance company.

**Albert Bandura** is Emeritus Professor of Psychology at Stanford University. He is a proponent of social cognitive theory, which is rooted in an agentic perspective. This theory accords a central role to cognitive, vicarious, self-regulatory, and self-reflective processes in human self-development, adaptation, and change. His diverse programs of research blend his theoretical interests with an abiding concern for the application of our knowledge for human enlightenment and betterment.

**Laura Borgogni** is Full Professor of Work and Organizational Psychology at University Sapienza of Rome, Italy. Her main topics of expertise concern perceptions of social context, goal setting, self- and collective efficacy, and job burnout.

**Claudia Buengeler** is a Research Associate and PhD Fellow at Jacobs University Bremen (Germany) in close collaboration with Vrije Universiteit Amsterdam (Netherlands). Her research focuses on leadership, team diversity (for instance with regard to personality, attitudes, or age) as well as motivation and goal orientation.

**Dan V. Caprar** is a Lecturer at the Australian School of Business, University of New South Wales. His research focuses on the interplay between self-leadership, identity, and culture. Dan teaches cross-cultural management in Sydney and leadership for the Australian Graduate School of Management in Hong Kong.

**Joseph T. Cooper** is an Assistant Professor of Management in the College of Business at the University of Wyoming. He earned his PhD in organizational behavior and human resources from The Ohio State University. His research interests include commitment, the salience and importance of multiple commitment targets, and organizational roles.

**Kitty Dahl,** PhD, is Clinical Researcher at the Centre for Child and Adolescent Mental Health in Oslo, Norway. She has a joint PhD degree in neurobiology and clinical psychology from the University of Washington. Her area of research is currently on treatment of anxiety disorders.

**David V. Day** is Winthrop Professor and Woodside Chair in Leadership and Management at The University of Western Australia Business School. Day has core research interests in the areas of self-regulation, leadership, and leadership development. He is a Fellow of the American Psychological Association and the Society for Industrial and Organizational Psychology.

**Silvia Dello Russo** received her PhD in Work and Organizational Psychology at University Sapienza of Rome, Italy. Currently she is a Researcher at ISCTE-IUL in Lisbon, Portugal. Her research interests include work motivation, particularly in the social cognitive theory perspective, perceptions of social context, and performance management.

**Katleen E. M. De Stobbeleir** is Assistant Professor of Organizational Behavior and Leadership at Vlerick Business School, Belgium. She earned her ICM-funded PhD in Applied Economics from Ghent University. During her doctoral research, she was a visiting fellow at the Ross School of Business, University of Michigan (United States). Her current research focuses on feedback, leadership, and creative processes.

**Rod K. Dishman** is Professor of Kinesiology and Adjunct Professor of Psychology at the University of Georgia, where he is a member of the Neuroscience Program in the Biomedical and Health Sciences Institute. He received his PhD at the University of Wisconsin-Madison and focused his research on neurobiological aspects of the mental health outcomes associated and determinants of physical activity.

**Marion B. Eberly** is an Assistant Professor in the Milgard School of Business at the University of Washington, Tacoma. She received her PhD in organizational behavior and human resources at the University of Washington, Seattle. Her research focuses on the influence of emotions and attributions within leader-follower relationships.

**Natalie C. Ebner** is an Assistant Professor in Psychology at University of Florida. Her research focuses on attention and memory biases for socially relevant information and cognition-emotion-motivation interactions in adults of different ages. She uses a multi-methods research approach with the aim to integrate introspective, behavioral, and neuropsychological data. Her research is published in various peer-reviewed journals and book chapters.

**Miriam Erez** is Professor emeritus of Organizational Psychology, Faculty of Industrial Engineering & Management, Technion, Israel. Her research is in three areas: (a) Cross-Cultural Organizational Behavior; (b) Work Motivation, focusing on goal-setting theory; and (c) Innovation at work. She has published about 100 journal articles, book chapters, and books.

**Michael Frese** holds a joint appointment at NUS, Business School (Singapore) and University of Lueneburg (Germany). His research based on action regulation theory spans a wide range of topics (e.g., unemployment, stress at work, personal initiative, errors and error management training, psychological success factors of entrepreneurs, and innovation).

**Shlomit Friedman,** formerly a Senior Manager for Training and Development, received her PhD in organizational behavior from Tel Aviv University, and was a postdoctoral fellow at Rotman School on Management, University of Toronto while writing this chapter. Her research interests include motivation, organizational training, and the impact of goals and plans on learning and behavior.

**Peter M. Gollwitzer** is Professor of Psychology at New York University and the University of Konstanz. His research pertains to a number of areas in social psychology, cognition and perception, neuropsychology, and industrial and organizational psychology. He has developed various theoretical models of action control: self-completion theory, the mindset model of action phases, and the theory of intentional action control distinguishing between goal intentions and implementation intentions.

**Erin C. Hastings** earned her PhD in Psychology from the University of Florida (UF) in 2011. While at UF, Erin received several national and departmental awards, and published in APA and other peer-reviewed journals. Currently, Erin coordinates clinical research for the UF Center for Movement Disorders and Neurorestoration.

**Peter A. Heslin** is an Associate Professor of Management at the University of New South Wales. He conducts research on motivation, leadership, and careers. Peter leads the Managerial Skills EMBA elective at the Australian Graduate School of Management and is the 2011–2012 Program Chair for the Academy of Management Careers Division.

**Ann Howard,** prior to her retirement in 2009, was Chief Scientist for Development Dimensions International (DDI), a global talent management company. She is the senior author (with Douglas W. Bray) of *Managerial Lives in Transition: Advancing Age and Changing Times*, which received the Academy of Management's George R. Terry Award of Excellence in 1989.

**Chun Hui** is a Professor of the School of Business in the University of Hong Kong. He has published in journals including the *Academy of Management Journal, Journal of Applied Psychology, Organization Science, Journal of International Business Studies,* and *Journal of Personality and Social Psychology.*

**Robert Jensen**, BSW, is working at Centre for Cognitive Practice in Asker, Norway. He works with therapy, teaching, and supervision in CBT. He is working on a project in the northern region of Norway implementing CBT to units of the Norwegian Directorate for Children, Youth, and Family Affairs.

**Steve Kerr** is Provost of Chancellor University. He has been a managing director at Goldman Sachs and GE's VP-leadership development, and has been on the faculties of the Ohio State University, the University of Michigan, and the University of Southern California. His most recent book is *Reward Systems* (Harvard Business Press, 2009).

**Howard J. Klein** is a Professor of Management and Human Resources in the Fisher College of Business at the Ohio State University. He received his PhD from Michigan State University. His research interests center on workplace commitments, socialization, motivation, and talent management to facilitate individuals and team performance.

**Nick Koenig** earned his Psychology BA in 2006 from the University of Missouri-Columbia, and is currently an I/O Psychology Doctoral Candidate at UCF. His main interests include motivation, performance measurement, psychometrics, and selection. His work has focused on motivation and the use of ProMES as a performance system in sports.

**William S. Kramer** is a doctoral student in the Industrial/Organizational Psychology program at the University of Central Florida. He is currently a graduate research assistant at the Institute for Simulation and Training, where his research interests include culture, teams, and adaptation to changes in situational context.

**Gamze Koseoglu** is a PhD Student in the Organizational Behavior Program at the Scheller College of Business at the Georgia Institute of Technology. Her current research interests are the effects of social networks on individual and team creativity, and the relationship between goal setting and creative performance.

**Ho Kwong Kwan** is an Assistant Professor in Human Resource Management with the School of International Business Administration at The Shanghai University of Finance and Economics. His research interests include mentoring, leadership, work-family issues, and deviant behavior.

**Cynthia Lee,** Professor, Management and Organizational Development Group, Northeastern University and Visiting Chair Professor, Department of Management and Marketing, The Hong Kong Polytechnic University. Her research interests include managing change, motivation, and managing relationships including group processes and effectiveness, understanding the changing nature of psychological contracts, innovation, and job insecurity.

**Thomas W. Lee** is the Hughes Blake Professor of Management and an Associate Dean at the Foster School of Business, University of Washington. Tom served as Editor of the *Academy of Management Journal* and President of the Academy of Management, and is a Fellow of the Academy of Management and the Society for Industrial and Organizational Psychology.

**Geoffrey J. Leonardelli** is an Associate Professor at the University of Toronto's Rotman School of Management and Department of Psychology. His research investigates how self-perception enhances human effectiveness in teams, leadership, and negotiations, with research published in the *Journal of Applied Psychology*, *Psychological Science*, and *Advances in Experimental Social Psychology*.

**Douglas M. LePelley**, PhD, is Associate Professor of Business, Nyack College, past Senior Director, Dean Graduate Studies, Professor of Business and Simulations for Chancellor University and the Jack Welch Management Institute, University of Phoenix School of Advanced Studies. He spent 34+ years in business development, many with IBM, including LRN's *Inspiring Principled Performance* solutions.

**Dong Liu** is an Assistant Professor at the Georgia Institute of Technology's Ernest Scheller Jr. College of Business. He received his PhD from the University of Washington's Foster School of Business. His research interests include creativity, turnover, leadership, and teams, with particular focus on exploring the multilevel interface between individuals and organizational context.

**Per Jostein Matre**, MSW, is working at the Centre for Cognitive Practice in Asker, Norway. He is responsible for therapy, teaching, and supervision in CBT. He is now Project Manager in the northern region of Norway, implementing CBT for units of the Norwegian Directorate for Children, Youth, and Family Affairs.

**Terence R. Mitchell** received a BA from Duke in 1964, and a PhD from Illinois in 1969. He is currently with the Foster School of Business at University of Washington. He is a fellow of AOM and SIOP. His research focuses on the topics of turnover, motivation, leadership, and decision making.

**Christina A. Monahan** is a doctoral student in organizational behavior in the Fisher College of Business at The Ohio State University. She earned her BA in psychology from The Ohio State University. Her research interests span group motivation, information sharing, diversity and performance, interpersonal trust, and affective influences on individual/group behavior.

**Dominique Morisano** is a Scientist, Assistant Professor of Public Health, and licensed clinical psychologist focused on both personal goal setting and the implementation of evidence-based practice in mental health, education, and addiction services. She is located at the Centre for Addiction and Mental Health (CAMH) and the University of Toronto in Canada.

**Hans M. Nordahl,** PhD, is professor of clinical psychology at Department of Psychology, Norwegian University of Science and Technology and the clinical director of the Trauma outpatient clinic, Østmarka Hospital, St.Olav, Trondheim.

**Gabriele Oettingen** is Professor of Psychology at New York University and the University of Hamburg. She investigates thinking about the future and its impacts on cognition, emotion, and behavior. Her theory of fantasy realization and her model of positive fantasies specify self-regulatory processes that lead to behavior change in different domains and cultural contexts. She works across disciplines conducting lab- and field-experimental studies as well as behavior change interventions.

**Ronald F. Piccolo** is an Associate Professor of Management and Academic Director of the Center for Leadership Development at Rollins College in Winter Park, Florida. His research on leadership, motivation, and personality has been published in the *Academy Management Journal, Journal of Applied Psychology*, and the *Journal of Organizational Behavior*.

**Stefanie A. Plemmons** is a Post-Doctoral Fellow in the Work Experience Laboratory at The Georgia Institute of Technology. She earned her PhD from Purdue University in 2012. Her research focuses on regulatory resources, burnout, and emotions and attention in the workplace.

**Robert D. Pritchard** is Professor Emeritus at the University of Central Florida. He has published in the areas of work motivation and productivity improvement. The intervention he and his students developed, the Productivity Measurement and Enhancement System (ProMES), has been applied in many work settings in various jobs in different countries.

**Lise M. Saari,** PhD, is Adjunct Professor at NYU and Baruch College. Prior to joining NYU and Baruch, Lise was director, global workforce research at IBM, senior manager people research at Boeing, and research scientist at Battelle. Lise serves on professional boards and is a Fellow in APA, APS, and SIOP.

**Eduardo Salas** is Trustee Chair and Pegasus Professor of Psychology at the University of Central Florida. Salas earned a PhD in Industrial/Organizational Psychology at Old Dominion University, and has since co-authored or authored over 350 journal articles and book chapters on topics such as teamwork, team training, and performance assessment

**Daniel Schmerling** earned his BA in Psychology from the University of Maryland. He is currently an Industrial-Organizational Psychology Doctoral Candidate at the University of Central Florida. His interests include motivation, performance measurement and feedback, and psychometrics. His work includes applications of ProMES, moderators of performance feedback, and motivation scale development.

**Frank L. Schmidt** is Fethke Leadership Professor in the Tippie College of Business at the University of Iowa. He was a co-inventor of validity generalization/psychometric meta-analysis methods and has published over 190 journal articles and book chapters. He received the Distinguished Scientific Contributions Award (with John Hunter) from the American Psychological Association (APA) and also from the Association for Psychological Science (APS). He received the Distinguished Career Award from the Human Resources Division of the Academy of Management, and the Michael R. Losey Human Resources Research Award from the Society for Human Resource Management (SHRM). He received his doctorate in Industrial/ Organizational Psychology from Purdue University.

**Gerard H. Seijts** is an Associate Professor of Organizational Behavior, and the Executive Director of the Ian O. Ihnatowycz Institute for Leadership, at the Richard Ivey School of Business at the Western University. He received his PhD in organizational behavior from the Rotman School of Management, the University of Toronto. His areas of research are leadership, teams, performance management, and organizational change.

**Christina E. Shalley** is Thomas R. Williams Professor in the Scheller College of Business at the Georgia Institute of Technology. Her PhD in Business Administration is from the University of Illinois, Urbana-Champaign. She is a Fellow of the Society for Industrial and Organizational Psychology. Her current research examines effects of social and contextual factors for individual and team creativity.

**Mical Kay Shilts**, PhD, is an Associate Professor at California State University, Sacramento, teaching community and cultural nutrition courses in the Family and Consumer Sciences Department. She received her doctorate in nutrition from the University of California, Davis. Her research interests concentrate on the development and evaluation of obesity prevention interventions applying "guided" goal setting targeting low-income, ethnically diverse audiences.

**Shu Hua Sun** is currently a PhD candidate at NUS Business School, National University of Singapore. He holds a master's degree in Applied Psychology. His research interests lie in the area of work motivation, teams, leadership, and job search. His work has been published in academic journals and books.

**Ken G. Smith** Professor of Strategy (emeritus) at the College of Business of the University of Rhode Island. He is well-known for his groundbreaking research on all areas of competition, competitive advantage, and competitive dynamics. He was editor of the Academy of Management Review from 1996–99, elected a fellow of the Academy of Management in 1998, served as president of the Academy of Management from 2006–07, and received the Academy's 2011 Outstanding Educator Award.

**Victor Sojo** is a Postdoctoral Research Fellow in the Centre for Ethical Leadership at the Melbourne Business School. He completed his PhD in the School of Psychology at University of Melbourne, which was a study of personality, coping, positive emotion and health. His current research examines the determinants of the fit, function, and growth of minorities in hostile and non supportive environments.

**Kevin Tasa** is Associate Professor of Organizational Behavior at the Schulich School of Business, York University. He received his doctorate from the Rotman School of Management at the University of Toronto and conducts research on group decision making, goal setting in negotiations, and dispositional influences on individual and group behavior.

**Amanda L. Thayer** is an Industrial-Organizational psychology doctoral student at the University of Central Florida and graduate research associate at the Institute for Simulation and Training. Her research focuses on various factors that impact team process and performance, including trust, cohesion, team composition, and culture.

**Marilyn S. Townsend**, PhD, RD, Nutrition Specialist, UC Davis, is an expert in program evaluation, intervention development, and assessment tool validation. Her obesity prevention research focuses on improving diets and physical activity of low-income families. Serving as a consultant with numerous federal/state agency professionals and university researchers, she is considered an expert on the development of valid assessment tools for risk assessment and program evaluation of USDA programs with special attention to low-literate participants.

**Cheryl J. Travers** is a Senior Lecturer and Head of Discipline in Human Resource Management and Organisational Behaviour in the School of Business and Economics at Loughborough University. Her research interests are in the area of occupational stress, self-management, and the practical use of goal setting and reflective diary keeping in personal development. She received her doctorate from the University of Manchester Institute of Science and Technology.

**Kerrie L. Unsworth** is a Professor at the University of Western Australia Business School. Her research interests include motivation, self-leadership, creativity, and well-being. Her current research focuses on the role of goal hierarchies and goal systems on both conscious and unconscious goal choice and pursuit.

**Karyn L. Wang** earned her bachelor's and master's degrees in Psychology before working in HR and Consulting. She is currently working toward her doctorate at the University of New South Wales in the School of Management, where she is investigating how employees' emotional experiences shape motivation, performance, and well-being.

**Jennifer Whelan** is a Postdoctoral Fellow in the Centre for Ethical Leadership at Melbourne Business School. Her research is focused on the measurement and functions of implicit attitudes toward gender diversity and the role of goals, implemented at targets and quotas in selection processes, on the impacts of gender diversity. Jennifer completed her PhD in social psychology at the University of Melbourne.

**Howard M. Weiss** is Professor and Chair of the School of Psychology at Georgia Tech. His research focuses on the first-person experiences of working, including emotional states and attentional focus. He is a Fellow of the Society for Industrial and Organizational Psychology, the Association for Psychological Science, and the American Psychological Association.

**Robin L. West** is Professor of Psychology at the University of Florida, and conducts research on memory aging, with an emphasis on self-regulatory factors such as strategies, goals, and self-efficacy. She was director of the Center for Gerontological Studies and associate director of the Institute on Aging. In addition to academic work, Dr. West authored two popular memory books: *Memory Fitness Over 40* and the *Everyday Memory Clinic Workbook*.

**Kevin J. Williams** is Dean of Graduate Studies and Professor of Psychology at the University at Albany, State University of New York. His research on human motivation and performance examines the self-regulatory processes that guide goal strivings and goal revision over time. He observed goal setting theory in action for 14 years as college a cross-country and track and field coach.

**Marion Wittchen** is a Research Fellow at NYU. Prior to her current position, she was an assistant professor of organizational psychology at the University of Muenster. She received her PhD in psychology from the University of Würzburg. Her research interests are motivation and effort in work groups.

**Moureen Wong** is a PhD student at Melbourne Business School. Her research interests are in the area of self-regulation and learning, including the study of mediation pathways in the transfer of learning on complex tasks for interventions such as goal setting, feedback, meta cognitive training and error management.

**Robert E. Wood** is Professor of Management and Director of the Centre for Ethical Leadership at Melbourne Business School and Adjunct Professor of Organizational Psychology in the School of Psychology, University of Western Australia. He received his PhD from the University of Washington. His research covers a range of topics all conducted within a social cognitive theory framework, including goal setting and feedback, personality dynamics, learning, and leadership.

**Meredith Woodwark** is a PhD student in Organizational Behaviour at the Richard Ivey School of Business, Western University. She holds an MBA from the Sauder School of Business, University of British Columbia and a BA from Dalhousie University. Her current research focuses on employee engagement.

**Glen Whyte** is Marcel Desautels Chair in Integrative Thinking and Professor, Organizational Behavior and Human Resource Management, at the Rotman School of Management, University of Toronto. His primary research interests are in the areas of individual and group decision making under uncertainty, and managerial negotiations.

**Phyllis L. Wright** earned her PhD in Leadership Studies from Dallas Baptist University, an MBA from the University of Dallas, and a MS with emphasis in Organization Development and Change Management from the University of Texas at Dallas. She has 28 years of human resources experience across multiple industries including banking, public education, health care, and manufacturing. In her most recent role, Phyllis, was responsible for the design and execution of talent strategies that were targeted at ensuring optimal engagement, growth, and career navigation of the organization's talent.

**Natalie Wright Dixon** earned her PhD in I/O Psychology from the University of Central Florida in 2012. Her research focuses on motivation, performance measurement, and occupational health. Her work includes the application of ProMES to individual lifestyle behavior change.

**Brandon L. Young** earned his master's degree in industrial/organizational psychology at the University of Colorado-Denver and is currently a doctoral candidate in industrial/organizational psychology at the University of Central Florida. His research interests include psychometrics, motivation, and performance measurement and feedback. His work includes several studies on the utility of ProMES.

**Greg Young** is Associate Professor of Strategy at the Poole College of Management at North Carolina State University. His research focuses on strategic activity, the competitive advantage of the firm, and organizational reputation. Greg served on the editorial board of the *Academy of Management Review* from 2000 through 2002.

# Part I
# The Basics

# 1 Goal Setting Theory, 1990

*Edwin A. Locke*  Robert H. Smith School of Business, University of
Maryland

*Gary P. Latham*  Rotman School of Management, University of Toronto

> *The tragedy of life doesn't lie in not reaching your goal. The tragedy lies in having no goals to reach.*
>
> —Robert H. Smith, real estate developer after
> whom the R. H. Smith School of Business was named

## Introduction

Goal setting theory is a theory of motivation that explains what causes some people to perform better on work-related tasks than others. At its deepest roots, goal-directed action is based in biology. All living organisms, from plants to animals to people, must engage in goal-directed actions in order to survive. Life is conditional; organisms have needs. Survival requires taking action that satisfies needs.

Some goal-directed action is automatic, built in through evolution. Such actions include the root growth of a tree or a plant in search of water and nutrients, or a leaf turning toward light or the sun. The bodily systems of lower-level animals and people also contain autonomic processes that promote life, such as homeostasis, the beating of the heart, the functions of the other internal organs, the immune system, and the digestion of food. Organisms lacking these autonomic functions do not survive.

People and animals have an added tool for survival not possessed by plants, namely, consciousness, an awareness of the world through the sense organs. They can also retain perceptual knowledge, and in doing so benefit from experience through learning. They develop conscious goals to guide their actions (e.g., seek food and water, escape danger).

People can go one large step beyond lower-level animals. They can make volitional choices. For example, they can choose to think (Binswanger, 1991) and thereby choose their goals, both short and long term. As a corollary, they can decide whether to commit to goals set for them by others. They can appraise their performance relative to their goals, possess varying levels of confidence to attain them, experience emotions regarding goal success and failure, and raise or lower their goals as a result.

This view of goals is different from the view conceptualized in the original presentation of control theory. Control theory has its roots not in biology, but in electromechanical engineering (Miller, Galanter, & Pribram, 1960). This explicitly reductionist model is based on how torpedoes and thermostats operate. There is a standard for the object to meet, there is electrical or mechanical feedback, there is a detector to spot discrepancies between the standard and the current state of the object, and there is an effector to take corrective action.

There are intractable problems with applying an engineering model to human beings. Consequently, the electromechanical language has been gradually replaced by terms pertaining to human action and consciousness (e.g., goal, conscious awareness of discrepancies, emotion, and an actual person who takes action). Some advocates of this theory have even introduced the concept of free will or volition (Lord & Levy, 1994). Such changes have moved control theory closer to goal theory. However, one major difference remains: the last vestige of a mechanical model. Control theorists view discrepancy reduction to be the motivating force for action, whereas goal-setting theory states that the goal itself is the primary source of a person's motivation.

This difference between the two theories may initially seem trivial in that striving to attain a goal typically reduces the discrepancy between an individual's present and desired performance. But here is the problem: If discrepancy reduction alone were the primary source of motivation, people would simply eliminate their goals in every way possible. But this is not the case. People volitionally create discrepancies between their current performance and a specific desired goal (Bandura & Locke, 2003). They do this because they need to attain goals in order to live; hence the biological focus we noted above.

Because goals are the primary source of an individual's motivation, discrepancy reduction is simply one correlate of goal-directed action—in fact, it is just another way of describing what it means to pursue a goal. The second correlate is discrepancy production, namely, setting a goal for something an individual desires. To repeat, if discrepancy reduction were "the" source of motivation, most if not all people would choose to abandon their goals—or have as easy ones as possible. This is because they would strive to live a life free of tension. Yet, few people make this choice. Life is a process of goal-produced action.

Some control theorists, such as Vancouver and his colleagues (e.g., Vancouver, Thompson, & Williams, 2001), have repeatedly denied the causal role of self-efficacy, which affects both the difficulty level of goals people choose to set and their commitment to attaining them. They assert that the relation between self-efficacy and performance is an artifact of past performance. This claim has been repeatedly refuted (e.g., Bandura, 1997; Bandura & Locke, 2003). They also claim that within-subjects experimental designs show that high self-efficacy actually harms performance. Bandura (2012) has re-analyzed the studies that make this claim and has shown that the claim is false. The denial of self-efficacy's power to motivate behavior is a holdover from the original mechanistic/reductionist development of control theory, an anomaly in that control theorists do not deny the causal efficacy of goals.

Our 1990 goal setting theory was based on systematic research conducted over a quarter of a century by ourselves and many others. The theory was developed inductively from nearly 400 studies (Locke & Latham, 1990). Below we explain this theory. At the end of this book, we summarize additions to this theory since 1990. Because goal setting is an open theory, it is to be expected that additional studies will expand and refine the original 1990 theory—and they have.

## Goal Setting Theory, 1990

The term *goal* is defined by goal setting theory as the object or aim of an action. In a work setting, it might be a level of performance to be attained. Goals have two main attributes, namely, content and intensity. Goal content refers to the object or result being sought (e.g., increase profit by 20%). The research up to 1990 focused on the effect of degree of goal specificity and difficulty level on scores of different tasks in many different settings. The concept of, and the benefits from, setting a specific challenging learning goal for the performance of a task, when the requisite knowledge and skill to perform it effectively had yet to be acquired, was unknown. Moreover, the setting of multiple goals and goals differing in time span had been studied only to a limited degree.

Goal intensity refers to the effort needed to set a goal, the position of a goal in an individual's goal hierarchy, and the extent to which a person is committed to goal attainment. Most research on goal intensity, prior to 1990, had focused on the determinants and effects of goal commitment on performance.

The two core findings from nearly 400 empirical studies that led to the development of goal setting theory in 1990 were as follows:

1.  There is a linear relationship between the degree of goal difficulty and performance. Locke (1967) found that the performance of participants with the highest goals was over 250% higher than those with the easiest goals. He (Locke, 1968) derived an empirical function based on the results of 12 separate studies. In all cases, the functions were linear except when the participants reached the limit of their ability. Ability, as pointed out below, is a moderator variable in goal setting theory. Subsequent meta-analyses provided additional support for the linear relationship (Mento, Steele, & Karren, 1987; Tubbs, 1986; Wood, Mento, & Locke, 1987).

2.  Specific, difficult goals lead to higher performance than no goals as well as vague, abstract goals such as "do your best." Support for this assertion was obtained from enumerative reviews of the literature (e.g., Latham & Yukl, 1975; Locke, Shaw, Saari, & Latham, 1981; Steers & Porter, 1974). For example, Locke et al. reported that 51 of 53 studies, or 96%, showed the benefit of setting a specific, high goal. These enumerative reviews were supported by meta-analyses (e.g., Chidester & Grigsby, 1984; Mento, Steele, & Karren, 1987; Tubbs, 1986; Wood, Mento, & Locke, 1987). The number of studies included in the meta-analyses ranges from 17 to 53 and the number of participants from 1278 to 6635. In percentage terms, the range in performance improvement is 8.4% to 16%.

The problem with a do-best goal is its ambiguity as to what constitutes performance effectiveness. It is defined subjectively. A specific, high goal eliminates ambiguity as to what constitutes high effective performance. It defines for an individual what constitutes an acceptable level of performance. Moreover, the attainment of a specific, high goal is usually instrumental in leading to outcomes that are important to an individual. Latham and Lee (1986) found that these two core findings generalize across laboratory and field settings, quantity and quality criteria, soft and hard criteria, individual and groups, and goals that are assigned, self-set, or set participatively.

The research that identified the two core findings described above also identified the mechanisms by which a specific, high goal increases performance, as well as the moderator variables that enhance or attenuate the goal–performance relationship.

## Goal Mechanisms

Goal setting theory states that the mechanisms by which a specific, high goal leads to high performance are fourfold. The three most direct goal mechanisms are primarily motivational. One is choice or direction. A specific, high goal has two directional effects, both of which are relatively automatic. First, a specific, high goal orients an individual's attention and effort toward goal-relevant activities and away from those that are deemed by that individual to be irrelevant. For example, Locke and Bryan (1969a) found that driving scores changed only on the dimension for which a goal was set. Terborg (1976) found that goal specificity resulted in participants paying more attention to the task than those in the control group.

In addition, a specific, high goal activates the knowledge and skills a person possesses that are necessary to attain the goal. Latham and Baldes (1975), for example, found that logging truck drivers with a specific, high goal to increase the total weight of the logs they were carrying made modifications to their truck so they could judge the weight of the truck accurately. Latham and Saari (1982) found that drivers given goals for the number of trips to the mill per day used their CB radios to coordinate with each other so that there was always a truck ready to be loaded.

A second mechanism or mediator of the goal–performance relationship is effort. Once an individual chooses a goal and chooses to act on it, effort and arousal vary with the demands of attaining it. In short, effort is mobilized and expended in proportion to the difficulty level of the goal (Latham & Locke, 1975; Locke, 1968). Related to this is the fact that a high goal makes self-satisfaction contingent on a high level of performance

A third mechanism is persistence, that is, the time spent to attain a goal. A specific, high goal leads people to work longer at a task than a vague or easy goal. Bavelas and Lee (1978) reported that participants with easier goals stopped working sooner than those with high goals. They also found that those with high goals worked for a longer amount of time. Huber (1985) found that participants with high goals worked longer to complete a maze than those with moderate, easy, or do-best goals.

The fourth mechanism, knowledge or task strategy, is more cognitive in nature than the other three. As previously noted, a specific, high goal cues an individual to draw upon the extant knowledge/skill required to attain it. When tasks are complex for an individual, the direct goal mechanism of *choice* to exert *effort* and to *persist* until the goal is attained may not be sufficient to ensure high performance. A high, specific goal on a task that is complex for an individual can cause that person to have tunnel vision, to focus more on expending effort to get immediate results before learning how to perform the task. In such instances, a do-best goal may work better than a specific, hard goal. Kanfer and Ackerman (1989) found that air cadets, who had yet to master an air-traffic control simulation, performed significantly better during the declarative stage of learning when they were given a do-best goal as opposed to those in the control group who were given a specific, high goal.

### Moderator Variables

#### Ability

Goal setting theory states that ability is a moderator variable that affects the goal–performance relationship. Ability affects the choice of goal because people cannot perform in accordance with a goal when they lack the knowledge and skill to obtain that level of performance. Locke (1982) found that the relationship between goal difficulty level and performance was .82 ($p$ <.001) for goals ranging from easy to difficult, and only .11 (n.s.) for goals that were impossible to attain. Moreover, goal setting was shown to have a greater positive effect on the performance of people with high as opposed to low ability.

## Performance Feedback

Feedback or knowledge of results is a second moderator of the goal–performance relationship because goals regulate performance far better when feedback is present than when it is absent. Feedback allows people to decide if more effort or a different strategy is needed to attain their goal. When performance feedback is withheld, goal setting is ineffective for increasing performance. However, the theory also states, and the empirical research shows, that goal setting is the mediating variable that explains why feedback gets translated into action (Locke, Cartledge, & Koeppel, 1968). If the feedback does not result in goal setting, if the feedback is ignored, performance does not improve.

## Goal Commitment

Commitment is a third variable that moderates the goal–performance relationship. Locke and Latham (1990, p. 124) stated that "it is virtually axiomatic that a goal that a person is not *really* trying for is not really a goal and therefore cannot have much effect on subsequent action." Commitment, it was argued, is a more inclusive term than goal acceptance in that it refers to one's attachment to or determination to attain the goal, regardless of its source (e.g., self-set vs. assigned goal). Acceptance refers specifically to commitment to an assigned goal (Locke et al., 1981). The theory states that commitment is a moderator variable because goal difficulty level has been shown to be more highly and positively related to performance for people with high rather than low goal commitment (Erez & Zidon, 1984).

The causes of commitment fall into two broad categories: factors that make goal attainment important and factors that make an individual confident that the goal can be attained. Factors that were found to affect an individual's desire to attain a specific, high goal include authority, peers, making the goal public, incentives, internal rewards, punishment, and instrumentality.

Commitment to assigned goals was frequently found to reflect compliance with legitimate authority. The relationship between commitment and authority was addressed years earlier by Barnard (1938). He stated that employees assent to authority if they understand the request, they believe the request is consistent with an organization's objectives and their personal interests, and they are mentally and physically able to comply with the order. Bernard coined the concept "zone of indifference" under which orders are accepted without objection. Bassett (1979) viewed goal commitment in laboratory and field settings as so routine that he argued that a theory of goal rejection rather than one of commitment should be developed. Support for Bernard and Bassett's assertions came from a study by Ronan, Latham, and Kinne (1973). They found that a supervisor's presence was related to the productivity of logging crews with specific, high productivity goals as opposed to crews where the supervisor did not remain on the job.

Latham and Saari (1979a) found that supervisory supportiveness led to high goals being set. Anderson and O'Reilly (1981) also found that perceived top management's support of the company's goal setting system was significantly related to the performance of managers in a manufacturing plant. In fact, assigned goals were found to be as effective as participatively set goals if both were at the same level of difficulty (Latham & Saari, 1979b) and, consistent with Bernard's observation, the rationale for them was explained as opposed to assigning them curtly (Latham, Erez, & Locke, 1988).

With regard to peer influence, Matsui, Kakuyama, and Onglatco (1987) found that commitment was higher for participants working in dyads who were assigned both group and individual goals rather than just the latter. Mueller (1983) tested the hypothesis that competitiveness increases performance only if it leads to the setting of a specific, high goal. Participants in the competitive condition set significantly higher goals and performed significantly better than those in the control group.

There is a benefit to making one's goal public. Lyman (1984) reported that public, not private, goal setting was effective in changing the class conduct of 11- to 15-year-olds with a conduct disorder. Hayes, Rosenfarb, Wulfert, Munt, Korn, and Zettle (1985) found that students who wrote down their behavioral goals, signed them, and then read them aloud to the group performed significantly better than those in the private goal or control condition on reading and answering questions from passages on the GRE exam. Hollenbeck, Williams, and Klein (1989) found a significant effect for a publicly self-set goal on students' GPA. Those in the public condition shared their goal with a significant other.

Although contradictory findings regarding the effect of incentives and rewards on goal commitment were obtained prior to 1990, most suggested that bonus pay for a moderately difficult goal is effective. But when goals are very difficult, pay for performance or goal progress should be used, rather than for goal attainment (Locke & Latham, 1990).

Latham and Saari (1982) reported that a goal setting program with unionized truck drivers was accepted by those employees and their union officers only if there was a formal agreement that no one would be punished for failure to attain their goals. The goal setting program was highly effective in improving productivity.

Yukl and Latham (1978) found that the perceived instrumentality of goal attainment was significantly related to the goal commitment of word processors. Oliver and Brief (1983) obtained similar results for sales managers. Expectancy of success, particularly self-efficacy, were found to affect goal commitment. A number of studies reported that commitment declines with increasingly difficult goals (e.g., Erez & Zidon, 1984). However, both Locke (1982) and Garland (1983) showed that even impossible-to-attain goals motivate performance in the short term. Self-efficacy, one's judgment of how well one can perform a given task, is likely key here. Bandura (1986) reported voluminous studies showing that self-efficacy plays a major role in helping people remain committed to a course of action, particularly in overcoming obstacles and remaining resilient following failure.

Finally, goal intensity, the amount of thought or mental effort that goes into setting a specific, high goal, affects commitment to it (Henderson, 1963; Gollwitzer, Heckhausen, & Ratajczak, 1990). This is likely due to the fact that such intense processing makes people more aware of how the goal might be attained, and thus leads to the formulation of well-thought-out plans that in turn increases self-efficacy for implementation and goal attainment.

*Task Complexity*

In addition to ability, feedback, and commitment, the complexity of the task was found to affect the goal–performance relationship (Wood, Mento, & Locke, 1987). Goal setting was found to have a greater positive effect on tasks that were straightforward for people, tasks that people had the knowledge and skills to perform well. The majority of the tasks used to test goal setting theory were those where ability would not be a confounding variable. The increase in productivity resulting from goal setting on low, moderate, and high levels of task complexity were shown by Locke and Latham (1990) to be 12.5%, 9.12%, and 7.79%, respectively.

*Situational Constraints/Resources*

As we noted in 1990, it should be self-evident that situational constraints hamper goal attainment. Without the necessary resources (e.g., requisite task information, materials, supplies), a goal is unlikely to be attained (Peters, Chassis, Lindholm, O'Connor, & Kline, 1982).

*Personality*

Mitchell (1979), in a review of the literature, reported that personality variables control little of the variance in organizational behavior. Adler and Weiss (1988) concluded that setting a specific, high goal creates what Mischel (1977) termed a "strong situation," a situation that is relatively structured. Such situations provide strong cues to guide behavior, thus masking the effects of individual differences in personality.

*Goals and Affect*

One cannot make blanket statements about the effect of goal setting on affect without knowing the nature of the goals and how the resulting performance is valued and appraised by an individual. Goal setting can lead to a negative as well as a positive appraisal. In general, the greater the success a person experiences in goal attainment, the greater the degree of satisfaction they experience. Similarly, dissatisfaction is experienced when goal attainment is blocked (Locke, 1976; Peters et al., 1982). This is because a goal is the value standard for appraising one's performance. The mean weighted correlation between goal success and satisfaction was shown to be $r = .51$ (Locke & Latham, 1990).

Goal setting increases interest and reduces boredom with a routine, repetitive task. In a laboratory experiment, Bryan and Locke (1967) found that specific challenging goals increased task interest and the intensity of mental focus on such tasks. Similarly, setting specific, high goals increased a sense of challenge and purpose for loggers in the forest products industry cutting down trees (Latham & Kinne, 1974).

Intuitively, time constraints cause stress from feeling pressure to perform effectively. However, a field experiment showed that when forest products companies reduced the number of days they would purchase wood from loggers, the logging crews cut and sold as much wood in three days as they normally did in five (Latham & Locke, 1975).

## Other Key Findings

Other issues that interested goal setting researchers prior to 1990 included the setting of multiple goals; the relative advantages of assigned, participatively set, and self-set goals; and the importance of self-efficacy with regard to performance.

### Multiple Goals

Nearly all goal setting studies prior to 1990 examined the effect of a goal on the performance of a single task. Exceptions include an experiment by Schmidt, Kleinbeck, and Brockman (1984) where participants worked on a tracking and a reaction time task. When participants were given a goal to improve their tracking performance, reaction time *decreased* even when the participants were attempting to maintain it. When they were *assigned* a goal to improve their reaction time, tracking errors increased. Erez, Gopher, and Arazi (1987) required participants to work simultaneously on a typing and classification task. Performance was proportional to goal difficulty level.

In a study of first-line supervisors, where there was strong support from senior management, Ivancevich (1974) found that goals were set and performance improved for quantity and quality of performance, grievances, and absenteeism. Nemeroff and Cosentino (1979) examined the effects of giving management trainees goals for improving 12 specific behaviors. Significant improvement occurred on all 12 behaviors relative to performance in the control group.

Locke and Latham (1990) concluded that people can systematically pursue multiple goals. This is because in most instances people are able to prioritize goals and behave accordingly within the limits of their cognitive capacity and ability.

### Assigned versus Participative versus Self-Set Goals

A series of 11 studies by Latham and his colleagues examined the effect of goals that are assigned versus those that are set participatively on performance. Four were conducted in the laboratory, and seven were conducted in work settings. The tasks involved felling trees (Latham & Yukl, 1975), typing (Latham & Yukl, 1976, performance appraisal (Latham, Mitchell, & Dossett, 1978), test scores in a selection battery (Dossett, Latham, & Mitchell, 1979), brainstorming (Latham & Saari, 1979b), basic arithmetic (Latham, Steele, & Saari, 1982), and performance in a business game (Latham & Steele, 1983). The time span ranged from 6 minutes to 6 months. The results showed that when goal difficulty is held constant, an assigned goal is as effective as one that is set participatively. The caveat is that the logic or rationale for the assigned goal must be given (Latham, Erez, & Locke, 1988). The advantage of a participatively set goal is that it may be significantly higher than the goal assigned by a supervisor, and, consistent with the theory, the higher the goal, the higher the performance (Latham, Mitchell, & Dossett, 1978). Moreover, participation can increase understanding of how to perform the task (Latham & Saari, 1979a).

By 1990, it was clear that, contrary to self-determination theory (Deci & Ryan, 1985), self-set goals are as effective, but not more effective in bringing about goal commitment and increasing performance than an assigned or a participatively set goal. For example, in a study involving government employees, Latham and Marshall (1982) found that goal difficulty, goal acceptance, goal attainment, and performance (defined as the number of ideas generated in a job analysis) were the same regardless of whether the goal was assigned, self-set, or set in a participatory manner. Hollenbeck et al. (1989) reported that commitment to a high goal with regard to a grade in a university class was not significantly higher in a self-set versus an assigned goal condition. Locke and Latham (1990) concluded that the error many behavioral scientists had made was not in overestimating the beneficial effects of choice and participation in decision making for increasing goal commitment and subsequently performance, but rather in underestimating the beneficial effects of legitimate authority and a supportive leadership style.

### Self-Efficacy

Social cognitive theory, developed by Bandura (1986), posits three variables that regulate behavior: goal setting; outcome expectancies regarding the outcome one can expect from one's performance (e.g., goal attainment/non attainment); and, most importantly, self-efficacy, that is, one's confidence that one can do what is required to perform a given task. Self-efficacy is based on a self-assessment of all personal factors that can affect one's performance. Self-efficacy is measured in relation to a range of performance levels.

The relationship of goals and self-efficacy to performance within and between groups was investigated by Locke, Frederick, Lee, and Bobko (1984) and Locke, Motowidlo, and Bobko (1986). Self-efficacy affected the level of a self-set goal, and affected performance independently of the goal that was set. Assigned goals affected self-efficacy and personal goals, while self-efficacy affected both self-set goals and performance. As noted previously, self-efficacy also affects goal commitment. In short, it was found that performance is affected not only by what one is trying to do (i.e., the goal), but also by how confident one is of being able to do it (i.e., self-efficacy).

## Conclusion

In summary, the 1990 theory of goal setting developed inductively from studies involving close to 40,000 participants in eight countries performing 88 different tasks in laboratory and field settings, using experimental and correlational designs, over a time span of one minute to three years where the goal was assigned, self-set, or set participatively with an individual or group is this: (1) A specific, high goal leads to higher performance than no goal, or an abstract goal such as to do your best, (2) there is a linear relationship between the difficulty level of the goal and job performance, (3) performance feedback, participation in decision making, and competition only affect performance to the extent that they lead to the setting of a specific, high goal.

The moderator variables in the theory that enhance or weaken the above statements include ability, feedback, commitment, task complexity, and situational constraints. The mediating variables that explain the positive goal–performance relationship include choice/direction, effort, persistence, and strategy.

The overall validity of goal setting and its practicality or usefulness in the workplace was attested to by enumerative reviews (e.g., Latham & Yukl, 1975), meta-analyses, and comparative analyses of goal setting with other theories of motivation. With regard to the latter, Pinder (1984, p. 169) concluded that "goal setting theory has demonstrated more scientific validity to date than any other theory or approach to work motivation ... Moreover, the evidence thus far indicates that it probably holds more promise as an applied motivational tool for managers than does any other approach." This theory culminated in the development of the High Performance Cycle discussed in Chapters 18 and 21.

## References

Adler, S., & Weiss, H. M. (1988). Recent developments in the study of personality and organizational behavior. In C. L. Cooper & I. T. Robertson (Eds.), *International review of industrial and organizational psychology* (pp. 307–330). Oxford, UK: John Wiley & Sons.

Anderson, J. C., & O'Reilly, C. A. (1981). Effects of an organizational control system on managerial satisfaction and performance. *Human Relations, 34,* 491–501.

Bandura, A. (1986). Social foundations of thought and action: A social-cognitive theory. Englewood Cliffs, NJ: Prentice-Hall.

Bandura, A. (1997). *Self-efficacy: The exercise of control.* New York: Freeman.

Bandura, A. (2012). On the functional properties of perceived self-efficacy revisited. *Journal of Management, 38,* 9–44.

Bandura, A., & Locke, E. A. (2003). Negative self-efficacy and goal effects revisited. *Journal of Applied Psychology, 88,* 87–99.

Barnard, C. I. (1938). *The functions of the executive.* Cambridge, MA: Harvard University Press.

Bassett, G. A. (1979). A study of the effects of task goal and schedule choice on work performance. *Organizational Behavior and Human Performance, 24,* 202–227.

Bavelas, J., & Lee, E. S. (1978). Effect of goal level on performance: A trade-off of quantity and quality. *Canadian Journal of Psychology, 32,* 219–240.

Binswanger, H. (1991). Volition as cognitive self-regulation. *Organizational Behavior and Human Decision Processes, 50,* 154–178.

Bryan, J. F., & Locke, E. A. (1967). Parkinson's law as a goal-setting phenomenon. *Organizational Behavior and Human Performance, 2,* 258–275.

Chidester, T. R., & Grigsby, W. C. (1984). A meta-analysis of the goal-setting performance literature. In J. A. Pearce & R. B. Robinson (Eds.), *Academy of management proceedings* (pp. 202–206). Ada, OH: Academy of Management.

Deci, E. L., & Ryan, R. M. (1985). The general causality orientation scale: Self-determination in personality. *Journal of Research in Personality, 19,* 109–137.

Dossett, D. L., Latham, G. P., & Mitchell, T. R. (1979). The effects of assigned versus participatively set goals, KR, and individual differences when goal difficulty is held constant. *Journal of Applied Psychology, 64,* 291–298.

Erez, M. (1977). Feedback: A necessary condition for the goal setting-performance relationship. *Journal of Applied Psychology, 62,* 624–627.

Erez, M., Gopher, D., & Arazi, N. (1987). Effect of self-set goals and monetary rewards on dual task performance. *Organizational Behaviour and Human Decision Processes, 47,* 247–269.

Erez, M., & Zidon, I. (1984). Effect of goal acceptance on the relationship of goal difficulty to performance. *Journal of Applied Psychology, 69,* 69–78.

Garland, H. (1983). Influence of ability, assigned goals, and normative information on personal goals and performance: A challenge to the goal attainability assumption. *Journal of Applied psychology, 68,* 20–30.

Gollwitzer, P. M., Heckhausen, H., & Ratajczak, K. (1990). From weighing to willing: Approaching a change decision through prior or postdecisional mentation. *Organizational Behavior and Human Decision Processes, 45,* 41–45.

Hayes, S. C., Rosenfarb, I., Wulfert, E., Munt, E. D., Korn, Z., & Zettle, R. D., (1985). Self-reinforcement effects: An artifact of social standard setting. *Journal of Applied Behaviour Analysis, 18,* 201–214.

Henderson, E. H. (1963). A study of individually formulated purposes for reading in relation to reading achievement comprehension and purpose attainment. Department of Psychology, University of Delaware, unpublished doctoral dissertation.

Hollenbeck, J. R., Williams, C. R., & Klein, H. J. (1989). An empirical examination of the antecedents of commitment to difficult goals. *Journal of Applied Psychology, 74,* 18–23.

Huber, V. L. (1985). Effects of task difficulty, goal setting and strategy on performance of heuristic task. *Journal of Applied Psychology, 70,* 492–504.

Ivancevich, J. M. (1974). Changes in performance in a management by objectives program. *Administrative Science Quarterly, 19,* 563–574.

Kanfer, R., & Ackerman, P. L. (1989). Motivation and cognitive abilities: an integrative approach to skill acquisition. *Journal of Applied Psychology—Monograph, 74,* 657–690.

Latham, G. P., & Baldes, J. J. (1975). The "practical significance" of Locke's theory of goal setting. *Journal of Applied Psychology, 60,* 122–124.

Latham, G. P., & Kinne, S. B. (1974). Improving job performance through training in goal setting. *Journal of Applied Psychology, 59,* 187–191.

Latham, G. P., & Lee, T. W. (1986). Goal setting. In E. A. Locke (Ed.), *Generalizing from laboratory to field settings.* Lexington, MA: Heath.

Latham, G. P., & Locke, E. A. (1975). Increasing productivity with decreasing time limits: A field replication of Parkinson's law. *Journal of Applied Psychology, 60,* 524–526.

Latham, G. P., & Marshall, H. A. (1982). The effects of self-set, participatively set, and assigned goals on the performance of government employees. *Personnel Psychology, 35,* 399–404.

Latham, G. P., Erez, M., & Locke, E. A. (1988). Resolving scientific disputes by the joint design of crucial experiments by the antagonists: Application to the Erez-Latham dispute regarding participation in goal setting. [Monograph]. *Journal of Applied Psychology, 73,* 753–772.

Latham, G. P., Mitchell, T. R., & Dossett, D. L. (1978). The importance of participative goal setting and anticipated rewards on goal difficulty and job performance. *Journal of Applied Psychology, 63,* 163–171.

Latham, G. P., & Saari, L. M. (1979a). The importance of supportive relationships in goal setting. *Journal of Applied Psychology, 64,* 151–156.

Latham, G. P., & Saari, L. M. (1979b). The effects of holding goal difficulty constant on assigned and participatively set goals. *Academy of Management Journal, 22,* 163–168.

Latham, G.P., & Saari, L.M. (1982). The importance of union acceptance for productivity improvement through goal setting. *Personnel Psychology, 35,* 781–787.

Latham, G. P., & Steele, T. P. (1983). The motivation effects of participation versus goal setting on performance. *Academy of Management Journal, 26,* 406–417.

Latham, G. P., Steele, T. P., & Saari, L. M. (1982). The effects of participation and goal difficulty on performance. *Personnel Psychology, 35,* 677–686.

Latham, G. P., & Yukl, G. A. (1975). Assigned versus participative goal setting with educated and uneducated wood workers. *Journal of Applied Psychology, 60,* 299–302.

Latham, G. P., & Yukl, G. A. (1976). Effects of assigned and participative goal setting on performance and job satisfaction. *Journal of Applied Psychology, 61,* 166–171.

Locke, E. A. (1967). Further data on the relationship of task success to liking and satisfaction. *Psychological Reports, 20,* 246.

Locke, E. A. (1968). Toward a theory of task motivation and incentives. *Organizational Behavior & Human Performance, 3,* 157–189.

Locke, E. A. (1976). Nature and causes of job satisfaction. In M. D. Dunnette (Ed.), *Handbook of industrial and organizational psychology* (pp. 1297–1349). Chicago: Rand McNally.

Locke, E. A. (1982). The ideas of a short work period and multiple goal levels. *Journal of Applied Psychology, 67,* 512–514.

Locke, E. A., & Bryan, J. F. (1969a). Knowledge of score and goal level as determinants of work rate. *Journal of Applied Psychology, 53,* 59–65.

Locke, E. A., & Bryan, J. F. (1969b). The directing function of goals in task performance. *Organizational Behavior and Human Performance, 4,* 35–42.

Locke, E. A., & Latham, G. P. (1990). *A theory of goal setting and task performance.* Englewood Cliffs, NJ: Prentice Hall.

Locke, E. A., Cartledge, N., & Koeppel, J. (1968). Motivation effects of knowledge of results: A goal setting phenomenon? *Psychological Bulletin, 70,* 474–485.

Locke, E. A., Frederick, E., Lee, C., & Bobko, P. (1984). Effect of self-efficacy, goals, and task strategies on task performance. *Journal of Applied Psychology, 69,* 241–251.

Locke, E. A., Motowidlo, S. J., & Bobko, P. (1986). Using self efficacy theory to resolve the conflict between goal setting theory and expectancy theory in organizational behavioral and industrial/organizational psychology. *Journal of Social and Clinical Psychology, 4,* 328–338.

Locke, E. A., Shaw, K. N., Saari, L. M., & Latham, G. P. (1981). Goal setting and task performance: 1969–1980. *Psychological Bulletin, 90,* 125–152.

Lord, R. G., & Levy, P. E. (1994). Moving from cognition to action: A control theory perspective. *Applied Psychology: An International Review, 43,* 335–367.

Matsui, T., Kakuyama, T., & Onglatco, M. (1987). Effects of goals and feedback on performance in groups. *Journal of Applied Psychology, 72,* 407–415.

Mento, A. J., Steele, R. P., & Karren, R. J. (1987). A meta-analytic study of the effects of goal setting on task performance: 1966–1984. *Organizational Behavior and Human Decision processes, 39,* 52–83.

Miller, G. A., Galanter, E., & Pribram, K. H. (1960). *Plans and the structure of behavior.* London: Holt, Rinehart & Winston.

Mischel, W. (1977). The interaction of person and situation. In D. Magnusson & N. S. Endler (Eds.), *Personality at the crossroads: Current issues in interactional psychology.* Hillsdale, NJ: Lawrence Erlbaum.

Mitchell, T. R. (1979). Organizational behavior. *Annual Review of Psychology, 30,* 243–281.

Mueller, M. E. (1983). The effects of goal setting and competition on performance: A laboratory study. University of Minnesota, unpublished master's thesis.

Nemeroff, W. F., & Cosentino, J. (1979). Utilizing feedback and goal setting to increase performance appraisal interviewer skills of managers. *Academy of Management Journal, 22,* 566–576.

Oliver, R. L. & Brief, A. P. (1983). Sales Managers' Goal Commitment Correlates. *The Journal of Personal Selling and Sales Management, 3,* 11–18.

Peters, L. H., Chassis, M. B., Lindholm, H. R., O'Connor, E. J., & Kline, C. R. (1982). The joint influence of situational constraints and goal setting on performance and affective outcomes. *Journal of Management, 8,* 7–20.

Pinder, C. C. (1984). *Work motivation: Theory, issues, and applications.* Glenview, IL: Scott Foresman.

Ronan, W. W., Latham, G. P., & Kinne, S. B. (1973). The effects of goal setting and supervision on worker behavior in an industrial situation. *Journal of Applied Psychology, 58,* 302–307.

Saari, L. M., & Latham, G. P. (1981). Hypotheses on reinforcing properties of incentives contingent upon performance. Technical Report GS-11, N00014-79-C-0690, Office of Naval Research.

Schmidt, K. H., Kleinbeck, U., & Brockman, W. (1984). Motivational control of motor performance by goal setting in a dual-task situation. *Psychological Research, 46,* 129–141.

Steers, R. M., & Porter, L. W. (1974). The role of task-goal attributes in employee performance. *Psychological Bulletin, 81,* 434–452.

Terborg, J. R. (1976). The motivational components of goal setting. *Journal of Applied Psychology, 61,* 613–621.

Tubbs, M. E. (1986). Goal-setting: A meta-analytic examination of the empirical evidence. *Journal of Applied Psychology, 71,* 473–483.

Vancouver, J. B., Thompson, C. M., & Williams, A. A. (2001). The changing signs in the relationships among self-efficacy, personal goals, and performance. *Journal of Applied Psychology, 86,* 605–620.

Winters, D., & Latham, G. P. (1996). The effect of learning versus outcome goals on a simple versus a complex task. *Group and Organization Management, 21,* 236–250.

Wood, R. E., Mento, A. J., & Locke, E. A. (1987). Task complexity as a moderator of goal effects: A meta analysis. *Journal of Applied Psychology, 72,* 416–425.

Yukl, G. A., & Latham, G. P. (1978). Interrelationships among employee participation, individual differences, goal difficulty, goal acceptance, goal instrumentality and performance. *Personnel Psychology, 31,* 305–324.

# 2 The Economic Value of Goal Setting to Employers

*Frank L. Schmidt* Tippie College of Business, University of Iowa

## The Economic Value of Goal Setting to Employers

The purpose of this chapter is to estimate the practical (i.e., economic) value of goal setting to employers by applying standard accepted utility analysis procedures (e.g., Hunter & Schmidt, 1982; 1983; Schmidt, Hunter, & Pearlman, 1982; Schmidt, Hunter, McKenzie, & Muldrow, 1979; Hunter, Schmidt, & Judiesch, 1990) to the available evidence showing the effect of goal setting in increasing job performance. This effect is the difference between "do your best" or no-goal conditions (i.e., the control condition) and the setting of specific, difficult goals. Economic value is expressed in two metrics: dollar value and percent increase in output. The dollar value metric is the dollar value as sold of the increase in output due to adoption of goal setting. That is, the dollar value figures represent increases in *revenue* from improved performance, not increases in profit. The percentage metric is the average percentage increase in output produced under goal setting conditions as compared to the baseline in the control condition. It has repeatedly been found that percentage increases in output that appear modest to some (e.g., 9%) correspond to very large figures in the dollar value metric (Hunter, Schmidt, & Judiesch, 1990). As we will see later, that is also the case for goal setting. The process of determining practical or economic value is called utility analysis.

## Overview of Utility Analysis

The methods of utility analysis used in industrial/organizational (I/O) psychology were originally developed in the 1940s for application to personnel selection procedures. The main contributor to these methods was Hubert Brogden (Brogden, 1946, 1949a, 1949b), but others also contributed (cf. Richardson, 1944; Jarrett, 1948). Two key quantities determining the economic value of selection procedures are the validity coefficient (the correlation between scores and later job performance) and the selection ratio (the proportion of job applicants who are hired.) Larger validity coefficients produce higher economic value, and smaller selection ratios create higher economic gains per employee selected.

These two quantities are not relevant to the practical value of workforce interventions or "treatment conditions," such as goal setting, training programs, or financial incentives. The standard utility procedures were modified for application to personnel or workforce interventions by Schmidt, Hunter, and Pearlman (1982) and Hunter and Schmidt (1983). A key quantity in determining the economic value of an intervention is the standardized increase in job performance that it produces. This is the difference in performance between those who get the intervention (here, goal setting) and those who don't (the control group), divided by the pooled standard deviation (SD) (which is close to the average of the SDs in the two groups). The value is called the *d*-value or effect size, and it is the effect of the intervention in SD units. For the purposes of this chapter, this value was computed as the sample-size-weighted average *d*-value for goal setting across four meta-analyses of the effectiveness of goal setting (Chidester & Grigsby, 1984; Mento, Steel, & Karren, 1987, Tubbs, 1986; and Wood, Mento, & Locke, 1987). All the effect sizes included in this average reflected the difference between the specific, difficult goal condition and a "do your best" or no-goal condition. These four meta-analyses included a total of 19,839 data points. The sample-size-weighted mean effect size (*d*-value) is .46. This means that on average goal setting increased job performance by nearly one-half of an SD. This is a fairly large effect. In a normally distributed distribution of job performance, this is the difference between the 50th percentile and the 68th percentile. The task of utility analysis is to translate this difference into metrics of practical or economic value.

## Factors Beyond the *d*-Value

Utility analysis requires some means of translating the effect size or *d*-value into dollar value of the performance increase. Doing this requires an estimate of the standard deviation of dollar value of output across employees (SDy). The dollar value of employee output as sold varies markedly across different employees in the same job. Schmidt et al. (1979) developed a method of quantifying SDy, and this method was subsequently supported empirically (Bobko, Karren, & Parkington, 1983; Judiesch, Schmidt, & Mount, 1992). After this method had been applied to a variety of different jobs, it became apparent that a lower-bound value for SDy for any given job could be expressed as 40% of the average salary for that job (Schmidt, Mack, & Hunter, 1984; Schmidt, Hunter, Outerbridge, & Trattner, 1986). This finding allowed a conservative translation of the effect size into dollar value. For example, if the average salary on a given job is $50,000, then SDy = (.40)($50,000) = $20,000. Then (*d*)($20,000) is the dollar value of the increase in job performance. This follows from the fact that *d* is the performance increase in SD units, and SDy is the dollar value of a one-SD increase in job performance. In the case of goal setting, *d* = .46, and so this is (.46)($20,000) = $9200/year. Thus, we would expect an average increase in output of employees of $9200/year as a result of the introduction of goal setting.

But this is not the whole story. The total value of the goal setting program also depends on other factors: (a) the number of employees who are given the goal setting "treatment"; (b) the number of years the goal setting program is continued (assuming the improvement will stop if the program is discontinued); and (c) the cost per employee of implementing the program (this will usually be small for goal setting). The final equation for the dollar value of the program is

Dollar Value = (T)(N)(SDy) − (N)(C),

where:

T   = the number of years the program is continued;
N   = the number of employees included in the goal setting program;
SDy = the SD of job performance in dollars, as described above; and
C   = the cost per employee of implementing the goal setting program.

In our example, SDy = $9200. Suppose the goal setting program lasts 5 years and there are 35 employees in the program. Suppose, further, that it costs $200 per employee to implement the program (or $40/year/employee). We then have

Value = (5)(35)($9200) – (35)($200) = $1,603,000.

Thus, this goal setting program is predicted to increase company revenues by a little over one and a half million dollars. But it is important to note that this is the increase in revenue resulting from increased production, not the increase in profit. Increased production may entail increased materials and other costs. For example, if employees are making jewelry, more productive employees will use more materials (silver, gold, diamonds, etc.). However, in many jobs these production costs are negligible. For example, if insurance salespeople sell more policies, there are only trivial increases in such materials costs (Schmidt et al., 1984, 1986).

Suppose our focus is on percent increase in output instead of the dollar value of output. We must have some way to convert the *d*-value into a percentage increase in output. To do this, we must know the SD of work output across employees as a percentage of mean output (SDp). This value can be computed only by using data on actual employee output; that is, counts of actual output. Supervisory ratings and other similar measures cannot be used. Hunter, Schmidt, and Judiesch (1990) compiled this kind of data from all available studies in the literature that presented actual counts of employee output on a variety of jobs, ranging from unskilled to professional-level jobs. They found that SDp varied with the level of the job. In round figures, these values were as follows: for unskilled jobs, SDp = .20; for mid-level jobs, SDp = .30; and for professional/managerial jobs, SDp = .50. This means that on unskilled jobs, employees one SD above the mean produce 20% more than the average employee. On a midlevel job, an employee one SD above average in performance (i.e., at the 84th percentile of output) produces 30% more than the average employee. For any job at one of these levels, these data allow one to convert the *d*-value to percentage increase in output. The percentage increase in output is (*d*)(SDp). Using our *d* of .46, for a midlevel job this will then be (.46)(.20) = .092; that is, a 9.2% increase in output. This percentage increase in output applies to each employee in the goal setting program and lasts as long as the employee remains in the program (i.e., until the program is discontinued or the employee leaves the job). As noted earlier, many people express surprise that the apparently large dollar value gains from a program are accounted for by what seems to be a modest percentage increase in output. However, a 9.2% increase in output is not modest. As productivity gains go, it is a large increase, as any economist will attest.

But what if an organization does not want to increase overall output (because, for example, there is no market for additional output)? The percentage increase in output can then be evaluated in terms of reduced labor costs (Hunter & Schmidt, 1983; Schmidt et al., 1986). That is, if each employee produces more, fewer employees are needed to produce the same output. Thus, the savings can be expressed as a reduction in labor costs. If there is a 9.2% increase in average output per employee, then there can be a reduction of 8.4% in the number of employees with no decrease in output. (The inverse of 1.092 is .916; 1.00 – .916 = .084 or an 8.4% decrease in the number of employees.) Suppose, for example, that there were initially 100 employees. Then after the introduction of the goal setting program, only 92 employees would be needed to produce the same amount of output. Now, suppose the employment costs per employee were $60,000 (which includes $50,000 in wages or salary plus the cost of health care and other benefits and other employment costs). Then the labor savings would be approximately (8) ($60,000) = $480,000 per year. Because labor costs average only about half or less as large as revenues in most companies (Hunter & Schmidt, 1983), the savings in labor costs are less than the gains in dollar value of output.

## Managerial Reactions to Utility Analysis

As can be seen from the presentation thus far, utility analysis is fairly straightforward. These procedures are widely accepted in industrial/organizational psychology and related areas and have been applied to evaluate selection programs and organizational interventions (Boudreau & Ramstad, 2002). However, in the 1990s, Latham and Whyte (Latham & Whyte, 1994; Whyte & Latham, 1997) published two studies in which they concluded that managers were skeptical of utility analysis to the point that presentation of utility analysis actually reduced their confidence that a program had practical value. However, subsequent studies of this sort failed to replicate these findings and in fact found that presentation of utility analyses increased managers' confidence in the value of workforce programs. In the Carson, Becker, and Henderson (1998) study, for example, the authors presented the utility analysis information in a manner that was easier for managers to understand in comparison to the complicated, formula-based presentation in the two earlier Latham and Whyte studies (see also Cronshaw, 1997.) In both their studies, Carson et al. (1998) found that presentation of utility analyses increased managers' confidence in the value of workforce programs. A subsequent study by Macan and Foster (2004) replicated the Carson et al. (1998) findings. In addition, in the Macan and Foster study, managers were asked afterward to rank the importance they placed on the different items of information they had been given (e.g., validity coefficients, expectancy tables, etc.) when making their decisions. The study found that the managers ranked the utility analysis information very highly. Rauschenberger and Schmidt (1987) describe in some detail a successful real-world use of utility analysis with managers in a steel company and offer suggestions as to the best ways to make utility analysis credible to managers. So overall, it appears that if utility information is presented in an appropriate manner, managers give it considerable weight in their decisions.

## Conclusion

There is strong evidence that the increases in job performance produced by goal setting have important economic and practical value. The gains in dollar value of output as sold are substantial under typical real-world conditions. The percentage increase in output is also substantial, and for organizations that do not want to increase total output, this percentage increase makes it possible to achieve important decreases in labor costs.

## References

Bobko, P., Karren, R., & Parkington, J. J. (1983). Estimation of stardard deviations in utility analysis: An empirical test. *Journal of Applied Psychology, 68,* 170–176.

Boudreau, J. W., & Ramstad, P. M. (2002). Strategic I/O psychology and the role of utility analysis models. Center for Advanced Human Resource Studies (CAHRS), Industrial and Labor Relations School, Cornell University, Ithaca, NY.

Brogden, H. E. (1946). On the interpretation of the correlation coefficient as a measure of predictive efficiency. *Journal of Educational Psychology, 37*, 65–76.

Brogden, H. E. (1949a). A new coefficient: Application to biserial correlation and to estimation of selective efficiency. *Psychometrika, 14*, 169–182.

Brogden, H. E. (1949b). When testing pays off. *Personnel Psychology, 2*, 171–184.

Carson, K. P., Becker, J. S., & Henderson, J. A. (1998). Is utility really futile? A failure to replicate and an extension. *Journal of Applied Psychology, 83*, 84–96.

Chidester, T. R., & Grigsby, W. C. (1984). A meta-analyis of the goal setting performance literature. *Academy of Management Proceedings*, 202–206.

Cronshaw, S. F. (1997). Lo! The stimulus speaks: The insider's view on Whyte and Latham's "The futility of utility analysis". *Personnel Psychology, 50*, 611–615.

Hunter, J. E., & Schmidt, F. L. (1982). Fitting people to jobs: Implications of personnel selection for national productivity. In E. A. Fleishman & M. Dunnette (Eds.) *Human performance and productivity*. Volume 1: *Human capability assessment*. Hillsdale, NJ: Earlbaum, 233–284.

Hunter, J. E., & Schmidt, F. L. (1983). Quantifying the effects of psychological interventions on employee job performance and workforce productivity. *American Psychologist, 38*, 473–478.

Hunter, J. E., Schmidt, F. L., & Judiesch, M. K. (1990). Individual differences in output variability as a function of job complexity. *Journal of Applied Psychology, 75*, 28–42.

Jarrett, R. F. (1948). Percent increase in output of selected personnel as an index of test efficiency. *Journal of Applied Psychology, 32*, 135–145.

Judiesch, M. K., Schmidt, F. L., & Mount, M. K. (1992). Estimates of the dollar value of job performance in utility analysis: An empirical test of two theories. *Journal of Applied Psychology. 77*, 234–250.

Latham, G. P., & Whyte, G. (1994). The futility of utility analysis. *Personnel Psychology, 47*, 31–46.

Macan, T. H., & Foster, J. (2004). Managers' reactions to utility analysis and perceptions of what influences decisions. *Journal of Business and Psychology, 19*, 241–253.

Mento, A. J., Steel, R. P., & Karren, R. J. (1987). A meta-analytic study of the effects of goal setting on task performance: 1966 – 1984. *Organizational Behavior and Human Decision Process, 39*, 52–83.

Rauschenberger, J., & Schmidt, F. L. (1987). Application of utility analysis to personnel programs. *Journal of Business and Psychology, 2*, 50–59.

Richardson, M. W. (1944). The interpretation of a test validity coefficient in terms of increased efficiency of a selected group of personnel. *Psychometrika, 9*, 245–248

Schmidt, F. L. Hunter, J. E., McKenzie, R. C., & Muldrow, T. W. (1979). The impact of a valid selection procedures on work-force productivity. *Journal of Applied Psychology, 64*, 609–626.

Schmidt, F. L., Hunter, J. E., Outerbridge, A. M., & Trattner, M. H. (1986). The economic impact of job selection methods on the size, productivity, and payroll costs of the Federal work-force: An empirical demonstration. *Personnel Psychology, 39*, 1–29.

Schmidt, F. L., Hunter, J. E., & Pearlman, K. (1982). Assessing the economic impact of personnel programs on workforce productivity. *Personnel Psychology, 35*, 333–347.

Schmidt, F. L., Mack, M. J., & Hunter, J. E. (1984). Selection utility in the occupation of U.S. Park Ranger for three modes of test use. *Journal of Applied Psychology, 69*, 490–497.

Tubbs, M. E. (1986). Goal setting: A meta-analytic examination of the empirical evidence. *Journal of Applied Psychology, 71*, 474–483.

Whyte, G., & Latham, G. P. (1997). The futility of utility analysis revisited: When even an expert fails. *Personnel Psychology, 50*, 601–610.

Wood, R. E., Mento, A. J., & Locke, E. A. (1987). Task complexity as a moderator of goal effects: A meta analysis. *Journal of Applied Psychology, 72*, 416–425.

# 3 Stretch Goals

## Risks, Possibilities, and Best Practices

*Steve Kerr*  Provost Chancellor University

*Douglas LePelley*  Associate Professor of Business Nyack College;
Senior Director and Dean of Graduate Studies,
Chancellor University

In our roles as leaders, managers, and decision makers, we are all confronted with numerous choices. Among the most important of these pertains to the nature of the goals we establish. Specifically, whether setting goals for ourselves or for others, we may elect to set small, continuous-improvement goals; realistic but challenging goals; or goals that are so daunting that no methodology for achieving them currently exists.

> *Impossible only defines the degree of difficulty.*
> —Herb Brooks, coach of the 1980 US Olympic hockey team
> that upset a heavily favored Soviet team to win the gold medal

> *I won't let you down.*
> *There's no way you can.*
> — communication between Colonel Potter and
> Frank Burns, MASH TV show

A great deal of research has been conducted on the relative merits of assigned versus jointly determined goals, quantitative versus qualitative goals, short-term versus long-term goals, and other important components of the goal setting process. One of the most important choices to be made is the level of goal difficulty, which has been found in numerous studies to exert significant influence on employee attitudes and performance.

One of the most consistent findings concerning the level of goal difficulty is that when goals are set too low, people often achieve them, but subsequent motivation and energy levels typically flag, and the goals are usually not exceeded by very much. Compared to easy goals, difficult goals are far more likely to generate sustained enthusiasm and higher levels of performance. However, this finding comes with an important caveat, namely, that the goals, though difficult, must be seen to be achievable by those who are supposed to attain them. The logic behind this finding is nicely expressed by Locke and Latham, who point out that

> Nothing breeds succeeds like success. Conversely, nothing causes feelings of despair like perpetual failure. A primary purpose of goal setting is to increase the motivation level of the individual. But goal setting can have precisely the opposite effect if it produces a yardstick that constantly makes the individual feel inadequate.

Consequently, the supervisor must be on the lookout for unrealistic goals and be prepared to change them when necessary.

(Locke & Latham, 1984, p. 39)

Consistent with Locke and Latham's observation, considerable research shows that overly difficult goals can cause people to view them as ridiculous and not take them seriously, or alternatively, to work harder and harder until they eventually conclude that the goals cannot be attained, whereupon they become demoralized and disengage (c.f. Reinertsen, 2000; Choo, 2011).

Yet, in the face of such definitive research, and against all common sense, some organizations persist in intentionally constructing goals whose performance levels are so high that the great majority of attempts to achieve them invariably end in failure. These goals, called "stretch goals," will be the primary focus of this chapter.

## Definition, Purposes, and Potential Benefits of Stretch Goals

The notion that stretch goals have the potential to increase an organization's aspirations and subsequent performance has been around for a long time. In one of the most influential business books of the 1960s, Cyert and March noted that most organizational goals are influenced primarily by three factors: the organization's past goal, the organization's past performance, and the past performance of other "comparable" organizations (Cyert & March, 1963, p. 115). Obviously, conceiving goals in such a manner is unlikely to stimulate innovation or result in breakthrough ideas. The authors pointed out that by establishing goals that are less tied to the past, and by recognizing that there is an interaction between the level of the goals that are set and resultant employee behavior, "an organization can induce behavior designed to confirm its prediction (goal)" (Cyert & March, 1963, p. 112).

In their discussion of the implications of Cyert and March's work, Sitkin et al. noted that "by forcing a substantial elevation in collective aspirations, stretch goals can shift attention to possible new futures and perhaps spark increased energy. They thus can prompt exploratory learning through experimentation, innovation, broad research, or playfulness as organizational actors seek new or varied approaches to reach the target" (Sitkin, See, Miller, Lawless, & Carton, 2011, p. 545). However, on the basis of their review, Sitkin et al. asserted that the business literature has overweighted the successes attributed to stretch goals and underreported the cases where setting stretch goals turned out to have no effect or were counterproductive.

The concern expressed by Locke and Latham—that employees can easily become demoralized if they believe the goals set for them are unachievable—is especially relevant to the concept of stretch goals, because such goals are not accidental overreaches that the supervisor "must be on the lookout for," but are *intentionally* set at levels that are "seemingly unattainable with present resources, … and not currently seen as possible" (T&D Guru, 2011). Talk about potential frustration! At GE, Jack Welch used to tell his managers: "If you're making most of your stretch goals, all that tells me is that you aren't setting them high enough" (Welch, 1990–1991).

Why, then, if stretch goals have such high potential to create dysfunctional outcomes, did some of the supposedly best-managed, most people-oriented organizations in the1990s persist in using them? As a partial response to this question, let's consider just a few of the experiences and reported results from companies that made use of stretch goals during this period—starting with GE.

## Goal Setting at GE

Despite the attention paid to the topic by Cyert and March and others, the concept of stretch goals did not attract widespread attention until its adoption by GE's then CEO, Jack Welch. When Welch first assumed the chairmanship of GE in 1981, the company had a very traditional approach to the goal setting process and the goals that were set. In common with many other corporations at the time, GE taught its new managers to adhere to the "SMART" model when setting and evaluating their goals. As employed by GE, the acronym START was intended to serve as a reminder to the company's managers to set goals that were Specific, Measurable, Attainable, Results-Oriented, and Timely, so that they could be achieved in a maximum of three months (General Electric, 1984, pp. 132–133). As a way to ensure that goals were attainable, GE told its managers to use the following questions as guidelines: "Is the goal realistic? Is it feasible? Can it be completed within the time allowed with the available resources?" GE managers were also presented with an example of an "unattainable" goal—something that was *not* to be used in GE. The example they were given was "to have no absenteeism for one full year" (p. 132).

As a result of this advice, GE's goals were primarily influenced by the same three elements that, according to Cyert and March (1963), so may other organizations depended on: the organization's past goal, the organization's past performance, and the past performance of other "comparable" organizations. Not surprisingly, setting goals in this manner failed to consistently generate the out-of-the-box thinking and breakthrough results that Welch felt were needed to attain or maintain GE's position as #1 or #2 in every market the company served.

For this and other reasons, by the early 1990s Welch had become very interested in some of the concepts and techniques of Japanese-style management. In particular, GE began to make extensive use of employee empowerment (called "Work-Out" in GE), continuous improvement (operationalized in GE as "finding a better way every day"), Six Sigma, and what Welch referred to as the "bullet train" method of goal setting. To underscore the importance of "bullet train thinking" in his discussions with his managers, he would often cite the following example:

> It used to take more than six hours to travel by train from Tokyo to Osaka. If the Japanese executives had said to their engineers "I want you to reduce the time to six hours," the engineers would have instinctively thought in terms of small improvements, perhaps in the way they boarded passengers and unloaded baggage. But instead, the Japanese executives set out a challenge to reduce the time of the journey to three and a half hours. Faced with such an "impossible" goal, the engineers and designers were forced to reexamine the most fundamental assumptions governing rail travel in Japan. The result of this reexamination was the bullet train.
>
> (Welch, 1990–1991)

To Welch, stretch goals were the mechanism through which he could use bullet train thinking, with all its attendant creativity, longer-term focus, and sense of daring, to fundamentally alter GE's business processes, thus permitting the company to better compete with its Asian and best American competitors. By using stretch goals as a supplement (Welch might say antidote) to GE's traditional goal setting and budgetary processes, he hoped to expand the unconscious upper limits he believed his managers were placing on productivity gains, quality improvements, cycle time reductions, inventory turns, and customer satisfaction. The ultimate purpose of stretch goals, he said, was "to reinvent how we do work" (Bartlett, 1999).

Well before the use of stretch goals became widespread in GE, Welch required that his most senior business leaders present updated results in a number of areas at each quarterly meeting of his Corporate Executive Council (CEC). These results were of three kinds:

1. Metrics that were considered to be permanent, critical indicators of the health and success of the company, and were equally pertinent to such widely different businesses as power systems, appliances, television, lighting, and financial services. Operating margin, earnings growth, market share, and indicators of customer satisfaction are examples of metrics that were considered to be common to all businesses and immutable over time.
2. Metrics to track the progress of the company's "initiatives." These were considered to be applicable to every business, but were centrally tracked and reported at the CEC meetings for a limited period (typically 2–3 years), after which they were entrusted to the business leaders for monitoring and control. Among the most important initiatives during Welch's years at the helm of GE were Work-Out, CAP (the Change Acceleration Process), and Six Sigma.
3. Metrics that were considered to be permanent indicators of a business's stability and growth, but were particular to one business or set of businesses. Examples of this kind include inventory turns, TV ratings, loan defaults, and cycle time.

As the use of stretch goals became increasingly prevalent in GE, they began to exert influence over all three types of metrics. *It is worth emphasizing that they were not employed as substitutes for the "regular" goals that GE managers absolutely had to meet, or risk losing their jobs. Rather, the stretch goals were intended to catalyze creative thinking and stimulate unconventional solutions.* It could be argued that, in Welch's mind, GE's traditional goal setting process would bring about high performance today, while the stretch goals were for the purpose of ensuring high performance tomorrow.

An early example of Welch's use of stretch goals was to announce to his managers that the new yardstick for return on equity (ROE), which he was certain they could achieve, was 20%. When he made that statement, GE's ROE had already risen to a remarkable 18.7%, compared to an industry norm of 13.2%. Although Welch himself might have been confident that such performance was achievable, to most of his managers, a 20% ROE in a company as highly diversified as GE seemed impossible (*The Economist*, 2011).

Many of GE's stretch goals pertained to increasing the quality of the company's products and services, and were expressed and quantified in Six Sigma terminology

(Harry & Schroeder, 2005). Welch observed at the time that "it is the struggle to meet stretch goals that helped US companies become world-class competitors again" (Litvan, 1997, p. A-1). GE managers rose to the challenge—surprising themselves in the process—and accomplished a high enough percentage of the established stretch goals so that, in Six Sigma quality initiatives alone, GE produced savings of $12 billion between 1996 and 2000 (Litvan, 1997). According to *The Economist* (2011), what Jack Welch and GE leaders learned from these early experiences was not to put any boundaries on productivity gains, quality improvements, or increases in market share. They concluded that if the right environment was created for the group, setting stretch goals and working toward what might seem to be impossible results often became reality.

During this period, a number of other organizations were also experiencing positive results from their stretch goal efforts. For example, in 1988, Commonwealth Health Corporation (CHC) formed a partnership with GE to improve their organization in a similar manner to what Welch accomplished in GE. As part of the process, CHC introduced their employees to various Six Sigma techniques, and established stretch goals in each of the following categories: customer satisfaction, timeliness of care, speed of care, convenience, quality of care/service, and overall cost. Beyond realizing improvements in each of these areas, by employing stretch goals in combination with Six Sigma, a culture of seeking significant improvement became a way of life at CHC. According to the company's calculations, $900,000 was invested in the first year of the stretch goal program and resulting Six Sigma projects. The first year payback was $3 million, which grew to $7 million after Year 2 (Thomerson, 2002). In reviewing the results of the program, Commonwealth's CEO John Desmarais noted: "It is amazing, the use of stretch goals and Six Sigma. It is just a different way to look at things" (Thomerson, 2002, p. 297).

Another company that was an early adopter of stretch goals, and had great success in applying the stretch goals concept to their Six Sigma quality initiatives, was Toyota Motors. From 1997 to 2001, Toyota employed stretch goals to induce their employees to look deeply into the underlying reasons behind the company's high supply chain, distribution, and inventory costs. Rather than setting specific improvement goals in these areas, Toyota leadership challenged their employees to "dream big." By their own calculations, the company realized more than $100 million in cost savings in these areas within two years (Oxnard, 2004).

For more recent examples of organizations that have enjoyed great success by employing stretch goals, see Simkin et al. (pp. 545–546). However, keep in mind Simkin et al.'s assertion that stretch goals are, in their view, equally likely to induce negative reactions on the part of employees.

## Potential Difficulties and Disadvantages of Stretch Goals

Up to this point we have noted that goals that are viewed as impossibly difficult may be dismissed as naïve or absurd, and simply ignored. If, instead, a stretch goal is taken seriously, employees may expend so much time and energy trying to meet it that they burn out in the attempt. If they do stay the course, experiencing continual failures may generate reduced self-confidence, and cause employees to become alienated from the organization.

## Negative Effects of Stretch Goals on Thoughts and Emotions

Consistent with this latter argument, some theorists and researchers have argued that the creation of stretch goals can be emotionally harmful to many employees. Recent neuroscience research shows that the brain works in a protective way, such that any goals that require substantial behavioral change or thinking-pattern change will automatically be resisted. The brain is wired to avoid pain or discomfort, including fear. Fear of failure initiates a desire to return to known, comfortable behavior and thought patterns. According to this line of reasoning, the best way to initiate changes that the human brain will support is via small and incremental improvements, accompanied by positive reinforcement (Williams, 2010).

Researchers have also observed that the psychological manifestations of not achieving goals may well be more damaging than would result from not having any goals at all. When people fail to attain something that they want and work for, their brains' nervous systems often trigger strong negative emotions. Since the goal setting metrics of many organizations effectively create an either-or polarity of success, whereby goals are viewed as either met (via 100% attainment) or missed, and since stretch goals are set at levels that make 100% attainment very unlikely, the process virtually ensures that organization members will experience a loss of self-confidence and other negative emotions (Williams, 2011).

## Adverse Impact of Stretch Goals on Work–Life Balance

A relatively obvious problem with stretch goals is that they are difficult to reconcile with the pursuit of work–life balance. If stretch goals are only utilized occasionally, for specified, limited periods, this may not be a big issue. However, in organizations that employ them on an ongoing basis, employees may be required to make fundamental choices between their work and home lives. In a 1995 *Fortune* interview, Steve Kerr, who was running GE-Crotonvillle at a time when numerous organizations were studying and seeking to copy GE's approach to stretch goals, observed that "it's popular for companies today to ask their people to double sales or increase speed to market threefold. But then they don't provide their people with the knowledge, tools, and means to meet such ambitious goals .... To meet stretch targets, people use the only resource that's not constrained, which is their personal time" (Sherman, 1995, p. 231).

In his book W*inning,* Jack Welch admitted to practicing "do as I say, not as I did" by coming out strongly in favor of work–life balance (Welch, 2005, p. 313). However, Welch went on to say that "your boss's top priority is competitiveness. Of course, he wants you to be happy, but only inasmuch as it helps the company win. In fact, if he is doing his job right, he is making your job so exciting that your personal life becomes a less compelling draw" (p. 316). Welch then described three "successful" work–life balancing acts during his days in GE, but in two cases the balance was achieved by the employee turning down big promotions, and in the third case the employee "balanced" his work and home lives by coming in very early every morning and not leaving until six pm. A skeptic might point out that these are not really examples of a balanced solution (except perhaps over a period of years), since in each case, the time and energy invested in the employee's career or home life came at the expense of the other.

*Technical Shortcomings of Stretch Goals*

Perhaps the most articulate spokesperson for this line of argument is Harry Levinson, who has long argued, with some empirical support, that to be effective, goals should be (a) team versus individually focused and (b) set by the group and/or by the employee and the manager jointly, but never solely by the manager (Levinson, 2003). With respect to the need for goals to be team focused, Levinson noted that:

> Most job descriptions are limited to what employees *do* in their work …. The more employees' effectiveness depends on what other people do, the less any one employee can be held responsible for the outcome of individual efforts …. The reason for having an organization is to achieve more together than each could alone. Why, then, emphasize and reward individual performance alone, based on static job descriptions?
>
> (Levinson, 2003, pp. 78 and 91)

Levinson's assertion that goals must be established with extensive employee involvement stems from his conviction that the most useful performance feedback comes from peers, in part because higher management will invariably be unaware of structural impediments and other significant barriers to achievement. Lacking such knowledge, attempts by one's boss to establish goals, and to assess and provide feedback about goal performance, are likely to generate employee cynicism. One of the implications of Levinson's ideas for stretch goals is that, since they are typically set by higher management with little or no input from those who have to achieve them, they are unlikely to generate feelings of employee ownership or buy-in.

Taken as a whole, the concerns about stretch goals articulated above are substantial, and are buttressed by theory, research, and common sense. They are, however, primarily criticisms of stretch goals *as they are typically conceived and employed*, rather than constituting inherent flaws that cannot be prevented or remedied. In the remainder of this chapter, we shall discuss a few ideas, already in use, for mitigating these concerns and making stretch goals more effective.

## Improving the Effectiveness of Stretch Goals

*Preserving Employees' Self-Esteem*

One of the most serious charges levied against stretch goals is that they are typically constructed within systems that measure employee performance in terms of goal attainment, but are set at levels that make goal attainment exceptionally difficult. Consequently, stretch goals tend to produce adverse physiological effects in people's brains and nervous systems, resulting in a variety of negative psychological consequences, including feelings of inadequacy and loss of self-esteem.

The truth and severity of these charges is undeniable, but remedies are available, and were successfully applied in a number of organizations. In GE, for example, it became evident very soon after the introduction of stretch goals that the company's usual (harsh) reaction to missed targets would be not only unfair, but unproductive. Consequently, a new set of metrics began to be taught to all GE managers, and became a part of the business reviews. These metrics were designed to replace the "goals met/goals missed" either-or mentality discussed earlier in this chapter. They were built around a mantra that was created as a guide to be employed when assessing performance against the company's stretch goals. The mantra said: "Don't punish failure."

Instead of asking whether an employee's stretch goals were made or missed, GE managers were asked to consider the following three questions:

- Has meaningful progress been made toward the stretch goal?
- How well are we doing in that area, as compared to our competitors?
- (Most subjective, but most important): What effect has the stretch goal had upon performance? That is, how does our performance compare to what it would have been had we not established a stretch goal in that area? Through the use of these metrics, GE was able to expand its use of stretch goals, while continuing to recognize, reward, and build the self-esteem of its high performers, thus preserving the essential elements of the company's pay-for-performance culture (Kerr & Landauer, 2004).

However, there is a caveat that accompanies employment of the mantra "don't punish failure." It is this: The mantra is only feasible when the stretch goals you set are well above the level of performance you must achieve to satisfy one of your stakeholders. If, for example, a new government regulation requires you to make substantial alterations to your company's financial reporting systems, or take immediate actions to improve product safety, "not punishing failure" is a luxury you can't afford. In such cases, it is essential that goals be set that at least minimally meet your stakeholders' requirements, and it may well be a good idea to let people know that in this case failure will, in fact, be punished—if not by you, then surely by the government. Since, by definition, any aspect of your business that is given special emphasis by your stakeholders is one in which you want to excel, it may make good sense for you to establish stretch goals in these areas as well, but these stretch goals cannot act as substitutes for goals that absolutely must be met.

### Recognizing Interdependencies and Permitting Involvement

The process of establishing goals, including stretch goals, has also been indicted for failing to recognize how interdependent most employees are upon one another, and for denying meaningful influence into the process by peers and subordinates. These flaws do exist, but are not inherent in the process.

By way of illustration, soon after initiating stretch goals in GE, it became apparent that decisions needed to be made regarding how one division or department should react when another department established stretch goals that affected both of them. For example, the regional offices in many GE businesses were induced to establish sales goals that went well beyond what had ever been done before. This posed a ticklish problem for Manufacturing. Should they reconfigure their plants and accumulate raw materials in anticipation of these sales materializing? If Manufacturing didn't do this, wouldn't they be inadvertently sabotaging whatever chance Sales had to meet their targets? On the other hand, if Manufacturing *did* increase production and the hoped-for sales didn't materialize, shouldn't the added manufacturing costs be transferred to someone else's budget—to Sales, perhaps, for failing to meet their goals, or to GE's executive office, which had caused the $#%#!! stretch goals to be set in the first place? And if the added manufacturing costs (and for that matter, the added costs incurred by the regional sales offices because of the stretch goals) were *not* transferred to the executive office, wouldn't that be a violation of the company's commitment to not punishing failure? (Kerr & Landauer, 2004).

As is so often the case, once these problems surfaced and were declared politically acceptable to talk about, the resolution was fairly straightforward, and turned out to be consistent with Levinson's recommendations (given that the stretch goals still came from Welch). Norms were developed, and mechanisms established, to require and permit regular interactions among all the parties who would be affected by a particular stretch goal. While admittedly not given equal weight, when future stretch goals were set by Welch, all the affected parties were informed and given an opportunity to voice their concerns and opinions before the goals were implemented.

## Conclusion

In this chapter, we have tried to present an objective overview of the concept of stretch goals. Our personal view is that the criticisms of stretch goals are fair and accurate, but in the main, they describe weaknesses in the way that stretch goals (indeed, goals in general) are typically conceived and implemented. Awareness of these weaknesses is a vital precursor to using them but should not be a deterrent.

There's an old saying that "if you do what you've always done, you'll get what you've always gotten." While the risks of using stretch goals on a widespread basis in an organization are real, so are the risks of not doing so. Most of us do not have readily available alternatives that promote risk taking, catalyze innovation, and stimulate people to come up with startlingly different ways to get things done. For all their risks and flaws, there is abundant evidence that, in a wide variety of circumstances, stretch goals have been successful at achieving such results.

In this regard, Jack Welch's own conclusion about his company's experiences with stretch goals bears repeating. He said "we have found that by reaching for what appears to be impossible, we often actually do the impossible; and even when we don't quite make it, we inevitably wind up doing much better than we would have done" (Subhnij, 2008).

Beyond the specific deliverables due to particular stretch goals, a wider point also seems worth making:

> Whatever their magnitude, the specific quantities of the goals that are set invariably turn out to be less important than the conversations, energy, and activities they stimulate The immediate purpose of stretch goals in GE was to try to achieve the designated targets (without punishing failure), but the broader purpose was to get employees to conceive of their jobs and perform their tasks in fundamentally different and innovative ways. The message that GE was trying to convey was that most people typically access only a small portion of their creative energy—that most people have a huge capacity to do things quicker, better, and cheaper.
>
> (Kerr & Landauer, p. 136)

## Appendix: A Neat Illustration of the Potential Power of Stretch Goals

Among the numerous events sponsored by GE-Crotonville in the 1990s were a series of "innovation days." At one of these events, one of the consultants staged a demonstration in which he gave a team of six or seven people an orange and told them that each person had to touch the orange, but only one at a time. He said that they could throw it to each other or do anything else they wanted, but the orange had to end up in the hands of the person who touched it first.

The team started throwing the orange back and forth, and the consultant timed it. The first time they did it in about nine seconds. When asked to improve, they stood a little closer, threw a little faster, and got it down to about seven seconds.

Then the consultant told them: "Many groups do this in less than a second, and it's possible to do it in less than half a second." After a short planning session, the team did it in less than a second, by stacking their hands. The person with the orange dropped it. It went *swoosh* through everybody's hands, and the first person caught it at the bottom (Kerr, 1997).

## References

Bartlett, C. A. 1999. *GE compilations: Jack Welch 1981–1999*. Video, Harvard Business School, Boston.

Choo, A. S. Impact of a stretch strategy on knowledge creation in quality improvement projects. *IEEE Transactions on Engineering Management*, February 2011, Vol. 58, Issue 1, pg. 87–96.

Cyert, R. M., & March, J. G. *A behavioral theory of the firm*. Englewood Cliffs, NJ: Prentice-Hall, 1963. The Economist. A work-out for corporate America. *Academic OneFile*. Web. June 28, 2011.

General Electric. *New Manager's Manual*. GE Company, 1984.

Harry, M., & Schroeder, R. *Six Sigma: The breakthrough management strategy revolutionizing the world's top corporations*. Doubleday: NY, 2005.

Kerr, S. *Ultimate Rewards: What Really Motivates People to Achieve.*, Boston, MA: Harvard Business School Press, 1997.

Kerr, S., & Landauer, S. Using stretch goals to promote organizational effectiveness and personal growth: general electric and Goldman Sachs. *Academy of Management Executive*, 2004. Vol. 18, No. 4.

Levinson, H. Management by whose objectives? *Harvard Business Review*, January 2003.

Litvan, L.M. Leaders & success General Electric's Jack Welch. *Investors Daily*. Los Angeles: August 20, 1997.

Locke, E. A., Latham, G. P. *Goal setting: A motivational technique that works*. Englewood Cliffs, NJ: Prentice Hall, 1984.

Oxnard, T. Stretch: How Toyota reaches for big goals. *Supply Chain Management Review*, March 2004.

Reinertsen, D. The design factory. Drastic stretch goals can do more harm than good. *Electronic Design*. June 12, 2000.

Sherman, S. Stretch goals: The dark side of asking for miracles. *Fortune*, November 13, 1995.

Sitkin, S. B., See, K. E., Miller, C. C., Lawless, M. W., & Carton, A. M. The paradox of stretch goals: Organizations in pursuit of the seemingly impossible. *Academy of Management Review*, 2011, Vol. 36, No. 3, 544–566, 22 pgs.

Subhnji, T. Winning the new-generation workforce. *Bangkok Post*. Bangkok: May 16, 2008.

Thomerson, L. D. Six Sigma intensified—is 99% good enough? *Annual Quality Congress Proceedings.* Milwaukee: 2002.

T&D Guru. Monkey business. *Training and Development in Australia.* Surry Hills: Apr 2011. Vol. 38, Issue 2; pg. 25, 1pg. www.1000ventures.com/business_guide/goals_stretch.html/

Welch, J. F. *Lectures at GE-Crotonville*, 1990–91, unpublished.

Welch, J. F. *Winning.* New York: Harper Business, 2005.

Williams, R. Why "stretch" goals are a waste of time. *Financial Post*, FP Entrepreneur blog, August 26, 2010.

Williams, R. Why goal setting doesn't work. *Psychology Today*, Wired for Success blog, April 11, 2011.

# Part II
# Mediators and Moderators

# 4 Attributions and Emotions as Mediators and/or Moderators in the Goal-Striving Process

*Marion B. Eberly* Milgard School of Business, University of Washington

*Dong Liu* Ernest Scheller Jr. College of Business, Georgia Institute of Technology

*Terence R. Mitchell and Thomas W. Lee* Foster School of Business, University of Washington

## Introduction

Understanding under what circumstances employees are motivated to perform desired work-related activities targeted at meeting organizational objectives is often considered critical to maximizing organizational performance, meeting strategic goals, and satisfying employees' needs (Mitchell & Daniels, 2003). Accordingly, work motivation has continued to be a heated research topic examined by countless researchers and practitioners alike (Latham, 2007; Latham & Pinder, 2005; Locke, 2004; Locke & Latham, 2004). While traditional goal setting research examining direction, intensity, persistence, and task strategies as goal mechanisms has provided compelling insights into the motivational dynamics underlying the effectiveness of goals (Locke & Latham, 1990, 2002, 2006), these mechanisms do not fully capture the complexities of reactions involved during the goal-striving and recalibration phases of the self-regulation process (Diefendorff & Lord, 2008; Gollwitzer, 1990). For example, while initial goal choice (and the subsequent initial goal–performance discrepancy) generally motivates effort and persistence, employees may choose to withdraw this effort upon gathering performance feedback that makes them realize that they have not met the goal and expect to not meet it in the future either (e.g., Cooper, 2007; Venables & Fairclough, 2009). There are cognitive and emotional reactions, which may explain both dedication to the original goal and goal abandonment. To solve part of this complex riddle, researchers increasingly attempt to explain goal-striving dynamics from an attributional perspective (Mitchell, Harman, Lee, & Lee, 2008).

Attributions often follow the receipt of feedback, especially when such feedback is negative or unexpected (Weiner, 1990; Weiner & Graham, 1999). Due to the influence of attributions on motivated action and their close link with success and failure expectancies, attribution theory may be particularly suitable for delineating individuals' nuanced reactions to goal–performance discrepancies (Weiner, 1985). Attribution theory has not been fully incorporated into organizational motivation theory, especially the self-regulation literature, although it has the potential to explain a wide range of human behavior associated with goals (Latham, 2007; Locke & Latham, 2004; Martinko, Harvey, & Dasborough, 2011). Hence, one purpose of our chapter is to depict the attributional contingencies that may explain under what circumstances people choose to devote additional effort to a goal or reduce their effort and ultimately withdraw.

In addition to identifying the attributional contingencies, another purpose of this research is to elaborate on the emotional dynamics inherent in the goal-striving process. Attribution research in general has shown that attributions and emotions are often intertwined and that affective reactions may mediate the relationship between attributions and behaviors (Weiner, 1985). Moreover, emotions have long been credited with having motivational properties, and researchers are calling for an increased integration of emotion and motivation theory (e.g., Erez & Isen, 2002; Ilies, Judge, & Wagner, 2010). Building on the extant literature on goals, attributions, and emotions, Figure 4.1 depicts the relationships described in this chapter and shows the process through which goal-performance discrepancies translate into goal revision. Specifically, the focus is on how goal–performance discrepancies and attributions interactively influence emotions and then self-efficacy, which in turn affect goal revision.

We approach this chapter in the following way. First, we offer an overview of the traditional mechanisms through which goals translate into performance with an emphasis on direction, intensity, and persistence (for details on task strategies as the fourth mechanism, see Chapter 7) in order to underscore the importance of investigating the contingent role of attributions. Second, we follow with an explanation of the range of attributions individuals make in response to goal–performance discrepancies. We summarize the existing empirical research demonstrating how these attributional reactions moderate the relationships between goal–performance discrepancies and goal striving. Here, we primarily focus on negative goal–performance discrepancies, because they are more likely to trigger attributional processing (Weiner & Graham, 1999). Third, we expand our discussion by describing the role of goal strivers' emotions in the motivational process. Finally, we conclude this chapter with a discussion on how attribution theory may inform other critical elements of the self-regulation process such as multiple goal pursuit and team-level goals.

Our model (Figure 4.1) is not intended to be complete or all-inclusive, but rather focuses on those elements and relationships that have only recently been added to self-regulation frameworks and have been tested empirically (i.e., attributions and emotions). And while we emphasize the importance of emotions in explaining how goal–performance discrepancies ultimately link to goal revision, we do not mean to suggest that emotions are the most critical mechanism. Goal–performance discrepancies clearly can operate via other mechanisms or have direct effects on self-efficacy and goal revision.[1]

## Traditional Goal Mechanisms

How exactly do goals translate into employee performance? Goal setting theory has traditionally emphasized three action-oriented mechanisms through which goals (and the associated goal–performance discrepancies) positively influence employee performance: direction, effort, and persistence (Locke & Latham, 1990). First, goals direct individuals' attention to goal-relevant activities and away from goal-irrelevant activities. Goals clarify what tasks need to be performed and hence direct focus toward them. Individuals cognitively and behaviorally pay more attention to a task that is associated with a goal than to a task that is not associated with a goal. Through a series of six studies where

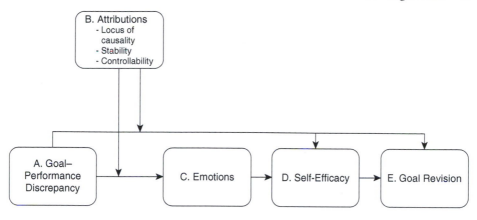

*Figure 4.1* The influence of attributions and emotions in the goal-striving process.

goals were either consciously generated by study participants or subconsciously primed, Shah, Friedman, and Kruglanski (2002) provided support for this goal-shielding effect and showed that the activation of certain goals inhibits the accessibility of alternative goals. In one of the studies, they also demonstrated that such goal shielding had positive effects on persistence and actual task performance. Johnson, Chang, and Lord (2006), in a recent meta-analysis, demonstrated that following goal choice, goal-relevant knowledge structures are automatically activated while irrelevant knowledge structures are simultaneously inhibited. When setting a goal, individuals may therefore quickly access relevant information and focus on their goal without cognitive interference or distractions.

Second, goals energize and generate effort toward goal accomplishment. The higher the goal, the more the effort exerted. Venables and Fairclough (2009), for instance, demonstrated that participants who received false negative feedback on a repeated-trial task attempted to make up for their perceived failure by investing higher levels of mental effort as evaluated via physiological measures. However, when these compensatory effects do not suffice to reach desired goals, they are likely going to diminish over time, eventually leading to effort withdrawal and goal abandonment. Venables and Fairclough (2009), for example, noticed that mental effort during the *latter* phase of the task trial declined for participants who received negative feedback, suggesting that they may have ultimately withdrawn completely had the task continued. Similarly, Cooper (2007) found that individuals with a difficult goal only continued to perform well when they received positive feedback. When faced with negative feedback, individuals with difficult goals quickly deteriorated in their performance.

This latter research highlights the fact that people receive feedback on their progress, and this feedback allows them to determine a discrepancy between their current standing and obtaining the goal. Interestingly, research generally has shown that the relationship between goal–performance discrepancies and effort and subsequent performance is nonlinear. Large negative discrepancies may lead to a withdrawal of effort when individuals are discouraged and perceive low likelihood of future goal attainment (Carver & Scheier, 1998). Further, research has revealed that individuals may not only react to negative goal–performance discrepancies by attempting to adjust their performance to match their goal, but also by adjusting their goal to match their performance (goal revision [Box E in Figure 4.1]; Donovan & Williams, 2003; Tolli & Schmidt, 2008). Goals are hardly ever static in nature. They are frequently changed as a function of past performance, success expectancies, and the availability of resources (Carver & Scheier, 2000; Kanfer, Chen, & Pritchard, 2008). These complexities may not be fully captured by the three traditional goal mechanisms. The interpretation of and reaction to discrepancies are major causes of continued goal pursuit. Thus, to understand exactly why and when people continue to pursue or revise their goals, Locke and Latham (2004) urged future motivation research to explicitly incorporate attribution theory. Below, we highlight the empirical research that has begun to describe the attributional processes underlying goal striving and recalibration.

## Attributional Dynamics in Goal Striving

According to attribution theory, people like to make sense of their surroundings by acting as naïve psychologists (Heider, 1958). When confronted with certain events, people often seek to determine and understand their causes. For instance, in the organizational context one might ask, "Why did I get passed over for promotion?" or "Why did my boss criticize me for my work on this project?" (e.g., Martinko, Douglas, & Harvey, 2006). Through the use of attributions, people attempt to (re)establish control over their lives and improve their ability to predict future events (Kelley, 1971; Thibaut & Walker, 1975). As research on attribution theory has demonstrated, attributions for performance can significantly influence individuals' affective, cognitive, and behavioral reactions to feedback and hence determine motivation levels post-feedback (Lam, Huang, & Snape, 2007). Attribution theory is therefore a particularly compelling theory within the context of goal striving, where feedback is sought, interpreted, and reacted to. When individuals fail to reach their goals or discover negative goal–performance discrepancies, attributional processes are usually triggered. The human desire to understand the underlying causes of events (e.g., missed goals) is particularly pronounced when the events are negative, novel, or unexpected (Weiner, 1990; Weiner & Graham, 1999). When individuals face negative goal–performance discrepancies, they will likely consider the reasons why they are behind, which systematically determines their subsequent behaviors. Attributions therefore are an important motivational mechanism that may explain under what circumstances individuals persist in goal pursuit or adjust their goal levels.[2]

## The Moderating Role of Attributions in the Goal-Striving Process

The above discussion makes it clear that the causes for events may be classified along multiple dimensions, which in turn influence individuals' expectancies for future success (Martinko et al., 2006). Attribution research suggests that in answering questions as to why an event occurred, people distinguish between (1) internal (self) and external (outside of self) explanations, (2) stable and unstable explanations (whether or not the cause persists over time), and (3) controllable or uncontrollable explanations (whether or not the cause is under the person's control [Heider, 1958; Kelley, 1967]).

Individuals' attributions about their goal pursuit failures or successes may determine their motivational and behavioral reactions through their influence on future success expectancies. As Weiner and colleagues have argued (Weiner, 1986; Weiner, Frieze, Kukla, Reed, Rest, & Rosenbaum, 1971), attributions about causes of performance moderate the relationship between performance outcomes and individuals' reactions such as self-efficacy (Box D) and goal revision (Box E). Following this logic, motivation researchers have increasingly conceptualized and tested the influence of the attributional dimensions (box B) on reactions to goal–performance discrepancies.

*Locus of Causality.* Empirical research demonstrates that reactions to negative goal–performance discrepancies vary as a function of whether one blames oneself for the discrepancy (internal attribution) or something outside the self (external attribution [e.g., peers, context]). Silver, Mitchell, and Gist (1995) showed that internal attributions for past successes were positively related to post-task self-efficacy, whereas internal attributions for past failures were negatively related to post-task self-efficacy. Due to self-efficacy's link to individual's personal goal levels and performance (e.g., Stajkovic & Luthans, 1998), causal attributions may ultimately determine, in conjunction with goal-performance discrepancies, whether individuals choose to leave their goal level unchanged or revise their goal downward. Tolli and Schmidt (2008), in an extension of this previous work, demonstrated exactly that; in their study, individuals who attributed failure to internal causes felt less self-efficacious, which in turn led them to revise their goals downward. Locus of causality attributions moderated the relationship between feedback and goal revision, and the effect was mediated by self-efficacy.

*Stability.* When individuals perceive the cause of the failure or negative goal–performance discrepancy to be stable and thus likely to remain the same in the future, they will likely expect the outcome (i.e., failure to reach their goal) to recur. Thus, individuals' expectations for future success will be lower and likely lead to a downward revision of the goal. For example, if an employee believes that being behind schedule on a project is due to a lack of ability and believes that such a lack of ability is not going to change over time (i.e., it is stable), the employee is likely to expect to not reach a similar goal in the future, and will therefore be motivated to adjust the goal downward. On the other hand, if the employee believes that the primary cause for failure is a lack of effort, this person may expect to reach the same goal in the future, because effort can be strengthened over time. This employee may therefore choose not to revise the goal downward. Empirical research provides consistent support for this logic.

Using samples of exam-taking students, Mone and Baker (1992) and Thomas and Mathieu (1994) showed that the relationship between goal attainment and positive self-efficacy change was strongest among those students who perceived the cause of their exam success to be stable. Although not measured in this particular study, this increase in self-efficacy may have translated into an upward revision of goals, as demonstrated by Donovan and Williams (2003) and Tolli and Schmidt (2008). In an earlier study, Donovan and Williams (1996) found that recreational cross-country runners were more likely to set easier goals following goal failure when they attributed their performance to stable causes. Corroborating this finding, Williams, Donovan, and Dodge (2000) documented in a sample of varsity track and field athletes that the negative relationship between goal–performance discrepancy and goal change was significant only for those athletes who perceived their performance to be a function of stable causes. Finally, in a study that tracked varsity-level college track and field athletes over the course of an 8-week competitive season, Donovan and Williams (2003) reported that goal revision was a function of both the direction and the magnitude of the goal–performance discrepancy. Specifically, when individuals encountered a negative discrepancy, they were likely to revise their goal downward in proportion to the magnitude of the discrepancy. Goal revision was greatest when individuals perceived the cause for their failure to be stable over time (see Chapter 24 on goals and sports).

*Controllability.* Similar to the stability dimension, if people believe that causes for failure are controllable, they will probably continue or renew their effort and commitment to their original goal, but be less likely to do so if the cause of a negative discrepancy or failure is perceived to be due to uncontrollable causes (Weiner, 1990). However, empirical research using the controllability dimension of attributions in the context of goal striving is rather limited. Jackson, Hall, Rowe, and Daniels (2009) conducted a study with students who had just completed unsuccessful employment interviews. Half of the students were randomly assigned to receive an attributional retraining where they were taught to perceive the causes of their past interview performance as controllable. Results revealed that students who underwent the attributional retraining increased their attributions for poor interview performance to their effort: a factor that is under their personal control. These controllable attributions in turn positively influenced students' feelings of regret, making it more likely that they stayed committed to the goal and increased their efforts to be successful during the interviewing process.

## Emotional Dynamics in Goal Striving

Clearly, feedback about the attainment or nonattainment of goals triggers attributional processes. In addition, there is evidence for affective reactions in individuals (Box C), which in turn also affect individuals' motivation, cognition, and behavior. The affective system plays a critical self-regulatory role as it can quickly interrupt and reorient individuals to focus their attention on what is most important at the moment. The motivational account of emotions proposes that emotions evoke behavioral impulses such as approach and avoidance, and therefore directly influence motivated behavior. But due to the cognitive nature of many motivational constructs, affect has only recently come to the forefront of motivation research (Richard & Diefendorff, 2011) and has recently been shown to play a critical role in understanding goal-oriented behavior (Brown & McConnell, 2011; Seo, Bartunek, & Barrett, 2010). An attributional model of goal striving is therefore not complete without considering the affective dynamics involved in resource allocation and goal revision decisions. We contend that attributional processes may influence emotions, which in turn may shape motivation-critical cognitions such as self-efficacy judgments.

At the most basic level, goals serve as standards by which to judge one's achievements and should therefore influence one's satisfaction levels (Locke & Latham, 1990). Generally, it has been shown that positive goal–performance discrepancies lead to satisfaction, whereas negative goal–performance discrepancies lead to dissatisfaction (Cron, Slocum, VandeWalle, & Fu, 2005; Ilies & Judge, 2005; Ilies et al., 2010). Early on, attribution researchers proposed and demonstrated that distinct attributions can lead to discrete affective reactions (e.g., Weiner, Russell, & Lerman, 1978, 1979), which in turn may drive distinct behavioral and motivational tendencies.

The positive or negative sign of the feedback or goal-performance discrepancy likely triggers immediate general positive or negative emotional reactions. This primary emotional appraisal, which happens fairly quickly and automatically (Locke, 2009; Smith, Haynes, Lazarus, & Pope, 1993), is followed by a more elaborate secondary appraisal where a cognitive analysis of the situation occurs (Frijda, 1993). It is during this secondary appraisal that the attributional process is initiated (Smith & Kirby, 2001; Weiner, 1985), which ultimately determines the specific emotional reaction (i.e., guilty or angry, proud or grateful). Because discrete emotions of the same valence may have very different consequences, it is critical to understand how attributions influence specific emotional reactions (Gooty, Gavin, & Ashkanasy, 2009). Thus, to fully understand the emotional dynamics of goal striving, an examination of the differential effects of discrete emotions following attributional processing is imperative.

In general, attribution research has demonstrated that individuals' perceptions of the locus of causality, stability, and controllability of causes systematically influence individuals' specific affective reactions. For instance, in a study examining students' reactions to goal achievement on two exams over the period of a semester, Thomas and Mathieu (1994) documented that students' locus of causality attributions in response to receiving their exam grades moderated their affective reactions. Specifically, students who attributed goal attainment to internal causes were more satisfied with their success than students who attributed goal attainment to external causes. Jackson and colleagues (2009) showed that attributing failures to controllable causes feelings of regret. Tracy and Robins (2006) found that internal attributions for failure were generally positively related to feelings of guilt and shame. When the internal attribution was stable or uncontrollable (e.g., ability), individuals tended to feel shame. When the internal attribution was unstable or controllable (e.g., effort), individuals tended to feel guilt. Other research has similarly shown that internal attributions for failure elicit feelings of shame and guilt, especially when the cause is also perceived as stable (Hareli & Hess, 2008; Turner, Husman, & Schallert, 2002). Van Overwalle, Mervielde, and De Schuyter (1995) documented that guilt may only arise when the attribution is internal and controllable, whereas shame may be independent of a controllability judgment.

Attributions about negative goal discrepancies may also influence other emotions beyond guilt and shame. For example, internal, stable, uncontrollable attributions for failure are associated with negative emotions such as helplessness and anxiety (Campbell & Martinko, 1998). In a scenario study examining students' reactions to outcomes on a project that was completed collaboratively with another student, students reported feeling more guilty if they made an internal, controllable attribution, whereas they reported feeling more angry with their partner if they made an external, controllable attribution (Peterson & Schreiber, 2006). In an examination of self-discrepancies (discrepancies between one's actual self and one's target self or one's ideal self), Petrocelli and Smith (2005) revealed that emotional reactions were a function of both the discrepancy and the causal attributions made for the discrepancies. Specifically, agitation-related emotions and dejection-related emotions were the highest when individuals made internal attributions for high self-discrepancies. Moreover, anger-related emotions were highest when individuals made external attributions for high self-discrepancies. Generally, it has been shown that external attributions for failure lead to the experience of anger toward the external cause (e.g., toward one's supervisor, a coworker [Russell & McAuley, 1986; Weiner et al., 1978, 1979]).

In their research on college students during the course of a semester, Mone and Baker (1992) showed that students' locus of causality attributions moderated the relationship between goal discrepancies and students' general positive affect. Students felt more positive about attaining a goal and more negative about failing to attain a goal when they primarily made internal attributions for their exam performance. Similarly, poor goal progress was related to higher negative affect in a sample of varsity athletes and musicians, especially for those individuals who were high in self-criticism and therefore more likely to make internal attributions for poor performance (Powers, Koestner, Lacaille, Kwan, & Zuroff, 2009). Allen, Jones, and Sheffield (2009) introduced an interesting temporal perspective on the attributional and emotional dynamics following achievement-related events. Using a sample of female golfers, they verified that golfers experienced anger for a longer period of time following competition when they attributed their poor performance to stable rather than unstable causes.

## The Mediating Role of Emotions

In combination, previous research on attributions and emotions suggests that affective reactions to performance feedback are a function of the feedback recipients' attributions. In turn, these reactions systematically impact the recipients' motivation and behaviors in general (e.g., Erez & Isen, 2002; Seo et al., 2010) and the goal-striving process in particular. Cron and colleagues (2005), for example, showed that ongoing negative emotional responses to negative goal–performance discrepancies resulted in setting a lower goal level for the next task. Using a sample of collegiate golfers, Schantz and Conroy (2009) found that the golfers' mood before teeing off influenced their achievement goals for that particular hole.

Ilies and Judge (2005) assigned a critical role to these ongoing affective reactions experienced while striving for goal accomplishment by demonstrating that they fully mediate the relationships between goal–performance discrepancy and goal revision. Specifically, participants who received negative feedback and subsequently felt negative affect revised their goals downward, whereas participants who received positive feedback and subsequently felt positive affect revised their goals upward. Positive affect mediated the relationship in all six of their samples, whereas negative affect mediated the relationship in only one sample. Ilies et al. (2010) showed that positive and negative emotions in response to performance–goal discrepancy feedback affect subsequent goal setting, either directly or indirectly through self-efficacy. Positive emotions led to higher goals, whereas negative emotions resulted in lower goals via a reduction in self-efficacy. Richard and Diefendorff (2011) similarly found that affect systematically influences goal levels, but did so in a study where participants did not receive any explicit feedback. Consistent with the mood-as-information model (Schwarz & Clore, 2003), the authors verified that positive affect led to an upward revision of goals, whereas negative affect was related to a downward revision. This finding extends the work by Ilies and Judge (2005) by showing that affect influences goal revision even when the experienced affect is independent of explicit performance feedback. This result may therefore be particularly relevant for the goal-striving phase when individuals may not frequently receive direct feedback.

Interestingly though, while affect had systematic effects on subsequent goal pursuit efforts in Richard and Diefendorff's (2011) research, the results were different from affect's effects on goal revision. Negative affect was positively related to next day's effort, whereas positive affect was negatively related to next day's effort. Positive affect may signal good progress and then lead individuals to reduce their efforts, while negative affect may signal problems in goal pursuit, which may then lead individuals to not only decrease their goals but also to increase their efforts to overcome the discrepancies.

While we mentioned that research generally supports the notion that negative goal-performance discrepancies can result in feelings of shame and guilt (e.g., Tracy & Robins, 2006), the research linking shame and guilt to goal-relevant outcomes is mixed. There is some evidence available that shame is more closely linked to avoidance tendencies (i.e., withdrawing effort), whereas guilt is more closely associated with approach tendencies (i.e., ramping up effort to overcome the guilt-eliciting event) (Ketelaar & Au, 2003; Tangney, Miller, Flicker, & Barlow, 1996), but more empirical research is needed to make sense of the mixed results present in the current literature.

In sum, this research supports a model where the attributions individuals make for their goal–performance discrepancies interact with the magnitude of the discrepancies to determine affective reactions, which in turn influence the goal-striving process (see Figure 4.1). Drawing on this model, we now present a number of summary comments and suggestions for further research.

## Discussion

Motivation theory has made great strides over the last few decades to explain goal-oriented behaviors in the workplace. Many different approaches have been advanced to shed light on the intricacies and complexities involved in human behavior associated with goals, and all of these approaches have added something interesting, unique, and important (Locke & Latham, 2004). This chapter shows that a valuable future research direction is to integrate attributional and affective dynamics into self-regulatory processes. As our chapter has demonstrated, studies focused on attribution or emotion have significantly advanced our understanding of the goal pursuit process. Individuals' reactions to goal–performance discrepancies are partially a function of their attributions, and their affective reactions systematically determine their motivated behaviors such as goal revision. Attributional and emotional dynamics are interconnected: any comprehensive understanding of goal striving should therefore incorporate both elements.

What our review of the applicable literature made apparent, however, is that no single study has examined the entirety of the model we put forth (see Figure 4.1). We thus believe there is an opportunity and a necessity to combine all aspects of our model into future empirical work to delineate exactly how they play out within and across individuals. For example, while affect has been extensively studied in conjunction with either attributions or motivation, the field would benefit from combining all of those elements into one study to test how emotions exactly operate (i.e., directly and indirectly, as a partial or full mediator, etc.). In addition, research would benefit from studying the attributional and emotional impacts on the traditional goal mechanisms of effort, direction, and persistence. Although we know that emotions have an influence on these three mechanisms (e.g., Seo et al., 2010), the existing empirical attribution research has not systematically included them, although theoretical propositions are available (e.g., Mitchell et al., 2004).

Furthermore, as discussed in the introduction, the empirical research conducted so far on goal–performance discrepancies has not clearly distinguished between the goal-striving phase and the recalibration phase (when the deadline is reached or a particular trial or task is completed and one resets the goal). However, there may be significant differences between the two phases that are currently ignored. For example, affective reactions during the recalibration phase may be stronger, because this phase may more often coincide with explicit, widely shared, and impactful feedback in the form of performance appraisals and public announcements of goal accomplishment (e.g., sales figures are published in the annual report, bonuses based on performance are handed out, etc.).

While attributional and emotional concepts have been given increasingly more consideration in motivation research, we believe there are areas where they could possibly have additional impact. To our knowledge, all the empirical research examining the attributional dynamics of goal striving has focused on the pursuit of a single goal. It is the reality of the modern workplace, however, that individuals simultaneously pursue multiple goals that compete for resources such as time and attention (DeShon & Gillespie, 2005; Lord, Diefendorff, Schmidt, & Hall, 2010; Schmidt, Dolis, & Tolli, 2009). As Schmidt and DeShon (2007: 928) noted, "little is known about how individuals dynamically allocate—and subsequently reallocate—their time and attention as they pursue multiple goals over time." Attributional and emotional processes contribute to our understanding of these highly complex and dynamic situations. Despite having initially set specific and difficult goals, individuals may reallocate significant resources or even entirely switch to the pursuit of another goal in the midst of goal pursuit (Mitchell et al., 2004). The attributional and affective dynamics described in this chapter may predict when this occurs. An obvious situation where one might switch focus to another task is when one gives up on the initial goal. This may commonly occur when faced with negative goal–performance discrepancies that are perceived to be difficult to overcome. This is because the individual makes internal, stable, and uncontrollable attributions and therefore feels helpless and discouraged. In this situation, the initial resource allocation plan may prove to be faulty, and an individual may quickly adjust and switch to a new task with high expectancy and value formulation (Mitchell et al., 2008).

The pursuit of multiple goals offers a completely new set of attributions that may affect reactions to goal progress such as "I am not good at multitasking" (internal attribution) or "My supervisor only inquires about my progress on project A, so I could not concentrate on project B" (external attribution). These attributions may uniquely contribute to (re)allocation decisions and therefore add to our understanding of goal pursuit in complex environments. Moreover, affective reactions may vary as a function of multiple goal pursuit. For example, individuals may feel both positive and negative affect when making good progress on (or meeting) one goal, but making poor progress on (or failing) another goal. The question arises as to which emotions are more pronounced and ultimately more impactful in predicting subsequent motivation and behaviors. Following Baumeister, Bratslavsky, Finkenauer, and Vohs' (2001) notion that "bad is stronger than good," individuals' negative affect may overshadow their joy from meeting at least one goal and therefore lead to withdrawal or downward goal revision for the remaining goal. Or, alternatively, the experience of simultaneously feeling positive and negative emotions (a state called emotional ambivalence) may trigger creative problem solving, which may help speed up the pursuit of the second goal (Fong, 2006). Nevertheless, affective reactions likely vary as a function of the attributions the individual makes for the two different goals. For example, positive affect may "win" when the individual makes an external attribution for the failure and an internal attribution for the success; whereas negative affect may "win" in the opposite scenario (internal attribution for failure and external attribution for success). We encourage future research on multiple goal pursuit to incorporate elements of attribution and emotion theory into theory development and empirical research (for a detailed treatment of the dynamics of multiple goal pursuit, see Chapter 12).

An attributional and emotional perspective on goal pursuit may also benefit from examining the interdependencies among goals nested within a goal hierarchy. Often, the accomplishment of a lower-level, short-term, and concrete goal (e.g., finishing a project on time) contributes to the achievement of a higher-level, long-term, and abstract goal (e.g., getting a promotion to middle management [Bateman, O'Neill, & Kenworthy-U'Ren, 2002; Lord et al., 2010]). When considering individuals' attributions and emotions in the process of reaching or failing to reach a subordinate goal, additional insight may therefore be gained by examining the nature of the superordinate goal. For example, when making an internal attribution for goal failure, an individual may be more likely to continue goal pursuit when the goal contributes significantly to a highly valued superordinate goal. The individual may be more likely to revise the goal downward when the goal is tangential to the superordinate goal's accomplishment.

Finally, we propose that attributions and emotions might uniquely contribute to the study of self-regulation at the team level. The research reviewed here describes individuals' reactions to individual goal-performance discrepancies. With an increasingly interdependent and team-oriented workplace, however, team goals are becoming prevalent (Ilgen, Hollenbeck, Johnson, & Jundt, 2005). Thus, it is imperative to understand how teams allocate their resources between and within team goals. We suggest that teams' attributions for their successes and failures can contribute to the understanding of team regulation processes. For example, research examining the attributions made by teams in response to feedback found that teams generally share credit for good performance but single out individuals as the cause of poor performance (Dorfman & Stephan, 1984; Naquin & Tynan, 2003). Research on the latter case often focuses on reactions to the poorest-performing member of the team, the "scapegoat" (Jackson & LePine, 2003; Taggar & Neubert, 2004). Little is known, however, about how these reactions determine the teams' subsequent goal pursuit. Under what circumstances may they withdraw from a goal or allocate additional resources to it? When do they revise their goals downward, or persist despite obvious challenges?

The way that the locus of causality, stability, and controllability attributions interact with goal–performance discrepancies at the individual level may be similar at the team level. Yet, these attributions are likely arrived at via different processes. Team members may or may not differ on their judgments of the causes of the events. Teams' shared mental models and team cohesion may contribute to a unified team attribution, whereas different personalities and high internal conflict may give rise to high attribution differentiation (Kozlowski & Ilgen, 2006). There is clearly a need to understand these attributional processes at the team level, and to link them to team regulation processes such as resource allocation, goal striving, and goal revision. The team setting may also evoke an entirely new set of attributions, which Eberly, Holley, Johnson, and Mitchell (2011) labeled *relational attributions*. Relational attributions capture performance explanations that perceive one's relationships with others as the cause of the event. Within a work team, members may attribute their failure as a team to the poor coordination between two members who are required to communicate and exchange information frequently to meet performance standards. Alternatively, coordination may be poor within the entire team and hence account for poor goal progress. Depending on whether team members feel efficacious about improving their coordination and communication processes (i.e., depending on stability and controllability judgments), these relational attributions may lead to increases or decreases in motivated actions.

## Conclusion

This chapter has highlighted the attributional and affective dynamics underlying goal striving. Clearly, motivation research has benefited greatly from incorporating components of attribution and emotion theory. At the same time, however, we believe there is an opportunity for additional and more comprehensive empirical research, including all elements of the self-regulation model specified in Figure 4.1 and beyond. Also, attribution research can and should be extended to other aspects of the self-regulation process such as multiple goal pursuit and team-level goals. We hope this chapter provides a platform from which such research may flourish, so that scholars may understand how and why goal–performance discrepancies lead to employees' subsequent goal revision and performance in the workplace.

## Notes

1. While self-regulation phase models clearly differentiate the goal-striving phase from the recalibration phase, our review of the literature indicates that the theoretical and empirical work has not made a clear (if any) distinction. The theoretical arguments for reactions to negative goal–performance discrepancies are essentially identical, whether these reactions occur during goal striving or during recalibration. Since empirical research often bundles the two phases together, we also do not distinguish between them in this chapter. We therefore use the terms *goal striving* and *recalibration* interchangeably.
2. We will mostly focus on the negative discrepancy change in goals, primarily because most of the research focuses on this pairing. However, it is important to point out that positive discrepancies can occur, where individuals are ahead of schedule or exceed their goal. In such cases, depending on their attributions, those individuals may reduce their effort on the current or next task or maintain (or increase) effort levels if they believe that progress or accomplishment are due to luck or external circumstances (Mitchell, Lee, Lee, & Harman, 2004).

## References

Allen, M. S., Jones, M. V., & Sheffield, D. 2009. Causal attribution and emotion in the days following competition. *Journal of Sports Sciences*, 227: 461–468.

Bateman, T. S., O'Neill, H., & Kenworthy-U'Ren, A. 2002. A hierarchical taxonomy of top managers' goals. *Journal of Applied Psychology*, 6: 1134–1148.

Baumeister, R. F., Bratslavsky, E., Finkenauer, C., & Vohs, K. D. 2001. Bad is stronger than good. *Review of General Psychology*, 5: 323–370.

Brown, C. M., & McConnell, A. R. 2011. Discrepancy-based and anticipated emotions in behavioral self-regulation. *Emotion*, 11: 1091–1095.

Campbell, C. R., & Martinko, M. J. 1998. An integrative attributional perspective of empowerment and learned helplessness: A multimethod field study. *Journal of Management*, 24: 173–200.

Carver, C. S., & Scheier, M. F. 1998. *On the self-regulation of behavior*. New York, NY: Cambridge University Press.

Carver, C. S., & Scheier, M. F. 2000. On the structure of behavioral self-regulation. In M. Boekaerts, P. R. Pintrich, & M. Zeidner (Eds.), *Handbook of self-regulation:* 41–84. San Diego, CA: Academic Press.

Cooper, S. 2007. *An examination of some temporal implications of goal setting.* Paper presented at SIOP.

Cron, W. L., Slocum, J. W., Jr., VandeWalle, D., & Fu, Q. 2005. The role of goal orientation on negative emotions and goal setting when initial performance falls short of one's performance goal. *Human Performance*, 18: 55–80.

DeShon, R. P., & Gillespie, J. Z. 2005. A motivated action theory account of goal oriented behavior. *Journal of Applied Psychology*, 90: 1096–1127.

Diefendorff, J. M., & Lord, R. G. 2008. Goal-striving and self-regulation processes. In R. Kanfer, G. Chen, & R. D. Pritchard (Ed.), *Work motivation: Past, present, and future:* 151–197. New York, NY: Routledge.

Donovan, J. J., & Williams, K. J. 1996. *Self-regulation and goal revision in cross-country runners: Effects of goal attainment and performance attributions.* Poster session presented at the 1996 Academy of Management Annual Meeting, Cincinnati, OH.

Donovan, J. J., & Williams, K. J. 2003. Missing the mark: Effects of time and causal attributions on goal revision in response to goal-performance discrepancies. *Journal of Applied Psychology*, 88: 379–390.

Dorfman, P. W., & Stephan, W. G. 1984. The effects of group performance on cognitions, satisfaction, and behavior: A process model. *Journal of Management*, 10: 173–192.

Eberly, M. B., Holley, E. C., Johnson, M. D., & Mitchell, T. R. 2011. Beyond internal and external: A dyadic theory of relational attributions. *Academy of Management Review,* 36: 731–753.

Erez, A., & Isen, A. M. 2002. The influence of positive affect on the components of expectancy motivation. *Journal of Applied Psychology*, 87: 1055–1067.

Fong, C. T. 2006. The effects of emotional ambivalence on creativity. *Academy of Management Journal*, 49: 1016–1030.

Frijda, N. H. 1993. The place of appraisal in emotion. *Cognition and Emotion,* 7: 357–387.

Gollwitzer P. M. 1990. Action phases and mind-sets. In E. T. Higgins, R. M. Sorrentino (Eds.) *Handbook of Motivation and Cognition*, 2: 53–92. New York: Guilford.

Gooty, J., Gavin, M., & Ashkanasy, N. M. 2009. Emotions research in OB: The challenges that lie ahead. *Journal of Organizational Behavior*, 30: 833–838.

Hareli, S., & Hess, U. 2008. The role of causal attribution in hurt feelings and related social emotions elicited in reaction to other's feedback about failure. *Cognition & Emotion*, 22: 862–880.

Heider, F. 1958. *The psychology of interpersonal relations.* Hillsdale, NJ: Lawrence Erlbaum.

Ilgen, D. R., Hollenbeck, J. R., Johnson, M., & Jundt, D. 2005. Teams in organizations: From I-P-O models to IMOI models. *Annual Review of Psychology*, 56: 517–544.

Ilies, R., & Judge, T. A. 2005. Goal regulation across time: The effects of feedback and affect. *Journal of Applied Psychology*, 90: 453–467.

Ilies, R., Judge, T. A., & Wagner. D. T. 2010. The influence of cognitive and affective reactions to feedback on subsequent goals. *European Psychologist*, 15: 121–131.

Jackson, S. E., Hall, N. C., Rowe, P. M., & Daniels, L. M. 2009. Getting the job: Attributional retraining and the employment interview. *Journal of Applied Social Psychology*, 39: 973–998.

Jackson, C. L., & LePine, J. A. 2003. Peer responses to a team's weakest link: A test and extension of LePine and Van Dyne's model. *Journal of Applied Psychology*, 88: 459–475.

Johnson, R. E., Chang, C., & Lord, R. G. 2006. Moving from cognition to behavior: What the research says. *Psychological Bulletin*, 132: 381–415.

Kanfer, R., Chen, G., & Pritchard, R. D. (Eds.) 2008. *Work motivation: Past, present, and future.* New York, NY: Routledge.

Kelley, H. H. 1967. Attribution theory in social psychology. *Nebraska Symposium on Motivation*, 15: 192–240.

Kelley, H. H. 1971. *Attributions in social interactions.* Morristown, NJ: General Learning Press.

Ketelaar, T., & Au, W. T. 2003. The effects of feelings of guilt on the behaviour of uncooperative individuals in repeated social bargaining games: An affect-as-information interpretation of the role of emotion in social interaction. *Cognition and Emotion*, 17: 429–453.

Kozlowski, S. W. J., & Ilgen, D. R. 2006. Enhancing the effectiveness of work groups and teams. *Psychological Science in the Public Interest*, 7: 77–124.

Lam, W., Huang, X., & Snape, E. 2007. Feedback-seeking behavior and leader-member exchange: Do supervisor-attributed motives matter? *Academy of Management Journal*, 50: 348–363.

Latham, G. P. 2007. *Work motivation: History, theory, research and practice.* Thousand Oaks, CA: Sage.

Latham, G. P., & Pinder, C. 2005. Work motivation theory and research at the dawn of the 21st century. *Annual Review of Psychology*, 56: 485–516.

Locke, E. A. 2004. Work motivation. In C. Spielberger (Ed.), *Encyclopedia of applied psychology*, Vol. 3: 709–714. Oxford, U.K.: Elsevier.

Locke, E. A. 2009. Attain emotional control by understanding what emotions are. In E. A. Locke (Ed.), *Handbook of principles of organizational behavior: Indispensable knowledge for evidence-based management*, 2nd Ed.: 145–160. West Sussex, U.K.: John Wiley & Sons.

Locke, E. A., & Latham, G. P. 1990. *A theory of goal setting and task performance.* Englewood Cliffs, NJ: Prentice-Hall.

Locke, E., & Latham, G. 2002. Building a practically useful theory of goal setting and task motivation: A 35-year odyssey. *American Psychologist*, 57: 705–717.

Locke, E. A., & Latham, G. P. 2004. What should we do about motivation theory? Six recommendations for the twenty-first century. *Academy of Management Review*, 29: 388–400.

Locke, E. A., & Latham, G. P. 2006. Further confusion in the study of self-regulation: Comments on Cervone, Shadel, Smith, and Fiori. *Applied Psychology: An International Review*, 55: 428–438.

Lord, R. G., Diefendorff, J. M., Schmidt, A. M., & Hall, R. J. 2010. Self-regulation at work. *Annual Review of Psychology*, 61: 543–568.

Martinko, M. J., Douglas, S. C., & Harvey, P. 2006. Attribution theory in industrial and organizational psychology: A review. *International Review of Industrial and Organizational Psychology*, 21: 127–187.

Martinko, M. J., Harvey, P., & Dasborough, M. T. 2011. Attribution theory in the organizational sciences: A case of unrealized potential. *Journal of Organizational Behavior*, 32: 144–149.

Mitchell, T. R., & Daniels, D. 2003. Motivation. In W. C. Borman, D. R. Ilgen, & R. J. Klimoski (Eds.), *Comprehensive handbook of psychology: Industrial organizational psychology*, 12: 225–254. New York: Wiley.

Mitchell, T. R., Harman, W. S., Lee, T. W., & Lee, D.-Y. 2008. Self-regulation and multiple deadline goals. In R. Kanfer, G. Chen, & R. D. Pritchard (Eds.), *Work motivation: Past, present, and future*: 197–233. New York, NY: Routledge.

Mitchell, T. R., Lee, T. W., Lee, D. Y., & Harman, W. 2004. Attributions and the action cycle of work. In M. Martinko (Ed.), *Advances in attribution theory*: 25–48. Greenwich, CT: Information Age.

Mone, M. A., & Baker, D. D. 1992. A social-cognitive, attributional model of personal goals: An empirical evaluation. *Motivation and Emotion*, 16: 297–321.

Naquin, C., & Tynan, R. 2003. The team halo effect: Why teams are not blamed for their failures. *Journal of Applied Psychology*, 88: 332–340.

Peterson, S. E., & Schreiber, J. B. 2006. An attributional analysis of personal and interpersonal motivation for collaborative projects. *Journal of Educational Psychology*, 98: 777–787.

Petrocelli, J. V., & Smith, E. R. 2005. Who I am, who we are, and why: Links between emotions and causal attributions for self- and group discrepancies. *Personality and Social Psychology Bulletin*, 31: 1628–1642.

Powers, T. A., Koestner, R., Lacaille, N., Kwan, L., & Zuroff, D. C. 2009. Self-criticism, motivation, and goal progress of athletes and musicians: A prospective study. *Personality and Individual Differences*, 47: 279–283.

Richard, E. M., & Diefendorff, J. M. 2011. Self-regulation during a single performance episode: Mood-as-information in the absence of formal feedback. *Organizational Behavior and Human Decision Processes*, 115: 99–110.

Russell, D., & McAuley, E. 1986. Causal attributions, causal dimensions, and affective reactions to success and failure. *Journal of Personality & Social Psychology*, 50: 1174–1185.

Schantz, L. H., & Conroy, D. E. 2009. Achievement motivation and intraindividual affective variability during competence pursuits: A round of golf as a multilevel data structure. *Journal of Research in Personality*, 43: 472–481.

Schmidt A. M., & DeShon R. P. 2007. What to do? The effects of discrepancies, incentives, and time on dynamic goal prioritization. *Journal of Applied Psychology*, 92: 928–941.

Schmidt A. M., Dolis C. M., & Tolli A. P. 2009. A matter of time: individual differences, contextual dynamics, and goal progress effects on multiple-goal self-regulation. *Journal of Applied Psychology*, 94: 692–709.

Schwarz, N., & Clore, G. L. 2003. Mood as information: 20 years later. *Psychological Inquiry*, 14: 296–303.

Seo, M., Bartunek, J. M., & Barrett, L. F. 2010. The role of affective experience in work motivation: Test of a conceptual model. *Journal of Organizational Behavior*, 31: 951–968.

Shah, J. Y., Friedman, R., & Kruglanski, A. W. 2002. Forgetting all else: On the antecedents and consequences of goal shielding. *Journal of Personality & Social Psychology*, 83: 1261–1280.

Silver, W. S., Mitchell, T. R., & Gist, M. E. 1995. Responses to successful and unsuccessful performance: The moderating effect of self-efficacy on the relationship between performance and attributions. *Organizational Behavior and Human Decision Processes*, 62: 286–299.

Smith, C., Haynes, K. N., Lazarus, R. S., & Pope, L. K. 1993. In search of the "hot" cognitions: Attributions, appraisals and their relation to emotion. *Journal of Personality and Social Psychology*, 65: 916–929.

Smith, C. A., & Kirby, L. D. 2001. Toward delivering on the promise of appraisal theory. In K. Scherer, A. Schorr, & T. Johnstone (Eds.), *Appraisal processes in emotion: Theory, methods, research*. Oxford: Oxford University Press.

Stajkovic, A., & Luthans, F. 1998. Self-efficacy and work-related performance: A meta-analysis. *Psychological Bulletin*, 124: 240–261.

Taggar, S., & Neubert, M. 2004. The impact of poor performers on team outcomes: An empirical examination of attribution theory. *Personnel Psychology*, 57: 935–968.

Tangney, J. P., Miller, R. S., Flicker, L., & Barlow, D. H. 1996. Are shame, guilt, and embarrassment distinct emotions? *Journal of Personality and Social Psychology*, 70: 1256–1269.

Thibaut, J., & Walker, L. 1975. *Procedural justice: A psychological analysis.* Hillsdale, NJ: Erlbaum.

Thomas, K. M., & Mathieu, J. E. 1994. Role of causal attributions in dynamic self-regulation and goal processes. *Journal of Applied Psychology*, 79: 812–818.

Tolli, A. P., & Schmidt, A. M. 2008. The role of feedback, causal attributions, and self-efficacy in goal revision. *Journal of Applied Psychology*, 93: 692–701.

Tracy, J. L., & Robins, R. W. 2006. Appraisal antecedents of shame and guilt: Support for a theoretical model. *Personality and Social Psychology Bulletin*, 32: 1339–1351.

Turner, J. E., Husman, J., Schallert, D. L. 2002. The importance of students' goals in their emotional experience of academic failure: Investigating the precursors and consequences of shame. *Educational Psychologist*, 37: 79–89.

Van Overwalle, F., Mervielde, I., & De Schuyter, J. 1995. Structural modelling of the relationships between attributional dimensions, emotions, and performance of college freshmen. *Cognition and Emotion*, 9: 59–85.

Venables, L., & Fairclough, S. H. 2009. The influence of performance feedback on goal-setting and mental effort regulation. *Motivation and Emotion*, 33: 63–74.

Weiner, B. 1985. An attributional theory of achievement motivation and emotion. *Psychological Review*, 92: 548–573.

Weiner, B. 1986. *An attributional theory of achievement motivation and emotion.* New York: Springer-Verlag.

Weiner, B. 1990. Attribution in personality psychology. In L. A. Perrin (Ed.), *Handbook of personality: Theory and research*: 465–485. New York: Guilford Press.

Weiner, B., Frieze, I., Kukla, A., Reed, L., Rest, S., & Rosenbaum, R. M. 1971. *Perceiving the causes of success and failure.* Morristown, NJ: General Learning Press.

Weiner, B., & Graham, S. 1999. Attribution in personality psychology. In L. A. Perrin & O. P. John (Eds.), *Handbook of personality: Theory and research*, 2: 605–628. New York: Guilford Press.

Weiner, B., Russell, D., & Lerman, D. 1978. Affective consequences of causal ascriptions. In J. H. Harvey, W. J. Ickes, & R. F. Kidd (Eds.), *New directions in attribution research*, 2: 59–90. Hillsdale, NJ: Erlbaum.

Weiner, B., Russell, D., & Lerman, D. 1979. The cognition-emotion process in achievement and related contexts. *Journal of Personality and Social Psychology*, 37: 1211–1220.

Williams, K. J., Donovan, J. J., & Dodge, T. L. 2000. Self-regulation of performance: Goal establishment and goal revision processes in athletes. *Human Performance*, 13, 159–180.

# 5   Feedback, Goal Setting, and Task Performance Revisited

*Susan J. Ashford*   Ross School of Business, University of Michigan

*Katleen E. M. De Stobbeleir*   Vlerick Business School,
Ghent University

Feedback is information that tells a performer how well he or she is performing a task or progressing with respect to a goal (Ashford & Cummings, 1983). Feedback plays two roles in goal setting processes (Locke and Latham, 1990). First, feedback stimulates individuals to set subsequent goals for their performance. In this way, goal setting mediates the relationship between feedback and performance. Second, feedback is thought to interact with goals such that performance is improved most when both feedback and goals are present. In this way, feedback moderates the relationship between goal setting and performance. Following Locke and Latham (1990), we divide this updated literature review along these two lines. We retain most of the nomenclature of their original chapter, but we broaden our sense of feedback beyond simply knowledge of results (typically indicative of quantitative feedback) or one's performance to also consider feedback more generally, from that existing in the environment, that available from multiple sources, that which is ambiguous as well as clear-cut, and that which is qualitative as well as quantitative.

## The Mediation Hypothesis

### What Have We Learned Since 1990?

Support for the mediation hypothesis can be found in a series of studies investigating the impact of feedback in the form of performance–goal discrepancy information on individuals' subsequent goal setting. A field study among college students by VandeWalle, Cron, and Slocum (2001) showed that positive feedback was positively associated with higher subsequent self-set goals. The effects of feedback on goal-setting were found to be mediated by students' self-efficacy, providing direct evidence for Locke and Latham's (1990) assertion that self-efficacy mediates the effects of feedback on subsequent goal setting.

Two studies by Ilies and Judge (2005) examined how performance feedback influenced subsequent goal setting for individuals receiving both negative and positive performance feedback. They also assessed the mediating role of affect in this relationship. In support of goal setting theory's predictions, results showed that people revised their goals downward when they received negative feedback and upward following positive feedback. Results further showed that individuals' general positive affective reactions (e.g., enthusiasm, alert or active) were an especially important psychological mechanism explaining these effects. Specifically, individuals tended to experience more positive affect after positive feedback, which in turn resulted in upwards goal revision. These effects occurred regardless of whether the feedback was based on and accurately reflected performance or whether it was randomly manipulated (Ilies & Judge, 2005). Negative feedback only resulted in positive affect and increased goal setting when the discrepancy between performance and the standard was relatively small.

A second field study by Cron, Slocum, VandeWalle, and Fu (2005) assessed the emotional reactions of college students who performed at a lower level than their initial self-set grade goal, and asked them to set a new grade goal for their next exam. The results showed that the affective reactions of students who failed to achieve their initial performance goals were not negative per se, but depended on their goal orientation, a personality trait reflecting personal preferences in achievement situations (Dweck, 1986). Students with an avoidance goal orientation (i.e., a preoccupation with not revealing a lack of ability and avoiding negative ability judgments from others) showed more negative initial reactions to negative performance feedback and lower subsequent self-set goals and task performance. A learning goal orientation (i.e., an orientation toward acquiring new skills), on the other hand, was unrelated to negative initial emotional reactions, but mitigated the detrimental effects of negative emotions on subsequent goal setting and fostered greater subsequent performance.

Ilies, Judge, and Wagner (2010) add to Cron et al.'s (2005) and Ilies and Judge's (2005) studies by showing that individuals' behavioral inhibition system (BIS), a disposition reflecting individual differences in the ways in which people process feedback information, influenced their resilience after receiving negative feedback and their subsequent goal setting. Individuals with a strong BIS tend to feel hurt and worry when they think they did something wrong. Results showed that small discrepancies yielded low levels of negative emotional reactions, regardless of individuals' BIS. However, when feedback indicated large negative discrepancies, individuals with highly sensitive behavioral inhibition systems had stronger negative emotional reactions than individuals with a less sensitive BIS. These negative emotional reactions, in turn, had a negative impact on self-efficacy and subsequent goal setting.

In a completely different setting, Williams, Donovan, and Dodge (2000) found that athletes' goal revision was predicted by the size of the discrepancy between their goals and current performance, and that these effects were moderated by the attributions that these athletes made for their performance. Large discrepancies that were attributed to uncontrollable causes resulted in downward goal revision. Goals were increased when discrepancies were small and attributed to controllable causes.

Extending these findings, Donovan and Williams (2003) studied athletes' goal-revision processes longitudinally over the course of an 8-week competitive season. They found that the extent to which athletes revised their goals also depended on their causal attributions (i.e., to internal versus external causes) and on how far they were in the season. As the season progressed, athletes with large negative goal–performance discrepancies did more downward goal revision.

Tolli and Schmidt (2008) showed that the moderating effect of causal attributions on goals was observed most clearly following positive feedback. Subjects who attributed successful performance to internal factors showed higher self-efficacy, which in turn led to upward goal revision. Those attributing success to external factors reported no increases in self-efficacy, and as a result, self-set goal difficulty remained largely the same. However, nearly all those who received negative feedback revised their goals downward, regardless of their attributions for the failure. They attributed this unexpected finding to their measure of self-efficacy, which included a projection of future attainments.

Finally, a field study of the impact of feedback-seeking behavior on performance by Renn and Fedor (2001) showed that such behavior only impacted performance when the feedback seeker set personal improvement goals based on the feedback.

In sum, there is strong evidence that the impact of feedback on performance is partially dependent on the goals that individuals set for themselves based on feedback. This research also confirms Locke and Latham's (1990) suggestion that feedback-based goal setting is not simply an automatic response to goal–performance discrepancies, but that context and individual attributions as well as affect and self-efficacy shape how individuals will respond to the feedback.

While these studies operationalized goal–performance discrepancies by manipulating the sign of the feedback, one's relative performance compared to others also may impact perceived goal–performance discrepancies. Giving subjects veridical feedback on their absolute performance, but providing them with false comparative feedback (i.e., how they scored relative to others), Bandura and Jourdan (1991) showed that subjects in a progressive mastery condition (i.e., subjects receiving feedback of gradually increasing performance relative to peers) set higher goals and were able to increase their performance more than those who were in the progressive decline condition (receiving feedback of gradually declining performance), superior condition (consistently surpassing their counterparts over the trials), or similar condition (matching their counterparts over the trials). These results suggest that comparative feedback can have both beneficial and detrimental effects depending on the sign of the implied feedback.

Johnson, Turban, Pieper, and Ng (1996) further examined this issue. They showed that two types of feedback, nominal feedback (that concerning one's own performance) and comparative feedback (that comparing one's performance to others) had differential effects on individuals' self-efficacy, intrinsic motivation, and goal setting. In the first trials, nominal, but not comparative feedback had a positive impact on personal goals. In later trials, both types of feedback positively impacted personal goals. The impact of nominal feedback on goal setting was mediated by self-efficacy. These researchers did not find a significant relationship between goal setting and subsequent performance. Also, this study included the sign of the comparative and nominal feedback but did not report results relevant to this variable.

Ilies and Judge (2005) assessed whether upward and downward goal revision would be more or less prevalent when positive or negative feedback was comparative or nominal. They examined this question using two versions of a word-generating task. In the first version, participants could choose between five different relative goals (e.g., I want to perform better than 70% of the participants in this study). In the second version, participants were asked to set nominal goals by estimating how many words they would generate in the task. After the first trial, participants received either nominal or comparative feedback. Individuals in the relative goal condition received relative feedback; those who were in the nominal goal condition received nominal feedback. Results showed that when the feedback message was negative, both nominal and comparative feedback predicted subsequent goal revisions. For positive feedback, the feedback–goal relationship was significant only in the combined nominal goals and feedback condition.

That is, after receiving positive feedback, people tended to further increase their goals when the goal and feedback were nominal. This pattern suggests that at least for positive feedback, the effects of feedback on subsequent goal setting are stronger when the feedback is provided in reference to the individual's own performance. Ilies and Judge did not directly test the impact of goals on actual performance, but from these results they conclude that higher self-set goals are likely to result in increased effort, and ultimately in increased performance.

In addition to the sign of the feedback, researchers also have begun to examine the impact of other facets of feedback on subsequent goal setting and performance. In one decision-making experiment conducted by Korsgaard and Diddams (1996) on the effects of ongoing process feedback (versus outcome feedback) on goal setting, results showed that when outcome feedback (i.e., feedback at the end of the task) was supplemented with ongoing process feedback on the strategies they used during the task, people tended to set more goals for themselves, which ultimately helped them to increase their performance. This effect was moderated by the complexity of the task, such that the availability of process feedback for simple tasks had little impact on subsequent goal setting, but when process feedback was available for complex tasks, the number of self-set personal goals and performance increased.

Kernan, Heimann, and Hanges (1991) assessed how two types of feedback (i.e., self-generated and feedback provided by an external source) impacted subsequent goal setting. Results showed no direct impact of whether the feedback was self-generated or externally provided on subsequent goal setting or performance. Under self-feedback, subjects in the assigned strategy condition set higher goals than subjects in the participative strategy conditions. These effects did not extend to subsequent performance, though. These results seem to suggest that self-generated feedback is not necessarily superior to feedback delivered by others, unless the individual has no discretion about how a goal should be pursued. The authors invoke self-determination theory and speculate that self-generated feedback may have positive effects in such an autonomy-limiting condition because individuals prefer that at least one of the factors (goals, strategy, or feedback) be imposed by an external source, and find it difficult to manage too much autonomy.

These studies have not addressed how people react when the feedback they receive from others conflicts with their self-generated feedback. Bono and Colbert (2005) provided suggestive data on this question using a multisource feedback intervention among MBA students. Results showed that individuals' reactions to situations where self-generated feedback was at odds with that provided by others depended on their level of core self-evaluations. Core self-evaluations represent individuals' enduring evaluations of themselves on four broad traits: self-esteem, generalized self-efficacy, locus of control, and emotional stability (Judge, Locke, & Durham, 1997). Individuals with positive core self-evaluations were most committed to development goals when their own evaluations and the feedback they received from others were discrepant. In contrast, individuals with low core self-evaluations were most committed to developmental goals when self and others' ratings were in agreement.

Though the initial research seems to indicate that how feedback is acquired does not affect subsequent goal setting, there is evidence suggesting that the specificity of the feedback does. In a field study, Tziner, Kopelman, and Joanis (1997) examined the effects of different types of rating formats used in performance appraisals on subsequent goal setting.

Their study showed that rating formats that provide employees with specific behavioral feedback (e.g., behavioral observation scales) yielded significantly higher goal specificity than formats that provided more general feedback (e.g., the general rating scale). According to goal setting theory, specific feedback should result in enhanced performance when the specific goals that individuals set for themselves based on the feedback are sufficiently challenging.

Examining this question at the group level, Mesch, Farh, and Podsakoff (1994) randomly assigned groups of three students to two feedback conditions (positive and negative). Groups that received negative feedback after their first performance session set higher goals and performed better in the second performance session than groups receiving positive feedback. What this study did not reveal, though, is why they did so. One reason why they may have performed better is that the negative feedback did not harm individuals' self-efficacy because it was only the first performance session and/or because they felt that increased effort would enhance their performance.

DeShon, Kozlowski, Schmidt, Milner, and Wiechmann (2004) developed a multilevel, multiple goal model of individual and team regulatory processes across individual and team goals. Their research showed that individual self-set goals were the highest for individuals who received individual-level feedback only, followed by a combination of individual and team feedback, and were lowest for those receiving only team feedback. It appears that providing group members with individual feedback made them strive for greater levels of individual performance.

The main conclusion that can be drawn from our review is that most studies we found provide strong support for Locke and Latham's (1990) assertions that goals mediate the impact of feedback on performance. That said, we note that most studies focused on isolated feedback interventions in controlled settings. We know very little about how the broader feedback environment that surrounds employees in natural settings impacts the development of goals, and performance (Ashford & Northcraft, 2003; Steelman, Levy, & Snell, 2004). That broader feedback environment consists of many different feedback interventions and many different feedback cues. How do these feedback cues work together in impacting the goals people pursue and performance? Given the increasingly complex nature of work, the time is ripe for a more in-depth assessment of how multiple feedback interventions and multiple facets of feedback interact in impacting goal setting and performance.

## The Moderation Hypothesis

### *What Have We Learned Since 1990?*

Support for the moderation hypothesis is found in studies since 1990 examining the joint effect of feedback and goal setting on performance. For example, examining the joint effects of goal difficulty and feedback on budgetary performance, Hirst and Lowy (1990) found that goal difficulty and feedback interacted to affect performance positively, whereas independently neither had a significant effect on performance.

A third study also examined the basic proposition that goals and feedback both are needed to optimally produce performance, but looked at feedback sought by the performer rather than that given by the supervisor or as part of a programmatic intervention.

Morrison and Weldon (1990) found that both observer and self-reports of feedback seeking increased substantially from Trial 1 to Trial 2 when a goal was assigned at Trial 2's onset. No increase was found in the absence of a goal. Their analysis also showed that subjects who sought this task feedback performed better (were more likely to reach their goal) than subjects who did not.

Much work since 1990 has focused on the moderators of the joint effect of goals and feedback on performance. Neubert's (1998) meta-analysis of 11 studies provided evidence for the role of task complexity and the source of feedback in moderating the joint effect of goals and feedback on task performance. The *d* value for complex tasks was more than double that for simple tasks (1.02 vs. .47). His results did not confirm a second hypothesis, that feedback from personal sources would be more impactful than that from impersonal sources (e.g., computers). The source did not moderate the incremental effect of adding feedback to goal setting.

Other studies examining moderator variables come from psychology. West, Bagwell, and Dark-Freudeman (2005) argued that younger people are more likely to believe they can meet a challenging goal even in the face of negative feedback, a belief they attributed to the greater sense of memory control in younger adults. They found that subjects performed better in the goals and feedback (combined) condition and the goals and positive feedback (combined) condition compared to a control condition and that this difference did not vary by age. The goals and positive feedback condition prompted the most goal commitment and subsequent goal setting and did so especially among older adults.

McCalley and Midden (2002) found that goal setting and feedback combined created the most energy-saving behavior in an experimentally created "laundry room." These authors also examined a personality variable, pro-self versus pro-social values and found that individuals with pro-self values did not respond well to feedback combined with experimenter-set goals (they saved less energy), whereas those with pro-social values saved significantly more energy when the goal was assigned and feedback provided. Several authors have added nuance and complexity to our understanding of the goals–feedback interaction by assessing different aspects of feedback. Shih and Alexander (2000) examined the effect of two types of feedback in interaction with goal setting as they affect the academic skill development of Taiwanese children. They compared four conditions: goal setting with self-referenced feedback, goal setting with social-referenced feedback, self-referenced feedback only, and social-referenced feedback only. All feedback was received privately, but was either self-referenced (information on their own performance in a pretest trial) or social-referenced (comparative information relative to peers). They found that children in the self-referenced feedback groups had higher self-efficacy and performed better than did those receiving socially referenced feedback. However, goal setting played a nonsignificant role in predicting both self-efficacy and performance. Like Locke and Latham (1990), they speculated that this finding may be due to students spontaneously setting goals on their own in the no goal setting condition.

Louro, Pieters, and Zeelenberg (2007) examined a different type of feedback. They followed people over the course of pursuing a weight loss goal and examined responses to positive versus negative feedback. They found that beginners increased their efforts in response to success (versus failure) feedback, but people who were more advanced in their pursuit of their goal tended to increase their efforts in response to failure (versus success) feedback. They examined this effect in a multiple goal context (comparing pursuit of a weight loss goal and a second personally specified goal) and found that positive feedback on distant goals causes individuals to allocate effort toward the goal for which that feedback is given. As the goal becomes proximal, the effect is reversed: negative feedback increases effort toward the now proximal goal. The authors speculate that positive feedback when goals are proximate cue performers that coasting is possible and their efforts get drawn on toward more novel goals on which more work is needed

Finally, other scholars have begun to examine the content of the goals being pursued. Cianci, Klein, and Seijts (2010) examined the interaction of learning versus performance goals and negative feedback on resulting tension and performance in a laboratory setting. They found that subjects with a learning goal both felt less tension and performed better following negative feedback than those assigned a performance goal. Perceived tension mediated the effects of the assigned goal on performance in their negative feedback context. Cianci, Schaubroeck, and McGill (2010) found that performance on a complex task in a lab study declined when positive feedback was combined with assigned learning goals, but had the opposite effect with assigned performance goals. Conversely, negative feedback favorably influenced performance for individuals assigned a learning goal, whereas performance declined when negative feedback was combined with performance goals. The authors do not provide an explanation for their findings, though their data rule out attributions about the causes of successful or unsuccessful performance in a prior task and emotional states during task performance as mediators. One possible explanation may be that positive feedback for people with a learning goal orientation may suggest that their goal of mastery within a situation has been achieved and further effort is less required.

Several studies have advanced our understanding of this process through their examination of attributes of goals and feedback simultaneously. For example, Earley, Northcraft, Lee, and Lituchy (1990) conducted a lab study using a stock-market simulation in which they crossed goal setting (specific and challenging versus general), outcome feedback, and process feedback (both general versus specific). They found that individuals with specific, challenging goals and specific outcome or process feedback performed better than did those working under any other goal-feedback condition. Self-confidence partially and task strategy quality fully mediated these effects. Their finding that self-confidence was high when individuals were given negative outcome feedback but a general goal suggests that this feedback alone might create a false sense of performance possibilities.

Latham and Seijts (1999) examined the effects of proximal and distal goals on performance of a complex task. They found that participants with proximal goals in addition to specific difficult distal goals performed better and argued that proximal goals provide clearer markers of progress than do distal goals. As they noted, "proximal goals may provide individuals with additional specific information about performance that is not present when only a distal goal is set" (Latham & Seijts, 1999, p. 422). Kernan and Lord (1990) looked at the interaction of specific versus general goals and feedback in an escalation of commitment context. They found that general goals led to greater escalation than did explicit or specific goals. They explained this result by arguing that specific goals enable subjects to use feedback information more precisely, whereas general goals allow individuals to give themselves the benefit of the doubt concerning the adequacy of performance (and thus to continue to escalate).

One group of field studies that seems to not interact with or draw on the OB goal setting literature very much are studies done under the rubric of Organizational Behavior Management. For example, Langeland, Johnson, and Mawhinney (1998) found that a joint program of feedback, goal setting, and praise from supervisors improved performance. In a similar study, Reber, Wallin, and Chhokar (1990) found that goals helped increase safety performance in a field setting when they were specific, difficult, and accepted, but that the goals were not consistently achieved until feedback was provided. Similar studies have shown that these practices combine to improve performance in therapy settings (Huberman & O'Brien, 1999), among university admissions officers (Wilk & Redmon, 1998), to increase safety on construction projects (Cooper, Phillips, Sutherland, & Makin, 1994; Lingard & Rowlinson, 1997), and the customer service of university student advisors (Tittelbach, DeAngelis, Sturmey, & Alvero, 2007). Unfortunately, these studies lump the planned interventions together, confounding effects and leaving us unable to examine their potential interactions.

## Our Suggestions for Future Research

While the literature has clearly progressed since Locke and Latham's (1990) review, many questions and topics require further exploration and testing. First, the moderation and mediation literatures do not seem to speak to each other extensively. For example, research on the mediation hypothesis looks primarily at goal level, whereas the moderation literature examines other aspects of a goal (e.g., its specificity, proximity, and content). The moderation literature looks at more attributes of feedback (e.g., source and content), whereas mediation simply assesses the feedback sign. In the moderation literature, process and outcome feedback are examined as they potentially interact with goal setting. These also could be examined as types of feedback stimulating subsequent goal setting and thereby performance on the mediation side.

Second, the goal setting literature has tended to focus on simple tasks, single goals, and individual, independent performers (Neubert, 1998). These are somewhat at odds with work as it is performed in today's organizations. For example, some authors have concluded that in complex tasks, feedback distracts the performer from coping with all the complexity of his or her work. However, this conclusion may only be true in the short burst over which the work is tracked in the laboratory. When complex work is done over a longer period of time, feedback may be welcomed and indeed essential. Also, we know little about how goals and feedback might best be combined effectively to promote creative performance in organizations. Recent work has shown that knowledge workers who seek more feedback and seek feedback more broadly were rated as exhibiting higher creative performance (De Stobbeleir, Ashford, & Buyens, 2011). How goals (of different types and levels) might interact with these findings is an important subject of future research.

Researchers since 1990 have complicated our image of task and task performance by examining multiple tasks/goals, tasks without explicit beginning and end points (much less trials), and tasks where performance is much more subjectively measured. This more complex portrayal of tasks, however, can certainly be mined for additional insights.

For example, the literature to date often portrays a single person performing by him or herself. However, people often work with others and sometimes on interdependent tasks where tight coordination is needed. How do those others affect this process? There may be emotional contagion as suggested by Barsade (2002) and interpretive influences communicated interpersonally that are important to understand. In addition, both goals and feedback can be singular or multiple, and clear or ambiguous. What are the performance consequences of various permutations of these two dimensions? What happens, for example, when goals are clear and feedback is ambiguous? Alternatively, whereas most goal setting studies have examined processes with respect to very clear standards of "good" performance, in organizations there often is more ambiguity and subjectivity in judging when someone has met a particular standard (e.g., of being a "good manager"; Ashford & Tsui, 1991). Does an ambiguous and subjective standard require more feedback?

Third, the attributes of goals seem much more nuanced and developed than are notions of feedback in this literature. We know a lot about goal level, specificity, the effects of who sets the goal, acceptance of the goal, and so forth. Although since 1990 people have begun to examine more nuanced feedback differences (e.g., whether the feedback is composed of self-comparisons versus comparisons to others (Shih & Alexander, 2000), whether it focuses on process versus outcomes of performance (Earley et al., 1990), whether it is given versus sought (Morrison & Weldon, 1990), and whether it is given verbally versus through a graphic objective presentation or virtually (Wilk & Redmon, 1998), more can be done. Goodman (1998) found that external feedback was detrimental to learning when the task itself provided little feedback, suggesting that any study of the role of feedback in the performance process needs to reference the various sources of feedback available to a performer. While there may be a single, identifiable person in the environment who assigns a goal, a performer can use a variety of different sources of feedback to assess his or her progress on that goal, including self-feedback, task feedback, coworker feedback, and cues derived from his or her observation of the environment and the supervisor (Ashford & Cummings, 1983; Herold & Greller, 1977). Given this, some authors suggest that we devote more attention to the conceptualization and measurement of task feedback, and consider the relationship between its dimensions and subsequent performance (Renn, 2003).

In addition to more research on these dimensions, future research could also examine the source of the feedback. Feedback from the boss might have a quite different effect from feedback from coworkers, for example. Also, what happens if feedback is multiple and especially if that multiple feedback conflicts? We know a bit about conflicts between self-generated and social feedback (Bono & Colbert, 2005). What happens when a performer detects or receives conflicting feedback from different evaluators, something we might expect to occur with some frequency in organizations? Do individuals interpret it anyway and is there any regularity in their interpretations that might be important to understand? The literature to date seems to presume that certain conditions allow people to "tell on their own" how they are performing (and thus feedback from others or the organization is not needed or may have less effect). Latham and Seijts (1999) argued that proximate goals allow for self-assessment, and Neubert (1998) proposed that clear-cut tasks do the same. We need studies, though, that explicitly test this presumption. Finally, feedback in this literature is often treated as a one-time event. And yet in organizations there are often historical patterns. If individuals have continuously and regularly been given positive feedback but suddenly do not receive feedback during a particular time period or for a particular performance trial, they may interpret that (non) event as feedback. A historical pattern of all positive feedback may lull a performer into a relatively mindless state in which he or she becomes less attentive to feedback cues and perhaps less concerned about performance. Feedback frequency may also have an effect. Feedback that comes too rarely will not give employees timely information. On the other hand, too frequent feedback can be redundant, time-consuming, and distracting, resulting in lower efficiency. This relationship may be moderated by the nature of the goal that they are pursuing, and by organizational and even industry contexts. For example, in a fast-changing industry, more frequent feedback may be seen as critical and appropriate.

Given that people and organizations often are pursuing multiple goals simultaneously (either across tasks or on different dimensions of the same task), feedback plays a directional role as well. Feedback in the environment, either that explicitly given by the organization or that naturally occurring in the task environment, makes certain tasks and goals more salient than others, thereby drawing individual's attention and efforts (Ashford & Northcraft, 2003; Northcraft, Schmidt, & Ashford, 2011). As shown by Northcraft et al. (2011), the more frequent and specific the feedback for a given task dimension, the higher the task's salience for the individual, the individual's efficacy for that task, and their performance.

Feedback also has affective consequences (Cianci et al., 2010). People feel joy or disappointment based in part on feedback regarding their success or failure to attain a goal. Thus, consideration of the interactive effects of goals and feedback is a perfect place to begin to answer Locke & Latham's (1990) call to begin focusing on affect as it plays a role in the goal setting process. While Locke and Latham (1990) focused primarily on satisfaction and dissatisfaction as affect, researchers since have begun to look at more nuanced affective reactions (e.g., Ilies & Judge, 2005). However, in most studies to date, affect is construed solely as a reaction to an experienced discrepancy (i.e., negative feedback). It is also possible, though, that independent emotions might play a role. For example, what role does mood play? Does mood or specific affective experiences influence the amount of feedback sought?

Feedback's affective consequences also suggest ways that feedback can be a reward for people. This is not to rule out the cognitive processes involved in the goal setting process, and certainly the cognitive processes involved in interpreting feedback and developing subsequent intentions regarding performance, but it is also to recognize that feedback, especially from supervisors, represents attention from a prominent person in the environment. As such, it can have reinforcing properties. The presence of feedback can represent supervisor consideration, concern, and caring. As such it may build affective commitment to the goal and thereby produce motivation. In organizations, people sometimes work for a long time before knowing if they have met a standard or are making progress toward it. In such conditions, the symbolic role of feedback may be more important (Neubert, 1998). Simply knowing that someone cares and is attending to a performer's progress may motivate him or her.

While various mediators and moderators of goal setting effects have been examined, there has been a decided emphasis on individual dispositions. However, in organizations, context will certainly also matter. For example, the goal revision of individuals receiving negative feedback but working in a context full of supportive colleagues might differ from that of individuals working on their own; individuals doing highly interdependent work might react differently from those working independently. The results of one study are suggestive here. Senko and Harackiewicz (2002) found that a performance goal undermined performance and intrinsic motivation only when pursued within an explicitly evaluative context by a person who characteristically avoids challenge. The effect of negative outcome feedback also varied by the evaluativeness of the context.

Finally, there is interesting research to be conducted at the group level too, especially given recent progress in research on groups. Identity processes and emotional contagion (Barsade, 2002) are just two possible mediating processes that may occur in groups under different goal/feedback conditions that might affect how feedback and goals impact performance at the individual and group level. We know that being in a group instantiates an identity that then motivates and constrains subsequent behavior (citation). Group feedback and goals may serve as an accelerator of those effects, given their motivational properties. Emotional contagion processes may amplify the effect of group feedback or goals as emotions experienced by one or another group member (perhaps due to their personalities) spread throughout the group. Of course, additional complexities may occur in groups. For example, when a group is given a goal but feedback is given at the individual level (perhaps in addition to group level), what happens? When individuals have goals but are interacting in a group where they receive group feedback, what happens? However, at least one study suggests that traditional moderation findings may still hold at the group level. Specifically, Jung, Schneider, and Valacich (2010) found that groups given feedback and an explicit difficult goal (versus do your best) outperformed all other groups in terms of both quantity and quality of ideas. While there is a lot to be worked out on a theoretical level, these questions are an attractive focus for future research in this area.

## Conclusion

Two decades of research on the role of feedback in goal setting provide strong support for Locke and Latham's (1990) basic premises. Consistent with Locke and Latham (1990), this review of studies across a range of settings and samples shows that feedback plays two roles in goal setting: It stimulates performers to set goals for themselves, and those feedback-based goals subsequently help them to improve their performance (mediation hypothesis); and it tells them how well they are doing in relation to those goals, thereby strengthening the impact of goals on performance (moderation hypothesis). In that sense, the progress that has been made to date has largely been incremental rather than radical, but it is still considerable. Our historical review highlights some of the boundary conditions for the effective delivery of feedback in the goal setting process (e.g., comparative versus nominal feedback, and positive versus negative feedback), and has identified a number of underlying individual and contextual mechanisms explaining the goal setting–performance relationship (e.g., performers' affective reactions and task complexity). Given the radical changes in the world of work and given the complex goals and feedback environments that individuals face today, we hope that this chapter will inspire researchers to continue to set increasingly difficult goals to answer the questions still remaining in this literature.

# References

Ashford, S. J., & Cummings, L. L. (1983). Feedback as an individual resource: Personal strategies of creating information. *Organizational Behavior and Human Performance*, 32, 370–398.

Ashford, S. J. & Northcraft, G. (2003). Robbing Peter to Pay Paul: Feedback environments and enacted priorities in response to competing task demands. *Human Resource Management Review*, 13, 537–559.

Ashford, S. J. & Tsui, A. S. (1991). Self-regulation for managerial effectiveness: The role of active feedback-seeking. *Academy of Management Journal*, 34(2), 251–280.

Bandura, A., & Jourdan, F. J. (1991). Self-regulatory mechanisms governing the impact of social comparison on complex decision making. *Journal of Personality and Social Psychology*, 60(6), 941–951.

Barsade, S. G. (2002). The ripple effect: Emotional contagion and its influence on group behavior, *Administrative Science Quarterly*, 47(4), 644–675.

Bono, J. E., & Colbert, A. (2005). Understanding responses to feedback: The role of core self-evaluations. *Personnel Psychology*, 58, 171–203.

Cianci, A. M., Klein, H. J., & Seijts, G. H. (2010). The effect of negative feedback on tension and subsequent performance: The main and interactive effects of goal content and conscientiousness. *Journal of Applied Psychology*, 95(4), 618–630.

Cianci, A., Schaubroeck, J., & McGill, G. (2010). Achievement goals, feedback, and task performance. *Human Performance*, 23(2), 131–154.

Cooper, M. D., Phillips, R. A., Sutherland, V. J., & Makin, P. J. (1994). Reducing accidents using goal setting and feedback: A field study. *Journal of Occupational and Organizational Psychology*, 67(3), 219–240.

Cron, W. L., Slocum, J. W., Jr., VandeWalle, D., & Fu, Q. (2005). The role of goal orientation on negative emotions and goal setting when initial performance falls short of one's performance goal. *Human Performance*, 18(1), 55–80.

De Stobbeleir, K. E. M., Ashford, S. J., & Buyens, D. (2011). Self-regulation of creativity at work: The role of feedback-seeking behavior in creative performance. *Academy of Management Journal*, 54(4), 811–831.

DeShon, R. P., Kozlowski, S. W. J., Schmidt, A. M., Milner, K. R., & Wiechmann, D. (2004). Multiple goal feedback effects on the regulation of individual and team performance in training. *Journal of Applied Psychology*, 89, 1035–1056.

Donovan, J., & Williams, K. J. (2003). Missing the mark: Effects of time and causal attributions on goal revision in response to goal-performance discrepancies. *Journal of Applied Psychology*, 88, 379–390.

Dweck, C. S. (1986). Motivational processes affecting learning. *American Psychologist*, 41, 1040–1048.

Earley, P. C., Northcraft, G. B., Lee, C., & Lituchy, T. R. (1990). Impact of process and outcome feedback on the relation of goal setting to task performance. *Academy of Management Journal*, 33(1), 87–105.

Goodman, J. S. (1998) The interactive effects of task and external feedback on practice performance and learning, *Organizational Behavior and Human Decision Processes*, 76(3), 223–252.

Herold, D., & Greller, M. (1977). Feedback: the definition of the construct. *Academy of Management Journal*, 20, 142–147.

Hirst, M. K., & Lowy, S. M. (1990). The linear, additive, and interactive effects of budgetary goal difficulty and feedback on performance. *Accounting Organizations and Society*, 15(5), 425–436.

Huberman, W. L., & O'Brien, R. M. (1999). Improving therapist and patient performance in chronic psychiatric group homes through goal-setting, feedback, and positive reinforcement. *Journal of Organizational Behavior Management*, 19(1), 13–36.

Ilies, R., & Judge, T. A. (2005). Goal regulation across time: The effects of feedback and affect. *Journal of Applied Psychology*, 90(3), 453–467.

Ilies, R., Judge, T. A., & Wagner, D. T. (2010). The influence of cognitive and affective reactions to feedback on subsequent goals: Role of behavioral inhibition/activation. *European Psychologist*, 15(2), 121–131.

Johnson, D. S., Turban, D. B., Pieper, K. F., & Ng, Y. M. (1996). Exploring the role of normative- and performance-based feedback in motivational processes. *Journal of Applied Social Psychology*, 26, 973–992.

Judge, T. A., Locke, E. A., & Durham, C. C. (1997). The dispositional causes of job satisfaction: A core evaluations approach. In L. L. Cummings & B. M. Staw (Eds.), *Research in organizational behavior*, 19, 151–188.

Jung, J. H., Schneider, C., & Valacich, J. (2010). Enhancing the motivational affordance of information systems: The effects of real-time performance feedback and goal setting in group collaboration environments. *Management Science*, 56(4), 724–742.

Kernan, M. C., & Lord, R. G. (1990). Effects of valence, expectancies, and goal-performance discrepancies in single and multiple goals environments. *Journal of Applied Psychology*, 75(2), 194–203.

Kernan, M. C., Heimann, B., & Hanges, P. J. (1991). Effects of goal choice, strategy choice, and feedback source on goal acceptance, performance, and subsequent goals. *Journal of Applied Social Psychology*, 21(9), 713–733.

Korsgaard, M. A., & Diddams, M. (1996). The effect of process feedback and task complexity on personal goals, strategies, and performance. *Journal of Applied Social Psychology*, 26, 1889–1911.

Langeland, K. L., Johnson, C. M., & Mawhinney, T. C. (1998). Improving staff performance in a community mental health setting: Job analysis, training, goal setting, feedback, and years of data. *Journal of Organizational Behavior Management*, 18(1), 21–43.

Latham, G. P., & Seijts, G. H. (1999). The effects of proximal and distal goals on performance on a moderately complex task. *Journal of Organizational Behavior*, 20(4), 421–429.

Lingard, H., & Rowlinson, S. (1997). Behavior-based safety management in Hong Kong's construction industry. *Journal of Safety Research*, 28(4), 243–256.

Locke, E. A., & Latham, G. P. (1990). *A theory of goal setting and task performance*. Prentice Hall, Englewood Cliffs, 413 p.

Louro, M. J. S., Pieters, R., & Zeelenberg, M. (2007). Dynamics of multiple goal pursuit. *Journal of Personality and Social Psychology*, 93(2), 174–193.

McCalley, L. T., & Midden, C. J. H. (2002). Energy conservation through product-integrated feedback: The roles of goal-setting and social orientation. *Journal of Economic Psychology*, 23(5), 589–603.

Mesch, D. J., Farh, J., & Podsakoff, P. M. (1994). Effects of feedback sign on group goal setting, strategies, and performance. *Group and Organization Management*, 19(3), 309–333.

Morrison, E. W., & Weldon, E. (1990). The impact of an assigned performance goal on feedback seeking behavior. *Human Performance*, 3, 37–50.

Neubert, M. J. (1998). The value of feedback and goal setting over goals setting alone and potential moderators of this effect: A meta-analysis. *Human Performance*, 11(4), 321–335.

Northcraft, G., Schmidt, A., & Ashford, S. (2011). Feedback and the rationing of time and effort among competing tasks. *Journal of Applied Psychology*, 96, 1076–1086.

Reber, R. A., Wallin, J. A., & Chhokar, J. S. (1990). Improving safety performance with goal setting and feedback. *Human Performance*, 3(1), 51–61.

Renn, R. W., & Fedor, D. B. (2001). Development and field-test of a feedback seeking, self-efficacy, and goal setting model of work performance. *Journal of Management*, 27(5), 563–583.

Renn, R. W. (2003). Moderation by goal commitment of the feedback-performance relationship: Theoretical explanation and preliminary study. *Human Resource Management Review*, 13(4), 561–580.

Senko, C., & Harackiewicz, J. M. (2002). Performance goals: The moderating roles of context and achievement orientation. *Journal of Experimental Social Psychology*, 38(6), 603–610.

Shih, S., & Alexander, J. M. (2000). Interacting effects of goal setting and self- or other-referenced feedback on children's development of self-efficacy and cognitive skill within the Taiwanese classroom. *Journal of Educational Psychology*, 92, 536–543.

Steelman, L. A.,Levy, P. E., & Snell, A. F. (2004). The feedback environment scale (FES): Construct definition, measurement, and validation. *Educational and Psychological Measurement*, 64(1), 165–184.

Tittelbach, D., DeAngelis, M., Sturmey, P., & Alvero, A. M. (2007). The effects of task clarification, feedback, and goal setting on student advisors office behaviors and customer service. *Journal of Organizational Behavior Management*, 27(3), 27–37.

Tolli, A. P., & Schmidt, A. M. (2008). The role of feedback, casual attributions, and self-efficacy in goal revision. *Journal of Applied Psychology*, 93(3), 692–701.

Tziner, A., Kopelman, R., & Joanis, C. (1997). Investigation of raters' and ratees' reactions to three methods of performance appraisal: BOS, BARS, and GRS. *Canadian Journal of Administrative Sciences*, 14(4), 396–404.

VandeWalle, D., Cron, W. L., & Slocum, J. W., Jr. (2001). The role of goal orientation following performance feedback. *Journal of Applied Psychology*, 86(4), 629–640.

West, R. L., Bagwell, D. K., & Dark-Freudeman, A. (2005). Memory and goal setting: The response of older and younger adults to positive and objective feedback. *Psychology and Aging*, 20(2), 195–201.

Wilk, L. A., & Redmon, W. K. (1998). The effects of feedback and goal setting on the productivity and satisfaction of university admissions staff. *Journal of Organizational Behavior Management*, 18(1), 45–68.

Williams, K. J., Donovan, J. J., & Dodge, T. L. (2000). Self-regulation of performance: Goal establishment and goal revision processes in athletes. *Human Performance*, 13, 159–180.

# 6   Goal Commitment

*Howard J. Klein*  Department of Management and Human Resources, The Ohio State University

*Joseph T. Cooper*  Department of Management and Marketing, University of Wyoming

*Christina A. Monahan*  Department of Management and Human Resources, The Ohio State University

## Goal Commitment

Because goals will not operate as intended without commitment, goal commitment plays a central role in goal theory. This essential moderator has been recognized since the inception of goal theory (Locke, 1968), and commitment's role has been clarified as the theory evolved (e.g., Locke & Latham, 1990). In this chapter, we focus on the published literature between 1989 and mid-2011 to highlight the advances made and the challenges that remain. We begin with a discussion of how commitment has been defined and measured. We then review the extant literature, summarizing what is known about the consequences of goal commitment and then its determinants. We give special attention to three research streams that have emerged or grown substantially since Locke and Latham (1990) and close with a research agenda to further our understanding and prediction of goal commitment and its consequences.

## Conceptual Definitions of Goal Commitment

Early reviews (Hollenbeck & Klein, 1987; Locke, Latham, & Erez, 1988) noted that goal commitment was typically assumed rather than assessed, not sufficiently understood or examined given its central role, and inconsistently defined and measured. The lack of definitional consistency remains today, and is an issue with all workplace commitments (Klein, Molloy, & Brinsfield, 2012). Becker, Klein, and Meyer (2009), discussing commitment in general, noted that a lack of consensus regarding the meaning, structure, and in turn, measurement of commitment is detrimental to more coherently and systematically advancing our understanding. Tubbs (1993) suggested that five related but distinct motivational concepts have been lumped together under the term *goal commitment:* motivational force, intention, intention strength, assigned goal adherence, and maintenance of that adherence. DeShon and Landis (1997) similarly suggested three distinct components within operationalizations of goal commitment: importance, determination to attain, and unwillingness to abandon the goal. Jaros (2009) also noted various elements in definitions of goal commitment and suggested that the definition be revised to be narrower in scope and remove confounding elements.

Looking across all workplace commitments (e.g., goals, individuals, organizations), Klein, Molloy, and Cooper (2009) identified eight distinct commitment conceptualizations; all but one (identification) have been used in describing goal commitment, as illustrated

Table 6.1 Variation in Goal Commitment Definitions in the Literature

| Commitment conceptualizations | Sample definitions |
| --- | --- |
| **Conceptualizations that are best viewed as determinants of commitment** | |
| Commitment as an *exchange*—one's reciprocal response to either promised or received benefits (economic or social). | " … degree to which an individual is willing to commit resources toward accomplishing a goal." (Naylor & Ilgen, 1984, p. 98). |
| Commitment as *congruence*—the internalization of a goal due to shared values or interests. | "… acceptance of it as your own personal goal …" (Yukl & Latham, 1978, p. 312)."… the use of or internalization of an assigned goal" (Tubbs, 1993, p. 87). |
| **Conceptualizations that are best viewed as consequences of commitment** | |
| Commitment as *motivation*—one's willingness to put forth effort toward a goal. | "… a determination to try for a goal (or to keep trying for a goal), …" (Locke et al., 1981, p. 143)."… motivation to pursue the goal …" (Hollenbeck & Brief, 1987, p. 397). "… determination to reach a goal, …" (Locke, Latham, & Erez, 1988, p. 24)."… the strength of one's intention to reach a goal …" (Tubbs, 1993, p. 87)."… the degree to which the individual … is determined to reach it by expending effort over time …" (DeShon & Landis, 1997, p. 106). |
| Commitment as *continuation*—the desire to continue to pursue or the unwillingness to abandon a goal. | "… an unwillingness to subsequently reduce goals …" (Campion & Lord, 1982, p. 268). "… persistence in pursuing it over time." (Hollenbeck, Williams, & Klein, 1987, p. 18)"… the degree to which the individual … is unwilling to abandon or lower the goal …" (DeShon & Landis, 1997, p. 106). |
| **Conceptualizations of commitment that are not confounded by antecedents or outcomes** | |
| Commitment as an *attitude*—one's summary evaluation of the goal. | "… the degree to which the individual considers the goal to be important, …" (DeShon & Landis, 1997, p. 106). |
| Commitment as a *force*—pressures that bind or oblige one to a goal. | "… a pre-choice attitudinal evaluation, similar or identical to motivational force …" (Tubbs, 1993, p. 86)."… a force that binds an individual to a course of action …" (Meyer & Herscovitch, 2001, p. 301). |
| Commitment as a *bond*—how strongly one is attached to a goal. | "… one's attachment to … reach a goal, …" (Locke, Latham, & Erez, 1988, p. 24). |

in Table 6.1. Klein et al. also noted that most commitment conceptualizations are confounded with the antecedents or outcomes of commitment. This is also noted in Table 6.1. Klein et al. concluded that viewing commitment as an attachment or bond was most defensible. Yet goal commitment is most often defined in terms of determination (motivation) and persistence (continuation): outcomes of commitment rather than commitment itself, according to Klein et al.

To address construct ambiguity within and across the study of workplace commitments, Klein et al. (2012) presented an alternative conceptualization and construct definition aimed at addressing key criticisms of the commitment construct. After reviewing the definition and operation of commitment across multiple literatures and disciplines with the goal of more precisely and distinctively conceptualizing commitment, they concluded that commitment is best viewed as a bond, consistent with Klein et al. (2009). However, they went further to specify commitment as a particular type of bond. Specifically, they defined commitment as a volitional psychological bond reflecting dedication to, and responsibility for, a particular target. Applied to goals, this definition essentially captures the pledging of oneself to a goal. We recommend that future theorizing and research regarding goal commitment adopt this definition.

## Measuring Goal Commitment

Early reviews (Hollenbeck & Klein, 1987; Locke et al., 1988) highlighted the need to assess goal commitment and led to increased attention to its measurement. In 1990, there was debate about the appropriate time (i.e., pre- or post-performance) to assess goal commitment. Locke and Latham (1990) concluded that measurement timing is unlikely to affect results, and subsequent research has supported that conclusion (Klein, Wesson, Hollenbeck, Wright, & DeShon, 2001). However, because commitment can change during goal striving, repeated measurement may be needed depending on the research question. Timing aside, several approaches and scales have been used to assess goal commitment as summarized below.

### Approaches

Goal commitment has been assessed using *self-reports* and inferred from both *discrepancies* between assigned and personal goals and *behavior*. The use of *self-reports* has been the most common measurement approach. We reviewed 144 studies published between 1989 and 2011 that empirically assessed goal commitment (or acceptance[1]). Self-reports were used in 95% of those studies. Because commitment is an internal psychological state (Klein et al., 2012), self-report is also the most appropriate means for assessing goal commitment. Using self-reports assumes that individuals have insight into their commitment. Although there are limitations to introspection (e.g., Schooler & Schreiber, 2004), it is the individual experiencing the state that is typically in the best position to describe their commitment. The limitations of other sources and approaches are usually greater, resulting in arguably less valid assessments. Self-reports capture a person's assessment of commitment to a particular goal at a given point in time. Self-reports of goal commitment do not capture the personal goals of those who are not committed to an assigned or participatively set goal, nor do they capture or preclude subsequent goal change, even if high commitment is reported. If goal change or personal goals are variables of interest, personal goals should be assessed when assessing commitment to an assigned, participatively set, or even previously self-set personal goal (Seijts & Latham, 2000a; Wright, O'Leary, Cortina, Klein, & Hollenbeck, 1994).

A few studies (i.e., 5% of those reviewed) have used the *discrepancy* between personal goals and assigned or participatively set goals, or even personal goals at two different points in time, to infer commitment. We do not dispute the claim by Tubbs (1994, p. 806) that the "discrepancy approach, though it has its limits, is the most direct and unambiguous way to assess the difference between assigned and personal goals." That difference, however, reflects a construct distinct from, and not necessarily related to, goal commitment. As a psychological state, commitment can change as conditions and perceptions change (Klein et al., 2012). The fact that a goal is revised does not mean the individual was not at a previous time committed to achieving it. In our opinion, the demonstrated divergence between self-report and discrepancy measures by Tubbs (1993) supports the fact that discrepancy measures are assessing something other than commitment rather than suggesting that self-report measures are invalid. There are also well-documented limitations of discrepancies (e.g., Edwards, 1994, 1995). The specific theoretical, practical, and empirical problems with using discrepancies to infer goal commitment, well described elsewhere (Seijts & Latham, 2000a; Wright et al., 1994), are not repeated here.

The final approach to assessing commitment has been to examine *behavior*. Locke and Latham (1990) suggested that commitment could be satisfactorily measured either attitudinally or behaviorally, and there is a long history of viewing commitment in behavioral terms (e.g., Becker, 1960; Salancik, 1977). The behavioral view of commitment, however, focuses on how behavior creates commitment to that course of action, and infers commitment from action. No recent studies have examined commitment in terms of behavior. Goal commitment should motivate goal striving and thus influence behavior. However, behavior does not always follow from commitment (e.g., when there are competing goals to which one is also committed, when one lacks ability, or when there are situational constraints). In the model presented by Klein et al. (2012), behavior is an indirect consequence of commitment that may or may not occur. In sum, the absence of behavior does not necessarily indicate an absence of goal commitment.

In most cases, self-reports will be the most valid approach to measuring goal commitment. In some instances (e.g., data collection limitations, study purpose), it may be necessary or sufficient to assess behavior or discrepancies as indicators of commitment. In such cases, those proxies should not be confused with goal commitment itself. It is time to move from debating whether self-reports versus discrepancy or direct versus indirect questions are best. Instead, attention should shift to better understanding the relationships between direct self-reports and alternatives so that when those alternatives must be used, the results can be interpreted appropriately. We next turn to the different self-report measures used in the recent literature.

### Alternative Self-Report Measures

**Single-item measures.** A single item was used in 8% of the studies we reviewed that measured goal commitment. In half of those studies, the item assessed commitment directly (e.g., "how committed are you …"). Another quarter of these studies used items reflecting intentions to pursue a goal, with the remaining items reflecting the conceptual variability discussed at the beginning of this chapter. Single-item measures are generally discouraged, but they are not necessarily invalid (e.g., Wanous & Hudy, 2001). In some instances (e.g., survey length limits), the use of a single-item measure may be justifiable if goal commitment is being assessed solely as a control variable or manipulation check. In such cases, we recommend that a direct, rather than an indirect, item be used for reasons discussed below.

*Idiosyncratic multi-item scales.* Of the studies measuring goal commitment, 22% used a multi-item (2–6 items) scale, but a scale that was not (a) used by more than 2 other studies or (b) not simply an adaptation of the commonly used scales discussed below. The items in these measures mirror the above-noted conceptual variability. Those not directly assessing commitment tend to reflect the following concepts: importance or urgency; intention, willingness, or determination; time or effort allocation; expectancy, doubt, or reasonableness; anticipated satisfaction or disappointment; investment, felt responsibility, or caring; planning intensity and persistence. Some of these concepts are consistent with the recommended definition of goal commitment. Most, however, are best viewed as belonging to distinct antecedent or outcome constructs.

A few researchers (e.g., Oettingen, Mayer, Sevincer, Stephens, Pak, & Hagenah, 2009) have suggested that assessing goal commitment indirectly, though still with self-reports, via concepts such as planning intensity or anticipated disappointment is more valid than direct assessments because they require less introspection and are less susceptible to social desirability bias. We are not aware of any evidence demonstrating that these have been issues with goal commitment measures. As such, we recommend that direct assessments be used unless there is a strong rationale, given the purpose of the study (e.g., assessing commitment to subconscious goals) or contextual features, suggesting that respondents will not respond accurately or have insight into their commitment. When indirect self-reports are used, the proxy construct (e.g., goal importance, frustration) should be articulated along with its theoretical relationship to goal commitment, and not labeled as, or confused with, goal commitment itself.

*Hollenbeck, Klein, and colleagues' scales.* The lack of consensus regarding how to best measure commitment, reflected in the variation that has remained in the above single and idiosyncratic multi-item scales, led Hollenbeck, Williams, and Klein (1989) to construct a 9-item measure based on original and previously used items. In that study, two items ("I am willing to put forth a great deal of effort ...") and "There is not much to be gained ...") were excluded from the analyses because they loaded on a separate factor. Hollenbeck, Klein, O'Leary, and Wright (1989) presented additional validation evidence for that 7-item scale, along with an alternative 4-item version. Eleven studies subsequently used the full 9-item scale, 28 studies used the 7-item scale, and 5 studies used the 4-item scale. Interestingly, another 27 studies used variations of this scale—not minor rewording of items, but alterations to the structure of the scale. In a few instances, those changes took the form of adding items to a scale (4 studies) or both adding and deleting items (3 studies). In most cases, however, the alteration involved deleting items (20 studies) resulting in varying configurations of the scales. This diversity in item usage raises concerns regarding the comparability of the results. Furthermore, when items are added or removed from a validated scale, the validity of the altered scale cannot be assumed.

These established scales were altered for conceptual (e.g., believing items are deficient and/or confounded) and empirical (e.g., multiple dimensions, reliability not meeting acceptable standards without item removal) reasons. Concerns regarding the structure and content of the scale (e.g., DeShon & Landis, 1997; Donovan & Radosevich, 1998;

Tubbs & Dahl, 1991) led Klein et al. (2001) to conduct a measurement model meta-analysis and multi-sample confirmatory factor analysis to evaluate the original 9 scale items. Based on their findings, a 5-item scale was recommended. That scale is a subset of the previously recommended 7-item measure, but contains only 2 items from the 4-item version. The Klein et al. (2001) 5-item scale has been used in 22 studies (15% of those reviewed). Seijts and Latham (2000a) concluded that the Klein et al. scale was the most promising of the available goal commitment measures. Indeed, 91% of the studies that have used the 5-item scale have done so without alteration. However, there have still been studies using only select items, and questions remain about whether all 5 items appropriately tap the commitment construct (e.g., Aube & Rousseau, 2005). Jaros (2009), for example, expressed concerns about the content validity of the items and recommended that motivational elements (effort, willingness, and persistence) be removed.

**Klein et al. unidimensional target-free (KUT) scale.** The previously discussed definitional variability and ambiguity are responsible for the variation in single and idiosyncratic multi-item scales and the debate about the validity of the various Hollenbeck and Klein scales. The Klein et al. (2012) reconceptualization of commitment addresses that inconsistency. Klein, Molloy, Cooper, and Swanson (2011) developed and validated a corresponding 4-item measure. In doing so, they sought to (a) avoid criticisms of prior commitment (goal, union, organizational) measures with respect to dimensionality and confounds, (b) capture all aspects of the construct definition, and (c) do so in a manner applicable to any target and with minimal length. Klein et al. (2011) presented validation evidence for the KUT scale (presented in Table 6.2), across multiple targets and a variety of organizations, occupations, and industries. The validation evidence presented by Klein et al. (2011) indicates that this scale is unidimensional, and sensitive to differences in commitment both within and between respondents.

Klein et al. (2011) found that the alpha reliability was higher for the KUT (.85) than for the Klein et al. (2001) measure (.71). The two scales were positively correlated ($r = .54$, $p < .01$), but a confirmatory factor analysis supported the distinctiveness of the two scales (despite sharing a similar core item directly assessing commitment). Additional validity evidence comes from the KUT measure relating to other variables as predicted in that study. A key advantage of the KUT measure is that it allows commitments to multiple targets to be examined in a directly comparable manner (e.g., the interplay

*Table 6.2* KUT Commitment Measure Items and Response Format[a]

How committed are you to [your/the/this] goal[b]?

To what extent do you care about [your/the/this] goal?

How dedicated are you to [your/the/this] goal?

To what extent have you chosen to be committed to [your/the/this] goal?

| 1 | 2 | 3 | 4 | 5 |
|---|---|---|---|---|
| Not at all | Slightly | Moderately | Quite a bit | Extremely |

[a]A 7-point response scale can also be used (Not at all, Slightly, Somewhat, Moderately, Mostly, Very, Completely) if restricted variance is a concern.

[b]Goal can be replaced with any other commitment target of interest (e.g., organization, team, supervisor, decision, value).

between organizational commitment, supervisor commitment, and goals assigned by or set with that supervisor; the relationship between team commitment and commitment to team goals). Additional evidence regarding the operation of the KUT measure as specified by goal theory is needed before we can indisputably recommend that this scale be used in future goal setting studies, but the preliminary evidence is highly supportive.

## Goal Commitment Outcomes

We next turn to the variables comprising the nomological network around goal commitment. We begin with the consequences of goal commitment, highlighting the value of this construct for understanding goal theory and task performance. Locke and Latham (1990) focused exclusively on performance in discussing goal commitment outcomes. Given that most goal setting studies examine goals for task performance, task performance has remained the principal outcome of interest. However, other outcomes have since received research attention.

### Performance

*Interaction with goal level.* In 1990, the evidence regarding goal commitment's primary role in goal theory (as a moderator of the goal level–performance relationship) was largely indirect. There were still relatively few studies directly testing the proposed moderating effect of goal commitment at the time of the Klein, Wesson, Hollenbeck, & Alge (1999) meta-analysis. That meta-analysis showed that the relationship between goal commitment and performance was significantly stronger for difficult goals relative to easy ones. This indirectly supports the expected interaction between goal commitment and goal level on performance. Klein et al. also clarified situations in which a goal level by goal commitment interaction would not be expected (i.e., insufficient variance in one or both variables). This recognition resolves much of the inconsistent findings in the literature. When there is sufficient variation in both goal level and commitment, direct support is found for the expected interaction between goal commitment and goal level (e.g., Heimerdinger & Hinsz, 2008; Tubbs, 1993). However, when variance is restricted, the interaction is not evident (e.g., Latham, Seijts, & Crim, 2008).

*Main effects.* Given the form of the expected interaction between goal level and goal commitment on performance (see Klein et al., 1999), a main effect for commitment on performance should generally be observed, even when a significant interaction is present. In addition, when goal level is held constant (or variance severely restricted) at a moderate or difficult level, a positive main effect of commitment on performance, rather than an interaction, should be evident. This positive main effect of commitment on performance has been supported time and again. Meta-analytic results indicate an average population effect size of .23 between goal commitment and performance (Klein et al., 1999). More recent studies have, with a few exceptions (e.g., Wood, Atkins, & Bright, 1999), continued to find this significant main effect of goal commitment on performance across a variety of tasks and contexts, including laboratory settings (e.g., Jarupathirun & Zahedi, 2007; Latham et al., 2008; Schweitzer, Ordóñez, & Douma, 2004), educational courses (e.g., Berenbroek, 2007), and work settings (e.g., Barrick, Mount, & Strauss, 1993; Erez & Judge, 2001; Piccolo & Colquitt, 2006).

*Extra-role performance.* Most studies have focused on in-role performance as goals are typically set for desired in-role rather than extra-role outcomes. Goals are thought to operate, in part, by directing attention to the tasks required for goal attainment. As such, there is no reason to expect commitment to a task goal to lead to extra-role or organizational citizenship behaviors (OCBs), unless individuals perceive such behaviors to be instrumental to their goal attainment. In fact, a negative relationship between goal commitment and OCBs could be expected if those behaviors are viewed as detrimental to goal attainment. Three studies have examined the effects of goal commitment on OCBs. In an experimental study by Wright, George, Farnswarth, and McMahon (1993), OCBs in the form of assisting "co-workers" were assessed by a confederate co-worker. Commitment to a specific task goal was predicted to be negatively related to OCBs, as helping others detracted from task performance, and that this effect was expected to be stronger for difficult goals. Results supported the predicted goal level by commitment interaction on OCBs. The other studies, both conducted in field settings, examined commitment to work goals in general (versus a specific goal). Häsänen, Hellgren, and Hansson (2011) found a significant positive relationship between goal commitment and self-reported OCBs, whereas Piccolo and Colquitt (2006) found the relationship between goal commitment and supervisor-reported OCBs to be nonsignificant. None of these studies directly examined the perceived instrumentality of OCBs for goal attainment, which likely explains these discrepant results.

## Nonperformance Outcomes

In addition to performance, other outcomes (e.g., motivation, affect, subsequent goal choice) have been examined. The goals in these studies, however, were still goals for task performance. As such, relationships between goal commitment and these nonperformance outcomes should only be expected if the outcomes are themselves related to task performance or goal attainment.

*Motivation.* Motivation is one of the primary outcomes of commitment to any target (Klein et al., 2012). Thus, it is not surprising that goal commitment has been shown to relate to motivation operationalized in terms of effort (e.g., Erez & Judge, 2001; Slocum, Cron, & Brown, 2002), persistence (e.g., Allen & Nora, 1995; Chang, Johnson, & Lord, 2010), and even motivation to learn in educational contexts (Colquitt & Simmering, 1998). In all of these forms, motivation should be operating as a mediator between commitment and performance. One study examining the degree of individual and team-focused effort (DeShon, Kozlowski, Schmidt, Milner, & Wiechmann, 2004), however, did not find commitment to be significantly related to effort. Another indicator of effort is the development of strategies for goal attainment. Earley, Shalley, and Northcraft (1992) found that goal commitment was significantly and positively correlated with the number of strategies developed by participants.

*Affect.* Studies have shown a consistent positive relationship between goal commitment and satisfaction with both the job (Häsänen et al., 2011; Leung, Chong, Ng, & Cheung, 2004; Roberson, 1990) and task (Chang et al., 2010). At a more general level, Busch (1998) found that employees who were more committed to their goals had more positive attitudes toward the management-by-objectives system that generated those goals. A somewhat related finding from the accounting literature is that commitment to a set of goals related to a client's preferred accounting method was related to viewing those methods positively (Kadous, Kennedy, & Peecher, 2003). In discussing commitment in general, Klein et al. (2012) noted that affect is both an antecedent and outcome of commitment. Affective evaluations are part of the initial decision to commit, and that commitment to a target biases one's subsequent evaluation of that target. A final study related to affect examined how goal attributes, including commitment, impacted the effects of goal striving on subjective well-being. Brunstein (1993) found that goal commitment moderated the goal attainability–subjective well-being relationship such that well-being was unaffected by goal attainability (whether or not conditions were favorable to attain personal goals) when goal commitment was low, but strongly related to attainability when commitment was high.

*Subsequent goal choice.* Goal commitment has also been examined as a predictor of subsequently chosen personal goals (e.g., Vance & Colella, 1990). Other studies have found goal commitment to moderate the effects on subsequent goal choice, with those having high commitment being less likely to change their goals. Mathieu (1992), for example, found that past goal attainment and commitment to that prior goal interacted in determining subsequent personal goals, such that chosen goals reflected goal attainment when commitment was low, but reflected prior goals with high commitment. Fishbach and Dhar (2005) found that individuals who focused on commitment to their goal were more likely to engage in further goal pursuit rather than pursue alternative goals when progress was satisfactory as compared to those who focused on goal progress. Similarly, Fishbach, Dhar, and Zhang (2006) found that individuals focused on commitment to a superordinate goal following initial subgoal success were more likely to engage in additional goal-related activity than individuals who were focused on subgoal completion.

## Determinants of Goal Commitment

Locke and Latham (1990) inferred many causes of goal commitment from relationships with performance or goal choice, as their effect on commitment had not been directly examined. Researchers have since given greater attention to the antecedents of goal commitment. Goal commitment has also been examined as a mediator between determinants of commitment and the above-reviewed outcomes. Those relationships are noted in our review of determinants. We organize those determinants using the Hollenbeck and Klein (1987) framework. In that model, the attractiveness and expectancy of goal attainment—as well as motivational force (the combination of the two)—are viewed as the most proximal determinants of goal commitment. Those evaluations, similar to Locke et al.'s (1988) desirability and perceived capability, are in turn each influenced by both situational and personal factors. In discussing these relationships, we begin with the findings of the Klein et al. (1999) meta-analysis and then note subsequent findings. There are other, earlier reviews and meta-analyses (e.g., Wofford, Goodwin, & Premack, 1992), but those findings are subsumed in the Klein et al. (1999) results.

### Attractiveness, Expectancy, and Motivational Force

*Expectancy of goal attainment.* Several studies have directly examined the relationship between self-efficacy or the expectancy of goal attainment and goal commitment.

We recognize that self-efficacy and expectancy should be measured in distinct ways given the conceptual distinctions between the two constructs. However, we discuss the two together as they have often been operationalized with nearly identical measures. The mean weighted correlation, corrected for unreliability (hereafter referred to simply as the average correlation), between efficacy/expectancy and goal commitment was .36 in the Klein et al. (1999) meta-analysis. More recent studies replicate this significant, positive relationship (e.g., Chang et al., 2010; Colquitt & Simmering, 1998; De Clercq, Menzies, Diochon, & Gasse, 2009; Harrison & Liska, 1994; Seijts & Latham, 2001; Slocum et al., 2002; Webb, 2004; Wood et al., 1999). There have also been studies demonstrating that goal commitment partially mediates the relationship between self-efficacy and performance (e.g., Johnson, 2005). Furthermore, consistent with Hollenbeck and Klein's (1987) model, the expectancy of goal attainment has been shown to be a proximal antecedent, mediating the relationships between goal commitment and several of the more distal antecedents discussed below (Ingledew, Wray, Markland, & Hardy, 2005).

*Attractiveness of goal attainment.* A significant positive correlation has consistently been observed between attractiveness and goal commitment, with Klein et al. (1999) reporting an average correlation of .29. Subsequent studies have consistently replicated that positive relationship (e.g., Colquitt & Simmering, 1998; De Clercq et al., 2009; Webb, 2004). Studies have also demonstrated that attractiveness mediates the relationships between more distal antecedents and goal commitment (e.g., Ingledew et al., 2005). In addition to attractiveness and expectancy, the product of the two, motivational force, has also been found to be significantly related to goal commitment. Klein et al. (1999) reported an average correlation of .33 between motivational force and goal commitment. No additional studies have subsequently examined this relationship.

## Situational Factors Affecting Attractiveness of Goal Attainment

*Volition.* The perceived volition for a goal is distinct from, but related to goal origin, and research has examined the effects of both on commitment. In general, volition should be highest for self-set goals, moderate for participatively set goals, and lowest for assigned goals (Hollenbeck & Klein, 1987). However, even with self-set goals, individuals can feel pressured to select a particular goal, and goals can be assigned in a way (i.e., "tell and sell") that allows for a sense of ownership. Volition is least certain for participatively set goals, given the variation that can occur in how those goals are actually determined. Furthermore, because of other commitment determinants, commitment can be higher to assigned goals than for participatively set goals regardless of perceived volition. In their meta-analysis, Klein et al. (1999) found an average correlation of .40 between volition/participation and goal commitment. Two studies have since examined the influence of goal origin. Renn (1998) found participation, assessed in terms of self-reported relative influence in determining the goal, to be related to commitment, which mediated the effects of participation on performance. Lozano and Stephens (2010) manipulated goal origin (assigned versus participative) and found goal commitment to be significantly higher for participatively set goals. Support was not found for commitment as a mediator of the participation–performance relationship in this study because goal origin was not significantly related to performance (a reduction in drinking behavior).

*Reward structure.* Locke and Latham (1990) suggested that incentives and rewards should influence goal commitment, but noted that very few goal and incentive studies measured goal commitment. The Klein et al. (1999) meta-analysis reported an average correlation of .20 based on only three studies, with two additional studies having since been conducted. In a series of three experiments, Wood et al. (1999) found no significant differences in goal commitment across two different incentive conditions (self-set goal attainment bonus vs. end-of-period bonus based on performance relative to other participants). On the other hand, Presslee, Vance, Webb, and Jeffrey (2011) found greater goal commitment associated with the possibility of tangible rewards (points redeemable for items including electronics and travel) than for cash rewards. Studies have also examined goal commitment as a mediator of the incentive–performance relationship. Wright (1992) found that goal commitment mediated the effects of incentives on performance, but Wright and Kacmar (1995) did not. Lee, Locke, and Phan (1997) found that goal commitment was related to performance, but did not find a mediating effect on the incentive–performance relationship. Presslee et al. (2011) similarly failed to support this mediation hypothesis. It thus appears that providing incentives generally increases goal commitment, but the extent of that impact and whether or not commitment mediates the effects of incentives on performance depends on the incentive type and other incentive system features. Additional research directly examining the mechanisms through which reward systems impact commitment is needed to more definitively understand the relationship between incentives and goal commitment.

*Leadership.* Klein et al. (1999) identified three studies examining relationships between leadership and goal commitment, and reported a nonsignificant average correlation of .12. One subsequent study examined transactional and transformational leadership and found both to be significantly and positively related to goal commitment (Bruch, Tekie, Voelpel, & Walter, 2006). These mixed results, likely due to focusing on different aspects and definitions of leadership, suggest the need for additional research to better pinpoint what leadership behaviors or elements consistently facilitate goal commitment among followers. Along these lines, Klein et al. reported one study demonstrating a positive significant relationship between procedural justice and goal commitment. Finally, Locke and Latham (1990) discussed the role of authority in influencing the desirability of goal attainment. There is considerable indirect evidence of this effect, given the high levels of commitment to assigned goals often observed in both organizational and laboratory settings, but no studies have directly tested this relationship.

*Other situational factors.* Klein et al. (1999) reported an average correlation of .19 between explicitness (goal specificity) and goal commitment. Recent studies have continued to find a positive relationship between goal specificity and goal commitment (Gauggel, Leinberger, & Richardt, 2001; Häsänen et al., 2011). Another goal characteristic, stability, is also positively related to goal commitment based on a single study reviewed by Klein et al., with no subsequent research examining that relationship. In their review, Klein et al. identified two studies examining the effects of publicness, and reported an average correlation of .19 indicating that making goals public resulted in higher goal commitment than keeping goals private. Ingledew et al. (2005) subsequently also found a significant positive correlation between publicness and goal commitment. That study also demonstrated that this relationship is mediated by the perceived value or attractiveness of goal attainment.

Locke and Latham (1990) reviewed studies demonstrating that competition leads to better performance, but again the effects on goal commitment were unknown. At the time of the Klein et al. (1999) meta-analysis, there were no studies that examined this relationship, and we identified only one subsequent study doing so. Allscheid and Cellar (1996) did not find a significant relationship between competition and goal commitment. In that study, competition did not significantly impact performance either, suggesting that additional research on the relationships among competition, goals, goal commitment, and performance is warranted. Finally, Piccolo and Colquitt (2006) found that individuals with more positive perceptions of core job characteristics were more committed to their goals, and that commitment mediated the job characteristics–performance relationship.

## Personal Factors Affecting Attractiveness of Goal Attainment

**Personality traits.** Locke and Latham (1990) suggested that personality factors should influence goal commitment, but noted that almost no research on such relationships had been conducted. Hollenbeck and Klein (1987) specifically identified three traits thought to relate to attractiveness of goal attainment—type A personality, need for achievement, and endurance—all of which have received some attention. Klein et al. (1999) found an average correlation of .12 between type A personality and goal commitment, based on only two studies, and we did not identify any subsequent studies examining this relationship. Need for achievement had an average correlation of .17 with goal commitment based on three studies, and one recent study similarly found a significant positive relationship (Slocum et al., 2002). Finally, Klein et al. reported a single study demonstrating a significant relationship between endurance and commitment with no subsequently published studies examining this relationship.

Four additional studies have been conducted looking at *conscientiousness*, a five-factor model trait that encompasses need for achievement. Significant, positive relationships were observed in all of these studies (Barrick et al., 1993; Bipp & Kleingeld, 2011; Colquitt & Simmering, 1998; Erez & Judge, 2001). Barrick et al. (1993) further found that goal commitment mediated the conscientiousness–performance relationship. Three additional traits have also each been examined once. The Klein et al. (1999) meta-analysis noted that perfectionism had been examined, but was not significantly related to goal commitment. Subsequently, failure avoidance was found to have a significant negative relationship with goal commitment (Heimerdinger & Hinsz, 2008), whereas future orientation has been shown to have a significant positive relationship with goal commitment (Chang et al., 2010).

**Job involvement and organizational commitment.** Hollenbeck and Klein (1987) suggested that individuals with high job involvement and high organizational commitment would be more likely to commit to difficult goals. These relationships are supported by one study each, based on Hollenbeck et al. (1989) and the Klein et al. (1999) meta-analysis. A recent study (Klein et al., 2011) found organizational commitment to be significantly and positively related to commitment to a stated organizational goal. Spillover from other workplace commitment targets (e.g., commitment to supervisors, top management team, organization strategy, change efforts) can also be expected to influence commitment to task goals.

*Affect.* Klein et al. (1999) reported an average correlation between affect and goal commitment of .22. Affect was also discussed above as an outcome of goal commitment, and the two should be considered as reciprocally related (Klein et al., 2012). No additional studies have examined relationships between satisfaction and commitment, but one study did examine mood states. Ingledew et al. (2005) did not expect mood to directly influence goal commitment, but found a positive relationship between one dimension (hostility) and commitment. The effect was explained in terms of hostile feelings about a goal providing a short-term energizing effect because of the desire to achieve that goal and overcome or avenge the source of that hostility.

*Other personal factors.* Three recent studies have examined the effects of goal activation and forming implementation intentions on goal commitment. Nenkov and Gollwitzer (2011) found that decision status (i.e., whether or not one has decided to pursue a goal) positively influenced commitment, and that commitment mediated the effect of decision status on goal-directed behavior. The decision to pursue a goal is a precursor to, but distinct from, implementation intentions: specific "if–then" plans developed to service goal intentions. Diefendorff and Lord (2003) did not find a significant relationship between the formation of implementation intentions and goal commitment. Similarly, Bayer, Gollwitzer, and Achtziger (2010) conducted a series of experiments to investigate the role of implementation intentions in shielding goal striving from disruptions. No significant differences in commitment were observed as a function of forming implementation intentions. Finally, there is no conceptual reason to expect demographic variables to influence goal commitment, but enough studies had reported these variables for two such relationships to be included in the Klein et al. (1999) meta-analysis. As expected, neither education (average correlation of .04) nor age (average correlation of .09) was significantly associated with goal commitment.

### Situational Factors Affecting Expectancy of Goal Attainment

*Goal difficulty.* Klein et al. (1999) reported a nonsignificant average correlation between goal commitment and goal difficulty of .04 accompanied by a large amount of unexplained variance, suggesting moderators. Goal origin was supported as a moderator (− .09 for assigned goals; .16 for self-set goals), but did not fully explain the variation, suggesting the presence of additional moderators. The potential role of expectancies and attractiveness were specifically suggested, but have not been examined. Wright (1992) found goal level to be negatively related to goal commitment, but this relationship varied depending on the incentive system. Wright (1992) also found that goal commitment mediated the effects of goal level on performance. Presslee et al. (2011) also found a significant negative relationship between goal level and goal commitment. In that study, goal commitment did not mediate the goal level–performance relationship.

**Feedback.** In their meta-analysis, Klein et al. (1999) reported significant positive relationships between goal commitment and both the provision of feedback (having knowledge of results; average correlation of .13 with more feedback associated with higher commitment) as well as type of feedback (a composite of attributes including specificity, quality, and whether the feedback was framed in terms of discrepancy from goal versus past performance; average correlation of .30 with commitment higher when feedback was more specific, higher quality, and framed in terms of goal discrepancy).

In a recent study, Chang et al. (2010) found that smaller discrepancies (less negative feedback) produced higher goal commitment than larger discrepancies (more negative feedback). In another study, DeShon et al. (2004) did not find a main effect for feedback level (individual, team, or both) on goal commitment. They did find a feedback by time interaction, with participants receiving individual feedback reporting greater individual goal commitment early in training. Individuals receiving team and both individual and team feedback demonstrating increases in goal commitment as training progressed and greater goal commitment by the end of training than those receiving only individual feedback. DeShon et al. (2004) also found a performance goal orientation by feedback interaction. Higher performance goal orientation was associated with higher goal commitment for trainees receiving only individual feedback, but lower goal commitment for trainees receiving only team feedback.

*Other situational factors.* Klein et al. (1999) reported an average correlation of .45 between social influence and goal commitment based on two studies. More recently, Ke and Zhang (2009) found a significant positive relationship between an individual's social identification with a workgroup and his or her goal commitment, with commitment mediating the relationship between identification and performance. Social influence can take multiple forms, and additional research appears warranted given the sizable demonstrated effects and small number of studies. Klein et al. reported an average correlation of .38 between supervisor supportiveness and goal commitment based on two studies. More recently, Häsänen et al. (2011) similarly found supervisor support to be positively related to goal commitment. Klein et al. reported an average correlation of −.50 between *task complexity* and goal commitment based on three studies. The relationship between performance constraints and goal commitment is significant and negative, based on a single study reported by Klein et al. (1999). No further studies have examined the effects of task complexity or performance constraints on goal commitment.

### Personal Factors Affecting Expectancy of Goal Attainment

*Personality traits.* Hollenbeck and Klein (1987) identified two personality traits that should impact commitment through expectancies. Those traits, self-esteem and locus of control, are components of core self-evaluations (CSE). The other components of CSE are neuroticism, and generalized self-efficacy. At the time of the Klein et al. (1999) meta-analysis, self-esteem and locus of control had each been examined once as predictors of goal commitment, with a significant effect found for locus of control (internals having higher commitment) and a nonsignificant effect for self-esteem. Subsequently, Erez and Judge (2001) found all four CSE components to be significantly related to goal commitment, as well as the composite CSE. Erez and Judge further demonstrated that goal commitment (combined with personal goal setting) mediated the effects of CSE on effort. Bono and Colbert (2005) replicated the significant relationship between CSE and commitment. One additional study has supported the relationship between general self-efficacy, a CSE component, and goal commitment (Theodorakis, 1996).

*Ability, knowledge, and conflict.* Klein et al. (1999) reported an average correlation between goal commitment and ability/past performance of .18, and between goal commitment and task experience of .24. These relationships have not been examined further. Klein et al. reported an average correlation, based on three studies, of .21 between strategy development and goal commitment. Perceived strategy quality has also been found to be significantly and positively related to goal commitment (Diefendorff & Lord, 2003). Locke and Latham (1990) suggested that goal conflict could be assumed to negatively influence goal commitment. Recent studies have confirmed this predicted negative relationship (Berenbroek, 2007; Häsänen et al., 2011; Slocum et al., 2002).

*Other personal factors.* Oettingen et al. (2009) suggested that when individuals engage in mental contrasting (contrasting positive fantasies about a desired future with thoughts of obstacles they actually face currently), it will energize the individual in such a way that if they have high expectations of success they will be more committed to the future goal than if they have low expectations of success. They found that high expectations of success led to higher levels of commitment than low expectations of success for individuals who engaged in mental contrasting, and that energization partially mediated the relationship between expectations and goal commitment. Finally, Sevincer and Oettingen (2009) suggested that alcohol consumption, because it interferes with attention and cognition, will lead individuals to strongly commit to their goals regardless of their expectations of actually attaining those goals. They found that expectations did not predict goal commitment in the alcohol condition, but did predict commitment in the placebo condition. Also, when expectations of success were low, participants felt more committed in the alcohol condition than did participants in the placebo condition; but, when expectations were high, commitment between the conditions did not significantly differ.

## New Developments

We conclude our review by highlighting three areas of research that have either emerged since Locke and Latham (1990) or have received considerably more attention over the past two decades: team goals, learning versus performance goals, and subconscious goals.

### Team Goal Commitment

With the increased use of team-based structures in organizations, considerable research has examined team goal setting. One unique aspect of team goal setting is that for any particular outcome, instead of a single goal, there can be multiple goals that may or may not be in alignment: the individual's goal for self, the individual's goal for the group, the group's goal for the individual, and the group's goal for itself. Several studies have examined the interplay between individual and team goals or differences in focus. Goals function in part by directing attention. Crown and Rosse (1995) demonstrated that assigning only a team or individual goal leads to participants focusing on and being more committed to maximizing performance at the level referenced by the assigned goal. Van Mierlo and Kleingeld (2010) found similar results. Individual and team goal commitment were associated with reduced and greater cooperation, respectively. In both the Van Mierlo and Kleingeld (2010) and Crown (2007) studies, levels of commitment to individual goals were similar across participants given just individual goals and those given both individual and team goals. Similarly, there was no difference in team goal commitment between those given only team goals and both individual and team goals. However, both across conditions (both studies) and within the combined goal condition (Crown, 2007) higher levels of commitment were evident for team goals than individual goals.

The nature of the task, particularly interdependence, appears to play a key role in the joint operation of individual and team goal commitment, as individual and team goal alignment becomes more crucial as interdependence increases. Hoegl and Parboteeah (2006) did not find a significant main effect for outcome interdependence on team goal commitment, but Aube and Rousseau (2005) found that task interdependence moderated the team goal commitment–team performance relationship, with that relationship being stronger under conditions of higher interdependence. Antoni (2005) did not find that same interaction, but speculated that there was not sufficient variation in the studied teams. Task interdependence is also an explanation for differences between studies that used largely independent (e.g., Weingart & Weldon, 1991) versus interdependent tasks (e.g., Van Mierlo & Kleingeld, 2010). Other unique aspects of team goal setting involve the influence of team attributes and processes on goal setting and striving. Two studies examined team size, with the expectation that commitment to team goals would be greater in smaller teams. This relationship was confirmed by Hoegl and Parboteeah (2006), but not by Seijts and Latham (2000b). Several studies have found positive effects of group norms for performance and cohesion on team goal commitment (e.g., Klein & Mulvey, 1995; Mulvey & Klein, 1998; Whiteoak, 2007; Whitney, 1994). Studies have further found that team goal commitment mediates the effects of cohesion on team performance (Klein & Mulvey, 1995) and turnover intentions (Whiteoak, 2007), whereas Podsakoff, MacKenzie, and Ahearne (1997) found a significant interaction between commitment and cohesion relating to team performance.

Finally, studies have examined whether findings at the individual level operate in a similar manner at the group level. Studies have generally supported the main effect of team goal commitment on team performance (e.g., Aube & Rousseau, 2005; Hoegl & Parboteeah, 2006; Klein & Mulvey, 1995), but we found no studies directly assessing the goal level by commitment interaction at the team level. The positive effects of collective efficacy (as well as team potency) on team goal commitment have been demonstrated (e.g., Durham, Knight, & Locke, 1997; Mulvey & Klein, 1998; Weldon & Weingart, 1993) paralleling findings for self-efficacy with individual goals. Studies have not, however, supported team goal commitment as a mediator of the team efficacy–performance relationship (e.g., Durham et al., 1997; Hecht, Allen, Klammer, & Kelly 2002; Latham, Winters, & Locke, 1994; Lin, Yang, Arya, Huang, & Li 2005), perhaps because of the number of other factors that can impact team performance. Turning to more distal antecedents, the effects of team goal difficulty on team goal commitment have been mixed (e.g., Durham et al., 1997; Weingart, 1992), paralleling findings at the individual level. Also consistent with individual-level findings, leadership (e.g., Durham et al., 1997; De Souza & Klein, 1995), participation in goal setting (Latham et al., 1994; Hoegl & Parboteeah, 2006), and feedback (Hoegl & Parboteeah, 2006) have all be found to be positively related to team goal commitment, though there have been some exceptions (e.g., Weingart & Weldon, 1991).

*Learning versus Performance Goal Commitment*

Early goal setting research focused almost exclusively on goals for task performance. A number of studies have subsequently looked at learning or mastery goals. The influence of goal content (learning versus performance) on goal commitment has been mixed.

Winters and Latham (1996) found no difference in goal commitment between partici-pants assigned learning goals and those assigned performance goals, a result replicated by Kozlowski, Gully, Brown, Salas, Smith, and Nason (2001). However, other studies have found significantly higher levels of goal commitment for learning goals than for performance goals (Seijts & Latham, 2001; Seijts, Latham, Tasa, & Latham, 2004). The results of these later studies suggest a possible explanation for these discrepant findings. The differences in commitment may result from differences in self-efficacy and the nov-elty of the task. Specifically, on tasks for which people have not yet acquired the requisite skills or identified appropriate task strategies, efficacy for learning is likely to be higher than efficacy for performance, and hence commitment to learning goals is generally higher. Seijts and Latham (2011) found that commitment was a moderator of the learn-ing goal–performance effect on a highly complex task.

### Subconscious Goal Commitment

Research on goal theory has historically focused on conscious goals (i.e., explicit goals that operate within an individual's awareness), but increasing attention has been given to subconscious goals (i.e., implicit goals that operate automatically, outside of immedi-ate awareness). Bittner (2011) examined the interaction between simultaneously acti-vated explicit and implicit goals in a series of three studies. In the first two studies, commitment to the explicit goal was assessed as a control variable, and there was no effect of priming the implicit goal on commitment to the explicit goal. Commitment was not assessed in the third study, but raised as a possible alternative explanation for the observed findings, which involved the assignment of extremely difficult goals to which all participants may not have been committed. Several additional studies have begun to examine the joint influence of conscious and subconscious goals (e.g., Stajkovic, Locke, & Blair, 2006; Latham & Piccolo, 2012), but those studies have not examined goal commitment. Doing so is needed to understand the effects, if any, of subconscious goals on commitment to conscious goals. In addition, assessing commitment to subconscious goals presents a number of interesting avenues for future research as well as challenges, which are discussed later in this chapter.

## Future Research

Great strides have been made in our understanding of goal commitment, but numerous gaps and questions remain. First, there is still a paucity of studies examining the central hypothesis that goal commitment and goal difficulty interact in relation to task perfor-mance, assuming sufficient variance in both variables. Another relatively basic relation-ship deserving additional attention is that between goal difficulty and goal commitment. Studies are needed directly examining the role of self-efficacy/expectancy and attractive-ness/valence in explaining this relationship, which may be nonlinear. Additional research is also needed on several goal commitment antecedents that have only be exam-ined in a single study, not at all, or appear to be more complex, with moderating effects needing to be identified or verified.

Another needed area of research pertains to understanding the influence of goal con-text on goal commitment. A few contextual factors have received attention, but many more, including goal origin, require further examination. A missing contextual consideration is goal domain. Some recent attention has been given to learning rather than performance goals, but social relationships and well-being are also relevant workplace domains along with numerous other nonwork domains. Another consideration is goal hierarchies. To what extent are commitments laddered within hierarchies the same ways as goals? To what extent does commitment to a higher-order goal influence commitment to subgoals? Goal frames and attributes other than difficulty (e.g., specificity, temporality, complexity) also warrant further consideration. Goal frames refer to how individuals view their goals in absolute or relative terms, as well as how the goal is defined (as a hope for versus expected versus minimal outcome).

Additional within-person studies are also needed examining how goal commitment changes during goal striving, particularly in response to setbacks and competing commitments. Such studies are needed to better understand when changes in commitment occur relative to goal change or abandonment. Such studies should ideally examine commitment to several goals simultaneously to examine the role goal commitment plays in the allocation of attention and effort between competing goals. The recent attention given to subconscious goals (e.g., Shantz & Latham, 2011; Stajkovic et al., 2006; Latham & Piccolo, 2012) opens another set of research questions relating to goal commitment, including how to best assess commitment to subconscious goals, examining commitment relative to subconscious versus conscious goals, and determining whether goal commitment itself can be subconsciously primed.

Another set of future research needs pertains to the broadening of the criterion space. To date, the primary dependent variable of interest has been task performance, but commitment likely impacts other outcomes important to individuals and organizations. The effects of goal commitment on stress, well-being, and affect require further exploration, as does the influence of positive and negative affect, mood, and emotion on goal commitment. The potential negative consequences of commitment have been occasionally recognized in the literature, but too often it is assumed that more commitment to a goal is better. The examination of commitment to macro goals is another area needing research. Organizations and units within organizations larger than teams have goals and individuals may or may not be committed to those goals. Locke and Latham (1990) devoted attention to issues relating to commitment to macro goals both in their goal commitment chapter and in a subsequent chapter on micro versus macro goal setting research. Yet in the intervening two decades, we did not locate a single published study that examined the commitment of individuals to macro goals, only a recent conference presentation, Klein et al. (2011), which found commitment to an espoused organizational goal was significantly and positively related to job satisfaction, motivation, engagement, and extra role behavior, and significantly negatively related to both turnover intentions and actual turnover.

## Conclusion

In this chapter, we summarized the advances that have been made in the study of goal commitment, and presented a research agenda for issues requiring examination or resolution. In 1990, there was tremendous variation in the definition and measurement of goal commitment, when it was measured at all. Today, there is still debate and variation in the meaning of goal commitment, and although it is reduced, measurement variability still persists. Hopefully, recent efforts (e.g., Klein et al., 2012, 2011) will provide conceptual and measurement consistency. Goal commitment is assumed less often today than twenty years ago, though it is often assessed as a manipulation check or control variable–important for ruling out alternative explanations, but not helpful in advancing our understanding, particularly when omitted from correlation tables.

Fortunately, sufficient attention has been paid in the interim to allow more definitive conclusions than was the case two decades ago regarding the operation of goal commitment and factors that facilitate goal commitment. There is more support, though still limited, for goal commitment moderating the effects of goal level on performance and considerable support, and a better understanding of the main effects of goal commitment on performance. In terms of antecedents, there is strong support for attractiveness and self-efficacy/expectancies as the most proximal determinants of commitment with several distal antecedents consistently receiving support (e.g., ability/experience, social influence/support, affect, conscientiousness, and volition). Many other antecedents, however, have received limited or mixed support. Goal commitment is deserving of greater attention as a variable of interest both because of the central role it plays in goal theory and because of the demonstrated main and interactive effects it has on variables of interest to both organizations and individuals.

## Note

1. We do not differentiate between goal commitment and acceptance in our review. Conceptual distinctions can be made, but measures are highly similar, and acceptance can be considered a special case of commitment (c.f. Locke, Shaw, Saari, & Latham, 1981).

## References

Allen, D., & Nora, A. (1995). An empirical examination of the construct validity of goal commitment in the persistence process. *Research in Higher Education, 36*(5), 509–533.

Allscheid, S. P., & Cellar, D. F. (1996). An interactive approach to work motivation: The effects of competition, rewards, and goal difficulty on task performance. *Journal of Business & Psychology, 11,* 219–237.

Antoni, C. (2005). Management by objectives—an effective tool for teamwork? International *Journal of Human Resource Management, 16*(2), 174–184.

Aube, C., & Rousseau, V. (2005). Team goal commitment and team effectiveness: The role of task interdependence and supportive behaviors. *Group Dynamics: Theory, Research, and Practice, 9*(3), 189–204.

Barrick, M. R., Mount, M. K., & Strauss, J. P. (1993). Conscientiousness and performance of sales representatives: Test of the mediating effects of goal setting. *Journal of Applied Psychology, 78,* 715–722.

Bayer, U. C., Gollwitzer, P. M., & Achtziger, A. (2010). Staying on track: Planned goal striving is protected from disruptive internal states. *Journal of Experimental Social Psychology, 46*(3), 505–514.

Becker, H. S. (1960). Notes of the concept of commitment. *American Journal of Sociology, 66,* 32–42.

Becker, T. E., Klein, H. J., & Meyer, J. P. (2009). Accumulated wisdom and new directions for workplace commitments. In H. J.Klein, T. E.Becker, &J. P.Meyer (Eds.), *Commitment in organizations: Accumulated wisdom and new directions.* Routledge/Taylor and Francis.

Berenbroek, A. (2007). *The pursuit of multiple parallel goals over time: Longitudinal investigation of language proficiency development.* Unpublished manuscript, Department of Economics and Business Administration, University Maastricht, Maastricht, Netherlands.

Bipp, T., & Kleingeld, A. (2011). Goal-setting in practice: The effects of personality and perceptions of the goal-setting process on job satisfaction and goal commitment. *Personnel Review, 40*(3), 306–323.

Bittner, J. V. (2011). Implicit processing goals combine with explicit goal standards to motivate performance through underlying comparison processes. *European Journal of Social Psychology, 41*(2), 210–219.

Bono, J. E., & Colbert, A. E. (2005). Understanding responses to multi-source feedback: The role of core self-evaluations. *Personnel Psychology, 58*(1), 171–203.

Bruch, H., Tekie, E., Voelpel, S. C., & Walter, F. (2006, August). Leadership and the aging workforce: The impact of leadership style on the motivation of older employees. Presented at the research workshop at the Annual Academy of Management Conference, Atlanta, GA.

Brunstein, J. C. (1993). Personal goals and subjective well-being: A longitudinal study. *Journal of Personality & Social Psychology, 65*, 1061–1070.

Busch, T. (1998). Attitudes towards management by objectives: An empirical investigation of self-efficacy and goal commitment. *Scandinavian Journal of Management, 14*(3), 289–299.

Campion, M. A., & Lord, R. G. (1982). A control systems conceptualization of the goal setting and changing process. *Organizational Behavior and Human Performance, 30*, 265–287.

Chang, C. D., Johnson, R. E., & Lord, R. G. (2010). Moving beyond discrepancies: The importance of velocity as a predictor of satisfaction and motivation. *Human Performance, 23*(1), 58–80.

Colquitt, J. A., & Simmering, M. J. (1998). Conscientiousness, goal orientation, and motivation to learn during the learning process: A longitudinal study. *Journal of Applied Psychology, 83*(4), 654–665.

Crown, D. F. (2007). Effects of structurally competitive multilevel goals for an interdependent task. *Small Group Research, 38*(2), 265–288.

Crown, D. F., & Rosse, J. G. (1995). Yours, mine, and ours: Facilitating group productivity through the integration of individual and group goals. *Organizational Behavior and Human Decision Processes, 64*, 138–150.

De Clercq, D., Menzies, T. V., Diochon, M., & Gasse, Y. (2009). Explaining nascent entrepreneurs' goal commitment: An exploratory study. *Journal of Small Business and Entrepreneurship, 22*(2), 123–140.

DeShon, R. P., Kozlowski, S. W. J., Schmidt, A. M., Milner, K. R., & Wiechmann, D. (2004). A multiple-goal, multilevel model of feedback effects on the regulation of individual and team performance. *Journal of Applied Psychology, 89*(6), 1035–1056.

DeShon, R., & Landis, R. S. (1997). The dimensionality of the Hollenbeck, Williams, and Klein (1989) measure of goal commitment on complex tasks. *Organizational Behavior & Human Decision Processes, 70*, 105–116.

De Souza, G., & Klein, H. J. (1995). Emergent leadership in the group goal-setting process. *Small Group Research, 26*, 475–496.

Diefendorff, J. M., & Lord, R. G. (2003). The volitional and strategic effects of planning on task performance and goal commitment. *Human Performance, 16*(4), 365–387.

Donovan, J. J., & Radosevich, D. J. (1998). The moderating role of goal commitment on the goal difficulty-performance relationship: A meta-analytic review and critical reanalysis. *Journal of Applied Psychology, 83*, 308–315.

Durham, C. C., Knight, D., & Locke, E. A. (1997). Effects of leader role, team-set goal difficulty, efficacy, and tactics on team effectiveness. *Organizational Behavior & Human Decision Processes, 72*, 203–231.

Earley, P. C., Shalley, C. E., & Northcraft, G. B. (1992). I think I can, I think I can: Processing time and strategy effects of goal acceptance/rejection decisions. *Organizational Behavior and Human Decision Processes, 53*, 1–13.

Edwards, J. R. (1994). The study of congruence in organizational behavior research: Critique and proposed alternative. *Organizational Behavior and Human Decision Processes, 58*, 51–100.

Edwards, J. R. (1995). Alternatives to difference scores as dependent variables in the study of congruence in organizational research. *Organizational Behavior and Human Decision Processes, 64*, 307–324.

Erez, A., & Judge, T. A. (2001). Relationship of core self-evaluations to goal setting, motivation, and performance. *Journal of Applied Psychology, 86*(6), 1270–1279.

Fishbach, A., & Dhar, R. (2005). Goals as excuses or guides: The liberating effect of perceived goal progress on choice. *Journal of Consumer Research, 32*, 370–377.

Fishbach, A., Dhar, R., & Zhang, Y. (2006). Subgoals as substitutes or complements: The role of goal accessibility. *Journal of Personality and Social Psychology, 91*, 232–242.

Gauggel, S., Leinberger, R., & Richardt, M. (2001). Goal Setting and Reaction Time Performance in Brain-Damaged Patients. *Journal of Clinical & Experimental Neuropsychology, 23*(3), 351–361.

Harrison, D. A., & Liska, L. Z. (1994). Promoting regular exercise in organizational fitness programs: Health related differences in motivational building blocks. *Personnel Psychology, 47*, 47–71.

Häsänen, L., Hellgren, J., & Hansson, M. (2011). Goal setting and plant closure: When bad things turn good. *Economic and Industrial Democracy, 32*(1), 135–156.

Hecht, T. D., Allen, N. J., Klammer, J. D., & Kelly, E. C. (2002). Group beliefs, ability, and performance: The potency of group potency. *Group Dynamics: Theory, Research, and Practice, 6*(2), 143–152.

Heimerdinger, S. R., & Hinsz, V. B. (2008). Failure avoidance motivation in a goal-setting situation. *Human Performance, 21*(4), 383–395.

Hoegl, M., & Parboteeah, K. P. (2006). Team goal commitment in innovative projects. *International Journal of Innovation Management, 10*(3), 299–324.

Hollenbeck, J. R., & Brief, A. P. (1987). The effects of individual differences and goal origin on goal setting and performance. *Organizational Behavior and Human Decision Processes, 40*, 392–414.

Hollenbeck, J. R., & Klein, H. J. (1987). Goal commitment and the goal-setting process: Problems, prospects, and proposals for future research. *Journal of Applied Psychology, 72*(2), 212–220.

Hollenbeck, J. R., Klein, H. J., O'Leary, A. M., & Wright, P. M. (1989). Investigation of the construct validity of a self-report measure of goal commitment. *Journal of Applied Psychology, 74*(6), 951–956.

Hollenbeck, J. R., Williams, C. R., & Klein, H. J. (1989). An empirical examination of the antecedents of commitment to difficult goals. *Journal of Applied Psychology, 74*, 18–23.

Ingledew, D. K., Wray, J. L., Markland, D., & Hardy, L. (2005). Work-related goal perceptions and affective well-being. *Journal of Health Psychology, 10*(1), 101–122.

Jaros, S. (2009). Measurement of commitment. In H. Klein, T. Becker, & J. Meyer (Eds.), Commitment in organizations: Accumulated wisdom and new directions. Mahwah, NJ: Lawrence Erlbaum.

Jarupathirun, S., & Zahedi, F. (2007). Exploring the influence of perceptual factors in the success of web-based spatial DSS. *Decision Support Systems, 43*(3), 933–951.

Johnson, R. D. (2005). An empirical investigation of sources of application-specific computer-self-efficacy and mediators of the efficacy–performance relationship. *International Journal of Human-Computer Studies, 62*, 737–758.

Kadous, K., Kennedy, S. J., & Peecher, M. E. (2003). The effect of quality assessment and directional goal commitment on auditors' acceptance of client-preferred accounting methods. *Accounting Review, 78*(3), 759–778.

Ke, W., & Zhang, P. (2009). Motivations in open source software communities: The mediating role of effort intensity and goal commitment. *International Journal of Electronic Commerce 13*(4), 39–66.

Klein, H. J., Molloy, J. C., & Brinsfield, C. T. (2012). Reconceptualizing workplace commitment to redress a stretched construct: Revisiting assumptions and removing confounds. *Academy of Management Review, 37*(1), 130–151.

Klein, H. J., Molloy, J. C., & Cooper, J. T. (2009). Conceptual foundations: Construct definitions and theoretical representations of workplace commitment. In H. J. Klein, T. E. Becker, & J. P. Meyer (Eds.), *Commitment in organizations: Accumulated wisdom and new directions.* New York: Routledge/Taylor and Francis.

Klein, H. J., Molloy, J. C., Cooper, J. T., & Swanson, J. A. (2011). Validation of a uni-dimensional, target-free self-report measure of commitment. Annual Meeting of the Academy of Management. San Antonio, Texas.

Klein, H. J., & Mulvey, P. W. (1995). Two investigations of the relationships among group goals, goal commitment, cohesion, and performance. *Organizational Behavior and Human Decision Processes, 61*(1), 44–53.

Klein, H. J., Wesson, M. J., Hollenbeck, J. R., & Alge, B. J. (1999). Goal commitment and the goal setting process: Conceptual clarification and empirical synthesis. *Journal of Applied Psychology, 84,* 885–896.

Klein, H. J., Wesson, M. J., Hollenbeck, J. R., Wright, P. M., & DeShon, R. P. (2001). The assessment of goal commitment: A measurement model meta-analysis. *Organizational Behavior and Human Decision Processes, 85,* 32–55.

Kozlowski, S. W. J., Gully, S. M., Brown, K. G., Salas, E., Smith, E. M., & Nason, E. R. (2001). Effects of training goals and goal orientation traits on multidimensional training outcomes and performance adaptability. *Organizational Behavior and Human Decision Processes, 85*(1), 1–31.

Latham, G. P., & Piccolo, R. F. (2012). The effects of context specific versus nonspecific subconscious goals on employee performance. *Human Resource Management, 51*(4), 511–523.

Latham, G. P., Seijts, G., & Crim, D. (2008). The effects of learning goal difficulty level and cognitive ability on performance. *Canadian Journal of Behavioural Science, 40,* 220–229.

Latham, G. P., Winters, D. C., & Locke, E. A. (1994). Cognitive and motivational effects of participation: A mediator study. *Journal of Organizational Behavior, 15*(1), 49–63.

Lee, T. W., Locke, E. A., & Phan, S. H. (1997). Explaining the assigned goal-incentive interaction: The role of self-efficacy and personal goals. *Journal of Management, 23*(4), 541–559.

Leung, M. Y., Chong, A., Ng, S. T., & Cheung, M. C. K. (2004). Demystifying stakeholders' commitment and its impacts on construction projects. *Construction Management & Economics, 22*(7), 701–715.

Lin, Z., Yang, H., Arya, B., Huang, Z., & Li, D. (2005). Structural versus individual perspectives on the dynamics of group performance: Theoretical exploration and empirical investigation. *Journal of Management, 31*(3), 354–380.

Locke, E. A. (1968). Toward a theory of task motivation and incentives. *Organizational Behavior and Human Performance, 3*(15): 157–189.

Locke, E. A., & Latham, G. P. (1990). *A theory of goal setting and task performance.* Englewood Cliffs, NJ: Prentice Hall.

Locke, E. A., Latham, G. P., Erez, M. (1988). The determinants of goal acceptance and commitment. *Academy of Management Review, 13,* 23–39.

Locke, E. A., Saari, L. M., Shaw, K. N., & Latham, G. P. (1981). Goal setting and task performance: 1969–1980. *Psychological Bulletin, 90,* 125–152.

Lozano, B. E., & Stephens, R. S. (2010). Comparison of participatively set and assigned goals in the reduction of alcohol use. *Psychology of Addictive Behaviors, 24*(4), 581–591.

Mathieu, J. E. (1992). The influence of commitment to assigned goals and performance on subsequent self-set goals and performance. *Journal of Applied Social Psychology, 22*, 1012–1029.

Meyer, J. P., & Herscovitch, L. (2001). Commitment in the workplace: Toward a general model. *Human Resource Management Review, 11*, 299–326.

Mulvey, P. W., & Klein, H. J. (1998). The impact of perceived loafing and collective efficacy on group goal processes and group performance. *Organizational Behavior and Human Decision Processes, 74*(1), 62–87.

Naylor, J. C., & Ilgen, D. R. (1984). Goal setting: A theoretical analysis of a motivational technology. In B. Staw & L. L. Cummings (Eds.), *Research in organizational behavior* (Vol. 6, pp. 95–140). Greenwich, CT: JAI.

Nenkov, G. Y., & Gollwitzer, P. M. (2011). Pre- versus post-decisional deliberation and goal commitment: The positive effects of defensiveness (Working Paper No. 1756906). Retrieved from Social Science Research Network website: http://ssrn.com/abstract=1756906.

Oettingen, G., Mayer, D., Sevincer, A. T., Stephens, E. J., Pak, H., & Hagenah, M. (2009). Mental contrasting and goal commitment: The mediating role of energization. *Personality and Social Psychology Bulletin, 35*, 608–622.

Piccolo, R. F., & Colquitt, J. A. (2006). Transformational leadership and job behaviors: The mediating role of core job characteristics. *Academy of Management Journal, 49*(2), 327–340.

Podsakoff, P. M., MacKenzie, S. B., & Ahearne, M. (1997). Moderating effects of goal acceptance on the relationship between group cohesiveness and productivity. *Journal of Applied Psychology, 82*(6), 974–983.

Presslee, A., Vance, T. W., Webb, A., Jeffrey, S. (2011, May). *The effects of reward type on Employee goal setting, goal commitment and performance.* Paper presented at the meeting of Canadian Academic Accounting Association Annual Conference, Toronto, Ontario.

Renn, R. W. (1998). Participation's effect on task performance: Mediating roles of goal acceptance and procedural justice. *Journal of Business Research, 41*, 115–125.

Roberson, L. (1990). Prediction of job satisfaction from characteristics of personal work goals. *Journal of Organizational Behavior, 11*, 29–41.

Salancik, G. R. (1977). Commitment and the control of organizational behaviour and belief. In B. M. Staw, & G. R. Salancik (Eds.), *New directions in organizational behavior* (pp. 1–54). Chicago: St.Clair Press.

Schooler, J., & Schreiber, C. A. (2004). Experience, meta-consciousness, and the paradox of introspection. *Journal of Consciousness Studies, 11*, 17–39.

Schweitzer, M. E., Ordoñez, L., & Douma, B. (2004). Goal setting as a motivator of unethical behavior. *Academy of Management Journal, 47*(3), 422–432.

Seijts, G. H., & Latham, G. P. (2000a). The construct of goal commitment: Measurement and relationships with task performance. In R. G. Goffin & E. Helmes (Eds.), *Problems and solutions in human assessment: Honoring Douglas N. Jackson at seventy.* Norwell, MA: Kluwer Academic Publishers.

Seijts, G. H., & Latham, G. P. (2000b). The effects of goal setting and group size on performance in a social dilemma. *Canadian Journal of Behavioural Science, 32*(2), 104–116.

Seijts, G. H., & Latham, G. P. (2001). The effect of distal learning, outcome, and proximal goals on a moderately complex task. *Journal of Organizational Behavior, 22*(3), 291–307.

Seijts, G. H., & Latham, G. P. (2011). The effect of commitment to a learning goal, self-efficacy, and the interaction between learning goal difficulty and commitment on performance in a business simulation. *Human Performance, 24*(3), 189–204.

Seijts, G. H., Latham, G. P., Tasa, K., & Latham, B. W. (2004). Goal setting and goal orientation: An integration of two different yet related literatures. *Academy of Management Journal, 47*(2), 227–239.

Sevincer, A. T., & Oettingen, G. (2009). Alcohol breeds empty goal commitments. *Journal of Abnormal Psychology, 118*(3), 623–633.

Shantz, A., & Latham, G. P. (2011). The effect of primed goals on employee performance: Implications for human resource management. *Human Resource Management, 50*, 289–299.

Slocum, J. W., Cron, W. L., & Brown, S. P. (2002). The effect of goal conflict on performance. *Journal of Leadership & Organizational Studies, 9(1)*, 77–89.

Stajkovic, A. D., Locke, E. A., & Blair, E. S. (2006). A first examination of the relationships between primed subconscious goals, assigned conscious goals, and task performance. *Journal of Applied Psychology, 91*, 1172–1180.

Theodorakis, Y. (1996). The influence of goals, commitment, self-efficacy and self-satisfaction on motor performance. *Journal of Applied Sport Psychology, 8*, 171–182.

Tubbs, M. E., & Dahl, J. G. (1991). An empirical comparison of self-report and discrepancy measures of goal commitment. *Journal of Applied Psychology, 76*, 708–716.

Tubbs, M. E. (1993). Commitment as a moderator of the goal-performance relation: A case for clearer construct definition. *Journal of Applied Psychology, 78*, 86–97.

Tubbs, M. (1994). Commitment and the role of ability in motivation: Comment on Wright, O'Leary-Kelly, Cortina, Klein, and Hollenbeck (1994). *Journal of Applied Psychology, 79*, 804–811.

Vance, R. J., & Colella, A. (1990). Effects of two types of feedback on goal acceptance and personal goals. *Journal of Applied Psychology, 75*, 68–76.

Van Mierlo, H., & Kleingeld, A. (2010). Goals, strategies, and group performance: some limits of goal setting in groups. *Small Group Research, 41*(5), 524–555.

Wanous, J., & Hudy, M. (2001). Single-item reliability: A replication and extension. *Organizational Research Methods, 4*, 361–375.

Webb, R. A. (2004). Managers' commitment to the goals contained in a strategic performance measurement system. *Contemporary Accounting Research, 21*(4), 925–958.

Weingart, L. R. (1992). Impact of group goals, task component complexity, effort, and planning on group performance. *Journal of Applied Psychology, 77*, 682–693.

Weingart, L. R., & Weldon, E. (1991). Processes that mediate the relationship between a group goal and group member performance. *Human Performance, 4*(1), 33–54.

Weldon, E., & Weingart, L. R. (1993). Group goals and group performance. *British Journal of Social Psychology, 32*(4), 307–334.

Whiteoak, J. W. (2007). The relationship among group process perceptions, goal commitment and turnover intention in small committee groups. *Journal of Business and Psychology, 22*(1), 11–20.

Whitney, K. (1994). Improving group task performance: The role of group goals and group efficacy. *Human Performance, 7*(1), 55–78.

Winters, D., & Latham, G. (1996). The effect of learning versus outcome goals on a simple versus a complex task. *Group and Organization Management, 21*, 236–250.

Wofford, J. C., Goodwin, V. L., & Premack, S. (1992). Meta-analysis of the antecedents of personal goal level and of the antecedents and consequences of goal commitment. *Journal of Management, 18*, 595–615.

Wood, R. E., Atkins, P. W. B., & Bright, J. E. H. (1999). Bonuses, goals, and instrumentality effects. *Journal of Applied Psychology, 84*(5), 703–720.

Wright, P. M. (1992). An examination of the relationships among monetary incentives, goal level, goal commitment, and performance. *Journal of Management, 18*, 677–693.

Wright, P. M., George, J. M., Farnswarth, S. R., & McMahon, G. C. (1993). Productivity and extra-role behavior: The effects of goals. *Journal of Applied Psychology, 78*, 374–381.

Wright, P. M., & Kacmar, K. M. (1995). Mediating roles of self-set goals, goal commitment, self-efficacy, and attractiveness in the incentive-performance relation. *Human Performance, 8*, 263–296.

Wright, P. M., O'Leary, A. M., Cortina, J. M., Klein, H. J., & Hollenbeck, J. R. (1994). On the meaning and measurement of goal commitment. *Journal of Applied Psychology, 79*(6), 795–803.

Yukl, G. A., & Latham, G. P. (1978). Interrelationships among employee participation, individual differences, goal difficulty, goal acceptance, goal instrumentality, and performance. *Personnel Psychology, 31*, 305–323.

# 7 Goals, Goal Orientations, Strategies, and Performance

*Robert E. Wood, Jennifer Whelan, Victor Sojo, and Moureen Wong* Melbourne Business School, University of Melbourne

## Introduction

The role of goals as determinants of performance has been a central topic of research in organizational behavior since goal setting was first proposed by Locke (1968) as a core component of work motivation. Over the ensuing decades, a range of robust findings in diverse settings have established that the presence and properties of goals combined with the right types of feedback produce improved performance (Locke & Latham, 1990; Locke, Shaw, Saari, & Latham, 1981; Mento, Steele, & Karren, 1987). Locke and Latham (1990) outlined a theory of goal setting based on a body of evidence that had already established the robustness of goal setting effects across over 80 different tasks, in culturally diverse settings and in field and laboratory studies, and in both correlational and experimental designs (Latham & Locke, 2007; Locke & Latham, 2006). Goals produce performance effect sizes that are second only to money as a motivational tool (Wood & Locke, 1990), and goal setting theory explains how and when these effects occur.

Following their review of the goal setting research up to 1980, Locke et al. (1981) proposed four mediating mechanisms to explain how goals influence performance. The first three of these mechanisms, focus, effort, and persistence, were supported by studies conducted up to the time of their review and have not received much attention since. The fourth mechanism proposed by Locke et al. (1981), strategy, has been the subject of studies conducted since 1980, which are the focus of this chapter.

Locke et al. (1981) argued that the effect of strategy, unlike the previous three factors, is an indirect one. Although strategy development is motivated by goals, it involves the development of skills and problem solving, and is thus cognitive in nature. Early goal setting studies of strategy development supported the argument that goals motivate strategies, which in turn lead to improved performance (Earley & Perry, 1987). Wood and Locke (1990) elaborated the argument for the strategy mechanism in a model that makes specific predictions about the nature of the relationships between goals, strategies, and performance on tasks of varying levels of novelty and complexity. They proposed that goals affect performance directly on simple tasks by activating a repertoire of general automatized task strategies that are stored in long-term memory. In the Wood and Locke (1990) model, the direction, effort, and persistence mechanisms described by Locke et al. (1981) are the most common general automatized task strategies. Although not mentioned by Wood and Locke (1990), general task strategies may also include self-regulation strategies such as goal setting and monitoring, which also relate to the regulation of effort across all tasks (Pintrich, 2000; Yoon, 2009).

When a person experiences a task as novel or complex, the effects due to general automatized task strategies are subsumed by task-specific strategies, which are the product of past learning and are also stored in long-term memory. If the task is novel or difficult such that previously learned task-specific strategies do not produce expected results, then an individual will undertake problem solving that can lead to the adaptation of existing task strategies or the development of new ones.

The first proposition of the model put forward by Wood and Locke (1990) is that when a person acquires a goal, they first activate strategies stored in long-term memory, including general automatized task strategies and, if the task is complex enough to require the allocation and/or coordination of effort across task components, task-specific strategies. The second proposition of the Wood and Locke models is that, when the recall and application of strategies stored in long-term memory does not produce the desired outcome expressed in the goal, attempts to solve the problem will include the creation of new task strategies through study, experimentation, and creative problem solving, some of which may be based on previously stored strategies and motivated by a desire to succeed in a particular goal, or a fear of failure. Thus, in summary, goals and performance are related because goals direct attention, effort, and persistence towards a goal-relevant outcome. That is, they motivate and guide the use of existing knowledge and skills (strategies) and, where necessary, they promote the acquisition of new skills through problem solving and learning, leading to new strategies.

Locke (2000) extended these arguments through a presentation of three different types of relationships between goals, task strategies, and task performance based on analyses of the results of existing studies, which he then argued could all be accounted for by one underlying model. The three types of relationships described by Locke (2000) included independent effects of goals and task strategies (e.g., Taylor, Locke, Lee, & Gist, 1984; Chesney & Locke, 1991), interactions between goals and task strategies (e.g., Durham, Knight, & Locke, 1997; Earley & Perry, 1987) and mediation of goal effects by task strategies (e.g., DeShon & Alexander, 1996, study 2; Locke & Kristof, 1996; Knight, Durham, & Locke, 2001). Locke's (2000) discussion of task strategies took into account the existence of subconscious knowledge, which had not been previously considered in studies of goals and task strategies and therefore, Locke argued, was present but unmeasured. All performance requires some form of knowledge. Studies that supported the interaction and mediation models were those in which knowledge was measured, whereas the studies that found direct effects for goals were those in which the application of task strategies drew on subconscious knowledge that was unmeasured (Locke, 2000).

A number of more recent developments are also relevant to the discussion of goals and strategies (Locke & Latham, 2006; Latham & Locke, 2007). A recent stream of research by Latham, Seijts, and colleagues has refined propositions surrounding the assertion that specific or difficult goals produce better performance than simply "trying one's best" through their analyses of how different goals influence strategy development. In an initial study, Mone and Shalley (1995) found that a "do your best" goal led to higher performance than a specific, challenging goal on a complex simulation task as a result of more systematic searching for correct task strategies by those with the "do your best" goal. Winters and Latham (1996) argued that the Mone and Shalley (1995) result was due to differential effects of goal criteria (goal content) on the application and search for task strategies. Specific, challenging performance goals can produce "tunnel vision" in which existing strategies are activated in preference to a search for new strategies, which may be required as tasks become more complex and when a person lacks the knowledge and skills for the task. Winters and Latham (1996) found that a learning goal, that is a goal to discover effective strategies, produced better performance on a more complex version of their study task than a performance goal. In a follow-up study, Seijts and Latham (2001) replicated the Winters and Latham (1996) result and established that the effects of the learning goal on a more complex task was partially mediated through the discovery of new strategies. Thus, it appears that a learning goal activates metacognitive processes such as the search, planning, monitoring, and evaluation of strategies, whereas performance goals activate pre-existing strategies, which may be applied either consciously or subconsciously. Specific, challenging goals work best when individuals either have the required knowledge and skills for a given level of task complexity (Locke & Latham, 2002) or have the necessary abilities to discover the required task strategies.

## Overview

As Locke and Latham (2006) point out, the success of goal setting theory is dependent on research attending to the mechanisms by which goals and performance are related, that is, the moderating and mediating effects of other factors. To that end, in this chapter, we present a review of studies conducted since 1980 that have studied either the mediating or moderating role of strategies in the relationship between goals and performance. The discussion of the mediating role is based on a meta-analysis of the findings from studies that have reported the information needed to calculate effect sizes for both the goals–strategies relationships and the strategies–performance relationships in a single model. The discussion of the moderating role of strategies is based on a narrative review of available studies. There were too few studies with the required information to calculate effect sizes for a meta-analysis.

In the analyses of the mediating model, we examine the goal property of challenge, which has been the focus of goal setting researchers since the original statement of the theory by Locke (1968) and has become firmly established as the key determinant of the effects of goals. We supplement the study of goal challenge with analyses of three types of goal orientation (GO): mastery approach, performance approach, and performance avoidance. Goal orientations have been the subject of a growing volume of organizational research over the past two decades (Payne, Youngcourt, & Beaubien, 2007). Approach and avoidance GOs were originally associated with mastery and performance orientations, respectively, until Elliot (1994) pointed out that the performance GO could be split into a performance approach GO and a performance avoidance GO, each with different determinants and different effects.

The following sections provide an overview of the arguments for the mediator and moderator roles of strategies in the goal–performance relationship, a description of the methods used in identifying the studies included in the analyses reported, and the results of the analyses. The results section includes a description of the goals, strategies, and performance constructs followed by presentation of the results of the analyses for the mediation and moderator models. The final section summarizes the main findings of our review and discusses some practical implications and possible future research of the relationship between goals, strategies, and performance.

## Models of the Goals, Strategies, and Performance Relationship

In this chapter, we evaluate the mediating and moderating models of the relationship between goals and strategy and their resulting impacts on performance. The third model in which goals and strategies each have direct effects on performance, which Locke (2000) argued was a result of unmeasured strategies, is not considered. The mediating and moderator models are complementary but assign different causal roles to goals and strategies and adopt different conceptualizations of the strategy variable. One argument treats strategies as a moderator of goal effects such that pre-existing strategies lead to higher performance for specific, challenging goals. In this argument, strategies are conceptualized as pre-existing knowledge that is either stored in long-term memory or is the product of a strategy training intervention (Northcraft, Neale, & Earley, 1994; Vollmeyer, Burns, & Holyoak,1996). The second argument treats strategies as a product of goals and as a mediator of the effects of goals on performance. In this approach, strategy has been conceptualized as the level and quality of selected strategies applied during task performance or as the levels of strategy development activities such as exploration and information processing as a result of goals (Elliot, McGregor, & Gable, 1999; Phan, 2009a, 2009b; Senko & Miles, 2008). The different conceptualizations of strategy in the two arguments overlap but also have some differences.

### The Mediator Model

In the most commonly tested model for the relationships between goals, strategies, and performance, strategies are treated as a mediator between goals and performance, one of the four mediating mechanisms identified by Locke et al. (1981). The mediator argument is that goals activate the application of or search for strategies as part of an individual's goal-striving efforts. Tests of the effects of goals on the application of pre-existing task strategies can be differentiated from the use of pre-existing task strategies in the tests of the moderator argument described below by focusing on the relationship between the properties of goals and levels of strategy applied during goal-striving processes. In the moderator argument, goals and pre-existing task strategies are treated as independent of one another. Tests of the mediator argument that have looked at the application of pre-existing strategies have included, for example, self-regulation strategies (Ford, Smith, Weissbein, Gully, & Salas, 1998; Yoon, 2009) and strategy effort levels (Greene & Miller, 1996; Phan, 2009a, 2009b, 2010).

A variant of the mediation argument has focused on how goals stimulate the search and information-processing activities required for the development of new task strategies. Search and information processing are most likely to occur when a task is novel or challenging for the individual or dynamically complex, such that existing strategies must be adapted or new ones developed to achieve a goal (Goodman, Wood, & Chen, 2011). Also, Seijts and Latham (2001) have shown that specific, challenging learning goals, such as learn five new strategies, promote greater search and discovery of new strategies than specific, challenging performance goals. This related informative line of research is discussed in Chapter 13 in this volume and will not be considered further here.

Although goals stimulate the application of strategies, they do not guarantee that a person will apply or discover the correct strategy. The effectiveness of strategies stimulated by goals will instead depend on prior knowledge of the task for the application of strategies and of meta-search strategies, such as hypothesis testing, for the discovery of new strategies.

## The Moderator Model

In the moderator model, strategies are treated as pre-existing knowledge that can be used to achieve a goal, through focus, effort, and persistence mechanisms (Locke et al., 1981). In tests of the moderator model, prior knowledge of task-specific strategies could be operationalized through measures of levels of existing knowledge or through manipulation. In all of the studies reviewed, manipulations of prior task strategy knowledge have been through training manipulations, including training in negotiation strategy (Northcraft et al., 1994), prediction strategy (Earley, Connolly, & Lee, 1989), and test-taking strategy (Whinnery & Fuchs, 1993). The moderator argument is that goals will have a greater impact on performance for individuals who have knowledge or strategies for performing the task than for those who either lack the knowledge or adopt faulty strategies. A conclusion from this argument is that more experienced and more expert performers, who will have more task-specific strategies available, will experience greater performance gains due to the focusing and persistence effects of goals than novices.

Several boundary conditions can be identified for this argument. First, it requires tasks of sufficient complexity that previously learned task-specific strategies will make a difference. Moderator effects are expected to be most pronounced when the general automatized task strategies described by Wood and Locke (1990), such as work hard, and self-regulation strategies, are not enough for successful task performance. Second, differences in the levels of knowledge or strategies of different individuals must be related to differences in performance levels of the task. These rather obvious conditions may not be satisfied if the different levels of experience in a sample are not reflected in different levels of learning of effective task strategies or if the performance on the criterion task is not sufficiently sensitive to measurable differences in experience or strategies within the ranges of expertise captured in a sample. For example, if task learning is best described by a step function in performance, with long plateaus between steps, significant differences in measurable levels of knowledge or experience may not be reflected in differences in performance. A third potential limiting condition is that the task remain sufficiently stable that the application of previously learned strategies still have a positive effect on performance and not impede adaptive responses, or the development of new task plans, when tasks are dynamic or vary from the source task.

## The Method

### Sample

A range of sources were used to collate research relating to the key concepts of interest: goals, strategy, and performance. Online reference databases searched included PsychInfo, ERIC, PubMed, and Sociological Abstracts. Google Scholar was also used to search any additional published material not included in the previously mentioned academic reference databases. Given the size of the goal setting literature, we restricted our attention to papers published in peer-reviewed publications. Thus, we did not solicit unpublished manuscripts, dissertations, or survey data. We also excluded any studies that did not report effect sizes, or provide sufficient data for reliable estimates of effect sizes to be calculated. Thus, the final sample for the analyses to produce the results reported in this chapter comprised 58 papers that included 63 studies, of which 18 were experimental studies, and 53 were correlational. In total, these studies yielded data from 21,931 people. The numbers of effects (K) used in the calculation of effect sizes and other statistics for each of the relationships are shown in Tables 7.1 to 7.7. Some studies included more than one effect.

The studies used to derive the results reported were coded as to the study design, (experimental, correlational, or field study design), the composition of the sample (i.e., student, community, organizational), the sample size, the independent variables, covariates, moderators, mediators, and the scales used for each. The studies were then further coded according to the conceptual definitions for strategies, goals, and performance used in the different studies. All coding was done by trained research assistants. Inter-rater reliability estimates were conducted on a subsample of 30% of the papers included in the analysis. This was computed on both the conceptual and statistical coding processes, and was assessed using kappa. The inter-rater reliability coefficients were high for both the conceptual ($k = .89$) and statistical ($k = .92$) coding process.

## Strategies, Goals, and Performance Criteria

The coding of the conceptual definitions of strategies revealed four types of strategies. As previously mentioned, goals were coded for specificity and challenge, and GOs were coded for mastery approach, performance approach, and performance avoidance. The performance measures reflect the criterion task used in each of the studies, which were collapsed into a single category for the reported analyses.

### Strategies

The primary distinction of the work reported in this chapter relative to other chapters in the book is the focus on strategies, and the way in which the relationship between goals and strategies affects performance. The term *strategy* has many different definitions, but most refer to a plan or pattern of decision making or actions designed or undertaken to achieve a goal. The studies reviewed for this chapter focus on individual task strategies that govern the allocation of personal resources during the execution of a task. At the individual level, strategic behavior includes the application of relevant task knowledge from long-term memory and the refinement and elaboration of that knowledge into new strategies (Wood & Locke, 1990). The application of knowledge from long-term memory can be either a conscious or subconscious process (Locke, 2000).

Four broad categories of strategies were identified in the studies reviewed. These included three strategies that were focused on the task and one that focused on the individual's self-regulation. The task strategies were categorized as task-specific strategies, as described by Wood and Locke (1990), strategy development, and search and information processing. The latter two strategy types refer to different types of activities undertaken in refinement of task-specific strategies or the development of new task-specific strategies.

*Task-specific strategies* are those that refer to knowledge that can be applied directly to judgments and actions on the specific task being performed. Operationalizations of task-specific strategies included measures of the repeated use of a strategy that had worked in the past (Audia, Locke, & Smith, 2000) and the degree to which participants followed a prescribed strategy for a task (He, 2008; Johnson, Graham, & Harris, 1997). In moderator studies, the knowledge of task-specific strategies was typically manipulated through a training intervention before the introduction of a goal (e.g., Northcraft et al., 1994; Earley et al., 1989; Whinnery & Fuchs, 1993).

*Strategy development* was assessed with self-report measures that tapped the amount of effort that was directly devoted to the development or refinement of task-specific strategies during performance of the task. These included self-reported levels of effort devoted to the development of strategies (Diefendorff & Lord, 2003; Locke, Frederick, Lee, & Bobko, 1984; Northcraft et al., 1994; Wright, 1990) and reported levels of imagination applied in developing novel strategies (Saavedra, Earley, & van Dyne, 1993), and practice on a similar task (Ford et al., 1998). These measures of strategy development differ from the search and information processing strategies discussed next in that they ask respondents specifically about the task being worked on and, in most cases, are collected ex post and therefore are confounded by the respondents' knowledge of their performance on the task.

*Search and information processing strategies* (SIPs) included measures of the actual cognitive processes that can lead to strategy development, such as hypothesis testing and critical thinking, as distinct from those that relied on self-reports of effort devoted to development of a specific task strategy. SIP strategies were operationalized through objective measures of how participants explored problem spaces and gathered information (Goodman et al., 2011) and self-reports of the levels of critical thinking processes (Liem, Lau, & Nie, 2008; Matos, Lens, & Vansteenkiste, 2007; Phan, 2008, 2009a, 2009b, 2010; Pintrich, 2000; Wolters, 2004). A common objective measure of SIP was the use of systematic hypothesis testing by varying one factor at a time (VOTAT, Cervone, Jiwani, & Wood, 1991; Vollmeyer et al., 1996, Study 1). SIP strategies based on self-reports of critical thinking processes included measures tapping the levels of surface versus deep thinking (Liem et al., 2008; Matos et al., 2007; Phan, 2008, 2009a, 2009b, 2010; Pintrich, 2000; Wolters, 2004).

*Self-regulatory strategies* included all strategies that were focused on the personal allocation of effort plus the management of emotions and self-evaluative reactions to the task. These included negative self-handicapping strategies (reverse scored) such as reduction of effort and procrastination in the face of difficult tasks, plus a range of positive strategies such as goal setting, time management, planning and scheduling activities, persistence, organization, risk taking, repeating tasks, positive self-talk, and gratification delay. Self-regulatory strategies such as self-talk have been shown to lead to significant improvements in the self-efficacy and performance of disadvantaged groups (e.g., Latham & Budworth, 2006; Yanar, Budworth, & Latham, 2009). The items used to assess participant self-regulation strategies included scales to tap emotional control (Bell & Kozlowski, 2008), goal setting and planning (Bong, 2009; Pintrich, 2000; Yoon, 2009), and monitoring of performance (Geddes, 2009). The items in the scales asked participants about the levels of self-regulatory activities they employed when learning or performing a task and not about the specific strategies for performing the task.

## Goals

In the broader psychological literature, goals refer to many different levels and scope of intentions. Within organizational psychology over the period covered by the review for this chapter, two different approaches have been most common in the description and operationalization properties of goals. The first approach focuses on the challenge and specificity properties of goals, as described by Locke et al. (1981). The second approach, which was adopted in the overwhelming majority of studies covered by this review, makes a distinction between approach and avoidance GOs (Elliott & Dweck, 1988).

Specific, challenging goals refer to intentions for a specific task, which may be of short or long duration, simple or complex, routine or novel. GO refers to a more general mindset that includes beliefs, values, and criteria that influence how people respond to achievement situations in general when operationalized as a trait, and to specific task situations when operationalized as a state (Dweck, 1986; Payne et al., 2007).

In the distinction between *approach* and *avoidance* goals, those who adopt an approach orientation strive to attain a goal or achieve success at a task, which may include a risk of failure. Those who adopt an avoidance orientation focus on avoiding failure and other negative outcomes. The distinction between mastery and performance orientations is based on the self-evaluative purpose that the task has for an individual. According to Dweck (1999), in achievement contexts, *performance goals* have the purpose of validating personal attributes, such as ability, and seeking positive evaluations of those attributes from others, while *mastery or learning goals* have the purpose of developing or acquiring an attribute, such as a specific task skill or knowledge. Three categories of goal orientation have been included in most studies of goals and strategies: mastery approach, performance approach, and performance avoidance (Day, Radosevich, & Chasteen, 2003; Ng, 2009). These three categories are reported in our analyses. The mastery-avoid orientation has been included in two studies (Bong, 2009; Neuville, Frenay, & Bourgeois, 2007). These are excluded from our analyses due to the small number of studies.

## Performance

Measures of performance included, in order of frequency, school or university subject grade, GPA, SAT score, nonacademic task performance, learning performance, work, and performance ratings. These were all combined in a single category in the analyses.

## Results

Research examining the relationship of goals, strategies, and performance has included a range of different types of goals, strategies, and performance tasks. Our categorizations of the different types for each of these variables are shown in Table 7.1.

Table 7.1 Performance Effects of Different Strategies

| Strategy | K | N | Nonsupportive Results | 95% CI | z | p | r |
|---|---|---|---|---|---|---|---|
| Self-Regulation | 23 | 10,068 | 3 | .182, .282 | 8.80 | .001 | .233 |
| Task Specific | 13 | 1523 | 6 | .166, .427 | 4.25 | .001 | .302 |
| Strategy Development Effort | 10 | 1462 | 4 | .139, .331 | 4.63 | .001 | .237 |
| Search & Information Processing | 31 | 13,504 | 15 | .044, .146 | 3.66 | .001 | .095 |

## Strategies and Performance

The first question we addressed is, "do strategies have a positive effect on performance?" The results of the analyses to address this question are shown in Table 7.1. Studies of the relationship between strategies and performance produced a total of 77 effects on tasks ranging from 2-hour experimental tasks to semester-long courses of study. The most common strategy studied has been the fundamental search and information processing (SIP) strategies, particularly levels of thinking that can contribute to learning of new knowledge such as task-specific strategies. The other frequently studied type of strategy was self-regulation.

The answer is clearly yes, strategies do enhance performance. All four types of strategies tested in different studies have a positive effect on performance, but the magnitude of that effect varies as a function of the proximity of the strategy content to the actual execution of task behaviors. Task-specific strategies that draw on pre-existing task-relevant knowledge from long-term memory have the greatest impact on task performance ($r = .302$, $p < .001$), followed by strategies in which effort is directed to the testing, refinement, and development of task-specific strategies ($r = .237$, $p < .001$). More fundamental strategy development processes, such as the effort devoted to SIP, have the least pronounced effect on performance ($r = .095$, $p < .001$) of all strategies. Fundamental processes such as search, information processing, and thinking are, of course, fundamental to learning and, therefore to the development of the knowledge that makes up task-specific strategies (Durham, Locke, Poon, & McLeod, 2000; Geddes, 2009). Therefore, it is possible that the effects of SIP strategies on performance are mediated through the resulting task-specific strategies, but this model has not been tested in the studies reviewed in this chapter.

Self-regulation strategies also had a strong positive effective on performance ($r = .233$, $p < .001$). Given that self-regulation may be a supplemental or coordinating strategy for other more task-specific strategies, it is possible that self-regulation and more task-specific strategies may have additive effects on performance for selected tasks. First, they are the product of a significant number of studies, a large total sample, and a wide range of tasks, including academic performance in a single task (e.g., Ng, 2008), general academic performance, such as SAT and GPA (e.g., Day et al., 2003; Shih, 2005), decision making during an experimental task (e.g., Ford et al. 1998), and knowledge transfer (e.g., Bell & Kozlowski, 2008; Yoon, 2009). Second, only 3 out of the 23 effect sizes for the studies of the relationship between self-regulation strategies and performance were not significant. Third, the lower limit of the 95% confidence interval does not approach zero, and the range of possible effects for self-regulation strategies on performance was quite narrow (*95% CI; .282 > r > .182*) compared to the ranges for the other four strategies shown in Table 7.1. The generalizable nature of self-regulation strategies may mean that they contribute much more to learning and performance across a range of tasks, such as those included in a job role or a program of study, than is evident in the studies of specific tasks reported here.

However, there is a caveat to this conclusion for the effects of self-regulatory strategies on performance. The assessment of self-regulation strategies in the studies reviewed for this chapter focused on self-regulatory processes such as planning, monitoring, time management, attention management, and emotional control. A recent meta-analysis of the effects of self-regulation on learning found that it was the self-regulatory states of goal level, persistence, effort, and self-efficacy that had the strongest effects on learning (Sitzmann & Ely, 2011). Self-regulatory processes did not have a significant effect on learning after controlling for cognitive ability and pre-training knowledge, which the authors pointed out may have been due to variations in the quality of the strategies used (Sitzmann & Ely, 2011). Sitzmann and Ely also found that the different self-efficacy constructs were highly inter-correlated. Therefore, it is possible that the self-regulatory motivational states were the most proximal predictors of learning and were products of the more distal self-regulatory processes captured by the strategies reported here and in the studies reviewed in the Sitzmann and Ely (2011) meta-analysis.

In summary, it can be said with some confidence that strategies do make a difference to performance. Individuals who regulate their task engagement in a strategic manner use prior knowledge about the task in selecting actions, and those who spend more effort in search and information processing activities that lead to the development of the knowledge of new task-specific strategies perform better than those who do not.

## Goals and Strategies

Results for the studies of the relationships between goals and strategies are shown in Tables 7.2 to 7.6. Each table shows the effects for one of the task goals or GO properties with each of the four strategies on which data were available. The results for the task goals and GO properties shown in the five tables will be discussed in turn, but first some general points can be made about the distribution of studies. First, of the 77 effect sizes included in the analyses, the effects of goal challenge and goal specificity on strategies have only been assessed in 12 studies and 2 studies, respectively. Thus, the two goal properties that were the primary focus of goal setting research in the decades leading up to the Locke and Latham (1990) book have received relatively little attention in the past two decades. This is particularly true for specificity, which has only been included in two studies, both of which examined the effects of goal specificity on the use of task-specific strategies. The well-established and consistent effects for goal specificity (Locke & Latham, 1990) are the most likely reason for lack of research on this goal property. Studies including goal challenge have primarily examined the effects on the use of task-specific strategies, which has been the relationship studied in 6 of the 12 studies that have included this goal property. Goal orientations have been the subject of many more studies and have been examined in relationships with strategies such as self-regulation strategies and SIP, which have received less attention in studies including goal challenge and goal specificity.

## Goal Challenge and Strategies

As shown in Table 7.2, studies with goal challenge as a predictor were identified for each of the four strategies. Half of the 12 studies of goal challenge examined the effect on the use of task-specific strategies, for which there was a significant and relatively large positive effect ($r = .373$, $p <.05$) but high variance in the results for different studies ($95\%$ $CI$; $.623 > r > .054$), suggesting the presence of moderators. Goal challenge also had a significant positive effect on effort spent on the refinement and development of task-specific strategies ($r = .290, p < .001$) in the two studies that reported that relationship. The positive effect of goal challenge from the two studies that included SIP strategies ($r = .271$, $p = .012$) was only supported in one study and had high variance across those two studies ($95\%$ $CI$; $.459 > r > .061$), suggesting either the presence of moderators or that the observed effect is not robust. Further studies are needed to confirm which.

## Goal Specificity and Strategies

The two studies that examined the effects of goal specificity focused on the relationship with the use of task-specific strategies, and both found a significant positive relationship. The effects for the two studies combined, shown in Table 7.3 ($r = .241$, $p < .001$; $95\%$ $CI$; $.356 > r > .118$), suggest that the effect is robust but, given the small number of studies reported, the accumulated results of further studies may either identify a moderator or lead to a different conclusion.

*Table 7.2* The Effects of Goal Challenge on Different Strategies

| Strategy | K | N | Nonsupportive Results | 95% CI | z | p | r |
|---|---|---|---|---|---|---|---|
| Self-Regulation | 2 | 615 | 1 | −.170, .820 | 1.45 | .150 | .456 |
| Task Specific | 6 | 918 | 2 | .054, .623 | 2.27 | .023 | .373 |
| Strategy Development Effort | 2 | 403 | 0 | .151, .418 | 3.30 | .001 | .290 |
| Search & Information Processing | 2 | 184 | 1 | .061, .459 | 2.51 | .012 | .271 |

*Table 7.3* The Effects of Goal Specificity on Different Strategies

| Strategy | K | N | Nonsupportive Results | 95% CI | z | p | r |
|---|---|---|---|---|---|---|---|
| Self-Regulation | – | – | – | – | – | – | – |
| Task Specific | 2 | 238 | 0 | .118, .356 | 3.80 | .001 | .241 |
| Strategy Development Effort | – | – | – | – | – | – | – |
| Search & Information Processing | – | – | – | – | – | – | – |

*Table 7.4* The Effects of Performance Avoidance Goal Orientation on Different Strategies

| Strategy | K | N | Nonsupportive Results | 95% CI | z | p | r |
|---|---|---|---|---|---|---|---|
| Self-Regulation | 13 | 7201 | 5 | −.292, .009 | −1.843 | .065 | −.145 |
| Task Specific | – | – | – | – | – | – | – |
| Strategy Development Effort | – | – | – | – | – | – | – |
| Search & Information Processing | 14 | 8785 | 7 | −.003, .146 | 1.890 | .059 | .072 |

## Performance Avoidance Goal Orientation and Strategies

Results for the research conducted on the relationships of a performance avoidance GO with self-regulation (13 studies) and SIP (14 studies) strategies are shown in Table 7.4. No studies were found for the relationships of performance avoidance GO with task-specific strategies and strategy development effort. Overall, performance avoidance GO had a small and nonsignificant effect (at $p < .05$, one-tailed test) on self-regulation and SIP strategies. The small overall relationship between performance avoidance GO and the use of effective self-regulation strategies was negative ($r = -.145$, $p = .065$; 95% CI; $.009 > r > -.292$). Interestingly, the two studies that included measures of mastery/learning avoidance goals (Bong, 2009; Neuville et al., 2007) both reported a significant, positive relationship between mastery avoidance GO and levels of self-regulation ($r = .19$, $p < .01$; $r = .085$, $p < .05$, respectively). The relationship between performance avoidance GO and the use of SIP strategies had a small positive effect ($r = .072$, $p = .059$; 95% CI; $.003 > r > .146$). Half of the studies (7 out of 14) reported a nonsignificant relationship, including one study that reported a significant negative relationship between performance avoidance GO and levels of SIP (Elliot et al., 1999; $r = -.167$; 95% CI; $-.021 > r > -.306$). Thus, the weight of evidence across the 14 studies reported in Table 7.4 indicates that a performance avoidance GO is not related to the greater use of SIP strategies. This result is consistent with the evidence that people with a performance orientation do not actively seek new knowledge but prefer to work on tasks they know they can already perform (Dweck, 2006; Seijts, Latham, Tasa, & Latham, 2004).

## Performance Approach Goal Orientation and Strategies

Studies of the relationship of a performance approach GO and the use of selected strategies includes 21 effects for self-regulation strategies and 26 effects for SIP strategies, as shown in Table 7.5. In summary, a performance approach GO has a small positive, nonsignificant relationship with the use of self-regulation strategies ($r = .069$, $p < .120$; 95% CI; $-.018 > r > .155$), and a small positive, significant relationship with the use of SIP strategies ($r = .191$, $p < .001$; 95% CI; $.131 > r > .250$).

The positive small effect for the relationship between a performance approach GO and SIP strategies may reflect the balancing or movement between the approach component of the orientation, which would promote the use of search for new knowledge in order to achieve a goal, and the performance component, which would predict a preference for existing strategies over the search for new approaches. Nearly a third (31%) of the 26 effects for SIP strategies reported in Table 7.5 did not report a significant positive relationship.

The weight of evidence presented in Tables 7.4 and 7.5 suggests that a performance approach GO is more likely to lead to greater use of effective self-regulation strategies and SIP strategies than a performance avoidance GO, but neither has consistent or large effects on the use of either strategy.

## Mastery Approach Goal Orientation and Strategies

The effects for the relationships between a mastery approach GO and the use of self-regulation strategies (22 effects) and SIP strategies (27 effects) are shown in Table 7.6. The results show that, of the three goal orientations, a mastery approach GO has the largest and most robust positive effects on the use of both self-regulation strategies ($r = .335$, $p < .001$; 95% CI; $.253 > r > .413$) and SIP strategies ($r = .348$, $p < .001$; 95% CI; $.288 > r > .404$). The overall pattern of results supports the conclusion that the observed positive effect of a mastery approach GO on the use of productive strategies for both managing the self and engaging in the development of new task strategies is generalizable and does not need to be qualified by considerations of potential moderators. Components of the pattern of results in Table 7.6 to support this conclusion include the relatively narrow confidence intervals, which are 24% and 17% of the effect sizes for self-regulation strategies and SIP strategies, respectively, plus the small number of

Table 7.5  The Effects of Performance Approach Goal Orientation on Different Strategies

| Strategy | K | N | Non-supportive Results | 95% CI | z | p | r |
|---|---|---|---|---|---|---|---|
| Self-Regulation | 21 | 9537 | 8 | −.018, .155 | 1.555 | .120 | .069 |
| Task Specific | – | – | – | – | – | – | – |
| Strategy Development Effort | – | – | – | – | – | – | – |
| Search & Information Processing | 26 | 12,542 | 8 | .131, .250 | 6.185 | .001 | .191 |

Table 7.6  The Effects of Mastery Approach Goal Orientation on Different Strategies

| Strategy | K | N | Nonsupportive Results | 95% CI | z | p | r |
|---|---|---|---|---|---|---|---|
| Self-Regulation | 22 | 9703 | 3 | .253, .413 | 7.556 | .001 | .335 |
| Task Specific | – | – | – | – | – | – | – |
| Strategy Development Effort | – | – | – | – | – | – | – |
| Search & Information Processing | 27 | 12,809 | 1 | .288, .404 | 10.782 | .001 | .348 |

nonsignificant effects. Of the four nonsignificant effects shown in Table 7.6, two were marginally significant positive effects ($p < .10$; He, 2008; Albaili, 1998), and there were no negative effects.

Therefore, we can conclude that individuals with a mastery approach GO are more likely to adopt strategies to regulate their emotions, attention, and effort during task performance and to engage in the search, information processing, and thinking processes that are considered critical to learning. This latter finding supports the argument that an approach GO focuses attention on how to improve and to master a task and produces a willingness to take the risks of failure implicit in the exploration and experimentation, while the mastery orientation focuses on learning and progress as the key indicator of success.

### Goals→Strategies→Performance

Table 7.7 shows the results of Sobel tests for all variations of the mediation model goals→strategies→performance that could be formed using combinations of the effects for the different sets of relationships reported in Tables 7.1 to 7.6. The mediational model for the direct effects of goal specificity on the use of task-specific strategies and goal challenge on the use of SIP strategies could not be tested as, in both cases, there was only one effect that included both steps of the mediational model.

Consistent with the arguments of Locke and Latham (Locke et al., 1981; Locke & Latham, 1990) the effects of goal challenge on performance were mediated through the application of existing task-specific strategies (Sobel's $Z = 2.21$, $p < .05$) and effort devoted to the development of strategies (Sobel's $Z = 3.84$, $p < .001$). Challenging goals encourage greater strategic effort, which in turn leads to greater performance.

Tests of the mediational models for the effects of the three goal orientations provide strong support for mediation of the effect of a mastery approach GO on performance through the greater use of self-regulation strategies (Sobel's $Z = 5.35$, $p < .001$) and SIP strategies (Sobel's $Z = 2.91$, $p < .01$). As noted earlier, the results reported in this chapter refer to the effects of mastery approach GO on the use of self-regulatory processes such as planning, time management, attention management, and emotional control. However, as reported in Sitzmann and Ely (2011) for learning and transfer, the effects of a mastery approach GO may be more strongly mediated through more proximal motivational states, such as persistence, effort, and self-efficacy.

Of the two performance GOs, the one significant mediation model was for the mediation of the effects of a performance approach GO on performance through the use of SIP strategies (Sobel's $Z = 2.83$, $p < .05$). As noted earlier, this effect was not large and was considerably smaller than the effects of a mastery approach GO on performance.

### Strategies as Moderators of Goals Effects

Studies of the interactions between goals and strategy have provided mostly positive support for the moderator model, but the support is less robust than that reported for the mediation model. The studies reviewed include a variety of manipulations of participants' prior knowledge of a strategy across a diverse range of tasks, which may account for the mixed results obtained in the different studies. The earliest publication

*Table 7.7* Tests of Mediation Pathways for Goals and Strategies to Performance Models

| Model | K | N | $A_{IV}$ $\rightarrow$M | $SE_A IV$ $\rightarrow$M | $B_M$ $\rightarrow$DV | $SE_B M$ $\rightarrow$DV | Sobel's Z | Exact p (two-tailed) |
|---|---|---|---|---|---|---|---|---|
| **Goal Challenge → Strategy → Performance** | | | | | | | | |
| Self-Regulation Strategy | 2 | 515 | .456 | .247 | .265 | .102 | 1.50 | .132 |
| Task-Specific Strategy | 6 | 918 | .373 | .143 | .457 | .110 | 2.21 | .027* |
| Strategy Development Effort | 2 | 403 | .290 | .067 | .418 | .050 | 3.84 | .001* |
| Search & Information Processing Strategy[1] | 1 | – | – | – | – | – | – | – |
| **Goal Specificity → Strategy → Performance** | | | | | | | | |
| Task-Specific Strategy[1] | 1 | – | – | – | – | – | – | – |
| **Performance Avoidance GO → Strategy → Performance** | | | | | | | | |
| Self-Regulation Strategy | 13 | 7201 | −.145 | .079 | .228 | .032 | 1.78 | .075 |
| Search & Information Processing Strategy | 14 | 8785 | .072 | .038 | .104 | .036 | 1.58 | .113 |
| **Performance Approach GO → Strategy → Performance** | | | | | | | | |
| Self-Regulation Strategy | 20 | 9387 | .067 | .046 | .232 | .029 | 1.43 | .152 |
| Search & Information Processing Strategy | 25 | 12,395 | .191 | .032 | .090 | .028 | 2.83 | .005* |
| **Mastery Approach GO → Strategy → Performance** | | | | | | | | |
| Self-Regulation Strategy | 21 | 9553 | .338 | .048 | .230 | .028 | 5.35 | .001* |
| Search & Information Processing Strategy | 26 | 12,659 | .350 | .034 | .085 | .028 | 2.91 | .010* |

1. Only one study included both steps of the mediation model.

*Significant at $p < .05$.

identified as including the provision of prior knowledge of a strategy in a study of the relationship between goals and performance was conducted by Latham and Steele (1983), who studied the effects of specific, challenging goals versus "do your best" goals on a toy assembly task. In their study, all participants received the same strategy knowledge regarding three choices about the assembly process before commencing the task. The strategy knowledge was provided through either a participative or an assigned decision-making process, which had no effect on performance, either direct or in interaction with goals. The fact that Latham and Steele (1983) carefully matched the prior strategy knowledge in the two decision conditions may have accounted for the lack of effect.

Interestingly, two subsequent studies in which strategy knowledge for a course-scheduling task was obtained through either a participative or an assigned decision-making process, as in Latham and Steele (1983), have both reported significant but opposite effects for the process of obtaining knowledge. Earley and Kanfer (1985) found that strategy choice combined with goal choice produced higher performance than conditions that included an assigned strategy plus an assigned goal or an assigned strategy plus goal choice. However, because their study lacked the condition that combined strategy choice with an assigned goal, the effect of how strategy knowledge was obtained could not be tested. Kernan, Heimann, and Hanges (1991) conducted a study with the two conditions fully crossed using the course-scheduling task from Earley and Kanfer (1985) and found that it was the *assigned* strategy combined with goal choice that produced higher performance than any of the other conditions.

Two sets of studies by Earley and his colleagues (Earley & Perry, 1987; Earley et al., 1989) and two studies by Locke and his colleagues (Chesney & Locke, 1991; Durham et al., 1997) have found varying levels of support for the moderator model. Three subsequent studies across a range of different tasks have not been able to replicate those results (Northcraft et al., 1994; Whinnery & Fuchs, 1993; Vollmeyer et al., 1996, Study 2). Earley and Perry (1987) reported two studies in which strategies were provided through instructions to participants prior to their undertaking three tasks. The strategy instruction, which was the suggestion to use the mental image of a room when identifying uses of an object, was relevant for two of the tasks but not for the third task, which was to identify numbers above a minimum. In both studies, the task-specific strategy instructions and goals interacted as predicted. The task-specific strategy instructions produced greater performance on the relevant tasks than the unrelated task when participants were assigned a specific goal, but had no differential effect when the assigned goal was "do your best" (Earley & Perry, 1987, Tables 2 & 4).

In a follow-up study, Earley et al. (1989) found a significant interaction effect for prior strategy knowledge and goals on performance of a stock price prediction task. Participants predicted stock prices of fictitious companies based on three cues under one of two goal conditions (specific, challenging or "do your best") and one of three sets of strategy training. The three training conditions were no training, training in a set of possible strategies, and training in a systematic method of strategy development. The results showed that participants who were assigned specific, challenging goals significantly outperformed those assigned a "do your best" goal, but only in the two strategy training conditions (Earley et al., 1989, Figure 1, p. 596). Without training or prior knowledge of a task-specific strategy for the stock price prediction task, specific, challenging goals did not lead to higher performance than "do your best."

In the studies by Locke and his colleagues, both the task used and the operationalization of strategy has differed from the tasks and measures of strategy used in other studies that have tested the moderator model. Both studies used complex simulations and measures of strategy that captured the quality of strategies used by participants, rather than manipulate participants' strategic knowledge. Also, one of the studies, (Durham et al., 1997), studied teams and used the levels of team-set goals in tests of the moderator model. Chesney and Locke (1991) found a significant interaction effect for one of their two performance criteria on a business strategy simulation. Specific, challenging goals had a significantly greater effect on performance when participants used good rather than poor strategies on the simulation. The quality of strategies used and assigned goals also had direct effects on performance, with strategy quality being the stronger of the two effects. In a later study of teams working on a battle simulation game, Durham et al. (1997) found that the interaction between team-set goals and quality of strategy used, which they called *team tactics*, has a significant effect on performance in the simulation.

Three subsequent studies in which knowledge of specific strategies has been provided through training have not found support for the moderator argument. These include studies of negotiation (Northcraft et al., 1994), test taking (Whinnery & Fuchs, 1993), and a rule induction task (Vollmeyer et al., 1996, Study 2). In two of the studies (Northcraft et al., 1994; Whinnery & Fuchs, 1993), descriptions of the strategy training provided suggest that participants did not receive sufficient specific knowledge that they could apply directly to the performance of the criterion task. Northcraft et al. (1994) manipulated strategy knowledge through a one-hour lecture, without any practice problems, which was intended to provide participants with "a generalized conceptual understanding of how to develop and evaluate negotiations strategies. The lecture did not provide task-specific knowledge that would sensitize subjects" (1994, p. 263). Thus, it appears that the strategy knowledge provided in the training was not sufficiently specific for the negotiation task, which was performed the following day. In the Whinnery and Fuchs (1993) study, the strategy training was limited to the instructions about how to interpret a graph that included a goal and feedback against the goal for students' test performance, but no specific instructions on how to complete the arithmetic items in the test task. As with Northcraft et al. (1994), the Whinnery and Fuchs (1993) strategy training did not provide task-specific strategies that included specific actions for performance of the criterion task (Wood & Locke, 1990).

In Vollmeyer et al. (1996, Study 2), strategy instructions (yes/no) were crossed with an assigned specific goal (yes/no) for the performance of a rule induction task known as the Biology Lab (see Funke, 1991). Participants in the strategy instruction conditions received written instructions that described the VOTAT hypothesis-testing strategy and included an example of how to apply the VOTAT strategy to the Biology Lab rule induction task that was used to obtain the criterion performance measures. The interaction between goals and task-specific strategy predicted by the moderator model was not significant; however, both goals and strategy instruction had independent main effects on performance (Vollmeyer et al., 1996, Study 2). Subjects may have been subconsciously using some unmeasured prior knowledge as a result of the assigned goal (Locke, 2000) and using the VOTAT hypothesis-testing strategy to generate new knowledge that also aided them in learning rules for the Biology Lab task. However, without measures of prior and post-task relevant knowledge, this hypothesis remains speculative.

In summary, support for the moderator model has been mixed, but the majority of studies have found a significant interaction effect for goals and strategy on performance. The diversity of tasks and operationalizations of strategy in the studies reviewed, which could be a strength with a larger number of studies, limits the conclusions that can be made about the moderator model until further research is conducted. This point is taken up in the next section.

# Discussion

Research on the effects of goals on strategies and performance is essentially the study of how goals affect the application of existing knowledge and the development of new knowledge, or learning, and of processes that support learning, such as search and information processing and self-regulation. Based on the available evidence, challenging goals (which are always also specific) continue to have a wide range of beneficial effects for the use of strategies, leading to better performance across a range of different tasks. The mediating role of strategies in goal setting effects outlined by Locke et al. (1981) has been strongly supported and much more generally than might have been expected when the argument was first put forward. Tests of the moderator model have, on balance, provided positive support for the argument that specific, challenging goals combined with appropriate strategies produce stronger performance effects than either alone.

Over the last 20 years, studies of the effects of the goal properties for specific tasks, such as specificity and challenge, have been far fewer in number than studies of GO. Goal orientations are more general in content and application than task-specific intentions contained in goals, but they form part of the broader nomological network that, along with task specific goals, influence task performance. Similar to task goals, the effects of GOs on performance are mediated through a range of strategies, in particular, the SIP and self-regulation strategies that support learning. There are no studies of how GOs affect the use of pre-existing knowledge in the form of task-specific strategies.

Several specific conclusions and some areas for possible future research can be taken from our review of the evidence for the mediator and moderator models.

Strategic effort makes a difference to performance. Task-specific strategies and strategies directed at the learning and development of strategic knowledge are beneficial. This is a rather obvious and expected conclusion, but it highlights the importance of considering the impacts on strategies and learning processes when studying and recommending interventions such as goals, feedback, error management, and the like. Also, the current findings identify a range of different strategies that include application of existing knowledge and the development of new knowledge, or learning, and of processes that support learning, such as search and information processing and self-regulation. The results for the effects of strategy on performance (Table 7.1) and the support for mediation models with strategy as the mediator (Table 7.7) provide robust and general support for the notion that all performance requires some form of knowledge (Locke, 2000). It also demonstrates that the knowledge can vary widely in how it is relevant to the task being performed, but the more directly it is related to the execution of the immediate task, the stronger the impact on performance.

An assumption of the studies in our analyses is that the relationship between strategic effort and performance is linear. However, this may not necessarily be the case (see Chapter 13). For example, for some tasks, the relationship between knowledge and task performance may be nonlinear because of the synergistic effects of knowing multiple strategies. As persons learn more strategies, they are able to make better use of their knowledge in a wider range of task situations and to combine different strategies in order to adapt to more challenges.

Among the issues relating to goals and strategies requiring further research, the study of how challenging goals interact with different levels of strategic expertise has potential to make useful contributions. For example, further tests of the moderator model could look at the benefits of different types of strategies and challenging goals on different types of tasks. These could include studies in which strategy knowledge manipulations include training in search and information processing skills, such as hypothesis testing, and the testing of goal effects on both novel and more routine complex tasks. Field studies of the same question could look at the benefits of goal setting across different levels of job or role expertise in complex and dynamic work environments.

The work on goal orientations suggest that of the three GOs reviewed, it is the positive effects of a mastery approach GO on the use of strategies that have the most beneficial effects for performance, particularly the use of self-regulation processes and the exploration and information processing that leads to strategy development and learning. A performance approach GO had a small positive effect on the use of SIP strategies, and this in turn had a positive effect on performance. However, while an approach orientation is consistent with the idea of the experimentation and risks of failure that typically are part of SIP strategies, a performance GO is generally expected to undermine such activities. Aside from the small effect of an approach performance GO on the use of SIP strategies, performance GOs did not have significant effects on the use of strategies. The studies of performance avoidance GO found nonsignificant effects for both self-regulation and SIP strategies. There was no evidence that a performance avoidance GO had a negative effect on the use of search and information processing strategies. Limitations of the goal orientation research to date include that it is not specific enough about the tasks and circumstances under which performance GOs could have differential effects on the use of strategies, and it has not examined how goal orientations affect the use of existing strategic knowledge or how prior knowledge moderates their effects on performance.

One question we were not able to address with our data is, "what is the relationship between goal orientation and task-specific goals?" Seijts et al. (2004) provide one answer to this question with their finding that assigning specific, challenging goals, for either learning or performance outcomes, creates a strong situation in which the goal orientation disposition has no relationship with performance, while in the weaker situation created by a "do your best" goal, goal orientation is significantly related to performance. Further research questions that might be considered could include, for example, "how does goal orientation affect the content and challenge of self-set goals?" and "how does goal orientation affect the interpretation of feedback against assigned performance goals?"

In the 10 reported tests of the moderator model, including the two studies in Earley and Perry (1987) and excluding Latham and Steele (1983) who did not manipulate task knowledge, 7 found a significant interaction effect for goals and strategy on performance. These 7 studies included manipulations of task-specific strategy knowledge through task instructions, training, and participative or directive decision making and measures of quality of the actual strategies used. The tasks on which significant performance effects were found for the goals and strategy interaction included the simple listing of objects, scheduling tasks, stock predictions, and complex simulations. In the three studies that failed to find a significant interaction, strategy knowledge was manipulated through training, and the tasks included negotiations, test taking, and rule induction. As previously noted, in two of the nonsignificant studies (Northcraft et al., 1994; Whinnery & Fuchs, 1993), the descriptions of the strategy knowledge training suggested that the manipulations were not strong enough to provide the knowledge required for task-specific strategies and, therefore, do not provide adequate tests of the moderator model. Future research on the moderator model needs to take into account the specific knowledge requirements for the study task and ensure that operationalizations of strategies create or capture that knowledge.

## Conclusion

In summary, the overall pattern of results for tests of the mediating and moderator models show that specific, challenging goals remain strong and general predictors of performance when strategies are taken into account. They encourage people to use their strategic knowledge to good effect, and when that knowledge is not sufficient, to engage in the activities needed to develop the required knowledge to achieve their goal. Approach GOs encourage the use of strategies that support learning and the development of new strategic knowledge. Understanding of how an approach GO and specific, challenging task goals work together to affect performance and learning awaits further research to build on the initial study by Seijts et al. (2004).

The existing body of work provides a platform for practice and future research, but we believe studies of the combined effects of specific, challenging goals and GOs on strategies should be conducted in natural work settings where the novelty or magnitude of a task challenge means that past experience does not provide the task-specific strategies needed to achieve the required levels of performance. Examples of such challenges might include transformational changes to organizations cultures, major product and service innovations, and development of affirmative action strategies that lead to greater representation of minorities *and* high performance.

## References

References marked with an asterisk indicate studies included in the meta-analysis.

*Albaili, M. (1998). Goal orientations, cognitive strategies and academic achievement among United Arab Emirates college students. *Educational Psychology, 18* (2), 195–203.

*Audia, P. G., Locke, E. A., & Smith, K. G. (2000). The paradox of success: An archival and a laboratory study of strategic persistence following radical environmental change. *Academy of Management Journal, 43* (5), 837–853.

*Bell, B. S., & Kozlowski, S. W. (2008). Active learning: Effects of core training design elements on self-regulatory processes, learning, and adaptability. *Journal of Applied Psychology, 93* (2), 296–316.

*Bong, M. (2009). Age-related differences in achievement goal differentiation. *Journal of Educational Psychology, 101* (4), 879–896.

*Cervone, D., Jiwani, N., & Wood, R. (1991). Goal setting and the differential influence of self-regulatory processes on complex decision-making performance. *Journal of Personality and Social Psychology, 61* (2), 257–266.

Chesney, A., & Locke, E. A. (1991) Relationships among goal difficulty, business strategies, and performance on a complex management simulation task. *Academy of Management Journal, 34*, 400–424.

*Day, E. A., Radosevich, D. J., & Chasteen, C. S. (2003). Construct- and criterion-related validity of four commonly used goal orientation instruments. *Contemporary Educational Psychology, 28* (4), 434–464.

DeShon, R. P., & Alexander, R. A. (1996). Goal setting effects on implicit and explicit learning of complex tasks. *Organizational Behavior and Human Decision Processes, 65* (1), 18–36.

*Diefendorff, J. M., & Lord, R. G. (2003). The volitional and strategic effects of planning on task performance and goal commitment. *Human Performance, 16* (4), 365–387.

*Durham, C. C., Locke, E. A., Poon, J. M., & McLeod, P. P. (2000). Effects of group goals and time pressure on group efficacy, information-seeking strategy, and performance. *Human Performance, 13* (2), 115–138.

Durham, C. C., Knight, D., & Locke, E. A. (1997). Effects of leader role, team-set goal difficulty, efficacy, and tactics on team effectiveness. *Organizational Behavior and Human Decision Processes, 72,* 203–231.

Dweck, C. S. (1986). Motivational processes affecting learning. *American Psychologist, 41,* 1040–1048.

Dweck, C. S. (1999). *Self-theories: Their role in motivation, personality, and development.* New York: Psychology Press.

Dweck, C. S. (2006). *Mindset: The New Psychology of Success.* New York: Random House.

*Earley, P. C., Connolly, T., & Lee, C. (1989). Task strategy interventions in goal setting: The importance of search in strategy development. *Journal of Management, 15* (4), 589–602.

Earley, P. C., & Kanfer, R. (1985). The influence of component participation and role models on goal acceptance, goal satisfaction, and performance. *Organizational Behavior and Human Decision Processes, 36,* 378–390.

*Earley, P. C., Lee, C., & Hanson, L. A. (1990). Joint moderating effects of job experience and task component complexity: relations among goal setting, task strategies, and performance. *Journal of Organizational Behavior, 11* (3), 3–15.

*Earley, P. C., & Perry, B. C. (1987). Work plan availability and performance: An assessment of task strategy priming on subsequent task completion. *Organizational Behavior and Human Decision Processes, 39,* 279–302.

*Earley, P. C., Shalley, C. E., & Northcraft, G. B. (1992). I think I can, I think I can ... Processing time and strategy effects of goal acceptance/rejection decisions. *Organizational Behavior and Human Decision Processes, 53* (1), 1–13.

Elliot, A. J. (1994). *Approach and avoidance achievement goals: An intrinsic motivation analysis.* Unpublished doctoral dissertation, University of Wisconsin-Madison.

Elliott, E. S., & Dweck, C. S. (1988) Goals: An approach to motivation and achievement. *Journal of Personality and Social Psychology, 54,* 5–12.

*Elliot, A. J., McGregor, H. A., & Gable, S. (1999). Achievement goals, study strategies, and exam performance: A mediational analysis. *Journal of Educational Psychology, 91* (3), 549–563.

*Fenollar, P., Román, S., & Cuestas, P. J. (2007). University students' academic performance: an integrative conceptual framework and empirical analysis. *British Journal of Educational Psychology, 77* (4), 873–891.

Ford, J. K., Smith, E. M., Weissbein, D. A., Gully, S. M., & Salas, E. (1998). Relationships of goal orientation, metacognitive activity, and practice strategies with learning outcomes and transfer. *Journal of Applied Psychology, 83* (2), 218–233.

Funke, J. (1991). Solving complex problems: Human identification and control of complex systems. In R. J. Sternberg & P. A.Frensch (Eds.), *Complex problem solving: Principles and mechanisms* (pp. 185–222). Hillsdale, NJ: Lawrence Erlbaum.

*Geddes, D. (2009). How am I doing? Exploring on-line gradebook monitoring as a self-regulated learning practice that impacts academic achievement. *The Academy of Management Learning and Education, 8* (4), 494–510.

Goodman, J., Wood, R. E., & Chen, Z. (2011). Feedback specificity, information processing, and transfer of training. *Organizational Behavior and Human Decision Processes, 115,* 253–267.

*Greene, B., & Miller, R. (1996). Influences on achievement: Goals, perceived ability, and cognitive engagement. *Contemporary Educational Psychology, 21,* 181–192.

He, T. H. (2008). Reading for different goals: the interplay of EFL college students' multiple goals, reading strategy use and reading comprehension. *Journal of Research in Reading, 31* (2), 224–242.

*Ho, I. T., & Hau, K. T. (2008). Academic achievement in the Chinese context: The role of goals, strategies, and effort. *International Journal of Psychology, 43* (5), 892–897.

*Johnson, L., Graham, S., & Harris, K. R. (1997). The effects of goal setting and self-instruction on learning a reading comprehension strategy: A study of students with learning disabilities. *Journal of Learning Disabilities, 30* (1), 80–91.

*Kennett, D., Young, A., & Catanzaro, M. (2009). Variables contributing to academic success in an intermediate statistics course: the importance of learned resourcefulness. *Educational Psychology, 29* (7), 815–830.

*Kernan, M. C., Heimann, B., & Hanges, P. J. (1991). Effects of goal choice, strategy choice, and feedback source on goal acceptance, performance and subsequent goals. *Journal of Applied Social Psychology, 21* (9), 713–733.

*Klein, H. J., Whitener, E. M., & Ilgen, D. R. (1990). The role of goal specificity in the goal-setting process. *Motivation and Emotion, 14* (3), 179–193.

Knight, D., Durham, C. C., & Locke, E. A. (2001). The relationship of team goals, incentives, and efficacy to strategic risk, tactical implementation, and performance. *Academy of Management Journal, 44,* 326–338.

*Korsgaard, M. A., & Diddams, M. (1996). The effect of process feedback and task complexity on personal goals, information searching, and performance improvement. *Journal of Applied Social Psychology, 26* (21), 1889–1911.

Latham, G. P., & Budworth, M-H (2006). The effect of training in verbal self-guidance on the self-efficacy and performance of native North Americans in the selection interview. *Journal of Vocational Behavior, 68,* 516–523.

Latham, G. P., & Locke, E. A. (2007). New developments in and directions for goal-setting research. *European Psychologist, 12,* 290–300.

*Latham, G. P., & Steele, T. P. (1983). The motivational effects of participation versus goal setting on performance. *Academy of Management Journal, 26* (3), 406–417.

*Leondari, A., & Gonida, E. (2007). Predicting academic self-handicapping in different age groups: The role of personal achievement goals and social goals. *British Journal of Educational Psychology, 77* (3), 595–561.

*Liem, A. D., Lau, S., & Nie, Y. (2008). The role of self-efficacy, task value, and achievement goals in predicting learning strategies, task disengagement, peer relationship, and achievement outcome. *Contemporary Educational Psychology, 33,* 486–512.

Locke, E. A. (1968). Toward a theory of task motivation and incentives. *Organizational Behavior and Human Decision Processes, 3,* 157–189.

Locke, E. A. (2000). Motivation, cognition and action: An analysis of studies of task goals and knowledge. *Applied Psychology: An International Review, 49* (3), 409–429.

*Locke, E. A., Frederick, E., Lee, C., & Bobko, P. (1984). Effect of self-efficacy, goals, and task strategies on task performance. *Journal of Applied Psychology, 69*, 241–251.

Locke, E. A., & Kristof, A. (1996). Volitional choices in the goal achievement process. In P. Gollwitzer & J. Bargh (Eds.), *The psychology of action: Linking cognition and motivation to behaviour* (pp. 365–384). New York: Guilford Press.

Locke, E. A., & Latham, G. P. (1990). *A theory of goal setting and task performance*. Englewood Cliffs, NJ: Prentice-Hall.

Locke, E. A., & Latham, G. P. (2002). Building a practically useful theory of goal setting and task motivation: A 35-year odyssey. *American Psychologist, 57*, 705–717.

Locke, E. A., & Latham, G. P. (2006). New directions in goal-setting. *Current Directions in Psychological Science, 15,* 265–268.

Locke, E. A., Shaw, K. N., Saari, L. M., & Latham, G. P. (1981). Goal setting and task performance: 1969–1980. *Psychological Bulletin, 90*, 125–152.

*Locke, E. A., Smith, K. G., Erez, M., Chah, D. O., & Schaffer, A. (1994). The effects of intra-individual goal conflict on performance. *Journal of Management, 20* (1), 67–91.

*Matos, L., Lens, W., & Vansteenkiste, M. (2007). Achievement goals, learning strategies and language achievement among Peruvian high school students. *Psychologica Belgica, 47* (1/2), 51–70.

Mento, A. J., Steele, R. P., & Karren, F. J. (1987). A meta-analytic study of the effects of goal setting on task performance: 1966–1984. *Organizational Behavior and Human Decision Processes, 39*, 52–83.

*Mesch, D. J., Farh, J.-L., & Podsakoff, P. M. (1994). Effects of feedback sign on group goal setting, strategies, and performance. *Group Organization Management, 19* (3), 309–333.

*Midgley, C., Arunkumar, R., & Urdan, T. C. (1996). If I don't do well tomorrow, there's a reason: Predictors of adolescents'use of academic self-handicapping strategies. *Journal of Educational Psychology, 88* (3), 423–434.

*Midgley, C., & Urdan, T. (2001). Academic self-handicapping and performance goals: A further examination. *Contemporary Educational Psychology, 26,* 61–75.

*Miller, R. B., Greene, B. A., Montalvo, G. P., Ravindran, B., & Nichols, J. D. (1996). Engagement in academic work: The role of learning goals, future consequences, pleasing others, and perceived ability. *Contemporary Educational Psychology, 21* (4), 388–422.

Mone, M., & Shalley, C. (1995). Effects of task complexity and goal specificity on change in strategy and performance over time. *Human Performance, 8* (4), 243–262.

*Neuville, S., Frenay, M., & Bourgeois, E. (2007). Task value, self-efficacy and goal orientations: Impact on self-regulated learning, choice and performance among university students. *Psychologica Belgica, 47* (1–2), 95–117.

*Ng, C. C. (2008). Multiple-goal learners and their differential patterns of learning. *Educational Psychology, 28* (4), 439–456.

*Ng, C. C. (2009). Profiling learners' achievement goals when completing academic essays. *Educational Psychology, 29* (3), 279–295.

*Northcraft, G. B., Neale, M. A., & Earley, P. C. (1994). Joint effects of assigned goals and training on negotiator performance. *Human Performance, 7* (4), 257–272.

*Payne, S. C., Youngcourt, S. S., & Beaubien, J. M. (2007). A meta-analytic examination of the goal orientation nomological net. *Journal of Applied Psychology, 92*, 128–150.

*Phan, H. P. (2008). Unifying different theories of learning: theoretical framework and empirical evidence. *Educational Psychology, 28* (3), 325–340.

*Phan, H. P. (2009a). Exploring students' reflective thinking practice, deep processing strategies, effort, and achievement goal orientations. *Educational Psychology, 29* (3), 297–313.

*Phan, H. P. (2009b). Relations between goals, self-efficacy, critical thinking and deep processing strategies: A path analysis. *Educational Psychology, 29* (7), 777–799.

*Phan, H. P. (2010). Students' academic performance and various cognitive processes of learning: An integrative framework and empirical analysis. *Educational Psychology, 30* (3), 297–322.

*Pintrich, P. R. (2000). Multiple goals, multiple pathways: The role of goal orientation in learning and achievement. *Journal of Educational Psychology, 92* (3), 544–555.

*Racicot, B. M., Day, D. V., & Lord, R. G. (1991). Type A behavior pattern and goal setting under different conditions of choice. *Motivation and Emotion, 15* (1), 67–79.

*Saavedra, R., Earley, P. C., & van Dyne, L. (1993). Complex interdependence in task-performing Groups. *Journal of Applied Psychology, 78* (1), 61–72.

*Schutz, P. A. (1997). Educational goals, strategies use and the academic performance of high school students. *The High School Journal, 80* (3), 193–201.

*Schutz, P. A., & Lanehart, S. L. (1994). Long-term educational goals, subgoals, learning strategies use and the academic performance of college students. *Learning Individual Differences, 6* (4), 399–412.

Seijts, G. H., & Latham, G. P. (2001). The effect of learning, outcome, and proximal goals on a moderately complex task. *Journal of Organizational Behavior, 22,* 291–307.

Seijts, G. H., Latham, G. P., Tasa, K., & Latham, B. W. (2004). Goal setting and goal orientation: An integration of two different yet related literatures. *Academy of Management Journal, 47,* 227–239.

*Senko, C., & Miles, K. M. (2008). Pursuing their own learning agenda: How mastery-oriented students jeopardize their class performance. *Contemporary Educational Psychology, 33,* 561–583.

*Shih, S. S. (2005). Taiwanese sixth graders' achievement goals and their motivation, strategy use and grades: An examination of the multiple goal perspective. *The Elementary School Journal, 106* (1), 39–58.

*Simons, J., Dewitte, S., & Lens, W. (2004). The role of different types of instrumentality in motivation, study strategies, and performance: know why you learn, so you'll know what you learn! *British Journal of Educational Psychology, 74* (3), 343–360.

Sitzmann, T., & Ely, K. (2011). A meta-analysis of self-regulated learning in work related training and educational attainment: What we know and where we need to go. *Psychological Bulletin, 137* (3), 421–442.

*Stipek, D., & Gralinski, J. H. (1996). Children's beliefs about intelligence and school performance. *Journal of Educational Psychology, 88* (3), 397–407.

Taylor, S., Locke, E. A., Lee, C., & Gist, M. E. (1984). Type A behavior and faculty productivity: What are the mechanisms? *Organizational Behavior & Human Performance, 34,* 402–418.

*Vollmeyer, R., Burns, B. D., & Holyoak, K. J. (1996). The impact of goal specificity on strategy use and the acquisition of problem structure. *Cognitive Science, 20* (1), 75–100.

*Whinnery, K. W., & Fuchs, L. S. (1993) Effects of goal and test-taking strategies on the computation performance of students with learning disabilities. *Learning Disabilities Research & Practice, 8* (4), 204–214.

*Winters, D., & Latham, G. P. (1996). The effect of learning versus outcome goals on a simple versus a complex task. *Group Organization Management, 21* (2), 236–250.

*Wolters, C. (2004). Advancing achievement goal theory: Using goal structures and goal orientations to predict students' motivation, cognition, and achievement. *Journal of Educational Psychology, 96* (2), 236–250.

*Wolters, C. A., Yu, S. L., & Pintrich, P. R. (1996). The relation between goal orientation and students' motivational self-regulated learning. *Learning and Individual Differences, 8* (3), 211–239.

Wood, R. E., & Locke, E. (1990). Goal setting and strategy effects on complex tasks. In B. Staw, & L. Cummings (Eds.), *Research in organizational behavior* (Vol. 12, pp. 73–109). Greenwich, CT: JAI Press.

*Wright, P. M. (1990). Monetary incentives and task experience as determinants of spontaneous goal setting, strategy development, and performance. *Human Performance, 3* (4), 237–258.

Yanar, B., Budworth, M-H., & Latham, G. P. (2009). The effect of verbal self-guidance training for overcoming employment barriers: A study of Turkish women. *Applied Psychology: An International Review, 58* (4), 509–728.

*Yoon, C. H. (2009) Self-regulated learning and instructional factors in the scientific inquiry of scientifically gifted Korean middle school students. *Gifted Child Quarterly, 53* (3), 203–216.

# Part III

# Special Goal Topics

# 8    Goals and Affect

*Stefanie A. Plemmons and Howard M. Weiss*
School of Psychology, Georgia Institute of Technology

## Goals and Affect

It is virtually impossible to discuss goal processes without reference to affect, just as it is impossible to discuss affect processes without reference to goals. All appraisal theories of emotion instigation start with the evaluation of events or circumstances as being either goal relevant (emotion ensues) or goal irrelevant (no emotional reaction) (e.g., Scherer, 1999; Smith & Kirby, 2001). Similarly, theories of the ways in which goals guide behavior frequently have affective reactions to goal progress and goal attainment as mediating motivational mechanisms (see Chapter 4). It is not surprising, therefore, that the literature on goals and affect is voluminous, too large for one book chapter to usefully summarize. Consequently, we have taken the liberty of narrowing the review in ways we think are most appropriate for likely readers of this volume.

First, we limit our discussion to the literature on affect and task goals. In doing so, we ignore the broader issues of life goals, career goals, life satisfaction, etc., in favor of a narrower focus on relatively immediate objectives and experiences. Obviously, this is not a statement of the relative importance of the topics, but rather an admission of an inability to cover all such topics in one chapter.

Second, we focus attention on true affective reactions, moods and emotions, and their relations to goals. In doing so, we intentionally removed from the discussion broader attitudinal constructs such as job satisfaction or organizational commitment, unless relevant to the narrower issues of affective experiences.

Discussions of the conceptual relationship between affective states and work attitudes have a long history (Weiss, 2002b). Clearly, attitudes that people have *about their jobs,* tasks, etc., are influenced by the emotional experiences they have *on their jobs* (Weiss, Nicholas, & Daus, 1999). Still, affective constructs such as emotions and moods refer to experiential states bounded in time and accompanied by subjective awareness of certain "feelings." Attitudes are evaluative judgments that, while changeable, are not properly states and have none of the subjective experiential content that accompanies true affect. Thus, we have taken the task of examining affect and goals seriously, leaving attitudes for another time.

We begin by summarizing the coverage of this topic in Locke and Latham (1990). The initial chapter focused most of its attention on the relationship between goal achievement/failure and subsequent experiences of satisfaction. This discussion was framed by Locke's (1969, 1970, 1976) enormously influential theory of job satisfaction. Indeed, approximately half of the original chapter is devoted to discussing the nature of values, satisfaction, and emotions and to documenting the relationships between value attainment, goal achievement, and performance on the one hand and satisfaction on the other. As was summarized by Locke and Latham (1990), those relationships are strong and consistent. In the ensuing years, interest has been stimulated, we believe, by the broad interest of self-regulatory processes and the role that goals and affect play in such processes. Consequently, our chapter covers research following from such perspectives as self-regulation, goal orientation, goal velocity, etc. As such, we present this chapter as a complement to the original one.

Even within these boundaries, the remaining literature is large and rather fragmented. An attempt has been made to organize that literature in terms of major topics and themes. We begin by addressing how affect researchers think about goals, focusing on how goals elicit affective states. We then spend more time addressing how goal researchers think about affect, focusing on how affect guides goal-related behaviors, since this is more relevant to the overall set of chapters at hand. After setting the stage, we move into the major themes of affect and goal choice, affect and goal pursuit, and affect and goal outcomes. Lastly, we address affect and goal orientation, which is a topic that has begun to work its way into the Industrial-Organizational literature and has important implications for the workplace.

## Goals and Emotion Elicitation

Almost all cognitive theories of emotion elicitation argue that emotions are a consequence of cognitive appraisal processes. As Scherer (1999) has stated: "A central tenet of appraisal theory is the claim that emotions are elicited and differentiated on the basis of a person's subjective evaluation or appraisal of the personal significance of a situation, object, or event on a number of dimensions or criteria" (p. 637). Of course, cognitive does not necessarily mean conscious, and the approaches vary in terms of how much emphasis is given to conscious versus automatic processes. Nonetheless, cognitive theories of emotion elicitation view emotion generation as the result of an appraisal of various aspects of the situation. An excellent summary is provided by Smith and Kirby (2001).

One heuristic that is popular among cognitive appraisal theorists has been to partition the appraisal process into primary and secondary appraisals (Weiss, 2002a). Primary appraisal focuses on whether the event is concerned with one's well-being and whether that relevance is positive or negative. It is relevant to the direction and intensity of the emotional experience. Secondary appraisal focuses on an additional set of dimensions (varying across theorists), such as coping potential or attribution of responsibility, seen as responsible for the particular discrete emotion that is experienced (anger, guilt, etc.).

Primary appraisal is where goals come in as goal achievement, whether relevant to task performance or broader life objectives, as part of the concept of well-being appraisal. Secondary appraisal is where the distinct emotions arise. It is interesting to note that since most appraisal theorists are interested in the nature of specific discrete emotions, and since discrete emotions arise from the secondary appraisal dimensions, they have seen little reason to look at the nature of goal processes in the generation of emotions. They just take it for granted that reaching one's goals is a good thing, not reaching one's goals a bad thing, and that emotion intensity is somehow related to goal importance. For them, the real interest is in why we feel angry or ashamed or proud, and this is more about secondary appraisal than primary appraisal.

## Affect in the Goal Process

Locke and Latham (1990) reviewed the literature between goal achievement/failure and ensuing satisfaction and quite convincingly showed the strength and consistency of that effect. It is perhaps a consequence of that strong and consistent effect that attention has shifted away from the influence of goals on emotions. Instead, more attention has been given to the role that affective reactions play in the processes involved in guiding goal-directed behavior. We now turn to a discussion of that literature.

Today, much of the thinking about the role of affect in goal processes is done within the framework of control theories of self-regulation. (See Chapter 11 for a review of goals and self-regulation. For a good overview of self-regulation in a work context, see Lord, Diefendorff, Schmidt, & Hall, 2010. For a good discussion of the specific role of affect in this framework, see Carver & Scheier, 2009.) We recognize the differences of opinion that exist in the field with regard to the control theory perspective (see Chapter 1). We also recognize that the goal setting perspective discusses the relationship between goals and affect. That said, with regard to affect, goal setting theory largely focuses on the implications of either completing or failing to complete a goal on an individual's level of affect, whereas control theory largely focuses on the role of affect in regulating ongoing goal-directed behavior. We present this perspective not as an endorsement, but rather because it has served as the most frequent and useful framework for recent work on affect and goals. In brief, this position sees goal-directed behavior as being directed by a feedback system with four subcomponents: (1) goals, or behavior standards, which exist at varying levels of abstraction and often exist in a nested structure; (2) input, which represents information about status with respect to the goal; (3) an internal comparator, which judges discrepancies between input and goals/standards; and (4) an output function that takes the information from the comparator and acts to modify discrepancies.

What is the role of affect in the control theory framework? Generally, in this framework, affect is seen as information in the system that keeps the system moving in the right direction. For Carver and Scheier (2009), affect is the phenomenological experience that accompanies the velocity of movement toward one's goal. It is the "feeling" that accompanies the feedback process and, as such, serves as a cue regarding goal progress. For Carver and Scheier, affect processes run in parallel to feedback processes "checking on how well the first process is doing." Yet it is unclear whether this subjective feeling has an effect over and above the feedback system that generated it. Lord and colleagues (2010) argued that effective regulation of behavior requires the integration of cognition and affect, with affect acting as the balancing force among multiple goals. This still fails to answer the question of the independent effect of feedback-prompted emotion in a single-goal paradigm. We leave this interesting question to future researchers, however, and return to the specifics of Carver and Scheier as they relate to the remainder of our chapter.

Positive and negative affect can arise with regard to both discrepancy-reducing motivation (needing to move toward a goal) and discrepancy-enhancing systems (needing to move away from an outcome to be avoided). Specifically, negative affect accompanies slow movement toward a positive goal and slow movement away from an avoidance goal. Positive affect accompanies fast movement toward a positive goal and away from an avoidance goal. However, they also argued that the discrete emotional experiences are different in such situations. Quickly approaching a positive goal leads to feelings of elation and eagerness, whereas slow movement toward a positive goal results in frustration and anger. High velocity away from an avoidance goal results in relief, whereas slow movement away from such a goal results in fear and anxiety.

In any case, the idea that affect serves as a cue within the general self-regulatory framework leads to general questions about the speed of goal progress (velocity) and affect, affect and goal switching, types of affect in response to types of comparisons, etc. In the next sections, we discuss the role of affect in the general processes of goal-directed behavior often, but not exclusively, guided by the processes just outlined.

In addition to the affect experienced as a result of velocity assessments, affect has implications for subsequent goal-directed behavior. Carver and Scheier (2009) argued that affect caused by velocity feedback signals an individual to adjust his or her rate of progress, deemed a "cruise control" model. When negative affect results from lower-than-expected progress, an individual is compelled to either allocate more resources to the goal and expend greater effort, or abandon the goal altogether. The effects of positive affect are the opposite. Positive affect signals that an individual is ahead of expectations, thereby leading him or her to temporarily coast, allowing resources to be reallocated toward different goals with lower velocities. Affect, in essence, acts as one mechanism for prioritizing effort among multiple goals.

It should be noted that the control-process view is not uniformly accepted. Gollwitzer and Rohloff (1999) contest the model put forth by Carver and Scheier (1990) and argued that positive and negative affect do not have uniform functions in directing goal effort. Gollwitzer and Rohloff argued that positive goal discrepancies should not lead to a reduction in effort, as suggested, but should instead lead to an increase in effort. The only time positive discrepancies should lead to a reduction in effort is when other important goals also need to be addressed. According to these authors, it is more functional for an individual to finish the current goal, as opposed to coasting, so that he or she may completely move onto the next goal. The authors also argued that negative affect is not necessary to spur effort when goal progress is slower than expected; a slowdown is contrary to goal commitment in and of itself, and should therefore lead to an increase in effort regardless of affect. Indeed, while it may be more functional for an individual to finish his or her goal, it is well established that people do not always behave in a logical manner. Additionally, while negative affect may not be necessary to spur goal effort, it may be the driving force behind the behavior. It thus seems that the criticisms put forth by Gollwitzer and Rohloff are minor at best.

As previously stated, the control-process view has important implications for managing multiple simultaneous goals. In addition to acknowledging that individuals work toward multiple goals at the same time, it must also be acknowledged that goals may exist in hierarchical form (Kruglanski, Shah, Fishbach, Friedman, Chun, & Sleeth-Keppler, 2002). Within the hierarchy, primary goals have related subgoals (also known as proximal goals) that aid in their attainment; for example, completing an outline (subgoal) moves one closer to completing a paper (primary goal). Thus, the completion of one goal can also act as forward progress for a larger goal. This has interesting implications for affect; the positive affect resulting from completing a subgoal may in turn hinder primary goal progress if the positive affect leads to coasting. If an individual focuses on the next subgoal, however, it is expected that effort towards the primary goal would be maintained.

We have yet to distinguish between moods and emotions in the goal process. Arguments have been made that mood may exert a longer-lasting effect on motivation, whereas emotions may exert a more immediate and stronger effect on goal behavior (Forgas & Laham, 2005). We agree that such distinctions are important, in line with general thinking on the differences between moods and emotions (see Weiss & Cropanzano, 1996), and translate well into research regarding the role of affect as information in the pursuit of goals. Emotions and moods are both affective states; however, moods may be distinguished from emotions in that they generally are less intense, are of a longer duration, and lack specific targets (Weiss & Cropanzano, 1996). Emotions should certainly play a larger informational role than diffuse mood states. We distinguish between the effects of moods and emotions in the subsequent sections wherever we are able to.

It seems appropriate to start at the beginning and work through the steps associated with goals from start to finish. The sequential structure begins with setting a goal, pursuing goal, and finally attaining or not attaining the goal. We digress from this structure, however, and begin with an update on the research pertaining to goal outcomes, the focus of the original chapter on goals and affect.

## Affect and Goal Outcomes

One of the most common relationships studied, if not the most common, is the relationship between affect and goal attainment. It is the oldest topic within the realm of goals and affect and, as we noted earlier, was well reviewed in the original chapter on goals and affect (Locke & Latham, 1990). Although many of the studies cited in that chapter examined satisfaction, an attitude, instead of a true affective state, the body of research leads to a clear conclusion that goal attainment leads to satisfaction and positive affect; failing to attain a goal leads to dissatisfaction and negative affect. Indeed, the original chapter found that these relationships were so robust that further demonstrations have been considered unnecessary in the ensuing years. Since then, the focus has largely shifted to affect and goal pursuit. Additional research has been conducted, however, on specific emotions elicited from goal completion and failure, including the achievement of subgoals; we will focus our attention on these studies.

Attaining one's goal leads to positive affect. This is not a shocking assertion, but it is so commonly found that it must be acknowledged. A sampling of studies shows that goal attainment leads to positive affect (Gollwitzer & Rohloff, 1999; Henkel & Hinsz, 2004) and reduced negative affect (Henkel & Hinsz, 2004) as measured by the Positive and Negative Affect Schedule (PANAS), as well as increased affective well-being as measured by mood adjectives (Harris, Daniels, & Briner, 2003). In addition, research by Bagozzi, Baumgartner, and Pieters (1998) suggests that the size of the achievement impacts the intensity of the emotion; larger achievements led to greater intensity of positive affect (e.g., feelings of excitement and delight). In short, goal completion is beneficial to affect and is moderated by the magnitude of the achievement.

In contrast, failing to attain one's goal, as expected, leads to negative affect. It has been argued, and supported, that goal failure leads one to experience negative affect and rumination (Martin, Tesser, & McIntosh, 1993; Moberly & Watkins, 2010). The thwarting of one's goals has been linked to both an increase in negative affect and a decrease in positive affect as measured by the PANAS (Henkel & Hinsz, 2004). Thus, goal attainment has positive effects on affect, whereas goal failure has negative effects on affect.

While overall goal attainment is an important topic, previously we noted that large goals tend to have subgoals. These subgoals have been referred to in the literature as goal activities; they are whole activities in and of themselves, yet the completion of each activity aids an individual in moving closer to a major goal. Logically, completion of a subgoal is itself a goal attainment, and subgoals are a means of major goal attainment. Fishbach, Shah, and Kruglanski (2004) have noted that affect can be associated with means; subgoals should thus be associated with affect.

Research findings support such an assertion. Goal-furthering activities have been shown to be associated with positive moods, decreased stress, and lowered negative affect, as measured by the Multidimensional Affect Scale (Hoppmann & Klumb, 2006). In addition, positive affect was found to mediate the relationship between goal-furthering activities and stress; goal-furthering activities increased positive affect, which in turn decreased cortisol levels. Conversely, goal-hindering activities and lack of progress toward one's goal leads to endorsement of negative affect words, such as discouraged, depressed, and agitated (Houser-Marko & Sheldon, 2011), as well as stress (Hoppmann & Klumb, 2006; Lavallee & Campbell, 1995). As with major goals, subgoal attainment has positive consequences for emotional states and subgoal failure has negative consequences.

As we examined research regarding affect and goal outcomes, it caught our attention that there is a lack of empirical research investigating discrete emotions. Researchers have largely focused on aggregates of positive and/or negative affective words. We believe that this oversight provides an area ripe for research, as discrete emotions provide particularly useful information. As we have argued above, emotions provide information. It is certainly possible that discrete emotions provide more information than generalized feeling states. Discrete emotions are associated with different action implications, thus resulting in potentially different outcomes in the goal process. Whether one feels angry or anxious or depressed has the potential to provide more useful information regarding subsequent behavior than simply knowing one has negative affect. There is a distinct difference between pride and relief, and it is not difficult to imagine that pride in completing one's goal results in remarkably different behavior e.g., setting higher goals in the future) than relief at completing one's goal (which one could imagine would not result in the setting of higher goals).

## Affect and Goal Choice

Affect is not only relevant to goal outcomes, but it also plays a role in the initial choice of performance goals. Multiple theories shed light on the underlying affective processes that may influence goal setting. For example, Forgas (1995) suggested that affect primes judgments, and that individuals make judgments that are consistent with their current mood states. Individuals experiencing positive affect are likely to set higher goals than those experiencing negative affect, as they are more likely to envision a successful outcome. Additionally, George and Brief (1996) posited that affect may influence distal motivation through goal choice; positive mood leads to positive expectation, thereby leading to the belief that one can accomplish more difficult tasks. A review by Forgas and George shows a remarkable amount of support for these assertions; affect has been demonstrated to influence information processing, which in turn influences judgments, such as goal choice (Forgas & George, 2001).

Research generally supports assertions that affect influences initial goal choice. Davis, Kirby, and Curtis (2007) found a significant positive relationship between mood and self-set goal; positive moods were associated with higher goals, whereas negative moods were associated with lower goals. Importantly, the impact of mood on goal level was unique from the effect of past performance on the goal level chosen. It should be noted, however, that a second study where a neutral mood group was added failed to find effects of mood on goal choice (Davis et al., 2007). A prior study by Saavedra and Earley (1991) also supports the idea that affect influences goal choice; the authors found that participants with induced positive affect were more likely to maintain their goal level when given the choice on a subsequent task, whereas participants with induced negative affect were more likely to decrease their goal level. The authors argued that their results support views put forth by Isen (1984): negative affect promotes mood repair. In this study, mood was believed to be repaired by choosing a lowered goal, as a lower goal presumably increases the likelihood of success and subsequent positive mood.

### Affect and Goal Pursuit

After a goal is set, affect continues to exert an influence. As we have said, it is argued that one of the many roles that affect takes within the goal process is to function as a signal of goal progress along with feedback. Affect plays two major roles during the time between adopting a goal and concluding it: (1) it serves to focus attention toward the goal itself, thus affecting aspects such as goal prioritization and maintenance, and (2) it helps determine the expectancy of goal attainment, affecting goal revision and persistence as one works toward a goal.

*Goal Prioritization and Shifting.* Emotions provide insight into goal attainment processes, signaling the need to reprioritize goals or adjust one's rate of progress. As early as 1967 (Simon, 1967), researchers had proposed that negative affect interrupts one's current goal and signals a need to reprioritize to an alternate goal. More recently, it has been proposed that negative affect leads to pessimism in regard to goal attainment, whereas positive affect leads to optimism (Carver, Lawrence, & Scheier, 1996). In a slightly different vein, Custers (2009) suggested that positive affect signals that the primed goal is desirable and is a goal worth pursuing. This optimism and desirable evaluation in turn lead to approaching the goal; conversely, negative emotions lead to avoiding the goal and redirecting motivational forces to alternate goals. Positive emotions result in approach outcomes, whereas negative emotions result in avoid outcomes (although these avoid outcomes ultimately result in approaching a different goal). Stated in a different way, positive emotions are presumed to prioritize effort toward a goal, whereas negative emotions are presumed to shift effort away from a goal to alternate goals.

It is not just that negative emotions are detrimental and positive emotions are beneficial. Specific emotions tend to provide different types of information that lead to different action tendencies. Roseman, Wiest, and Swartz (1994), in a study examining negative emotions, found that discrete emotions were associated with distinct goal-related behaviors. Sadness, dislike, and fear signaled a need for avoidance actions; individuals ceased goal pursuit, distanced one's self, and escaped to a safe place, respectively. Frustration, regret, and guilt, on the other hand, signaled approach actions. Individuals viewed such emotions as a sign that more effort should be expended and behaviors should be changed. In essence, emotions that trigger avoidance reactions orient an individual away from the goal (presumably toward another goal), whereas emotions that trigger approach reactions focus attention toward continuing the current goal. Taken as a whole, negative emotions have both negative and positive effects on goal effort. There is a subtlety to the signals that needs to be taken into account. Certain negative emotions lead to prioritizing effort toward the goal, whereas other negative emotions lead to shifting effort and attention away from the goal. Unfortunately, the nuances of negative emotion proposed by Roseman and colleagues have neither been adequately acknowledged nor tested.

It appears that distance from one's goal based on feedback may determine the effect that positive emotions have on goal reprioritization. Importantly, positive emotions signal different behaviors based on how far one is from accomplishing one's goal. Louro, Pieters, and Zeelenberg (2007) found support for their assertion that emotions signal the effectiveness of goal-relevant behavior and provide individuals with an estimate of goal performance, influencing subsequent goal-related behavior. Positive emotions led individuals to determine they were performing well, leading to greater effort exertion when far from the goal, but less effort exertion when close to goal attainment. Participants who were close to goal attainment, and were feeling good about it, were thus able to reallocate goal-related resources to other tasks. Similarly, Orehek, Bessarabova, Chen, and Kruglanski (2011) found that positive affect acted as goal feedback and resulted in an increase in goal activation, but only when competing goals were not present. When competing goals existed, positive affect led to a decrease in goal activation. These studies support Carver and Scheier's (2009) suggestion that affect can signal one to adjust rate of progress toward a goal: positive emotion signals that progress is being made and efforts can be reallocated to a goal further behind, whereas negative emotion signals that more effort needs to be directed to the current goal or that it needs to be abandoned entirely in extreme cases.

Interestingly, negative emotion, along with goal-performance discrepancy and rate of progress, signals a need for increased effort when viewed as a signal of goal progress, yet the same emotion signals a need to change goals when viewed as a signal of goal reprioritization. It appears that the lens through which the individual interprets the emotion is important in determining goal-related outcomes.

*Goal Revision.* As an individual progresses toward a goal, he or she experiences goal-related feedback (for a more thorough review on feedback, see Chapter 5). This feedback often results in affect, which in turn results in revising one's goal upward or downward. Similar to results found for goal choice, positive affect leads to higher goals, or revising upward; negative affect leads to lowering goals, or revising downward.

Drawing upon the distinction between behavioral approach and behavioral inhibition, Ilies and Judge (2005) argued that positive feedback leads to positive affect, which is associated with approach activation; approach activation results in an individual setting a significantly higher goal. They also argued that negative feedback would lead to negative affect, in turn resulting in an individual lowering his or her goal. The authors found support for their assertion of positive affect acting as a mediator, but failed to find support for the role of negative affect in revising goals downward. In a separate study, Richard and Diefendorff (2011) followed students for two weeks prior to a course exam. Daily measures of mood and expected exam grade were collected. Results support the assertion that momentary mood related to goal revision. A significant positive relationship was found between positive affect and goal revision. A significant negative relation between negative affect and goal revision was also found. Not only were significant relationships found, but mood accounted for 22% of within-person variance above and beyond the level of the previous goal, course-related effort, and how many days the student was from taking the exam.

It thus appears that individuals not only set goals in line with their current affective state, but they revise goals in a similar manner. Affect influences one's expectations of goal attainment. Positive affect increases one's expectations for goal performance, resulting in the setting of higher goals. Negative affect has the opposite effect; it leads to a lowering of goals. An important question arises: How does affect differ from self-efficacy in the revision process?

Only two studies to our knowledge have examined the independent roles of affect and self-efficacy in the goal process; both studies examined affect as a mediator in the feedback–self-efficacy relationship. Seo and Ilies (2009) found that positive and negative affect influence self-efficacy, which in turn influences goal level. In addition, Ilies, Judge, and Wagner (2010) found that the effect of feedback on self-efficacy was largely mediated by emotional states associated with the feedback. This is an area of few studies where much remains to be done.

*Goal Persistence.* Lastly, affect also plays a role in commitment to the goal, but in a unique way (for an examination of goal commitment, see Chapter 6). Individuals create and modify emotions in the service of goal persistence. Carver and Scheier (2009) argued that individuals may modify their emotions to persist at a goal. Specifically, individuals may shut down positive emotions they are experiencing in order to aid in goal persistence. By preventing or ignoring positive affect, an individual creates a setting conducive for continuing effort toward the goal. Alternately, an individual may artificially create a feeling of anger or frustration to fuel effort toward a goal.

Recently, researchers have also begun to examine how anticipatory emotions affect goal attainment. Anticipatory emotions occur when individuals look forward to the completion of a goal and develop perceptions and emotions regarding its attainment (Harvey & Victoravich, 2009). In essence, the prospect of goal attainment or failure leads one to experience emotions in anticipation of the imagined outcome (Bagozzi et al., 1998). It has been found that positive anticipatory emotions increase goal commitment to a failing project, as individuals believe that goal attainment is likely (Harvey & Victoravich, 2009). It is unclear whether this is an adaptive function; however, it suggests that anticipatory emotions can be as important to goal attainment as goal attainment is to the experience of emotion.

## Affect and Goal Orientation

An aspect of the goals–affect relationship that has garnered a large quantity of research concerns the relationship between goal orientation and affect. While goal orientation originated, and continues to be largely studied, in educational settings, it has made its way into the I-O literature and informs workplace research; it is thus worth devoting some time and space to this topic. The majority of the studies summarized occurred within a classroom learning environment, although a few are of a more traditional work-related context and involve specific tasks. While the goal orientation literature is vast, we are interested in how orientation relates to affect, which has not been a major part of goal orientation research. However, certain authors have devoted time to the study of goal orientation and affect; in this section, we review their theories and findings. We begin with an overview of goal orientation before focusing on one theoretical model, the Asymmetrical Bidirectional Model (ABM; Linnenbrink & Pintrich, 2002), which makes explicit predictions of goal orientation and affective states. We then conclude by summarizing the research involving goal orientation and affect.

Goal orientation, defined as "two types of superordinate goals people can hold during task performance" (Steele-Johnson, Beauregard, Hoover, & Schmidt, 2000, p. 724), includes both between-person and within-person differences. Goal orientation research began in the 1970s, revolving around two key frameworks: Dweck (1975), who differentiated between learning and performance goals; and Nicholls (1975), who differentiated between task-involvement and ego-involvement goals. Learning goals, or task-involvement goals, are concerned with developing competence and learning for the purpose of increasing knowledge. In these goals, individuals compare themselves to an internal standard and view ability as an attribute that can be changed with effort. Performance goals, or ego-involvement goals, on the other hand, are concerned with demonstrating competence and result in individuals comparing themselves to others. It is believed that these individuals view ability as a fixed entity.

Goal orientations are not only divided into mastery and performance, but have also been further delineated into approach and avoidance goals. It is commonly accepted that performance goal orientations can be distinguished between performance-approach and performance-avoidance goals. Elliot (1994) pointed out the distinction, defining performance-approach as focusing on performing well and performance-avoidance as focusing on not performing poorly. VandeWalle (1996) arrived at similar conclusions, labeling the dimensions as "prove" and "avoid" goals. Recently, Linnenbrink and Pintrich (2002) argued for the partitioning of mastery goals into approach and avoidance, as well, resulting in a 2 × 2 model of mastery–performance and approach–avoidance.

The ABM (Linnenbrink & Pintrich, 2002) offers a comprehensive theory concerning goal orientation, taking into consideration both the mastery–performance distinction and the approach–avoidance distinction. We focus on this model as it makes explicit reference to and prediction of affective states. The model hypothesizes that mood influences goal orientation and that goal orientation in turn influences discrete emotions. Specifically, it is predicted that positive mood leads to a mastery goal structure within the perceived environment; it is also predicted that, within personal goal adoption, positive mood leads to approach goals, whereas negative mood leads to avoid goals. Predictions regarding discrete emotions can be found in Table 8.1.

*Table 8.1* Affective Predictions of the Asymmetrical Bidirectional Model

|  | *Mastery* | *Performance* |
|---|---|---|
| *Approach* | • Increased positive emotions<br>• Decreased negative emotions | • Unrelated to positive emotions<br>• Increased negative emotions |
| *Avoid* | • Decreased positive emotions<br>• Increased negative emotions | • Decreased positive emotions<br>• Increased negative emotions |

In general, research has provided mixed support for the assertions put forth by the ABM; however, this is not to be taken as an indicator of the usefulness of the model. Most studies were not conducted to test the ABM, and they are being forced upon the structure for the purposes of summarizing the literature. Admittedly, the focus within the literature has largely revolved around the role that goal orientation plays in influencing affect, not the influence of affect on goal orientation.

Only one study to our knowledge has looked at how affect informs goal orientation. Hopefulness and helplessness were examined as predictors of mastery and performance goals (Daniels, Stupinsky, Pekrun, Haynes, Perry, & Newall, 2009). Hopefulness was found to positively predict the adoption of both mastery and performance goals. Helplessness was found to negatively predict mastery goals. In short, positive affect led to goal adoption, while negative affect undermined the adoption of mastery goals. Unfortunately, no other studies were identified that have examined this influence of affect on orientation. It appears that this is an area where further research would be useful, as it has potential implications for goals in training programs and continuing education.

The majority of research relevant to the ABM focuses on the influence of goal orientation on affective states. Before examining the research, it should be noted that the mastery goal orientation is generally conceptualized in an approach manner. Recently, studies have started to differentiate between mastery-approach and mastery-avoidance goal orientations; however, studies examining mastery-avoidance are still relatively rare, and thus conclusions drawn are tenuous and in need of further empirical support.

Mastery-approach goals were hypothesized by the ABM to lead to an increase in positive emotions and a decrease in negative emotions. Linnenbrink and Pintrich (2002) argued that progress toward a goal of learning should result in happiness and pride as an individual gains knowledge. When an individual makes slow progress, he or she will view the situation as challenging, not frustrating. Indeed, these relationships have been supported across studies. Having a mastery goal has been found to positively predict enjoyment (Daniels, Stupinsky, Pekrun, Haynes, Perry, & Newall, 2009; Pekrun, Elliot, & Maier, 2006), hope (Pekrun et al., 2006; Pekrun, Elliot, & Maier, 2009), and pride (Pekrun et al., 2006, 2009). Individuals with such goals also appear to be similarly satisfied, regardless of task difficulty (Steele-Johnson et al., 2000). A mastery goal orientation has also been found to negatively predict boredom (Daniels et al., 2009; Pekrun et al., 2006, 2009), anxiety (Daniels et al., 2009; Payne, Youngcourt, & Beaubien, 2007), anger (Pekrun et al., 2006, 2009), and shame (Pekrun et al., 2006, 2009). Mastery-approach goal orientations increase positive emotions and decrease negative emotions.

As stated previously, research on mastery-avoid goal orientation is still relatively new. Perhaps one reason for the lack of research is that mastery-avoidance orientations do not appear to be strongly related to performance outcomes (Elliot & McGregor, 2001). However, mastery-avoidance goals do appear to be related to affect within classroom settings. These orientations have been found to relate to an increase in negative affect, including worry, anxiety, and emotionality (Elliot & McGregor, 2001; Sideridis, 2008; Witkow & Fuligni, 2007). In addition, Witkow and Fuligni (2007) found that mastery-avoidance goals were negatively related to positive affect. The limited research on mastery-avoidance goals paints a negative picture, with the goal orientation increasing negative affect outcomes and decreasing positive affect.

In general, performance goal orientations were expected to lead to increased negative emotions, with different predictions about positive emotions for performance-approach and performance-avoid orientations. Results for general performance goals support this hypothesized relationship within the ABM. Performance orientations have been found to positively predict anxiety (Daniels et al., 2009). In addition, the performance orientation–satisfaction relationship has been found to be moderated by task difficulty, with greater levels of satisfaction found for performance-oriented participants working on a simple task than those performance-oriented participants who were working on a difficult task.

Performance-approach goal orientations were predicted to increase negative feelings and to have no relationship with positive feelings. Linnenbrink and Pintrich (2002) asserted that dismay and anxiety typically result for performance-approach–oriented individuals as they compare themselves to other individuals and attempt to gain self-worth from outperforming peers. These goals were found to positively relate to anxiety (Payne et al., 2007) and negatively relate to helplessness (Pekrun et al., 2009). It appears as though performance-approach orientations increase certain negative emotions and decrease others. Although not expected, performance-approach goals were also found to relate positively to pride (Pekrun et al., 2006, 2009) and hope (Pekrun et al., 2009).

Similar to performance-approach orientations, the ABM hypothesizes that performance-avoidance orientations should lead to an increase in negative emotions; it also predicts a decrease in positive emotions associated with this goal orientation. The authors argued that avoid-oriented individuals will not be able to move quickly enough away from undesired outcomes, resulting in anxiety and negative emotions. In addition, success at the avoid goal may simply lead to relief, not pride or joy. Results clearly support the predicted relationships. Performance-avoid orientations have been found to positively predict anxiety (Payne et al., 2007; Pekrun et al., 2006, 2009), boredom (Pekrun et al., 2006), hopelessness (Pekrun et al., 2006, 2009), and anger (Pekrun et al., 2009). In addition, an avoid-orientation was positively related to the intensity of negative emotional reaction in a study by Cron, Slocum, VandeWalle, and Fu (2005). Positive emotions such as hope and pride (Pekrun et al., 2009) were negatively predicted by performance-avoid orientations.

Affect has been shown to play a role in how individuals develop goals, including how they develop goal orientations. In addition, the way in which one views a goal has large implications for subsequent affect experienced. It appears that, in general, approach goal orientations lead to positive emotions, whereas avoid goal orientations lead to negative emotions. In addition, performance orientations lead to negative emotions, and a curious effect is created for those with performance-approach goals; they experience an increase in both positive and negative emotions. Perhaps goal outcome mediates the specific emotions experienced. Regardless, goal orientation is a topic that does much to inform the relationship between goals and affect, yet still has fruitful areas to be explored.

## Summary

We hope that the current chapter provides an informative, if brief, introduction to major topics with regard to goals and affect research. We have reviewed how emotion researchers generally think about goals and how goal researchers generally think about emotions, have highlighted the importance of goal attainment on affective outcomes, have explored the research on affect throughout the goal process, and have brought to light the literature on goal orientation and affect, which has largely remained within the realm of educational psychology.

The relationship between goals and affect has been a productive area of research, yet many questions still remain. As previously stated, very few studies examine discrete emotions within the goal process, instead focusing on general positive and negative affect. Given that discrete emotions lead to different actions, an examination of nuanced emotions may shed additional light on the goal process. Distinguishing between the effects of moods and discrete emotions on the goal process may also prove to be fruitful. If we take the signaling function of affect seriously, it seems clear that particular discrete emotions can have quite different meanings and behavioral implications even when they fall within the same broad classes of positive or negative emotions. Related to this, we think that understanding the affective implications of the nested nature of goal struc-tures, goals at one level that serve the accomplishment of objectives at a broader level, deserves serious study. Additionally, work on goal orientation and emotion within the workplace appears to be an exceptionally good area for future studies. Initial research into the topic suggests that affect may influence goal orientation, which may translate well into the literature on training.

These are just a small set of research questions within the broader agenda of under-standing the relationship between affect and goals. Overall, the literature tells us quite convincingly that although the specific topics may have changed since the first Locke and Latham chapter, the importance and viability of affect and goals as a research topic has not diminished.

## References

Bagozzi, R., Baumgartner, H., & Pieters, R. (1998). Goal-directed emotions. *Cognition and Emotion, 12*, 1–26.

Carver, C. S., Lawrence, J. W., & Scheier, M. F. (1996). A control-process perspective on the origins of affect. In L. L. Martin & A. Tesser (Eds.), *Striving and feeling: Interactions among goals, affect, and self-regulation* (pp. 11–52). Mahwah, NJ: Lawrence Erlbaum.

Carver, C. S., & Scheier, M. F. (1990). Origins and functions of positive and negative affect: A control-process view. *Psychological Review, 97*, 19–35.

Carver, C. S., & Scheier, M. F. (2009). Action, affect, and two-mode models of functioning. In E. Morsella, J. A. Bargh, & P. M. Gollwitzer (Eds.), *Oxford handbook of human action* (pp. 298–327). New York: Oxford University Press.

Cron, W. L., Slocum, J. W., VandeWalle, D., & Fu, Q. (2005). The role of goal orientation on negative emotions and goal setting when initial performance falls short of one's performance goal. *Human Performance, 18*, 55–80.

Custers, R. (2009). How does our unconscious know what we want? The role of affect in goal representations. In G. B. Moskowitz & H. Grant (Eds.), *The psychology of goals* (pp. 179–202). New York: The Guilford Press.

Daniels, L. M., Stupnisky, R. H., Pekrun, R., Haynes, T. L., Perry, R. P., & Newall, N. E. (2009). A longitudinal analysis of achievement goals: From affective antecedents to emotional effects and achievement outcomes. *Journal of Educational Psychology, 101*, 948–963.

Davis, M. A., Kirby, S. L., & Curtis, M. B. (2007). The influence of affect on goal choice and task performance. *Journal of Applied Social Psychology, 37,* 14–42.

Dweck, C. S. (1975). The role of expectations and attributions in the alleviation of learned helplessness. *Journal of Personality and Social Psychology, 31,* 674–685.

Elliot, A. J. (1994). *Approach and avoidance achievement goals: An intrinsic motivation analysis.* Unpublished doctoral dissertation, University of Wisconsin–Madison.

Elliot, A. J., & McGregor, H. A. (2001). A 2 x 2 achievement goal framework. *Journal of Personality and Social Psychology, 80,* 501–519.

Fishbach, A., Shah, J. Y., & Kruglanski, A. W. (2004). Emotional transfer in goal systems. *Journal of Experimental Social Psychology, 40,* 723–738.

Forgas, J. P. (1995). Mood and judgment: The affect infusion model (AIM). *Psychological Bulletin, 117,* 39–66.

Forgas, J. P., & George, J. M. (2001). Affective influences on judgments and behavior in organizations: An information processing perspective. *Organizational Behavior and Human Decision Processes, 86,* 3–34.

Forgas, J. P., & Laham, S. M. (2005). The interaction between affect and motivation in social judgments and behavior. In J. P. Forgas, K. D. Williams, & S. M. Laham (Eds.), *Social motivation: Conscious and unconscious processes* (pp. 168–193). Cambridge: Cambridge University Press.

George, J. M., & Brief, A. P. (1996). Motivational agendas in the workplace: The effects of feelings on focus of attention and work motivation. In B. M. Staw & L. L. Cummings (Eds.), *Research in organizational behavior* (Vol. 18, pp. 75–109). Greenwich, CT: JAI Press.

Gollwitzer, P. M., & Rohloff, U. B. (1999). The speed of goal pursuit. In R. S. Wyer (Ed.), *Perspectives on behavioral self-regulation* (pp. 147–159). Mahwah, NJ: Lawrence Erlbaum.

Harris, C., Daniels, K., & Briner, R. B. (2003). A daily diary study of goals and affective well-being at work. *Journal of Occupational and Organizational Psychology, 76,* 401–410.

Harvey, P., & Victoravich, L. M. (2009). The influences of forward-looking antecedents uncertainty and anticipatory emotions on project escalation. *Decision Sciences, 40,* 759–782.

Henkel, J. M., & Hinsz, V. B. (2004). Success and failure in goal attainment as a mood induction procedure. *Social Behavior and Personality, 32,* 715–722.

Hoppmann, C. A., & Klumb, P. L. (2006). Daily goal pursuits predict cortisol secretion and mood states in employed parents with preschool children. *Psychosomatic Medicine, 68,* 887–894.

Houser-Marko, L., & Sheldon, K. M. (2008). Eyes on the prize or nose to the grindstone? The effects of level of goal evaluation on mood and motivation. *Personality and Social Psychology Bulletin, 34,* 1556–1569.

Ilies, R., & Judge, T. A. (2005). Goal regulation across time: The effects of feedback and affect. *Journal of Applied Psychology, 90,* 453–467.

Ilies, R., Judge, T. A., & Wagner, D. T. (2010). The influence of cognitive and affective reactions to feedback on subsequent goals: Role of behavioral inhibition/activation. *European Psychologist, 15,* 121–131.

Isen, A. M. (1984). The influence of positive affect on decision making and cognitive organization. *Advances in Consumer Research, 11,* 534–537.

Kruglanski, A. W., Shah, J. Y., Fishbach, A., Friedman, R., Chun, W. Y., & Sleeth-Keppler, D. (2002). A theory of goal systems. *Advances in Experimental Social Psychology, 34,* 331–378.

Lavallee, L. F., & Campbell, J. D. (1995). Impact of personal goals on self-regulation processes elicited by daily negative events. *Journal of Personality and Social Psychology, 69,* 341–352.

Linnenbrink, E. A., & Pintrich, P. R. (2002). Achievement goal theory and affect: An asymmetrical bidirectional model. *Educational Psychologist, 37,* 69–78.

Locke, E. A. (1969). What is job satisfaction? *Organizational Behavior and Human Performance, 4,* 309–336.

Locke, E. A. (1970). Job satisfaction and job performance: A theoretical analysis. *Organizational Behavior and Human Performance, 5,* 484–500.

Locke, E. A. (1976). The nature and causes of job satisfaction. In M. D. Dunnette (Ed.), *Handbook of industrial and organizational psychology* (pp. 1297–1349). Chicago: Rand McNally.

Locke, E. A., & Latham, G. A. (1990). *A theory of goal setting and task performance.* Englewood Cliffs, NJ: Prentice Hall.

Lord, R. G., Diefendorff, J. M., Schmidt, A. M., & Hall, R. J. (2010). Self-regulation at work. *Annual Review of Psychology, 61,* 543–568.

Louro, M. J., Pieters, R., & Zeelenberg, M. (2007). Dynamics of multiple-goal pursuit. *Journal of Personality and Social Psychology, 93,* 174–193.

Martin, L. L., Tesser, A., & McIntosh, W. D. (1993). Wanting but not having: The effects of unattained goals on thoughts and feelings. In D. M. Wegner & J. W. Pennebaker (Eds.), *Handbook of mental control* (pp. 552–572). Englewood Cliffs, NJ: Prentice-Hall.

Moberly, N. J., & Watkins, E. R. (2010). Negative affect and ruminative self-focus during everyday goal pursuit. *Cognition and Emotion, 24,* 729–739.

Nicholls, J. G. (1975). Causal attributions and other achievement-related cognitions: Effects of task outcomes, attainment, value, and sex. *Journal of Personality and Social Psychology, 31,* 379–389.

Orehek, E., Bessarabova, E., Chen, X., & Kruglanski, A. W. (2011). Positive affect as informational feedback in goal pursuit. *Motivation and Emotion, 35,* 44–51.

Payne, S. C., Youngcourt, S. S., & Beaubien, J. M. (2007). A meta-analytic examination of the goal orientation nomological net. *Journal of Applied Psychology, 92,* 128–150.

Pekrun, R., Elliot, A. J., & Maier, M. A. (2006). Achievement goals and discrete achievement emotions: A theoretical model and prospective test. *Journal of Educational Psychology, 98,* 583–597.

Pekrun, R., Elliot, A. J., & Maier, M. A. (2009). Achievement goals and achievement emotions: Testing a model of their joint relations with academic performance. *Journal of Educational Psychology, 101,* 115–135.

Richard, E. M., & Diefendorff, J. M. (2011). Self-regulation during a single performance episode: Mood-as-information in the absence of formal feedback. *Organizational Behavior and Human Decision Processes, 115,* 99–110.

Roseman, I. J., Wiest, C., & Swartz, T. S. (1994). Phenomenology, behaviors, and goals differentiate discrete emotions. *Journal of Personality and Social Psychology, 67,* 206–221.

Saavedra, R., & Earley, P. C. (1991). Choice of task and goal under conditions of general and specific affective inducement. *Motivation and Emotion, 15,* 45–65.

Scherer, K. R. (1999). On the sequential nature of appraisal processes: Indirect evidence from a recognition task. *Cognition and Emotion, 13,* 763–793.

Seo, M., & Ilies, R. (2009). The role of self-efficacy, goal, and affect in dynamic motivational self-regulation. *Organizational Behavior and Human Decision Processes, 109,* 120–133.

Sideridis, G. D. (2008). The regulation of affect, anxiety, and stressful arousal from adopting mastery-avoidance goal orientations. *Stress and Health, 24,* 55–69.

Simon, H. A. (1967). Motivational and emotional controls of cognition. *Psychological Review, 74,* 29–39.

Smith, C. A., & Kirby, L. D. (2001). Toward delivering on the promise of appraisal theory. In K. R. Scherer, A. Schorr, & T. Johnstone (Eds.), *Appraisal processes in emotion: Theory, methods, research* (pp. 121–138). New York: Oxford University Press.

Steele-Johnson, D., Beauregard, R. S., Hoover, P. B., & Schmidt, A. M. (2000). Goal orientation and task demand effects on motivation, affect, and performance. *Journal of Applied Psychology, 85,* 724–738.

VandeWalle, D. (1996). *Are students trying to prove or improve their ability? Development and validation of an instrument to measure academic goal orientation.* Paper presented at the annual meeting of the Academy of Management, Cincinnati, OH.

Weiss, H. M. (2002a). Conceptual foundations for the study of affect at work. In R. G. Lord, R. Klimoski, & R. Kanfer (Eds.), *Emotions at Work* (pp. 20–63). New York: Jossey-Bass.

Weiss, H. M. (2002b). Deconstructing job satisfaction: Separating evaluations, beliefs and affective experiences. *Human Resource Management Review, 12,* 173–194.

Weiss, H. M., & Cropanzano, R. (1996). Affective events theory: A theoretical discussion of the structure, causes and consequences of affective experiences at work. In B. M. Staw & L. L. Cummings (Eds.), *Research in organizational behavior* (Vol. 18, pp. 1–74). Greenwich, CT: JAI Press.

Weiss, H. M., Nicholas, J. P., & Daus, C. S. (1999). An examination of the joint effects of affective experiences and job beliefs on job satisfaction and variations in affective experiences over time. *Organizational Behavior and Human Decision Processes, 78,* 1–24.

Witkow, M. R., & Fuligni, A. J. (2007). Achievement goals and daily school experiences among adolescents with Asian, Latino, and European American backgrounds. *Journal of Educational Psychology, 99,* 584–596.

# 9 Determinants of Goals[1]

*Peter A. Heslin and Karyn L. Wang* School of Management,
Australian School of Business,
University of New South Wales

In light of the consequential nature of goals, considerable research has investigated the antecedents of goal setting. Goals can be either self-initiated, participatively-set, or assigned by an authority figure such as a manager, experimenter, or parent. When self-initiated, goals tend to be guided by personal needs, values, and higher-order goals (Lord, Diefendorff, Schmidt, & Hall, 2010), as well as social, contextual (Locke, 1991), and sometimes unconscious cues (Latham, Stajkovic, & Locke, 2010). Following Locke and Latham (1990), this chapter focuses on what leads people to set and pursue high goals in valued domains.

The processes of choosing and committing to a goal are related, though conceptually and empirically distinct (see Chapter 6). For instance, some factors that influence goal choice (e.g., self-efficacy and conscientiousness) also influence goal commitment (Bandura, 1997; Barrick, Mount, & Strauss, 1993). On the other hand, goal commitment can be operationalized by examining the magnitude of any discrepancy between the level of assigned goals and personally chosen goals (Tubbs, 1993); the lower the discrepancy, the higher the personal commitment to the assigned goal. In addition, self-set goals often fully mediate the relationship between assigned goals and effort (e.g., Fu, Richards, & Jones, 2009). Finally, life is filled with institutional and social inducements to adopt goals that often conflict with each other, thereby requiring decisions about what goals to pursue. It is thus important to examine the determinants of personal goals.

We begin by reviewing what empirical research conducted over the last two decades has revealed about individual differences, psychological states, and contextual factors that drive goal setting. We then briefly discuss the emerging literature on the determinants of subconscious goals. We conclude by summarizing what is known about goal determinants and discuss some future research opportunities.

## Determinants of Conscious Goals

In the first edition of this book, Locke and Latham (1990, p. 122) concluded that goal choice is largely a function of "what the individual thinks *can be* achieved and what he or she *would like to* achieve or thinks *should be* achieved." Over the last two decades, empirical research has continued to explore what leads people to set and pursue high goals. This chapter reviews the key individual and contextual determinants of high personal goal setting revealed by empirical studies published since 1989. As summarized in Table 9.1, we organized our review into the *individual difference, psychological state,* and *contextual* determinants of goals.

*Table 9.1* Conscious Goal Determinants Documented Between 1989 and 2011

| Individual differences | Psychological states | Contextual determinants |
|---|---|---|
| • Competitiveness | • Self-efficacy | • Feedback |
| • Conscientiousness | • Affect | • Goal anchors |
| • Core-self evaluations | • Perceived controllability | • Groups |
| • Gender | • Implicit theories | • Incentives |
| • Goal Orientation | | • Leadership |
| | | • Management by objectives |
| | | • Time |

## Individual Differences

*Competitiveness.* Brown, Cron, and Slocum (1998) examined the main and interactive effect of trait competitiveness and competitive organizational climate levels on personal goal setting. Those high in trait competitiveness set the highest goals when in a competitive climate. Those with low trait competitiveness set lower goals, regardless of the organizational climate.

*Conscientiousness.* In a study of when people proactively set goals, Barrick et al. (1993) found that when sales representatives had high conscientiousness, they set personal goals and subsequently had higher sales volumes and supervisor-rated job performance. Owing to the focus on whether participants set goals, Barrick et al. did not examine the level at which they set them. To investigate this issue, Gellatly (1996) examined how conscientiousness influenced personal goal levels on an arithmetic task. Those higher in conscientiousness tended to set higher goals, although this relationship was indirect and mediated by expectancy. That is, conscientious individuals set higher goals as a function of being more confident in their ability to perform effectively. The measure of expectancy in this study overlaps with the concepts of self-efficacy and control discussed below.

*Core-Self Evaluations.* Core-self evaluations (CSEs) are a higher-order trait referring to positive self-regard in terms of high self-esteem, generalized self-efficacy, internal locus of control, and neuroticism (Judge, Locke, Durham, & Kluger, 1998). Erez and Judge (2001) demonstrated that high CSEs are associated with engaging in goal setting, as well as high subsequent job performance and productivity. Judge, Bono, Erez, and Locke (2005) showed that high CSEs increase one's tendency to set self-concordant goals (i.e., goals that are concordant with personal interests and values), which enhances life satisfaction both directly and through increased goal attainment.

CSEs have not been studied directly in relation to personal goal levels, though the individual traits that make up CSEs, such as self-efficacy and self-esteem, have been investigated with regard to personal goals. Chen, Gully, Whiteman, and Kilcullen (2000) found that generalized self-efficacy influences task-specific self-efficacy, which in turn predicts the setting of high personal goals. However, the findings are less consistent with regard to self-esteem. For example, whilst several studies report that people with higher levels of self-esteem typically set more difficult goals (Levy & Baumgardner, 1991; Pilegge & Holtz, 1997), other studies indicate that self-esteem has negligible effects on goal setting (Hollenbeck, 1987; Mone, Baker, & Jeffries, 1995). The inconsistencies associated with the main effects of self-esteem may be partly due to its interactive effects. For example, Pilegge and Holtz (1997) found that self-esteem interacted with social identity, such that only those with high self-esteem and strong social identification with coworkers set themselves more difficult goals. Baumeister, Heatherton, and Tice (1993) discovered that under ego-threat conditions, those with higher levels of self-esteem set higher and riskier goals. However, when individuals were not exposed to ego-threat conditions, there was no discernable difference in goal setting between high- and low self-esteem individuals. Levy and Baumgardner (1991) observed that self-esteem also interacts with gender, such that only males with higher self-esteem set higher goals.

*Gender.* Several researchers have found that, compared to women, men are more likely to set higher goals (Levy & Baumgardner, 1991; Stevens, Bavetta, & Gist, 1993; Tolli & Schmidt, 2008), as men tend to have higher self-esteem (Levy & Baumgardner, 1991) and higher self-efficacy (Tolli & Schmidt, 2008). Stevens et al. investigated how MBA students' salary negotiations are affected by two types of training: goal setting training and self-management training. Prior to any training, women had lower self-efficacy, largely saw the negotiation process as uncontrollable, set lower salary goals, and negotiated lower salaries than men. Following goal-setting training, although both men and women negotiated higher salaries, men still managed to negotiate higher salaries than women. This was again due to women setting lower salary goals. Following self-management training, however, both men and women increased their salaries and the pre-training salary difference between them was no longer apparent. Analysis revealed that following self-management training, women managed to close the salary gap by (a) setting higher goals and (b) perceiving the negotiation situation as controllable, but unexpectedly (c) not as a result of having increased self-efficacy.

*Goal Orientation.* Goal orientation refers to the type of goals that people typically adopt in achievement contexts (Dweck, 1985). Individuals with a learning goal orientation (LGO; Dweck, 1985) approach tasks with the goal of learning how to perform more effectively. Individuals with a performance-prove goal orientation (PPGO) attempt to demonstrate their abilities to gain favorable judgments from others, while those with a performance-avoid goal orientation (PAGO) attempt to avoid negative judgments from others (VandeWalle, 1997).

A meta-analysis by Payne, Youngcourt, and Beaubien (2007) revealed that LGO had a positive relationship with self-set goal levels, whereas PAGO had a negative effect on self-set goal levels. However, PPGO had a trivial negative effect on personal goal setting, with the confidence interval containing zero.

### Psychological States

*Self-Efficacy.* Self-efficacy is one of the most widely researched constructs in the goal setting literature. As mentioned in the original book chapter (Chapter 5, Locke & Latham, 1990), those with high self-efficacy set high goals. Since then, self-efficacy has been primarily examined as a mediator between the variable of interest and personal goal setting. For example, research has examined the effects of variables such as affect (Seo & Ilies, 2009), perceived controllability (Bandura & Wood, 1989), implicit theories (Wood & Bandura, 1989), feedback (Bandura & Jourden, 1991), and time (Earley & Erez, 1991) on self-set goals via self-efficacy. The influence of these variables, along with their relationship with self-efficacy, is discussed next. For further discussion regarding the nature of self-efficacy and its role in the goal setting process, see Chapter 10.

*Affect.* An important development in the goal-setting literature concerns the influence of affect, which encompasses concepts such as general mood and momentary emotions. Richard and Diefendorff (2011) examined student goal revisions leading up to a course exam by using diary methods. Daily positive affect predicted upward goal revision, whereas negative affect predicted downward goal revision. In explaining the findings, Richard and Diefendorff suggested that positive affect may have inflated self-efficacy, hence resulting in upward goal revision. On the other hand, those experiencing negative affect may have believed that they were not progressing toward their goal, and thus revised their goal downward. Richard and Diefendorff also demonstrated that goals and affect had reciprocal effects, such that upward goal revision positively predicted positive affect. However, the impact of affect on goal levels was larger than the impact of goal levels on affect.

The effects of positive and negative affect on personal goals is also apparent in a study by Seo and Ilies (2009), in which private stock investors participated in online stock investment simulations. Seo and Ilies observed that positive affect predicted higher personal investment return goals, whereas negative affect predicted lower personal investment return goals. The relationship between affect and personal goals was largely mediated by changes in self-efficacy. Ilies and Judge (2005) found that positive affect largely mediated the effects of feedback on subsequent goal setting. Following negative feedback, there was a decrease in positive affect, and participants adjusted their goals downward. Following positive feedback, there was an increase in positive affect, and participants adjusted their goals upward.

*Perceived Controllability.* In a laboratory simulation, Bandura and Wood (1989) portrayed organizations as either difficult to control, or quite controllable. Despite performing the same production management task, participants in the high-controllability condition had higher self-efficacy and subsequently set higher goals, compared to those in the low-controllability condition. Bandura and Wood thus demonstrated that people's self-efficacy is fostered when they construe their environments as controllable, resulting in higher goals. On the other hand, apparently uncontrollable environments erode self-efficacy, thereby resulting in lower goals.

Tolli and Schmidt (2008) gave undergraduate students bogus performance feedback following the completion of an anagram task. When participants made internal attributions about the controllability, stability, and causality of performance, they engaged in upward goal revision following positive feedback and downward goal revision following negative feedback. Those who held external attributions about performance, implying less controllability, did not adjust their goals following feedback. These studies suggest that encouraging people to frame their challenges as controllable can foster the high goal setting and self-efficacy that are often a precursor to effective action.

*Implicit Theories.* Implicit theories embody the assumptions people hold about the plasticity of their abilities. An *entity* implicit theory reflects the assumption that abilities are essentially fixed endowments, while an *incremental* implicit theory construes abilities more as acquirable skills that are amenable to being cultivated (Dweck, 1986).

Wood and Bandura (1989) induced these different implicit theories via the framing of a complex managerial decision-making task. Incremental theories were cultivated by informing experimental participants that "decision-making skills are developed through practice. In acquiring a new skill, people do not begin with faultless performance.

However, the more they practice making decisions the more capable they become" (p. 410). Entity theories were induced by informing other participants that "… decision making reflects the basic cognitive capabilities that people possess. The higher their underlying cognitive-processing capacities, the better is their decision making" (p. 410). By virtue of introducing evaluative concerns that can undermine a range of self-regulatory processes (e.g., self-efficacy and analytical thinking) while completing a challenging task, participants in the entity condition set lower goals and were more likely to lower their goals over time than those induced to adopt an incremental theory.

Implicit theories also affect the type of goals that people set. Among entering students at the University of Hong Kong (where English proficiency is a necessity), those with an incremental theory were more likely to set relevant self-development goals, as evidenced by expressing interest in taking a remedial English class from which they could benefit (Hong, Chiu, Dweck, Lin, & Wan, 1999). Besides fostering avoidance of developmental opportunities, entity theories also lead to dysfunctional goals—such as the goal to avoid expending effort (Hong et al., 1999)—and methods of goal attainment, such as being willing to cheat in order to appear capable (Blackwell, Trzesniewski, & Dweck, 2007). For more details about the nature and nomological network of implicit theories, see Dweck (1999; Dweck & Grant, 2008).

We have reviewed individual differences and psychological states that give rise to goal setting and revision. Unlike with individual differences, initiatives can be employed to foster the high self-efficacy (Bandura, 1997), positive affect (Fredrickson, 2009), perceived controllability (Seligman, 2011), and incremental implicit theories (Heslin, Latham, & Vandewalle, 2005) that are associated with setting high goals. Next we consider how facets of the work context can influence personal goals.

## Contextual Determinants

*Feedback.* Positive performance feedback generally leads to upward goal revision, whereas negative performance feedback typically precipitates downward goal revision (Donovan & Hafsteinsson, 2006; Donovan & Williams, 2003; Vance & Colella, 1990; Williams, Donovan, & Dodge, 2000). Bandura and Jourden (1991) gave participants bogus feedback regarding their performance on an organizational decision-making task and examined how such feedback influenced subsequent goal setting. In the four bogus feedback conditions, participants were told that their performance: (a) was similar to that of others (similar capabilities condition), (b) was superior to others (superior capabilities condition), (c) increased over time compared with others (progressive mastery condition), or (d) decreased over time compared with others (progressive decline condition). The results show that those in the similar and superior capabilities condition maintained their self-efficacy. Participants in the progressive mastery group exhibited a sharp increase in self-efficacy, whereas those in the progressive decline group showed deterioration of self-efficacy across time. Consistent with social cognitive theory (Bandura, 1986), only those in the progressive mastery condition had increased self-efficacy and subsequently higher goals.

Feedback affects self-efficacy and thus the new goals that people set. Tolli and Schmidt (2008) found that positive feedback regarding performance on a anagram task increased self-efficacy and subsequent goals, whereas negative feedback decreased self-efficacy and subsequent goals. Self-efficacy also influences how people revise goals following feedback. Donovan and Hafsteinsson (2006) found that positive performance-goal discrepancies (i.e., when performance exceeded initial goals) predicted subsequent upward goal revision, such that greater discrepancies predicted more upward goal revision and smaller discrepancies predicted less upward goal revision. However, those with higher self-efficacy revised their goals upward to a greater extent, compared to those with lower self-efficacy.

*Goal Anchors.* Assigned goals influence personal goal levels, not only by conveying normative information about what is expected, but also via anchoring. Hinsz, Kalnbach, and Lorentz (1997) conducted an experimental study in which students were encouraged to do their best, adopt a goal, or were given an extremely high arbitrary anchor in a brainstorming task. In the arbitrary anchor condition, students were instructed to "set a challenging and specific goal for the number of uses you will generate this next period—for example, 320 uses." Heinz et al. found that compared to the self-set goal condition, those in the arbitrary anchor condition had significantly higher goals, sometimes almost twice as high, and performed better on the brainstorming task across performance trials. In subsequent experiments, when the anchor was manipulated from low (e.g., 10 uses) to high (e.g., 120/240 uses), people exposed to high anchors set higher goals and performed better than those exposed to the low anchors. This research shows that simply suggesting a goal may influence the level of personal goals that people set.

*Groups.* Group membership and goals serve as a referent point for personal goal setting. Hinsz (1991, 1995) demonstrated that individually set goals tend to be more difficult than goals that result from groups reaching a consensus regarding questions such as, "What would be an appropriate goal for the task performance of each group member?" Hinsz (1991, 1995) explained these findings in terms of a social comparison process, whereby collectively establishing lower goal expectations increases the scope for individuals to exceed group targets and performance. Another explanation involves evaluation apprehension concerns within group contexts, whereby individuals can lose confidence in their abilities (Hinsz, 1992), a similar dynamic to how self-efficacy and subsequent goals can be undermined by an entity implicit theory (Wood & Bandura, 1989) or a PAGO (VandeWalle, Cron, & Slocum, 2001).

Pilegge and Holtz (1997) experimentally investigated the effects of social identification and self-esteem on personal goal setting. They manipulated individuals' social identification with co-workers by creating in-groups. Stronger social identification with co-workers resulted in higher individual performance goals, compared to those with weaker social identification with co-workers. In addition, social identity interacted with self-esteem such that those with higher self-esteem and strong social identities set the most difficult goals.

Feedback also plays a role in establishing goals in group settings. DeShon, Kozlowski, Schmidt, Milner, and Wiechmann (2004) investigated the effects on individual-only, team-only, or individual and team-based feedback on subsequent goal levels. Individual feedback resulted in higher *individual* goals, higher self-efficacy, and increased focus on individual performance. At the team level, teams receiving only individual feedback established the highest *team* goals, followed by teams that received both individual and team feedback. The lowest goals were set by teams that received only team feedback.

*Incentives.* Individuals set the highest goals under piece-rate plans compared to bonus plans or fixed-rate plans (Farh, Griffeth, & Balkin, 1991; Guthrie & Hollensbe, 2004; Moussa, 1996). Goals are highest under piece rates because there is strong extrinsic motivation to perform when payment is contingent on performance. On the other hand, there is no such motivation to set higher goals for those on flat rates. Receiving a bonus for arriving at a personal goal encourages people to set lower goals, thus making the goal easier to achieve and maximizing the chance of receiving payment (Moussa, 2000; Wright & Kacmar, 1995).

Lee, Locke, and Phan (1997) found that under a bonus pay system, students performed better with medium assigned goals than with difficult assigned goals. Under a piece-rate system, participants performed better with difficult rather than medium-level goals, as fully mediated by personal goals and self-efficacy.

Guthrie and Hollensbe (2004) observed that variable pay (i.e., performance-contingent pay) resulted in higher team goal levels than flat rate pay. In addition, teams with the most contingent pay set significantly higher goals than other groups.

The effects of incentives on personal goal setting can depend on task-specific self-esteem and norms. Moussa (1996) discovered that individuals set higher goals under piece-rate plans, compared to flat-rate plans, only when they have high task-specific self-esteem. Individuals with low task-specific self-esteem set comparable goal levels under piece rates and flat rates. The effects of incentives on personal goal levels also depend on whether people choose the method of payment or are assigned the payment method. Moussa (2000) documented a positive relationship between piece rates and personal goal levels, but only when the experimenter encouraged participants to set difficult goals. Piece rates did not have a positive effect on personal goal setting when the experimenter did not suggest a norm, or when easy goals were encouraged.

The reward systems that people prefer are a function of their ability. Farh et al. (1991) found that only high performers on a pre-test chose piece rate or bonus rewards more often than fixed rates of pay. Participants who chose piece rates also had higher goals than those who were assigned piece rates. Individuals who selected fixed rates set lower personal goals than those who were assigned the fixed-rate condition. Finally, individuals who chose a bonus plan set their goals at about the same level as those who were assigned the bonus plan.

*Leadership.* Leaders affect motivation by shaping the nature of the goals that followers set. In an experimental study, Kirkpatrick and Locke (1996) found that when leaders communicated task cues (i.e., suggestions for improving productivity), followers set quantity-related goals. When leaders communicated a vision of quality, followers adopted quality-related goals. Leaders' traits and skills also affect company goals and subsequent venture growth (Kirkpatrick & Locke, 1996). In a field study of architectural woodwork firms, Baum and Locke (2004) reported that entrepreneur-CEO skills and traits are positively associated with CEO goal setting. Specifically, CEOs set higher annual sales and employment goals when they have passion for work, tenacity, and high ability to find new resources.

Leaders not only affect individual goal setting but also how goals function within groups. When leaders foster the acceptance of group goals, group cohesiveness has a positive relationship with commissions and employees meeting sales quotas. However, when leaders do not foster the acceptance of group goals, group cohesiveness was negatively related to commissions and employees reaching their quotas (Podsakoff, MacKenzie, & Ahearne, 1997).

*Management by Objectives.* By virtue of signaling management expectations, management by objectives (MBO) can stimulate goal setting by employees (Drucker, 1954). A meta-analysis by Rodgers and Hunter (1991) showed that when top-management commitment is high, the average gain in productivity from MBO is 56%, compared to just 6% when top management commitment is low. Fu et al. (2009) predicted that company-assigned goals would be a precursor of personal goals. Their study of 802 salespeople working in the construction and building maintenance industries revealed that territory-based individual sales quotas predicted 19% of the variance in the level of individuals' self-set sales goals.

Nonetheless, goal systems that are not prudently designed can readily elicit unintended goal-directed behavior that directly undermines organizational objectives (Kerr, 1975). Useful guidelines for aligning personal goals with organizational objectives are provided by Kerr (1999), Latham and Locke (2006), and Locke (2004).

*Time.* Goals tend to be revised as a function of the time remaining for them to be attained. In a study of athletes, Donovan and Williams (2003) tracked fluctuations in goal levels across the track and field competition season. At the beginning of the season, athletes set their season's goals at a level slightly lower than their previous season's personal best. Over time, athletes adjusted their competition goals upwards such that it became less discrepant with their distal performance goals. Greater discrepancies between competition goals and actual performance predicted downward seasonal goal revision, but this effect was mediated by time with greater seasonal downward goal adjustment at the end of the season compared to the beginning of the season.

Richard and Diefendorff (2011) demonstrated that goal levels initially remain relatively stable but are revised downward as deadlines approach. Downward goal revision may reflect an increasing need to be accurate as a deadline approaches, to maintain self-esteem, or protect oneself from experiencing failure.

Earley and Erez (1991) found that the relative impact of assigned goals and normative information on personal goals depends on when the information is presented. In an experiment addressing whether assigned goals influence personal goals via primacy or recency effects, business students were either assigned goals on day 1 and received normative information on day 8, or received normative information on day 1 and assigned goals on day 8. Self-efficacy and personal goal setting were assessed on day 8. The data supported the recency effect as the most temporally proximal cue, regardless of whether it was an assigned goal or normative information, had the strongest influence on the level of personal goals.

The preceding discussion has addressed individual differences, psychological states, and contextual factors that are precursors of conscious goal setting. Next we consider how subconscious goals can influence goal-directed behavior.

## Determinants of Subconscious Goals

Bargh and Chartrand (1997) argued that environmental features can activate automatic goals that affect goal-directed cognition and behavior without conscious awareness. Such subconscious goals can produce similar performance outcomes as conscious goal assignment (Bargh, Gollwitzer, Lee-Chai, Barndollar, & Trötschel, 2001; Stajkovic, Locke, & Blair, 2006) and can supplement (Shantz & Latham, 2009) conscious goal setting to increase performance. Subconscious goals can increase a person's motivation to engage in goal-directed behavior (Ferguson, 2008; Shantz & Latham, 2009, Shantz & Latham, 2011) or make an already valued goal seem even more desirable (Aarts, Custers, & Holland, 2007; Ferguson, 2008).

By virtue of operating outside conscious awareness, subconscious goals can stimulate performance without exerting the cognitive load imposed by the self-regulatory processes associated with conscious goals (Anderson, 1985). Thus, besides the potential motivational benefits of using subconscious goals to supplement conscious goals, subconscious goals may also enhance the cognitive capacity available for adapting to novel situations and for complex knowledge and skill learning (Latham et al., 2010).

Research in this area typically activates subconscious goals via methods that are either subliminal (below the threshold of awareness) or supraliminal (i.e., using a seemingly unrelated task such as scrambled sentence or word search). Because subliminal stimuli rarely occur naturally and are typically too weak or brief in natural settings to affect behavior (Bargh & Morsella, 2008), most subconscious goal research uses supraliminal primes.

Many types of behaviors can be cued by subconscious goals. For example, well-mannered behavior has been increased by having people complete a scrambled sentence task priming politeness (e.g., patient, cautious, sensitive; Bargh, Chen, & Burrows, 1996). Performance on an intelligence test can be improved by people rating the intelligence and knowledgeability of professors, and diminished by rating the intelligence and knowledgeability of soccer hooligans (Dijksterhuis & van Knippenberg, 1998). Shah (2003) demonstrated that self-efficacy, persistence, and performance on an anagram task can be enhanced by having people recall the name of someone who holds high expectations of them. Even cleaning-related behaviors (i.e., picking up their biscuit crumbs) can be increased by exposure to a citrus-scented cleaner (Holland, Hendriks, & Aarts, 2005).

Within an organizational context, Shantz and Latham (2009, 2011) increased the productivity of call center workers by using an achievement prime—a photograph of a woman winning a race—on a page of instructions. Latham and Piccolo (2012) found that only a task-relevant achievement prime—such as photograph of engaged call center workers—increased call center workers' productivity across the course of a work week; an achievement prime that was not task-relevant did not have the same positive impact on employee productivity. A fuller discussion of how subconscious goals can influence behavior and performance is provided in Chapters 29 and 30.

## Conclusion

This chapter has reviewed the empirical literature on the individual and contextual precursors of conscious goal setting, as summarized in Table 9.1. Individual determinants of high, conscious goals include being conscientious; being a competitive person in a competitive environment; having high generalized self-efficacy; being male (unless gender differences are ameliorated via self-management training); having high self-esteem combined with identifying with one's workgroup; and have a high LGO and a low PAGO. Psychological states that trigger high goal setting include having high self-efficacy, positive affect, perceiving performance domains as controllable, and holding an incremental theory of ability. In terms of context, positive feedback generally predicts upward goal revision, whereas negative feedback precipitates downward goal revision. Personal goals are also influenced by goal anchors, group dynamics, incentives, leadership styles, management by objectives, and the passage of time.

Future research could usefully follow the lead of Wood and Bandura (1989) and Stevens et al. (1993) in examining how interventions can create the states (e.g., self-efficacy, perceived controllability, and/or incremental implicit theories) that lead people to set and sustain their commitment to attaining high goals. Further research might also fruitfully utilize multi-level methods to investigate how external inducements to adopt goals are manifested on a personal level (e.g., Fu et al., 2009), and/or latent growth modeling methods to map how personal goals fluctuate over time (e.g., Richard & Diefendorff, 2011).

The scope for cuing subconscious goals presents great opportunities for supplementing the motivational benefits of conscious goals without incurring the additional cognitive load that can impede learning and conscious self-regulation. Much is yet to be learned, however, about issues such as how long primes remain effective, how different types of primes interact and can be used in conjunction with each other, and also regarding how to manage the potential ethical issues associated with manipulating others' behaviors via mechanisms that operate outside conscious awareness.

## Note

1. This research was supported in part by a grant to the first author from the Australian School of Business, UNSW.

## References

Aarts, H., Custers, R., & Holland, R. W. (2007). The nonconscious cessation of goal pursuit: When goals and negative affect are coactivated. *Journal of Personality and Social Psychology, 92*, 165–178.

Anderson, J. R. (1985). *Cognitive psychology and its implications.* New York: Freeman.

Bandura, A. (1986). *Social foundations of thought and action: A social cognitive theory.* Englewood Cliffs, NJ: Prentice Hall.

Bandura, A. (1997). *Self-efficacy: The exercise of control.* New York: W.H. Freeman.

Bandura, A., & Jourden, F. J. (1991). Self-regulatory mechanisms governing the impact of social comparison on complex decision making. *Journal of Personality and Social Psychology, 60*, 941–951.

Bandura, A., & Wood, R. (1989). Effect of perceived controllability and performance standards on self-regulation of complex decision making. *Journal of Personality and Social Psychology, 56*, 805–814.

Bargh, J. A., & Chartrand, T. L. (1997). Studying the mind in the middle: A practical guide to priming and automaticity research. In H. Reis & C. Judd (Eds.), *Research methods in social psychology* (pp. 253–285). New York: Cambridge University Press.

Bargh, J. A., & Morsella, E. (2008). The unconscious mind. *Perspectives on Psychological Science, 3*, 73–79.

Bargh, J. A., Chen, M., & Burrows, L. (1996). Automaticity of social behavior: direct effects of trait construct and stereotype-activation on action. *Journal of Personality and Social Psychology*, *71*, 230–244.

Bargh, J. A., Gollwitzer, P. M., Lee-Chai, A., Barndollar, K., & Trötschel, R. (2001). The automated will: Nonconscious activation and pursuit of behavioral goals. *Journal of Personality and Social Psychology*, *81*, 1014–1027.

Barrick, M. R., Mount, M. K., & Strauss, J. P. (1993). Conscientiousness and performance of sales representatives: Test of the mediating effects of goal setting. *Journal of Applied Psychology*, *78*, 715–722.

Baum, J. R., & Locke, E. A. (2004). The relationship of entrepreneurial traits, skill, and motivation to subsequent venture growth. *Journal of Applied Psychology*, *89*, 587–598.

Baumeister, R. F., Heatherton, T. F., & Tice, D. M. (1993). When ego threats lead to self-regulation failure: Negative consequences of high self-esteem. *Journal of Personality and Social Psychology*, *64*, 141–156.

Blackwell, L., Trzesniewski, K., & Dweck, C. (2007). Implicit theories of intelligence predict achievement across an adolescent transition: A longitudinal study and an intervention. *Child Development*, *78*, 246–263.

Brown, S. P., Cron, W. L., & Slocum, J. W. (1998). Effects of trait competitiveness and perceived intraorganizal competition on salesperson goal setting and performance. *Journal of Marketing*, *62*, 88–98.

Chen, G., Gully, S. M., Whiteman, J. A., & Kilcullen, R. N. (2000). Examination of relationships among trait-like individual differences, state-like individual differences, and learning performance. *Journal of Applied Psychology*, *85*, 835–847.

DeShon, R. P., Kozlowski, S. W. J., Schmidt, A. M., Milner, K. R., & Wiechmann, D. (2004). A multiple-goal, multilevel model of feedback effects on the regulation of individual and team performance. *Journal of Applied Psychology*, *89*, 1035–1056.

Dijksterhuis, A., & van Knippenberg, A. (1998). The relation between perception and behavior, or how to win a game of trivial pursuit. *Journal of Personality and Social Psychology*, *74*, 865–877.

Donovan, J. J., & Hafsteinsson, L. G. (2006). The impact of goal-performance discrepancies, self-efficacy, and goal orientation on upward goal revision. *Journal of Applied Social Psychology*, *36*, 1046–1069.

Donovan, J. J., & Williams, K. J. (2003). Missing the mark: Effects of time and causal attributions on goal revision in response to goal-performance discrepancies. *Journal of Applied Psychology*, *88*, 379–390.

Drucker, P. F. (1954). *The practice of management*. New York: HaperCollins.

Dweck, C. S. (1985). Intrinsic motivation, perceived control, and self-evaluation maintenance: An achievement goal analysis. In C. Ames & R. Ames (Eds.), *Research on motivation in education: Vol. 2. The classroom milieu* (pp. 289–305). New York: Academic.

Dweck, C. S. (1986) Motivational processes affecting learning. *American Psychologist*, *41*, 1040–1048.

Dweck, C. S. (1999). *Self-theories: Their role in motivation, personality, and development*. Philadelphia: Psychology Press.

Dweck, C. S., & Grant, H. (2008). Self-theories, goals, and meaning. In J. Shah, & W. Gardner (Eds.), *The handbook of motivational science* (pp. 345–371). New York: Guilford.

Earley, P. C., & Erez, M. (1991). Time-dependency effects of goals and norms: The role of cognitive processing on motivational models. *Journal of Applied Psychology*, *76*, 717–724.

Erez, A., & Judge, T. A. (2001). Relationship of core self-evaluations to goal setting, motivation, and performance. *Journal of Applied Psychology, 86*, 1270–1279.

Farh, J. L., Griffeth, R. W., & Balkin, D. B. (1991). Effects of choice of pay plans on satisfaction, goal setting, and performance. *Journal of Organizational Behavior, 12*, 55–62.

Ferguson, M. J. (2008). On becoming ready to pursue a goal you don't know you have: effects of nonconscious goals on evaluative readiness. *Journal of Personality, 95*, 1268–1294.

Fredrickson, B. L. (2009). *Positivity: Discover the ratio that tips your life toward flourishing.* New York: Crown Book.

Fu, F. Q., Richards, K. A., & Jones, E. (2009). The motivation hub: Effects of goal setting and self-efficacy on effort and new product sales. *Journal of Personal Selling and Sales Management, 29*, 277–292.

Gellatly, I. R. (1996). Conscientiousness and task performance: Test of a cognitive process model. *Journal of Applied Psychology, 81*, 474–482.

Guthrie, J. P., & Hollensbe, E. C. (2004). Group incentives and performance: A study of spontaneous goal setting, goal choice and commitment. *Journal of Management, 30*, 263–284.

Heslin, P. A., Latham, G. P., & Vandewalle, D. (2005). The effect of implicit person theory on performance appraisals. *Journal of Applied Psychology, 90*, 842–856.

Hinsz, V. B. (1991). Individual versus group decision making: Social comparison in goals for individual task performance. *Journal of Applied Social Psychology, 21*, 987–1003.

Hinsz, V. B. (1992). Social influences on the goal choices of group members. *Journal of Applied Social Psychology, 22,* 1297–1317.

Hinsz, V. B. (1995). Group and individual decision making for task performance goals: Processes in the establishment of goals in groups. *Journal of Applied Social Psychology, 25*, 353–370.

Hinsz, V. B., Kalnbach, L. R., & Lorentz, N. R. (1997). Using judgmental anchors to establish challenging self-set goals without jeopardizing commitment. *Organizational Behavior and Human Decision Processes, 71*, 287–308.

Holland, R. W., Hendriks, M., & Aarts, H. (2005). Smells like clean spirit. Nonconscious effects of scent on cognition and behavior. *Psychological Science, 16*, 689–693.

Hollenbeck, J. (1987). The effects of individual differences and goal origin on goal setting and performance. *Organizational Behavior and Human Decision Processes, 40*, 392–414.

Hong, Y. Y., Chiu, C. Y., Dweck, C. S., Lin, D. M. S., & Wan, W. (1999). Implicit theories, attributions, and coping: A meaning system approach. *Journal of Personality and Social Psychology, 77*, 588–599.

Ilies, R., & Judge, T. A. (2005). Goal regulation across time: the effects of feedback and affect. *Journal of Applied Psychology, 90*, 453–467.

Judge, T. A., Bono, J. E., Erez, A., & Locke, E. A. (2005). Core self-evaluations and job and life satisfaction: The role of self-concordance and goal attainment. *Journal of Applied Psychology, 90*, 257–268.

Judge, T. A., Locke, E. A., Durham, C. C., & Kluger, A. N. (1998). Dispositional effects on job and life satisfaction: The role of core evaluations. *Journal of Applied Psychology, 83*, 17–34.

Kerr, S. (1975). On the folly of rewarding A, while hoping for B. *The Academy of Management Journal, 18*, 769–783.

Kerr, S. (1999). Organizational rewards: Practical, cost-neutral alternatives that you may know, but don't practice. *Organizational Dynamics, 28*, 67–70.

Kirkpatrick, S. A., & Locke, E. A. (1996). Direct and indirect effects of three core charismatic leadership components on performance and attitudes. *Journal of Applied Psychology*, *81*, 36–51.

Latham, G. P., & Locke, E. A. (2006). Enhancing the benefits and overcoming the pitfalls of goal setting. *Organizational Dynamics*, *35*, 332–340.

Latham, G. P., & Piccolo, R. F. (2012). The effect of context specific versus nonspecific subconscious goals on employee performance. *Human Resource Management, 51*, 511–524.

Latham, G. P., Stajkovic, A. D., & Locke, E. A. (2010). The relevance and viability of subconscious goals in the workplace. *Journal of Management*, *36*, 234–255.

Lee, T. W., Locke, E. A., & Phan, S. H. (1997). Explaining the assigned goal-incentive interaction: The role of self-efficacy and personal goals. *Journal of Management, 23*, 541–559.

Levy, P. E., & Baumgardner, A. H. (1991). Effects of self-esteem and gender on goal choice. *Journal of Organizational Behavior*, *12*, 529–541.

Locke, E. A. (1991). The motivation sequence, the motivation hub, and the motivation core. *Organizational Behavior and Human Decision Processes*, *50*, 288–299.

Locke, E. A. (2004). Linking goals to monetary incentives. *Academy of Management Executive*, *18*, 130–133.

Locke, E. A., & Latham, G. P. (1990). *A theory of goal setting and task performance*. Englewood Cliffs, NJ: Prentice Hall.

Lord, R. G., Diefendorff, J. M., Schmidt, A. M., & Hall, R. J. (2010). Self-regulation at work. In S. T. Fiske (Ed.), *Annual review of psychology* (pp. 543–568). Chippewa Falls, WI: Annual Reviews.

Mone, M. A., Baker, D. D., & Jeffries, F. (1995). Predictive validity and time dependency of self-efficacy, self-esteem, personal goals, and academic performance. *Educational and Psychological Measurement*, *55*, 716–727.

Moussa, F. M. (1996). Determinants of process of the choice of goal difficulty. *Group & Organization Management*, *21*, 414–438.

Moussa, F. M. (2000). Determinants, process, and consequences of personal goals and performance. *Journal of Management*, *26*, 1259–1285.

Payne, S. C., Youngcourt, S. S., & Beaubien, J. M. (2007). A meta-analytic examination of the goal orientation nomological net. *Journal of Applied Psychology*, *92*, 128–150.

Pilegge, A. J., & Holtz, R. (1997). The effects of social identity on the self-set goals and task performance of high and low self-esteem individuals. *Organizational Behavior and Human Decision Processes*, *70*, 17–26.

Podsakoff, P. M., MacKenzie, S. B., & Ahearne, M. (1997). Moderating effects of goal acceptance on the relationship between group cohesiveness and productivity. *Journal of Applied Psychology*, *82*, 974–983.

Richard, E. M., & Diefendorff, J. M. (2011). Self-regulation during a single performance episode: Mood-as-information in the absence of formal feedback. *Organizational Behavior and Human Decision Processes*, *115*, 99–110.

Rodgers, R., & Hunter., J. E. (1991). Impact of management by objectives on organizational productivity. *Journal of Applied Psychology, 76*, 322–336.

Seligman, M. E. P. (2011). Building resilience. *Harvard Business Review*, *89*, 100–106.

Seo, M., & Ilies, R. (2009). The role of self-efficacy, goal, and affect in dynamic motivational self-regulation. *Organizational Behavior and Human Decision Processes*, *109*, 120–133.

Shah, J. (2003). The motivational looking glass: how significant others implicitly affect goal appraisals. *Journal of Personality and Social Psychology, 85,* 424–439.

Shantz, A., & Latham, G. P. (2009). An exploratory field experiment of the effect of subconscious and conscious goals on employee performance. *Organizational Behavior and Human Decision Processes, 109,* 9–17.

Shantz, A., & Latham, G. P. (2011). The effect of primed goals on employee performance: Implications for human resource management. *Human Resource Management, 50,* 289–299.

Stajkovic, A. D., Locke, E. A., & Blair, E. S. (2006). A first examination of the relationships between primed subconscious goals, assigned conscious goals, and task performance. *Journal of Applied Psychology, 91,* 1172–1180.

Stevens, C. K., Bavetta, A. G., & Gist, M. E. (1993). Gender differences in the acquisition of salary negotiation skills: The role of goals, self-efficacy, and perceived control. *Journal of Applied Psychology, 78,* 723–735.

Tolli, A. P., & Schmidt, A. M. (2008). The role of feedback, casual attributions, and self-efficacy in goal revision. *Journal of Applied Psychology, 93,* 692–701.

Tubbs, M. E. (1993). Commitment as a moderator of the goal-performance relation: A case for clearer construct definition. *Journal of Applied Psychology, 78,* 86–97.

Vance, R. J., & Colella, A. (1990). Effects of two types of feedback on goal acceptance and personal goals. *Journal of Applied Psychology, 75,* 68–76.

VandeWalle, D. (1997). Development and validation of a work domain goal orientation instrument. *Educational and Psychological Measurement, 57,* 995–1015.

VandeWalle, D., Cron, W. L., & Slocum, J. W. (2001). The role of goal orientation following performance feedback. *Journal of Applied Psychology, 86,* 629–640.

Williams, K. J., Donovan, J. J., & Dodge, T. L. (2000). Self-regulation of performance: Goal establishment and goal revision processes in athletes. *Human Performance, 13,* 159–180.

Wood, R. E., & Bandura, A. (1989). Impact of conceptions of ability on self-regulatory mechanisms and complex decision making. *Journal of Personality and Social Psychology, 56,* 407–415.

Wright, P. M., & Kacmar, K. M. (1995). Mediating roles of self-set goals, goal commitment, self-efficacy, and attractiveness in the incentive-performance relation. *Human Performance, 8,* 263–296.

# 10 The Role of Self-Efficacy in Goal-Based Motivation

*Albert Bandura* Stanford University

People's beliefs in their capabilities regulate the quality of their functioning through four separable processes: cognitive, motivational, affective, and decisional (Bandura, 1997). In the cognitive mode, self-efficacy beliefs affect whether people think optimistically or pessimistically, in self-enhancing or self-debilitating ways. In the motivational mode, such beliefs influence the goal challenges people set for themselves, how much effort they invest in the endeavor, and their perseverance in the face of difficulties and setbacks. In the affective mode, people's beliefs in their coping capabilities affect the quality of their emotional life and their vulnerability to stress and depression. In the decisional mode, based on beliefs in their capabilities, people set the slate of options they consider the decisions they make, and how well they implement them. The choices made at critical decision points shape the course lives take. The present chapter reviews the effect of self-efficacy on the goals people set for themselves and the strength of their commitment to them. However, before examining the empirical evidence, I will comment briefly on the forms that goals take and the scope of self-efficacy assessment. For linguistic brevity, perceived self-efficacy as a belief in one's capabilities is represented throughout the chapter in a shorter form as self-efficacy.

## Scope of Self-Efficacy Beliefs and Goals

Self-efficacy theory does not subscribe to a decontextualized all-purpose measure of self-efficacy. Given the conditional nature of human behavior, such measures sacrifice explanatory and predictive power (Bandura, 1997, 2012). Assessment of self-efficacy relies on a sound conceptual analysis of the relevant domain of functioning. Knowledge of the activity domain specifies the types of self-efficacy that should be measured. Attainments are the products of multiple determinants. Multicausality requires multidimensional assessment of self-efficacy. Self-management of weight is a good case in point. Weight is determined by eating habits that govern calorie intake, level of exercise that burns calories, and by genetic factors that regulate metabolic processes. Multifactor assessment that includes perceived capability to regulate food purchases, eating habits, and physical exercise provides a more accurate estimate of the contribution of self-efficacy to self-management of weight than if the assessment is confined to eating habits, as is typically the case. In eating disorders, self-efficacy to regulate aversive affective states and to manage troublesome interpersonal relationships, both of which often trigger binge-eating, also come into play (Love, Ollendick, Johnson, & Schlezinger, 1985; Schneider, O'Leary, & Agras, 1987).

Self-efficacy accounts for a larger share of the variance in performance when included as a constellation of theoretically relevant forms of self-efficacy operating in concert than only in partial form (Bandura, Barbaranelli, Caprara, & Pastorelli, 2001; Bandura, Barbaranelli, Gerbino, & Pastorelli, 2003; Bandura, Caprara, Barbaranelli, Pastorelli, & Regalia, 2001). In addition to incomplete assessment, measuring self-efficacy as a decontexualized trait-like factor also detracts from predictiveness.

Many areas of functioning are primarily concerned with self-regulatory efficacy. These take three forms. One form concerns self-efficacy to get oneself to do what one knows how to do. The issue is not whether one can do the activities occasionally but whether one has the efficacy to get oneself to do them regularly in the face of varied dissuading conditions. For example, consider the measurement of perceived self-efficacy to stick to a health-promoting exercise routine. Individuals judge how well they can get themselves to exercise regularly under various impediments, such as when they are under pressure from work, are tired, or are depressed; in foul weather; and when they have other commitments or more interesting things to do. The second self-regulatory form concerns self-efficacy to resist pressures to engage in behavior that violates one's standards, as in antisocial activities or an abstinence goal in addiction behavior. The stronger the perceived self-regulatory efficacy, the higher the success rates in curbing undesired behaviors (Annis & Davis, 1989; Bandura, 1997; Bandura et al., 2003).

The latter two forms of self-regulatory efficacy target established behaviors per se, in one case enhancing desired behaviors and in the other case curbing undesired ones. The third form of self-regulatory efficacy centers on belief in one's capabilities to mobilize the means and resources to produce desired achievements. For example, in research on self-efficacy for self-directed learning, students judged their efficacy to create environments conducive to learning, to plan and organize their academic activities, to use cognitive strategies to gain better understanding and memory of the material being taught, to obtain information and get teachers and peers to help them when needed, to motivate themselves to do their schoolwork, to get themselves to complete scholastic assignments within deadlines, and to pursue academic activities when there are competing interesting things to do. Students registered the highest self-efficacy to manage the content aspects of instruction, but a low sense of efficacy to manage themselves to get their academic activities done. Belief in one's efficacy for academic achievement was grounded in the more generic self-management efficacy. The effect of self-regulatory efficacy on achievement efficacy remained after controlling for ability and past performance (Zimmerman & Bandura, 1994; Zimmerman, Bandura, & Martinez-Pons, 1992). Self-regulatory efficacy assesses the process, whereas self-efficacy for eventual attainment addresses the destination.

Belief in one's learning self-efficacy is another form that is especially relevant to activities oriented toward acquisition of knowledge and skills. Individuals with a strong sense of learning efficacy exploit opportunities to cultivate their knowledge and competencies. Because one learns from mistakes, for those of high learning self-efficacy, errors are informative rather than demoralizing. Schunk and Hanson (1985) examined the contribution to mathematical achievement of children's beliefs in their learning efficacy to acquire arithmetic skills. This form of self-efficacy was varied experimentally by social modeling. Based on perceived similarity, children gained a stronger belief in their learning self-efficacy by observing a peer model than teacher model, even though the same arithmetic operations were modeled in both conditions. The stronger children believed in their learning efficacy, as instilled at the beginning the faster they acquired skills and the higher the proficiency they achieved in the subject matter.

The route to tough goals is often strewn with failures, setbacks, and a host of environmental stressors. These conditions can be highly distressing and cognitively disruptive. Performers begin to doubt their capabilities, and dwell on possible failures and ensuing adverse consequences (Meichenbaum, 1977; Beck, 1976). The inward self-focus detracts from effective management of the task at hand. It is not the aversive rumination per se but the perceived helplessness to turn them off that is the main source of distress (Bandura, 1997; Edwards & Dickerson, 1987). The relevant form of self-efficacy for managing aversive inner life centers on affect regulation and exercise of control over ruminative thinking. Because self-efficacy operates through multiple processes, its relationship with performance is usually partially rather than completely mediated through goals.

Goals are studied most extensively in acquisition of competencies and enhancement of productivity. In these activities, goals are progressively raised as knowledge and skills are acquired and performance challenges are met. In other areas of functioning, goals represent standards of merit that serve as the basis for self-evaluating one's performance. Such standards are typically set relatively high because easy accomplishments hold no interest. The issue is whether self-efficacy affects standards of merit. Research on creative writing indicates that it does (Zimmerman & Bandura, 1994). The stronger the students' beliefs in their self-regulatory efficacy, the higher the quality standard they set for self-satisfaction with their creative performances. Given evidence that self-regulatory efficacy affects quality standards, the nature of this relationship warrants more detailed study.

## Role of Self-Efficacy in the Motivating Potential of Goals

Social cognitive theory posits dual control systems in the regulation of motivation and action. They include proactive discrepancy production operating in concert with reactive discrepancy reduction (Bandura, 1991). People are aspiring and proactive, not just reactive to the shortfalls of their performance. They motivate and guide themselves through proactive control by setting themselves challenging goals and performance standards that create negative discrepancies to be mastered. Reactive feedback control comes into play in the motivation and resources needed to realize the challenging goals. After people attain the goals they have been pursuing, those with high self-efficacy set a higher standard for themselves (Bandura & Cervone, 1986). The adoption of further challenges creates new motivating discrepancies to be mastered.

Goals have been verified as one of the most reliable motivators in countless laboratory and field studies (Locke & Latham, 1990). Social cognitive theory grounds the motivating potential of goals in affective self-reactions to one's performances. Goals motivate by enlisting self-investment in the activity rather than directly. Once people commit themselves to certain goals, they seek self-satisfaction from fulfilling them and intensify their efforts by dissatisfaction with substandard performance. Most any activity can get invested with self-evaluative significance.

The way in which self-efficacy and affective self-reaction operate in concert in goal-based motivation is illustrated in situations in which performances fall short of one's goals. In one such study, individuals were arbitrarily informed that they failed to accomplish an assigned challenging goal (Bandura & Cervone, 1986). Those who were dissatisfied with the substandard performance but judged themselves efficacious to meet the challenge redoubled their efforts (Figure 10.1). Neither dissatisfaction with a low sense

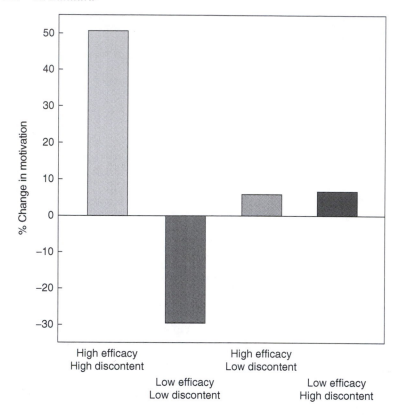

*Figure 10.1* Level of motivation as a function of the joint influence of self-efficacy and discontent with substandard performance. (Drawn from data in Bandura, A., & Cervone, D. (1986). *Organizational Behavior and Human Decision Processes, 38*, 92–113.).

of self-efficacy nor high self-efficacy but being untroubled by deficient performance boosted the level of motivation. Those who judged themselves inefficacious to meet the challenging goal and couldn't care less about their mediocre performance slackened their effort and just coasted along apathetically. These different motivational effects of the same assigned goal were obtained with control for prior performance.

The goals that are motivating are the type that engage self-reactive influences to the match between goals and performance. They include explicitness, level of challenge, and temporal proximity. Explicit goals motivate because they specify the type and amount of effort needed to realize them. Vague goals are too general and noncommitting to arouse any self-reaction. In her stage show, Lily Tomlin provides a familiar example of the ineffectiveness of vague, noncommitting goals. Her character Chrissy never quite manages to get her act together. She says, "I vowed to make something of myself when I grew up." Then she reflects, "I guess I should have been more specific."

Interest and gratifying self-reactions are sparked by challenges. To mountaineers, crawling on slippery rocks in foul weather is not inherently joyful. It is personal triumphs over lofty peaks that rouse exhilaration. Easy goals are unmotivating because they are too easy to attain, so they bring few self-evaluative and social benefits such as pride and job benefits (Mento, Locke, & Klein, 1992). The effectiveness of goals in regulating motivation also depends on how far into the future they are projected. Long-range goals provide the vision of a desired future. However, there are too many competing influences in the present for distant futures to regulate current behavior. It is too easy to put off matters in the present under the illusion that one will have more time later. The temporizing strategy is captured well in the Spanish proverb: "Manana is the busiest day of the week."

Under distant goals, people put off what needs to be done until looming deadlines spur them into a flurry of activity. Nowadays, computers and wireless devices provide, with instant access, a handy limitless source of alluring detours requiring an exercise of self-regulatory efficacy. This boundless electronic environment presents an ever-present strain on goal adherence. Short-term goals provide continuing challenges in the here and now to get one to where one wishes to go. Proximal subgoals that lead to a valued future produce higher accomplishments than distal goals alone (Bandura & Schunk, 1981; Latham & Seijts, 1995; Stock & Cervone, 1990). The performance gains under interim goals are mediated through increases in self-efficacy.

There are several ways in which self-efficacy contributes to the motivating potential of goals (Bandura, 1997). People who are beset with self-doubts about their capabilities do not go around setting challenging goals for themselves and sticking for long in the face of difficulties to the goals they adopted. People's beliefs in their capabilities influence the level of goals they set for themselves. The stronger the self-efficacy, the higher the goals people set for themselves. This positive relationship remains after controlling for ability and past performance (Bandura & Cervone, 1986; Phillips & Gully, 1997; Seo & Ilies, 2009). In addition, self-efficacy beliefs foster strategic thinking, productive enlistment of resources, and perseverance in difficult undertakings (Schunk, 1989; Wood & Bandura, 1989b). Firm belief that one has what it takes to succeed provides the necessary staying power in the face of failures and setbacks. Self-efficacy beliefs affect not only goal levels and resilience in their pursuit, but also the quality standards by which individuals judge the merit of their performance (Zimmerman & Bandura, 1994). Although less often considered in the contribution of self-efficacy to goal-related activities, the self-management of intrusive thinking and disruptive emotional states come into play as well, especially in arduous goal pursuits. Self-regulatory efficacy enables performers to stay on course in the face of tenacious intrapersonal and situation distracters.

## Role of Self-Efficacy in the Effects of Goal Orientations

People's conceptions of intelligence and corresponding goal orientations figure prominently in Carol Dweck's (1991, 2006) theory of motivation. She identifies two mindsets. Some people view intelligence as an inherent ability that is unchangeable. For them achievement tasks carry high threat. Poor performance, having to work hard, and seeking help show that one is not smart. Others view intelligence as an acquirable skill. This is a highly functional mindset because intelligence is viewed as improvable by taking on challenges and developing one's competencies through hard work. The corresponding goal orientations to the two mindsets are performance goals for the inherent group and learning goals for the acquirable one. Individuals who prefer performance goals tend to avoid activities where they may not look good in favor of those they can do well to demonstrate their competence. These self-protective strategies come at the cost of retarding one's skill development. By contrast, those preferring learning goals take advantages of opportunities to enhance their competence. Learning goals generally serve one better than self-hampering performance ones.

To test the mechanisms through which these mindsets produce their effects, Wood and Bandura (1989a) had business graduates manage a complex simulation of an organization. They made managerial decisions for a series of projects with feedback on how well their organization performed. At periodic intervals, we measured their perceived managerial self-efficacy, their organizational goals and the quality of their analytic thinking. Before they began, half of the managers were led to believe that the simulation measured their innate ability for complex decision making. The other half was told that it measured an acquirable skill. They were given tough productivity goals to fulfill. We measured the quality of their functioning over a series of production projects.

Managers in the acquirable skill condition remained resilient in their managerial self-efficacy in the face of difficulties, they set challenging organizational goals, and used efficient analytic strategies. This self-efficacious orientation paid off in high organizational productivity. For managers in the innate ability condition, their self-efficacy plummeted as they encountered problems, they lowered their aspirations for the organization, and because more and more erratic in their analytic thinking. They produced a progressive decline in organizational productivity.

The causal structure was tested by path analysis computed on the combined data from a set of studies using the organizational simulation with a variety of experimental interventions (Wood & Bandura, 1989b). In the initial projects, self-efficacy enhanced organizational performance through its effects on managers' goal setting and analytic strategies, both of which enhanced performance. The causal structure was replicated in the subsequent projects except that the contribution of prior performance was weaker, and managerial self-efficacy played a larger causal role in organizational performance, affecting it both directly as well as through manager's goal setting and analytic strategies. Thus, when initially faced with managing a complex, unfamiliar environment, managers relied on performance information in judging their efficacy and in setting their personal goals. However, as they began to form a self-schema of their self-efficacy through further experience, they based their goal setting on self-efficacy and regulated their performance more strongly and intricately by their view of their self-efficacy.

There is a big difference between performance goal orientation and setting goals for performance. Hampering oneself by playing it safe and avoiding new challenges for fear of looking incompetent stunts self-efficacy development and constricts the acquisition of knowledge and skills. By contrast, setting for oneself performance goals gives direction for one's pursuits and serves as a motivator for performance attainments. The importance of this distinction is verified empirically by Seitz and his collaborators in a comparative test of the influence of goal orientation and goal setting on performance on a complex simulation in which participants sought to increase market share under rapidly evolving changes in the phone business (Seijts, Latham, Tasa, & Latham, 2004). Participants were led to set the challenging learning goal to discover and use a specified number of strategic options or a challenging performance goal to achieve a certain level of market share. Participants' goal orientation predicted performance only under a vague goal to do one's best. Adding a challenging learning goal or a challenging performance goal reduced the effect of learning goal orientation on performance. Self-efficacy and information search mediated the effect of a learning goal on performance.

Potosky and Ramakrishna (2002) examined the mediating role of self-efficacy in learning goals in a field study with employees in an information technology firm with contrasting organizational support for innovation. Under an organizational climate conducive to innovation, the relationships between learning goals and performance was entirely mediated through learning self-efficacy. Organizations that are inhospitable to innovative initiatives that threaten the status quo in how the system is run put a damper on innovativeness. It is perhaps for that reason that a learning goal did not predict performance in such an organizational climate.

Phillips and Gully (1997) found that self-efficacy was positively related to a learning goal orientation, but negatively related to a performance goal orientation aimed at impressing others with what one can do well. The effect of goal orientation on performance was entirely mediated through self-efficacy. Evidence that goal orientation works mainly through self-efficacy carries implication for the locus of change and how to structure interventions for best results. Advocates of the goal orientation approach focus on persuading individuals that ability is acquirable and rewarding effort as the main vehicle of change. This presupposes a supportive environment conducive to change so that effort pays off, otherwise unsuccessful effort can instill a sense of futility. As noted in the study by Potosky and Ramakrishna, in an unsupportive environment a learning orientation alone does not aid performance.

Self-efficacy theory provides a variety of enabling aids for developing a resilient self-efficacy that serves the acquisition of competencies (Bandura, 1997). Some of the efforts are directed at building collective efficacy that enables people to work together to transform inequitable and dysfunctional social systems. Changes in social systems that expand opportunity structures provide substantial leeway for self-development and change.

It should be noted in passing that research into how goal orientations work raises the broader issue of dispositions. Dweck characterizes goal orientations as a mindset, not a dispositional trait (Dweck, 2011). Mindsets are readily teachable and modifiable. However, some researchers treat it as a disposition. After a determinant is elevated to a disposition, it is invested with generalized power that allegedly regulates behavior regardless of time, situational conditions, and activity domains. Because of the generalized conception, dispositional traits are typically measured with decontextualized items that mask significant variability in behavior. Therefore, decentralization sacrifices predictiveness (Bandura, 2012; Bing, Whanger, Davison, & VanHook, 2004; Hunthausen, Truxillo, Bauer, & Hammer, 2003; Schmit, Ryan, Stierwalt, & Powell, 1995). It does so because people do not behave in an unconditional way. Indeed, human behavior is socially situated, richly contextualized, and conditionally manifested. The conception of disposition in social cognitive theory as conditional (Bandura, 1999; Mischel & Shoda, 1999) is in keeping with the empirical evidence. Dweck's conception of goal orientation is in accord with the latter view. A learning orientation is not a monolithic dispositional trait. One and the same individual can view ability as acquirable in a given activity domain and as innate in another. For example, women whose self-efficacy for quantitative and technical activities is socially undermined (Bandura, 1997) are likely to view linguistic ability as acquirable but mathematical ability as largely inherent.

## Disconnect of Self-Efficacy from Goals in Affective Disorders

Conditions that disconnect self-efficacy from stringent self-set goals can give rise to affective disorders. Depression, which touches most everyone from time to time, is a good example. In a laboratory test, students performed a cognitive task allegedly indicative of innate intelligence and were led to believe that they fell far short of an improvement goal compared to their peers (Bandura & Abrams, 1986). Those who had a high sense of efficacy to fulfill the goal and continued to strive for it had no adverse emotional reactions to the apparent failure. Those who judged themselves inefficacious to realize the goal and abandoned it responded apathetically. Those who continued to demand of themselves attainment of the goal but were beset with self-doubt in their capability to do so reacted despondently.

Kanfer and Zeiss (1983) further verify that self-demanding standards of worth with perceived inefficacy to fulfill them is conducive to depression. Here the goal is to live up to a performance standard of self-worth. People rated their perceived social self-efficacy to manage interpersonal relationships in occupational, social, and familial transactions. They also rated the minimal standard of performance with which they would be self-satisfied. Depressed and nondepressed individuals did not differ in the self-evaluative standards they set for themselves. Rather, they differed in the discrepancy between their self-efficacy and their standards. For the nondepressed, their standards were congruent with their self-efficacy. For the depressed, their self-efficacy fell far short of the standards by which they judge their worthiness. Belief in one's inefficacy to fulfill what is minimal for a sense of self-worth can create a life plagued with despondency.

It remains to be determined how self-evaluative standards get disconnected from self-efficacy in an emotionally perturbing way. A case report by Jackson (1972) sheds some light on how detrimental child-rearing practices may do so. The case involved a young woman who suffered from chronic depression, self-disparagement, and feelings of unworthiness that proved refractory to traditional psychotherapy. She was raised by a hypercritical mother who imposed on her stringent standards of self-worth, but undermined her efficacy to fulfill them. She constantly lectured to her on her shortcomings and compared her unfavorably with others. A program of realistic performance goals with self-reward for fulfilling or surpassing them raised the client's level of positive self-regard with an accompanying decline in depression. The client spontaneously generalized the self-enhancing practices to different aspects of her life. In a follow-up assessment, positive self-regard rooted in realistic goals supplanted depression. The notion that imposing stringent standards while deflating self-efficacy to fulfill them is depressogenic calls for systematic study.

Continued progress in a valued activity does not necessarily bring self-satisfaction. Simon (1979) demonstrated that the pace of attainments can drastically alter self-evaluative reactions to one's performance attainments. Accomplishments that surpass earlier ones bring a continued sense of self-satisfaction. However, people derive little satisfaction from smaller accomplishments, or even devalue them after having made larger strides. People who are prone to depression display even greater affective reactivity to their rate of progress. They are more self-satisfied with accelerating strides, but they find little satisfaction in modest improvements after large attainments. This is a possible consequence of early extraordinary accomplishments.

Individuals who experience spectacular early successes often find themselves wrestling with self-doubt and despondency if their later work falls short of their earlier triumphs. The playwright Arthur Miller was haunted by this comparative self-devaluation problem because his later works never measured up to his acclaimed first play, *Death of a Salesman*. The Nobel Laureate Linus Pauling prescribed the absolute remedy for the woes of belittling self-comparison. When asked what one does after winning a Nobel Prize, he replied, "Change fields, of course!" It remains to be determined how self-efficacy, goal setting, and the relationship between these two determinants change over the temporal pattern of accomplishments and the effects these determinants have on self-satisfaction and productivity.

## Concluding Remarks

The present chapter reviewed the role of self-efficacy as a determinant of goals and as a mediator of their effects. These functional relationships were examined within the context of different types of self-efficacy conceptually linked to the multicausality of behavior. The review also examined the relation between self-efficacy and a broadened conception of goals that encompasses the standards people strive to live up to. This extension expands the scope of goal theory.

## References

Annis, H. M., & Davis, C. S. (1989). Relapse prevention. In R. K. Hester & W. R. Miller (Eds.), *Handbook of alcoholism treatment approaches: Effective alternatives* (pp. 170–182). New York: Pergamon.

Bandura, A. (1991). Self-regulation of motivation through anticipatory and self-reactive mechanisms. In R. A. Dienstbier (Ed.), *Perspectives on motivation: Nebraska symposium on motivation* (Vol. 38, pp. 69–164). Lincoln: University of Nebraska Press.

Bandura, A. (1997). *Self-efficacy: The exercise of control.* New York: Freeman.

Bandura, A. (1999). A social cognitive theory of personality. In L. Pervin & O. John (Ed.), *Handbook of personality* (2nd ed., pp. 154–196). New York: Guilford Publications.

Bandura, A. (2012). On the functional properties of self-efficacy revisited. *Journal of Management, 18*, 9–44.

Bandura, A., & Abrams, K. (1986). Self-regulatory mechanisms in motivating, apathetic, and despondent reactions to unfulfilled standards. Manuscript, Stanford University, Stanford, CA.

Bandura, A., Barbaranelli, C., Caprara, G. V., & Pastorelli, C. (2001). Self-efficacy beliefs as shapers of children's aspirations and career trajectories. *Child Development, 72*, 187–206.

Bandura, A., Caprara, G. V., Barbaranelli, C., Gerbino, M. G., & Pastorelli, C. (2003). Role of affective self-regulatory efficacy in diverse spheres of psychosocial functioning. *Child Development, 74*, 769–782.

Bandura, A., Caprara, G. V., Barbaranelli, C., Pastorelli, C., & Regalia, C. (2001). Sociocognitive self-regulatory mechanisms governing transgressive behavior. *Journal of Personality and Social Psychology, 80*, 125–135.

Bandura, A., & Cervone, D. (1986). Differential engagement of self-reactive influences in cognitive motivation. *Organizational Behavior and Human Decision Processes, 38*, 92–113.

Bandura, A., & Schunk, D. H. (1981). Cultivating competence, self-efficacy, and intrinsic interest through proximal self-motivation. *Journal of Personality and Social Psychology, 41*, 586–598.

Beck, A. T. (1976). *Cognitive therapy and the emotional disorders.* New York: International Universities Press.

Bing, M. N., Whanger, J. C., Davison, H. K., & VanHook, J. B. (2004). Incremental validity of the frame-of-reference effect in personality scale scores: A replication and extension. *Journal of Applied Psychology, 89*, 150–157.

Dweck, C. S. (1991). Self-theories and goals: Their role in motivation, personality and development. In R. Dienstbier (Ed)., *Nebraska symposium on motivation*, (Vol. 38, pp. 199–235). Lincoln, Nebraska: University of Nebraska Press.

Dweck, C. S. (2006). *Mindset: The new psychology of success.* New York: Random House.

Dweck, C. S. (2011). Personal communication.

Edwards, S., & Dickerson, M. (1987). On the similarity of positive and negative intrusions. *Behaviour Research and Therapy, 25*, 207–211.

Hunthausen, J. M., Truxillo, D. M., Bauer, T. N., & Hammer, L. B. (2003). A field study of frame-of-reference effects on personality test validity. *Journal of Applied Psychology, 88*, 545–551.

Jackson, B. (1972). Treatment of depression by self-reinforcement. *Behavior Therapy, 3*, 298–207.

Kanfer, R., & Zeiss, A. M. (1983). Depression, interpersonal standard-setting, and judgments of self-efficacy. *Journal of Abnormal Psychology, 92*, 319–329.

Latham, G. P., & Seijts, G. H. (1995). The effects of proximal and distal goals on performance on a moderately complex task. *Journal of Organizational Behavior, 20*, 421–429.

Locke, E. A., & Latham, G. P. (1990). *A theory of goal setting and task performance.* Englewood Cliffs, NJ: Prentice-Hall.

Love, S. Q., Ollendick, T. H., Johnson, C., & Schlezinger, S. E. (1985). A preliminary report of the prediction of bulimic behavior: A social learning analysis. *Bulletin of the Society of Psychologists in Addictive Behavior, 4*, 93–101.

Meichenbaum, D. H. (1977). *Cognitive-behavior modification: An integrative approach.* New York: Plenum Press.

Mento, A. J., Locke, E. A., & Klein, H. J. (1992). Relationship of goal level to valence and instrumentality. *Journal of Applied Psychology, 77*, 395–405.

Mischel, W., & Shoda, Y. (1999). *Integrating dispositions and processing dynamics within a unified theory of personality: The cognitive-affective personality system.* In L. Pervin & D. John (pp. 197–218). New York: Gilford Press.

Phillips, J. M., & Gully, S. M. (1997). Role of goal orientation, ability, need for achievement, and locus of control in the self-efficacy and goal-setting process. *Journal of Applied Psychology, 82*, 792–802.

Potosky, D., & Ramakrishna, H. V. (2002). The moderating role of updating climate perceptions in the relationship between goal orientation, self-efficacy, and job performance. *Human Performance, 15*, 275–297.

Schneider, J. A., O'Leary, A., & Agras, W. S. (1987). The role of perceived self-efficacy in recovery from bulimia: A preliminary examination. *Behaviour Research and Therapy, 25,* 429–432.

Schunk, D. H. (1989). Self-efficacy and cognitive skill learning. In C. Ames and R. Ames (Eds.), *Research on motivation in education: Goals and cognitions* (Vol. 3, pp. 13–44). San Diego: Academic.

Schunk, D. H., & Hanson, A. R. (1985). Influence of peer-model attributes on children's beliefs and learning. *Journal of Educational Psychology, 81*, 431–434.

Schmit, M. J., Ryan, A. M., Stierwalt, S. L., & Powell, S. L. (1995). Frame-of-reference effects on personality scores and criterion-related validity. *Journal of Applied Psychology, 80*, 607–620.

Seijts, G. H., Latham, G. P., Tasa, K., & Latham, B. W. (2004). Goal setting and goal orientation: An integration of two different yet related literatures. *Academy of Management Journal, 47*, 227–239.

Seo, M., & Ilies, R. (2009). The role of self-efficacy, goal, and affect in dynamic motivational self-regulation, organizational behavior, and human decision processes. *Organizational Behavior and Human Decision Processes, 109*, 120–133.

Simon, K. M. (1979). *Effects of self comparison, social comparison, and depression on goal setting and self-evaluative reactions.* Unpublished manuscript, Stanford University, Stanford CA.

Stock, J., & Cervone, D. (1990). Proximal goal-setting and self-regulatory processes. *Cognitive Therapy and Research, 14*, 483–498.

Wood, R. E., & Bandura, A. (1989a). Impact of conceptions of ability on self-regulatory mechanisms and complex decision making. *Journal of Personality and Social Psychology, 56*, 407–415.

Wood, R., & Bandura, A. (1989b). Social cognitive theory of organizational management. *Academy of Management Review, 14*, 361–384.

Zimmerman, B. J., Bandura, A., & Martinez-Pons, M. (1992). Self-motivation for academic attainment: The role of self-efficacy beliefs and personal goal-setting. *American Educational Research Journal, 29*, 663–676.

Zimmerman, B., & Bandura, A. (1994). Impact of self-regulatory factors on writing course attainment. *American Educational Research Journal, 31*, 845–862.

# 11 Goals and Self-Regulation

## Emerging Perspectives across Levels and Time

*David V. Day*  Winthrop Professor, Woodside Chair in Leadership
and Management, University of Western Australia
Business School

*Kerrie L. Unsworth*  Professor, University of Western Australia
Business School

There has been extensive interest in and research activity on the general topic of goals and self-regulation in the 20 years since the publication of the breakthrough theory of goal-setting and task performance (Locke & Latham, 1990). The purpose of this chapter is to provide a focused update on advancement in the topics of self-regulation/ self-management as they pertain to goal setting since 1990. It is an interesting historical note that the topics of self-regulation and self-management covered only three pages in the Locke and Latham book; however, the amount of research that has been published on these topics directly and indirectly in the intervening time is impressive. Given the sheer volume of available research, it is not possible to review every published study. Instead, we will focus on research that we consider to be noteworthy, especially as they forge new areas of understanding. In addition, we broaden the focus from the effects of goals and self-regulation on task (or job) performance to also address areas associated with long-term development, learning, and individual change.

Before reviewing this recent research, brief attention needs to be given to construct clarification issues. There are several related concepts used in the literature, sometimes interchangeably. *Self-control* can be considered a foundational construct as much of the early theory and research in the field adopted that label, as well as being linked with other key processes such as self-efficacy (Bandura, 1997). According to pioneers in the area (Thoresen & Mahoney, 1974), self-control is demonstrated when an individual engages in behavior that originally had lower probability than that of a more desirable behavior in the absence of immediate external constraint or encouragement. As such, the focus is on the external application of control mechanisms to engage in behaviors that are thought to lead to better (e.g., healthier or more productive) outcomes. F.H. Kanfer (1980) portrayed self-control as a specialized case of self-management, whereas others have associated it with conscious impulse control (e.g., Vohs & Baumeister, 2004).

*Self-regulation* is the most widely used term referring to various processes involved in attaining and maintaining regular goals, where goals are internally represented desired states (Vancouver & Day, 2005). It has been noted that self-regulation is implicit in goal setting theory because "the setting of goals and their translation into action is a volitional process" (Latham & Locke, 1991, p. 233). *Self-management* is a highly similar term that pertains to individual efforts to exert control over specific aspects of decision making and behavior (Frayne & Geringer, 2000). Others have conceptualized self-management in terms of self-influence processes targeted at meeting standards and objectives (i.e., goals) that are externally set (Manz, 1991). *Self-leadership* is also considered to be a self-influence process and set of strategies that address what is to be done (e.g., standards and objectives), why it is to be done (e.g., strategic analysis), and how it is to be done, incorporating intrinsic motivation and a focus on cognitive processes (Manz, 1991). Thus, self-leadership is considered by proponents of the construct to be more encompassing than self-management in terms of the influence over the what, how, and why of work using both intrinsic and extrinsic incentives (Stewart, Courtright, & Manz, 2011). Critics, on the other hand, might see the term *self-leadership* as somewhat misleading, given that leadership usually involves leading others rather than oneself.

Nonetheless, these are not discrete construct categories; rather, they range along an implicit continuum from behavior that is mainly externally managed (self-control), to how individuals regulate or manage the way in which particular tasks are carried out (self-regulation and self-management), to incorporate what should be done and why it should be done (self-leadership; Stewart et al., 2011). The focus of the present review will be on the middle range of this proposed continuum, in which we use self-regulation and self-management interchangeably (with a preference for the former, which is consistent with the literature; Karoly, 1993; Lord, Diefendorff, Schmidt, & Hall, 2010). An additional distinction is that we will focus on the self-regulation and self-management processes mainly of individuals. Although the terms self-management and self-leadership are applied increasingly to teams as well as to individuals (Stewart et al., 2011), other chapters in this volume address goal setting processes in groups and at the macro level of analysis (see Chapters 15 and 17).

## Goals and Self-Regulation: What Is New?

Self-regulation involves four key processes: (a) Goal *establishment* (adopting, adapting, or rejecting a goal), (b) *planning* (processes involved in preparing to pursue a goal), (c) *striving* (moving toward or maintaining a goal), and (d) *revision* (processes involved in changes or disengagement from a goal; Austin & Vancouver, 1996). Research on self-regulation focuses on constructs that are thought to predict or influence these key processes (Vancouver & Day, 2005). The available research on these various related processes and constructs is truly voluminous, which is why the present review will focus on new and emerging trends in the literature. More comprehensive treatments can be found in the following reviews.

Since the publication of the 1990 book by Locke and Latham, there have been a number of reviews on core self-regulation topics published in major outlets, including a summary of 35 years of empirical research on goal setting theory (Locke & Latham, 2002). These include reviews of the self-regulation literature (Baumeister & Vohs, 2004; Karoly, 1993; Lord et al., 2010; R. Kanfer, 2005; Vancouver & Day, 2005; Wood, 2005), self-regulated learning (Sitzmann & Ely, 2011), and self-regulatory processes (e.g., Austin & Vancouver, 1996; Diefendorff & Lord, 2008; Sonnentag, 2002).

One particular issue that has yet to be comprehensively addressed, however, is the recognition that self-regulation processes occur over time, and relatedly, at different levels of abstraction (Lord et al., 2010). Lower levels of abstraction in which a goal is attempted and feedback is received quickly may involve just a few minutes or hours. Conversely, setting and managing goals and other resources to acquire expert-level performance may take years or even decades to achieve (Ericsson, Krampe, & Tesch-Römer, 1993). But the key issue is that a fuller consideration of time as well as levels of abstraction appears to add another layer of richness to understanding self-regulation processes.

Research on Locke and Latham's (2002) goal setting theory has shown that setting specific and difficult goals increases performance on over 100 different tasks across more than 40,000 participants with time spans ranging from 1 minute to 25 years. This is clearly a remarkable record of empirical support for the theory. And what may even be more remarkable is that researchers continue to uncover interesting and novel—and controversial—effects with further consideration of time. A big part of this discovery has come about through the development, availability, and application of multilevel modeling procedures (e.g., Raudenbush & Bryk, 2002) and computational modeling (Vancouver, Weinhardt, & Schmidt, 2010) that, among other things, allow researchers to accurately estimate within- and between-person changes over time. The implications of these advancements can be seen in the recent literature on self-efficacy.

### Self-Efficacy over Time

One of the most important constructs in predicting self-regulation processes and performance outcomes is self-efficacy, which is the belief in one's capacity to perform a particular behavior or a certain level in a task (Bandura, 1986). Self-efficacy is target specific and therefore varies across tasks. In general, self-efficacy enhances goal commitment (Locke & Latham, 2002) and is positively related to task performance; however, this has been mainly tested using cross-sectional and correlational research designs. Thus, an important question is whether the between-person effects of self-efficacy are similar to within-person effects over time. The answer to this question is surprising and has proved to be quite provocative.

Across a series of longitudinal, repeated measures studies, researchers have noted that self-efficacy may be related to overconfidence in one's ability and thus show a negative relationship with task performance when estimated as a longitudinal, within-person effect (Vancouver & Kendall, 2006; Vancouver, Thompson, Tischner, & Putka, 2002; Vancouver, Thompson, & Williams, 2001). In particular, overconfidence associated with heightened self-efficacy has been shown to result in an increased likelihood of committing logical errors on a task where feedback does not facilitate task mastery. It is also possible that with heightened self-efficacy, there is a tendency to "coast" or not put forth as much effort in goal-striving activities over time as those with lower confidence levels. Although high self-efficacy individuals are still better overall performers than those with lower self-efficacy (between-person comparison), when the level of analysis is within-person, the relationship between self-efficacy and task performance has been shown to be negative in some studies. It is important to keep in mind that these findings do not negate or otherwise invalidate those studies showing strong self-efficacy–performance relationships between individuals. Instead, these findings highlight the potential importance of incorporating time in the study of self-regulation processes both between and within individuals (also see Yeo & Neal, 2006) as well as distinguishing between tasks with different levels of possible mastery.

In terms of controversy, it is important to note that the negative effects of self-efficacy on dynamic self-regulation and performance have not been found in every published study. Seo and Ilies (2009) found that self-efficacy was positively related to effort and performance over time, and that goal level partially mediated the relationship between efficacy and performance. One issue to consider in attempting to make sense of these inconsistent results is the nature of the task, especially because some of the earlier work has been criticized for using "trivial research tasks" (Bandura, 2012). Seo and Ilies, on the other hand, developed and ran an Internet-based stock investment simulation over 20 consecutive business days, with participants starting with a bankroll of $10,000 in hypothetical cash. The overarching objective was to invest in ways to grow this bankroll to be as large as possible, in which real cash was awarded based on an algorithm associated with investment gains. Thus, the task was thought to be complex and difficult, as well as very engaging to participants (although it might have also encouraged more than the usual amount of risk taking). Whereas a number of the dynamic self-regulation studies have used relatively simple or sterile laboratory tasks, at least one found the negative effects for self-efficacy over time using exam scores as the outcome (Vancouver & Kendall, 2006). Presumably, scores on course exams would be of keen interest to students.

Adding to the controversial nature of this line of research, the studies finding negative effects for self-efficacy on performance over time have been roundly criticized on theoretical, methodological, and empirical grounds (Bandura, 2012). In particular, Bandura criticized this dynamic self-efficacy research in terms of having a deficient assessment of self-efficacy, using trivial research tasks, having a lack of variance in goals for testing performance effects, failing to measure key mediators, not including goal comparator mechanisms, among other things. A recent response to these criticisms by one of the original authors (Vancouver, 2012) suggests that the debate regarding the longitudinal within-person effects for self-efficacy on goal striving and performance will likely continue for some time.

Putting aside the effects of self-efficacy on performance over time, other research has examined how manipulated performance feedback affects self-efficacy and goal revision over time (see also Chapter 5). In an experimental laboratory study (Tolli & Schmidt, 2008), support was found for the hypothesized model in which performance feedback and causal attributions interacted in influencing self-efficacy, which subsequently influenced goal revision. The important role of self-efficacy in the dynamic goal revision process across time has long been assumed but apparently never been formally evaluated. This adds further complexity to the picture with regard to self-efficacy, self-regulation, and performance over time; however, these studies taken together further emphasize the importance of self-efficacy as a causal construct in goal setting research.

### Feedback over Time

Research has also examined self-regulation across time and across studies, with a particular focus on feedback. It has been argued that people need feedback for goals to be effective; otherwise it may not be possible to adjust their effort or performance strategies (Locke & Latham, 2002). Thus, feedback is an important construct to study with regard to goal setting and self-regulation. In a repeated-measures laboratory study, the role of feedback and affect were examined, with results suggesting that participants adjusted goals in a downward manner following negative feedback but raised goals in creating positive goal-performance discrepancies after receiving positive feedback (Ilies & Judge, 2005). This research also demonstrated that participants' positive/negative affect mediated the feedback–goal relationship within individuals.

## Goal Revision

Most of the research discussed thus far has been conducted in laboratory settings using experimental designs. These are powerful approaches for assessing causal relationships; however, it is important to understand self-regulation processes "in the wild" as well. In a longitudinal study, the effects of goal-performance discrepancies on goal establishment and revision were studied with men and women track and field athletes ($N = 25$) across the course of a competitive season (Williams, Donovan, & Dodge, 2000). Results indicated that the majority of the athletes created positive goal-performance discrepancies by setting initial goals higher than their previous best performance, with goal revision during the season used to maintain rather than reduce or eliminate goal discrepancies. In subsequent research with a larger number of athletes ($N = 100$), it was found that goal-performance discrepancies predicted the amount of goal revision engaged in by the athletes (Donovan & Williams, 2003). Large discrepancies and a failure to achieve goals were associated with lowered proximal (competition) and distal (season) goals. Significant moderators were noted with regard to attributions of stable causes and the particular time of the season. That is, the relationships between goal-performance discrepancies and goal revision (both proximal and distal) were stronger when individuals attributed performance to stable rather than unstable causes, and when examined during the second half of the season. As noted in the studies on dynamic self-regulation and performance, the role of time was shown again to be an important factor in the self-regulation process.

Also investigating self-regulation processes in field settings, the process of goal revision and effort allocation were studied over a single, relatively lengthy performance episode (exam preparation) in which no formal feedback was provided (Richard & Diefendorff, 2011). Using a daily diary methodology and growth curve modeling, the researchers found that the daily goal (the outcome) showed a curvilinear trend in which it was stable and relatively high near the beginning of preparations but declined steeply as the exam approached. Daily effort showed just the opposite pattern: low and stable near the beginning and increasing dramatically as the exam date approached. Given that no formal feedback was provided, a particular concern was how did participants gauge their progress toward their exam performance goal over time?

Based on the mood-as-information model (Schwarz & Clore, 1983), Richard and Diefendorff (2011) proposed that participants used information about their current affective state (i.e., mood) as diagnostic information about progress toward their exam goal. The results of within-person growth modeling found that, as hypothesized, there was a positive relationship between state positive affect on goal revision and a negative relationship between state negative affect on goal revision. Positive moods were associated with setting more difficult goals, whereas negative moods were associated with revising goals downward over time. These results suggest that in everyday situations in which formal performance feedback is unavailable, individuals will use other personal information such as their mood in assessing progress toward important goals and engage in self-regulatory behaviors based on this informal feedback.

It can be seen from this overview that the role of time is clearly important in self-regulation and goal processes. Furthermore, self-efficacy may play different roles when looking at one individual across time compared to the traditional between-persons perspective (although see Bandura, in press). Feedback and goal revision by definition imply a temporal component. Research is emerging that examines the predictors and moderators of these processes over time. On the other hand, what is striking is the relative lack of research on goal disengagement. Again, the temporal dimension is a key to understanding when and why individuals—particularly employees and older adults—disengage from their goals. We strongly urge researchers to fully examine this final stage in the self-regulatory process.

## Self-Management Training

Besides its extensive empirical support, a particular strength of goal setting theory is that it has many possible practical applications. We will present in this section a brief review of several high-quality studies that have examined different forms of self-management training on performance-related outcomes at work and school. The point has been made that everyone practices self-management, but not everyone is an effective self-manager (Karoly, 1993; Locke & Latham, 2002). So what does it take to enhance the effectiveness of individual self-management? One possible option is to provide self-management training.

In general, training in self-management teaches people how to (a) assess problems, (b) set specific and difficult goals in relation to those problems, (c) monitor how situational factors facilitate or impede goal attainment, and (d) identify and administer reinforcement for goal striving and attainment (Frayne & Geringer, 1994). Early studies of self-management training demonstrated their effects in increasing attendance, compared to a control group, up to nine months following training (Frayne & Latham, 1987; Latham & Frayne, 1989). Related to the findings from these studies, an especially noteworthy test of self-management training for improving the job performance of insurance salesmen adopted a control-group field experiment with a reversal design (Frayne & Geringer, 2000). Results showed that, compared with a control condition, training in self-management skills (i.e., self-awareness, goal-setting, self-monitoring, and self-evaluation) significantly improved job performance assessed objectively (e.g., calls made, policies sold, revenue generated) and subjectively (e.g., performance appraisal ratings). The authors suggested that self-management training offers the potential for achieving improved development and use of human resources in organizations. This recommendation needs to be considered in light of other research on self-management training that examined its effectiveness for individual performance across different types of work teams (Uhl-Bien & Graen, 1998). This study found that within a functional team environment (i.e., discipline sections), individuals' use of self-management strategies (e.g., self-assessment, goal-setting, self-rehearsal, self-observation and evaluation, and self-reinforcement) was associated with increased ratings of team performance and team dynamics; but in a cross-functional team environment, the use of such individually focused strategies was not related to higher team performance. Thus, this cross-sectional study suggests that there may be some potential boundary conditions (i.e., moderators) with self-management training, but it is important to note that it was not a field experiment.

On the other hand, a number of experimental field studies have been conducted. For instance, employees from five banks were randomly assigned to a self-management training condition or a waiting-list control condition (Pattni, Soutar, & Klobas, 2007). The results indicated that the training group significantly improved both their self-reported self-management behaviors (i.e., self-observation, goal-setting, self-monitoring, self-evaluation, and self-reinforcement) and their self-efficacy at 4 weeks and 24 weeks following the training; however, there were no differences between the supervisor-rated performance of the training group and the control group over time.

In two studies, a two-stage training program targeted at enhancing the effectiveness of participants' salary negotiation skills was used to compare goal setting training with self-management training. Specifically, the two-stage design was used to evaluate effects beyond goal-setting alone in training participants to identify obstacles and ways to overcome them (Stevens, Bavetta, & Gist, 1993): The goal-setting training focused specifically on the processes and principles of goal setting, while the self-management training covered, in addition to goal-setting, developing plans for overcoming obstacles to success, self-monitoring, and self-reinforcement. In the first study, whereas both supplementary training interventions improved salary negotiations, self-management training was needed to get the female negotiators to the same level as the males. The type of supplemental training did not matter for the male negotiators—both types were equally effective (Stevens et al., 1993). In a similar study, those with initially low to medium self-efficacy were able to use the negotiation training to improve their salaries when they underwent self-management training as well, while those with initially high self-efficacy benefited most from additional goal setting training (Gist, Stevens, & Bavetta, 1992). Thus, in salary negotiation contexts, gender and self-efficacy may moderate the effectiveness of self-management training compared to training in goal-setting techniques alone.

Morin and Latham (2000) conducted a field experiment investigating whether mental practice combined with goal setting would enhance the transfer of training back to the job and improve observed communication behavior. The sample consisted of supervisors and process engineers ($N = 41$) employed in a Canadian pulp and paper mill participating in a one-day training workshop. Results, measured six months after training, demonstrated that self-efficacy was significantly higher for the supervisors who engaged in either mental practice or mental practice combined with goal setting as compared with goal setting alone or a no-treatment control group. Self-efficacy correlated significantly with goal commitment and on-the-job communication skills. In addition, improved communication behavior was observed only for those supervisors who received mental practice training or that training plus goal setting. No change in communication behavior was noted for supervisors who set goals but did not engage in mental practice or were assigned to the control group.

Also using a field experimental design, researchers implemented a computerized goal setting and self-regulation program for students experiencing academic difficulties in college (Morisano, Hirsh, Peterson, Pihl, & Shore, 2010). Students with academic difficulties were recruited and randomly assigned to either a goal setting and self-regulation intervention or to a control task group with intervention-quality face validity. After four months, the students in the intervention group displayed significant improvements in academic performance, measured in terms of grade point average, compared with the control group participants. Given that approximately 25% of university students never complete their degree, this intervention shows considerable promise as a relatively quick, inexpensive, and effective program for struggling college students.

A specific type of self-management training, called verbal self-guidance (VSG), was examined across two separate studies. VSG is a classroom-based training program that is targeted at raising the self-efficacy of participants using a number of different techniques (e.g., positive self-talk, skills training, modeling, and practice). In one study, VSG was targeted to improve self-efficacy for employment interviews among Native North American (i.e., indigenous) participants (Latham & Budworth, 2006). Classrooms were randomly assigned to either the VSG or control conditions, and the employment interview performance on which participants were assessed was "for a job in a retail organization" (p. 519). Both self-efficacy and interview performance were significantly higher in the VSG as compared to the control condition.

The second VSG study examined the effects of a four-day program for Turkish women over the age of 40 with regard to re-employment outcomes (Yanar, Budworth, & Latham, 2009). A randomized experimental design with a control group was used. As hypothesized, those women in the VSG treatment group reported higher levels of self-efficacy for re-employment, greater job search behavior, and marginally higher levels ($p < .08$) of securing employment. Although the sample sizes in the two recent VSG studies are relatively small (total $N = 66$ and 55, respectively), the rigorous experimental designs allow for straightforward causal inferences to be made with regard to VSG training effectiveness.

One particular challenge to the various results discussed in this section is that it is not completely clear which aspects (or combinations) of these multifaceted training programs are driving their respective effectiveness (Vancouver & Day, 2005). Nonetheless, it could be that it is this "package," going beyond goal setting on its own, that creates these effects (e.g., Azrin, 1977; Rousseau, 1997). Regardless, we agree with the assessment that "few would argue the tremendous impact that [self-management] research findings ... have had on the development of managerial practices designed to enhance work motivation through goal setting and the provision of developmental feedback" (R. Kanfer, 2005, p. 189).

## Goals and Self-Regulation in Other Domains

In this section, we examine aspects of self-regulation as they pertain to emerging areas of interest involving issues of higher levels of abstraction and longer cycle times (Lord et al., 2010) as compared with typical laboratory studies of goals and self-regulation. Specifically, issues related to self-regulation across the lifespan, identity and self-regulation, and self-regulated learning are briefly reviewed (see also Chapter 27).

## Self-Regulation across the Lifespan

Perhaps one of the most important aspects of self-regulation is in enhancing well-being and "successful aging" across the lifespan. The notion of successful aging has been the focus of research for over 20 years. It is based on fundamental self-regulation processes associated with prioritizing goals (*selection*) according to their importance for increasing gains (*optimization*) and managing or avoiding losses (*compensation*). The overall strategy associated with successful aging is that of maximizing gains and minimizing losses (Baltes, 1997; Baltes & Baltes, 1990). This general model has been termed the selection–optimization–compensation (SOC) approach to lifespan development. A somewhat different way of conceptualizing this process is one of successful aging through the effective management of resources across the lifespan (Freund, 2008). When presented in this form, the connection between self-regulation and successful aging is readily apparent. Because readers who are interested in general goal setting research and theory may not be as familiar with this research from lifespan developmental psychology, a brief review of several key studies that have tested aspects of SOC are presented (also see Heckhausen, Wrosch, & Schulz, 2010, for a review of the empirical evidence on a related approach to motivation across the lifespan).

A basic and important concern with any model is in measuring its underlying processes. An early study in the SOC research program examined self-reported levels of the various processes and correlated them with subjective indicators of successful aging (Freund & Baltes, 1998). Results suggested that those who reported using SOC processes had higher scores on the indicators of successful aging associated with subjective well-being, positive emotions, and the absence of feelings of loneliness. These relationships were found to hold even after controlling for other measures associated with successful mastery such as intelligence, personality (neuroticism, extraversion, and openness to experience), control beliefs, subjective health, and age. Although causality cannot be inferred given the correlational nature of the research design, the findings provided preliminary support of a positive association between SOC processes and aspects of successful aging.

A subsequent study by the same pair of authors examined the construct validity of a 48-item SOC self-report questionnaire (Freund & Baltes, 2002). Results suggested acceptable psychometric properties for the measure (e.g., factor structure, retest reliability, criterion-related validity) as well as age-based predictions that supported the general SOC model perspective. Overall, the results from these studies (Freund & Baltes, 1998, 2002) suggest that the SOC model and its measure have the potential to enhance a deeper understanding of how people regulate goals across the lifespan and why this is an important concern.

A key tenet in the SOC model is that there are age-related differences in goal focus when it comes to optimization versus compensation. Specifically, whereas younger adults are generally on a trajectory of growth or gains in resources, older adults experience increased losses as they age. These differences should result in younger adults attempting to accumulate resources (increasing gain) and older adults focusing on minimizing losses (avoiding loss). It is important to note that both younger and older adults focus on goals to some degree on both optimization and compensation, but the relative amount or importance of this focus is expected to differ systematically by age. This assumption was tested across four studies comparing the goal focus of younger versus older adults on a sensorimotor task (Freund, 2006). Results supported the hypothesis that younger adults are more persistent when the task offers possibilities for optimizing performance than when the task requires counteracting a loss in performance (i.e., compensation). Older adults were more persistent in the compensation than in the optimization condition. These findings suggest that situating motivational (i.e., self-regulation) research in a lifespan context is not only relevant but important in studying and understanding successful aging.

The final sets of studies to be reviewed investigated aspects of the SOC approach in early adolescence and in old age. Longitudinal data from the 4-H Study of Positive Youth Development demonstrated the construct and predictive validity of a 9-item short form of the SOC Scale in a sample of 5th and 6th grade students (Gestsdóttir & Lerner, 2007). The measure was shown to be a valid assessment of intentional self-regulation in early adolescence, and was related to indicators of positive and negative development in predicted directions. These results suggest that intentional self-regulation is a foundational process even in early adolescence and that it contributes to positive youth development. At the other end of the age continuum, the question of whether SOC life-management strategies buffer the effects of resource deficits in old age was examined in a cross-sectional and longitudinal study (Jopp & Smith, 2006). The participants in both studies were between the ages of 70 and 92, and overall the results suggested that some resource-poor individuals used the SOC processes and benefited from them in terms of enhanced subjective well-being, whereas others did not engage in or benefit from SOC processes. It is unclear from these data why only some of the participants engaged and profited from using these life-management (i.e., self-regulation) strategies; however, the results hold promise for the design and implementation of SOC-based interventions with the hope of enhancing subjective well-being and successful aging across the lifespan.

## Identity and Self-Regulation

From the long-term perspective of goals across the lifespan, we now turn to a more medium-term approach to address the question of how a sense of self influences goal setting processes. This is a very relevant question given that research has shown that one's self-concept changes across the lifespan as well as in more short- to medium-term time frames (Ashforth, 2001; Ashforth & Mael, 1989; Ibarra, 1999). Each person's self-concept potentially contains a number of different identities held in the subconscious; however, given the limited attentional resources in humans, it is generally acknowledged that we are only able to consciously focus on a small portion of this "self space" at any one point in time (Markus & Wurf, 1987). As such, an individual's salient identity becomes a self-regulatory mechanism that can change in the near term, as well as over longer periods of time. Additional research has shown how influential others such as leaders can influence follower self-identities, which shapes follower self-regulation and behavior (Lord & Brown, 2004). Furthermore, Slotter and Gardner (2011) found that in the realm of social relationships, participants were more likely to choose potential friends on the basis of who would be able to help them with their identity-related goals. Given the volitional nature of self-regulation (Locke & Latham, 2002), who we choose to follow and befriend can be important identity-based actions. We propose, therefore, that at any given point in time, an individual's identity will affect self-management processes such as goal choice, goal commitment, goal interpretation, goal setting, and goal pursuit.

Most approaches that deal with multiple goals suggest that an individual's higher-order goals such as one's identity influence goal choice and commitment to lower-order task goals (Klein, Austin, & Cooper, 2008; Kruglanski et al., 2002). Nonetheless, very little work has been done to test this proposition in organizational contexts, with the exception of Ibarra (1999), who found that employees experimented with possible career identities by engaging in different tasks and, although she did not measure them, presumably different goals. Additional empirical support for this suggestion can be found from laboratory work examining social dilemmas (e.g., Kramer & Brewer, 1984). In these studies, participants' identities were manipulated experimentally and participants then placed in a situation where they must choose between a group- and an individual-welfare goal. For instance, De Cremer and colleagues (De Cremer & van Dijk, 2002; De Cremer & Van Vugt, 1999) have found strong support for the hypothesis that when individuals have stronger group identities they are more likely to see the group goal as important and thus are more likely to engage in cooperative behavior. From a self-management perspective, this suggests that focusing on one's role in the group (i.e., creating a salient group identity) will affect the goals to which one commits.

Interestingly, identity may affect not only the choice of goals but even the interpretation of assigned goals. Austin and Vancouver (1996) proposed that the processes surrounding an assigned goal (including higher-order identities) affect goal interpretation. In support of this assertion, MBA students interpreted the same assignment in different ways depending on which identity was salient (Brett & VandeWalle, 1999). Furthermore, members of different departments within manufacturing companies were also found to interpret goals differently (Nauta & Sanders, 2001). Across 11 manufacturing organizations, each department placed a different level of importance on six overall goals of manufacturing (efficiency, quality, delivery speed, delivery reliability, flexibility, and customer service). Although the empirical evidence is still emerging—and the role of identity not always clearly tested—this could be an interesting avenue for future research examining how goal setting within self-management is affected by identities.

Goal systems theory (Kruglanski et al., 2002) also suggests that identity should regulate goal pursuit and the amount of effort produced. The self-concordance literature, in particular, proposes that goals that are in line with an individual's higher-order identities and values are more likely to lead to better performance on those identity-related tasks (see, e.g., Sheldon & Elliot, 1999). Researchers in the areas of health and social psychology have found clear relationships between self-concordance and self-reported physical activity (e.g., Chatzisarantis, Hagger, & Thogersen-Ntoumani, 2008), between manipulated self-concordance and vitamin intake (Chatzisarantis, Hagger, & Wang, 2010), and between self-concordance and self-reported progress toward attaining personal goals (e.g., Koestner, Lekes, Powers, & Chicoine, 2002; Sheldon & Elliot, 1998). Despite these encouraging findings, the results from organizational settings are not as clear. The results of qualitative research suggested that, as predicted by the theory, goals that conflict with personal and team identities (i.e., the opposite of self-concordance) led to poorer performance and a failure to attain an overall organizational goal

(Ezzamel & Willmott, 1998). Quantitatively based research results demonstrated that laboratory participants with self-concordant goals had better task performance, but that employees' self-concordance did not relate to performance in the workplace (Bono & Judge, 2003). This is consistent with other research demonstrating that whereas self-concordance was related to overall job performance, it was not related to the direct attainment of the goals to which it was linked (Greguras & Diefendorff, 2010). Furthermore, Judge, Bono, Erez, and Locke (2005) found only a marginally significant relationship ($p <.10$) between self-concordance and goal attainment in their employee sample.

Interestingly, the level of identification (i.e., group or personal) also appears to influence goal pursuit following feedback. De Cremer and van Dijk (2002) manipulated the identity of undergraduate students and then provided them with feedback on the group's performance. When participants were provided with positive feedback, identification had no effect on subsequent contributions; however, participants whose identification was at the group level were more likely to contribute to the group's goal pursuit (and to contribute more than those who had been provided with positive feedback) following failure feedback. Those whose identification was at the individual level contributed less to the goal-striving process following failure feedback than following positive feedback. Although this study is limited in its use of ad hoc student groups that generally do not have the same level of development as intact teams in organizations, it is interesting to consider the potential implications of these findings in organizational contexts.

Taking a different approach, Houser-Marko and Sheldon (2006) looked at a particular type of personal identity termed the "do-er" identity. They found that the degree to which undergraduate students felt that the do-er version of their goals was self-descriptive (e.g., earn a 3.8 GPA turns into a do-er identity of a good grade-getter) were more likely to get high grades by the end of semester even after accounting for variance attributable to self-concordance, goal commitment, goal expectancy, neuroticism, and openness to experience. Furthermore, this finding was replicated using a sample of self-identified exercisers, weight lifters, and runners in that those who believed that the respective do-er identities described them well were more likely to rate their goal progress higher in biweekly follow-up questionnaires.

It should also be noted that identity also has a potential downside in the regulation of goals. Specifically, identity can impede an individual from seeing alternatives that may lead to better performance. An experimental study with undergraduate business students in which participants' social identities were manipulated (shared superordinate identity versus no shared superordinate identity) examined the effects of changing group membership part-way through a manufacturing task (Kane, Argote, & Levine, 2005). Importantly, the new group member had knowledge of a superior routine that would improve the group's performance; however, this knowledge was transferred and the performance benefits reaped only when the new member came from a group that shared a superordinate identity (i.e., the groups were told they were all part of the same, larger group that shared the same name). When the new member came from a group in which there was no shared superordinate identity (i.e., all the groups had different names and were not part of a larger entity), knowledge and goal pursuit performance were much less likely to be transferred and improved.

Finally, the relationship between identity and goals is not a simple, unidirectional path from identity to goals and goal striving. Instead, goals can affect the individual identities through bottom-up processing (Shah & Kruglanski, 2003). At a dyadic level, Rink and Ellemers (2007) demonstrated that undergraduate students who were experimentally manipulated to have different task goals (such as gaining practical experience in the organization or gaining research experience) still created a common identity based on those goals, particularly when the goals were either very similar or very different.

Overall, the literature on identity and self-regulation has provided an emergent and interesting set of empirical findings. These results indicate the effects of identity of self-regulation activities crosses various levels of abstraction and time cycles from more overarching and long-term processes associated with the development of provisional selves to more momentary and immediate effects resulting from the activation of a working self-concept. Areas for future research focus should fully examine and test the ways in which high-level identities shape specific self-regulation processes. For instance, longitudinal research on leader development has shown that adopting a leader identity is associated with more effective developmental trajectories (Day & Sin, 2011). Closely linking this type of identity development with specific self-regulation activities would help provide greater insight into processes with lengthy cycle times such as leader development. In particular, the role of self-regulated learning might be especially important in areas in which issues of individual development and goal achievement are relevant.

## Self-Regulated Learning

A crucial role of self-regulation is in maximizing the long-term best interest and well-being of an individual, which is highly dependent on acquiring new knowledge and skills needed to reach a desired level of achievement. A term for the individual modulation of cognitive, affective, and behavioral processes in a learning experience is called *self-regulated learning* (Sitzmann & Ely, 2011). It is a particular form of self-regulation that encompasses goal-oriented behavior operating through multiple processes to reach a desired level of achievement within a work-related learning context.

A recent meta-analysis examined 30 years of research on self-regulated learning incorporating 430 independent samples and over 90,000 participants (Sitzmann & Ely, 2011). In organizing the research literature, the researchers turned to self-regulation theory to derive a heuristic framework consisting of 16 fundamental constructs that are thought to constitute self-regulated learning. These constructs consist of one regulatory agent (goal level) that initiates self-regulated learning toward goal attainment; 12 specific regulatory mechanisms (planning, monitoring, metacognition, attention, learning strategies, persistence, time management, environmental structuring, help seeking, motivation, emotional control, and effort); and three regulatory appraisals (self-evaluation, attributions, and self-efficacy) that are used to evaluate progress and determine whether individuals in a learning context will begin or continue with their goal-striving activities.

One of the objectives of the meta-analysis was to examine the interrelations among self-regulation constructs across studies. Results suggested that about 30% of the various constructs had population (i.e., meta-analytic corrected) correlations of .50 or above and that the strongest relationships ($p \geq .70$) were between pairs of regulatory mechanisms. Thus, the data suggest that the self-regulation constructs are indeed interrelated. In terms of the relationships with learning outcomes, those self-regulation constructs with the strongest effects were goal level ($p = .44$, $k = 24$), self-efficacy ($p = .35$, $k = 160$), effort ($p = .28$, $k = 61$), and persistence ($p = .27$, $k = 30$). Taken together, these four constructs accounted for 17% in the variance in learning after controlling for cognitive ability and pre-training knowledge. It should be noted that the four constructs that were statistically significant were those specifically connected to goal-setting theory, while several other regulatory mechanisms—planning, monitoring, help seeking, and emotion control—had no significant effects on learning.

From these results, Sitzmann and Ely (2011) presented an inductively derived "parsimonious framework of adult self-regulated learning" (see p. 436, Figure 1) focusing on nine self-regulatory processes that had significant effects on learning. In that framework, goal level and self-efficacy emerged as the moderate to strong predictors of learning and were not redundant with other self-regulatory processes. Those identified as weak to moderate predictors of learning were (a) attributions, (b) effort, (c) motivation, (d) environmental structuring, (e) time management, (f) attention, and (g) metacognitive strategies (a combination of metacognition, planning, and monitoring). The authors proposed that these nine self-regulatory processes provide a more parsimonious and empirically grounded explanation of how trainees regulate their learning activities.

Another interesting finding from this meta-analysis was that only 12 studies in the review examined whether self-regulation during training predicted transfer of training. Of these available studies, only 3 of the 16 self-regulation constructs (i.e., metacognition, motivation, and self-efficacy) have been examined in more than two training transfer studies. Clearly, there is strong need for more primary studies investigating trainees' self-regulation processes and transfer of training (e.g., Morin & Latham, 2000).

Although only one study was reviewed in this section, we believe it is an important one. In reviewing and summarizing more than 30 years of research on self-regulated learning, Sitzmann and Ely (2011) have provided valuable insights into what has been shown to best facilitate learning (goal level and self-efficacy), what processes add little to the achievement of learning (planning, monitoring, help seeking, and emotion control), and what areas are in great need of additional research (self-regulated transfer of training). Finally, the authors noted the need to better understand the within-person unfolding of self-regulation over time and to determine the most appropriate episodic unit of analysis in different learning situations.

## Cnclusions and Future Directions

In this focused review of the self-regulation and self-management literature over the previous 20 years, it is apparent that the topics hold a great deal of interest to researchers. Self-management, as a package of self-regulatory techniques including but going beyond goal setting, appears to have both theoretical and practical importance. It will be interesting as research moves forward to identify the conditions under which various aspects of the training package are shown to be most important, compared to when the respective individual components such as goal setting and mental practice are most important. Furthermore, while there have been particular foci on issues of self-efficacy, feedback, and self-management interventions in the literature to date, research is also emerging in areas associated with self-regulation across the lifespan, the role of identity in shaping and being shaped by self-regulation processes, as well as the important practical concern of understanding and enhancing self-regulated learning. These are important new directions in that they generally address issues of higher levels of abstraction as well as longer cycle times in the self-regulation of behavior (Lord et al., 2010).

In looking ahead to the next 20 years of research on goals and self-regulation, we encourage further examinations of the role of time. It is also important to continue to expand the focus beyond the effects of goal setting and self-regulation processes on task performance to also consider life-related concerns such as successful aging, the development of long-term identities, as well as individual learning and change. Although we know quite a bit about the self-regulation processes that enhance performance, it is also clear that there is still much knowledge to gain with the consideration of various levels of abstraction and time cycles associated with self-regulation in work and life.

## References

Ashforth, B. E. (2001). *Role transitions in organizational life: An identity-based perspective.* Mahwah, NJ: Erlbaum.

Ashforth, B. E., & Mael, F. (1989). Social identity theory and the organization. *Academy of Management Review, 14,* 20–39.

Austin, J. T., & Vancouver, J. B. (1996). Goal constructs in psychology: Structure, process, and content. *Psychological Bulletin, 120,* 338–375.

Azrin, N. H. (1977). A strategy for applied research: Learning based outcome oriented. *American Psychologist, 32,* 140–149.

Baltes, P. B. (1997). On the incomplete architecture of human ontogeny: Selection, optimization, and compensation as foundation of developmental theory. *American Psychologist, 52,* 366–380.

Baltes, P. B., & Baltes, M. M. (1990). Psychological perspectives on successful aging: The model of selective optimization with compensation. In P. B. Baltes & M. M. Baltes (Eds.), *Successful aging: Perspectives from the behavioral sciences* (pp. 1–34). New York: Cambridge University Press.

Bandura, A. (1986). *Social foundations of thought and action: A social cognitive theory.* Englewood Cliffs, NJ: Prentice-Hall.

Bandura, A. (1997). *Self-efficacy: The exercise of control.* New York: Freeman.

Bandura, A. (2012). On the functional properties of perceived self-efficacy revisited [Guest Editorial]. *Journal of Management, 38,* 9–44.

Baumeister, R. F., & Vohs, K. D. (Eds.). (2004). *Handbook of self-regulation: Research, theory, and applications.* New York: Guilford.

Bono, J. E., & Judge, T. A. (2003). Self-concordance at work: Toward understanding the motivational effects of transformational leaders. *Academy of Management Journal, 46,* 554–571.

Brett, J. F., & VandeWalle, D. (1999). Goal orientation and goal content as predictors of performance in a training program. *Journal of Applied Psychology, 84,* 863–873.

Chatzisarantis, N. L. D., Hagger, M. S., & Thogersen-Ntoumani, C. (2008). The effects of self-disconcordance, self-concordance and implementation intentions on health behavior. *Journal of Applied Biobehavioral Research, 13,* 198–214.

Chatzisarantis, N. L. D., Hagger, M. S., & Wang, J. C. K. (2010). Evaluating the effects of implementation intention and self-concordance on behaviour. *British Journal of Psychology, 101,* 705–718.

Day, D. V., & Sin, H.-P. (2011). Longitudinal tests of an integrative model of leader development: Charting and understanding developmental trajectories. *The Leadership Quarterly, 22,* 545–560.

De Cremer, D., & van Dijk, E. (2002). Reactions to group success and failure as a function of identification level: A test of the goal-transformation hypothesis in social dilemmas. *Journal of Experimental Social Psychology, 38,* 435–442.

De Cremer, D., & Van Vugt, M. (1999). Social identification effects in social dilemmas: A transformation of motives. *European Journal of Social Psychology, 29,* 871–893.

Diefendorff, J. M., & Lord, R. G. (2008). Goal-striving and self-regulation processes. In R. Kanfer, G. Chen & R. D. Pritchard (Eds.), *Work motivation: Past, present, and future* (pp. 151–196). New York: Routledge.

Donovan, J. J., & Williams, K. J. (2003). Missing the mark: Effects of time and causal attributions on goal revision in response to goal-performance discrepancies. *Journal of Applied Psychology, 88,* 379–390.

Ericsson, K. A., Krampe, R. T., & Tesch-Römer, C. (1993). The role of deliberate practice in the acquisition of expert performance. *Psychological Review, 100,* 363–406.

Ezzamel, M., & Willmott, H. (1998). Accounting for teamwork: A critical study of group-based systems of organizational control. *Administrative Science Quarterly, 43,* 358–396.

Frayne, C. A., & Geringer, J. M. (1994). A social cognitive approach to examining joint venture general manager performance. *Group & Organization Management, 19,* 240–262.

Frayne, C. A., & Geringer, J. M. (2000). Self-management training for improving job performance: A field experiment involving salespeople. *Journal of Applied Psychology, 85,* 361–372.

Frayne, C. A., & Latham, G. P. (1987). Application of social learning theory to employee self-management of attendance. *Journal of Applied Psychology, 72,* 387–392.

Freund, A. M. (2006). Age-differential motivational consequences of optimization versus compensation focus in younger and older adults. *Psychology and Aging, 21,* 240–251.

Freund, A. M. (2008). Successful aging as management of resources: The role of selection, optimization, and compensation. *Research in Human Development, 5,* 94–106.

Freund, A. M., & Baltes, P. B. (1998). Selection, optimization, and compensation as strategies of life management: Correlations with subjective indicators of successful aging. *Psychology and Aging, 13,* 531–543.

Freund, A. M., & Baltes, P. B. (2002). Life-management strategies of selection, optimization, and compensation: Measurement by self-report and construct validity. *Journal of Personality and Social Psychology, 82,* 642–662.

Gestsdóttir, S., & Lerner, R. M. (2007). Intentional self-regulation and positive youth development in early adolescence: Findings from the 4-H Study of Positive Youth Development. *Developmental Psychology, 43,* 508–521.

Greguras, G. J., & Diefendorff, J. M. (2010). Why does proactive personality predict employee life satisfaction and work behaviors? A field investigation of the mediating role of the self-concordance model. *Personnel Psychology, 63,* 539–560.

Gist, M. E., Stevens, C. K., & Bavetta, A. G. (1992). Effects of self-efficacy and post-training intervention on the acquisition and maintenance of complex interpersonal skills. *Personnel Psychology, 44,* 837–861.

Heckhausen, J., Wrosch, C., & Schulz, R. (2010). A motivational theory of life-span development. *Psychological Review, 117*, 32–60.

Houser-Marko, L., & Sheldon, K. M. (2006). Motivating behavioral persistence: The self-as-doer construct. *Personality and Social Psychology Bulletin, 32*, 1037–1049.

Ibarra, H. (1999). Provisional selves: Experimenting with image and identity in professional adaptation. *Administrative Science Quarterly, 44*, 764–791.

Ilies, R., & Judge, T. A. (2005). Goal regulation across time: The effects of feedback and affect. *Journal of Applied Psychology, 90*, 453–467.

Jopp, D., & Smith, J. (2006). Resources and life-management strategies as determinants of successful aging: On the protective effect of selection, optimization, and compensation. *Psychology and Aging, 21*, 253–265.

Judge, T. A., Bono, J. E., Erez, A., & Locke, E. A. (2005). Core self-evaluations and job and life satisfaction: The role of self-concordance and goal attainment. *Journal of Applied Psychology, 90*, 257–268.

Kane, A. A., Argote, L., & Levine, J. M. (2005). Knowledge transfer between groups via personnel rotation: Effects of social identity and knowledge quality. *Organizational Behavior and Human Decision Processes, 96*, 56–71.

Kanfer, F. H. (1980). Self-management methods. In F. H. Kanfer & A. P. Goldstein (Eds.), *Helping people change: A textbook of methods* (2nd ed., pp. 334–389). New York: Pergamon Press.

Kanfer, R. (2005). Self-regulation research in work and I/O psychology. *Applied Psychology: An International Review, 54*, 186–191.

Karoly, P. (1993). Mechanisms of self-regulation. *Annual Review of Psychology, 44*, 23–52.

Klein, H. J., Austin, J. T., & Cooper, J. T. (2008). Goal choice and decision processes. In R. Kanfer (Ed.), *Work motivation: Past, present and future* (pp. 101–150). Hoboken, NJ: Routledge.

Koestner, R., Lekes, N., Powers, T. A., & Chicoine, E. (2002). Attaining personal goals: Self-concordance plus implementation intentions equals success. *Journal of Personality and Social Psychology, 83*, 231–224.

Kramer, R. M., & Brewer, M. B. (1984). Effects of group identity on resource use in a simulated commons dilemma. *Journal of Personality and Social Psychology, 46*, 1044–1057.

Kruglanski, A. W., Shah, J. Y., Fishbach, A., Friedman, R., Chun, W. Y., & Sleeth-Keppler, D. (2002). A theory of goal systems. *Advances in Experimental Social Psychology, 34*, 331–378.

Latham, G. P., & Budworth, M.-H. (2006). The effect of training in verbal self-guidance on the self-efficacy and performance of Native North Americans in the selection interview. *Journal of Vocational Behavior, 68*, 516–523.

Latham, G. P., & Frayne, C. A. (1989). Self-management training for increasing job attendance. *Journal of Applied Psychology, 74*, 411–416.

Latham, G. P., & Locke, E. A. (1991). Self-regulation through goal setting. *Organizational Behavior and Human Decision Processes, 50*, 212–247.

Locke, E. A., & Latham, G. P. (1990). *A theory of goal setting and task performance*. Englewood Cliffs, NJ: Prentice Hall.

Locke, E. A., & Latham, G. P. (2002). Building a practically useful theory of goal setting and task motivation: A 35-year odyssey. *American Psychologist, 57*, 705–717.

Lord, R. G., & Brown, D. J. (2004). *Leadership processes and follower self-identity*. Mahwah, NJ: Erlbaum.

Lord, R. G., Diefendorff, J. M., Schmidt, A. M., & Hall, R. J. (2010). Self-regulation at work. *Annual Review of Psychology, 61*, 543–568.

Manz, C. C. (1991). Leading employees to be self-managing and beyond: Toward the establishment of self-leadership in organizations. *Journal of Management Systems, 3*, 15–24.

Markus, H. R., & Wurf, E. (1987). The dynamic self-concept: A social psychological perspective. *Annual Review of Psychology, 38*, 299–337.

Morin, L., & Latham, G. P. (2000). The effect of mental practice and goal setting as a transfer of training intervention on supervisors' self-efficacy and communication skills: An exploratory study. *Applied Psychology: An International Review, 49*, 566–578.

Morisano, D., Hirsh, J. B., Peterson, J. B., Pihl, R. O., & Shore, B. M. (2010). Setting, elaborating, and reflecting on personal goals improves academic performance. *Journal of Applied Psychology, 95*, 255–264.

Nauta, A., & Sanders, K. (2001). Causes and consequences of perceived goal differences between departments within manufacturing organizations. *Journal of Occupational and Organizational Psychology, 74*, 321–342.

Pattni, I., Soutar, G. N., & Klobas, J. E. (2007). The impact of a short self-management training intervention in a retail banking environment. *Human Resource Development Quarterly, 18*, 159–178.

Raudenbush, S. W., & Bryk, A. S. (2002). *Hierarchical linear models: Applications and data analysis methods* (2nd ed.). Thousand Oaks, CA: Sage.

Richard, E. M., & Diefendorff, J. M. (2011). Self-regulation during a single performance episode: Mood-as-information in the absence of formal feedback. *Organizational Behavior and Human Decision Processes, 115*, 99–110.

Rink, F., & Ellemers, N. (2007). Defining the common feature: Task-related differences as the basis for dyadic identity. *British Journal of Social Psychology, 46*, 499–515.

Rousseau, D. M. (1997). Organizational behavior in the new organizational era. *Annual Review of Psychology, 48*, 515–546.

Schwarz, N., & Clore, G. L. (1983). Mood, misattribution, and judgments of well-being: Informative and directive functions of affective states. *Journal of Personality and Social Psychology, 45*, 513–523.

Seo, M., & Ilies, R. (2009). The role of self-efficacy, goal, and affect in dynamic motivational self-regulation. *Organizational Behavior and Human Decision Processes, 109*, 120–133.

Shah, J. Y., & Kruglanski, A. W. (2003). When opportunity knocks: Bottom-up priming of goals by means and its effects on self-regulation. *Journal of Personality and Social Psychology, 84*, 1109–1122.

Sheldon, K. M., & Elliot, A. J. (1998). Not all personal goals are personal: Comparing autonomous and controlled reasons as predictors of effort and attainment. *Personality and Social Psychology Bulletin, 24*, 546–557.

Sheldon, K. M., & Elliot, A. J. (1999). Goal striving, need satisfaction, and longitudinal well-being: The self-concordance model. *Journal of Personality and Social Psychology, 76*, 482–497.

Sitzmann, T., & Ely, K. (2011). A meta-analysis of self-regulated learning in work-related training and educational attainment: What we know and where we need to go. *Psychological Bulletin, 137*, 421–442.

Sonnentag, S. (2002). Performance, well-being, and self-regulation. In S. Sonnentag (Ed.), *Psychological management of individual performance* (pp. 405–424). New York: Wiley.

Slotter, E. B., & Gardner, W. L. (2011). Can you help me become the "me" I want to be? The role of goal pursuit in friendship formation. *Self and Identity, 10*, 231–247.

Stevens, C. K., Bavetta, A. G., & Gist, M. E. (1993). Gender differences in the acquisition of salary negotiation skills: The role of goals, self-efficacy, and perceived control. *Journal of Applied Psychology, 78*, 723–735.

Stewart, G. L., Courtright, S. H., & Manz, C. C. (2011). Self-leadership: A multilevel review. *Journal of Management, 37*, 185–222.

Thoresen, C. E., & Mahoney, M. J. (1974). *Behavioral self-control.* New York: Holt, Rinehart, and Winston.

Tolli, A. P., & Schmidt, A. M. (2008). The role of feedback, causal attributions, and self-efficacy in goal revision. *Journal of Applied Psychology, 93*, 692–701.

Uhl-Bien, M., & Graen, G. B. (1998). Individual self-management: Analysis of professionals' self-managing activities in functional and cross-functional work teams. *Academy of Management Journal, 41*, 340–350.

Vancouver, J. B. (2012). Rhetorical reckoning: A response to Bandura [Guest Editorial]. *Journal of Management, 38*, 465–474.

Vancouver, J. B., & Day, D. V. (2005). Industrial and organisation research on self-regulation: From constructs to applications. *Applied Psychology: An International Review, 54*, 155–185.

Vancouver, J. B., & Kendall, L. N. (2006). When self-efficacy negatively relates to motivation and performance in a learning context. *Journal of Applied Psychology, 91*, 1146–1153.

Vancouver, J. B., Thompson, C. M., Tischner, E. C., & Putka, D. J. (2002). Two studies examining the negative effect of self-efficacy on performance. *Journal of Applied Psychology, 87*, 506–516.

Vancouver, J. B., Thompson, C. M., & Williams, A. A. (2001). The changing signs in the relationships among self-efficacy, personal goals, and performance. *Journal of Applied Psychology, 86*, 605–620.

Vancouver, J. B., Weinhardt, J. M., & Schmidt, A. M. (2010). A formal, computational theory of multiple-goal pursuit: Integrating goal choice and goal-striving processes. *Journal of Applied Psychology, 95*, 985–1008.

Vohs, K. D., & Baumeister, R. F. (2004). Understanding self-regulation: An introduction. In R. F. Baumeister & K. D. Vohs (Eds.), *Handbook of self-regulation: Research, theory, and applications* (pp. 1–9). New York: Guilford.

Williams, K. J., Donovan, J. J., & Dodge, T. L. (2000). Self-regulation of performance: Goal establishment and goal revision processes in athletes. *Human Performance, 13*, 159–180.

Wood, R. E. (2005). New frontiers for self-regulation research in IO psychology. *Applied Psychology: An International Review, 54*, 192–198.

Yanar, B., Budworth, M.-H., & Latham, G. P. (2009). The effect of verbal self-guidance training for overcoming employment barriers: A study of Turkish women. *Applied Psychology: An International Review, 58*, 586–601.

Yeo, G. B., & Neal, A. (2006). An examination of the dynamic relationship between self-efficacy and performance across levels of analysis and levels of specificity. *Journal of Applied Psychology, 91*, 1088–1101.

# 12 Multiple Goal Pursuit

*Shu Hua Sun*  NUS Business School, National University of Singapore
*Michael Frese*  NUS Business School, National University of Singapore,
Leuphana University of Lueneburg, Germany

## Introduction

It is normal to pursue multiple goals at work and in our everyday life. Consider the case of college professors, who may set themselves several specific, difficult goals: publishing three articles in one year in high-impact journals with a high rejection rate, earning course evaluations from students of say 5.0 on a 7-point scale, and serving on two committees. Similarly, CEOs of business organizations have to pursue multiple goals, for example, market share, strategy implementation, innovation, customer service, cost control, ethical actions, the hiring and development of talent, legal issues, the organization's profitability, and more. The issue of multiple goals had not been well researched at the time of Latham and Locke's 1990 book; most goal setting studies at that time concentrated on the effect of single goals on various types of task performance (Latham & Locke, 2007). Recently, there has been a growing body of research examining multiple goals. In this chapter, we review the major findings generated from these studies spanning more than 20 years.

## A Framework of Multiple Goals

Before we move on to the review, we first present a framework to organize the studies (see Figure 12.1).

In the first category (Figure 12.1, I), the multiple goals are independent of each other, yet need common resources. These resources include attention, time, money, people, and various types of physical resources (e.g., technology). Because these common resources are finite (despite some elasticity), there is potential for goal conflict when different goals draw on these resources. As a result, there are often trade-offs so that progress in pursuing one goal has a detrimental effect on the pursuit of other goals. Except for drawing from the same pool of limited resources, the goals involved are separate (they are not logically connected to one another). We label this first category *Multiple, Separate Goals*. There are two subcategories: First, people can have two or more goals that they have to work on simultaneously (i.e., they work on them at the same time)—we call this form *Simultaneous Separate Goals*. This has mostly been studied using a dual-task paradigm. Second, people may have multiple goals that can be worked on at different times (called *Nonsimultaneous Separate Goals*).

A second category we call *Sequentially Interdependent Goals* (Figure 12.1, II). In this case, the degree of the interdependence among multiple goals is high in that the

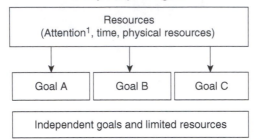

**I. Multiple separate goals**

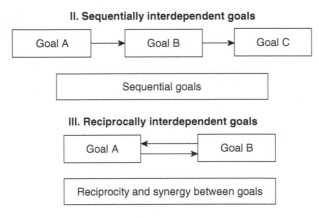

[1]Attention is used as a short descriptor for the concept of central processing capacity

*Figure 12.1* A typology of multiple goals. I. Multiple Separate Goals; II. Sequentially Interdependent Goals; III. Reciprocally Interdependent Goals.

attainment of one goal contributes to or is required for the attainment of another. Specifically, attaining goal A may be a prerequisite or a step for attaining goal B, which in turn is needed to attain goal C. The sequence is temporally unidirectional and cannot be reversed. An example is the relation of proximal goals or subgoals to long-term or distal goals (Locke & Latham, 1990). A related example is a goal hierarchy (Frese & Zapf, 1994). Each lower-level goal is the means to achieving the next higher-level goal, and so on.

In the third category (Figure 12.1, III), the interdependence among multiple goals is highest as reciprocal and synergic interrelationships exist. We call this category *Reciprocally Interdependent Goals*. These goals are usually pursued over a longer period of time. As shown in the figure, the progress in pursuing one goal tends to facilitate the pursuit of the other, but the effect is reciprocal in that attaining the second goal can in turn further help the attainment of the first, and so on. As Locke and Latham (1990, p. 53) put it, "goals are often causally interrelated in a positive way so that actions taken to attain one goal help rather than hinder the attainment of other goals." For example, attracting and developing human talent could help companies to better attain financial goals, which in turn help them to attract new talent and further develop the employees.

# Multiple Separate Goals

## Simultaneous Separate Goals

This type of multiple goal situation (Figure 12.1, I) occurs when people have to do more than one thing at the same time. When multiple independent tasks need to be done, performance decrements may result (Humphreys & Revelle, 1984). The problem of simultaneous separate goals is that working on these goals requires resources that are limited in nature, such as attention, time, or physical resources. Limited attention has been studied using the dual-task paradigm. Within this paradigm, the central research question concerns information processing capabilities and the underlying neurobiological processes. A common assumption is that people have limited cognitive resources (Anderson, 1983; Kanfer & Ackerman, 1989). In a typical dual-task study, participants are instructed to focus primarily on the performance of a given task while also performing a secondary task which consumes some of the attentional resources (Erez, Gopher, & Arazi, 1990). Examining the performance trade-offs, researchers can evaluate the extent to which performance in the primary task is reduced because the secondary task also consumes limited resources.

Attentional resources lie at the heart of the problem of simultaneous task performance. Kanfer and Ackerman (1989) found that specific, high-performance goals can have a negative effect on performance in a task requiring new learning. Learning while performance goals are pursued is often contradictory because learning and performing effectively use the same pool of attentional resources. The higher the performance goal when learning to perform the task, the higher the demands on the common pool of attentional resources, which may lead to giving up learning and "scrambling" unsystematically in an attempt to perform effectively. As a result, setting a specific, difficult goal can lead to lower performance than no goal setting or setting a vague goal. Recent research reveals several solutions to this problem: One is to set specific, high learning rather than performance goals (Latham & Locke, 2006); another is to set proximal goals rather than a distal goal alone (Latham & Seijts, 1999). This is discussed in the section on multiple goals with sequential interdependence.

Resource allocation theory maintains that while there may be variance across people in their attention resources, attention resources are limited for every person (Anderson, 1983; Kahneman, 1973; Kanfer & Ackerman, 1989). This is not to say that people cannot learn to work on two tasks at once. People have been trained to master seemingly impossible multiple tasks such as writing something down via dictation while reading and understanding something else, but participants had to be trained for 70 hours or more (Spelke, Hirst, & Neisser, 1976). Thus, there is elasticity within the pool of resources; enhanced dual-task achievement can be trained. However, a particular pair of tasks to be performed needs to be trained for a very long time, and there is no generalizable positive effect on other dual tasks (Oberauer & Kliegl, 2004); thus, one does not learn the meta-skill of how to do two tasks simultaneously.

In addition, other resources such as physical resources and time (Figure 12.1, I) may also play a role in multi-tasking, but they usually are not a major concern in research on multi-tasking. Our capability to manage multiple tasks is usually constrained by physical resources. Time is another resource. If time is lost, it is not retrievable. As a non-elastic variable, time constraint is certainly an important reason for the problem of multiple goals. Since each goal accomplishment requires a certain amount of time, multiple goals have conflicting requirements for time. Fortunately, time sharing allows a certain amount of elasticity vis-à-vis this scarce resource. However, time sharing usually requires split attention to multiple goals; thus, it produces displaced effects in sharing scarce attentional resources.

In sum, research utilizing the dual-task paradigm shows that multiple tasks often lead to performance decrements, although there is a certain elasticity that helps to deal with multiple tasks. This implies, from a practical perspective, that working on multiple tasks may be a learnable skill. On the other hand, there are costs associated with multiple tasks. For instance, there are "switch costs" in both reaction time (RT) and error rates when switching between multiple tasks (Kiesel et al., 2010). However, the exact process has yet to be determined.

While the dual-task paradigm has generated interesting insights into human information processing, there is less research examining the dual-tasking of individuals from a motivational perspective. Only a few studies have focused on the motivational effects on dual-task performance; one is by Erez, Gopher, and Arazi (1990). This study tested the effects of goal difficulty, goal origin (self-set vs. assigned), and monetary rewards (present vs. absent) on the simultaneous performance of two tasks: a computerized task of letter typing with the right hand and digit classification with the left hand. Their results indicated that self-set goals without monetary rewards led to the highest joint performance levels, whereas the combination of self-set goals and monetary rewards was detrimental to performance, particularly when goals were of either moderate or high difficulty. On the hand, the group of assigned goals without monetary rewards had the lowest performance even though their goals were higher than groups with monetary incentives. The result on this interaction between sources of the goal (self-set vs. assigned) and monetary rewards is interesting because it found that self-set goals and monetary rewards did not synergistically produce high performance. The authors proposed two explanations for the detrimental effect of monetary rewards on self-set goals: (1) monetary rewards reduce the intrinsic motivational potential of self-set goals and (2) self-set goals and monetary rewards combine to produce overarousal, which is detrimental to performance.

Even though we have mainly discussed experimental studies on simultaneous performance of multiple tasks, we should note the warning by Locke and Latham (1990, p. 53): "In most real-life situations goals do not have to be pursued simultaneously. ... Goals normally extend over a period of weeks, months, or years, and the individual can pursue the goals sequentially and/or cyclically." In the section that follows, research on multiple goals that people pursue within a certain period of time is reviewed. These concurrent multiple goals do not need to be pursued simultaneously as those studied within the framework of the dual-task paradigm.

## Nonsimultaneous Separate Goals and Goal Conflicts

In normal real-world organizational settings, the time period to attain multiple goals is typically longer than in the dual-task paradigm discussed above. A CEO can be working on a dozen different goals but can space them out within and across days. But there can still be conflict because the CEO has to decide how much time to allocate to each goal and which goal or goals to focus on for any given day or week. Time is still finite for him, and thus goal conflicts can exist.

Goal conflicts can arise for two reasons: First, there may be two-task environments that demand the fulfillment of goals. For example, there may be two bosses who pose conflicting demands; thus, pleasing one boss means displeasing the other. Second, one goal may be aversive and attractive at the same time. For example, an entrepreneur may need to raise funds but really dislikes this kind of task compared to working on a new product.

Strivings that are ambivalent (i.e., having both aversive and attractive qualities) produce negative affect (Emmons, 1986) and even depression (Kelly, Mansell, & Wood, 2011). In a longitudinal study, Kehr (2003) demonstrated that persistent goal conflict reduced attainment of new goals by managers. Another study differentiated multiple goals from a lifespan development perspective into goals that conflict with each other and goals that facilitate each other (Wiese & Salmela-Aro, 2008). Specifically, they found that facilitation of goals occurred more frequently than goals that conflicted and hindered each other; moreover, when there was more facilitation than hindrance, there was more satisfaction and higher engagement in work and family. Thus, the ratio of goal facilitation to hindrance made a difference for well-being and engagement.

Goal conflict can lead to performance decrements (Locke, Smith, Erez, Chah, & Schaffer, 1994). The performance decrement may be caused by limited attentional resources, as discussed in the dual-task paradigm, but they can also appear due to time constraints.

### Solving Goal Conflicts: Goal Prioritization

Goal conflict implies that people are drawn to different goals that cannot be reconciled. They cannot be reconciled because their pursuit is dependent on limited resources. Thus, the central question faced when confronted with multiple-goal pursuit that hinges on limited resources is priority management (Kernan & Lord, 1990). Goal prioritization is a function of goal importance, goal difficulty, self-efficacy, planning, and affect (cf. Figure 12.2). We review research on each of these factors below.

*Goal importance.* Kernan and Lord (1990) showed that goal importance is a critical factor influencing goal priority. Specifically, they compared the effects of

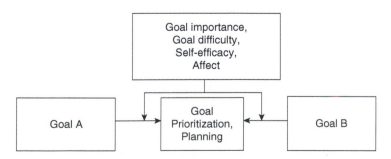

*Figure 12.2* Goal Prioritization among Nonsimultaneous Separate Goals.

goal-performance discrepancy, valences, and expectancies in both single-goal and multiple-goal environments. They found that goal-performance discrepancy, defined as the distance from current performance to the goal, was a significant predictor of effort and performance in a single-goal context; valences and expectancies had only minimal effects. However, in a multiple-goal context, valences and expectancies played significant roles in affecting goal prioritization and resource allocation; goal-performance discrepancy played a role only when both valences and expectancies were high.

Hollenbeck and Williams (1987) examined multiple goals in a natural environment. Goal importance per se did not relate to future performance. However, if goal importance was high, and if self-focus was high (high self-reflectivity), there was a significant relationship between goal level (low vs. high goal) and future performance.

*Goal difficulty.* Erez et al. (1990) found that differences in goal difficulty of the two tasks predicted differences in performance. Specifically, in a dual-goal context, resources are drawn to the more difficult goal, which results in higher performance in the difficult goal. However, they also showed that the joint performance (which is calculated by the sum of two task performances weighted by the bonus given for maintaining equal distances from the goal) was lower for the difficult goal condition than for the moderate goal condition.

*Self-efficacy.* Research evidence has indicated that self-efficacy raises goal levels and strengthens goal commitment (see Chapter 10). Little empirical information is available to date on the role of self-efficacy in multiple goal contexts. Thus, it is not clear how self-efficacy for multiple goal attainments affects resource allocation. On the one hand, it is likely that people will prioritize goals that they feel they can successfully reach. Support for this position is provided by Kernan and Lord (1990): Their participants prioritized the tasks that carried higher expectancies to be reached. Additional evidence for this prediction comes from an unpublished study by Byrd and Donovan (2004). They found that participants allocated more time to the task for which they had higher self-efficacy.

On the other hand, high self-efficacy can also reduce goal priority under certain conditions. Vancouver, More, and Yoder (2008) argued that in multiple-goal situations people allocate resources commensurate with their perceived task capability: higher self-efficacy would signal a reduced need for effort expenditure for the focal goal. As a result, people may free up some resources from the focal goal and redirect those resources to other goals. From this perspective, the prediction is that high self-efficacy for the focal goal lowers its priority, whereas relatively low self-efficacy would signal a greater need for attention and effort and would thus lead to higher priority.

Currently, there is a lively debate between Bandura (2012) and Vancouver (2005). However, the debate is not anchored explicitly in a multiple-goal approach. A few comments may be useful from a multiple-goal perspective. High self-efficacy signals that new challenges can be approached (Bandura, 1997). If there is only one task, then people search for challenges by increasing goal difficulty (Stoeber, Hutchfield, & Wood, 2008). If however, there is a task conflict, and one of the tasks is characterized by high self-efficacy and the other one by low self-efficacy, then the low self-efficacy for the other task signals that there is a challenge and then the low self-efficacy task will be prioritized. On the other hand, the high self-efficacy task is prioritized under task conflict conditions if the low self-efficacy task is relatively unimportant or if there is low affect when doing this task. An added complication may be how much self-efficacy beliefs people have for dealing with goal conflicts—Bandura (2012) refers to self-efficacy for self-regulation, and this may also apply to goal conflicts. We think that these are areas that require further research.

*Goal-performance discrepancy.* Goal-performance discrepancy has been recognized to trigger self-regulating attention and motivation (Bandura & Locke, 2003). After establishing one's goals by creating discrepancies, individuals monitor their progress and act to minimize and reduce any perceivable discrepancies between current performance and their goals by working to attain their goals. Larger goal-performance discrepancy indicates greater needs for attention and effort, leading people to allocate corresponding resources to the goal with larger goal-performance discrepancy (Lord & Levy, 1994). In multiple-goal contexts, however, there have been conflicting findings on the role of goal-performance discrepancy on resource allocation.

Kernan and Lord (1990) found that a large goal-performance discrepancy on one goal leads people to tentatively disengage from pursuing that goal, and prioritize other goals with smaller goal-performance discrepancies. Such a resource allocation decision is considered adaptive because it can help an individual to avoid negative affect associated with a larger goal-performance discrepancy and potential futile efforts to achieve an unattainable goal. Likewise, Byrd and Donovan (2004) found that participants invested more effort on tasks with smaller goal-performance discrepancies. In contrast, larger goal-performance discrepancy also indicates greater need for effort (Klein, 1989); Schmidt and DeShon (2007) found that participants prioritized goals with large goal-performance discrepancies.

These opposing findings highlight that the relationship between goal-performance discrepancy and resource allocation may be contingent upon other personal and contextual factors. Indeed, even in single-goal research, scholars have pointed out that the relationship between goal-performance discrepancy and effort allocation is not monotonically linear (Bandura, 1997). For example, although a large goal-performance discrepancy frequently has high motivational potential, it can also lead to reduced goal commitment and even goal disengagement due to reduced self-efficacy expectations (Bandura, 1986; Carver & Scheier, 1998; Locke & Latham, 1990).

Through a series of studies, Schmidt and his colleagues (Schmidt & DeShon, 2007; Schmidt & Dolis, 2009; Schmidt, Dolis, & Tolli, 2009) discovered that financial incentives, dual-task difficulty, and environmental uncertainty moderated the relationship between goal-performance discrepancy and resource allocation in multiple-goal contexts. For example, Schmidt and Dolis (2009) found that dual-goal expectancy, which they defined as individuals' beliefs regarding the likelihood of meeting both goals within a specified time period, moderated the relationship between goal-performance discrepancy and time expenditure. Specifically, the goal with larger goal-performance discrepancy is prioritized when dual-goal expectancy is high, whereas the other goal with smaller goal-performance discrepancy is allocated more time when dual-goal expectancy is low. Low dual-task expectancy signals that people are not sure whether they can attain both of their concurrent goals and, therefore, they choose by taking the safer option and pursuing the easier goal. In addition, recent research (Northcraft, Schmidt, & Ashford, 2011) showed the moderating role of feedback quality in terms of timeliness and specificity on the allocation of resources in multiple-goal pursuit processes.

This suggests that quality feedback is an important moderator variable for multi-goal pursuits.

Finally, it should be noted that goal-performance discrepancy is not a static concept, but changes dynamically (Bandura & Locke, 2003) as people often increase the goal difficulty after having achieved a goal (Locke & Latham, 2006). Self-efficacy has been shown to be a factor that leads to an increase in goal difficulty (Bandura, 2001; Stoeber, Hutchfield, & Wood, 2008).

In summary, goal conflicts have different effects depending on whether people believe that they can attain both goals. If they believe that they can attain both goals, they concentrate on the more difficult one; the opposite effect appears when they do not believe that they can attain both goals. Thus, for practical purposes, when setting multiple goals for employees, managers should ensure that the difficulty level of these goals corresponds with their ability and confidence levels. As Latham and Locke (2006) suggested, "before assigning ... goals, give employees the training and resources necessary for them to be prepared for the challenges they will encounter in pursuing these goals" (p. 337).

*Affect.* The role of affect in multiple-goal pursuits is relatively underexplored; however, it may influence resource allocation (Lord, Diefendorff, Schmidt, & Hall, 2010). Affect signals which goal is more important: Using a multiple-goal context, Louro, Pieters, and Zeelenberg (2007) found differences depending on whether or not a focal goal was remote or near. When the focal goal was remote, positive emotions increased the effort in that domain by decreasing resources from other goal pursuit. In contrast, negative emotions led to disengagement from the focal goal and an increase of effort for competing goals. However, if the goal was near, these relationships were reversed; in this case, negative affect signaled the need for additional effort (consistent with the Rubicon theory of Gollwitzer, 1999).

In another experience sampling study, Fulford, Johnson, Llabre, and Carver (2010) found that participants increased their subsequent effort toward the goal when they fell short of the expected rate of progress, but reduced their subsequent effort toward the goal when their rate of progress exceeded what they expected. However, this study did not measure affect directly; instead, affect was inferred from the calculated difference between perceived and expected rate of goal process (Carver, 2003).

Thus, affect provides information (Schwarz, 1990). When we feel bad about pursuing one goal, we may change to another one, except if we are already close to achieving the goal. Whenever we feel good about pursuing two goals, this information provides us a motivational impetus to greater achievement in both goals, except when we are already very close to having achieved it. Goal conflict may lead to giving up goal striving. This is practically important as it speaks for the importance of overarching goals and visions that provide us with a common idea that reduces goal conflict (Baum, Locke, & Kirkpatrick, 1998).

*Planning.* Planning produces a set of steps to accomplish a multiplicity of tasks (Frese & Zapf, 1994a). Planning is one way to deal with goal conflict because planning tells us in which way the goals can be secured in spite of their apparent goal conflict. Planning can have a number of functions, and different research traditions have emphasized different aspects of planning: (a) it produces steps and substeps to attain goals; in this case, the different goals are ordered, and substeps are suggested to attain the multiple goals. (b) It produces if-then commands (Miller, Galanter, & Pribram, 1960; Newell & Simon, 1975)—for example, if I achieve goal 1, I will attend to goal 2; (c) It is a mental simulation of actions toward a goal (Hacker, 1985); this means that we can simulate the optimal order in which we pursue multiple goals, and thereby detect synergy effects among the multiple goals. (d) Planning means thinking through potential actions and operations, and potential responses by the environment—again, this could lead to finding synergy effects among seemingly conflicting goals. (e) It automatizes the response to an opportunity; in other words it, reduces cognitive load (Gollwitzer, 1999), which allows us to make better use of resources. Goal setting theory has argued that plans are of particular importance in complex task environments (Wood, Mento, & Locke, 1987), that new tasks lead to deliberate planning (Locke & Latham, 2002), that comprehensive planning is necessary (Smith, Locke, & Barry, 1990), and that process characteristics of plans need to be considered (Wood & Locke, 1990).

In summary, planning is of particular importance in multiple-goal environments. Research on the first type of multiple goals (Figure 12.1, I) focuses on how people prioritize and plan these goals. We can summarize the major findings presented above into a conceptual model shown in Figure 12.2. Goal importance, goal difficulty, self-efficacy, and affect have an influence on how we prioritize and plan our goals. For purposes of simplicity, we assume two goals to be operative in the model. In the next section, we review research on multiple, sequentially interdependent goals (Figure 12.1, II).

## Sequentially Interdependent Goals

The sequentially interdependent goal structure implies that attaining one goal is the means or intermediate step to attaining another goal. In the existing literature, the most studied sequential and interdependent goals are proximal goals and distal goals (Locke & Latham, 1990). Any distal or long-term goal can be segmented into several smaller and more immediate subgoals. These subgoals are intermediate steps to attaining the distal end goal and can be pursued in a sequential way. Existing research tends to show that complementing distal goals by developing proximal goals facilitates performance (Bandura, 1997; Frese & Zapf, 1994; Latham & Seijts, 1999; Steel & König, 2006). Setting proximal goals facilitates goal pursuit by increasing motivation, by developing higher self-efficacy, by better detection and management of errors, and by learning. Proximal goals are particularly helpful when distal goals are far removed in time and when they are complex (Latham & Locke, 2007). Below we will discuss the effects of proximal goals on each of these processes.

*Goal proximity, motivation, and performance.* In general, theory and empirical research tend to support the proposal that the combination of distal and proximal goals leads to higher task persistence and better performance than distal goals alone (Latham & Seijts, 1999; Stock & Cervone, 1990; Weldon & Yun, 2000). Proximal goals can provide immediate incentives for current performance, whereas distal goals are too far removed in time to effectively motivate action (Bandura, 1997). Indeed, the "goal gradient hypothesis" (Brown, 1948; Hull, 1934; Lewin, 1935), the "goal looms larger" effect (Brendl & Higgins, 1996; Förster, Higgins, & Idson, 1998), and temporal discounting (Steel & König, 2006) all suggest that motivational strength increases as distance from the goals decreases.

Using a complex problem-solving task called "missionaries and cannibals," Stock and Cervone (1990) compared the effects of the distal goal alone, the distal goal coupled with attainable proximal subgoals, and the distal goal accompanied by unattainable subgoals on task persistence. Results revealed that participants in the attainable subgoal condition persisted significantly longer than those in the other two conditions.

In a study conducted by Latham and Seijts (1999), young adults were paid on a piece-rate basis to make toys under three experimental conditions: "do your best"; distal goal alone; and a combination of distal goals and proximal goals. The task consisted of six 10-minute sessions. Participants in the distal goal alone condition were assigned distal overall goals to be attained after completing all six sessions. Participants in the proximal goal condition were assigned subgoals for each session that helped them to reach the distal goals. Those participants who were assigned proximal subgoals in addition to distal goals showed the highest performance. The proximal goals oriented attention on task-appropriate strategies.

Attention on task strategies may be one factor that leads people who have both proximal and distal goals to perform better than people in a distal goal condition. But people who have proximal goals may also increase the difficulty level of their goals. Weldon and Yun (2000) compared the relative effects of proximal subgoals and distal goals alone on team task performance in terms of accuracy of reports among 31 teams of nurse surveyors working for a US state department of health over a period of 6 to 9 months. In this experimental study, 15 teams were assigned to the condition of distal goal accompanied by proximal goals, whereas the other teams were instructed to only develop distal goals. The teams in the distal plus proximal goals condition were asked to self-set two to three proximal goals to achieve their long-term goal. The authors found that teams in the proximal plus distal goals condition outperformed those in the distal-only goals conditions because the teams in the distal plus proximal goals condition ultimately set themselves more difficult distal goals.

Thus far, we have reviewed the literature on the advantages of proximal goals. They lead to higher performance because the long time frame for attaining a distal goal is reduced. Steel and König (2006) emphasized that proximal goals increase the urgency and immediacy of distal goals, thus increasing the perceived utility and motivational potential of distal goals. However, there are also potential disadvantages of dividing a distal goal into proximal subgoals. If too many proximal subgoals are set, the difficulty level of these subgoals is reduced and, thus, goal attainment is made less challenging and less self-satisfying (Steel & König, 2006). It pays to repeat Locke and Latham's (1990) warning that extensive subgoal setting by a superior may be seen as patronizing. For superiors to be setting many proximal subgoals as intermediate steps to distal goals signals little faith in the direct reports' competence, leading to lower direct reports' self-efficacy and an increased impression of a highly controlling superior (Manderlink & Harackiewicz, 1984). Conceptually, there should be an optimal point where the maximum motivational potential of subgoals is achieved by balancing the immediacy and challenge level of these subgoals (Steel & König, 2006). Future research might examine this optimal point of segmenting distal goals to maximize the motivational potential of subgoals.

While temporal proximity is not always positive, the dominant finding is that a long-term distal goal is more effectively pursued if it includes proximal goals, and that a distal goal alone is often too far removed in time to develop a high degree of motivation to pursue it (Steel & König, 2006). It should be noted, however, that these studies should not be taken to imply that long-term goal setting produces detrimental effects. The data only suggests that long-term goal setting coupled with proximal goals produces better performance than distal goals alone. Developing distal goals also has positive effects as long as there are also proximal goals; proximal goals alone can lead to a certain short-sightedness of perspective. Indeed, in the area of planning, there is evidence that long-term planning has positive effects on performance in multiple-goal environments (Frese, Krauss et al., 2007).

*Proximal goals and the development of self-efficacy.* According to Bandura (1997), progress in goal attainments of subgoals can lead to mastery experiences that increase self-efficacy. However, when the same progress is evaluated against a distal goal, the result can be disappointing because of the remaining large discrepancies between the current performance and the distal end goals. Thus, setting proximal subgoals can facilitate the development of self-efficacy. The research findings are quite consistent with this proposition (e.g., Stock & Cervone, 1990; Latham & Seijts, 1999).

A study by Stock and Cervone (1990) suggested that setting a proximal goal boosted the initial perception of self-efficacy. Attaining a proximal goal further enhanced self-efficacy. Latham and Seijts (1999) found that perceived self-efficacy was only significantly increased for those participants whose distal goals were accompanied by proximal sub-goals. There were no significant changes in perceived self-efficacy in the "do your best" or distal goals alone condition.

Although subgoal attainment can produce self-satisfaction and boost self-efficacy, there may be individual differences in people's preferences for proximal goal setting. Steel and König (2006) suggested that impulsiveness and need for achievement may affect people's preference for proximal subgoals and distal goals. Specifically, impulsive individuals may prefer frequent and more attainable subgoals, whereas individuals with high need for achievement may prefer less frequent and harder goals. Future research needs to empirically test the role of such individual differences in preferences for proximal goals and distal goals.

*Proximal goals, task strategy development, and learning.* Bandura (1986) argued that performance is optimal when there are proximal goals for a complex task. Proximal goals provide clear markers of goal progress, whereas distal goals are too far removed to sufficiently gauge one's advancement. Building on this, Latham and Seijts (1999, p. 422) suggested that proximal goals can provide "additional specific information about performance that is not present when only a distal goal is set" because setting proximal goals increases the frequency of feedback. This additional feedback information can facilitate task strategy development, which ultimately contributes to performance. Latham and Seijts found that participants in the distal plus proximal goal condition outperformed those in the distal-goal-only condition.

Latham and Locke (2007) further suggested that proximal goals contribute to performance because they facilitate error management (Keith & Frese, 2008). Since setting proximal goals increases the frequency of feedback (Latham & Seijts, 1999), people are able to learn from errors; error management leads to an improvement of strategy and, ultimately, to higher performance. Seijts and Latham (2001) evaluated the effect of proximal goals on strategy development and found that individuals with proximal goals indeed generated a greater number of strategies than those with distal goals only.[1]

Up to this point, we concentrated on studies in which the goals were set by the superior or the experimental condition. However, we still know little about people's tendency to develop proximal goals when they pursue distal goals. People do not always spontaneously develop proximal subgoals even if this is effective in achieving distal goals. Indeed, one research group has deemed deficient division of global goals into subgoals as a typical error in problem-solving situations (Dörner & Schaub, 1994). Borrelli and Mermelstein (1994) examined the role of self-efficacy, motivation to quit, and stress among smokers in a smoking cessation program over seven time points in 3 months. Surprisingly, they found self-efficacy to be negatively related to proximal subgoal development at all seven time points; motivation to quit was also significantly and negatively correlated with subgoal development at five of seven time points (Borrelli & Mermelstein, 1994). This result stands in contrast to the general findings that self-efficacy is positively related to goal achievement. The authors suggested that this was because highly efficacious abstainers may feel less need to set proximal subgoals, while abstainers with low self-efficacy for quitting may have a higher need for setting more subgoals to facilitate quitting and prevent relapse.

Donovan and Williams (2003) examined how athletes set and revise proximal and distal goals over the course of an 8-week competitive season. Here, the distal goal was the goal for the entire season, whereas proximal goals were the goals for each competition. They found that goal-performance discrepancies predicted the amount of goal revision: athletes faced with large goal-performance discrepancies for both competition (proximal) and season (distal) goals tended to revise these goals in a downward manner in proportion to the size of the discrepancies; in contrast, participants who surpassed their goals revised their goals in an upward manner. After controlling proximal goal-performance discrepancy, people with a large discrepancy between their distal goal and their performance raised their proximal goals. The authors suggested that this upward revision of proximal goals was an attempt to reduce the large discrepancy between the distal goal and performance. This interpretation is consistent with the argument that proximal goals are instrumental to achieving distal goals.

In conclusion, (1) when the distal goals are short term and relatively simple, there is little performance difference between proximal and distal goal setting; (2) when the distal goals are long term or complex, additional proximal goal setting outperforms the distal goals alone through goal persistence or effective strategy development or both. It is safe to conclude that setting proximal goals when pursuing a long-term goal is beneficial to both motivation and performance. However, supervisor setting of subgoals may sometimes be seen as patronizing and controlling and can actually reduce distal goal attainment. Moreover, the process of how people use self-developed proximal subgoals has not been studied enough to present clear conclusions. The literature so far suggests, however, that people should be encouraged to develop proximal subgoals, although this should not necessarily be the task of the supervisor (Oldham & Hackman, 2010).

## Reciprocally Interdependent and Synergetic Goals

It is possible that goals are not nested in each other, but are reciprocally interdependent and even synergetic. Thus, the multiple goals produce mutually beneficial effects (cf. Figure 12.1, III). The optimization of the attainment of these multiple goals may require knowledge of their interrelationships, strategic coordination, and self-regulatory strategies such as metacognitive activities. Thus, the research question examines how people construct a portfolio of goals that have the potential to benefit each other, and thus produce an overall positive effect on performance. Constructing a portfolio of synergistic goals is akin to solving a complex problem (Blech & Funke, 2010); this can also be viewed as a type of coping strategy to deal with potentially conflicting goals. Metacognitive strategies (i.e., thinking about one's goal setting, about one's planning, etc.) probably help to think of synergy between goals that are in principle distinct from each other. Although research in this area is limited, there are a few studies that may provide avenues for stimulating future research.

In a little-known paper on the metacognitive strategy of choosing synergetic goals, Resch and Oesterreich (1987) showed that people search to optimize two criteria when they chose proximal goals: First, the proximal goals should open up the highest number of options, and people should think that they have the requisite knowledge and skills to pursue them with a high degree of efficiency (they called it the principle of divergence-efficiency). For example, if people make career decisions, it makes sense for them to pursue career steps that allow more options later on, but where each action path can be pursued with optimal efficiency, given one's knowledge and skills. An example is to prefer a job in a big company as a first job after university because one is liable to get good training in such a company. This training allows the person to learn skills that are then useful in a wide range of areas in the job market.

Another way to increase perceived coherence among multiple goals is to change one's construal of those goals (Freitas, Clark, Kim, & Levy, 2009). People can construe the same action or goal either in high-level, abstract terms or in low-level, concrete terms (Dewitte & Lens, 2000; Vallacher & Wegner, 1989). For example, for the same goal of "writing a paper," some people might construe it as "typing sentences sitting in front of a computer" (i.e., a low-level or task-level construal), where others may construe it as "producing new theory" (i.e., high-level, abstract construal). Freitas et al.'s (2009) research suggests that, when facing multiple goals that on the surface may be unrelated and even competing, changing the construal levels of these goals from the concrete level to an abstract level allows people to perceive these goals as synergetic. For example, an individual may have a work goal (e.g., to get promoted this year) and a family goal (e.g., to spend $x$ hours of quality time per week with the family). These two goals are quite distinct because they belong to different life domains. However, when construing them in high-level terms, both goals can be construed to be subgoals for an abstract goal such as leading a happy and successful life. By construing the two goals in terms of the abstract and broader aim they serve, people can perceive the potential synergy that the two goals can create rather than perceive them as conflicting with each other. A change of the construal of multiple goals from low to high level facilitated perceiving coherence in them and in turn promoted positive affective experiences (Freitas et al., 2009). This may be one of the reasons for the positive performance effects of high-level visions for companies: visions make it possible to combine lower-level goals and to perceive them as synergetic (Baum et al., 1998).

Another metacognitive approach to produce a new perspective and to increase potential synergy between different goals is to set a learning goal: an emphasis on thinking of tasks as a chance to learn something new (Payne, Youngcourt, & Beaubien, 2007).

Adopting a learning goal facilitates the use of cognitive strategies such as learning and understanding, and metacognitive strategies for planning and monitoring (Suárez Riveiro, Cabanach, & Arias, 2001). Similarly, research on goal setting demonstrated that setting a learning goal leads to high performance through improving self-efficacy and information search (Seijts & Latham, 2001; Seijts, Latham, Tasa, & Latham, 2004). As a result, people with a learning goal may be more likely to engage in balanced goal pursuits, which ultimately optimizes overall performance. Taken together, these studies suggest that a learning goal could increase individuals' awareness of interrelationships among multiple ongoing goals, possibly through increased information search and thoughts about common themes of different goals.

Given the benefits of constructing synergistic relationships among multiple goals, future research on the mechanisms or strategies that people use to construct beneficial relationships among multiple goals is needed.

## Conclusion

People often pursue multiple goals in their work and everyday life. There has been growing interest in studying issues related to multiple-goal pursuits. In this chapter, we used a typology of multiple separate goals that draw on limited resources, sequentially interdependent goals, and reciprocal and synergetic goals. For each type of multiple goal, we identified research questions, reviewed the major research findings, and proposed future research.

When preparing this chapter, we were surprised to find that some research areas of multiple goals were primarily interested in their effects on well-being and that other research areas of multiple goals were primarily using performance as dependent variables. For example, research on goal conflicts is primarily interested in well-being or strain effects, but shows little interest in performance issues (e.g., role conflicts, King & King, 1990; or the area of work–family conflicts, Amstad, Meier, Fasel, Elfering, & Semmer, 2011; Ford, Heinen, & Langkamer, 2007). Specifically, in the most recent meta-analysis of the influence of work–family conflict on its various outcomes (Amstad, Meier, Fasel, Elfering, & Semmer, 2011), the number of effect sizes available for the analyses were 10 for work-related performance and 3 for family-related performance, which is rather small compared with 54 effect sizes for work satisfaction and 25 for marital and family satisfaction. It would be interesting to know more about the effects of goal conflicts on performance.

On the other hand, multiple-goal studies within the goal setting literature have been primarily interested in performance-related dependent variables although the high-performance cycle (Latham, Locke, & Fassina, 2002) includes job satisfaction as an indicator of well-being. We believe that it would also be interesting to examine the well-being consequences in more detail (e.g., Brunstein, 1993).

## Note

1. In contrast, Weldon and Yun (2000) did not find this effect of proximal goals on strategy development. However, they used a subjective measure of strategy development in contrast to the measure used by Seijts and Latham (2001).

# References

Amstad, F. T., Meier, L. L., Fasel, U., Elfering, A., & Semmer, N. K. (2011). A meta-analysis of work-family conflict and various outcomes with a special emphasis on cross-domain versus matching-domain relations. *Journal of Occupational Health Psychology, 16*(2), 151–169.

Anderson, J. R. (1983). *The architecture of cognition.* Cambridge, MA: Harvard University Press.

Bandura, A. (1986). *Social foundations of thought and action: A social cognitive theory.* Englewood Cliffs, NJ: Prentice-Hall.

Bandura, A. (1997). *Self-efficacy: The exercise of control.* New York: Freeman.

Bandura, A. (2001). Social cognitive theory: An agentic perspective. *Annual Review of Psychology, 52,* 1–26.

Bandura, A. (2012). On the functional properties of perceived self-efficacy revisited. *Journal of Management, 38,* 9–44.

Bandura, A., & Locke, E. A. (2003). Negative self-efficacy and goal effects revisited. *Journal of Applied Psychology, 88,* 87–99.

Baum, J.R., Locke, E.A., & Kirkpatrick, S.A. (1998). A longitudinal study of the relation of vision and vision communication to venture growth. *Journal of Applied Psychology, 83,* 43–54.

Blech, C. & Funke, J. (2010). You cannot have your cake and eat it, too: How induced goal conflicts affect complex problem solving. *Open Psychology Journal, 3,* 42–53.

Borrelli, B., & Mermelstein, R. (1994). Goal setting and behavior change in a smoking cessation program. *Cognitive Therapy and Research, 18*(1), 69–83.

Brendl, C. M., & Higgins, E. T. (1996). Principles of judging valence: What makes events positive or negative? *Advances in Experimental Social Psychology, 28,* 95–160.

Brown, J. S. (1948), Gradients of approach and avoidance responses and their relation to level of motivation. *Journal of Comparative and Physiological Psychology, 41*(6), 450–465.

Brunstein, J. C. (1993). Personal goals and subjective well-being: A longitudinal study. *Journal of Personality and Social Psychology, 65,* 1061–1070.

Byrd, T. G., & Donovan, J. J. (2004, April). Task prioritization in a multiple-goal setting: What determines our division of resources between simultaneous goals? *Symposium presented at the 19th annual conference of the society of industrial and organizational psychology,* Chicago, IL.

Carver, C. (2003). Pleasure as a sign you can attend to something else: Placing positive feelings within a general model of affect. *Cognition & Emotion, 17*(2), 241–261.

Carver, C. S., & Scheier, M. (1998). *On the self-regulation of behavior.* New York: Cambridge University Press.

Dewitte, S., & Lens, W. (2000). Procrastinators lack a broad action perspective. *European Journal of Personality, 14*(2), 121–140.

Donovan, J. J., & Williams, K. J. (2003). Missing the mark: Effects of time and causal attributions on goal revision in response to goal-performance discrepancies. *Journal of Applied Psychology, 88,* 379–390.

Dörner, D., & Schaub, H. (1994). Errors in planning and decision-making and the nature of human information processing. *Applied Psychology: An International Review, 43,* 433–454.

Emmons, R. A. (1986). Personal strivings: An approach to personality and subjective well-being. *Journal of Personal and Social Psychology, 51,* 1058–1068.

Erez, M., Gopher, D., & Arazi, N. (1990). Effects of goal difficulty, self-set goals, and monetary rewards on dual task performance. *Organizational Behavior and Human Decision Processes, 47*(2), 247–269.

Ford, M. T., Heinen, B. A., & Langkamer, K. L. (2007). Work and family satisfaction and conflict: A meta-analysis of cross-domain relations. *Journal of Applied Psychology, 92*(1), 57–80.

Förster, J., Higgins, E. T., & Idson, L. C. (1998). Approach and avoidance strength during goal attainment: Regulatory focus and the "goal looms larger" effect. *Journal of Personality and Social Psychology, 75*(5), 1115–1131.

Freitas, A. L., Clark, S. L., Kim, J. Y., & Levy, S. R. (2009). Action-construal levels and perceived conflict among ongoing goals: Implications for positive affect. *Journal of Research in Personality, 43*(5), 938–941.

Frese, M., Krauss, S., Keith, N., Escher, S., Grabarkiewicz, R., Luneng, S. T. et al. (2007). Business owners' action planning and its relationship to business success in three African countries. *Journal of Applied Psychology, 92*, 1481–1498.

Frese, M., & Zapf, D. (1994). Action as the core of work psychology: A German approach. In H. C. Triandis, M. D. Dunnette, & L. Hough (Eds.), *Handbook of industrial and organizational psychology* (Vol. 4, pp. 271–340). Palo Alto, CA: Consulting Psychologists Press.

Fulford, D., Johnson, S. L., Llabre, M. M., & Carver, C. S. (2010). Pushing and coasting in dynamic goal pursuit: Coasting is attenuated in bipolar disorder. *Psychological Science, 21*(7), 1021–1027.

Gollwitzer, P. M. (1999). Implementation intentions: Strong effects of simple plans. *American Psychologist, 54*, 493–503.

Hacker, W. (1985). Activity: A fruitful concept in industrial psychology. In M. Frese & J. Sabini (Eds.), *Goal directed behavior: The concept of action in psychology* (pp. 262–283). Hillsdale, NJ: Erlbaum.

Hollenbeck, J. R., & Williams, C. R. (1987). Goal importance, self-focus, and the goal-setting process. *Journal of Applied Psychology, 72*, 204–211.

Hull, C. L. (1934). The rats' speed of locomotion gradient in the approach to food. *Journal of Comparative Psychology, 17*(3), 393–422.

Humphreys, M. S., & Revelle, W. (1984). Personality, motivation, and performance: A theory of the relationship between individual differences and information processing. *Psychological Review, 91*, 153–184.

Kahneman, D. (1973). *Attention and effort*. Englewood Cliffs, NJ: Prentice Hall.

Kanfer, R., & Ackerman, P. (1989). Motivation and cognitive abilities: An integrative/aptitude-treatment interaction approach to skill acquisition. *Journal of Applied Psychology, 74*(4), 657–690.

Keith, N., & Frese, M. (2008). Performance effects of error management training: A meta-analysis. *Journal of Applied Psychology, 93*, 59–69.

Kehr, H. M. (2003). Goal conflicts, attainment of new goals, and well-being among managers. *Journal of Occupational Health Psychology, 8*, 195–208.

Kelly, R. E., Mansell, W., & Wood, A. (2011). Goal conflict and ambivalence interact to predict depression. *Personality and Individual Differences, 50*, 531–534.

Kernan, M. C., & Lord, R. G. (1990). Effects of valence, expectancies, and goal-performance discrepancies in single and multiple goal environments. *Journal of Applied Psychology, 75*(2), 194–203.

King, L. A., & King, D. W. (1990). Role conflict and role ambiguity: A critical assessment of construct validity. *Psychological Bulletin, 107*(1), 48–64.

Kiesel, A., Steinhauser, M., Wendt, M., Falkenstein, M., Jost, K., Philipp, A. M., et al. (2010). Control and interference in task switching—A review. *Psychological Bulletin, 136*, 849–874.

Klein, H. J. (1989). An integrated control theory model of work motivation. *The Academy of Management Review, 14*(2), 150–172.

Latham, G. P., & Locke, E. A. (2006). Enhancing the benefits and overcoming the pitfalls of goal setting. *Organizational Dynamics, 35*(4), 332–340.

Latham, G. P., & Locke, E. A. (2007). New developments in and directions for goal-setting research. *European Psychologist, 12,* 290–300.

Latham, G. P., Locke, E. A., & Fassina, N. E. (2002). The high performance cycle: Standing the test of time. In S. Sonnentag (Eds.), *The psychological management of individual performance. A handbook in the psychology of management in organizations* (pp. 201–228). Chichester, England: Wiley.

Latham, G. P., & Seijts, G. H. (1999). The effects of proximal and distal goals on performance on a moderately complex task. *Journal of Organizational Behavior, 20*(4), 421–429.

Lewin, K. (1935) *A dynamic theory of personality.* New York: McGraw-Hill.

Locke, E. A., & Latham, G. P. (1990). *A theory of goal setting & task performance.* Englewood Cliffs, NJ: Prentice Hall.

Locke, E. A., & Latham, G. P. (2002). Building a practically useful theory of goal setting and task motivation: A 35-year odyssey. *American Psychologist, 57*(9), 705–717.

Locke, E. A., & Latham, G. P. (2006). New directions in goal-setting theory. *Current Directions in Psychological Science, 15,* 265–268.

Locke, E. A., Smith, K. G., Erez, M., Chah, D. O., & Schaffer, A. (1994). The effects of intra-individual goal conflict on performance. *Journal of Management, 20*(1), 67–91.

Lord, R. G., Diefendorff, J. M., Schmidt, A. M., & Hall, R. J. (2010). Self-regulation at work. *Annual Review of Psychology, 61,* 543–568.

Lord, R. G., & Levy, P. E. (1994). Moving from cognition to action: A control theory perspective. *Applied Psychology,* An International Review, *43,* 335–367.

Louro, M. J., Pieters, R., & Zeelenberg, M. (2007). Dynamics of multiple-goal pursuit. *Journal of Personality and Social Psychology, 93*(2), 174–193.

Manderlink, G., & Harackiewicz, J. M. (1984). Proximal versus distal goal setting and intrinsic motivation. *Journal of Personality and Social Psychology, 47*(4), 918–928.

Miller, G. A., Galanter, E., & Pribram, K. H. (1960). *Plans and the structure of behavior.* London: Holt.

Newell, A., & Simon, H. A. (1975). Computer science as empirical inquiry: Symbols and search. *Communications of the ACM. 19,* 113–126.

Northcraft, G., Schmidt, A., & Ashford, S. (2011). Feedback and the rationing of time and effort among competing tasks. *Journal of Applied Psychology, 96,* 1076–1086.

Oberauer, K., & Kliegl, R. (2004). Simultaneous cognitive operations in working memory after dual-task practice. *Journal of Experimental Psychology: Human Perception and Performance, 30,* 689–707.

Oldham, G. R., & Hackman, J. R. (2010). Not what it was and not what it will be: The future of job design research. *Journal of Organizational Behavior, 31,* 463–479.

Payne, S. C., Youngcourt, S. S., & Beaubien, J. M. (2007). A meta-analytic examination of the goal orientation nomological net. *Journal of Applied Psychology, 92,* 128–150.

Resch, M., & Oesterreich, R. (1987). Bildung von Zwischenzielen in Entscheidungsnetzen [Formulation of intermediate goals in decision networks]. *Zeitschrift für Experimentelle und Angewandte Psychologie, 34,* 301–317.

Schmidt, A. M., & DeShon, R. P. (2007). What to do? The effects of discrepancies, incentives, and time on dynamic goal prioritization. *Journal of Applied Psychology, 92*(4), 928–941.

Schmidt, A. M., & Dolis, C. M. (2009). Something's got to give: The effects of dual-goal difficulty, goal progress, and expectancies on resource allocation. *Journal of Applied Psychology, 94*(3), 678–691.

Schmidt, A. M., Dolis, C. M., & Tolli, A. P. (2009). A matter of time: Individual differences, contextual dynamics, and goal progress effects on multiple-goal self-regulation. *Journal of Applied Psychology, 94*(3), 692–709.

Schwarz, N. (1990). Feelings as information: Informational and motivational functions of affective states. In E. T. Higgins & R. M. Sorrentino (Eds.), *Handbook of motivation and cognition* (pp. 527–561). New York: Guilford Press.

Seijts, G. H., & Latham, G. P. (2001). The effect of distal learning, outcome, and proximal goals on a moderately complex task. *Journal of Organizational Behavior, 22*(3), 291–307.

Seijts, G. H., Latham, G. P., Tasa, K., & Latham, B. W. (2004). Goal setting and goal orientation: An integration of two different yet related literatures. *The Academy of Management Journal, 47*(2), 227–239.

Smith, K. G., Locke, E. A., & Barry, D. (1990). Goal setting, planning, and organizational performance: An experimental simulation. *Organizational Behavior and Human Decision Making Processes, 464*, 118–134.

Spelke, E. S., Hirst, W. C., & Neisser, U. (1976). Skills of divided attention. *Cognition, 4*, 215–230.

Steel, P., & König, C. J. (2006). Integrating theories of motivation. *The Academy of Management Review 31*(4), 889–913.

Stock, J., & Cervone, D. (1990). Proximal goal-setting and self-regulatory processes. *Cognitive Therapy and Research, 14*(5), 483–498.

Stoeber, J., Hutchfield, J., & Wood, K. V. (2008). Perfectionism, self-efficacy, and aspiration level: Differential effects of perfectionistic striving and self-criticism after success and failure. *Personality and Individual Differences, 45*, 323–327.

Suárez Riveiro, J. M., Cabanach, R. G., & Arias, A. V. (2001). Multiple goal pursuit and its relation to cognitive, self-regulatory, and motivational strategies. *British Journal of Educational Psychology, 71*(4), 561–572.

Vallacher, R. R., & Wegner, D. M. (1989). Levels of personal agency: Individual variation in action identification. *Journal of Personality and Social Psychology, 57*(4), 660–671.

Vancouver, J. B. (2005). The depth of history and explanation as benefit and bane for psychological control theories. *Journal of Applied Psychology, 90*, 38–52.

Vancouver, J. B., More, K. M., & Yoder, R. J. (2008). Self-efficacy and resource allocation: Support for a nonmonotonic, discontinuous model. *Journal of Applied Psychology, 93*(1), 35–47.

Weldon, E., & Yun, S. (2000). The effects of proximal and distal goals on goal level, strategy development, and group performance. *Journal of Applied Behavioral Science, 36*(3), 336–344.

Wiese, B. S., & Salmela-Aro, K. (2008). Goal conflict and facilitation as predictors of work-family satisfaction and engagement. *Journal of Vocational Behavior, 73*, 490–497.

Wood, R. E., & Locke, E. A. (1990). Goal setting and strategy effects on complex tasks. *Research in Organizational Behavior, 12*, 73–109.

Wood, R. E., Mento, A. J., & Locke, E. A. (1987). Task complexity as a moderator of goal effects: A meta-analysis. *Journal of Applied Psychology, 72*, 416–425.

# 13 Learning Goals

## A Qualitative and Quantitative Review

*Gerard H. Seijts*  Richard Ivey School of Business, Western University
*Gary P. Latham*  Rotman School of Management, University of Toronto
*Meredith Woodwark*  Richard Ivey School of Business,
Western University

The beneficial effects of learning goals, a state, on self-regulation and performance were unknown when Locke and Latham (1990) published their theory and the research on which it is based. Hence, the purpose of this chapter is threefold. First, we review empirical research on learning goals. These studies show that both individuals and groups perform better with learning than performance goals on tasks that are complex for them. Second, the results of a meta-analysis on these studies are described. Third, this chapter concludes with a discussion of the practical implications of the research findings, limitations in research designs, and areas for future research on learning goals.

## Goal Setting for Complex Tasks

More than 1000 studies—in a wide variety of settings and around the globe, using widely different tasks in both laboratory and field settings—have been conducted on the internal and external validity of goal setting theory (e.g., Latham & Locke, 2007; Locke & Latham, 2002; Mitchell & Daniels, 2003). These studies have shown that specific, challenging goals lead to higher levels of performance than an easy goal or an abstract one such as an exhortation to do your best. Hence, researchers have concluded that goal setting theory is among the most robust, valid, and practical motivation theories of organizational behavior (e.g., Miner, 2003; Pinder, 1998).

Despite these robust findings for the goal–performance relationship, the complexity of the task affects this relationship. Resource allocation theory (e.g., Kanfer & Ackerman, 1989; Ackerman, Kanfer, & Goff, 1995; Kanfer, Ackerman, Murtha, Dugdale, & Nelson, 1994) explains why the setting of a specific, challenging goal can lead to a decrement in performance. This theory states that when individuals are in the declarative stage of learning, that is, when they have yet to acquire appropriate performance routines, their direction of thought should be on discovering ways of mastering the processes required to perform the task effectively rather than on ways of attaining a specific level of performance. People who lack the requisite knowledge and skills are distracted by factors that are not relevant to learning, and hence they are unable to devote the cognitive resources necessary to mastering the task. In other words, focusing on a specific, challenging goal interferes with learning appropriate strategies or procedures that will enable individuals to accelerate their effectiveness. Thus individuals should avoid setting a specific, challenging goal until they have acquired the ability (i.e., knowledge and skill) to perform the task. Ability is a moderator variable in goal setting theory (e.g., Locke & Latham, 1990, 2002). Empirical research supports this contention.

Mone and Shalley (1995) examined the interaction between goal condition (specific, challenging goal; do-your-best goal) and task complexity (simple; complex) on a human resources staffing simulation that took place over three consecutive days (performance periods). The results showed that a specific, challenging goal led to higher performance on an index of performance quality—total hiring, placement, and salary decisions— than a do-your-best goal on a simple version of the simulation. But the setting of a do-your-best goal, which is vague rather than specific, led to higher performance than a specific, challenging goal on a complex version of the simulation. Undergraduate business students who had a do-your-best goal searched systematically for effective task strategies, which in turn increased their performance.

Winters and Latham (1996) explained these findings in terms of the content of the goal, namely, one that focuses attention on a specific performance outcome rather than focusing on specific ways to learn to perform the task. A performance goal frames the goal instructions so that an individual's focus is on a specific task outcome (e.g., attain an increase of 15% market share by the end of the next fiscal year). A performance goal cues individuals to use performance routines or strategies that the individual has previously learned are effective in performing the task. In contrast, a learning goal frames the goal instructions in terms of knowledge or skill acquisition (e.g., discover five effective strategies to increase market share). Consequently, a learning goal draws attention away from a specific end result in that the emphasis is on discovering or mastering appropriate strategies, processes, or procedures necessary to perform a given task. Future research needs to explore whether learning goals should be followed by performance goals, or whether there are situations in which learning goals can coexist with performance goals to achieve optimal performance.

## Narrative Review of Research on Learning Goals

Relative to performance goals, only a few studies have been conducted on the effects of learning goals on performance (Latham, 2012). We review these studies here and explain how each has contributed to knowledge about when learning goals should be set. Programmatic research with replications and extensions enables scholars and practitioners to understand when and how learning goals affect self-regulation processes and performance in a positive way. The practical significance of these findings is important because individuals and groups have to continuously master new tasks, as many organizations operate in a highly complex environment characterized by rapid change.

Winters and Latham (1996) used a 3 (goal condition) × 2 (task complexity) × 3 (trials) design to test the effect of learning versus performance goals on performance. A specific, challenging performance goal ("complete 10 or more correct class schedules") led to higher performance than both a learning goal and a do-your-best goal on a class scheduling task that was straightforward. But the assignment of a do-your-best goal led to higher performance than a performance goal on a complex version of this task. This finding replicated the results obtained earlier by Mone and Shalley (1995).

The unique finding in the Winters and Latham experiment was that the assignment of a learning goal ("discover and implement 4 shortcuts to performing this scheduling task") led to even higher performance than urging individuals do their best. Participants with a learning goal also had significantly higher self-efficacy and they identified more task strategies than participants who had a performance goal. This was the first goal setting study that suggested that individuals should set specific, challenging learning goals as opposed to performance goals when performing a task that is complex for them.

Seijts and Latham (2001) showed that the learning goal effect was mediated by self-efficacy and the discovery of task strategies. Their results showed that undergraduate students with a specific, challenging learning goal had higher performance on a complex scheduling task than those with either a do-your-best goal or a specific, challenging performance goal. This finding is consistent with that obtained by Winters and Latham (1996). Commitment to the goal was higher in the learning goal condition than it was in the performance goal condition. The repeated measures design also showed that self-efficacy decreased significantly for participants with a performance goal, yet increased significantly for those with a learning goal. The latter finding reflects the fact that individuals were discovering or learning the strategies necessary to complete the task successfully. Self-efficacy mediated the relationship between strategies and performance. And the discovery of task strategies increased subsequent self-efficacy through an increase in performance. In short, self-efficacy and the discovery of task strategies had a reciprocal effect on one another, and both variables mediated the learning goal–performance relationship on this complex task.

Brown and Latham (2002) studied the effects of learning goals, behavioral goals, and do-your-best goals on teamwork behaviour in a group problem-solving task. Peers conducted behavioural assessments of one another using behavioral observation scales or BOS (Latham & Wexley, 1977). Business students who were assigned behavioral goals (a numerical score on the BOS) scored higher on teamwork behavior than did individuals with a learning goal ("discover ideas or strategies that will enable you to demonstrate the teamwork behaviors listed on the BOS") and a do-your-best goal ("do your best to demonstrate the behaviors listed on the BOS"). Self-efficacy correlated positively with the demonstrated teamwork behaviors; and self-efficacy was higher in both specific goal conditions than it was in the do-your-best goal condition. Brown and Latham concluded that a behavioral goal that is set on the basis of a systematic job analysis mitigates the necessity to discover the requisite desired behaviors to do well on the task. When people have been given the effective task procedures or processes, a learning goal needlessly focuses attention on rediscovering the task-relevant strategies (e.g., the individual may spend cognitive resources on the wrong activities). In short, a learning goal is not necessary when the requisite behaviors for task performance are known.

Drach-Zahavy and Erez (2002) used a 3 (goal assignment) × 2 (stress) × 2 (trials) design to examine the effect of goals on the performance of a complex stock market prediction task under conditions of stress. The setting of a specific, difficult goal often results in stress. But, stress can be appraised as either a challenge (e.g., there are opportunities for self-growth) or a threat (e.g., failure is possible). The results showed that participants with a learning goal had higher performance on the complex task than those with either a performance or a do-your-best goal. Participants with a do-your-best goal, however, outperformed those with a performance goal. But no significant differences were observed among the three goal conditions in the condition where the participants appraised the task as an opportunity for self-development. Moreover, a substantial change introduced to the task (Trial 2) had a negative effect on performance only in the condition appraised as a threat by participants who had a specific, high performance goal. There were no changes in performance for those with a learning or do-your-best goal. The results of this study show that learning goals are particularly beneficial when individuals appraise a task as a threat.

Dweck (1999) has studied the effect of goal orientation as a dispositional variable. She found that children with a learning goal orientation tend to choose tasks where they can increase their knowledge and skills. Failures or setbacks are viewed by them as inherent in the learning process. Children with a performance goal orientation, however, prefer tasks where they anticipate they will look good in the eyes of others.

Seijts, Latham, Tasa, and Latham (2004) investigated the effects of a specific, challenging learning goal in a complex business simulation to see if it masks the effect of goal orientation. Specific, high goals, a state rather than a disposition, create a strong situation (e.g., Meyer, Dalal, & Hermida, 2010; Mischel, 1977) in that they make clear what is expected of employees. Thus, they mask individual differences (e.g., Adler & Weiss, 1988; Latham, Ganegoda, & Locke, 2011). Seijts et al. found that a specific, challenging learning goal ("identify and implement 6 or more strategies to increase market share") led to higher performance than a do-your-best goal ("achieve as much market share as possible") as well as a specific, high performance goal ("achieve 21% or more market share"). As was found in previous studies, participants with a do-your-best goal had higher performance than those with a specific, high performance goal. However, performance increased across trials for participants with a learning goal. These individuals also spent more time in the simulation acquiring the knowledge to perform the task; and they reported higher commitment to the goal than participants in the other two goal conditions. The correlations between goal orientation and performance were significant only in the do-your-best goal condition, a weak situation. Setting a specific goal attenuated these correlations regardless of whether the goal that was set was a performance goal or a learning goal. The exception was a positive and significant correlation ($r = .35$) between a learning goal orientation and performance in the learning goal condition. This suggests that the effect of a learning goal, a state, is further enhanced when individuals have a learning goal disposition. The results also showed that self-efficacy and information search mediated the effect of a learning goal on performance.

Latham and Brown (2006) conducted a field experiment on the effect of learning versus performance goals on students' self-efficacy, satisfaction with their MBA program, and grade point average. The setting of a learning goal as well as a distal outcome goal that included proximal outcome goals led to a higher grade point average than the setting of a distal outcome goal only. Participants who set a learning goal had higher satisfaction with the MBA program than those in the other goal setting conditions. Latham and Brown concluded that the setting of a learning goal, by its very nature, appears to have focused the students' attention on developing ways to address the mental challenges of performing well in the business school which, in turn, increased their satisfaction with the program.

Noel and Latham (2006) studied the effect of learning goals in an entrepreneurial setting. Students from an entrepreneurship class performed a complex simulation: Launching a High-Risk Business. A learning goal ("generating strategies for improving performance in the upcoming trial") led to higher performance than setting a performance goal ("to keep the firm running for a specified number of months"). The results also showed that strategies mediated the relationship between self-efficacy and performance; and that self-efficacy mediated the relationship between the use of strategies and performance. These results are consistent with those obtained by Seijts and Latham (2001).

Kozlowski and Bell (2006) conducted an experiment to tease apart the effects of goal content (learning goal; performance goal), goal frame (acquire knowledge and skills; demonstrate competency) and goal proximity (proximal; distal) on self-regulation processes. Participants completed a complex computer radar-tracking simulation. Although all three factors (goal content; goal frame; and goal proximity) had a significant effect on self-regulation, goal content had the strongest influence "explaining almost twice as much variance in self-regulation activity as each of the other two factors" (p. 908). Congruence between learning frame and goal content was more beneficial for self-regulation activities (e.g., higher self-efficacy, less negative affect, more exploratory behavior) than congruence between performance frame and goal content. Participants with a learning goal reported a greater exploratory practice focus than did those with a performance goal. Finally, the results showed a significant correlation between goal content and basic performance (or the number of correct and incorrect decisions in the simulation): participants with a learning goal had higher basic performance than those with a performance goal. Kozlowski and Bell concluded that training interventions should focus on learning goals, use a learning goal frame for instructions, and ensure there is congruence among these factors.

Goal setting theory states that given adequate ability and given goal commitment, the higher the goal, the higher the performance. Latham, Seijts, and Crim (2008) studied the effect of learning goal difficulty on performance of a complex task. Consistent with the theory, the findings revealed a significant, positive correlation between commitment to the learning goal and task performance. Consistent with the theory, participants with a high learning goal also produced more class schedules than those with an easier learning goal. This was because a more difficult learning goal leads to greater cognitive effort to acquire task-relevant strategies than easier learning goals.

The results of a regression analysis showed a goal level × cognitive ability interaction on performance. Contrary to what has been found for high performance goals (Locke, 1965), participants with lower cognitive ability benefited more from the setting of a learning goal that increased in goal difficulty than did participants with higher cognitive ability. The latter group was relatively unaffected by the difficulty level of the learning goal; and they outperformed their counterparts with lower cognitive ability. Nevertheless, individuals with low cognitive ability assigned a high learning goal approached the performance level of high cognitive ability participants. Latham et al. speculated that a learning goal prompts individuals with lower cognitive ability to take the time to reflect on what went wrong with one or more strategies, and it encourages them to search for alternative solutions to the problem. The search for appropriate strategies is obviously important for both intelligent and less intelligent individuals. The benefit of a challenging learning goal is that it appears to cue the less intelligent to do so. Intelligent people likely do the above intuitively or automatically. Thus, it would appear that for individuals to do well on a task that requires the acquisition of knowledge and skill they must either have high cognitive ability or a high learning goal.

Seijts and Crim (2009) investigated whether cognitive ability affects the relationship between goal content and performance. Participants with higher cognitive ability benefited more from a performance goal as opposed to a learning goal; the reverse pattern was obtained for participants with lower cognitive ability. Participants with higher cognitive ability learned the task faster and hence progressed further through the phases of knowledge and skill acquisition as compared to those with lower cognitive ability. This is likely due to the fact that those with higher cognitive ability can devote more of their cognitive resources to task performance, whereas the latter must devote attentional resources toward learning how to perform the task. In sum, cognitive ability is a moderator of learning goal effects. This study provided evidence that the beneficial effects of performance goals and learning goals on task performance depends in part on cognitive ability, whereas Latham et al. (2008) found that the nature or strength of the learning goal difficulty–performance relationship depends in part on cognitive ability.

Cianci, Klein, and Seijts (2010) examined the interplay of goal content (learning goal; performance goal), conscientiousness, and tension on performance of a cognitive task following negative feedback indicating poor performance. Participants assigned a specific learning goal experienced less tension following negative feedback, and performed better on the subsequent performance trial, than did their counterparts who had been assigned a performance goal. Consistent with Dweck's (1999) work with children, individuals assigned a learning goal viewed errors and negative feedback as a natural part of their learning process. Those with a performance goal wanted to demonstrate their competence. They also became worried about the consequences of failure. The negative feedback and their resulting thoughts concerning the consequences of failure had a negative effect on their subsequent performance. High conscientiousness amplified the detrimental effect of a performance goal on tension, which in turn led to lower performance. This is because conscientious individuals have a desire to achieve, and as such are more vulnerable to experiencing feelings of tension and frustration to goal blockage. Yet, conscientiousness enhanced the performance of participants assigned a learning goal. These individuals exerted effort to develop their skills, to master the task rather than to focus on attaining a specific performance outcome. Thus, these results indicate that high conscientiousness does not help to elevate performance unless the person understands what it takes to perform at a high level. The results of this study also suggest that a learning goal appears to be a buffer against negative performance feedback. This finding further reinforces findings from previous studies that indicate that a specific, high learning goal should be set when individuals are in the process of learning how to perform a task that is complex for them. These results also speak to the importance of taking into account when and for whom the different types of goals—learning versus performance—are most effective.

Porter and Latham (in-press) studied the effect of learning goals, performance goals, and do-your-best goals on departmental performance during the 2009 financial and economic crisis. They surveyed both employees and managers working in various industries (e.g., financial, technology, and manufacturing). These individuals had learning goals, performance goals, do-your-best goals, or a combination of these goals. Hierarchical linear modeling showed a significant effect for learning goals on departmental performance. Learning goals explained more of the variance in a department's performance than did both performance goals and do-your-best goals. Porter and Latham explained that employees were likely searching for new strategies and procedures that would enhance the department's competitiveness during the environmental turbulence.

Seijts and Latham (2011) studied the interaction between the level of the learning goal and goal commitment on performance of a complex task. The correlation between commitment to the learning goal and performance was significant in the low as well as in the high learning goal conditions. Consistent with goal setting theory, commitment was also shown to be a moderator of the learning goal level–task performance relationship. Participants who reported high commitment to the high learning goal outperformed individuals who reported low commitment to the high learning goal. Commitment made less of a difference on the performance of participants in the low learning goal condition. This was the first study that showed that goal commitment moderates the learning goal–performance relationship. Evidence was also obtained for the cyclical effect among self-efficacy, commitment, and performance. For example, an increase in performance had a positive effect on both self-efficacy and commitment to the learning goal; and self-efficacy and commitment, in turn, facilitated subsequent performance. A serendipitous finding was that 75% of the participants self-set a performance goal even though they were committed to a learning goal. The regression analysis showed that the self-set performance goal was a significant predictor of performance.

Masuda and Locke (2011) observed that employees in organizations are often expected to learn while, at the same time, urged to attain difficult performance goals. Thus, they designed the first study that examined what happens when difficult learning and performance goals are assigned at the same time for performing the same complex task. They conducted two laboratory studies. In both studies, participants received four goals on an excel task: distal learning goal; distal performance goal; proximal learning goal; and proximal performance goal. The results of both studies showed that performance improved as a result of the learning and performance goals that were set simultaneously. But the improvement in performance was contingent on the total difficulty level of the goal (the average of proximal and distal learning goals and proximal and distal performance goal difficulty across trials). Neither all easy or all hard goals worked as well as an intermediate level of difficulty. Cognitive overload occurred when the goal difficulty level was too great. There was little motivation when all the goals were easy. Total learning goal difficulty (the average of self-set proximal and distal learning goal difficulty) was significantly related to the total number of strategies discovered and implemented by the participants. Goal effects were mediated either by strategies or self-efficacy.

## Meta-Analysis of Studies on Learning Goals

The previous section described the design and results of individual studies on learning goals. We combined the results of these studies to obtain the effect size for learning goals relative to specific, challenging performance and do-your-best goals. Both approaches—individual studies and aggregation—are part of the scientific method.

### Identification of Relevant Learning Goal Studies

The studies included in the meta-analysis were primarily identified using computerized keyword searches in managerially relevant databases including PsychINFO, Business Source Complete, ProQuest Plus, Dissertation Abstracts, Scholars Portal, ABI-Inform Global, PsychArticles, and Web of Science (formerly Social Sciences Citation Index). The reference lists of all the relevant goal setting studies were scanned for additional articles. We also contacted researchers who have conducted research on learning goals to request any unpublished studies including dissertations available for inclusion. To be included in the meta-analysis, a study had to include a learning goal condition as well as either a performance goal condition or a do-your-best goal condition; performance data for each experimental condition (including means, standard deviations, and sample sizes), ideally broken down by performance trial; a description of the experimental task sufficient to determine its level of complexity; and a description of the performance measures used. The authors of the studies were contacted to obtain the required performance data if it was not reported in the article in the required format.

The final sample size was 12 studies, all of which were peer-reviewed and published as none of the unpublished studies identified met the inclusion criteria. For example, Porter and Latham's field study (in-press) did not allow the required comparisons since all conditions had combinations of learning, performance, and do-your-best goals. The same was true for the two laboratory experiments conducted by Masuda and Locke (2011). The Winters and Latham (1996) study included both a complex and simple task condition. Thus, the final database contained 13 effect sizes.

All of the included studies were laboratory experiments with the exception of Latham and Brown (2006), who conducted a field experiment with MBA students. The sample sizes for the studies ranged from 29 to 542. The total sample size was 1567.

The studies used individual tasks, with the exception of Brown and Latham (2002). Most studies utilized objective measures of performance. The exception was the team survival scenario (Brown & Latham, 2002), where performance was based on peer ratings of teamwork behavior. The scheduling task used the number of correct schedules completed correctly as the performance measure. Latham and Brown's (2006) field experiment with MBA students used grade point average at the end of the first year as one measure of performance. The reading comprehension task used the number of correct responses to reading comprehension and analogy questions as the measure of performance (Cianci et al., 2010). The computer simulations used a performance measure based on the simulation's algorithms such as the number of months in business (Noel & Latham, 2006); the percentage of market share attained (Seijts et al., 2004; Seijts & Latham, 2011); the number of correct contact decisions (Kozlowski & Bell, 2006); and the accuracy of stock price predictions (Drach-Zahavy & Erez, 2002).

Table 13.1 provides an overview of the studies included in the meta-analysis. The table includes relevant characteristics of each study.

## Coding of Studies

In addition to examining the effect of learning goals relative to performance goals and do-your-best goals, we also examined whether the effect of learning goals on performance was contingent on the number of performance trials (would the effect of learning goals on performance decrease over time?), task complexity (would the effect of learning goals be stronger on more complex tasks?) and task length (are learning goals helpful in particular on tasks of longer duration in part because these tend to be more dynamic and based on actual events?).

*Performance trials.* Several of the studies had repeated measures designs. Five of the studies had one performance trial; three studies had two trials; and the remaining four studies had three trials. Separate effect sizes were calculated for each trial to examine how the effect sizes changed over time or performance trials.

*Task complexity.* The set of studies used a range of different tasks including four different computer-based simulations (high-risk business launch, radar war game, cellular industry business game, and stock market prediction task), a class scheduling task, a reading comprehension and analogies task, a team survival scenario, and performance during a first year MBA program. All of the simulations were coded as high in complexity because they met all three dimensions of Wood's (1986) definition of task complexity, namely, component, coordinative, and dynamic. Similarly, the first year MBA program experience in Latham and Brown's (2006) study and the team survival scenario in Brown and Latham's study (2003) were also coded as high in complexity. In contrast, the class scheduling tasks and the reading comprehension task were coded as medium in complexity because they lacked dynamic complexity, yet possessed the other two aspects of task complexity. Only one study had an experimental design that included a task that was straightforward. Winters and Latham's (1996) class scheduling task, where participants were told the strategies for them to perform effectively, was coded as low in complexity because it lacked all three dimensions of task complexity. The final result therefore was seven effect sizes coded as high in task complexity, five as moderate in complexity, and one as low in complexity.

*Task length.* The length of the tasks ranged from 24 minutes for the class scheduling task to a full academic year for the MBA field experiment. We split the tasks into those that were less than one hour in total (N = 4 studies) and those that were one hour or longer (N = 8 studies).

## Meta-Analytic Procedure

We used specialized meta-analytic software to conduct our analysis: the Comprehensive Meta-Analysis Version 2 (Borenstein, Hedges, Higgins, & Rothstein, 2005). The means, standard deviations, and sample sizes by experimental condition and performance trial were entered into the database and coded per the above criteria above and outlined in Table 13.1. For the Kozlowski and Bell (2006) study, the correlations were used instead of means and standard deviations.

Table 13.1 Learning Goal Studies and Design Characteristics

| Authors | Study design | Sample size | Task used | Task complexity | Task length | Trials | Participants | Performance | Effect size d (combined trials)* |
|---|---|---|---|---|---|---|---|---|---|
| Winters & Latham (1996) | 3 (PG, LG, DYB) × 2 (low, high task complexity) × 3 (trials) | 114 | Class scheduling | Low and moderate | 30 minutes or 10 minutes for each trial | 3 | Third and fourth year undergraduate business students | Number of correct schedules | High complex task: −0.429 for PG −0.413 for DYB Low complex task: +0.420 for PG −0.548 for DYB |
| Seijts & Latham (2001) | 2 (PG, LG) × 3 (distal goal, proximal goals plus distal goal, DYB) × 3 (trials) | 96 | Class scheduling | Moderate | 24 minutes or 8 minutes for each trial | 3 | Undergraduate business students | Number of correct schedules | −0.321 for PG |
| Brown & Latham (2002) | Behavioral outcome goal, LG, DYB | 50 | Team survival ranking exercise | High | 1 hour | 1 | Senior undergraduate business students | Peer ratings of teamwork behaviors | +1.026 for behavioral outcome goal −0.132 for DYB |
| Drach-Zahavy & Erez (2002) | 3 (PG, LG, DYB) × 3 (low, high stress threat, high stress challenge) × 2 (trials) | 51 | Stock market prediction | High | 2 hours | 2 | Undergraduate students | Stock price prediction accuracy | −1.321 for PG −1.484 for DYB |
| Seijts et al. (2004) | PG, LG, DYB | 170 | Cellular industry business game | High | 2 hours | 3 | Fourth year undergraduate business students | Total market share attained | −0.506 for PG −0.431 for DYB |
| Noel & Latham (2006) | PG, LG | 29 | Launching a high-risk business | High | 2.5 hours | 3 | Undergraduate entrepreneurship students | Number of months in business | −0.254 for PG |

| Study | Conditions | N | Task | Goal difficulty | Duration | Trials | Sample | Dependent variable | Effect size |
|---|---|---|---|---|---|---|---|---|---|
| Kozlowski & Bell (2006) | 2 (PG, LG) × 2 (performance, learning frame) × 2 (distal goal, proximal goals) | 542 | TANDEM (a radar tracking simulation) | High | 1.5 hours | 1 | Undergraduate psychology students | Number of correct and incorrect decisions about contacts | −0.181 for PG |
| Latham & Brown (2006) | Distal outcome goal, distal goal plus proximal outcome goals, LG, DYB | 120 | 1st year MBA program courses | High | School year | 1 | Full-time MBA students | Grade point average at end of 1st year | −0.167 for PG; −0.319 for DYB |
| Latham et al. (2008) | Low, high LG | 92 | Class scheduling | Moderate | 24 minutes or 12 minutes for each trial | 2 | First and second year pre-business undergraduate students | Number of correct schedules | −0.194 for goal level |
| Seijts & Crim (2009) | PG, LG | 105 | Class scheduling | Moderate | 24 minutes or 12 minutes for each trial | 2 | First and second year pre-business undergraduate students | Number of correct schedules | +0.178 for PG |
| Cianci et al. (2010) | PG, LG | 70 | Reading comprehension and analogies | Moderate | 1 hour | 1 | Undergraduate students | Number of correct responses to reading comprehension questions | −0.839 for PG |
| Seijts & Latham (2011) | Low, high LG | 128 | Cellular industry business game | High | 2 hours | 1 | Undergraduate business students | Total market share attained | −0.254 for goal level |

*Note:* DYB = do-your-best goal, LG = learning goal, PG = performance goal.

*Learning goals were coded as the control condition. In the case of low versus high learning goals, high is coded as the control condition.

We used a random effects model for all the effect size estimates because our set of studies consisted of independently published studies using a range of tasks and performance measures. A random effects model assumes that the individual study effect sizes are a random sample from a distribution of effect sizes, and seeks to estimate the mean of that distribution. Random effects models take into account both between-study and within-study variance in the estimates of the effect size. The random effects model assigns the appropriate weights to the studies to minimize both types of variance and therefore maximizes the precision of the effect size estimates. All confidence intervals reported are set at 95%.

Random effects models also minimize the impact of having a wide range of study sample sizes (as was the case in our analysis where $N$ ranged from 29 to 542) so that smaller studies are weighted more and larger studies are weighted less than in a fixed effects model. This procedure prevents the estimates from being skewed by one large study (i.e., Kozlowski & Bell, 2006; $n = 542$) and allows a small study (i.e., Noel & Latham, 2006; $n = 29$) to have an impact, and therefore permits a relatively balanced weighting of studies. When the overall number of studies is relatively small, as in our case, it is especially important that all the studies have an impact on the analysis, and that no one study dominates the results.

For all the effect size estimates, the standard mean difference $d$ (or Cohen's $d$) as the effect size measure is reported. The standard mean difference $d$ is calculated by estimating both the within-study and the between-study variance. The final point estimate effect size represents the estimated mean of the distribution of effect sizes of the sample population. A $z$-value and $p$-value are also included to test the null hypothesis that the mean effect size in the population is zero.

When completing the subgroup analyses, we followed the recommendations by Borenstein, Hedges, Higgins, and Rothstein (2009) to pool the within-group estimates of between-study variance (tau squared) to increase the precision of the point estimate when the number of studies in the subgroup analysis is five or fewer. In other words, our subgroup analysis model assumed a common between-study variance component for each subgroup analyzed. We then proceeded with the subgroup analysis using a random effects model.

### Results and Conclusions

The results of the meta-analysis are shown in Table 13.2. It shows the overall effect for learning versus performance goals, and for learning versus do-your-best goals. The results are broken down by goal level, complexity of the task, trials, and length of task. The significance of the findings are at least fivefold.

First, the benefit of learning versus performance goals on task performance is relatively small as defined by Cohen, yet significant ($d = -.275$, $p = .043$); the incremental benefit of learning goals over do-your-best goals is medium and significant ($d = -.507$, $p = .007$). Second, the effect for learning goal level on performance is small ($d = .229$, $p = .09$). Caution, however, is warranted given that this estimate is based on only two studies. Third, the effect of learning relative to performance goals is strengthened under conditions of high task complexity. The $d$-statistic for high task complexity is significant ($d = -.393$, $p = .012$). The low task complexity condition only had one study;

Table 13.2 Effect Sizes for Learning Goals versus Performance Goals and Do-Your-Best Goals

| | N studies | d statistic | S.E. | Variance | Low limit | High limit | Z value | P value |
|---|---|---|---|---|---|---|---|---|
| LG versus PG | 10 | −.275 | .136 | .019 | −.543 | −.008 | −2.020 | .043 |
| LG versus DYB | 5 | −.507 | .187 | .035 | −.872 | −.141 | −2.716 | .007 |
| LG level | 2 | .229 | .136 | .018 | .495 | −.037 | 1.691 | .091 |
| For LG versus PG: | | | | | | | | |
| Low complexity | 1 | .420 | .328 | .108 | −.223 | 1.063 | 1.280 | .200 |
| Medium complexity | 4 | −.331 | .225 | .051 | −.772 | .110 | −1.471 | .141 |
| High complexity | 5 | −.393 | .156 | .024 | −.699 | −.088 | −2.525 | .012 |
| Trial 1 | 6 | −.427 | .196 | .038 | −.811 | −.042 | −2.176 | .030 |
| Trial 2 | 6 | −.382 | .170 | .029 | −.716 | −.047 | −2.238 | .025 |
| Trial 3 | 4 | −.374 | .122 | .015 | −.614 | −.134 | −3.058 | .002 |
| <1 hour | 4 | −.150 | .196 | .038 | −.533 | .234 | −.765 | .444 |
| ≥1 hour | 8 | −.475 | .155 | .024 | −.779 | −.171 | −3.058 | .002 |

Note: DYB = do-your-best goal, LG = learning goal, PG = performance goal.

and performance goals led to higher performance than learning goals as discussed earlier. Fourth, the performance improvement of learning over performance goals is most pronounced on the first trial ($d = -.427, p = .03$) and then declines somewhat; but still the performance benefit holds over multiple trials ($d = -.382, p = .025$ for Trial 2; and $d = -.374, p = .002$ for Trial 3). Fifth, the beneficial effects of learning over performance goals become stronger as the task length increases. The $d$-statistic for tasks that last over one hour is $-.475$ ($p = .002$) and $-.150$ ($p = .444$) for tasks that last one hour or less.

## Practical Implications

Research has shown that it is important to distinguish between learning and performance goals. If individuals lack the knowledge or skills to perform a task effectively (e.g., new hires, recently promoted employees, and managers put on task forces to solve complex or ill-defined organizational challenges), then a specific, challenging learning goal rather than a specific, challenging performance goal should be set. This is because a learning goal focuses the individual's attention on acquiring the knowledge or skills necessary to attain the desired outcome rather than on the outcome itself. Setting a specific, challenging performance goal on a complex task may lead to even worse performance than urging an individual to do his or her best. The focus on learning goals increases self-efficacy and leads to an increased search for task-relevant information required for mastering the task. Learning goals also buffer against negative feedback and subsequent tension or frustration; this in turn facilitates task performance. Only after individuals have acquired the knowledge and skills necessary to perform the task effectively should a specific, challenging performance goal be set. A specific, challenging performance goal encourages individuals to use the knowledge gained and skills acquired in order to attain a desired performance outcome.

Tasks that require learning how to perform them are commonplace in organizations. Organizations face turbulent, changing environments, and hence employees are continuously required to adapt to new organizational realities. Such situations add complexity to jobs. Individuals continuously need to discover new and better ways to achieve both personal and organizational excellence and, in the process, stretch themselves. Hence, the findings reported in this chapter have relevance to areas such as innovation and idea generation, mergers and acquisitions, performance management and coaching, professional or leadership development, building high performance teams, establishing organizational cultures of learning, and so forth (e.g., Seijts & Latham, 2005, 2012).

The studies reviewed in this chapter also show that learning and performance goals do not have a uniform effect for individuals, and that dispositional variables may moderate the goal effect (Latham et al., 2011). Hence, managers should always consider how contextual and dispositional variables facilitate or undermine the effect of goals on performance. For example, high conscientiousness can be an asset when learning goals are set, but a burden when performance goals are assigned. The implication therefore is that managers should be flexible in their ways to motivate and develop their employees for high performance.

## Limitations of Studies and Future Research Opportunities

Goal setting theory was developed by induction (e.g., Latham & Locke, 2007; Locke & Latham, 1990, 2002). The theory is still evolving (Latham, 2007). Research on learning goals has made a valuable contribution to our knowledge base concerning goals and their effect on self-regulation and performance. This section discusses limitations of prior studies on learning goals, and offers avenues for future research.

First, most studies on learning goals have used simulations and business students as participants. Latham and Lee (1986) found that the results obtained in laboratory settings on goal setting generalize to field settings. Generalization can never be taken for granted and, in the end, is an empirical question. There is a need for more field studies in organizational settings using dependent variables that have organizational relevance. Organizational contexts are more complex than laboratory settings. Differences include the demands on employees' time, potential for conflict between goals, tangible rewards and punishers associated with performance, access to multiple sources of feedback, access to colleagues for advice and support, among others. The current business environment and the abrupt changes in today's organizations offer interesting opportunities to examine the effect of learning goals. Field studies should continue to investigate whether learning goals are effective for teams and departments. And field studies should also explore the effect of learning goal level on self-regulation and performance. Is this relationship curvilinear as it is with performance goals?

Second, prior studies have shown the mediating effect of self-efficacy, task strategies and information search, and goal commitment. Future studies should explore in depth the mediating and moderating variables of the learning goal effect. Examples of these variables, and which have organizational relevance, include incentives, participation in goal setting, job satisfaction, normative comparisons, feedback, and dispositional variables beyond goal orientation. These studies would help researchers to better understand why, when, and how learning goals affect performance. These insights can then be used in the design of interventions to enhance learning and subsequent job performance. For example, traits affect goal choice. Are there traits that predispose individuals to commit to specific, challenging learning goals?

Third, the existing studies on learning goals have used feedback that focused on outcome measures. No studies have investigated whether performance is enhanced when learning goals include process feedback, such as feedback on task- and relationship-related aspects. For example, are learning goals still effective when individuals receive ongoing negative feedback? Negative feedback is part of the learning process; and there is often a time lag before the effects of goals on complex or ill-defined tasks are noticeable. Should feedback be focused more on process as opposed to outcomes under conditions of learning?

Fourth, most studies have focused on assigned learning goals. Employees, of course, can self-set, revise learning goals, or switch their focus to performance goals. What variables or situations account for such switches in goals? The effect of assigned and self-set performance and learning goals warrants further investigation. Consonance or conflict between the content and level of goals can enhance or undermine performance. Masuda and Locke (2011) were the first to explore what happens when challenging learning and performance goals are set on the same task at the same time. Seijts and Latham (2011) found that participants self-set performance goals after having been assigned learning goals. Additional studies on the effects of goal combinations will further enhance understanding of when and how goals have a positive or negative effect on performance. For example, should learning goals be followed by performance goals, or are there situations where learning goals can co-exist with performance goals to achieve optimal performance?

Fifth, studies on performance goals have shown the importance of supervisor and managerial support to achieve high levels of performance. It is likely that in most organizations the focus of employees will be on meeting performance expectations. How then can supervisors and managers create a climate where individuals feel that they can spend time in a learning mode to discover the best way to perform a task, or discover strategies to achieve organizational effectiveness? What tangible and intangible aspects of support encourage employees to commit to a learning goal?

## Conclusion

Research on learning goals has shown that the core findings are all but the same as those of performance goals. Consistent with goal setting theory, challenging learning goals lead to higher performance than low learning goals. Performance is higher when commitment to the learning goal is high rather than low. Goal commitment is a moderator of the relationship between the difficulty level of a learning goal and task performance. Self-efficacy and the search for strategies mediate the effect of learning goals on performance. The mediating relationship between self-efficacy and strategy on task performance is reciprocal. Individual differences regarding goal orientation, cognitive ability, and conscientiousness moderate the effect of learning goals. Learning goals are particularly beneficial when individuals receive negative feedback on their performance on a task that is complex for them, a task they appraise as a threat. Both laboratory and field studies have shown the positive effects of learning goals on self-regulation and performance on complex tasks. Finally, there is evidence that learning goals are not only beneficial for individuals, but they have a beneficial effect on the performance of teams and departments as well.

# References

Ackerman, P. L., Kanfer, R., & Goff, M. (1995). Cognitive and non-cognitive determinants and consequences of complex skill acquisition. *Journal of Experimental Psychology: Applied, 1*, 270–304.

Adler, S., & Weiss, H. (1988). Recent developments in the study of personality and organizational behavior. In: C. L. Cooper & I. T. Robertson (Eds.), *International review of industrial and organizational psychology, 3*, 307–330. Chichester, England: Wiley.

Borenstein, M., Hedges, L.V., Higgins, J. P. T., & Rothstein, H. R. (2005). Comprehensive meta-analysis (Version 2) [Computer software]. Englewood, NJ: Biostat. Retrieved July 14, 2011. Available from http://www.meta-analysis.com/

Borenstein, M., Hedges, L. V., Higgins, J. P. T., & Rothstein, H. R. (2009). *Introduction to meta-analysis*. Chichester, England: Wiley.

Brown, T. C. (2003). The effect of verbal self-guidance training on collective efficacy and team performance. *Personnel Psychology, 56*, 935–964.

Brown, T. C., & Latham, G. P. (2002). The effects of behavioural outcome goals, learning goals, and urging people to do their best on an individual's teamwork behaviour in a group problem-solving task. *Canadian Journal of Behavioural Science, 34*, 276–285.

Cianci, A. M., Klein, H. J., & Seijts, G. H. (2010). The effect of negative feedback on tension and subsequent performance: The main and interactive effects of goal content and conscientiousness. *Journal of Applied Psychology, 95*, 618–630.

Drach-Zahavy, A., & Erez, M. (2002). Challenge versus threat effects on the goal–performance relationship. *Organizational Behavior and Human Decision Processes, 88*, 667–682.

Dweck, C. S. (1999). *Self-theories: Their role in motivation, personality, and development.* Philadelphia, PA: Psychology Press.

Kanfer, R., & Ackerman, P. L. (1989). Motivation and cognitive abilities: An integrative/aptitude-treatment interaction approach to skill acquisition. *Journal of Applied Psychology, 74*, 657–690.

Kanfer, R., Ackerman, P. L., Murtha, T. C., Dugdale, B., & Nelson, L. (1994). Goal setting, conditions of practice, and task performance: A resource allocation perspective. *Journal of Applied Psychology, 79*, 826–835.

Kozlowski, S. W.J., & Bell, B. S. (2006). Disentangling achievement orientation and goal setting: Effects on self-regulatory processes. *Journal of Applied Psychology, 91*, 900–916.

Latham, G. P. (2012). *Work motivation: History, theory, research and practice.* Thousand Oaks, CA: Sage.

Latham, G. P., & Brown, T. C. (2006). The effect of learning versus outcome goals on self-efficacy and satisfaction in an MBA program. *Applied Psychology: An International Review, 55,* 623.

Latham, G. P., Ganegoda, D. B., & Locke, E. A. (2011). Goal setting: A state theory but related to traits. In: T. Chamorro-Premuzic, S. von Stumm, & A. Furnham (Eds.), *The handbook of individual differences* (pp. 579–587). Oxford, England: Blackwell-Wiley.

Latham, G. P., & Lee, T. (1986). Goal setting. In: E.A. Locke (Ed.), *Generalizing from laboratory to field settings* (pp. 101–117). Lexington, MA: Lexington Books.

Latham, G. P., & Locke, E. A. (2007). New developments and directions for goal setting. *European Psychologist, 12,* 290–300.

Latham, G. P., Seijts, G. H., & Crim, D. (2008). The effects of learning goal difficulty level and cognitive ability on strategy development and performance. *Canadian Journal of Behavioural Sciences, 40,* 220–229.

Latham, G. P., & Wexley, K. N. (1977). Behavioral observation scales for performance appraisal purposes. *Personnel Psychology, 30,* 255–268.

Locke, E. A. (1965). Interaction of ability and motivation in performance. *Perceptual and Motor Skills, 21,* 719–725.

Locke, E. A., & Latham, G. P. (1990). *A theory of goal setting and task performance.* Englewood Cliffs, NJ: Prentice-Hall.

Locke, E. A., & Latham, G. P. (2002). Building a practically useful theory of goal setting and task motivation: A 35-year odyssey. *American Psychologist, 57,* 705–717.

Masuda, A., & Locke, E. (2011). The effects of having simultaneous learning and performance goals on performance: An inductive exploration. *Paper presented at the annual meeting of the academy of management,* San Antonio, Texas.

Meyer, R. D., Dalal, R. S., & Hermida, R. (2010). A review and synthesis of situational strength in the organizational sciences. *Journal of Management, 36,* 121–140.

Miner, J. B. (2003). The rated importance, scientific validity, and practical usefulness of organizational behaviour theories: A qualitative review. *Academy of Management Learning and Education, 2,* 250–268.

Mischel, W. (1977). The interaction of person and situation. In D. Magnusson & N. S. Endler (Eds.), *Personality at the crossroads: Current issues in interactional psychology.* Hillsdale, NJ: Lawrence Erlbaum.

Mitchell, T. R., & Daniels, D. (2003). Motivation. In: W. C. Borman, D. R. Ilgen, & R. J. Klimoski (Eds.), *Handbook of psychology, vol. 12: Industrial organizational psychology* (pp. 225–254). New York, NY: John Wiley & Sons.

Mone, M. A., & Shalley, C. E. (1995). Effects of task complexity and goal specificity on change in strategy and performance over time. *Human Performance, 8,* 249–262.

Noel, T. W., & Latham, G. P. (2006). The importance of learning goals versus outcome goals for entrepreneurs. *International Journal of Entrepreneurship and Innovation, 7,* 213–220.

Pinder, C. C. (1998). *Work motivation in organizational behaviour.* Upper Saddle River, NJ: Prentice Hall.

Porter, R., & Latham, G. P. (in-press). The effect of employee learning goals and goal commitment on departmental performance. *Journal of Leadership and Organizational Studies.*

Seijts, G. H., & Crim, D. (2009). The combined effects of goal type and cognitive ability on performance. *Motivation and Emotion, 33,* 343–352.

Seijts, G. H., & Latham, G. P. (2001). The effect of distal learning, outcome, and proximal goals on a moderately complex task. *Journal of Organizational Behavior, 22,* 291–302.

Seijts, G. H., & Latham, G. P. (2005). Learning versus performance goals: When should each be used? *Academy of Management Executive, 19,* 124–131.

Seijts, G. H., & Latham, G. P. (2011). The effect of commitment to a learning goal, self-efficacy, and the interaction between learning goal difficulty and commitment on performance in a business simulation. *Human Performance, 24,* 189–204.

Seijts, G. H., & Latham, G. P. (2012). Knowing when to set learning versus performance goals. *Organizational Dynamics, 41,* 1–7.

Seijts, G. H., Latham, G. P., Tasa, K., & Latham, B. W. (2004). Goal setting and goal orientation: An integration of two different yet related literatures. *Academy of Management Journal, 47,* 227–239.

Winters, D., & Latham, G. P. (1996). The effect of learning versus outcome goals on a simple versus a complex task. *Group and Organization Management, 2,* 235–250.

Wood, R. E. (1986). Task complexity: Definition of the construct. *Organizational Behavior and Human Decision Processes, 37,* 60–82.

Wright, J. C., & Mischel, W. (1987). A conditional approach to dispositional constructs: The local predictability of social behavior. *Journal of Personality and Social Psychology, 53,* 1159–1177.

# 14 Goals and Self-Efficacy as Mediators[1]

*Peter A. Heslin and Dan V. Caprar*  *School of Management,*
*Australian School of Business,*
*University of New South Wales*

It is well known that goals and self-efficacy influence performance, but how do they relate to other factors that predict performance? Goal setting theory (Locke & Latham, 1990) asserts that goals are an immediate impetus for the focused, persistent effort required for task performance. In contrast to other behavioral antecedents such as needs, values, and (subconscious) motives that are several steps removed from the action, Locke and Latham construe goals and self-efficacy as the most situationally specific, as well as temporarily and causally proximate conscious motivational determinants of performance.

According to Locke's (1991) motivation sequence framework, needs (e.g., Deci & Ryan, 1985; Maslow, 1954) are the prime antecedent of the "motivation core", made up of values (e.g., Miner, 1978) and motives (e.g., McClelland, 1961). Within the third element in the sequence, labeled the "motivation hub" and depicted as being triggered by the motivation core, goals influence performance directly, and self-efficacy influences performance both directly and indirectly via goal setting and commitment. For example, valuing money is modeled as most likely to result in the accumulation of wealth if it cues the mediating processes of setting goals, developing self-efficacy, and thus taking action aimed at making money.

The answer provided by the motivation sequence framework to the question that opens this chapter is that dispositional and environmental factors that influence performance tend to do so via goals and self-efficacy, which are the key elements of the motivation hub.

Locke (2001) elaborated on his 1991 motivation sequence framework by suggesting additional factors that affect performance via the hub variables. Specifically, Locke's (2001) mediation-linking model conceived of the immediate antecedents of performance (self-set goals and self-efficacy) as being a product of personal needs, values, motives, and personality, as well as the external incentives to act that are provided by assigned goals, participation, feedback, money, job design, and leadership. This chapter reviews highlights from the research literature between 1990 and 2011 on motivational factors that influence performance via self-set goals, goal commitment, and self-efficacy, as depicted in Figure 14.1. These studies are essentially empirical tests of what Locke and Latham (1990) labeled the *mediation hypothesis*.

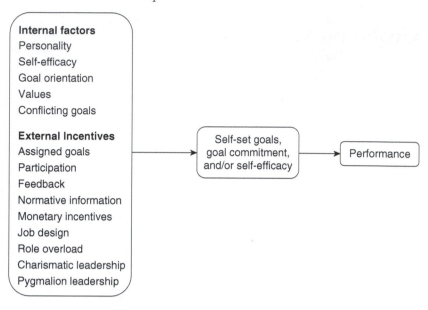

*Figure 14.1* Motivational factors that influence performance via self-set goals, goal commitment, and/or self-efficacy.

## Internal Factors

### Personality

Given that personality involves an individual's characteristic patterns of thought, emotion, and behavior (Funder, 2001), it is intuitively evident that personality will be directly and/or indirectly related to work performance. The relationship between personality and performance has been largely empirically confirmed (Barrick & Mount, 1991). This begs the question of the mechanisms that link personality to performance.

Studies addressing this question have often revealed the important mediating role of goals, goal commitment, and self-efficacy. For instance, in a field study of sales personnel by Barrick, Mount, and Strauss (1993), conscientiousness predicted both sales volume and performance ratings provided by supervisors. The relationship between conscientiousness and sales volume was partially mediated by autonomous sales goal setting. Similarly, the association between conscientiousness and performance ratings was partially mediated by goal commitment. These observations of partial mediation, rather than full mediation, highlight that other variables such as self-efficacy (which was not measured in this study) probably also intervene between conscientiousness and performance outcomes. Subsequent studies confirmed this idea. For instance, within a sports-exercise context, Lerner and Locke (1995) found that personal (self-set) goals and self-efficacy fully mediated the relationships between students' competitiveness, goal orientation, and their subsequent sit-up performance. Goal commitment also predicted performance, subsequent self-set goals, and self-efficacy, though it did not explain any performance variance beyond that attributable to the other two mediators.

The pattern of full mediation by self-set goals and self-efficacy predicted by Locke (1991) was often replicated. In a laboratory study involving undergraduate business students doing simple arithmetic, Gellatly (1996) found that the prediction of performance by conscientiousness was completely mediated by goal choice and performance expectancy (essentially a measure of self-efficacy). Klein and Lee (2006) investigated whether the difficulty of self-set academic goals and commitment to those goals mediates the effect on academic performance of three dispositions: conscientiousness, openness to experience, and a learning goal orientation. Goal commitment completely mediated the relationship between conscientiousness and performance, though the other two hypothesized mediated relationships were not supported.

Spurk and Abele (2011) explored whether Big Five personality factors predict professionals' annual salary over a four-year period, as mediated by occupational self-efficacy, career advancement goals, and contractual work hours. The results showed that except for openness to experience, the other Big Five personality traits significantly predicted the subsequent annual salary of masters graduates from several German universities. Career-advancement goals (measured via the rated importance of items such as "I want to gain high occupational reputation") mediated the positive influence of conscientiousness and extraversion, as well as the negative influence of agreeableness. Occupational self-efficacy also mediated the positive influence of conscientiousness and the negative influence of neuroticism on annual salary. Because the influence of occupational self-efficacy on annual salary was fully mediated by contractual work hours, the indirect influence of personality on salary via occupational self-efficacy included contractual work hours.

There are two notable features of this impressive field study that limit its relevance to the mediation hypothesis focus of this chapter. First, "career advancement goals" were measured in a way that seems more indicative of commitment to the goal of career advancement than to the level of self-set career advancement goals. In addition, although the salary criterion is often a function of work performance, the two variables are not synonymous. Spurk and Abele (2011) might thus be viewed as showing that goal commitment, along with self-efficacy, plays an important role in how personality is related to subsequent work outcomes.

In most studies, the effect of personality on performance is mediated by goals, goal commitment, and/or self-efficacy. This suggests that performance can be cultivated by selecting employees who are conscientious and possess other relevant personality traits for the task at hand (Barrick & Mount, 1991), as well as by ensuring that the context in which they work does not impede the natural process of their developing high self-efficacy, together with setting and committing to appropriately challenging goals.

## Self-Efficacy

Self-efficacy is the belief in one's capability to do what it takes to attain a certain level of performance within a given domain (Bandura, 1997). As noted above, when mediating the relationship between personality and performance, goals often work in tandem with self-efficacy. In this section, we consider the evidence that self-efficacy affects performance via goal setting.

In three studies with undergraduates, Earley and Lituchy (1991) observed that ability at solving mathematics problems, working on a complex game simulation, and completing a required general management course predicted subsequent performance in these respective domains, as consistently mediated by the level of relevant self-set goals. In two out of the three studies, goal setting also mediated the relationship between self-efficacy and performance.

Mone (1994) investigated how well academic goal setting and performance is predicted by *academic process* self-efficacy, versus *academic outcome* self-efficacy. Wood and Locke (1987) conceptualized academic process self-efficacy in terms of self-efficacy for tasks such as concentration, note-taking, understanding, memorization, explaining concepts, and discriminating concepts. Academic outcome self-efficacy pertains to perceptions of one's capability to attain certain levels of academic performance (i.e., grades). Mone (1994) observed that introductory management students' academic outcome self-efficacy predicted their personal grade goals and subsequent actual grades more strongly than academic process self-efficacy (Mone, 1994). Academic process self-efficacy was nonetheless a significant predictor of outcome self-efficacy.

A follow-up study by Mone, Baker, and Jeffries (1995) observed that college students' self-efficacy was significantly predictive of their academic grade goals and actual subsequent performance, while self-esteem was not. Interestingly, these results were invariant to whether self-efficacy, self-esteem, and grade goals were measured in a distal (2 weeks before exams) or proximal (2 days before each exam) manner. This highlights that although self-efficacy is a temporal and causal proximate performance determinant, its predictive power is not contingent on being measured right before subsequent goal setting and performance occurs.

Self-efficacy leads to performance not only by stimulating the setting of (high) goals, but also by influencing the type of goals people adopt and how committed they are to them. For instance, Seijts and Latham (2011) reported that the relationship between self-efficacy and performance on a complex business simulation was partially mediated by commitment to a challenging, assigned learning goal.

While goals often play an important role in mediating the effect of self-efficacy on performance (Pi-Yueh & Wen-Bin, 2010; Seo & Ilies, 2009), this does not always occur. For instance, Fort, Jacquet and Leroy (2011) reported that, as expected, job seekers' self-efficacy directly influenced their job search planning and job search behaviors. Contrary to the authors' expectations, however, employment goals did not mediate these relationships.

Notwithstanding these results, the evidence is compelling in support of Locke's (1991) motivation hub depiction of self-efficacy influencing performance indirectly via cuing people to set and strive to attain high goals, as well as directly (Bandura, 1997). For further details about the nature of self-efficacy and its relationship to goal setting and performance, see Chapter 10.

## Goal Orientation

Goal orientations are people's characteristic goal preferences in achievement situations. People with a learning goal orientation tend to choose tasks in which they can acquire knowledge and skill. Those with a performance goal orientation tend to choose easy tasks in which they can look good in the eyes of others and to avoid tasks where others may judge them unfavorably if they make mistakes. Seijts, Latham, Tasa, and Latham (2004) observed that a learning goal orientation predicted complex task performance via the setting of a learning goal.

In a longitudinal field study of experienced medical supplies salespeople, self-regulation tactics of goal setting, effort, and planning mediated the relationship between learning goal orientation and sales performance (VandeWalle, Brown, Cron & Slocum, 1999). VandeWalle, Cron, and Slocum (2001) found that undergraduate business students with a high learning goal orientation (i.e., a focus on developing one's competence) performed better on exams both before and after receiving performance feedback. A proving goal orientation (i.e., a focus on demonstrating one's competence) predicted performance only before feedback was received. An avoiding goal orientation (i.e., a focus on avoiding negative competence judgments) had a negative effect on performance regardless of whether feedback had been received. In all cases, the effect of goal orientation on performance was mediated by goal level, self-efficacy, and effort. These findings show that goal orientation affects behavior via the intermediate steps of having specific intentions, setting goals, and making plans regarding how to attain them.

Goal orientation also influences the content of goals that are set. In a study of MBA students working on improving their presentation skills, Brett and VandeWalle (1999) observed that a learning goal orientation led to skill improvement and refinement goals (better presentation skills), performance-prove orientation led to positive comparison goals (present better than others), and performance-avoid orientation led to avoidance goals (not looking bad or incompetent). Only the first two sets of content goals (improvement and positive comparison) had a (positive) impact on performance. This shows that trait goal orientation can influence performance by cuing a state inclination to self-set concrete learning goals within a particular context.

Heimerdinger and Hinsz (2008) investigated the mechanisms whereby performance is influenced by failure avoidance, a nonspecific motive limited to achievement situations that is assessed via self-reports regarding whether statements such as "I do what I can to avoid situations where I might experience failure" are "like me" (Heggestad & Kanfer, 2000). Heimerdinger and Hinsz observed that the relationship between undergraduate psychology students' failure avoidance and idea generation performance (regarding potential uses of a coat hanger) was partially mediated by self-efficacy and self-set goals.

It is important to note that although goal orientation is usually construed as a trait, it can also be modified (DeShon & Gillespie, 2005). This begs the question of what sets the stage for goal orientations. An answer is suggested by self-determination theory, which proposes that individuals are motivated by feeling that their behavior is freely chosen and driven by their personal values (Deci & Ryan, 1985), partly as a function of three personality characteristics: control, amotivated, and autonomy orientations. A *control orientation* is associated with an awareness of constraints, such as the expectations of authority figures or societal standards, which tend to undermine intrinsic motivation and enjoyment (Koestner & Zuckerman, 1994), as well as commitment and performance (Wong, 2000). An *amotivated orientation* involves sensitivity to signals that one is incompetent and likely to be unsuccessful, typically leading to perceived inability to control one's emotional state and performance (Deci & Ryan, 1985; Koestner &

Zuckerman, 1994). Finally, an *autonomy orientation* inclines people to making choices on the basis of their personal needs and preferences (Deci & Ryan, 1985).

Lee, Sheldon, and Turban (2003) observed that a control orientation is associated with both avoidance and approach goal orientations, with the latter predicting higher goals and performance. An amotivated orientation, on the other hand, is associated with goal-avoidance motivation, lower goal levels, and lower subsequent performance. An autonomy orientation also predicted performance, though via mastery goal orientation and enhanced mental focus rather than goal setting. This study shows that traits influence performance not only via the hub mediators of goals, goal commitment, and self-efficacy, though also via mental focus.

## Values

Can personal values predict performance, via goals, beyond the role of personality? Parks and Guay (2012) observed that undergraduates' achievement values predicted their management course grades, even after controlling for the potentially relevant personality factors of conscientiousness, emotional stability, and extraversion. Moreover, goal content (i.e., the anticipated future likelihood of pursuing achievement goals such as "Impressing others by doing a good job"; p. 160) and goal striving (i.e., effort and persistence) mediated the relationships between individual characteristics (personality and values) and academic performance. To the extent that this novel measure of goal content taps academic goal commitment, this result is consistent with Locke and Latham's (1990) mediation hypothesis.

## Conflicting Goals

At any given moment, people often have a range of goals that can pull them in different directions (Locke & Latham, 1990). Locke et al. (1994) conducted both a laboratory study with student teams in which conflicting goals were assigned (quantity versus quality), and a field study with college professors experiencing intra-individual goal conflict (teaching versus research). In both studies, goal conflict was negatively associated with at least one performance outcome, though these effects were surprisingly not mediated by goal commitment, goal priority, goal level, or strategies.

Ohbuchi and Tedeschi (1997) reported that during a social conflict, social goals (e.g., to form or maintain a good relationship, express hostility, etc.) were more strongly activated than resource goals (e.g., to secure the other person's assistance or permission, or to obtain something that is economically valued). Participant's tactical behaviors (e.g., integrating, appeasing or avoiding) were determined by their social goals. Finally, the effects of personal (e.g., gender) and situational (e.g., whether or not the conflict was with a friend) variables on tactical choice were mediated by activated social and resource goals.

Seijts and Latham (2000) showed that alignment of personal goals and group goals (and by extrapolation, potentially assigned or organizational goals) had a positive effect on performance. These studies raise interesting questions about the mechanisms whereby goal conflict can diminish subsequent performance related to one or more of the conflicting goals. We provide further comment on this topic in the concluding section of the chapter.

Overall, research on the internal factors that influence performance via goal setting and self-efficacy has yielded results that are consistent with Locke and Latham's (1990) mediation hypothesis. In the following section, we review the empirical literature on how the external incentives shown in Figure 14.1 are associated with goal setting, self-efficacy, and subsequent performance.

## External Incentives

### Assigned Goals

According to goal setting theory (Locke & Latham, 1990), assigned goals affect performance through their influence on self-set goals and self-efficacy. Although assigned and self-set goals are typically correlated, there may be discrepancies between them because individuals are not always fully committed to what others ask them to accomplish. Assigned goals can also affect self-efficacy, for example, because being assigned a difficult goal is an expression of confidence that may increase self-efficacy via persuasion (Bandura, 1997) or a Pygmalion effect (Eden, 1990).

Consistent with this theorizing, Earley and Lituchy (1991) found that personal goals and self-efficacy partially mediated the significant effects of assigned goal difficulty on performance. Zimmerman, Bandura, and Martinez-Pons (1992) explored the interesting question of whether and how 9th- and 10th-grade students are affected by the grade that their parents want them to earn. Student's personal grade goals fully mediated the effects of their parents' grade goals on the actual grades that the students attained.

Mediation processes may vary, however, with the nature of the goals, as revealed by Audia, Brown, Kristof-Brown, and Locke (1996). Using a multipath assembly task that allowed for setting both quality- and quantity-focused outcomes, Audia et al. found that personal goals and work processes completely mediated the goal-performance relationship for the quantitative goals, but only partially mediated the relationship for the quality-related goals. It is important to note that the task included work processes that were mainly quantity related. If more quality-related processes were included, perhaps the mediation effects would have been stronger for the quality goals as well.

Gibbons and Weingart (2001) observed that familiarity with the task determined whether task-specific self-efficacy had a direct or indirect effect on performance, such that on a rather familiar task (checking English grammar), self-efficacy affected performance only indirectly via personal goals. Gibbons and Weingart also examined the role of two additional levels of self-efficacy: general efficacy and domain efficacy. These variables also predicted performance, but their effect was mediated by task-specific self-efficacy. The overall motivational hub model, with task-specific self-efficacy and personal goals playing a mediating role between assigned goals and performance, was therefore supported.

Finally, in a longitudinal investigation of industrial sales performance, Fu, Richards, and Jones (2009) observed that self-set goals fully mediated the relationship between company-assigned goals (i.e., quotas) and selling effort, which in turn predicted new product sales.

Together, the results reported in this section reveal that assigned goals have clear potential to enhance performance by prompting personal goal setting and raising self-efficacy. Assigned goals are not always, however, set without input from the goal recipient. Next, we consider the role of participation in goal setting and performance.

## Participation

Are commitment and performance higher when people participate in setting their goals? There is a long and controversial literature on this issue (Locke & Latham, 1990). Two highlights that are relevant to the focal topic of goals as mediators are the studies by Erez, Earley, and Hulin (1985) and Latham, Erez, and Locke (1988). In a laboratory study involving making up class schedules, Erez et al. (1985) varied both the degree of partici-pative decision making (PDM) and whether or not the participants set personal goals. Participants in the PDM condition significantly outperformed those given assigned goals, as mediated by high levels of goal acceptance (commitment). Latham et al. (1988) observed that an assigned goal is as effective as one that is set participatively, as long as the purpose or rationale for the goal is given: that is, as long as the goal is "told and sold." On the other hand, if the goal is merely assigned tersely (e.g., "Do this …") without explana-tion, it leads to performance that is significantly lower than for a participatively set goal.

Renn (1998) proposed that setting goals has an impact on performance via the mediating roles of goal acceptance and procedural justice perception. In a study of 200 employees who participated in a two-year goal setting program, procedural justice perceptions were not related to performance (nor to goal acceptance), though goal acceptance mediated the relationship between participation and task performance.

Sue-Chan and Ong (2002) observed that participatively set goals result in higher self-efficacy, goal commitment, and performance than assigned goals. In addition, both self-efficacy and goal commitment mediated the goal assignment–performance rela-tionship. Most interestingly, power distance moderated the goal assignment–goal commitment and the goal assignment–performance relationships, though not the goal assignment–self-efficacy relationship. In essence and not surprisingly, participation is more motivating to individuals with a low power distance than a high power distance, probably as a function of the former expecting to be involved in the setting of their goals. Sue-Chan and Ong's results suggest that further research might usefully explore the extent to which the well-established mediation relationships reported in this chapter generalize across other dimensions of cultural difference. For additional evidence and suggestions for conducting this research, see Chapter 35.

Since Locke and Latham (1990), more research has focused on the potential cognitive rather than motivational impact of participation. For example, Latham et al. (1994) documented how participation in task strategy formulation significantly affects perfor-mance via task strategies and self-efficacy. Specifically, undergraduates' participation in strategy formulation improved the quality of their task strategies, which in turn increased their self-efficacy and subsequent class scheduling performance. Goal level was not assessed in this study. Similarly, Scully, Kirkpatrick, and Locke (1995) observed that high performance results from participation if the supervisor has the correct infor-mation or if at least one party has correct information and neither has incorrect or conflicting information.

To summarize, participation increases performance by building commitment better than curtly assigned goals, though not significantly better than goals that are explained and sold: These effects are likely to be culturally contingent. On complex tasks, the prime value of participation seems to be in building people's strategy formulation skills or giving them the information available to perform effectively. Next we consider the related topic of feedback.

## Feedback

At the time when Locke and Latham (1990) produced their synthesis of the goal-setting literature, feedback was the most studied incentive with regard to the mediation hypothesis. The relationships between feedback and goal setting are explored in detail in Chapter 5, so here we outline just a few key studies on the mediation of feedback effects by goals and self-efficacy.

Mesch, Farh, and Podsakoff (1994) reported that student groups set higher goals and performed better after receiving negative rather than positive feedback. Korsgaard and Diddams (1996) examined the role of feedback as an antecedent of goal setting and performance improvement, as a function of task complexity. They observed that the extent to which performance is enhanced by utilizing feedback to set goals is a positive function of task complexity.

In a field study looking at the relationship between feedback-seeking and performance, Renn and Fedor (2001) showed that feedback seekers improved the quality and quantity of their performance by setting relevant goals in these domains, inspired by the feedback received. The effect of self-efficacy on work performance was also mediated by these feedback-based goals.

## Normative Information

Goal setting and performance are influenced not only by feedback on one's performance, but also feedback about performance relative to that of other people. Consistent with social cognitive theory, Bandura and Jourdan (1991) reported that participants who received progressive *mastery feedback* (indicating gradually increasing performance relative to peers) set higher goals and were able to increase their performance more than those who received feedback indicating *progressive decline, consistent superiority,* or *similar performance* relative to their counterparts. Gibbons and Weingart (2001) also observed that normative information affected performance via self-efficacy and personal goals. These studies show that the trajectory of social comparative feedback affects goal setting, self-efficacy, and performance in a similar manner to individual feedback (cf. Locke & Latham, 1990).

## Monetary Incentives

With regard to how hub variables mediate the effect of monetary incentives on performance, Locke and Latham (1990) concluded that monetary incentives strengthen goal commitment if people value money, the amount is significant, and the associated goals are not perceived as unachievable.

Wood, Atkins, and Bright (1999) investigated the motivational dynamics of performance pay schemes in which awards are based on end-of-period assessments of performance, such as appraisal ratings. They observed that bonuses based on end-of-period determinations of standards led to setting more challenging goals but lower performance than a control condition in which bonuses were based on the achievement of self-set goals. Although self-set goals and self-efficacy were significant predictors of performance within both the bonus and control conditions, the incentive effects were mediated by instrumentality (outcome expectations), rather than by goals and efficacy.

Lee, Locke, and Phan (1997) examined the interaction between three types of incentives (piece rate, bonus, and hourly) and three levels of assigned goals. Following performance feedback (given after the first trial), a significant interaction was found. Specifically, under piece-rate pay, performance was higher with a hard goal than with a medium assigned goal. Under bonus pay, performance was higher with a medium goal than with a hard goal. Although commitment was not significantly affected by the experimental treatments, consistent with Locke's (1991, 2001) motivational hub theory, personal (self-set) goals and self-efficacy (which were significantly correlated with commitment) were. Indeed, goals and self-efficacy completely mediated the interaction effect. Specifically, when participants tried to attain hard-to-impossible assigned goals, personal goals and self-efficacy dropped or failed to increase under bonus pay, though they increased under piece-rate pay. People clearly became discouraged and disinclined to set challenging personal goals if they sense being unable to perform at the level needed to receive the bonus. With piece-rate incentives, at least incremental performance improvement and attainments would be rewarded. Practical implications for designing rewards systems based on these findings are outlined by Locke (2004).

Moussa (2000) observed a two-way interaction between (a) being assigned to self-set a low, high, or any goal, and (b) methods of payment (straight piece rate, differential piece rate with goal attainment step bonus, and hourly flat rate) in influencing personal goals, subsequent personal goals, and goal valences. The highest level of personal goals was set under straight piece rate (pay for performance) in which instructions were given to set a high goal. Self-set goals also completely mediated (1) the effects of goal valences on performance; and (2) the main effects of assigned goals, as well as the interactive effects of both assigned goals and methods of payment, on subsequent personal goals. This research shows that organizational contextual variables, such as the reward systems and assigned goals, significantly interact to influence self-set goals and performance.

## Job Design

The premise of Hackman and Oldham's (1980) job characteristics model (JCM) that enriched jobs increase job satisfaction has been well supported (e.g., Oldham, 1996), though the evidence that applying it enhances performance has been more equivocal, especially when actual productivity rather than satisfaction-related actions such as absenteeism and turnover are considered (Parker & Wall, 1998). An exception is Kirkpatrick (1992), who isolated the performance-enhancing elements of job design by varying levels of autonomy and responsibility within a laboratory-based proofreading task. Manipulated responsibility enhanced the level of personal goals (measured directly and in terms of anticipated satisfaction with various levels of performance) and goal commitment. Personal goals in turn enhanced performance. Goal commitment was only related to satisfaction. Although manipulated responsibility strongly affected experienced responsibility, the latter was unrelated to performance. These results suggest that it may be motivation hub variables (goals in this case) rather than critical intervening states (Hackman & Oldham, 1980) that link job redesign to motivational performance improvements.

Another potentially important variable in determining motivation and performance is the nature of the performance rating system. Bartol, Durham, and Poon (2001) investigated the impact of rating segmentation—specifically, whether feedback was provided on a 3-point or 5-point rating scale—on motivation and perceived fairness. Receiving feedback on a 5-point scale resulted in higher self-efficacy, goals, and subsequent performance, as partially mediated by self-efficacy and personal goals. Although the five-category system was more effective than the three-category system in motivating performance improvements, it resulted in lower perceptions of fairness on the part of individuals who were rated in the lower categories.

## Role Overload

Role overload occurs when role demands create the perception that available resources are inadequate to deal with them, often resulting in distraction and stress (Kahn, Wolfe, Quinn, & Snoek, 1964). Brown, Jones, and Leigh (2005) reported a pattern of moderated mediation whereby self-set goals mediated the indirect effect of self-efficacy on performance when role overload was low, but not when role overload was high. Although the self-efficacy and goal-level relationship remained strong even when role overload was high, the relationship between goal level and performance broke down under high role overload. These results suggest that performance does not necessarily benefit from setting high goals when people feel overloaded, even if their self-efficacy is high.

This finding is consistent with the evidence that performance can be harmed by excessively difficult goals (Locke & Latham, 1990). For discussions of when extremely difficult, "stretch" goals are likely to either help or hinder performance, see Kerr and Landauer (2004), Latham and Locke (2006), and especially Chapter 3 in this volume.

## Charismatic Leadership

In contrast to the substantial popular literature on charismatic or transformational leadership, most relevant studies have not investigated the mechanisms whereby this leadership style potentially produces beneficial organizational outcomes (Yukl, 2009). A laboratory study by Kirkpatrick and Locke (1996), using a clerical task used by a real organization, isolated three elements of charismatic leadership: vision, charismatic personality style (divorced from vision content), and task information (which is akin to intellectual stimulation). Vision was the most potent of the three components. Specifically, vision stressing quality significantly affected both personal goal level and self-efficacy for quality, which in turn significantly affected the quality of task performance. Task strategy information affected performance quantity through its effects on quantity goals and efficacy, and also directly. Vision had the most potent effects on a variety of attitude measures, including trust in the leader, congruence between own beliefs and vision, inspiration, and perceived charisma. Charismatic personality style had few effects of any kind. These results suggest that charismatic leadership substance (vision *content*) counts more than *style* and that vision operates, in part, through its effects on followers' goals and self-efficacy.

Leadership can have a particularly powerful impact on the trajectory of emerging firms. Baum and Locke (2004) studied the performance of small-venture entrepreneurs over a 6-year period. Entrepreneurs' passion for the work and tenacity predicted future sales and employment growth within their small ventures, as fully mediated by their growth goals, organizational vision for growth, and self-efficacy; these results essentially replicate those of an earlier study by Baum, Locke, and Smith (2001).

## Pygmalion Leadership

A Pygmalion Leadership Style (PLS) involves the "... consistent encouraging, supporting, and reinforcing of high expectations resulting in the adoption, acceptance, or internalization of high expectations on the part of the subordinates. In the simplest and most straightforward instance, it is a manager reassuringly telling a subordinate 'I know you can do this well.' This message can be transmitted in an endless variety of ways. The hallmark of an effective leader is his [sic] ability to get this message across convincingly and to inspire high self-confidence among the other persons around him" (Eden, 1990, p. 125). Bezuijen, van den Berg, van Dam, and Thierry's (2009) investigation of how this message can be conveyed revealed that assigned goal difficulty, goal specificity, and leaders providing learning opportunities each mediated the process through which high leader expectations influenced employees engaging in learning activities. Bezuijen, van Dam, van den Berg, and Thierry (2010) reported that goal difficulty and specificity also mediate the relationship between leader-member exchange (LMX) and employees' learning activities.

## Conclusions and Future Research

This chapter has reviewed highlights of empirical research conducted since Locke and Latham (1990) on how goal setting and commitment, as well as self-efficacy, mediate the relationship between core motivational variables and performance. Overall, this considerable literature strongly supports Locke and Latham's mediation hypothesis. It also provides the basis for suggesting a range of potentially theoretically enlightening and practically useful directions for future research.

A realm in which there is much more to learn pertains to the interaction between the factors that stimulate goal setting and performance. For example, although intrinsic motivation and incentives can each influence performance, external incentives can also diminish intrinsic motivation (Deci, Koestner, & Ryan, 1999). Research is needed on how the motivational core variables might interact in ways that potentially nullify, reverse, or amplify their effects on goal setting and performance. These interactions might be within and/or between the core motivational factors depicted in Figure 14.1. Research examining what moderates the effects outlined in this chapter would enhance our understanding and scope for applying what is known about the levers of performance via increased goal setting, commitment, and self-efficacy.

A growing area of research pertains to the extent to which the dynamics discussed in this chapter generalize to group-level goals (see Chapter 19) and processes (cf., Kozlowski & Klein, 2000). Guthrie and Hollensbe (2004) explored the impact of three forms of group incentives on group goal setting and group performance. They found that pay risk prompts spontaneous group goal setting, with the goal level mediating the group incentives–group performance relationship. Bray (2004) similarly reported that the group goals established by sports teams mediate the relationship between collective efficacy and group performance. Research might fruitfully investigate the potential role of the other antecedents of individual goal setting outlined in Figure 14.1 in stimulating group goal setting and performance. Related theorizing and research will likely also reveal group level constructs (e.g., group diversity, shared mental models, and emotional contagion) beyond the largely individual level causes of goal setting, self-efficacy, and performance addressed in this review.

Intra-individual and intra-team conscious goal conflict has been the topic of research attention for a while (e.g., Locke et al., 1994; Ohbuchi & Tedeschi, 1997). There is renewed interest in this area, especially regarding the alignment between conscious and subconscious goals. Stajkovic, Locke, and Blair (2006) examined the effect of aligned conscious and unconscious goals and observed that the effects of conscious difficult and do-best goals were enhanced by subconscious goals, although conscious easy goals were not affected. Shantz and Latham (2009) similarly showed how subconscious goals can supplement conscious goal setting to increase performance (see also Shantz & Latham, 2011 and Chapter 13 for more on subconscious goals). To our knowledge, however, no research has empirically examined a conceptually driven approach to how conscious versus subconscious goal conflicts could be managed.

Educational psychologists Kegan and Lahey (2001, 2009) have developed an insightful five-step competing commitments methodology for unearthing and addressing the subconscious values that can hold people back from attaining their conscious, self-set goals. Such an analysis can reveal, for example, that a conscious self-set goal to delegate more is often impeded by a deeply held subconscious commitment to not lose control of one's sense of power, discretion, and/or control. Research might usefully investigate the scope for deploying Kegan and Lahey's (2001, 2009) methodology to surface subconscious values that conflict with conscious behavioral intentions and goals, before assessing the impact of their intervention protocol on subsequent performance via the hub variables of goal setting, goal commitment, and self-efficacy.

Beyond conflicting goals, research is needed on the effects of conflicting feedback from different sources (see Chapter 5) such as one's boss, colleagues, customers, and spouse, as well as from incentive systems and the task itself (Northcraft, Schmidt, & Ashford, 2011). Hypotheses might be readily developed about how the core motivational factors could guide the relative salience and impact of different sources of feedback (e.g., feedback on quality should be more salient and impactful if quality is being rewarded). Studies are needed to examine how core factors interact to influence the salience and impact of different courses of conflicting feedback in influencing goal setting and performance.

Another interesting approach for future research pertains to the comparative effects of different types of motivational factors previously observed independently, together with the associated mediation processes. In a study aimed at investigating the effect of multiple motivational sources on task performance, Callahan, Brownlee, Brtek, and Tosi (2003) explored the relationship between assigned goals, monetary incentives, intrinsic motivation, and subsequent task performance in a rather interesting setting – people striving to improve their golf putting. After controlling for prior golf putting ability, each source of motivation independently contributed to performance, but not in the same way. Self-set goals and self-efficacy mediated the effect of assigned goals on performance, but did not mediate the impact of incentives. Intrinsic motivation had both direct and mediated effects (via self-set goals and self-efficacy) on performance, and was associated with the largest performance gains among the tested motivators. We conclude by underscoring that further examining the interaction between the internal factors and external incentives that influence performance is a promising area for future research.

## Note

1  This research was supported in part by a grant to the first author from the Australian School of Business, UNSW.

## References

Audia, P. G., Brown, K. G., Kristof-Brown, A., & Locke, E. A. (1996). Relationship of goals and microlevel work processes to performance on a multipath manual task. *Journal of Applied Psychology, 81*, 483–497.

Bandura, A. (1997). *Self-efficacy: The exercise of control.* New York: Freeman.

Bandura, A., & Jourdan, F. J. (1991). Self-regulatory mechanisms governing the impact of social comparison on complex decision making. *Journal of Personality and Social Psychology, 60*, 941–951.

Barrick, M. R., & Mount, M. K. (1991). The big five personality dimensions and job performance: A meta-analysis. *Personnel Psychology, 44*, 1–26.

Barrick, M. R., Mount, M. K., & Strauss, J. P. (1993). Conscientiousness and performance of sales representatives: Test of the mediating effects of goal setting. *Journal of Applied Psychology, 78*, 715–722.

Bartol, K. M., Durham, C. C., & Poon, J. L. (2001). Influence of performance evaluation rating segmentation on motivation and fairness perceptions. *Journal of Applied Psychology, 86*(6), 1106–1119.

Baum, J. R., & Locke, E. A. (2004). The relationship of entrepreneurial traits, skill, and motivation to subsequent venture growth. *Journal of Applied Psychology, 89*, 587–598.

Baum, J. R., Locke, E. A., & Smith, K. G. (2001). A multidimensional model of venture growth. *Academy of Management Journal, 44*, 292–303.

Bezuijen, X. M., van Dam, K., van den Berg, P. T., & Thierry, H. (2010). How leaders stimulate employee learning: A leader-member exchange approach. *Journal of Occupational & Organizational Psychology, 83*, 673–693.

Bezuijen, X. M., van den Berg, P. T., van Dam, K., & Thierry, H. (2009). Pygmalion and employee learning: The role of leader behaviors. *Journal of Management, 35,* 1248–1267.

Bray, S. R. (2004). Collective efficacy, group goals, and group performance of a muscular endurance task. *Small Group Research, 35,* 230–238.

Brett, J. F., & VandeWalle, D. (1999). Goal orientation and goal content as predictors of performance in a training program. *Journal of Applied Psychology, 84,* 863–873.

Brown, S. P., Jones, E., & Leigh, T. W. (2005). The attenuating effect of role overload on relationships linking self-efficacy and goal level to work performance. *Journal of Applied Psychology, 90,* 972–979.

Callahan, J., Brownlee, A. L., Brtek, M. D., & Tosi, H. L. (2003). Examining the unique effects of multiple motivational sources on task performance. *Journal of Applied Social Psychology, 33,* 2515–2535.

Deci, E. L., Koestner, R., & Ryan, R. M. (1999). A meta-analytic review of experiments examining the effects of extrinsic rewards on intrinsic motivation. *Psychological Bulletin, 125,* 627–668.

Deci, E. L., & Ryan, R. M. (1985). *Intrinsic motivation and self-determination in human behavior.* New York: Plenum.

DeShon, R. P., & Gillespie, J. Z. (2005). A motivated action theory account of goal orientation. *Journal of Applied Psychology, 90,* 1096–1127.

Earley, P. C., & Lituchy, T. R. (1991). Delineating goal and efficacy effects: A test of three models. *Journal of Applied Psychology, 76,* 81–98.

Eden, D. 1990. *Pygmalion in management: Productivity as a self-fulfilling prophecy.* Lexington, MA: D.C. Heath and Company.

Erez, M., Earley, P. C., & Hulin, C. L. (1985). The impact of participation on goal acceptance and performance: A two step model. *Academy of Management Journal, 28,* 50–66.

Fort, I., Jacquet, F., & Leroy, N. (2011). Self-efficacy, goals, and job search behaviors. *Career Development International, 16,* 469–481.

Fu, F. Q., Richards, K. A., & Jones, E. (2009). The motivation hub: Effects of goal setting and self-efficacy on effort and new product sales. *Journal of Personal Selling & Sales Management, 29,* 277–292.

Funder, D. C. (2001). *The personality puzzle* (2nd. ed.). New York: Norton.

Gellatly, I. R. (1996). Conscientiousness and task performance: Test of a cognitive process model. *Journal of Applied Psychology, 81,* 474–582.

Gibbons, D. E., & Weingart, L. R. (2001). Can I do it? Will I try? Personal efficacy, assigned goals, and performance norms as motivators of individual performance. *Journal of Applied Social Psychology, 31,* 624–648.

Guthrie, J. P., & Hollensbe, E. C. (2004). Group incentives and performance: A study of spontaneous goal setting, goal choice and commitment. *Journal of Management, 30,* 263–284.

Hackman, J. R., & Oldham, G. R. (1980). *Work redesign.* Reading, MA: Addison-Wesley.

Heggestad, E. D., & Kanfer, R. (2000). Individual differences in trait motivation: Development of the motivational trait questionnaire. *International Journal of Educational Research, 33,* 751–776.

Heimerdinger, S. R., & Hinsz, V. B. (2008). Failure avoidance motivation in a goal-setting situation. *Human Performance, 21,* 383–395.

Kahn, R. L., Wolfe, D., Quinn, R., & Snoek, J. D. (1964). *Organizational stress: Studies in role conflict and ambiguity.* New York: Wiley.

Kegan, R., & Lahey, L. L. (2001). The real reason people won't change, *Harvard Business Review, 79*(6), 85–92.

Kegan, R., & Lahey, L. L. (2009). *Immunity to change: How to overcome it and unlock the potential in yourself and your organization.* Boston, MA: Harvard Business School Publishing.

Kerr, S., & Landauer, S. (2004). Using stretch goals to promote organizational effectiveness and personal growth: General electric and Goldman Sachs. *Academy of Management Executive, 18*(4), 134–138.

Kirkpatrick, S. A. (1992). *The effect of psychological variables on the job characteristics-work outcomes relations.* Paper presented at Eastern Academy of Management.

Kirkpatrick, S., & Locke, E. (1996). Direct and indirect effects of three core charismatic leadership components on performance and attitudes. *Journal of Applied Psychology, 81*, 36–51.

Klein, H. J., & Lee, S. (2006). The effects of personality on learning: The mediating role of goal setting. *Human Performance, 19*, 43–66.

Koestner, R., & Zuckerman, M. (1994). Causality orientations, failure, and achievement. *Journal of Personality, 62*, 321–346.

Korsgaard, M. A., & Diddams, M. (1996). The effect of process feedback and task complexity on personal goals, strategies, and performance. *Journal of Applied Social Psychology, 26*, 1889–1911.

Kozlowski S. W. J., & Klein. K. J. (2000). A multilevel approach to theory and research in organizations: Contextual, temporal, and emergent processes. In K. Klein, & S. W. J. Kozlowski (Eds.), *Multilevel theory, research, and methods in organizations: Foundations, extensions, and new directions* (pp. 3–90). San Francisco, CA: Jossey-Bass.

Latham, G. P., Erez, M., & Locke, E. A. (1988). Resolving scientific disputes by the joint design of crucial experiments: Applications to the Erez-Latham dispute regarding participation in goal setting. *Journal of Applied Psychology, 73*, 753–772.

Latham, G. P., & Locke, E. A. (2006). Enhancing the benefits and overcoming the pitfalls of goal setting, *Organizational Dynamics, 35*, 332–340.

Latham, G. P., Winters, D., & Locke, E. (1994). Cognitive and motivational effects of participation: A mediator study. *Journal of Organizational Behavior, 15*, 49–63.

Lee, T. W., Locke, E. A., & Phan, S. H. (1997). Explaining the assigned goal-incentive interaction: The role of self-efficacy and personal goals. *Journal of Management, 23*, 541–559.

Lee, F. K., Sheldon, K. M., & Turban, D. (2003). Personality and the goal-striving process: The influence of achievement goal patterns, goal level, and mental focus on performance and enjoyment. *Journal of Applied Psychology, 88*, 256–265.

Lerner, B. S., & Locke, E. A. (1995). The effects of goal setting, self-efficacy, competition, and personal traits on the performance of an endurance task. *Journal of Sport and Exercise Psychology, 17*, 138–152.

Locke, E. A. (1991). The motivation sequence, the motivation hub and the motivation core. *Organizational Behavior and Human Decision Processes, 50*, 288–299.

Locke, E. A. (2001). Self-set goals and self-efficacy as mediators of incentives and personality. In M. Erez, U. Kleinbeck, & H. Thierry (Eds.), *Work motivation in the context of a globalizing economy*. Mahwah, NJ: Lawrence Erlbaum.

Locke, E. A. (2004). Linking goals to monetary incentives. *Academy of Management Executive, 18*, 130–133.

Locke, E. A., & Latham, G. P. (1990). *A theory of goal-setting and task performance.* Englewood Cliffs, NJ: Prentice Hall.

Locke, E. A., Smith, K. G., Erez, M., Dong-Ok, C., & Schaffer, A. (1994). The effects of intra-individual goal conflict on performance. *Journal of Management, 20,* 67–91.

Maslow, A. (1954). *Motivation and personality.* New York: Harper.

McClelland, D. C. (1961). *The achieving society.* New York: The Free Press.

Mesch, D. J., Farh, J., & Podsakoff, P. M. (1994). Effects of feedback sign on group goal setting, strategies, and performance. *Group and Organization Management, 19,* 309–333.

Miner, J. B. (1978). Twenty years of research on role-motivation theory of managerial effectiveness. *Personnel Psychology, 31,* 739–760.

Mone, M. A. (1994). Comparative validity of two measures of self-efficacy in predicting academic goals and performance. *Educational and Psychological Measurement, 54,* 516–529.

Mone, M. A., Baker, D. D., & Jeffries, F. (1995). Predictive validity and time dependency of self-efficacy, self-esteem, personal goals, and academic performance. *Educational and Psychological Measurement, 55,* 716–727.

Moussa, F. M. (2000). Determinants, process, and consequences of personal goals and performance. *Journal of Management, 26,* 1259–1285.

Northcraft, G. B., Schmidt, A. M., & Ashford, S. J. (2011). Feedback and the rationing of time and effort among competing tasks. *Journal of Applied Psychology, 96,* 1076–1086.

Ohbuchi, K. I., & Tedeschi, J. T. (1997). Multiple goals and tactical behaviors in social conflicts. *Journal of Applied Social Psychology, 27,* 2177–2199.

Oldham, G. R. (1996). Job design. In C. Cooper & I. Robertson (Eds.), *International review of industrial and organizational psychology* (Vol. 11, pp. 33–60). New York: Wiley.

Parker, S. K., & Wall, T. (1998). *Job and work design: Organizing work to promote wellbeing and effectiveness.* London: Sage.

Parks, L., & Guay, R. P. (2012), Can personal values predict performance? Evidence in an academic setting. *Applied Psychology: An International Review, 61,* 149–173.

Pi-Yueh, C., & Wen-Bin, C. (2010). Achievement, attributions, self-efficacy, and goal setting by accounting undergraduates. *Psychological Reports, 106,* 54–64.

Renn, R. W. (1998). Participation's effect on task performance: Mediating roles of goal acceptance and procedural justice. *Journal of Business Research, 41*(2), 115–125.

Renn, R. W., & Fedor, D. B. (2001). Development and field test of a feedback seeking, self-efficacy, and goal setting model of work performance. *Journal of Management, 27,* 563–583.

Scully, J. A., Kirkpatrick, S. A., & Locke, E. A. (1995). Locus of knowledge as a determinant of the effects of participation on performance, affect and perceptions. *Organizational Behavior and Human Decision Processes, 61,* 276–288.

Seijts, G. H., & Latham, G. P. (2000). The effects of goal setting and group size on performance in a social dilemma. *Canadian Journal of Behavioural Science, 32,* 104–116.

Seijts, G. H., & Latham, G. P. (2011). The effect of commitment to a learning goal, self-efficacy, and the interaction between learning goal difficulty and commitment on performance in a business simulation. *Human Performance, 24,* 189–204.

Seijts, G. H., Latham, G. P., Tasa, K., & Latham, B. W. (2004). Goal setting and goal orientation: An integration of two different yet related literatures. *Academy of Management Journal, 47,* 227–239.

Seo, M., & Ilies, R. (2009). The role of self-efficacy, goal, and affect in dynamic motivational self-regulation. *Organizational Behavior & Human Decision Processes, 109,* 120–133.

Shantz, A., & Latham, G. P. (2009). An exploratory field experiment of the effect of subconscious and conscious goals on employee performance. *Organizational Behavior and Human Decision Processes, 109,* 9–17.

Shantz, A., & Latham, G. P. (2011). The effect of primed goals on employee performance: Implications for human resource management. *Human Resource Management, 50,* 289–299.

Spurk, D., & Abele, A. (2011). Who earns more and why? A multiple mediation model from personality to salary. *Journal of Business & Psychology, 26*(1), 87–103.

Stajkovic, A. D., Locke, E. A., & Blair, E. S. (2006). A first examination of the relationships between primed subconscious goals, assigned conscious goals, and task performance. *Journal of Applied Psychology, 91,* 1172–1180.

Sue-Chan, C., & Ong, M. (2002). Goal assignment and performance: Assessing the mediating roles of goal commitment and self-efficacy and the moderating role of power distance. *Organizational Behavior & Human Decision Processes, 89,* 1140–1161.

VandeWalle, D., Brown, S. P., Cron, W. L., & Slocum, J. W. (1999). The influence of goal orientation and self-regulation tactics on sales performance: A longtitudinal field test. *Journal of Applied Psychology, 84,* 249–259.

VandeWalle, D., Cron, W. L., & Slocum, J. W. (2001). The role of goal orientation following performance feedback. *Journal of Applied Psychology, 86,* 629–640.

Wong, M. M. (2000). The relations among causality orientation, academic experience, academic performance, and academic commitment. *Personality and Social Psychology Bulletin, 26,* 315–326.

Wood, R. E., Atkins, P. B., & Bright, J. H. (1999). Bonuses, goals, and instrumentality effects. *Journal of Applied Psychology, 84,* 703–720.

Wood, R. E., & Locke, E. A. (1987). The relation of self-efficacy and grade goals to academic performance. *Educational and Psychological Measurement, 47,* 1013–1024.

Yukl, G. A. (2009). *Leadership in organizations.* Upper Saddle River, NJ: Prentice Hall.

Zimmerman, B., Bandura, A., & Martinez-Pons, M. (1992). Self-motivation for academic attainment: The role of self-efficacy beliefs and personal goal setting. *American Educational Research Journal, 29,* 663–676.

Part IV

# Long Term and Large Scale Goal Setting Programs and Studies

# 15 Long-Term Effects of Goal Setting on Performance with the Productivity Measurement and Enhancement System (ProMES)

*Robert D. Pritchard, Brandon L. Young,*
*Nick Koenig, Daniel Schmerling, and*
*Natalie Wright Dixon* University of Central Florida

This chapter focuses on organizational productivity, and the research on a highly effective goal setting–feedback intervention for increasing and maintaining it. While many aspects of goal setting have been addressed in this book up to this point, one aspect that is especially worth examining is the effect goals have on performance over the long term. Long-term effects are important because sustained, elevated performance is what is typically important in the work place.

## The Literature

In this summary of the literature, we consider a long-term goal setting study as one that examines the effect of goals on performance for a year or longer. The earliest empirical study on this issue was conducted by Latham and Baldes (1975) on the effect of setting a specific, high goal for truck drivers in a logging company. Goal setting had a positive effect on the drivers' performance for nine months and also decreased the company's costs. G.P. Latham (personal communication, 2011) reported that this positive effect lasted for several years. Krause, Seymour, and Sloat (1999) implemented a goal setting intervention targeted at reducing behaviors that lead to accidents. They used this intervention in 73 organizations. Goal setting resulted in a substantial reduction in accidents for five consecutive years. Finally, Howard (see Chapter 16) examined longitudinal data from AT&T in regard to the effect of employees setting a specific goal for job promotions. An individual's goal for reaching a specific management level was significantly related to actual job advancement 25 years later.

In short, the extant literature is sparse on the longitudinal effects of goal setting but what is available suggests that specific, high goals have a positive effect on long-term job-related performance.

## Purpose and Chapter Structure

This chapter adds to this literature by examining the long-term effects of an intervention, the Productivity Measurement and Enhancement System (ProMES), which contains important goal setting components including a measurement/feedback system for tracking progress toward goal attainment. Feedback is a moderator variable in goal setting theory (Locke & Latham, 1990, 2002). ProMES, unlike typical goal setting interventions, most often focuses on a group's rather than an individual's performance. The chapter addresses four research questions:

(1)  Does ProMES result in improvements in performance over long periods of time?
(2)  Are positive effects on performance maintained over time?
(3)  Are there variables that moderate the strength of the effects of ProMES over time?
(4)  What lessons can be learned about goal setting from this intervention?

To answer these four questions, we describe the ProMES intervention. We then examine data on the long-term performance effects of ProMES. Finally, we discuss the lessons learned about goal setting, and close with some conclusions.

## ProMES

Before discussing how ProMES incorporates goal setting, we need to describe ProMES. A more complete description can be found in Pritchard, Weaver, and Ashwood (2012).

ProMES is a measurement and feedback intervention designed to improve work productivity. The theoretical basis of ProMES is the NPI theory of motivation (Naylor, Pritchard, & Ilgen, 1980). This theory states that people are motivated by expectations of how their effort applied to actions will satisfy their needs (Pritchard & Ashwood, 2008; Pritchard, Weaver, & Ashwood, 2012).

To illustrate the ProMES process, we will reference a small production unit working in an electronics assembly plant producing printed circuit boards. The unit is composed of technicians who are responsible for the final steps in the production process. The first step in the ProMES process is to form a design team composed of people doing the work, their supervisors, and one or two ProMES facilitators to guide them through the process.

Next, the design team identifies their overall objectives. Once the objectives have been identified, the next step is to develop indicators of these objectives. An indicator is a measure of how well the unit is achieving the objective in question. Typical objectives with their indicators are shown below. This is a subset of the actual objectives and indicators developed in this project. Typically, there are 4–6 objectives and 8–12 indicators.

   Objective 1. Maintain High Production
      Indicator 1. *Output*—Percentage of boards completed. Number of boards completed, divided by number received to work on.
      Indicator 2. *Meeting Priorities*—Number of high-priority boards completed, divided by number needed.

   Objective 2. Make Highest Quality Boards Possible
      Indicator 3. *Inspections Passed*—Percentage of boards passing inspection.

   Objective 3. Maintain High Attendance
      Indicator 4. *Attendance*—Total hours worked divided by maximum hours possible to work.

Objective 4. Correctly Follow Housekeeping and Maintenance Procedures
   Indicator 5. *Audit Violations*—Number of violations of a general audit of house-
         keeping and maintenance procedures.

Once the objectives and indicators are finalized by the design team, they are presented to higher management for review and approval. When that is finished, the
next step is to establish what are called contingencies. A contingency is a graphical representation of the relationship between the amount of the indicator and the effectiveness
of that amount of the indicator. It is a way of expressing how much contribution different amounts of the indicator make to the overall functioning of the organization.
Contingencies can be seen as a type of utility function; that is, a way to indicate the
relative value of different levels or amounts of a given indicator. Figure 15.1 is an
example contingency. The horizontal axis is the *amount* of the indicator, which ranges
from its worst feasible level to the best level that is realistically possible. On the vertical
axis of the figure are the *effectiveness values* of the various levels of the indicator.
Effectiveness is defined as the amount of contribution made to the organization. It is
the value to the organization of that level of the indicator. The scale ranges from +100,
which is maximum effectiveness, to −100, minimum effectiveness. It also has a zero
point that is defined as the minimum expected level of effectiveness. This minimum
level is seen as neither good nor bad, but the level that just meets minimum expected
performance.

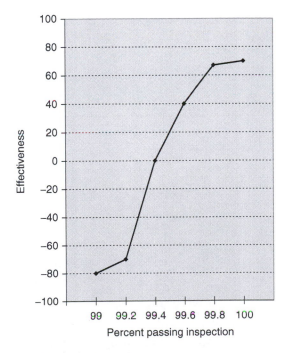

*Figure 15.1*  Example contingency.

The example in Figure 15.1 shows the contingency for the percentage of boards passing inspection, the first indicator the team developed for their objective to Make the Highest Quality Boards possible. The design team goes through a process of discussion to consensus when determining the values in the contingencies. This process is described in detail in Pritchard, Weaver, and Ashwood (2012). A contingency such as the one depicted in Figure 15.1 is done for each indicator, and when the contingency set is completed, it is reviewed by higher management for accuracy and consistency with organizational policy.

Contingencies have several advantages. They capture the relative importance of each indicator by the range of effectiveness values. More important indicators have larger ranges in their effectiveness scores. The one in the figure ranges from −80 to +70. Others in the contingency set could range from −30 to +40. Contingencies also convert performance scores on each indicator into a common metric, the effectiveness contributed by that level of the indicator. The effectiveness scores from each indicator can then be added to form an overall performance score, the overall effectiveness score. Finally, they can be used to determine improvement priorities. One can calculate the gain in effectiveness that would occur with a given improvement in each indicator. The indicators with the greatest potential gain should be given highest priority for improvement efforts.

Once the contingencies are approved, the measurement system is complete. The next step is to use this measurement system for the feedback system. This is accomplished by first collecting the indicator data for a given period of time, most often a month. Then, based on the contingencies, effectiveness scores would be calculated for each indicator. This information is arranged into a standardized feedback report. This is illustrated in Table 15.1. For example, if the maintenance unit had 99.8% of its boards pass inspection, this value of the indicator is associated with an effectiveness value of +62 on the vertical axis of the contingency in Figure 15.1. Continuing this process

*Table 15.1*  Basic Feedback Report: Circuit Board Manufacturing Unit

| Date: July | Indicator Data: July | Effectiveness Score |
|---|---|---|
| *I. Production* | | |
| A. Percentage of Boards Completed | 98% | +40 |
| B. Percentage of High Priority Boards Completed | 85% | −5 |
| *II. Quality* | | |
| A. Percentage Passing Inspection | 99.8% | +62 |
| *III. Attendance* | | |
| A. Percentage of Max Hours | 97% | 0 |
| *IV. Housekeeping and Maintenance* | | |
| A. Number of Violations | 10 | −5 |
| Overall Effectiveness | | +92 |

would give an effectiveness value for each indicator, as illustrated in Table 15.1. The overall effectiveness score is the sum of the effectiveness scores for each indicator.

The above table gives the most basic feedback from ProMES. Other desirable feedback information such as changes from past performance periods, amount of gain possible in each indicator as an index of priority for improvement, and graphical presentations of the feedback are also used.

Once the feedback report is prepared, a feedback meeting is held with all unit personnel and the supervisor. They discuss the report with special attention to indicators that changed and why they changed. This leads to plans to make changes that will improve the indicators. The feedback report is prepared for each feedback period, and a meeting is held to review it. This process is repeated over time; the feedback system uses a continuous improvement model in which feedback meetings continue to identify possible areas for improvement and use the feedback to assess the actual effectiveness of these improvements.

## ProMES and Goals

Developing a unit's measurement/feedback system involves converting broad objectives into specific goals (i.e., indicators). The choice by a unit's employees to use an indicator increases the probability of their commitment to exert effort to improve it, and goal setting theory suggests that commitment is a moderator between goal setting and performance. The contingencies also involve goal setting. The act of specifying the level of effectiveness for each level of an indicator clearly delineates what constitutes good and poor performance. This is essentially what assigning specific levels of performance in goal setting does. It specifies the level of performance, that is, the goal that is considered good performance (Naylor, Pritchard, & Ilgen, 1980; Naylor & Ilgen, 1984). The ProMES contingencies take this step further by specifying how good all levels of performance are. For example, the contingency in Figure 15.1 shows that 99.4% of boards passing inspection meet minimum expectations, an effectiveness score of 0. Having 99.6% pass inspection is very good performance with an effectiveness value of +40, and 99.8% is excellent performance. Conversely, 99.2% is very, very poor performance.

Once the measurement system has been developed by a unit's employees and approved by senior management, it is used for giving employees feedback on a recurring, agreed-upon schedule. In the feedback meetings, employees focus on the behaviors necessary to attain desired end states. Specifically, employees discuss what they need to start doing, stop doing, or continue doing to achieve a desired end state (i.e., one or more performance goals). For example, if a maintenance unit sees that repair time is suffering because of delays in getting spare parts, they might develop a new strategy for ordering parts. This new strategy may entail making an initial diagnosis of needed parts earlier in the repair process, and more coordination with the procurement process to ensure the parts are delivered on time. The benefits of focusing on behavioral goals have been discussed elsewhere (e.g., Brown & Latham, 2002; Latham, Mitchell, & Dossett, 1978). In brief, they make explicit what employees must do to attain one or more performance outcomes. Thus, through the feedback meetings, the group's participation in setting goals and deciding what they must do to attain them improves goal commitment by the employees in an organization unit.

Finally, and arguably most importantly, ProMES encourages the setting of specific learning goals. A learning goal focuses attention on the discovery of strategies or processes for attaining a desired outcome (Latham, 2007; Winters & Latham, 1996). Learning goals increase performance on complex tasks (Seijts & Latham, 2001; Seijts, Latham, Tasa, & Latham, 2004), as these types of tasks require knowledge acquisition for effective performance. ProMES incorporates learning goals in at least two ways. First, ProMES stresses that productivity measurement and improvement are long-term processes. Hence, performance is likely to be affected by environmental uncertainty. Second, the ProMES measurement/feedback process encourages discussion of current priorities, and development of strategies for attaining them.

Among the advantages of this intervention is that ProMES allows employees to focus on their unit's overall goal (e.g., Pritchard, Jones, Roth, Stuebing, and Ekeberg, 1988; Pritchard, Jones, Roth, Stuebing, & Ekeberg, 1989). In fact, having a single overall index of performance, such as that provided by ProMES, often makes goal pursuit more focused than having to deal with each goal for a number of different aspects of performance effectiveness such as quantity, quality, meeting deadlines, and customer satisfaction. Thus, with ProMES feedback, unit personnel can focus both on the overall goal and the more specific goals contained in the indicators. Performance on the indicators is the primary focus of the feedback meetings. Finally, while the ProMES intervention does not include formal goal setting in the form of publicly agreed-upon levels of target performance between supervisors and employees, it does make such formal goal setting easier. The goal can be set on the overall effectiveness score rather than separate goals on each indicator of performance.

## Long-Term Goal Effects

Because of the significant presence of goal setting in ProMES, it is appropriate to look at the effects of this intervention on long-term performance as evidence of the long-term effects of goal setting. Meta-analytic findings provide clear evidence that ProMES improves productivity across myriad industries (e.g., military, nonprofit, sales, service, manufacturing) and countries (e.g., Australia, Germany, Netherlands, Poland, Sweden, Switzerland, United States), and for different jobs ranging from entry level to top management (Pritchard, Harrell, DiazGranados, & Guzman, 2008). ProMES effectiveness was operationalized as the change in the overall effectiveness score from baseline to the time periods where feedback was provided. An effect size was calculated, for each ProMES project, by dividing the difference in the overall effectiveness score between the feedback and baseline periods by the pooled standard deviation.

Data from 83 ProMES projects revealed that, on average, productivity under ProMES was 1.16 standard deviations higher than productivity during baseline. To assess the effect of ProMES on long-term performance, we focused on projects with 20 or more feedback periods. The time between the vast majority of these feedback periods was one month. Twenty periods were selected as the cutoff because it was the longest time interval that still had a large enough number of projects for ascertaining meaningful conclusions.

Twenty-three such projects were identified from the ProMES database. The average number of baseline periods for these projects was 4.7 with a range from 1 to 12 baseline periods. The average number of feedback periods was 30.7 with a range from 20 to 59 feedback periods. The mean overall effectiveness scores across these 23 projects over time are plotted in Figure 15.2. Time periods are displayed along the horizontal axis, the B's along this axis are baseline periods and the F's are feedback periods. The plot only includes feedback periods up to 38. The number of projects with more than 38 feedback periods was quite small ($n = 4$), so their means are somewhat unstable. The overall trend shows a large increase in a unit's performance from the initiation of the feedback/measurement system, which generally improved over the 3+ years shown in the figure.

Caution is warranted in interpreting this figure. ProMES projects had varying numbers of baseline and feedback periods. The number of projects at each data point in the figure is not equal. For example, all ProMES projects had at least 20 feedback periods, but only 6 had the full 38 periods. This means that projects drop out of the plotted means when the time period goes beyond their number of feedback periods.

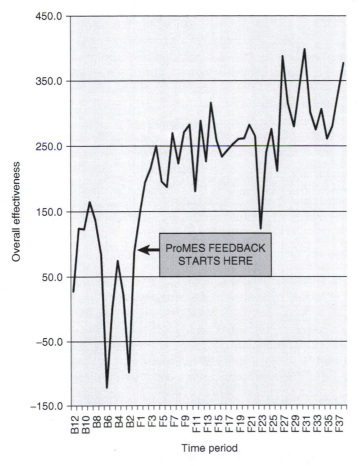

*Figure 15.2*  Performance effects over time (N = 23).

This dropping out of specific studies accounts for some of the large variability in mean overall effectiveness scores shown in the figure.

To get a clear picture of the long-term effects of ProMES, effect sizes were calculated for each project. The mean effect size for these long-term projects is 1.65, substantially greater than the average effect size for all projects (1.16). This effect size is very large. To get a feel for its magnitude, it means that a performance level at the 95th percentile during baseline has become the average performance level under ProMES feedback.

Thus, to answer the first question posed at the beginning of this chapter, a goal setting intervention such as ProMES does have an enduring long-term effect on an organizational unit's performance.

## Improvement Sustainability

The second question was whether the positive performance effects are maintained over time. It may be that the overall improvement is present, but the effect diminishes as ProMES continues. Figure 15.2 suggests this is not the case. To look at this issue more carefully, two effectiveness scores were calculated for each of the 23 projects. An effectiveness score was calculated for the first half of the feedback periods beyond 12, and another for the second half. For example, if a project had 25 feedback periods, there were 13 periods beyond 12. A mean was calculated for feedback periods 13 through 18, and a second mean was calculated for feedback periods 19 through 25. The purpose of this analysis was to explore what happens after a program had been operating for a year. Do the effects start to diminish?

While mean overall effectiveness scores decrease slightly from the first half ($M = 273.30$, $SD = 232.26$) to the second half ($M = 242.93$, $SD = 293.30$) of the later feedback periods, the difference is small, just over a tenth of the average standard deviation. Results of a paired samples $t$-test indicate the change was not significant ($t(22) = .77$, $p = .45$).

This finding provides an answer to the second research question. The positive performance effects of ProMES are indeed maintained over time.

## Moderating Variables

Are there moderating variables that affect the long-term performance effects of ProMES? While the average effect size is large, there is considerable variability; the effect sizes range from −.96 to 5.3. This variability suggests the presence of moderators.

The meta-analysis of ProMES (Pritchard et al., 2008) found a number of moderators. Specifically, the amount of performance improvement was positively related to how closely the study followed the original ProMES methodology, the quality of feedback given, and centralization of the organization. Performance improvement was negatively related to the amount of changes made in the feedback system, the amount of feedback prior to the intervention, and the degree of interdependence of the work group. Effect size was also influenced by country where the project was done, type of organization, type of worker, and ownership (profit versus nonprofit organization). The following sections focus on two previously unexplored ProMES moderators that have direct implications for goal setting.

*Goal Difficulty.* A core aspect of goal setting theory is that given sufficient ability, the higher the goal, the higher the performance. Part of the ProMES meta-analysis database is composed of questions answered by the facilitator of each project. One question deals with the minimum expected performance level used in contingencies (i.e., the zero effectiveness point). Design teams can set the performance level where they wish, as long as it is approved by higher management.

The issue is how high units set their goals. ProMES facilitators were asked, "In your opinion, how high were expected levels set?" with response anchors on a 5-point scale from 1 (quite low) to 5 (quite high). Thus, higher ratings of the expected levels signify more difficult goals. If one group saw a fairly low level of performance as minimally acceptable while another saw a higher level as minimally acceptable, the second group had set a higher goal. So the question was whether, as goal setting theory (Locke & Latham, 1990, 2002) suggests, more difficult goals led to greater performance improvement than easier goals. Consistent with goal setting theory, the results revealed a strong and positive relationship between goal difficulty and ProMES effectiveness as measured by effect size ($r = .42, p = .05$).

*Process versus Outcome Goals.* The type of feedback a unit received is a second potential moderator of the long-term performance effects of goal setting. Some researchers have made a distinction between two types of feedback: outcome versus process feedback (e.g., Earley, Northcraft, Lee, & Lituchy, 1990; Leung & Trotman, 2005). Outcome feedback typically refers to information regarding the end result of a task process performed by employees. Conversely, process feedback refers to information regarding the task process used to produce an end result: the actual actions of the employees (van de Geer, van Tuijl, Rutte, DiazGranados, Harrell, & Pritchard, 2010).

Although outcome feedback identifies where improvements are or are not needed, it often does not provide specific information about what actions or behaviors to change in order to improve a unit's performance (Earley et al., 1990; Latham & Wexley, 1994). For example, if the goal is to build 20 computers per day, the outcome feedback would simply be the actual number produced that day. This feedback only gives information on how far a unit's employees are from reaching their daily goal: it suggests nothing to help employees develop efficient performance strategies.

Process feedback, on the other hand, usually focuses on the behaviors that generate an outcome. Examples include quality checks on the computer as it is being assembled, successful identification of nonworking parts, etc. This type of feedback should be more meaningful and motivating as individuals can see what modifications are to be made and ways to change their behavior to obtain a desired end result. Process feedback is typically less influenced by external factors that cannot be controlled by the unit receiving the feedback, thus resulting in more meaningful feedback. Process feedback points out what the unit should start, stop, or do differently to attain its goals.

The distinction between process and outcome feedback is similar to the distinction between learning and outcome goals (e.g., Seijts & Latham, 2001; Latham, 2007). When a group is urged to discover strategies or processes for attaining a desired outcome, unit performance on complex tasks improves. Both process/learning goals and performance/outcome goals have been shown to improve performance. However, feedback focused on process is more effective on tasks that require knowledge acquisition because the individuals in a unit can focus on identifying specific behaviors to improve.

To explore feedback type, indicators from each ProMES study were independently coded by three raters as either a process feedback indicator or an outcome feedback indicator. The percentage of process indicators was then calculated for each study. For example, if a ProMES system consisted of 12 indicators and 3 of them were coded as process indicators, the percentage of process indicators for this study would be 25%. Sufficient indicator information was available for 22 of the 23 long-term studies. Details of the coding process and inter-rater reliability (.85 across 3 raters) can be found in Koenig, Young, and Schmerling (2010).

There were 8 feedback systems with greater than 50% process indicators and 14 with less than 50%. For those projects with fewer than 50% process indicators, the range for percent process indicators was 0% to 47% with a mean of 27%. For those projects with more than 50% process indicators, these values were 50%, 93%, and 69%, respectively.

The percentage of process indicators in the long-term ProMES systems was then correlated with the effect size for that study, ($r = .32$, $p = .08$). While the correlation is only marginally significant, it is moderately large. The small sample size likely explains the fact that this finding is of marginal statistical significance.

Another way to examine this relationship is to consider the difference between effect sizes. An independent samples $t$-test between the mean effect size for the systems with more than 50% process indicators ($M = 2.23$, $SD = 2.04$) and the mean effect size for the systems with less than 50% process indicators ($M = 1.07$, $SD = 1.84$) indicates a marginally significant difference, $t(20) = 1.37$, $p = .09$ (one-tailed). The actual mean effect size for the studies high in process indicators was more than twice the size of those low in process indicators. These findings suggest that process feedback is an important factor in how effective ProMES will be in the long term.

## Lessons Learned about Goal Setting

One important lesson from research on ProMES is that the productivity improvements endure over a long time period without the need for additional incentives or other interventions. The satisfaction derived from doing a good job along with the increased recognition and possible job security appear to be sufficient incentives for sustaining a unit's performance.

Another lesson is that when a unit's performance has been sustained for long periods of time, there is often a decision by organizational decision makers that the goal setting and feedback are no longer necessary. Specifically, the cost of collecting performance data and having the feedback meetings are erroneously viewed as no longer worth it. This is a bad decision. In a ProMES study by Janssen, van Berkel, & Stolk (1995), the unit's computer system was not operational for four months. Thus, it was not possible to get the data necessary for the ProMES feedback reports. When the computer system was again functioning, it was possible to go back and reconstruct the data. Janssen et al. found that without ProMES feedback, productivity decreased dramatically. When feedback and goal setting based on this feedback was reinstated, productivity improved very quickly to the previous level.

A more frequent reason for a ProMES project to stop is the introduction of a new manager. New managers often want to do something for which they can take credit. An existing program, even when successful, does not allow this.

Arguably, the most important lesson about goal setting from ProMES projects is the importance of assessing a unit's performance rather than goal attainment. In our experience, managers often set goals, and when it is time to review performance, they focus on the goal rather than on the performance. So if the goal was to improve from 400 to 500 units completed and the subordinate improved to 485, the supervisor focuses on why the person did not achieve the goal. For the subordinate, this is a failure experience: he or she did not make the goal, even though performance increased substantially. If a manager does this, it can lead to subordinates trying to set goals as low as possible so that they can be sure to achieve that goal. One somewhat cynical manager summarized this problem as, "Goal setting is a process where a smarter subordinate convinces a less smart supervisor to set goals as low as possible." This problem can occur when feedback and goals are at the unit level as well.

If this occurs, it is an incorrect application of the goal setting process. In the above example, the manager should congratulate the individual or unit on improving from 400 to 485. The review session should celebrate the achievement, discuss what was done to make these improvements, and explore how the manager could help provide support for attaining even further improvements in productivity.

## Conclusions

This chapter focused on the effect of long-term goals on group and individual performance in the ProMES research program. Four research questions can now be answered. First, a goal setting intervention, such as ProMES, does produce productivity improvements when done over long time periods. Second, the positive effects are maintained over time. Third, the evidence suggests that goal difficulty and the number of process goals enhance the amount of improvement. Finally, the long-term beneficial effects of goal setting can be sustained without added incentives; and most importantly, in formal review sessions, managers should focus on performance improvement rather than goal attainment. If the reverse is done, employees may attempt to set low goals that will be more easily achieved.

## References

Brown, T. C., & Latham, G. P. (2002). The effects of behavioural outcome goals, learning goals, and urging people to do their best on an individual's teamwork behaviour in a group problem-solving task. *Canadian Journal of Behavioural Science/Revue canadienne des sciences du comportement, 34(4)*, 276–285. doi:10.1037/h0087180.

Earley, P., Northcraft, G. B., Lee, C., & Lituchy, T. R. (1990). Impact of process and outcome feedback on the relation of goal setting to task performance. *Academy of Management Journal, 33(1)*, 87–105. doi:10.2307/256353.

Janssen, P., van Berkel, A., & Stolk, J. (1995). ProMES as part of a new management strategy. In R. D. Pritchard (Ed.), *Productivity measurement and improvement: Organizational case studies.* (pp. 43–61). New York, NY: Praeger.

Koenig, N., Young, B. L., & Schmerling, D. (2010). *The impact of feedback type on productivity improvement.* Unpublished manuscript, Department of Psychology, University of Central Florida, Orlando, Florida.

Krause, T. R., Seymour, K. J., & Sloat, K. C. M. (1999). Long-term evaluation of a behavior-based method for improving safety performance: a meta-analysis of 73 interrupted time-series replications. *Safety Science, 32,* 1–18.

Latham, G. P. (2007). *Work motivation: History, theory, research, and practice.* Thousand Oaks, CA: Sage.

Latham, G. P., & Baldes, J. J. (1975). The "practical significance" of Locke's theory of goal setting. *Journal of Applied Psychology, 60,* 122–124.

Latham, G. P., Mitchell, T. R., & Dossett, D. L. (1978). Importance of participative goal setting and anticipated rewards on goal difficulty and job performance. *Journal of Applied Psychology, 63(2),* 163–171. doi:10.1037/0021-9010.63.2.163.

Latham, G. P., & Wexley, K. N. (1994). *Increasing productivity through performance appraisal.* Reading, MA: Addison-Wesley.

Leung, P. W., & Trotman, K. T. (2005). The effects of feedback type on auditor judgment performance for configural and non-configural tasks. *Accounting Organizations and Society, 30(6),* 537–553.

Locke, E. A., & Latham, G. P. (1990). *A theory of goal setting and task performance.* Englewood Cliffs, NJ: Prentice Hall.

Locke, E. A., & Latham, G. P. (2002). Building a practically useful theory of goal setting and task motivation: A 35-year odyssey. *American Psychologist, 57(9),* 705–717. doi:10.1037/0003-066X.57.9.705.

Naylor, J. C., & Ilgen, D. R. (1984). Goal setting: A theoretical analysis of a motivational technology. *Research in Organizational Behavior, 6,* 95–140. Retrieved from EBSCO*host.*

Naylor, J. C., Pritchard, R. D., & Ilgen, D. R. (1980). *A theory of behavior in organizations.* New York, NY: Academic Press.

Pritchard, R. D., & Ashwood, E. L. (2008). *Managing motivation: A manager's guide to diagnosing and improving motivation.* New York, NY: Routledge, Taylor & Francis.

Pritchard, R. D., Harrell, M. M., DiazGranados, D., & Guzman, M. J. (2008). The productivity measurement and enhancement system: A meta-analysis. *Journal of Applied Psychology, 93(3),* 540–567. doi:10.1037/0021-9010.93.3.540.

Pritchard, R. D., Jones, S. D., Roth, P. L., Stuebing, K. K., & Ekeberg, S. E. (1988). Effects of group feedback, goal setting, and incentives on organizational productivity. *Journal of Applied Psychology, 73(2),* 337–358. doi:10.1037/0021-9010.73.2.337.

Pritchard, R. D., Jones, S. D., Roth, P. L., Stuebing, K. K., & Ekeberg, S. E. (1989). The evaluation of an integrated approach to measuring organizational productivity. *Personnel Psychology, 42(1),* 69–115.

Pritchard, R. D., Weaver, S. J., & Ashwood, E. L. (2012). *Evidence-based productivity improvement: A practical guide to the Productivity Measurement and Enhancement System.* New York: Routledge, Taylor & Francis.

Seijts, G. H., & Latham, G. P. (2001). The effect of distal learning, outcome, and proximal goals on a moderately complex task. *Journal of Organizational Behavior, 22(3),* 291–307. doi:10.1002/job.70.

Seijts, G. H., Latham, G. P., Tasa, K., & Latham, B. W. (2004). Goal setting and goal orientation: An integration of two different yet related literatures. *Academy of Management Journal, 47(2),* 227–239. Retrieved from EBSCO*host.*

van de Geer, E., van Tuijl, H. F. J. M., Rutte, C. G., DiazGranados, D., Harrell, M. M., & Pritchard, R. D. (2010). *Task uncertainty as a moderator for feedback effectiveness: A meta-analysis.* Unpublished manuscript, Department of Technology Management, Eindhoven University of Technology, The Netherlands.

Winters, D., & Latham, G. P. (1996). The effect of learning versus outcome goals on a simple versus a complex task. *Group & Organization Management, 21(2),* 236–250. doi:10.1177/1059601196212007.

# 16  The Predictive Validity of Conscious and Subconscious Motives on Career Advancement

*Ann Howard*  Development Dimensions International

Once upon a time two professors engaged in a scholarly debate about the relative contributions of conscious and subconscious motives in determining long-term success. Dr. David C. McClelland argued that because subconscious motives reveal what people enjoy doing, they should be relevant to a variety of tasks over time; by contrast, conscious motives such as goals relate to specific tasks and are short-lived. Dr. Edwin A. Locke countered that intentions are closest to action, and a meaningful goal might predict success better than more remote characteristics, even over a long period of time. Projective tests measure general traits, whereas goals are task- and situation-specific states; states are usually superior to traits in predicting performance.

Both types of motives had been demonstrated to relate empirically to work performance. The power of conscious motivation is evident from the vast body of work on goal setting summarized by Locke and Latham (1990, 2002) and in this volume. The importance of subconscious motives, measured by coding stories written to pictures in the Thematic Apperception Test (TAT), was extensively reported by McClelland and his colleagues (McClelland, D. C., 1975; McClelland, Atkinson, & Clark, 1953).

To help resolve this debate, Drs. Locke and McClelland invited me to engage in the research described in this chapter. The data came from the Management Progress Study (MPS), AT&T's longitudinal study of the lives and careers of managers initiated by Dr. Douglas W. Bray. The study had previously found that motivation was a significant predictor of the number of promotions a manager attained over a period of 20 years (Howard & Bray, 1988). Moreover, MPS used a variety of subconscious and conscious motivation measures, including the TAT and other projective tests, paper-and-pencil personality tests, and interview questions.

Previous MPS findings offered some support to both sides of the debate. The subconscious leader motive pattern, coded from responses to TAT stories according to McClelland's theoretical formulations, was associated with advancement for nontechnical managers after 16 years (McClelland & Boyatzis, 1982). On the side of conscious goals, one of the highest predictors of managerial success after 20 years was a composite ambition factor that was strongly influenced by interviews probing into managers' aspirations (Howard & Bray, 1988).

The research reported in this chapter involved coding additional MPS data and analyzing how various motivation measures related to advancement in management after 25 years.

## The MPS Sample

The original MPS sample included 422 male managers employed in six telephone companies that were part of the former Bell System. Nearly two-thirds of the participants were college graduates hired directly into management shortly before the data collection. The remaining participants were previously hired vocational employees who had been promoted into management at a young age (i.e., 32 or younger). All participants underwent a variety of tests, simulations, and other exercises in three 3-day assessment centers—the first at the beginning of the study, a second eight years later, and a third after 20 years. The original assessments took place in the summers of 1956 through 1960.

Table 16.1 shows the size of the sample at the first two assessments and after 25 years.

Attrition was substantial for the college group, such that by year 25 the sample was equally represented by college and noncollege men. The primary analyses for this research were conducted with the year 25 sample.

## Motivation Measures

The participants completed the motivation measures analyzed here during both the initial assessment and the second assessment eight years later. The motivation techniques ranged on a continuum from subconscious to conscious, as shown in Figure 16.1.

Most remote from consciousness were the themes identified in stories written to the TAT pictures. Other projective scores came from a summary of clinical impressions of

*Table 16.1* MPS Sample

| Year | College | Non-college | Total |
|------|---------|-------------|-------|
| 0 | 274 | 148 | 422 |
| 8 | 167 | 142 | 309 |
| 25 * | 139 | 138 | 277 |

* Includes retirees

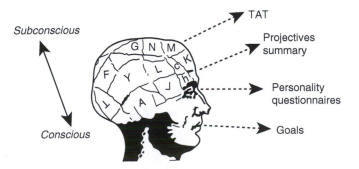

*Figure 16.1* Continuum of Motivation Measures.

the TAT stories and two tests using incomplete sentences. Further toward consciousness were traits scored from several personality tests. Most accessible to consciousness were the MPS participants' stated advancement goals. Each of these measures is described more fully below.

### Thematic Apperception Test (TAT)

At the first telephone company in the original assessment center (MPS:0), participants wrote stories to four TAT pictures (7BM, 8BM, 2, 14). Those from the remaining five companies wrote stories to six pictures (the four above plus 6BM and 16). The same six stories were used for all participants in the eighth year assessment (MPS:8). All test administrators gave the participants standard TAT instructions.

The McClelland and Boyatzis (1982) study used only the 6-picture stories from the original assessment. The present research added the 4-picture stories in order to take advantage of the full sample. Also included were the stories from the eighth year assessment.

### Coding

McClelland had identified a subconscious leader motive pattern that enables people to be effective managers at high levels in an organization (McClelland, 1975). He also theorized that need for achievement (McClelland, Atkinson, & Clark, 1953) would be related to success in small business or in sales, where people do most of the work themselves. In large organizations, he anticipated that need for achievement would have a curvilinear relationship to management level; that is, it would be important for lower-level success, where individual accomplishment mattered, but not for higher-level roles, where leading others is more critical.

An experienced coder for McClelland's consulting firm coded each story for both the original study (MPS:0) and this research (MPS:8). Coded scores used for this research included need achievement (n ach), need affiliation (n aff), need power (n pow), and activity inhibition (AI). The number of words was also counted. Scores were summed across the stories.

### Adjustments

Cognitive ability tests have repeatedly shown high validities in predicting job performance, particularly for jobs of higher complexity such as those studied here (Ones, Dilchert, Viswesvaran, & Salgado, 2010). Thus, for accurate evaluations and comparisons, the motivational measures needed to be free from potential contamination by cognitive ability. An adjustment was made to the coded TAT scores by applying a regression equation, developed for specific samples, to correct the scores for the number of words managers used in their stories. The first company of MPS:0 was treated separately from the remaining companies because of the different number of pictures. The MPS:8 sample was treated separately from the two samples at MPS:0.

The standardized residual scores, indicating motives not predicted by word length, were transformed to T scores (by multiplying the z-score by 10 and adding 50).

The resulting scores were checked to be sure that they had a zero correlation with word length.

Individuals who averaged fewer than 40 words per story were singled out as possibly producing unreliable codes. At MPS:0 this pertained to only one individual, who was left in the sample. There were 11 such individuals at MPS:8. Eliminating them did not, however, change the correlations with the criteria, so the brief story writers were left in the sample for the analyses reported here.

Correcting the scores for word length reduced their covariance with cognitive ability as measured by the School and College Ability Test (SCAT), administered to the MPS participants in each assessment center. For the MPS:0 sample (excluding the first company because of its variant word length), the correlation of raw n pow with the Total score of the SCAT (SCAT-T) was .19; the adjusted n pow correlated .12 with SCAT-T. The before and after correlations of Activity Inhibition with SCAT-T were .18 and .08. Neither n ach nor n aff correlated significantly with cognitive ability, before or after the transformations. The leader motive pattern adjusted for word length correlated .13 with SCAT-T.

## Leader Motive Pattern

The following formula defined the leader motive pattern.

- T-score of n pow $\geq$ 45.
- T-score of n pow $\geq$ T-score of n aff.
- AI $\geq$ median for the sample.

In other words, the theory stipulated that more successful leaders would be concerned with influencing others, have less concern about being liked, and have a moderate to high degree of self-control. Individuals who met the above criteria were assigned a leader motive pattern of 2; those who did not meet the criteria were scored 1. Because previous research had uncovered some problems with AI, a second leader motive pattern was computed without AI.

## Projectives Summary

In addition to the TAT, the MPS assessment centers used two other projective techniques: the Rotter Incomplete Sentences Blank (Rotter & Rafferty, 1950) and the Management Incomplete Sentences Blank (constructed by Walter Katkovsky, Vaughn C. Crandall, and Julian B. Rotter). The latter test contained 57 sentence stems related to various management attitudes, such as achievement orientation, level of aspiration, job involvement, and attitudes toward different types of assignments (Grant, Katkovsky, & Bray, 1967).

A clinical psychologist formulated impressions and hypotheses about each individual based on responses to all three instruments and summarized these in a written report. The same psychologist (Dr. Walter Katkovsky) wrote most of the reports at MPS:0 and MPS:8. The summaries emphasized characteristics that might influence the participant's management career, including attitudes and feelings about his job, career, family, and self. These reports were read aloud to the assessment staff in the assessment center integration session for each participant.

## Coding

Two psychologists who had not participated in the assessment center independently coded the summary reports on nine variables; the means of their ratings were used as final scores. Based on congruence with the other motivation measures under study, four of these variables were selected for this research.

- **Achievement/Advancement**—Ambition; motivation for and interest in advancement and success.
- **Affiliation**—Interest in being liked and accepted by others, being a part of groups, helping others, and avoiding arguments and friction with others; participating in group situations and being outgoing.
- **Willingness to Assume a Leadership Role**—Readiness to make decisions and accept leadership or supervisory responsibility; having dominance or leadership needs.
- **Willingness to Accept a Subordinate Role**—Willingness to act as a follower or subordinate in relationships with others; suggestibility and submissiveness.

### Personality Tests

Three paper-and-pencil tests of personality measured aspects of motivation that were considered relevant to long-term managerial success.

### Guilford-Martin Inventory

This questionnaire measures five personality characteristics, one of which was consistent with the type of motivation studied here.

- **Ascendance.** High scorers are eager to voice their own opinions, even if others disagree, and risk confrontation to protect their rights.

### Sarnoff Survey of Attitudes Toward Life

This short questionnaire, developed by Dr. Irving Sarnoff, evaluates conventional ambition for upward mobility and financial rewards. Two independent raters later defined three subscales, of which one was used in this research: **Motivation for Advancement**.

### Edwards Personal Preference Schedule

This forced-choice inventory measures 15 motivational needs. The following scales were selected for their congruence with relevant needs in the TAT.

- **Need for Dominance.** Motivation to lead and direct others. High scorers seek positions of leadership and want recognition as leaders.

- **Need for Affiliation.** Motivation to make and enjoy friends. Individuals scoring high form new friendships readily and would rather do things in friendly groups than alone.
- **Need for Achievement.** Motivation to do a difficult job well. Persons scoring high have a need to do their best and seek to solve difficult problems.

Following McClelland's theory that needs for achievement are important for lower-level positions but not high-level positions in organizations, a curvilinear relationship of need for achievement with attained management level was also tested.

### Goals

*Coding*

Interviewers repeatedly asked participants the highest management level they wanted to attain in their career. These interviews were conducted at the assessment centers as well as in follow-up activities conducted annually between the first two assessments. Goals could range from 1 (the lowest level of management) to 7 (president of a telephone company). The telephone companies considered levels 1 and 2 to be supervisory; levels 3 and 4 constituted middle management; and levels 5 through 7 were executive positions. Two experienced study administrators read interviews with the managers and coded their goals. Any ambiguities were resolved by discussion between the two coders.

The initial goal was taken from the interview at the first assessment. If no goal was given at that time, the goal stated in a follow-up interview one year later was used. The goal at year 8 was taken from participants' interviews at the year 8 assessment center.

If managers stated that they did not want to progress further up the hierarchy, their current level was used as the goal. If no ultimate level was indicated, the goal was considered missing. A few noncollege men stated that their ultimate goal was 1 1/2 level (an intermediate level used in a few telephone companies); these were coded as level 1.

*Adjustments*

Goals were adjusted for their correlation with cognitive ability using a regression equation with SCAT-T. The residual goals were transformed to T-scores in the same manner used for the TAT motives.

By year 8 of the study, more than three-fourths of the managers had been promoted at least one level. More specifically, 48% were at level 2, 26% at level 3, and 2% at level 4. This would undoubtedly create a bias in the stating of their goals. Two adjustments were made to compensate for this fact:

- **Goal partialing level 8 predictions.** Goal at year 8 was correlated with level year 25, partialing out that part of level 8 not predicted by the initial goal (year 0 or 1). The variable to be partialed was created by a regression equation of level 8 on the original goal.

- **Goal partialing level 8.** Goal at year 8 was correlated with level year 25, partialing out the level at year 8. This is a very conservative estimate because the year 8 level reflects multiple determinants of the year 25 level.

## Criteria

### Advancement of Managers Staying with Bell (Stayers)

The primary criterion for stayers was **management level at year 25**. By this time 38 managers had retired; if they had stayed with the Bell System for at least 20 years before retirement, their level at retirement was used.

### Adjustments

There were 43 men who had progressed beyond level 1 by the first year of the study, when the initial goals were measured. Of these, 39 had progressed to level 2, and 4 to level 3. Because these early promotions could constitute a bias in setting goals, management level at year 25 was adjusted to reflect what could not be predicted by the managers' year 1 level. This adjustment was made by a regression equation of the year 25 level on the year 1 level.

### Advancement of Managers who Left Bell (Leavers)

All except three managers who left the Bell System were college graduates. To avoid inadvertent contamination, the three noncollege managers were eliminated from the "leaver" sample.

One measure of advancement for leavers was their **management level at year 25**. This information was obtained by personal interview. If there was no year 25 interview, the immediately preceding interview (year 21) was used instead. Levels among the leavers ranged from 1 (specialist or first-level supervisor) to 5 (officer). Twenty-two leavers could not be classified into a management level. They included professionals, students, and people in one- or two-person businesses.

A second measure of leavers' progress was **salary at year 25**. This came from the same interview sources as the advancement data. Salaries were adjusted for inflation, using as 100 the consumer price index of 1982–1984, which was approximately 25 years after the original assessments.

## Findings

### Dichotomous Predictions from the TAT

Consistent with the earlier study by McClelland and Boyatzis (1982), the predictive power of the leader motive pattern was tested in a $2 \times 2$ design. That is, whether or not a participant had the leader motive pattern was compared to whether or not he had advanced as far as middle management (Level 3 in the 7-level hierarchy). Table 16.2 shows the results.

Table 16.2 Dichotomous Predictions from TAT Leader Motive Pattern

| Dichotomize above Level 2 | | Technical | | | | | Nontechnical | | | | |
|---|---|---|---|---|---|---|---|---|---|---|---|
| Year 0 Predictions | | Level 1 or 2 | Level 3+ | Total | Chi-square | p | Level 1 or 2 | Level 3+ | Total | Chi-square | p |
| A. After 16 years | Not LMP | 43 | 29 | 72 | 2.66 | ns | 58 | 75 | 133 | 4.78 | .03 |
| | LMP | 23 | 7 | 30 | | | 12 | 35 | 47 | | |
| | Total | 66 | 36 | 102 | | | 70 | 110 | 180 | | |
| B. After 25 years | Not LMP | 41 | 31 | 72 | .03 | ns | 52 | 76 | 128 | 1.49 | ns |
| | LMP | 16 | 13 | 29 | | | 14 | 32 | 46 | | |
| | Total | 57 | 44 | 101 | | | 66 | 108 | 174 | | |

| Dichotomize above Level 3 | | Technical | | | | | Nontechnical | | | | |
|---|---|---|---|---|---|---|---|---|---|---|---|
| Year 0 Predictions | | Level 1–3 | Level 4+ | Total | Chi-square | p | Level 1–3 | Level 4+ | Total | Chi-square | p |
| C. After 25 years | Not LMP | 66 | 6 | 72 | .06 | ns | 101 | 27 | 128 | 3.41 | .065 |
| | LMP | 27 | 2 | 29 | | | 30 | 16 | 46 | | |
| | Total | 93 | 8 | 101 | | | 131 | 43 | 174 | | |

Section A of Table 16.2 replicates the findings of McClelland and Boyatzis at year 16 with the augmented sample (including the 4-picture stories). At that point in time, participants in nontechnical positions with the leader motive pattern were significantly more likely to be in middle management than those who did not have the leader motive pattern. The lack of a similar finding with technical personnel was attributed to their promotions being more dependent on technical skills than on leadership qualities (McClelland and Boyatzis, 1982).

When these results were re-analyzed using advancement after 25 years (Section B of Table 16.2), the leader motive pattern no longer distinguished those in middle management and higher. A possible explanation is that many college graduates eventually rose into middle management, seemingly regardless of their abilities and motivation, a phenomenon dubbed the "upward seep of mediocrity" (Howard & Bray, 1988). After 25 years, then, it is reasonable to differentiate the more successful participants as those at the fourth level or higher rather than the third. These results are shown in Section C of Table 16.2. The chi-square increased for the nontechnical participants using this higher standard, but it did not quite reach a level of statistical significance ($p < .065$).

## Linear Predictions of Bell System Advancement

Independent predictors of advancement among the stayers are shown in Table 16.3. The criterion in all cases was the year 25 level, independent of what was predicted from the year 1 level.

## Predictions from MPS:0

The TAT leader motive pattern showed no significant linear relationship with management level 25 years later, even for the nontechnical group. However, low n affiliation was significantly related to advancement for both the nontechnical and total samples. Multiple regression equations tested the interactions of the various terms in the leader motive pattern (n pow × n aff; n pow × AI; n pow × n aff × AI), but none was statistically significant. Also lacking significance was the hypothesized curvilinear relationship of n ach with management level.

The projectives summary ratings showed small but significant relationships with advancement for both achievement/advancement motivation and unwillingness to assume a subordinate role.

Several of the paper-and-pencil test scores (GAMIN Ascendancy, Sarnoff Advancement, and Edwards need for dominance) also showed modest relationships with advancement. Surprisingly, need for affiliation from the Edwards test had a positive relationship to advancement, compared to a negative relationship for the same construct on the TAT. However, the correlation with the Edwards scale was quite small ($r = .14$).

In contrast to the other measures, goals showed a very strong correlation with advancement ($r = .54$), even when the influence of cognitive ability was eliminated ($r = .43$). The strong relationship held for both the technical and nontechnical samples.

Table 16.3 Predictors of Bell System Advancement: Correlations with Year 25 Level Partialing Out Year 1 Level

| | MPS:0 Assessment | | | MPS:8 Assessment | | |
|---|---|---|---|---|---|---|
| | Total | Tech (Yr. 25) | Nontech (Yr. 25) | Total | Tech (Yr. 25) | Nontech (Yr. 25) |
| **TAT** | | | | | | |
| Leader Motive Pattern | .07 | .01 | .13 | -.08 | -.15 | -.08 |
| Leader Motive without AI | .09 | .01 | .16 | -.05 | -.10 | -.05 |
| n pow T score | .05 | .08 | .03 | -.01 | -.04 | .01 |
| n aff T score | -.19** | -.09 | -.25** | .03 | .06 | .03 |
| Activity Inhibition T score | .04 | -.07 | .11 | .04 | -.03 | .07 |
| n ach T score | .11 | .10 | .12 | .10 | .11 | .13 |
| **PROJECTIVES SUMMARY** | | | | | | |
| Achievement/Advancement | .17** | .21* | .09 | .36** | .31** | .33** |
| Leader role | .11 | .19 | .05 | .27** | .17 | .27** |
| Subordinate role | -.14* | -.15 | -.12 | -.26** | -.20* | -.24** |
| Affiliation | .07 | .01 | .08 | -.11 | -.12 | -.12 |
| **PERSONALITY TESTS** | | | | | | |
| GAMIN Ascendancy | .22** | .11 | .24** | .21** | .06 | .25** |
| Sarnoff Advancement | .18** | .35** | .04 | .26** | .31** | .21** |
| Edwards n dom | .18** | .25* | .10 | .27** | .23* | .29** |
| Edwards n aff | .14* | .18 | .09 | -.05 | .00 | -.11 |
| Edwards n ach | .10 | .14 | .03 | .29** | .21* | .28** |
| **GOALS** | | | | | | |
| Goal (desired level) | .54** | .55** | .48** | .67** | .70** | .63** |
| Goal without Scat T | .43** | .40** | .38** | .56** | .56** | .54** |
| Goal partialing level 8 prediction | | | | .46** | .62** | .38** |
| Goal partialing level 8 | | | | .32** | .46** | .22** |

* p < .05; ** p < .01

*Predictions from MPS:8*

None of the TAT motives measured in year 8 came close to correlating significantly with the year 25 level. Test-retest reliability estimates (Spearman-Brown) for the MPS:0 and MPS:8 scores were quite low for the T-scores of all motives. Need power was especially unreliable at .18, and the leader motive pattern had a reliability of only .13. Even among the raw scores uncorrected for word length, test-retest reliability was quite low.

In contrast to the collapse of the motives from the TAT alone, scores derived from the projectives summary gained considerably in predictive power. For the total group, measures at year 8 of achievement/advancement motivation (r = .36), acceptance of a leader role (r = .27), and rejection of a subordinate role (r = .26) each correlated significantly with level at year 25. Moreover, the correlations remained significant regardless of whether the participant was in a technical or nontechnical position. Only need for affiliation was unrelated to advancement (r = .11 for total group).

Similar to the projectives summary ratings, the paper-and-pencil tests generally gained predictive power at MPS:8 compared to MPS:0. An enhanced relationship with year 25 management level was shown by Edwards need dominance (year 0 r = .18; year 8 r = .27), Edwards need achievement (year 0 r = .10; year 8 r = .29), and the Sarnoff advancement scale (year 0 r = .18; year 8 r = .26). The GAMIN ascendancy scale maintained about the same relationship to year 25 level (year 0 r = .22; year 8 r = .21). Edwards need for affiliation became unrelated to management level at year 25 (year 0 r = .14; year 8 r = −.05), replicating the finding for affiliation from the projectives summary.

As might be expected, uncorrected goals at year 8 showed a very high correlation with level at year 25 (.67 for the total group). This dropped to .56 without the influence of cognitive ability. However, conscious goals are dependent on progress to date, so these estimates contain a bias.

A better estimate comes from the correlations of year 8 goals with year 25 level, partialing out that part of year 8 level that was not predicted by the original goals. This dropped the correlation for the total group to .46, somewhat lower than that from the MPS:0 goal to year 25 level (.54). The most conservative estimate eliminates the influence of level 8 entirely. Even with this step, goals at year 8 correlated .32 with level at year 25 for the total group.

The pattern of results from Table 16.3 suggests that the more conscious the motivation measure, the better it predicts later advancement. Returning to Figure 16.1, the continuum of motivation measures directly paralleled the continuum of predictability found in this research.

*Combinations of Predictors*

Multiple regression analyses evaluated whether the different measures of motivation made independent contributions to the prediction of later advancement. The one or two strongest predictors from each category of motivation measures were entered stepwise into an equation to predict management level at year 25. Table 16.4 summarizes the results.

Whether measured at MPS:0 or MPS:8, goals, projective measures, and paper-and-pencil personality measures contributed independent variance to the prediction of

*Table 16.4* Multiple Regressions on Bell System Advancement: Predicting Year 25 Level Partialing Out Year 1 Level

| MPS:0 Assessment | R | R square | F Change |
| --- | --- | --- | --- |
| Goal without Scat T | .437 | .191 | 62.92** |
| TAT n aff T score (negative) | .458 | .210 | 6.16* |
| Edwards n dom | .472 | .223 | 4.5* |
| MPS:8 Assessment | R | R square | F Change |
| Goal partialing level 8 prediction | .453 | .205 | 68.35** |
| Projectives Achievement/Advancement | .549 | .302 | 36.46** |
| Edwards n dom | .577 | .333 | 12.41** |

advancement. Goals were the most powerful predictor and entered the equation first. While the TAT added to the prediction at the original assessment (though not in the hypothesized pattern), it was superseded by the projectives summary eight years later. Among the paper-and-pencil personality scales, the Edwards need for dominance at both assessments added significantly to the predictions of later advancement.

### Predictions of Success in Other Organizations

Table 16.5 shows correlations of motives with salary and advancement criteria among those who left the Bell System and moved into other organizations. The total group is shown as well as two subgroups who were employed either in a large organization or in their own business.

The sample size for the leavers was small, yet all categories of motives showed significant correlations with at least one of the criteria of success. For those who moved to other large organizations, the personality measures related to advancement. Among the entrepreneurs, goals were a strong predictor of salary. The TAT leader motive without the controlling influence of AI also related to salary. However, McClelland's theory suggested that it should be achievement rather than the leader motive that had the strongest influence on entrepreneurial success. Thus, while the correlation was significant, it did not support his theory. Moreover, other empirical research has supported his theory about achievement motivation. A meta-analysis found that self-report and projective measures of need for achievement were independently and equally correlated with entrepreneurial success (Collins, Hanges, & Locke, 2004).

The results for the leavers suggest that the relationship of conscious and subconscious motives to managerial success might generalize beyond the Bell System. Replication with a more robust sample is needed to be more definitive.

## Discussion

All three types of measures—subconscious projectives, personality questionnaires, and conscious goals—made independent contributions to the forecast of advancement in management. Apparently each method captured an aspect of motivation that the others

Table 16.5 MPS:0 Predictors of Success in Other Organizations: Correlations with Year 25 Hierarchical Level and Salary Adjusted for Inflation

| | Total | | Large Organization | | Own Business |
|---|---|---|---|---|---|
| | Level | Salary | Level | Salary | Salary |
| **TAT** | | | | | |
| Leader Motive Pattern | -.03 | .10 | -.08 | -.01 | .29 |
| Leader Motive without AI | .01 | .11 | -.15 | .08 | .36* |
| n pow T score | .00 | -.01 | -.07 | .16 | .28 |
| n aff T score | .04 | -.03 | .00 | .18 | -.28 |
| Activity Inhibition T score | .01 | -.05 | .18 | .04 | .12 |
| n ach T score | .05 | -.02 | .05 | -.07 | -.04 |
| **PROJECTIVES SUMMARY** | | | | | |
| Achievement/Advancement | .00 | .05 | .04 | .08 | .07 |
| Leader role | .26* | .12 | .12 | .18 | -.06 |
| Subordinate role | -.14 | .05 | .03 | .06 | .20 |
| Affiliation | .01 | .06 | .10 | -.20 | .26 |
| **PERSONALITY TESTS** | | | | | |
| GAMIN Ascendancy | .28** | .19* | .36* | .24 | .18 |
| Sarnoff Advancement | .17 | .13 | .35* | .19 | .07 |
| Edwards n dom | .07 | .13 | .07 | .02 | .30 |
| Edwards n aff | -.13 | .00 | -.06 | -.08 | .06 |
| Edwards n ach | .12 | .09 | .02 | .15 | -.07 |
| **GOALS** | | | | | |
| Goal (desired level) | .11 | .38** | .02 | .10 | .49** |
| Goal without Scat T | .08 | .27* | -.05 | -.01 | .42* |
| N | 90 | 111 | 47 | 47 | 34 |

did not. The constructs of importance centered on dominance, leadership, and power. Whether needs for achievement and affiliation also play a role remained unclear.

The constructs that related to advancement did so in a straightforward, positive way. Tests of constructs hypothesized to relate to advancement in different directions, whether curvilinear (achievement) or negative (affiliation), did not produce consistent results.

Although each type of measure helped to predict managerial advancement, the results formed a continuum of predictability. The more conscious the motivation measure, the greater its ability to predict job advancement. Goals were particularly strong, and the TAT and other projective measures particularly weak. Personality tests fell in between.

The situational constraint imposed for the TAT leader motive pattern—that it would apply only to advancement of managers in nontechnical positions—did not hold true when other measures were used, including other projective measures. The reason for this discrepancy is not immediately apparent.

Nor is it clear why the TAT failed so completely at the MPS:8 assessment. McClelland (personal communication) offered the explanation that test-retest reliability was often low because people tried to write different stories when exposed to the same picture a second time. However, it seems unlikely that the MPS managers would remember the stories they wrote eight years previously.

One challenge for theory and research is why the other motivation measures became better predictors after the passage of eight years. The increase in predictive power was of a magnitude of 50%, from accounting for 22% of the variance in advancement to 33% (see Table 16.4). Some clues to interpretation can be found in mean scores on the motivation measures for those at each management level in year 25, shown in Table 16.6. (Because only a handful of men had reached levels 6 and 7, they were combined with those at level 5.)

Between years 0 and 8, the lower-level men reduced their goals and their achievement/advancement motivation (from the projectives summary), while the higher-level men increased both (see the arrows in Table 16.6). On the Edwards need for dominance scale, the supervisory and middle-management groups increased slightly over time but the higher-level men increased more.

These findings are consistent with other MPS results described as "the rich get richer and the poor get poorer" (Howard & Bray, 1988). That is, better differentiation among the participants was often a combination of the high-level men enlarging their abilities and brightening their attitudes while the lower-level men declined. Perhaps those at the lower rungs of the ladder felt that the die was cast after eight years, and concluded that aspiring for a larger leadership role was futile. At the same time, those who were progressing nicely through the management ranks might have tasted power, liked it, and hungered for more.

Another challenge for motivation theory and research is why goals are such a potent predictor of job advancement 25 years later. A target such as organizational level likely includes not only drive to get ahead, but also expectation of success. In fact, expectation of attaining the desired level, measured from the same interviews, added no independent variance to goals in predicting advancement.

Table 16.6 Mean Scores on Motivation Measures by Year 25 Level

| Year 25 Level | N | Goal | | | Projectives Ach/Adv | | | Edwards n dom | | |
|---|---|---|---|---|---|---|---|---|---|---|
| | | Year 0 | Year 8 | | Year 0 | Year 8 | | Year 0 | Year 8 | |
| 1 | 41 | 2.23 | 1.95 | ⇩ | 26.10 | 23.85 | ⇩ | 18.02 | 18.25 | ⇑ |
| 2 | 86 | 3.19 | 2.96 | ⇩ | 30.06 | 25.00 | ⇩ | 19.98 | 20.26 | ⇑ |
| 3 | 103 | 3.74 | 3.81 | ⬆ | 31.32 | 29.80 | ⇩ | 20.78 | 21.80 | ⇑ |
| 4 | 38 | 4.32 | 4.32 | = | 32.67 | 32.11 | ⇩ | 21.24 | 21.84 | ⇑ |
| 5+ | 15 | 4.93 | 5.21 | ⬆ | 30.39 | 38.33 | ⬆ | 20.80 | 22.93 | ⬆ |
| Total | 283 | | | | | | | | | |

There were marked differences between the college and noncollege samples in terms of their expectations of success and their ultimate advancement, which could potentially bias the findings. Yet MPS:0 and MPS:8 goals significantly predicted job advancement after 25 years for the college and noncollege groups separately, so education level alone cannot fully explain the results. Perhaps a goal such as ultimate management level represents a self-assessment in the context of a particular organizational environment— a sizing up of oneself much like a good assessor does from an array of assessment center data.

It is questionable whether the power of goals to predict later advancement would be replicated with more recent data. The MPS research began within a very large hierarchical organization in the 1950s, when management level was clearly defined and highly desired as the ultimate mark of success. The subsequent flattening of organizations and growing employee cynicism about organizational life could seriously dampen hierarchical aspirations.

Given their predictive power, goals might be seen by eager industrial-organizational psychologists as a potential tool for selecting executives. Unfortunately, such use is limited. Once the "secret" was out that hierarchical goals were a selection tool, easy faking would inevitably be their undoing.

## Acknowledgments

With special thanks to Drs. Edwin A. Locke and David C. McClelland for their stimulation, advice, encouragement, and patience.

## References

Collins, C., Hanges, P., & Locke, E. A. (2004). The relationship of achievement motivation to entrepreneurial behavior: A meta-analysis. *Human Performance, 17,* 95–117.

Grant, D. L., Katkovsky, W., & Bray, D. W. (1967). Contributions of projective techniques to assessment of management potential. *Journal of Applied Psychology, 52* (3), 226–232.

Howard, A., & Bray, D. W. (1988). *Managerial lives in transition: Advancing age and changing times.* New York: Guilford.

Locke, E. A., & Latham, G. (1990). *A theory of goal-setting and task performance.* Englewood Cliffs, NJ: Prentice-Hall.

Locke, E. A., & Latham, G. (2002). Building a practically useful theory of goal setting and task motivation. *American Psychologist, 56,* 705–717.

McClelland, D. C. (1975). *Power: The inner experience.* New York: Irvington-Halsted-Wiley.

McClelland, D. C., Atkinson, J. W., & Clark, R. A. (1953). *The achievement motive.* New York: Appleton-Century-Crofts.

McClelland, D. C., & Boyatzis, R. E. (1982). Leadership motive pattern and long-term success in management. *Journal of Applied Psychology, 67* (6), 737–743.

Ones, D. S., Dilchert, S., Viswesvaran, C., & Salgado, J. F. (2010). Cognitive abilities. Chapter 12 in Farr, J. L., & Tippins, N. T. (Eds.), *Handbook of employee selection.* New York: Routledge, pp. 255–275.

Rotter, J. B., & Rafferty, J. E. (1950). *The manual for the Rotter incomplete sentences blank.* New York: Psychological Corporation.

# 17  Goal Setting and Organizational Transformation

*Lise M. Saari*  *Baruch College and New York University*

Goal setting research, conducted extensively over the past four decades, has shown that goal setting methods can be highly effective for energizing and increasing task performance (Locke & Latham, 1990; Locke, Shaw, Saari, & Latham, 1981). These findings have been well documented in hundreds of studies, many of which are carefully controlled laboratory experiments.

The purpose of this chapter is to go beyond the backdrop of the extensive research on goal setting to describe its actual use in a company undergoing large-scale change. This company is IBM. The author worked at IBM, as director of global workforce research, and observed the use of goal setting as an important part of IBM's transformation from the early 1990s and into the 2000s.

The case described here is representative of the types of change issues faced by many organizations today. We live in a world of constant change, and organizations—more precisely the people in them—must adapt and perform at high levels to be successful in the context of continually changing business realities.

This chapter describes a real-life case, observed by the author over 11 years and corroborated by other published accounts (Garr, 2000; Gerstner, 2002), of how goal setting worked in a company undergoing change and transformation. What was at stake was whether IBM would continue to exist. In 1993, IBM was described as a dinosaur with little chance of survival (Loomis, 1993).

This chapter describes how goal setting worked and its value for motivating hundreds of thousands of employees around the globe toward a common direction. Descriptions of how goal setting was actually carried out and reflections on its use are provided. Summaries of the use of goals in two other organizations, with which the author is also highly familiar, are briefly described. It should be noted that the information and perspectives provided in this chapter are the author's and do not reflect official information from the companies described.

## How was Goal Setting Used in IBM's Transformation?

IBM is a 100-year-old global IT company that provides computer technology products and services. IBM was in serious financial trouble in the early 1990s. In 1993, Lou Gerstner was brought in as the new CEO to attempt to turn it around. This case study describes how goal setting was used by Gerstner in the turnaround and as part of large-scale organizational change. Interestingly, throughout his career, Gerstner is said to have has a specific, challenging, self-set goal to improve his personal productivity by 30% annually (Cook, 1996).

The primary way goal setting was used at IBM was to align all employees to a new common company direction. This started with defining and communicating a set of eight principles for the company (e.g., "The marketplace is the driving force behind everything we do," "We think and act with urgency") as well as defining and providing feedback on eleven new requirements of leaders (e.g., straight talk, decisiveness, customer insight). However, these efforts, by the new CEO's own admission, did not move the company forward. Consequently, the transformation stalled. In addition, Gerstner received feedback that people were confused by so much to focus on. This may have been a type of goal overload or conflict from too many goals (Pritchard, Jones, Roth, Stuebing & Ekeberg, 1988). To address this, Lou Gerstner defined three superordinate goals for every IBM employee worldwide that defined the new company direction.

The three overall goals were: Win, Execute, and Team. As simple as these may seem, they came from a deep understanding of the business and organizational culture issues that were hindering IBM's success. They came from Lou Gerstner's analysis of and insights on IBM, and therefore were strategic and relevant for IBM. An essential element was having *appropriate* overall goals that supported *relevant company strategy*; motivating performance toward the wrong goals would *not* have resulted in the ultimate success of IBM's transformation.

The three overall goals were communicated by the CEO, by top leadership, via multiple company media, and through immediate managers to define each employee's specific performance objectives. They were part of all employees' Personal Business Commitments (PBCs) worldwide (Garr, 2000). Win, Execute, and Team were defined behaviorally so that everyone understood that they meant: winning in the marketplace, executing fast and effectively, and teaming across the business for the customer. According the Gerstner (2002), "Those three words … summed up the most important criteria I thought all IBMers needed to apply in setting their goals." (p. 211).

Within the three overall goals—Win, Execute, and Team—each employee had specific goals for his or her job. Specific Win, Execute, and Team goals were developed by each employee with his or her manager to ensure alignment, relevance, and most importantly to ensure that the goals were challenging. This was done at the beginning of each year, with specific goals defined for what the employee was going to focus on during the upcoming year. Highly communicated themes, such as customer focus, speed to market, accountability, and cross-division teaming, were made explicit in these specific, challenging goals. The goals varied by job, but the broad approach was uniform. As examples, a salesperson might have a quantified sales goal under Win, on-schedule delivery to the customer under Execute, and working with sales experts in other company areas under Team. A researcher might have investigating the viability of a new technology within a specified time period under Win, efficiency of research methods used under Execute, and collaborating with researchers in other laboratories under Team.

The PBC program was designed to align and motivate everyone toward a common company direction, one that was customer-focused and aimed at success in the marketplace. The importance of defining and aligning employees' focus to new goals has been noted extensively in the organization change literature. For example, Beer (2009) described the need to mobilize energy for change; an essential first step to achieving this change is for leaders to articulate demanding goals for organizational members.

The goal deployment at IBM, via the three overall goals of Win, Execute, and Team, was across the board, around the globe, for all IBM employees. There were some negotiations in a few countries (such as Works Council reviews in several European countries), but ultimately there was a consistent alignment of all employees globally. No matter where in the world an IBM employee worked, in one of hundreds of countries, each person had specific, challenging goals for Win, Execute, and Team.

The goals set in each of the three areas, Win, Execute, and Team, were assessed by an employee's manager at the end of the year, and an overall rating (1, 2, or 3) of the employee's performance was given. This rating (along with overall company and unit performance) determined the amount of variable pay, which was the year-end bonus that Gerstner implemented as part of IBM's transformation.

During the transformation, employees who were consistently assessed as low performers across these three goals (i.e., an overall rating of 3 over time) were likely to be downsized or part of a resource action (IBM term for layoffs). This, along with early across-the-board downsizing, was perhaps an unfortunate, though needed, part of the transformation. The departure of low performance from IBM was an important aspect of ensuring goal commitment on the part of an employee who remained with the company. This helped to ensure a good fit between organizational members and "the new IBM."

During this time, people also chose to voluntarily leave IBM or retire. Those choices also may have had incompatible goals and lack of organization fit as underlying explanations. As Schneider (1988) pointed out, people are attracted to or leave an organization based on fit to the organization. Furthermore, he stated (p. 443) that "it is goals to which people are attracted, it is goals with which they interact, and if they don't fit, they leave." To the extent that the new goals at IBM were not a good fit for people, they likely decided to leave. Schneider also posited that as organizations evolve, the behavior of all the people in them defines an organization's direction; it was precisely the organization's new direction that was addressed as part of the transformation of IBM.

## How Did the use of Goals Relate to Changing IBM's Culture?

The organizational culture of IBM was also addressed as part of its transformation. Historically, IBM had a culture that was considered strong and that helped make it great; however, it had become a hindrance to the changes IBM now had to make in order to survive (Gerstner, 2002).

A major issue contributing to IBM's difficulties was having, for many years, generally content employees. However, it was a contentment derived from an organization that promised lifelong employment and had a strong internal focus without customer-focused goals (Gerstner, 2002). Happy employees *without* goals will not lead to productive employees (Lucas & Diener, 2003). This appeared to be part of IBM's troubles; it was seen as a company with a lot of smart people on a wandering ship when Gerstner became the CEO. Employees needed customer-focused goals that were relevant to the new marketplace realities.

The PBC goals described above were part of the efforts to change IBM's culture. According to Gerstner, "Win, Execute, and Team summed up the most important criteria I thought all IBMers needed to apply in setting their goals ... This would, at our most basic level, define our new culture." (Gerstner, 2002, p. 211). Thus, the goal setting implemented at IBM was seen as essential for ultimately changing IBM's culture.

In order to change IBM's culture, Gerstner focused on "creating conditions for transformation by providing incentives and defining marketplace realities and *goals.*" (Gerstner 2002, p. 187). Consistent with Schneider's (1988) view that "people make the place," Gerstner stated "… in the end, management doesn't change culture. Management invites the workforce itself to change the culture." An interesting, complex, and counterintuitive challenge for Gerstner was that, as part of the new culture at IBM, he wanted employees to stop being followers, yet to achieve the new culture, he needed employees to follow in a new direction toward it.

## Goal Setting at IBM and the High-Performance Cycle

The High Performance Cycle (Latham, Locke, & Fassina, 2002; see Chapter 18) is a model that integrates goal setting theory with other theories of work motivation. This integrated model of goal setting also applies to the story of IBM and its transformation.

The High Performance Cycle (HPC) model starts with demands being made of the individual, group, and/or organization. In the case of IBM, there clearly were significant demands on the company and the people in it—starting with the company needing to survive. The model asserts that there should be demands or challenge in the form of goals. This was very much the case at IBM with the three overarching goals of Win, Execute, and Team. Also, the model suggests that specific, challenging goals should come about through a joint discussion between the immediate manager and the employee. This was also very much the case at IBM with the setting of specific, relevant goals within Win, Execute, and Team for each employee.

The HPC model incorporates social cognitive theory with its emphasis on the concept on self-efficacy and outcome expectancy (Bandura, 1986). High outcome expectancy and high self-efficacy are important because they lead to high goal commitment (Latham, Locke, & Fassina, 2002). Social cognitive theory states that people will be motivated when they see the relationship between what they are doing and the attainment of goals that are important to them. As part of the IBM transformation, goal achievement was tied to performance bonuses for all employees, thus aligning with this part of the model. Also, there was frequent communication on a clear and common company direction, giving the employees hope and confidence that they could work together to enable the company survive—thus enhancing an employee's self-efficacy.

The model also proposes several moderators that can enhance (or diminish) goal attainment and therefore performance. These are ability, commitment, feedback, task complexity, and situational constraints. These also applied to the IBM transformation. With the setting of challenging goals (which were tied to performance outcomes), individuals who did not have the ability or commitment to achieve them received low performance ratings, which in turn meant they likely left the company. The organization also became feedback-rich in many ways: from more communications regarding customer feedback to methods that increased individual feedback, such as 360's for managers, and regular PBC meetings between managers and employees to discuss goal progress.

The moderator, task complexity, was a deeply embedded problem at IBM, so much so that it had become part of its organizational culture (Gerstner, 2002). IBM was, in fact, a large, complex company that over the years had become even more bureaucratic and complex than it needed to be or should have been based on customer need. The clarity of the three overarching goals, Win, Execute and Team, as well as a "maniacal focus" on the customer, helped to reduce many of the complexities. The author recalls a meeting where someone asked Lou Gerstner a question that essentially involved competing internal views, and his response was to the effect: "... start with the customer— that drives all that we do."

For the moderator of situational constraints within the HPC, there were many such constraints in IBM as a company struggling to survive. The advantage of setting challenging goals (especially with high commitment and self-efficacy) is that they motivate people to overcome obstacles through tenacity and perseverance (Huber & Neale, 1987). Employees were strongly encouraged to eliminate bureaucracy and other nonessential factors that made accomplishing tasks overly difficult.

The HPC model proposes that if a person has challenging goals and the above moderating variables are in place to enhance goal attainment, then the person will enjoy high performance. The model also explains the mediators, the mechanisms by which goals actually affect performance, namely, direction of attention, effort, persistence, and task strategies.

Goals direct attention, effort, and persistence and by doing so keep people focused. This benefit of goals became very important at IBM during the transformation. Initially there was confusion, chaos, and churn. By having clear goals, people could stay on task with the most important things to be accomplished, and do so in a coordinated, strategic way. Also, employees developed new task-specific strategies (Wood & Locke, 1990) to carry out their work, because the overly complex, resource-intensive, time-consuming strategies of the past were discarded.

The HPC model states that once performance is demonstrated, rewards become an important inducement to continue. These rewards can be both external as well as internal. As discussed earlier, monetary bonuses were tied to an individual's goal attainment (as well as to the attainment of company/unit level goals). Internal rewards include a sense of achievement and feelings of success. These in turn can affect job satisfaction and self-efficacy, which in turn affect future success and goal attainment. These concepts relate to Hackman & Oldham's (1980) job characteristics theory that states task significance, task identity, responsibility/autonomy, and feedback contribute to greater meaningfulness of work, satisfaction, and motivation. All these factors came into play at IBM—from the new company direction and from connecting each employee to it via specific, challenging goals to the specific feedback received by each employee on goal progress and achievement. These external and internal rewards are important for their effects on job satisfaction and future job performance as part of the HPC. Indeed, the change efforts at IBM incorporated the key components of the HPC, the end result being a company that transformed successfully, as discussed next.

## Did Goal Setting Make a Difference?

As stated in the introduction, this chapter is descriptive in nature. However, there were several indications that goal setting was implemented successfully at IBM—and certainly there was the overall success of the company's survival—for which no one part of the intervention, be it goals or the company's strategies to attain them, can be clearly attributed.

The author had global responsibility at IBM for measuring employee attitudes during the time of the transformation, and therefore is knowledgeable about the trends of employee attitudes during the use of these goal setting approaches as part of the large-scale change initiative.

The trends on the global employee survey demonstrated both highly practical and statistically significant improvements over the period of the IBM transformation. This included trends on relevant questions such as "I have a clear understanding of my company's strategic direction" and "I see a clear link between my work and company objectives." (Given the proprietary nature of the survey data, specific results cannot be presented). What was fascinating with the IBM employee attitude data was that the question on "clarity of company direction" not only trended significantly upward during the transformation, but it actually surpassed other IT companies—based on IT industry benchmarks on the exact same question. All the other IT companies were smaller and more focused in their work (e.g., one company focused only on software development), which should have given them an advantage on an employee survey question related to clarity of company direction. The fact that IBM employees perceived greater clarity of company direction than smaller and more focused IT companies is a testament to the power of the clarity the goals provided. It also shows that creating a clear, common direction can be done successfully for even a large, complex global company with hundreds of thousands of employees in hundreds of countries.

During the period of the transformation (1993–2002), IBM also showed significant improvements on business performance measures. From 1993 to 2003, revenue increased by 30%, net income doubled, and IBM's stock price went from $13 to $120 (IBM annual financial reports). Also during this time, IBM earned more patent awards than any other company. IBM's supercomputer, Deep Blue, even defeated the then world chess champion Garry Kasparov. While many factors undoubtedly impacted these business measures, they were the result of the totality of the change efforts that include goal setting and the development of strategies to attain them.

## Other Examples of Effective use of Goals in Large-Scale Organization Change

There are two other company cases of which the author has direct knowledge that will briefly be reviewed here. These include Boeing (where the author worked for eight years as senior manager of people research) and Ford (where the author's former head of Boeing Airplane is now the CEO, and thus the author has been kept informed of the changes there). The use of goals at these companies again indicates how valuable goal setting and the alignment of employees to common goals are to company transformations. Both cases are briefly described next.

Boeing is a global manufacturer of commercial airplanes and defense and space systems. Goals were used at Boeing extensively as part of the 777 airplane design and build in the early 1990s. The primary, aligning, specific, challenging goal was "design, build, and deliver the first 777 airplane in 24 months." This was communicated widely and clearly. Project plans and all activities were aligned to this goal. A very important and highly communicated subgoal was "working together to achieve this goal." In fact, the first 777 built was named *Working Together*. This focus on teamwork is consistent with research showing the importance of group cooperation and information exchange for achieving group goals (Weldon & Weingart, 1988). In the end, the goal was achieved at Boeing with the 777 launched on schedule. As of 2011, the 777 is the world's largest twinjet airplane, is Boeing's best-selling airplane, and is the one with the largest single order at $18 billion (*Wall Street Journal*, Nov 13, 2011).

The leader of the 777 effort, Alan Mulally, subsequently left Boeing in 2006 to become the CEO of Ford Motor Company. Ford, a multinational automaker, was struggling at that time. Conditions got much worse by 2008. At Ford, among the first things Mulally did was interview employees, customers, dealers, and suppliers. From the insights he gained from those interviews, he developed and then assigned three company objectives: One Team, One Goal, One Plan. Each of these, defined by specific behaviors, was deployed throughout the company. As with Boeing and IBM, teamwork was determined to be critical, again pointing to research on the importance of group coordination for attaining organizational goals. At the time this chapter was written, Ford was the fifth most profitable automaker in the world, and the only US automaker to not take government bailout money during the economic crisis that began in 2008.

## Closing Remarks and Conclusions

This chapter describes how goal setting was used as part of large-scale organizational change efforts. Relevant organizational goals were translated into specific, challenging goals for employees to achieve higher levels of performance and organizational success. While cause and effect cannot be demonstrated with case studies, it is hoped that the information presented here on the value of goal setting for actual organizational change is helpful.

In Locke and Latham's (1990) book, *A Theory of Goal Setting and Task Performance*, the chapter on *organizational goals* was one of the smallest—due to the limited research on organizational goals at that time. Two decades later, as described by Pritchard et al. (see Chapter 15), research on organizational goals is more extensive, and there is more evidence that the goal setting can be used effectively in today's organizations.

More research on *multiple goals*, which is a reality in organizations, and other features of organizational goal setting would be valuable. The real world uses goal setting in complex environments with multiple demands. Having witnessed the value of goal setting in organizations that were successfully transformed, I would propose that future goal setting research would best be focused on understanding the factors that lead to effective real-world applications of goal setting in contemporary organizations.

Based on the strength and wealth of goal setting research, along with the workplace examples described here, it is reasonable to conclude that goal setting is an important part of organizational change efforts and is essential for companies undergoing a transformation.

## References

Bandura, A. (1986). *Social foundations of thought and action: A social-cognitive view*. Englewood Cliffs, NJ: Prentice Hall.

Beer, M. (2009). Sustain organizational performance through continuous learning, change and realignment. In E. A. Locke (Ed.), *Handbook of principles of organizational behavior: Indispensable knowledge for evidence-based management*. Chichester, UK: Wiley.

Cook, W. J. (1996). The turnaround artist: Louis Gerstner is creating a hard-driving new corporate culture at IBM. *U.S. News & World Report*, June 17.

Garr, D. (2000). *IBM redux: Lou Gerstner and the business turnaround of the decade.* Chichester, UK: Wiley.

Gerstner, L. V. (2002). *Who says elephants can't dance: Inside IBM's historic turnaround.* New York: Harper Business.

Hackman, J. R., & Oldham, G. R. (1980). *Work redesign.* Reading, MA: Addison-Wesley.

Huber, V. L., & Neale, M. A. (1987). Effects of self- and competitor-goals on performance in an integrated bargaining task. *Journal of Applied Psychology, 72,* 197–203.

Latham, G. P., Locke, E. A., & Fassina, N. E. (2002). The high performance cycle: Standing the test of time. In S. Sonnentag (Ed.), *The psychological management of individual performance. A handbook in the psychology of management in organizations* (pp. 201–228). Chichester, UK: Wiley.

Locke, E. A., & Latham, G. P. (2002). Building a practically useful theory of goal setting and task motivation: A 35-year odyssey. *American Psychologist, 57*(9), 705–717.

Locke, E. A., & Latham, G. P. (1990). *A theory of goal-setting and task performance.* Englewood Cliffs, NJ: Prentice Hall.

Locke, E. A., Shaw, K. N., Saari, L. M., & Latham, G. P. (1981). Goal setting and task performance: 1969–1980. *Psychological Bulletin, 90*(1), 125–152.

Loomis, C. J. (1993). Dinosaurs? They were a trio of the biggest, most fearsome companies on earth. Here's how earnest executives managed them into historic decline. *Fortune Magazine,* May 3.

Lucas, R. E., & Diener, E. (2003). The happy worker: Hypotheses about the role of positive affect in worker productivity. In A. M. Ryan and M. Barrick (Eds.), *Personality and work* (pp. 30–59). San Francisco: Jossey-Bass.

Pritchard, R. D., Jones, S. D., Roth, P. L., Stuebing, K. K., & Ekeberg, S. E. (1988). Effects of group feedback, goal setting, and incentives on organizational productivity. *Journal of Applied Psychology, 73*(2), 337–358.

Schneider, B. (1987). The people make the place. *Personnel Psychology, 40,* 437–453.

*Wall Street Journal* (Nov 13, 2011). *Boeing, Emirates announce historic order for 50 777-300ERs.* Retrieved Nov 1, 2011 from: http://online.wsj.com/article/PR-CO-20111113-900363.html.

Weingart, L. R., & Weldon, E. (1991). Processes that mediate the relationship between a group goal and group member performance. *Human Performance, 4,* 33–54.

Wood, R. E., & Locke, E. A. (1990). Goal-setting and strategy effects on complex tasks. In E. A. Locke and G. P. Latham (Eds.), *A theory of goal-setting and task performance* (pp. 293–319). Englewood Cliffs, NJ: Prentice Hall.

# 18 A Quantitative Analysis of the High Performance Cycle in Italy

*Laura Borgogni*  Department of Psychology, Sapienza University of Rome

*Silvia Dello Russo*  Business Research Unit, ISCTE-IUL

The High Performance Cycle (HPC), developed by Locke and Latham (1990), is a meta-theory, based on principles and empirical findings supporting goal setting theory, that predicts, explains, and influences an employee's job performance and satisfaction (see Figure 18.1). At the model's core is the relationship between specific, difficult goals (demands) and these two dependent variables. This relationship is mediated by four mechanisms. Boundary conditions are also specified regarding the extent to which demands/goals lead to high performance. The HPC shows that job performance leads to both intrinsic and extrinsic rewards and, through these, to job satisfaction. Job satisfaction, in turn, is related to organizational commitment that leads to the setting of and commitment to high goals and hence the recursive nature of the HPC. Latham, Locke, and Fassina (2002) provided an enumerative review of the literature and found strong support for the HPC.

In this chapter, we provide a brief overview of the literature on the HPC published after Latham et al.'s (2002) review. This is followed by the presentation of a questionnaire developed to quantitatively assess the HPC, and empirical data that tested the validity of aspects of the HPC's predictions for employees in Italy.

## The HPC Mediators

The HPC states that a goal's specificity and level of difficulty, which are referred to as demands, affect job performance positively through three motivational mechanisms, namely, direction, effort, and persistence (Latham et al., 2002). As noted by Latham and Locke (2007), goals focus attention on and direct subsequent behavior to relevant aspects of tasks; this typically leads to ignoring performance dimensions for which goals are not set (Latham & Locke, 2006). Second, goals serve an energizing function. This is because people expend effort in pursuing their goals. Therefore, higher demands propel employees forward through greater effort to attain higher performance. Moreover, goals prolong effort over time, thus affecting persistence.

In addition to these three motivational mechanisms, a fourth mediator is primarily cognitive in nature. When pursuing a goal, employees automatically use their existing skills and knowledge to execute well-established action plans. If the extant knowledge is inadequate for performing a new task, goal setting stimulates the discovery and development of new strategies (Latham, Seijts, & Crim, 2008).

## The HPC Moderators

Five factors moderate the goal–performance relationship.

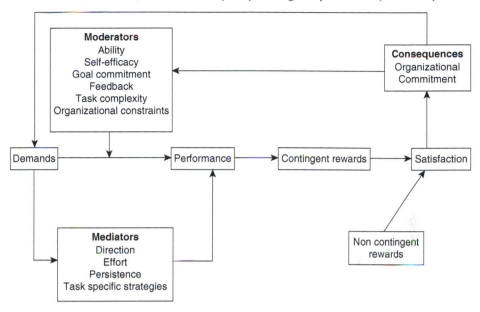

*Figure 18.1* The High Performance Cycle.

*Ability* and *self-efficacy*. Specific, difficult goals lead to higher performance only if people possess the ability to perform the task, and believe they can use their knowledge and skill when required. Self-efficacious employees interpret difficult goals as challenges rather than obstacles (Bandura, 2011). This is because the underlying properties of self-efficacy are anticipation, self-regulation, and self-reflection, which enable people to direct and adjust their behaviors. Self-efficacy is positively correlated with the development of task-related strategies and, through these, to performance (Seijts & Latham, 2001).

*Goal commitment.* Goal commitment is an individual's determination to pursue a goal over time. It implies a psychological bind to a goal (See Chapter 6). "It is virtually axiomatic that if there is no commitment to goals, then goal setting will not work" (Locke, Latham, & Erez, 1988, p. 23). Factors that bring about commitment to difficult goals are both situational (such as receiving support from the organization) and personal (particularly individual motives and the anticipation of rewards). Empirical research has shown that goal commitment not only moderates the relationship between difficult goals and performance, but it can also have a main effect on performance (Seijts & Latham, 2011).

*Feedback.* Feedback can lead to revising, either downward or upward, the goals set by an individual (Tolli & Schmidt, 2008). Feedback can increase or decrease a person's self-efficacy, in particular when internal rather than external attributions are made. Consistent with social cognitive theory (Bandura, 2011), this typically leads to adjusting one's level of aspirations. In fact, feedback activates goal regulation, such that employees generate a positive discrepancy by setting a higher goal as a result of positive feedback, whereas they often reduce a negative discrepancy following negative feedback by lowering their goal (Ilies & Judge, 2005).

*Task complexity.* Task complexity encompasses component, coordinative, and dynamic complexity (Wood, 1986). Hence, complexity is due to (a) the number of elements included in the task (e.g., acts to be executed or information to be processed), (b) the relationship among those elements, and (c) the evolution of this relationship over time, that requires monitoring and adapting one's behavior. On complex tasks, performance increases are due to the development of effective strategies appropriate to the difficulty of required actions. The resulting improvement in performance often involves a time lag (Seijts & Latham, 2005). This is because of the need to develop cognitive strategies, as well as the acquisition of new competencies and skills.

*Situational constraints.* In their discussion of factors that must be taken into account when setting goals, Latham and Locke (2006) stressed the necessity for (a) adequate resources (e.g., financial, technical) for employees to attain their goals, (b) the establishment of organizational systems and culture to support the goal setting process, (c) the provision of technical, operative, and emotional support by the immediate supervisor, (d) the minimization of conflicting goals (e.g., individual versus group goals; the activation of competitive dynamics among colleagues), and (e) the avoidance of increasing pressure on employees to achieve higher standards after the goal had been accomplished.

## Performance and its Consequences

The HPC states that job performance leads to contingent rewards and, through these, to job satisfaction. Contingent rewards include pay, promotion, career opportunities, recognition, and feelings of accomplishment. In two meta-analyses, a moderate correlation ($p = .29$) was found between an individual's actual pay and pay level satisfaction, whereas a significant but weak correlation ($p = .15$) was highlighted between level of pay and his or her overall job satisfaction (Judge, Piccolo, Podsakoff, Shaw, & Rich, 2010; Williams, McDaniel, & Nguyen, 2006). This suggests that there are a variety of factors that enhance job satisfaction. For example, intrinsic rewards (e.g., pride in accomplishment) following goal attainment increases job satisfaction (Latham, 2007). A central point in the HPC is that job satisfaction is related to job performance *only* if the latter is perceived as instrumental for attaining valued outcomes.

Job satisfaction is not just dependent on performance rewards but also "noncontingent" benefits, namely, positive returns to employees that are not linked to goal attainment, yet are connected to the nature of employment relationship (Jacobsen & Skillman, 2008). These include base-pay, benefits, job security, flexible hours, amount of leave, and congenial co-workers. They affect job satisfaction when they satisfy different needs, such as autonomy, pride, and work flexibility. There is evidence linking each of these noncontingent rewards to job satisfaction: fringe benefits (Artz, 2010); job security (OECD, 1997); and flexible work arrangements through the mediation of work–family enrichment (McNall, Masuda & Nicklin, 2010).

Finally, the HPC model states that job satisfaction affects organizational commitment. Job dissatisfaction leads an employee to reduce his or her commitment to the organization, namely, the identification with the company's values, a desire to strive for the organizational goals, and the willingness to maintain membership in the organization.

## HPC in the US Federal Government

Although the single paths of the model have been extensively studied and supported (Latham & Locke, 2007), only one study has empirically tested the overall HPC model. Selden and Brewer (2000) conducted a study involving over 2000 senior executives in US federal agencies. This sample was chosen because of its homogeneity in terms of pay plans based on performance compared to employees in other agencies. The authors selected items from data collected in the Survey of US Federal Government Employees to analyze the HPC. That is, they selected from that survey items that could be used as proxy variables for the HPC's theoretical concepts to test the model. Because they could not match responses to the questionnaire items with external sources of information about an employee's performance, they had to rely on self-report measures of job performance. Overall support for the hypothesized paths of influence were found. Specifically, the positive relationship between demands and performance was supported, as well as the positive association between performance and contingent rewards. The moderators, goal commitment and feedback, were significantly related to demands. However, the mediators were either not significant or negatively related to demands (i.e., persistence).

Selden and Brewer concluded that the HPC has practical significance for policy makers and managers in the public sector. This is especially true regarding the connections among job performance, contingent rewards, and job satisfaction. They also emphasized that financial incentives alone are not motivating variables; rather, they are effective only when high performance is in response to high goals, together with internal rewards (e.g., feelings of accomplishment and personal recognition).

In conclusion, the above-cited study suggests that the HPC has internal and external validity. Nevertheless, empirical data concerning an accurate operationalization of HPC constructs are needed, as is a test of its validity in the private sector.

## The Research on the HPC in Italy

In the remainder of this chapter, we report two empirical studies of the HPC conducted in an organization in Italy. The purpose of the first study was to develop a reliable and valid questionnaire to measure the variables in the HPC. The purpose of the second study was to test the model's validity in a private multinational telecommunication company.

### The Italian Context

During the past 20 years many changes have occurred in Italy with regard to the business environment. There is an ongoing growth and competition between multinational companies in the country and local companies. These changes have affected Italian HR management practices, in that there is a shift:

- from a management style emphasizing task fulfillment to a style promoting goal attainment with an emphasis on results;
- from a traditional role of the immediate manager who is responsible for controlling and exercising power over his or her team, to a manager who supports employee development, motivation, and the necessity for taking responsibility for goal attainment; and

- from an organizational culture that fosters "paternalistic" relationships to a culture that rewards competence, exercising autonomy, and taking initiative.

As a result of these changes, goal setting is increasingly implemented in Italian organizations. Therefore, Italy provides an interesting context to investigate the validity of the HPC model, and to make recommendations for practice derived from the research results.

## Study 1

### Development of Measures for the HPC

A questionnaire was developed by combining previously validated scales in the literature, and developing new items worded specifically to assess HPC constructs for which validated scales were not available. The questionnaire was tested in two samples in two private organizations, as described below.

### Participants

The first sample consisted of 322 middle managers in a telecommunications organization. This sample consisted of 23% females and 77% males. Sixty-one percent of them ranged in age between 36 and 45 years old; 92% had more than 6 years of tenure in this organization.

The participants were employed in a company that was formed in 1997, during the "new economy." It was the first provider in Italy of integrated wireless, fixed-line, and Internet services. From its beginning, this company has stood out in the marketplace for its innovative technological, organizational, and marketing skills. This led to the decision to acquire two additional telecommunication companies. In 2005, the majority shareholder, an Italian privatized company, sold the organization to an Egyptian telecommunication business. Major changes subsequently occurred with regard to organizational structure as well as in the senior management team. The senior management team was in place for two years when the present study was conducted. This management team focused on reducing costs and maximizing revenues. They downsized personnel and set demanding goals in terms of the results to be attained. This led the company to making a profit for the first time in its history.

The second sample consisted of 173 employees and managers from a multinational insurance company. The sample comprised 35% females and 65% males. Forty-four percent were 45 years old or more; 47% had between 1 and 5 years of tenure in the organization.

The company was founded in 2007 as a joint venture between a French multinational group and an Italian bank. As such, it is still in the start-up stage with regard to HR practices. The HR department has introduced several innovations in terms of procedures and tools for organizational development, including climate and culture surveys, leadership style assessment, talent management, and pay for performance.

### Procedure

A web-based questionnaire was delivered to both samples. Each participant received a personal code from the company's HR department to voluntarily access the web site. Confidentiality of individual responses was guaranteed, because the HR department assigned random codes to employees, and the researchers who accessed and processed the data were unaware of the association between each code and an individual's name.

## Measures

A 53-item questionnaire was developed to measure the constructs in the HPC model. Each item was assessed using a 7-point Likert-type response format (1 = strongly disagree; 7 = strongly agree).

Demands. Consistent with Lee and Bobko's (1992) argument that "perceptions of self-referenced goal difficulty may be more appropriate in ipsative models" (p. 1425), goal difficulty was measured using three of their five items (e.g., "The goals I am given require as much attention and effort as I can give").

Mediators. Twelve items measured an employee's (a) direction, (b) effort, (c) persistence, and (d) strategy in relation to their goals.
  a) Three items measured the attention and action elicited by the goals (e.g., "My goals indicate to me the direction to follow in my job").
  b) Three items were reworded from Earley, Wojnaroski, and Prest (1987) to measure effort (e.g., "I work very hard to attain the goal").
  c) Three items measured an individual's persistence in pursuing goals (e.g., "I strive to achieve my goal even when I'm faced with obstacles").
  d) Three items measured the availability of and the search for suitable strategies to attain the goals (e.g., "I reflect on the most suitable strategy to follow before taking action toward the goal").

Moderators
  Self-efficacy. The 8-item scale by Chen, Gully, and Eden (2001) was used to measure self-efficacy (e.g., "I will be able to attain my goals").
  Goal commitment. Goal commitment was measured using three items from the scale developed by Hollenbeck, Klein, O'Leary, and Wright (1989) (e.g., "Quite frankly, I don't care if I achieve this goal or not").
  Feedback. In order to assess the extent to which the supervisor gives feedback to employees in relation to their goals, four items were adapted from Locke and Latham's (1990) questionnaire (e.g., "I get regular feedback indicating how I am performing in relation to my goals", Reversed).
  Task complexity. Consistent with Wood's (1986) definition, three items were worded to assess task complexity (e.g., "In my job I perform complex tasks").
  Situational constraints. We operationalized this construct as the lack of constraints and the presence of opportunities in the organizational context that facilitate the goal setting process. Specifically, we used two scales: support by supervisor and organizational support. Three items measured the extent to which the supervisor is perceived as supportive of an employee's goal attainment (e.g., "My boss is supportive when I face obstacles in my job"). Organizational support regarding the resources needed for attaining a goal was measured using three items (e.g., "Company policies here help rather than hurt goal attainment"). In both cases, items were adapted from Locke and Latham's (1990) questionnaire.

Consequences

>   Contingent rewards. Three items were used to measure both tangible (i.e., pay raise) as well as intangible (i.e., supervisory appreciation) rewards employees anticipate if their goals are attained. Two of these items were selected from Locke and Latham's (1990) questionnaire (e.g., "If I reach my goals, it increases my chances for a pay raise").
>
>   Noncontingent rewards. Three items measured rewards not dependent upon goal attainment (e.g., "I have good working conditions").
>
>   Job satisfaction. Three items were adapted from Judge and colleagues (Judge, Locke, Durham, & Kluger, 1998) to measure overall job satisfaction (e.g., "Overall, I am satisfied with my job").
>
>   Organizational commitment. Five items were adapted from the Italian version (Pierro, Lombardo, Fabbri, & Di Spirito, 1995) of Allen and Meyer's (1990) affective commitment scale (e.g., "The organization where I work has great meaning for me").

*Statistical Analyses*

In order to test the multidimensionality of the questionnaire, a PAF exploratory factor analysis with direct oblimin rotation was conducted that allowed for correlations among factors (Fabrigar, Wegener, MacCallum, & Strahan, 1999). This was followed by a confirmatory factor analysis (CFA), conducted using Mplus (Muthén & Muthén, 1998) and the maximum likelihood estimation. Both analyses were conducted on the two samples combined, for a total sample size of 495 individuals.

## Results

After the exploratory analysis, items that did not load strongly on the intended factor ($< .30$), or cross-loaded on multiple factors were deleted. Thus, two items from the self-efficacy scale and two items from the noncontingent rewards scale were not included in subsequent analyses. The results showed that each theoretical construct in the HPC was represented by an empirical factor. The exception was items measuring feedback and support by the supervisor; these loaded on the same factor. In the confirmatory factor analysis, we estimated this new pattern of loadings.

Overall, fit indices from the CFA satisfied the recommended standards (e.g., Bagozzi & Yi, 1988; Browne & Cudeck, 1993). This suggests that the 14-factor model fit the data ($\chi^2 = 2586.66$, df $= 1037$, $p < .01$, N $= 491$; CFI $= .90$; RMSEA $= .05$ (CI .05–.06); SRMR $= .05$).

The standardized factor loadings, shown in Table 18.1, are all above .45. Moreover, the Cronbach alpha coefficients ranged from .65 to .93 (Table 18.2). Each empirical factor had adequate internal consistency. The corrected item-total correlations ranged between .44 and .84.

## Discussion

The scales assessing the HPC variables were shown to have adequate internal consistency. The factor loadings suggest that the HPC measures are valid. With only one exception,

*Table 18.1* Items and Item Loadings from the First Confirmatory Factor Analysis

| Factor | Items | Loadings |
|---|---|---|
| 1. Demands (.77) | The goals I am given require as much attention and effort as I can give | .79 |
| | The goals I am given are such that I often have to push myself to capacity to attain the goal | .83 |
| | The goals I am given require some hard thinking on my part to attain them | .56 |
| 2. Goal Commitment (.65) | It's hard to take this goal seriously (R) | .48 |
| | Quite frankly, I don't care if I achieve this goal (R) | .56 |
| | I am strongly committed to pursuing this goal | .78 |
| 3. Feedback & Supervisory support (.93) | My supervisor updates me regularly concerning my advancement towards my goal | .81 |
| | My supervisor tells me both the positive and negative aspects of my performance | .83 |
| | I get regular feedback indicating how I am performing in relation to my goals | .81 |
| | In performance appraisal sessions with my boss, problem-solving rather than criticism is stressed | .63 |
| | My boss is supportive with respect to encouraging me to reach my goals | .84 |
| | My boss gives me all the information necessary to perform well on my job | .88 |
| | My boss is supportive when I face obstacles in my job | .83 |
| 4. Self-Efficacy (.88) | I will be able to achieve most of the goals that I have set for myself | .68 |
| | When facing difficult tasks, I am certain that I will accomplish them | .74 |
| | I believe I can succeed at most any endeavour to which I set my mind | .75 |
| | I will be able to successfully overcome many challenges | .83 |
| | I am confident that I can perform effectively on many different tasks | .72 |
| | Even when things are tough, I can perform quite well | .71 |
| 5. Task Complexity (.80) | In my job I perform complex tasks | .70 |
| | In my job I regularly encounter novel tasks | .80 |
| | In my job I perform a wide variety of tasks | .79 |
| 6. Organizational Support (.84) | Company policies here help rather than hurt goal attainment | .78 |
| | This organization provides sufficient resources (e.g. time, money, equipment, co-workers) to make goal setting work | .83 |
| | This organization treats all employees fairly | .78 |
| 7. Direction (.85) | My goals focus my actions on relevant aspects of my job | .74 |
| | My goals indicate to me what I should spend my time on | .84 |
| | My goals indicate to me the direction to follow in my job | .87 |
| 8. Effort (.84) | I work very hard to attain the goal | .87 |
| | I put forth a lot of effort into my work to attain the goal | .83 |
| | In my job I increase my efforts toward attaining my goal if need be | .69 |

*(Continued)*

*Table 18.1* Cont'd.

| Factor | Items | Loadings |
|---|---|---|
| 9. Persistence (.86) | I strive to achieve my goal even when I'm faced with obstacles | .85 |
| | In my job I keep trying even when things are not going well | .86 |
| | In my job I intensify my efforts after failure | .78 |
| 10. Strategy (.84) | I have a strategy for attaining my goals | .81 |
| | I reflect on the most suitable strategy to follow before taking action toward the goal | .84 |
| | I usually feel that I have a suitable or effective action plan or plans for reaching my goals | .76 |
| 11. Contingent Rewards (.82) | My supervisor shows me appreciation when I perform well | .81 |
| | I get credit and recognition when I attain my goals | .85 |
| | If I reach my goals, it increases my chances for a pay raise | .69 |
| 12. Non contingent Rewards | I have good working conditions | 1 |
| 13. Job satisfaction (.87) | Overall, I am satisfied with my job | .84 |
| | Most days I am enthusiastic about my work | .89 |
| | I find real enjoyment in my work | .77 |
| 14. Affective Commitment (.90) | I feel a strong sense of belonging to my organization | .89 |
| | This organization has a great deal of personal meaning for me | .90 |
| | I really feel as if this organization's problems are my own | .76 |
| | I do not feel emotionally attached to this organization | .85 |
| | I am willing to commit more than one expects to contribute to the success of my organization | .64 |

*Note:* Beside each factor name, values in parentheses indicate Cronbach's alpha coefficients.

the items loaded on the appropriate latent factor, thus providing empirical support for the HPC constructs. It is worth noting that the finding that feedback and supervisory support loaded on the same factor is consistent with previous goal setting field research (Ronan, Latham, & Kinne, 1973). Consequently, a second study was conducted to empirically test the HPC model.

## Study 2

After developing the questionnaire for assessing the HPC, we assessed the relationships among the variables included in the first part of the HPC model; that is, the antecedents of job performance were assessed.

### Participants and Procedure

A subsample of managers from the telecommunication sample (n = 101) who participated in the previous study was used in this second study. These managers had been assigned quantitative goals. Individual responses to the HPC questionnaire were collected nearly two months after each manager had been given goals for the year, and then matched with supervisory appraisals of job performance conducted at the end of the year. The evaluations of their job performance were provided by the HR department to the researchers.

Table 18.2 Bivariate Correlations

| Dimensions | 1 | 2 | 3 | 4 | 5 | 6 | 7 | 8 | 9 |
|---|---|---|---|---|---|---|---|---|---|
| 1. Demands | | | | | | | | | |
| 2. Goal commitment | 0, 26** | | | | | | | | |
| 3. Feedback & Support | 0, 31** | 0, 35** | | | | | | | |
| 4. Self-efficacy | 0, 03 | 0, 28** | 0, 18 | | | | | | |
| 5. Organizational Support | 0, 25* | 0, 40** | 0, 59** | 0, 16 | | | | | |
| 6. Direction | 0, 29** | 0, 50** | 0, 35** | 0, 33** | 0, 41** | | | | |
| 7. Effort | 0, 47** | 0, 26** | 0, 23* | 0, 18 | 0, 24* | 0, 40** | | | |
| 8. Persistence | 0, 17 | 0, 44** | 0, 22* | 0, 44** | 0, 28** | 0, 37** | 0, 55** | | |
| 9. Strategy | 0, 15 | 0, 37** | 0, 21* | 0, 55** | 0, 23* | 0, 37* | 0, 43** | 0, 51** | |
| 10. Job Performance | 0, 08 | 0, 27** | 0, 15 | 0, 19 | 0, 04 | 0, 19 | 0, 21* | 0, 31** | 0, 12 |

** $p < .01$
* $p < .05$

## Measures

Job Performance. The performance appraisal was expressed as the percentage of goal attainment at the end of the year, as a composite of the quantitative goals (maximum three) assigned to each manager.

## Analyses and Results

Table 18.2 presents the correlations among HPC scales and job performance.

Structural equation modeling (SEM) of the HPC model was conducted using the software Mplus (Muthén & Muthén, 1998). Following an iterative approach, we tested a model that could fit the observed data and could be considered a reliable representation of them. Thus, we chose a revised model, shown in Figure 18.2, in which some modifications to the original theoretical paths were implemented in order to improve the fit to an acceptable degree. These relationships held together theoretically.

We estimated a latent factor encompassing the four mediators, which was affected by demands. Demanding goals led managers to specify the direction of their actions, exert considerable effort, persevere in the face of obstacles, and search for suitable strategies. Consistent with the HPC model, these four mechanisms mediated the relationship between demands and job performance, as suggested also by a significant indirect link. Self-efficacy and goal commitment also exerted a main rather than a moderating effect on the mediators. Again, the indirect paths were significant. Therefore, the more confident managers were about their abilities and the more committed they were to their goals, the more they pursued their goals and the better their actual performance. Task complexity did not play a significant role in the model.

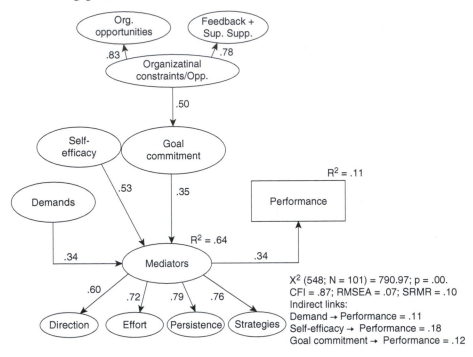

*Figure 18.2*   Empirical model tested in the telecommunication sample.

We estimated a latent factor that includes the dimension in which feedback merged with support from the supervisor, and organizational support. This second-order factor was derived from our conceptualization of organizational opportunities and was related to goal commitment. This finding is consistent with Hollenbeck and Klein's (1987) argument that supervisory support and situational constraints are antecedents of goal commitment. Receiving timely feedback and support from one's supervisor, in conjunction with organizational support, encouraged the managers to commit to their goals.

## Discussion

A revised model of the HPC was derived inductively. The variables in this model are related to one another. The relationships are consistent with previous findings (DeShon, Kozlowski, Schmidt, Milner, & Wiechmann, 2004; Donovan & Radosevich, 1998; Klein & Kim, 1998; Renn, 2003; Seijts & Latham, 2001). In particular, feedback, support by the supervisor, and organizational support are related to goal commitment. Goal commitment together with self-efficacy affected the mediating variables that are related to job performance. That is, the level of commitment to the goals and one's confidence to succeed are related to (a) the pursuit of one's goals, (b) the expenditure of effort and persistence, (c) the discovery of suitable strategies, and (d) high performance.

Overall, the results of the structural equation modeling show that the main tenets of the HPC model are valid. To the extent to which a manager received difficult goals, his or her self-efficacy and goal commitment affected his or her motivation, by activating the four motivational mechanisms specified in the HPC. These results, obtained in the private sector in Italy, support those obtained in the public sector in the United States (Selden & Brewer, 2000). However, it was not possible to verify the second part of the model concerning the consequences of job performance, namely contingent rewards, job satisfaction, and organizational commitment, because the data collected for these variables were only cross-sectional.

The limitations of this study are at least threefold. Although the questionnaire and the performance appraisals were collected during different time periods, we were not able to test the overall model and its recursive nature. Future research should investigate in the private sector the paths connecting job performance to contingent rewards, job satisfaction, and organizational commitment. Second, the sample size was relatively small. Finally, the revised HPC model should be replicated in different contexts in order to assess its generalizability.

## Practical Implications

The present results led the company to implement three interventions. First, top management now purposively acts as a role model for setting goals. They provide people the resources for goal attainment. For example, they supply equipment, information, money, as well as the time for people to attain their goals. They give managers freedom to develop strategies for pursuing their goals rather than prescribing specific action plans. Finally, they have instituted a meritocratic culture whereby rewards are now contingent on performance.

Second, training in self-efficacy is being conducted. Employees are given the opportunity to put themselves to the test and strengthen their self-efficacy through a series of successful experiences in daily work activities. Progressively more complex goals are set to increase employees' self-efficacy. Managers also learn from colleagues, by observing their behaviors in the face of difficult situations, and discerning the underlying strategy that led them to succeed. A third source of self-efficacy is verbal persuasion, through which managers encourage themselves (and are encouraged by others) to engage in challenging activities. In this regard, verbal self-guidance has proved to be a useful method for increasing self-efficacy (Millman & Latham, 2001).

A third intervention concerns top management giving the necessary information to perform well and delivering timely feedback to subordinates. The company has also implemented a well-structured training program focused on leadership skills development. Rather than traditional training on leadership styles, they have started to promote self-awareness with regard to leaders' perception of their role in general, particularly in relation to the goal setting process.

## References

Allen, N. J., & Meyer, J. P. (1990). The measurement and antecedents of affective, continuance and normative commitment to the organization. *Journal of Occupational Psychology, 63*, 1–18.

Artz, B. (2010). Fringe benefits and job satisfaction. *International Journal of Manpower, 31*, 6, 626–644. doi: 10.1108/01437721011073346.

Bagozzi, R. P., & Yi, Y. (1988). On the evaluation of structural equation models. *Journal of the Academy of Marketing Science, 16*, 74–94.

Bandura, A. (2011). On the functional properties of perceived self-efficacy revisited. *Journal of Management.* Doi: 10.1177/0149206311410606.

Browne, M. W., & Cudeck, R. (1993). Alternative ways of assessing model fit, In K. A. Bollen & J. S. Long (Eds.), *Testing structural equation models* (pp. 136–162). Thousand Oaks, CA: Sage.

Chen, G., Gully, S. M., & Eden, D. (2001). Validation of a new general self-efficacy scale. *Organizational Research Methods, 4*, 62–83. Doi: 10.1177/0013164406288171.

DeShon, R. P., Kozlowski, S. W. J., Schmidt, A. M., Milner, K. R., & Wiechmann, D. (2004). A multiple-goal, multilevel model of feedback effects on the regulation of individual and team performance. *Journal of Applied Psychology, 89*, 6, 1035–1056. Doi: 10.1037/0021-9010.89.6.1035.

Donovan, J. J., & Radosevich, D. J. (1998). The moderating role of goal commitment on the goal difficulty-performance relationship: A meta-analytic review and critical reanalysis. *Journal of Applied Psychology, 83*, 308–315.

Earley, C. P., Wojnaroski, P., & Prest, W. (1987). Task planning and energy expended: Exploration of how goals influence performance. *Journal of Applied Psychology, 72*, 1, 107–114.

Fabrigar, L. R., Wegener, D. T., MacCallum, R. C., & Strahan, E. J. (1999). Evaluation of the use of exploratory factor analysis in psychological research. *Psychological Methods, 4*, 272–299.

Hollenbeck, J. R., Klein, H. J., O'Leary, A. M., & Wright, P. M. (1989). Investigation of the construct validity of a self-report measure of goal commitment. *Journal of Applied Psychology, 74*(6), 951–956. Doi: 10.1037//0021-9010.74.6.951.

Hollenbeck, J. R., & Klein, H. J. (1987). Goal commitment and the goal-setting process: Problems, prospects, and proposals for future research. *Journal of Applied Psychology, 72*(2), 212–220. doi:10.1037//0021-9010.72.2.212.

Ilies, R., & Judge, T. A. (2005). Goal regulation across time: the effects of feedback and affect. *Journal of Applied Psychology, 90*(3), 453–67. doi:10.1037/0021-9010.90.3.453.

Jacobsen, J. P., & Skillman, G. L. (Eds.) (2008). *Labor markets and employment relationships: A comprehensive approach.* Malden, MA: Blackwell.

Judge, T. A., Locke, E. A., Durham, C. C., & Kluger, A. N. (1998). Dispositional effects on job and life satisfaction: The role of core evaluations. *Journal of Applied Psychology, 83*, 17–34.

Judge, T. A., Piccolo, R. F., Podsakoff, N. P., Shaw, J. C., & Rich, B. L. (2010). The relationship between pay and job satisfaction: A meta-analysis of the literature. *Journal of Vocational Behavior, 77*(2), 157–167. Doi: 10.1016/j.jvb.2010.04.002.

Klein, H. J., & Kim, J. S. (1998). A field study of the influence of situational constraints leader-member exchange, and goal commitment on performance. *Academy of Management Journal, 41*(1), 88–95. Doi:10.2307/256900.

Latham, G. P. (2007). *Work motivation: Theory, research and practice.* Thousand Oaks, CA: Sage.

Latham, G. P., & Locke, E. A. (2006). Enhancing the benefits and overcoming the pitfalls of goal setting. *Organization Dynamics, 35*, 4, 332–340. Doi:10.1016/J.Orgdyn.2006.08.008.

Latham, G. P., & Locke, E. A. (2007). New developments in and directions for goal setting. *European Psychologist, 12*, 290–300. Doi: 10.1027/1016-9040.12.4.290.

Latham, G. P., Locke, E. A., & Fassina, N. E. (2002). The high performance cycle: Standing the test of time. In S. Sonnentag (Ed.), *The psychological management of individual performance. A handbook in the psychology of management in organizations* (pp. 201–228). Chichester: Wiley.

Latham, G. P., Seijts, G., & Crim, D. (2008). The effects of learning goal difficulty level and cognitive ability on performance. *Canadian Journal of Behavioural Science, 40*, 4, 220–229. doi:10.1037/a0013114.

Lee, C., & Bobko, P. (1992). Exploring the meaning and usefulness of measures of subjective goal difficulty. *Journal of Applied Social Psychology, 22*, 1417–1428. Doi: 10.1111/j.1559-1816.1992. tb00957.x.

Locke, E. A., & Latham, G. P. (1990). *A theory of goal setting and task performance.* Englewood Cliffs: Prentice Hall.

Locke, E. A., Latham, G. P., & Erez, M. (1988). The determinants of goal commitment. *Academy of Management Review, 13*, 23–39. http://www.jstor.org/stable/258352.

McNall, L. A., Masuda, A. D., & Nicklin, J. M. (2010). Flexible work arrangements, job satisfaction, and turnover intentions: The mediating role of work-to-family enrichment. *Journal of Psychology, 144*, 1, 61–81. Doi: 10.1080/00223980903356073.

Millman, Z., & Latham, G. P. (2001). Increasing re-employment through training in verbal self-guidance. In M. Erez, U. Kleinbeck, & H. K. Thierry (Eds.), *Work motivation in the context of a globalizing economy* (pp. 87–99). Hillsdale, NJ: Lawrence Erlbaum.

Muthén, L., & Muthén, B. O. (1998). *Mplus user's guide.* Los Angeles, CA: Muthén & Muthén.

OECD (1997). *Is Job Insecurity on the Rise in OECD Countries?* OECD Employment Outlook.

Pierro, A., Lombardo, I., Fabbri, S., & Di Spirito, A. (1995). Evidenza empirica della validità delle misure di job involvement e organizational commitment: modelli di analisi fattoriale confermativa (Empirical evidence of job involvement and organizational commitment scales' validity: models of confermative factorial analysis). *TPM, 2*, 1, 5–18.

Renn, R. W. (2003). Moderation by goal commitment of the feedback–performance relationship: Theoretical explanation and preliminary study. *Human Resource Management Review, 13*, 4, 561–580. Doi:10.1016/J.Hrmr.2003.11.003.

Ronan, W. W., Latham, G. P., & Kinne, S. B. (1973). The effects of goal setting and supervision on worker behavior in an industrial situation. *Journal of Applied Psychology, 58*, 302–307.

Seijts, G. H., & Latham, G. P. (2001). The effect of learning, outcome, and proximal goals on a moderately complex task. *Journal of Organizational Behavior, 22*, 291–307. DOI: 10.1002/job.70.

Seijts, G. H., & Latham, G. P. (2005) Learning versus performance goals: When should each be used? *Academy of Management Executive, 19*, 124–131.

Seijts, G. H., & Latham, G. P. (2011). The effect of commitment to a learning goal, self-efficacy, and the interaction between learning goal difficulty and commitment on performance in a business simulation. *Human Performance, 24*, 189–204. Doi: 10.1080/08959285.2011.580807.

Selden, S. C., & Brewer, G. A. (2000). Work motivation in the senior executive service: Testing the high performance cycle theory. *Journal of Public Administration Research and Theory, 10*, 531–550.

Tolli, A. P., & Schmidt, A. M. (2008). The role of feedback, casual attributions, and self-efficacy in goal revision. *Journal of Applied Psychology, 93*(3), 692–701. Doi: 10.1037/0021-9010.93.3.692.

Williams, M. L., McDaniel, M. A., & Nguyen, N. T. (2006). A meta-analysis of the antecedents and consequences of pay level satisfaction. *Journal of Applied Psychology, 91*, 2, 392–413. Doi: 10.1037/0021-9010.91.2.392.

Wood, R. E. (1986). Task complexity: Definition of the construct. *Organizational Behavior and Human Decision Processes, 37*, 60–82. Doi: 10.1016/0749-5978(86)90044-0.

Part V

# Goals in Groups and at the Macro Level

# 19 Goal Setting in Teams

*William S. Kramer, Amanda L. Thayer, and Eduardo Salas*  Department of Psychology, Institute for Simulation & Training, University of Central Florida

Over the last twenty years, organizations have shifted their structures from hierarchical, individualized work to flatter, team-based work structures. While these flatter structures are beneficial to organizational outcomes in many circumstances, there are also a number of additional considerations to be made. First, as noted in multilevel theory, not all constructs and relationships operate in the same fashion across levels (e.g., as work structure moves from the individual to the team level; Kozlowski & Klein, 2000). For instance, effectiveness at the individual and team levels may look the same in terms of results or outcomes (i.e., functional equivalence), but the structure of the construct is rather different. In team-based structures, individuals do not operate in a vacuum. Rather, they must engage in interpersonal interaction and various other processes in order to accomplish the team's goal. For instance, various team processes such as a communication and coordination that simply do not exist within individual tasks are required for successful task accomplishment at the team level. Furthermore, the social factors inherent to teams as social entities can impact outcomes as evidenced by numerous studies on team process and performance (e.g., Kozlowski & Ilgen, 2006; LePine, Piccolo, Jackson, Mathieu, & Saul, 2008).

Much of the literature uses the terms *group* and *team* interchangeably. However, we adopt the definition of teams put forth by Salas, Dickinson, Converse, and Tannenbaum (1992): "a team is defined as a distinguishable set of two or more people who interact, dynamically, interdependently, and adaptively toward a common and valued goal/objective/mission, who have been assigned specific roles or functions to perform, and who have a limited lifespan of membership" (p. 4). Teams are generally assembled in order to capitalize on the unique knowledge, skills, and abilities of the members. In contrast, groups are simply multiple individuals clustered together but not necessarily interdependent in nature, having any specific roles or functions, or sharing a common and valued goal. Without a purpose (as defined by the team goals), there is no marker to guide the definition of roles or determine how to engage in team processes. For the purposes of this chapter, we will discuss *team* goal setting, as it is these distinctions between the definitions of groups and teams that make team goal setting inherently different than with individuals or nondependent groups of people.

Research on goal setting indicates that there are, in fact, structural differences between goal setting with individuals and teams. Locke and Latham's (1990) goal setting theory, one of the most widely accepted and supported theories in the motivation literature, argues that compared to vague goals or no goals at all, specific and difficult goals coupled with feedback result in higher performance. Difficult goals serve to focus and direct attention, energize individuals to work harder, increase persistence, and lead to strategy development for attaining the goal. However, the relationship between goals and performance depends on several factors, including the level of goal commitment, characteristics of the task, feedback, and situational factors (Locke & Latham, 2002).

A plethora of research has supported the propositions posed in goal setting theory. However, until recently research in this arena had focused primarily upon goal setting in individuals. With the increased prevalence of team-based structures within the workplace, research on goal setting theory in the last couple of decades has begun to test the generalizability of goal setting theory to team contexts as well as examine *additional* factors (above and beyond the factors that influence individual goal setting) that come into play when goal setting is transposed into a social arena. Because team settings are inherently more social in nature than individual tasks, social influence and emergent states (i.e., affective or cognitive states that emerge or arise from the interaction of members) are key factors in explaining why the structure of goal setting and task performance is different at the individual and team levels.

To our knowledge, this chapter is one of the first attempts to provide a comprehensive discussion of how goal setting differs in teams from individuals, specifically delineating the characteristics that impact goal setting at the team level, along with a discussion of how these characteristics influence the application of goal setting in a variety of team types common in today's workplace. In this chapter, we first explore goal setting in teams and its major departures from goal setting with individuals, taking into account the interactions among members and the processes and emergent states that make teams unique from individuals. Second, we present various factors to be considered when setting goals in a social context. Third, we apply these factors to a discussion of goal setting in a variety of teams such as virtually distributed teams, teams in extreme environments, and multi-team systems. Finally, we present goal setting and feedback interventions designed for team contexts.

## Goal Setting at the Team Level

Team goal setting allows for goal setting at multiple levels (Van Mierlo & Kleingeld, 2010). While the intention may be for all individuals in the company to contribute to a larger organizational goal, alone each person can only work toward a measurable goal at the individual level. For example, it makes little sense for the goal of an individual to be centered around the overall profit of the organization, as individuals cannot work toward that goal with measurable feedback on their own performance. However, team-based structures do allow for goals at multiple levels (i.e., individual, team). Within a team, each member may have a goal for his or her own performance in addition to a larger goal for the team. For instance, within a sales team, each member may have a specific number of sales calls he or she is striving to make as well as a team goal of some number of closed sales. Just as individual goals contribute to team goals, team-level goals in turn promote action toward the organization's goals and mission. For example, a logging company may set a goal to increase its profit by 25%; however, the accomplishment of this goal results from successful goal accomplishment at the team level among many different logging crews (Latham & Kinne, 1974). Therefore, if each of these teams sets and attains its respective goals, the logging company will have greater potential to reach its goals, though this would not be achieved if goals were not also set at the lower team level.

Furthermore, teams utilize social dynamics to enforce motivation toward the team's goals. Team emergent states represent the characteristics of a team, including member attitudes, values, cognitions, and motivations (Marks, Mathieu, & Zaccaro, 2001) that result from team interaction. Emergent states such as team cognition (e.g., shared mental models, transactive memory), cohesion, and trust are all important factors in team goal attainment and have each been found to be predictive of team process and team performance because of their influence on team motivational states (DeChurch & Mesmer-Magnus, 2010; Dirks, 1999; LePine, Piccolo, Jackson, Mathieu, & Saul, 2008). Consider XYZ Widget Company. Suppose the component teams each have performance goals. Now, let's consider what factors might motivate the teams to strive for achievement of those goals. Perhaps the members feel that they have a bond and want to ensure that the team succeeds so that it can continue working as an intact team (i.e., cohesion), so their bond motivates the members to work together to achieve the goals. Similarly, the members may trust that each member is competent and will not intentionally engage in any acts that might harm the team, and thus are motivated to succeed because they feel they have good relationships with each of the members. While these emergent states represent only a small portion of the emergent characteristics of a team, it is important to note that organizations which foster emergent states that drive team motivation are more likely to obtain desired results.

Finally, in discussing team goals, it is important to consider team processes that result as a function of the social nature of teams (i.e., the interactions and resulting emergent states). Team process is defined as the members' interdependent acts that convert inputs to outputs (Marks et al., 2001). For instance, Marks and colleagues outlined a framework and taxonomy of team processes including goal specification, strategy formulation, coordination, and team monitoring and backup, among others, across three phases of a performance episode (transition, action, interpersonal). Many models of team effectiveness include team process as a mediator of the relationship between group goal setting and performance (e.g., Hackman, 1987; McGrath, 1964). However, because teams cycle through phases of transition and action, it also stands to reason that team process may also influence group goal setting via a reciprocal input–mediator–output–input (IMOI) loop (Ilgen, Hollenbeck, Johnson, & Jundt, 2006). In other words, team process may be the driving mechanism that allows teams to effectively carry out their goal setting and strategy implementation and thus perform at an optimal level to achieve goals. However, it may also be the case that team processes such as communication and conflict management may in turn impact goal setting when the team moves into the next transition phase. Research has also found that teamwork quality (of interactions; coordination, sharing of information, utilization of knowledge and expertise, mutual support, effort, team spirit, and cohesion) moderates the relationship between goal setting and goal performance in innovation teams (Hoegl & Parboteeah, 2003).

## Goal–Performance Relationship

Now that a clear, fundamental understanding of goal setting has been put in place, the following question may now be asked: Why is it important? The answer to this question can be found when examining the plethora of scholarly journal articles, books, and symposia that have covered the topic in the past. Most of these resources point to the fact that there is some relationship that exists between group goal setting/commitment and performance. For instance, Aubé and Rousseau (2005) explicitly stated that team goal commitment is not only positively tied to performance but also to the other two criteria of team effectiveness (quality of experience and viability). Additional research by Wegge and Haslam (2005) found that, dependent on the manner in which the goals were created, they could lead to improved performance for brainstorming exercises.

To provide an understanding of why this happens, one must take a step back and examine one of the general beliefs of goal setting theory on an individual level; if a specific, difficult goal is set by an individual, he or she will perform better than if the goal is nonspecific or easy (Robbins & Judge, 2009; Hollenbeck & Klein, 1987). It is also important to note that both goal setting theory and empirical research have pointed to the fact that, without commitment to the aforementioned goals, the increase in performance would not be seen (Klein, Wesson, Hollenbeck, & Alge, 1999; Locke & Latham, 1990; for more information, see Chapter 6). Therefore, goal difficulty, specificity, and commitment interact with one another to determine how much of an increase in performance will be seen due to goal setting. For individual goals, this happens mainly due to the fact that difficult, specific goals provide direction as to where attention needs to be aimed, create motivation for the individual to develop a set plan or strategies in pursuing goals, and energizes one to be persistent in his or her actions. Based on findings in the recent literature, it has been found that all of these ideas can be extrapolated from the individual level to a team level (Kleingeld, Van Mierlo, & Arends, 2011).

These ideas are best represented by the work of DeShon, Kozlowski, Schmidt, Milner, and Wiechmann (2004). They found that that team goals, goal commitment, and efficacy interact with one another to determine how much action will be taken by the team to enact strategies and focus effort on obtaining their set goals, and that this, in turn, will directly affect performance on a team level. Additionally, their findings serve to add preexisting and situational factors that have direct and interactive effects on how an individual or team will formulate goals as well as their feelings of efficacy. For instance, the situational factor of providing feedback to a team based on their performance has been shown to lead to the setting of new goals or the alteration of old goals (Locke & Latham, 1990). Furthermore, there has been evidence to show that feedback provided to a team will have a positive relationship with their efficacy (Prussia & Kinicki, 1996).

Finally, despite the fact that much support can be found for the idea that goal setting will have a direct effect upon performance on a task, it is important to note that there have been findings that show little to no relationship between the two variables (Sagie, 1996; Wegge & Haslam, 2005). Therefore, in an effort to obtain a better understanding of the aforementioned relationship, we can turn to two meta-analyses that have been performed on this topic.

O'Leary-Kelly, Martocchio, and Frink (1994) examined 163 groups and found that the performance of teams with specific, difficult group goals was almost one standard deviation (d =.92) higher than the performance of teams that were simply told to do their best to complete the task. These findings are comparable to those of Kleingeld, Van Mierlo, & Arends (in press), who examined 38 groups and found a standard deviation of d =.80 for teams with specific, difficult goals. Therefore, based on these two meta-analyses, there appears to be a significant relationship between team goal setting and performance on a task throughout the previous scholarly literature.

The meta-analysis by Kleingeld and colleagues (in press) discussed earlier noted a separate multilevel finding. The effect that individual goals have upon team performance is dependent upon the focus of the goal itself. Two specific foci have been defined and examined by Crown and Rosse (1995): egocentric and groupcentric individual goals. Egocentric individual goals are set by individuals to maximize their own performance on the task and can potentially contradict and undermine the team goals. Furthermore, they can lead to an increase in competition if all of the individuals in the team set the same type of goals. Groupcentric individual goals, on the other hand, are set by individuals to maximize the performance of the team. These goals ultimately lead to cooperation and collaboration (Crown & Rosse, 1995). Findings from the meta-analysis showed that, for teams that created egocentric goals, there was a significant decrease in team performance ($d = -1.75$, $k = 6$); for those teams that created group centric goals, there was a significant increase in performance ($d = 1.20$, $k = 4$). This is an important finding because it is evidence that there are multilevel effects that should be addressed in team goal setting.

Pieterse, van Knippenberg, and van Ginkel (2011) highlighted an extremely important point that should be considered when applying goal setting in teams: the composition of the team affects how the individuals perform. Specifically, Pieterse et al. (2010) explained that diversity of learning and performance orientations within a team works against the team, and ultimately leads to a decrease in team performance. This is because in a team with a number of differing orientations, it is unlikely that there is socially shared cognition among the team members. For their purposes, the authors defined socially shared cognition as the "sharedness of representations/mental models and how the sharedness of representations/mental models may feed into team performance" (p. 155). Therefore, they found that the lower the levels of representations/mental models among the team, the less likely that the team will effectively coordinate with one another (Mathieu, Heffner, Goodwin, Cannon-Bowers, & Salas, 2005; Mathieu, Heffner, Goodwin, Salas, & Cannon-Bowers, 2000). Only one prescription was given as to how the effect of diversity in a team might be alleviated: increasing team reflexivity (i.e., the constant assessment of a team environment and adaptation to changes). The reasoning behind this is that if everyone in the team is reflexive enough to perform one another's tasks, then they have a shared understanding of what everyone is doing and, in a sense, are creating socially shared cognitions.

In summary, group goal setting should be examined using multilevel analysis to explain how differing contextual factors hinder the positive effect of goal setting on performance. In the following section, the contextual factors that impact group goal setting are presented.

## Factors That Impact Team Goal Setting

Team contexts are inherently social in nature, and thus we now turn to the most influential factors within teams that impact goal setting. This list is by no means exhaustive; it represents the most researched issues within the group and team goal setting literature.

## Interdependence

As discussed previously, one factor that makes teams unique from individuals and groups is interdependence. Task interdependence is the degree to which members must rely upon each other to successfully complete the task (Saavedra, Earley & Van Dyne, 1993). Saavedra and colleagues proposed four degrees of interdependence, namely, pooled (i.e., each member makes a contribution without the need for interaction with other members), sequential (i.e., one member must act before another one can), reciprocal (i.e., two-way interactions in which one member's output becomes another's input and vice versa), and team/intensive (i.e., mutual interactions among all members of the team).

Interdependence is an important variable for consideration in team performance. For instance, a meta-analysis by Gully, Incalcaterra, Joshi, and Beaubien (2002) found that task interdependence moderated the relationship between collective efficacy and team performance such that the relationship was stronger in teams with highly interdependent (i.e., reciprocal or team/intensive) tasks. Furthermore, in tasks that require high interdependence (i.e., team), team goal commitment is an important factor in goal accomplishment. Aubé and Rousseau (2005) found that task interdependence moderates the relationship between team goal commitment and team performance such that the higher the task interdependence, the more important team goal commitment is to team performance. This is because the task cannot be accomplished without the collective effort of the team (as opposed to pooled interdependence in which the outcome is simply the sum of individual efforts).

## Goal Type

Related to interdependence, goal type is an important factor in team goal setting. As described previously, team contexts allow for goal setting at multiple levels. Individual goals may be set to motivate members to attain a goal of their own, whereas team goals may be utilized to attain goals for each individual on the team, which would create interdependence between members to accomplish the goal (i.e., goal interdependence; Saavedra et al., 1993). However, there are problems that can arise in setting goals in this manner. Individual goals can interfere with cooperation and team performance such that a goal referent triggers either cooperation or competition (Mitchell & Silver, 1990; Van Mierlo & Kleingeld, 2010). Cooperative team goals promote interdependence and collaboration and thus foster teamwork and successful *team* goal accomplishment, whereas competitive individual goals promote competition and result in the accomplishment of *individual* tasks.

Seijts & Latham (2000) found that when faced with a social dilemma, teams in which individuals set personal goals compatible with the assigned group goal performed better than did those teams in which individuals' personal goals were incompatible (i.e., the participants were greedy). This finding supports the notion that competitive goals among individuals undermine the objectives of the team as a whole, whereas cooperative (i.e., compatible) goals further the team mission. Furthermore, Tjosvold & Yu (2004) found that setting cooperative goals instead of competitive or independent goals resulted in members applying their abilities (i.e., utilize each others' diverse set of expertise and KSAs) more for the mutual benefit of the team/members, which in turn

improved team performance. Finally, Wong, Tjosvold, & Liu (2009) found that cooperative goals help teams develop a sense of confidence in team efficacy and initiative to
persist, two critical mechanisms driving the goal setting–performance relationship
(Locke & Latham, 2002).

## Organizational Culture

Organizational culture is a critical factor in the successful implementation of goal setting. Culture is defined as the assumptions about humans' relationships, and the environment that is shared among an identifiable group of people (e.g., the organization).
It is manifested in individuals' values, beliefs, norms for social behavior, and artifacts
(Gibson, Maznevski, & Kirkman, 2009) and has implications for organizationally relevant outcomes. Beyond goal type, cooperative versus competitive *norms* within an
organization have been found to have a significant impact on goal setting (Taggar &
Ellis, 2007). There are several means through which organizations can promote and reinforce cooperative norms beyond the goals themselves (i.e., cooperative or competitive
goals), such as evaluating cooperative behaviors in formal job appraisals, providing recognition for engaging in cooperative behaviors, and regularly highlighting common and
cooperative goals. Quigley, Tesluk, Locke, and Bartol (2007) found that beyond team
incentives and cooperative goals, clear norms for sharing reinforced motivation to share
knowledge within teams. Further, Taggar and Ellis (2007) found that collaborative
norms significantly predicted goal setting and performance management. However,
these norms may be strong or weak, and the degree to which teams adopted collaborative
norms depended on the leader and staff expectations. Much like variability among individuals in adopting values, beliefs, and norms of a national culture, teams may vary in the
degree to which they adopt organizational norms due to a variety of contextual factors
and team characteristics (e.g., team composition and individual differences, leadership).

Goal setting has received some scrutiny for its potential to cause harm if the wrong
outcomes are reinforced, including dysfunctional competition, corrosion of organizational culture, and a rise in unethical behavior (e.g., Ordóñez, Schweitzer, Galinsky, &
Bazerman, 2009). However, on the other side of the coin, scholars have argued that
ethical organizational cultures prevent dishonesty and corrupt practices in obtaining
goals (Locke & Latham, 2009; Latham & Locke, 2009). Furthermore, an ethical climate
may attenuate the potential for competing goals to lead to unethical behavior in reaching organizational goals. In sum, organizational culture is an important factor in instill-
ing collaborative and ethical goal setting in team contexts.

## Reward Systems

Reward systems (e.g., pay-for-performance, bonuses, recognition) serve to reinforce
goals through goal commitment. Much like goal type, rewards can be set at the individual or team levels, which in turn can have implications for goal attainment. This is
due to the interdependent nature of team reward attainment; if the reward is intended
for the team as a whole rather than a separate reward for each of the members, the team
as a collective must work toward the goal to obtain the reward (Pearsall, Christian, &
Ellis, 2010). Some researchers have suggested that hybrid reward systems which reward

both individual and team performance may promote optimal performance. However, hybrid rewards have the potential to create a social dilemma wherein members defect from the team to secure their own interests (Barnes, Hollenbeck, Jundt, DeRue, & Harmon, 2011). Barnes and colleagues found that while hybrid structures increased the speed with which members accomplished the task as compared to individual or team-based reward structures, individuals were more likely to commit errors, less likely to engage in back-up behaviors, and more focused on their own individual taskwork than the team's. Furthermore, Quigley and colleagues (2007) found that when strong sharing norms are in place, team incentives promote knowledge sharing among dyads engaged in a decision-making task.

Furthermore, the significance of the incentive can play a role in the degree to which teams engage in challenging goals. Guthrie and Hollensbe (2004) examined the group incentive–group performance relationship and found that teams the greatest at risk in terms of incentives (i.e., highly variable pay) were more likely to set higher, more challenging, and spontaneous goals than were those teams with either low-variable pay or fixed pay. This suggests that risk in rewards needs to be significantly noticeable to have an impact on the difficulty level of goals spontaneously set by teams.

## Team Size

More than three decades ago, research on social loafing found that as team size increases, members are more likely to engage in social loafing (Latané, Williams, & Harkins, 1979; Harkins & Petty, 1982; Karau & Williams, 1993). Social loafing is the decreased effort exerted by team members. Stated differently, as team size increases, an individual member's effort is reduced.

Furthermore, as the team grows larger, both reward dilution and "free riding" increase. The more members there are within a team, the more the team goals will be split among members, leaving little incentive for team members to work toward the overall team goal. Thus, individuals in larger teams generally are less committed to group goals. In smaller teams, in which behavior can be monitored and incentives are worthwhile, commitment to group goals is enhanced (Hollensbe & Guthrie, 2000) In addition, individuals in larger teams have been found to be less cooperative and to have lower collective efficacy, outcome expectancies, and commitment to the group goal than do individuals in smaller teams (Seijts & Latham, 2000; Seijts, Latham, & Whyte, 2000).

## Leadership

Leadership in teams has been identified as an important component of team motivation and effective team performance (Zaccaro, Rittman, & Marks, 2001). Zaccaro and colleagues (2001) defined team leaders as those "individuals who are primarily responsible for defining team goals and for developing and structuring the team to accomplish these missions" (p. 452). In fact, several leadership theories have incorporated motivation as a key aspect of the leader's purpose. For example, House's path-goal theory (1971) essentially combined classic leadership theory and expectancy theory to theorize that the purpose of leaders is to align the goals of followers with goals of the organization by providing followers with the information and resources to achieve goals and clarifying the path toward achievement of those goals. House identified four types of leaders, namely, directive (providing task structure and clarifying effort and rewards in goal attainment), supportive (focusing on worker well-being), participative (includes followers in decision-making) and achievement-oriented (sets challenging goals for the followers). Teams with coordinators (whose job is to ensure communication and coordination among members) who supported participatory decision making implement higher-quality tactics than those teams with commanders who made decisions for the team, which in turn impacted overall team performance (Durham, Knight, & Locke, 1997). Therefore, there is evidence that participatory goal setting and decision making may be indirectly beneficial for team goal attainment and performance.

Wu, Tsui, and Kinicki (2010) examined the effect of group-focused versus individual-focused leadership using a three-phase survey. They found that differentiated leadership (i.e., individual-focused; leader-member exchange theory; Graen, Novak, & Sommerkamp, 1982) in teams diminished team effectiveness by creating divergence in leader identification (i.e., only some members identifying with the leader) as well as both lower member self-efficacy and collective efficacy. However, group-focused leadership facilitated group identification and collective efficacy, which positively influenced team effectiveness overall. These findings suggest that in team contexts, leaders should direct specific attention to the team as a whole to maintain collective efficacy. This, in turn, promotes goal achievement and team performance. However, if leaders must give individual feedback, it should be in reference to how individuals perform as a member of the team.

## Identity

Identity plays an important role in goal setting and performance within teams. Identity refers to the aspect of one's self-concept that is based upon group membership (Tajfel & Turner, 1979). Tajfel and Turner's social identity theory argued that categorization into a group results in one identifying with that group. This translates into social comparison and in-group distinctiveness. Further, self-categorization (a related theory) leads to self-stereotyping and depersonalization (Turner, 1984) such that people see themselves as a representation of the group.

Goal setting serves as a mechanism to build social identity within teams (Haslam, Wegge, & Postmes, 2009; Oakes, Haslam, Morrison, & Grace, 1995). Team-level goals provide a common purpose, such that members develop and define themselves in terms of a shared social identity. Haslam and colleagues (2009) argued that for group goals to be effective, those goals must be aligned with the norms and interests of the in-group. They found that goals set participatively by the in-group (as opposed to being imposed upon the team by an external leader) and at the team level become increasingly beneficial to team performance as the goals become more difficult.

The degree to which members identify with the team can have implications for attainment of team goals and overall performance. In five studies that evaluated contributions to group idea generation and disaster victim support, Fishbach, Henderson, and Koo (2011) found that those individuals who identify with the group at a low level model the contributions of others. However, those individuals who highly identify with the group compensate for the contributions of other members. In other words, when members do not highly identify with the team, they are more likely to put forth the same amount of effort as their teammates. Therefore, if their teammates are barely contributing to the team goal, they will model that level of effort. However, members who highly identify with the team are more likely to compensate for low contributions by increasing their own effort. This is because those who identify at a high level value the shared goal and its purpose. An emphasis on tasks (or portion thereof) that have been completed increases the contributions of low identifiers because this provides them a baseline to mimic the contributions of others; conversely, an emphasis on what has been left incomplete increases the contributions of high identifiers because they want to see the goal attained.

## Individual Differences

The majority of the factors discussed in this chapter have focused on team structure and contextual variables that impact goal setting in teams. Individual differences also play a role in goal setting and performance in team contexts. There is evidence for a number of factors that predict motivation to learn in training. These include locus of control, organizational commitment, outcome valence, supervisor and peer support, and a positive organizational climate (Colquitt, LePine, & Noe, 2000). Goal orientation, or the predisposition to adopt certain goals in achievement contexts, has been widely cited as an important factor in a team's performance (Dweck & Leggett, 1988; Pieterse, van Knippenberg, & van Ginkel, 2011; VandeWalle, 1997). People with a learning goal orientation value the process of learning and possess an internal motivation to achieve some standard relative to one's own standards of improvement, often actively setting their own goals and seeking feedback (Phillips & Gully, 1997; VandeWalle & Cummings, 1997). Conversely, those with a performance goal orientation are primarily concerned with outcomes that prove their competence to others, and tend to make normative comparisons of their own performance against that of others.

Towler and Dipboye (2001) found that those individuals with a mastery (learning) orientation have a higher motivation to learn. These findings at the individual level also extrapolate to the team level. High-performance goal orientation teams are much less likely to be able to adapt in challenging situations than are high-learning goal orientation teams, which are much more likely to be able to adapt and perform (LePine, 2005). Porter (2005) found that high-learning-oriented teams are also more likely to engage in backing up behaviors, have higher collective efficacy beliefs, and are more committed to the team; performance-oriented teams have higher collective efficacy beliefs only when task performance is high. Recent research on team composition and goal setting has begun to take a compilational approach (as described by Kozlowski & Klein, 2000) to evaluate differences within teams as opposed to simply evaluating team averages. Pieterse, van Knippenberg, and van Ginkel (2011) found that diversity (differences between members) in performance and learning orientation within teams is negatively related to team performance as a result of strategy differences among members.

It is also noteworthy that much of the goal setting research to date has been conducted in Western, namely American and Canadian, populations (Sanchez-Runde, Lee, & Steers, 2009; Erez, Kleinbeck, & Thierry, 2001). However, there is sufficient evidence that culture may be an important moderator when discussing reward structures and incentives, which are important reinforcers of team goal accomplishment (cf. Sanchez-Runde et al., 2009). For instance, Pennings (1993) found that American managers are more comfortable with risky compensation methods than are Europeans, likely due to being able to tolerate uncertainty and ambiguity (i.e., uncertainty avoidance). Therefore, individuals and teams that are more risk averse may be less likely to respond favorably to pay-for-performance incentives. Furthermore, Earley (1989) found that social loafing occurred less in collectivistic teams than individualistic, suggesting team size (as discussed previously) may be less important of a factor for highly collectivistic teams. The important point here is that there is sufficient research on most of these factors described when focusing on Western cultures; however, further research is needed to determine if these results are generalizable to non-Western cultures.

## Goal Setting in Contextually Different Teams

Despite the aforementioned factors being important to team goal setting in general, recent research on teams points to the fact that not all teams are created equal. For instance, it is exceedingly common to see that there is an increase in distributed teams working together via a virtual communication tool (Bell & Kozlowski, 2002). Additionally, due to the increase in globalization and expatriation, it is not uncommon for individuals to be working in a team that is culturally diverse. In each of these situations, it is plausible that goal setting should be approached from a different perspective. Therefore, in this section, an examination of goal setting in four different types of teams will be given: virtual/distributed teams, intercultural teams, teams in extreme environments, and multi-team systems.

### Virtual/Distributed Teams

For our purposes, virtual/distributed teams will be defined as those that consist of two or more individuals who work together to achieve a common goal despite being in different locations and having to communicate via virtual methods (i.e., e-mail, video conferencing, telephone, etc.). In teams such as these, it has been shown that it is difficult to establish and maintain a set of common team goals (Hertel, Konradt, & Orlikowski, 2004). This, in turn, has the ability to significantly decrease goal commitment and collaboration within the team. Throughout the virtual teams literature, there are three major themes that might serve as hindrances to proper goal setting and commitment. The first lies in the fact that certain individuals in virtual teams might feel that their work is not important and will be overlooked, or that others will take care of the work for them if they do not perform effectively. Essentially, in these situations, the individual is not feeling that there are pressing consequences that will affect him or her, so they ignore their goals.

The second major theme is that working in a virtually distributed team can increase the feeling of anonymity among team members. This can make people act differently than if they were in a face-to-face team. For instance, anonymity in teams has been shown to decrease social control and increase social loafing (Shepherd, Briggs, Reinig, Yen, & Nunamaker, 1996; Karau & Williams, 1993). Finally, the last important factor that can affect goal setting in virtual teams is that team members might not trust one another as much as they would if they were working face to face. This can cause individuals to look out for themselves and strive to obtain individual goals that might conflict with team goals or ignore team goals all together.

In an effort to provide an understanding of how this can be avoided, Hertel, Konradt, and Orlikowski (2004) explained that the highest-performing virtual teams were those that implemented both high-quality goal setting processes and formulated the task to have a very high interdependence among team members. This interdependence helped create a shared understanding of what everyone's role on the team was and served to diminish feelings that one's work and input do not ultimately matter to the goal. Furthermore, the authors explained that, if coupled with team-based rewards, the team would be much more likely to strive to achieve shared goals. Finally, one last prescription for virtual teams is that when the team goals are set, it is beneficial to create the goals through a participatory process instead of a directive process. This allows the individuals in the team to feel ownership of the goals and provide a shared understanding as to what everyone is responsible for (Wegge, Bipp, & Kleinbeck, 2007). It is for these reasons we suggest that when creating shared goals in a virtual/distributed team, it is best to use a participative method where everyone is involved in creating the goals, and then teaching the team that interdependent goals are important for their success.

## Intercultural Teams

Focusing specifically on teams of individualists and collectivists, it is apparent that goals might be perceived differently by these two groups. For instance, based on the very definition of individualists as being primarily concerned with themselves, and collectivists as being concerned primarily with the best interests of their in-groups (Hofstede, 1980), one can deduce that when left to their own devices, each group would create different types of goals, which could potentially harm the team. This is specifically the case for individualists who might create individual goals and ignore those shared by the team. However, research has found that when provided with a difficult, specific group goal, the focus of individualists shifts from competition and the creation of individual goals to being more cooperative (Crown & Rosse, 1995; Mitchell & Silver, 1990).

Collectivists, on the other hand, have the predisposition to aim their sights at team goals. However, this does not mean that no direction should be given to a team of collectivists. Instead, in an effort to form a strong, shared bond among the team, it has been found that team-oriented training and goal setting has been beneficial in increasing the efficacy and commitment of the individuals on the team (Gibson, 2001). If this is not carried out when there are collectivists on the team who feel that other team members are not part of their in-group, collectivists have been shown to have less commitment to team goals than individualists (Earley, 1993). Furthermore, research has also shown that the creation of group goals is equally beneficial for teams that consist of both individualists and collectivists. This is because individualists are more likely to feel that they need to look out for the best interest of the team, and collectivists are more likely to accept the individualists into their in-group (Crown, 2007). Therefore, we suggest that in intercultural teams, team-oriented goal setting training should be given to all members, and it should focus on providing the team with difficult, specific goals such that no one person on the team could attain them on his or her own.

### Teams in Extreme Environments

Unlike all of the other teams presented here, these do not always function within typical organizational conditions. Whenever a small team is confined and isolated for long durations, they are considered to be functioning within an "extreme environment" (Stuster, 1998). Examples of teams operating in extreme conditions include space flight, submarine teams, and Arctic missions. In high-stress situations such as these, where teams are under constant external threat, both cohesion and the hierarchical structure of teams strengthen (Kansas, Salnitskiy, Grund, Weiss, Gushin, Kozerenko, Sled, & Marmar, 2001). This, in turn, causes the team to turn to the leader for guidance, and increases the likelihood that the leader will not take the input of his or her team into consideration (Klein, 1976; Driskell & Salas, 1991). Therefore, we can see that leadership maps onto teams in extreme environments. For the purposes of this chapter, not all of the impacts will be mapped onto the different contexts; however, for a visual representation of how the impacts map, refer to Table 19.1.

Therefore, it might be said that it is important for the leader to provide constant reminders to a team as to what their mission is. The more specific and detailed the leader is, the greater the identification that the team will feel with the mission. This identification will have a negative relationship with stress and a positive relationship with mission culture, pro-mission organizational behavior (OCB), recognition, goal sharing, and motivation (Gromer, Frischauf, Soucek, & Sattler, 2006). However, the following findings should be addressed, which show that specific, difficult goals in situations where individuals are under high time pressure can cause individuals to take more risks (Van Mierlo & Kleingeld, 2010). For these types of teams, an increase in risk taking could potentially be disastrous. Therefore, it might be typical to find that the mission/goal of teams in extreme environments is vague and leaves room for interpretation which changes based on the situation that the team finds itself in. It is for these reasons that we propose that goal setting in teams in extreme environments should be performed by the leader. He or she should be trained to know that in times of little time pressure or stress, it is best to provide detailed goals to the team whereas, in high-stress and time pressure circumstances, it is better to provide broad, overarching goals to the team.

### Multi-Team Systems

A multi-team system (MTS) is typically defined as two or more teams that work together to achieve a collective, interdependent goal (Marks, Mathieu, & Zaccaro, 2001). Moreover, despite goals being in the forefront of the MTS definition, the topic of goal setting in MTSs has not been greatly examined throughout previous research. However, it is important to note that regardless of the type of goal setting that occurs in MTSs, it is important that team goals should be interdependent and ultimately merge with the overarching goal of the MTS (Marks, DeChurch, Mathieu, Panzer, & Alonso, 2005; Bateman, O'Neill, & Kenworthy-U'Ren, 2002). Similar to the aforementioned research

Table 19.1 Factors Impacting Goal Setting in Various Team Contexts

| Teams in differing contexts | Interdependence | Goal type | Reward systems | Team size | Leadership | Identity | Individual differences | Organizational culture |
|---|---|---|---|---|---|---|---|---|
| Virtual/distributed teams | X | | X | X | | | X | X |
| Intercultural teams | X | | X | | | | X | X |
| Teams in extreme environments | X | X | | | X | X | | |
| Multi-team systems | X | X | | X | X | X | | X |

in teams in extreme environments, it is recommended that the team should be constantly monitored by a leader who keeps the individual teams on track towards achieving the superordinate goal (DeChurch & Marks, 2006). This may be due to the fact that if the team is worrying about the goals of other teams within the MTS, they have the potential to be overwhelmed, and then focus their energies outside of where they should be. Some researchers might feel that focusing on a team's own goal and not focusing on the MTS goal might be detrimental. However, as explained by Latham (2004), the pursuit of individual goals will not be detrimental to the superordinate goal as long as the teams realize that both goals are beneficial for goal attainment and hence increase performance. Therefore, we suggest that to decrease cognitive load on the team members, goal setting in teams in MTSs should mainly be performed by the leader. Specifically, the leader should set individual and team goals that correspond with the ultimate goal of the MTS.

## Training Team Goal Setting

At this point, we have determined the factors that influence team goal setting and examined a number of other contexts. We now ask the question: How do we take these things we have learned and apply them to the production of an effective training program? For individuals, it has been shown through previous research that goal setting training is capable of increasing job performance, attendance, and efficacy (Latham & Kinne, 1974; Gibson, 2001; Ivancevich, 1976; Earley & Kanfer, 1985; Latham & Frayne, 1989). One possible reason for this is that training in setting goals serves to clarify what is expected of each individual (Mitchell, 1973). Typically, individual goal setting training consists of guiding each person through the process of setting and establishing goals (Frayne & Latham, 1987). It is extremely important that during this process the individuals are always involved so that they feel attached to the goals that they have set and have a sense of ownership (Erez & Kanfer, 1983). This positive outlook regarding the goals that have been set, in turn, will increase the individual's goal commitment (Latham, Erez, & Locke, 1988).

However, at the team level of analysis, there is very little research that has been done to test how goal setting training affects teams. However, what research has shown is that team goal setting training will increase group efficacy, which in turn will increase team effectiveness (Gibson, 2001). Group efficacy is thought to increase in these situations because the training establishes a set of norms that the team will follow in the future. These norms will cause the team to process information more effectively and promote cooperation among the members of the team.

To provide an example of how team goal setting training might be put together, one can turn to the procedures given by Gibson (2001), which based the training on the works of Locke and Latham (1990). The training was broken down into two specific parts. First, the teams would, with the direction of the trainer, come up with team goals that were personalized to their profession and goals that they might experience. Second, the trainer would talk through with the team ideas regarding what might aid or hamper them in attaining their goal. This minimizes ambiguity and allows the team to have some idea as to what they can expect. Additionally, much as in individual training, it is important to ensure that the trainer is not specifically doing the work for the teams, but leading them in the proper direction to learn on their own.

Additionally, a form of team goal setting training can be found in guided team self-correction. This training is designed to be a structured format in which to brief and debrief teams with the ultimate goal of allowing for self-correction within the team (Smith-Jentsch, Cannon-Bowers, Tannenbaum, & Salas, 2008). The process consists of a pre-task brief in which the team is informed that it will be critiquing its own performance and is provided with overarching goals, an observation session where the team performs a task and is observed, and a debrief where the facilitator guides the team through the process of critiquing its own performance. Typically, those who facilitate the training are subject matter experts on the topic so that they can provide useful observations based on how they saw the team perform. Furthermore, if done properly, guided team self-correction has been found to improve team members' taskwork skills, teamwork, performance, and collective efficacy (Smith-Jentsch, Cannon-Bowers, Tannenbaum, & Salas, 2008).

There are five main goals of the guided team self-correction process: (1) teaching team members how to self-correct, (2) creating an open, participative team climate, (3) teaching how to create relevant team learning goals, (4) organizing team discussion around a model of effective teamwork, and (5) providing analysis of positive and negative performance (Tannenbaum, Smith-Jentsch, & Behson, 1998). For the purposes of this chapter, the most important is teaching teams how to create learning goals (Seijts & Latham, 2005). These learning goals are typically focused around team processes that are performed during typical performance situations. Therefore, it is important to note that this is different from other methods of team goal setting training in that it does not teach the team to create goals that are directly tied to performance outcomes, but rather ties the goals to the processes that affect team performance. This is particularly useful for teams that are constantly adapting to new situations (e.g., teams in extreme environments) because their performance goals have a tendency to change based on the situation that they are presented.

Similarly, a debriefing method of providing feedback to teams is typically used in teams that often are faced with crisis situations that require quick thinking and adaptation (Hoare, 1996). Created and implemented by the US Army, debriefings take many forms that can range from short brainstorming sessions with the team to extremely long discussion sessions, based on the amount of time that the team can allot to feedback. The most important goals of the feedback provided are increasing team learning, integrity, and building team trust (Schindler & Eppler, 2003). Debriefing training differs from guided team self-correction training in that most of the feedback concerning performance and team goal attainment is provided directly by a commanding officer or leader. It is for this reason that one of the most common criticisms of debriefing methods is that the leaders who provide feedback fail to use questions to lead the process and do not let the team learn from one another (Morrison & Meliza, 1999).

From these different types of training programs, we can deduce a number of important best practices in creating goal-setting training. First, it is vital to provide the team members with the chance to take an active role in the training process. Doing so ensures that the team has some ownership over the created goals in addition to promoting learning, performance, and facilitating adaptive transfer (Keith & Frese, 2005; Debowski, Wood, & Bandura, 2001). Furthermore, it is important to remember that teams should not be left on their own to create goals during training. It is important to have an expert as a guide, particularly for teams that operate in extreme environments or MTSs. This is because of how close and often they interact with the leader of their team. This expert should ensure that the team is not setting the wrong goals, getting caught up in unnecessary steps, provide positive and negative goal examples, and provide performance feedback to the team. This will focus teams on the expert model, and create a shared understanding at the construct level (Smith-Jentsch, Cannon-Bowers, Tannenbaum, & Salas, 2008). Finally, it should be explained to the team that they are encouraged to make mistakes. In doing so, they will become more adaptive and capable of transferring what they learned to new, novel experiences in their work (Keith & Frese, 2008).

## Conclusion

Over time, goal setting theory and research have evolved greatly. The research has moved beyond an individual level. The theory is now being examined at a team level and at a multi-team level. Our research shows that there are eight specific influencing factors that affect team goal setting, and that each of these has differential power based on the context in which the team operates. Therefore, in Figure 19.1 we propose a theoretical model that mirrors this fact. Additionally, it is important to note that there are other types of teams that exist which should also be taken into consideration in future team goal setting research (e.g., impromptu teams, multidisciplinary teams).

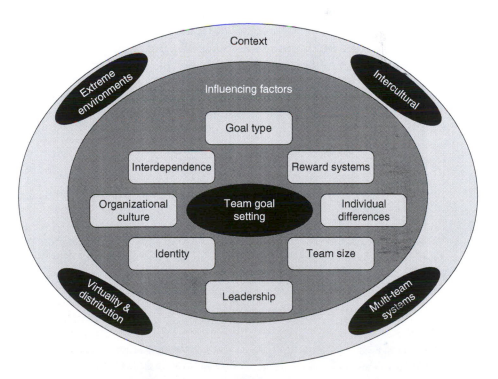

*Figure 19.1* Framework of Goal Setting in Teams.

Despite the amount of research that has been done in these settings, there are still many questions that are left to be answered. For instance, what is the best type of team goal setting training? Research provides us with examples of training programs and pre-scriptions concerning what should be done. However, there is no research to show that one type of training works best for a specific type of team. One of the next steps in goal setting training research should be to test the aforementioned propositions to determine if teams in different contexts benefit from differential goal setting training. Doing so will ensure that organizations are not wasting valuable time and money on training that either does not work or could be significantly strengthened, and then determine if there is a significant increases in performance across teams. This is particularly salient for teams whose wrong decisions could mean life or death for team members.

Additionally, one factor that has not been examined within the team goal setting literature is team tenure. Tenure homogeneity has been found to increase communication and member attraction within teams (Ancona & Caldwell, 1992). Future research should elaborate upon this by examining team lifespan and determining if there a relationship with goal commitment. Or, in these situations, could it potentially be the case that novelty is driving the team's motivation and performance? Furthermore, research might look toward examining goal setting in ad hoc or swift action starting teams where trust might be low among team members who are not familiar with one another.

Finally, whereas goal setting in teams is not a new idea, goal setting in a multi-team system is a new area of research that has not been fully developed. There are still a number of factors within an MTS that should be examined. For instance, we know from previous research that leaders are extremely important in guiding an MTS and maintaining shared goals. However, we do not know what other factors influence those goals across teams. For instance, is the situation where one team does not trust another to complete their task function the same as the situation where two individuals do not trust one another? Future research should bring team goal setting to this new, higher level of analysis and provide insight as to how it differs from previously, well-established team and individual levels.

## Acknowledgments

This work was partially supported by funding from the National Science Foundation grant to Dr. Matthew W. Ohland, Principal Investigator, Purdue University (0817403-DUE), subcontract to UCF (4101-25418) and by NASA Grant NNX09AK48G to Eduardo Salas, Principal Investigator; and Kimberly Smith-Jentsch and Stephen M. Fiore, Co-Principal Investigators, of the University of Central Florida. The views expressed in this work are those of the authors and do not necessarily reflect the organizations with which they are affiliated or their sponsoring institutions or agencies.

## References

Ancona, D.G., & Caldwell, D.F. (1992). Bridging the boundary: External activity and performance in organizational teams. *Administrative Science Quarterly, 37*(4), 634–665.

Aubé, C., & Rousseau, V. (2005). Team goal commitment and team effectiveness: The role of task interdependence and supportive behaviors. *Group Dynamics: Theory, Research, and Practice, 9,* 189–204.

Barnes, C. M., Hollenbeck, J. R., Jundt, D. K., DeRue, D. S., & Harmon, S. J. (2011). Mixing individual incentives and group incentives: Best of both worlds or social dilemma? *Journal of Management, 37,* 1611–1635.

Bateman, T. S., O'Neill, H., & Kenworthy-U'Ren, A. (2002). A hierarchical taxonomy of top managers' goals. *Journal of Applied Psychology, 87,* 1134–1148.

Bell, B. S., & Kozlowski, W. J. (2002). Goal orientation and ability: Interactive effects on, self-efficacy, performance, and knowledge. *Journal of Applied Psychology, 87,* 497–505.

Colquitt, J. A., LePine, J. A., & Noe, R. A. (2000). Toward an integrative theory of training motivation: A meta-analytic path analysis of 20 years of research. *Journal of Applied Psychology, 85*(5), 678–707.

Crown, D. F. (2007). The use of group and groupcentric individual goals for culturally heterogeneous and homogeneous task groups: An assessment of European work teams. *Small Group Research, 38,* 489–508.

Crown, D. F., & Rosse, J. G. (1995). Yours, mine, and ours: Facilitating group productivity through the integration of individual and group goals. *Organizational Behavior and Human Decision Processes, 64,* 138–150.

DeChurch, L. A., & Marks, M. A. (2006). Leadership in multiteam systems. *Journal of Applied Psychology, 91,* 311–329.

DeChurch, L. A., & Mesmer-Magnus, J. R. (2010). The cognitive underpinnings of effective teamwork: A meta-analysis. *Journal of Applied Psychology, 95,* 32–53.

DeShon, R. P., Kozlowski, S. W. J., Schmidt, A. M., Milner, K. R., & Wiechmann, D. (2004). A multiple-goal, multilevel model of feedback effects on the regulation of individual and team performance. *Journal of Applied Psychology, 89,* 1035–1056.

Debowski, S., Wood, R. E., & Bandura, A. (2001). Impact of guided exploration and enactive exploration on self-regulatory mechanisms and information acquisition through electronic search. *Journal of Applied Psychology, 86,* 1129–1141.

Dirks, K. (1999). The effects of interpersonal trust on work group performance. *Journal of Applied Psychology, 84*(3), 445–455.

Driskell, J. E., & Salas, E. (1991). Group decision making under stress. *Journal of Applied Psychology, 76,* 273–478.

Durham, C. C., Knight, D., & Locke, E. A. (1997). Effects of leader role, team-set goal difficulty, efficacy, and tactics on team effectiveness. *Organizational Behavior and Human Decision Processes, 72*(2), 203–231.

Dweck, C. S., & Leggett, E. L. (1988). A social-cognitive approach to motivation and personality. *Psychological Review, 95,* 256–273.

Earley, P. C. (1989). Social loafing and collectivism: A comparison of the United States and the People's Republic of China. *Administrative Science Quarterly, 34* (4), 565–581.

Earley, P. C. (1993). East meets west meets Mideast: Further explorations of collectivistic and individualistic work groups. *Academy of Management Journal, 36,* 319–348.

Earley, P. C., & Kanfer, R. (1985). The influence of components of participation and role models on goal acceptance, goal satisfaction, and performance. *Organizational Behavior and Human Decision Processes, 36,* 378–390.

Erez, M., & Kanfer, F. H. (1983). The role of goal acceptance in goal-setting and task performance. *Academy of Management Review, 8,* 454–463.

Erez, M., Kleinbeck, U., & Thierry, H. (2001). *Work Motivation in the Context of a Globalizing Economy.* Mahwah, NJ: Lawrence Erlbaum.

Fishbach, A., Henderson, M. D., & Koo, M. (2011). Pursuing goals with others: Group identification and motivation resulting from things done versus things left undone. *Journal of Experimental Psychology: General, 140,* 520–534.

Frayne, C. A., & Latham, G. P. (1987). Application of social learning theory to employee self-management of attendance. *Journal of Applied Psychology, 72,* 387–392.

Gibson, C. B. (2001). Me and us: Differential relationships among goal-setting training, efficacy and effectiveness at the individual and team level. *Journal of Organizational Behavior, 22,* 789–808.

Gibson, C. B., Maznevski, M. L., & Kirkman, B. L. (2009). When does culture matter? In R. S. Bhagat & R. M. Steers (Eds.) *Cambridge handbook of culture, organizations, and work* (pp. 46–68). New York: Cambridge University Press.

Graen, G.B., Novak, M., & Sommerkamp, P. (1982). The effects of leader-member exchange and job design on productivity and satisfaction: Testing a dual attachment model. *Organizational Behavior and Human Performance, 30,* 109–131.

Gromer, G., Frischauf, N., Soucek, A., & Sattler, B. (2006). AustroMars—a simulated high-fidelity human Mars analogue mission. *Proceedings of the Mars 2030 Workshop,* 4–12.

Gully, S. M., Incalcaterra, K. A., Joshi, A., & Beaubien, J. M. (2002). A meta-analysis of team-efficacy, potency, and performance: Interdependence and level of analysis as moderators of observed relationships. *Journal of Applied Psychology, 87,* 819–832.

Guthrie, J. P., & Hollensbe, E. C. (2004). Group incentives and performance: A study of spontaneous goal setting, goal choice and commitment. *Journal of Management, 30,* 263–284.

Hackman, J. R. (1987). The design of work teams. In J. Lorsch (Ed.), *Handbook of organizational behavior.* Englewood Cliffs, NJ: Prentice-Hall.

Harkins, S. G. & Petty, R. E. (1982). Effects of task difficulty and task uniqueness on social loafing. *Journal of Personality and Social Psychology, 43*(6), 1214–1229.

Haslam, S. A., Wegge, J., & Postmes, T. (2009). Are we on a learning curve or treadmill? The benefits of participative group goal setting become apparent as tasks become increasingly challenging over time. *European Journal of Social Psychology, 39,* 430–446.

Hertel, G., Konradt, U., & Orlikowski, B. (2004). Managing distance by interdependence: Goal setting, task interdependence, and team-based rewards in virtual teams. *European Journal of Work and Organizational Psychology, 13,* 1–28.

Hoare, R. (1996). From debrief to after action review (AAR). *Modern Simulation and Training, 6,* 13–17.

Hoegl, M., & Parboteeah, K. P. (2003). Goal setting and team performance in innovative projects: On the moderating role of teamwork quality. *Small Group Research, 34,* 3–19.

Hollenbeck, J. R., & Klein, H. J. (1987). Goal commitment and the goal setting process: Problems, prospects, and proposals for future research. *Journal of Applied Psychology, 74,* 212–220.

Hollensbe, E. C., & Guthrie, J. P. (2000). Group pay-for-performance plans: The role of spontaneous goal setting. *Academy of Management Review, 25,* 864–872.

Hofstede, G. (1980). *Culture's consequences: National differences in thinking and organizing.* Beverly Hills, CA: Sage.

Ilgen, D. R., Hollenbeck, J. R., Johnson, M., & Jundt, D. (2005). Teams in organizations: From input-process-output models to IMOI models. *Annual Review of Psychology, 56* (1), 517–543.

Ivancevich, J. M. (1976). Effects of goal setting on performance and job satisfaction. *Journal of Applied Psychology, 61,* 605–612.

Kansas, M., Salnitskiy, V., Grund, E. M., Weiss, D. S., Gushin, V., Kozerenko, O., Sled, A., & Marmar, C. R. (2001). Human interactions in space: Results from shuttle/Mir. *Acta Astronautica, 49,* 243–260.

Karau, S. J., & Williams, K. D. (1993). Social loafing: A meta-analytic review and theoretical integration. *Journal of Personality and Social Psychology, 65,* 681–706.

Keith, N., & Frese, M. (2005). Self-regulation in error management training: Emotion control and metacognition as mediators of performance effects. *Journal of Applied Psychology, 90,* 677–691.

Keith, N., & Frese, M. (2008). Effectiveness of error management training: A meta-analysis. *Journal of Applied Psychology, 93,* 59–69.

Klein, A. L. (1976). Changes in leadership appraisal as a function of the stress of a simulated panic situation. *Journal of Personality and Social Psychology, 34,* 1143–1154.

Klein, H. J., Wesson, M. J., Hollenbeck, J. R., & Alge, B. J. (1999). Goal commitment and the goal-setting process: Conceptual clarification and empirical synthesis. *Journal of Applied Psychology, 84,* 885–896.

Kleingeld, A., Van Mierlo, H., & Arends, L. (2011). The effect of goal setting on group performance: A meta-analysis. *Journal of Applied Psychology,* in print.

Kozlowski, S. W. J., & Ilgen, D. R. (2006). Enhancing the effectiveness of work groups and teams. *Psychological Science in the Public Interest, 7*(3), 77–124.

Kozlowski, S. W. J., & Klein, K. J. (2000). A multilevel approach to theory and research in organizations: Contextual, temporal, and emergent processes. In K. J. Klein & S. W. J. Kozlowski (Eds.), *Multilevel Theory, Research, and Methods in Organizations: Foundations, Extensions, and New Directions* (pp. 3–90). San Francisco: Jossey-Bass.

Latané, B., Williams, K., & Harkins, S. (1979). Many hands make light the work: The causes and consequences of social loafing. *Journal of Personality and Social Psychology, 37,* 822–832.

Latham, G. P. (2004). The motivational benefits of goal-setting. *Academy of Management Executive, 18,* 126–129.

Latham, G. P., Erez, M., & Locke, E. A. (1988). Resolving scientific disputes by the joint design of crucial experiments by the antagonists: Application to the Erez-Latham dispute regarding participation in goal-setting. *Journal of Applied Psychology, 73,* 753–772.

Latham, G. P., & Frayne, C. A. (1989). Self-management training for increasing job attendance: A follow-up and a replication. *Journal of Applied Psychology, 74,* 411–416.

Latham, G. P., & Kinne, S. B. (1974). Improving job performance through training in goal setting. *Journal of Applied Psychology, 59,* 187–191.

Latham, G. P., & Locke, E. A. (2009). Science and ethics: What should count as evidence against use of goal setting? *Academy of Management Perspectives, 23*(3), 17–21.

LePine, J. A. (2005). Adaptation of teams in response to unforeseen change: Effects of goal difficulty and team composition in terms of cognitive ability and goal orientation. *Journal of Applied Psychology, 90,* 1153–1167.

LePine, J. A., Piccolo, R. F., Jackson, C. L., Mathieu, J. E., & Saul, J. R. (2008). A meta-analysis of teamwork processes: Tests of a multidimensional model and relationships with team effectiveness criteria. *Personnel Psychology, 61,* 273–307.

Locke, E. A., & Latham, G. P. (1990). *A theory of goal setting and task performance.* Englewood Cliffs, NJ: Prentice-Hall.

Locke, E. A., & Latham, G. P. (2002). Building a practically useful theory of goal setting and task motivation: A 35-year odyssey. *American Psychologist, 57,* 705–717.

Locke, E. A., & Latham, G. P. (2009). Has goal setting gone wild, or have its attackers abandoned good scholarship? *Academy of Management Perspectives, 23,* 17–23.

Marks, M. A., DeChurch, L. A., Mathieu, J. E., Panzer, F. J., & Alonso, A. (2005). Teamwork in multiteam systems. *Journal of Applied Psychology, 90,* 964–971.

Marks, M. A., Mathieu, J. E., & Zaccaro, S. J. (2001). A temporally based framework and taxonomy of team processes. *Academy of Management Review, 26,* 356–376.

Mathieu, J. E., Heffner, T. S., Goodwin, G. F., Cannon-Bowers, J. A., & Salas, E. (2005). Scaling the quality of teammates' mental models: Equifinality and normative comparisons. *Journal of Organizational Behavior, 26,* 37–56.

Mathieu, J. E., Heffner, T. S., Goodwin, G. F., Salas, E., & Cannon-Bowers, J. A. (2000). The influence of shared mental models on team processes and performance. *Journal of Applied Psychology, 85,* 273–283.

McGrath, J. E. (1964). *Social psychology: A brief introduction.* New York: Holt, Rinehart, & Winston.

Mitchell, T. R. (1973). Motivation and participation: An integration. *Academy of Management Journal, 16*(4), 670–679.

Mitchell, T. R., & Silver, W. S. (1990). Individual and group goals when workers are interdependent: Effects on task strategies and performance. *Journal of Applied Psychology, 75,* 185–193.

Morrison, J. E., & Meliza, L. L. (1999). Foundations of the after action review process. *United States Army Research Institute for the Behavioral and Social Science, 1*–71.

O'Leary-Kelly, A. M., Martocchio, J. T., & Frink, D. D. (1994). A review of the influence of group goals in group performance. *Academy of Management Journal, 37,* 1285–1301.

Oakes, P. J., Haslam, S. A., Morrison, B., & Grace, D. (1995). Becoming an in-group: Reexamining the impact of familiarity on perceptions of group homogeneity. *Social Psychology Quarterly, 58,* 52–61.

Ordóñez, L. D., Schweitzer, M. E., Galinsky, A. D., & Bazerman, M. H. (2009). Goals gone wild: The systematic side effects of overprescribing goal setting. *Academy of Management Perspectives, 23,* 6–16.

Pearsall, M. J., Christian, M. S., & Ellis, A. P. J. (2010). Motivating interdependent teams: Individual rewards, shared rewards, or something in between? *Journal of Applied Psychology, 95,* 183–191.

Pennings, J. M. (1993). Executive reward systems: A cross-national comparison. *Journal of Management Studies, 30,* 261–280.

Phillips, J. M., & Gully, S. M. (1997). Role of goal orientation, ability, need for achievement, and locus of control in the self-efficacy and goal-setting process. *Journal of Applied Psychology, 82*(5), 792–802.

Pieterse, A. N., van Knippenberg, D., & van Kinkel, W. P. (2011). Diversity in goal orientation, team reflexivity, and team performance. *Organizational Behavior and Human Decision Processes, 114,* 153–164.

Porter, C. O. L. H. (2005). Goal orientation: Effects on backing up behavior, performance, efficacy, and commitment in teams. *Journal of Applied Psychology, 90,* 811–818.

Prussia, G. E., & Kinicki, A. J. (1996). A motivational investigation of group effectiveness using social-cognitive theory. *Journal of Applied Psychology, 81,* 187–198.

Quigley, N. R., Tesluk, P. E., Locke, E. A., & Bartol, K. M. (2007). A multilevel investigation of the motivational mechanisms underlying knowledge sharing and performance. *Organization Science, 18*, 71–88.

Robbins, S. P., & Judge, T. A. (2009). *Organizational behavior.* New Jersey: Prentice Hall.

Saavedra, R., Earley, P. C., & Van Dyne, L. (1993). Complex interdependence in task-performing groups. *Journal of Applied Psychology, 78*, 61–72.

Sagie, A. (1996). Effects of leader's communication style and participative goal setting on performance and attitudes. *Human Performance, 9*, 51–64.

Salas, E., Dickinson, T. L., Converse, S. A., & Tannenbaum, S. I. (1992). Toward an understanding of team performance and training. In R. W. Swezey & E. Salas (Eds.), *Teams: Their training and performance* (pp. 3–29). Westport, CT: Ablex Publishing.

Sanchez-Runde, C., Lee, S. M., & Steers, R. M. (2009). Cultural drivers of work behavior: Personal values, motivation, and job attitudes. In R. S. Bhagat & R. M. Steers (Eds.), *Cambridge handbook of culture, organizations, and work* (pp. 46–68). New York: Cambridge University Press.

Schindler, M., & Eppler, M. J. (2003). Harvesting project knowledge: A review of project learning methods and success factors. *International Journal of Project Management, 21*, 219–228.

Seijts, G. H., & Latham, G. P. (2000). The effects of goal setting and group size on performance in a social dilemma. *Canadian Journal of Behavioural Science, 32*, 104–116.

Seijts, G. H., & Latham, G. P. (2005). Learning versus performance goals: When should each be used? *Academy of Management Executive, 19*, 124–131.

Seijts, G. H., Latham, G. P., & Whyte, G. (2000). Effect of self- and group-efficacy on group performance in a mixed-motive situation. *Human Performance, 13*, 279–298.

Shepherd, M., Briggs, R. O., Reinig, B., Yen, J., & Nunamaker, J. F. (1996). Invoking social comparison to improve brainstorming: Beyond anonymity. *Journal of Management Information Systems, 12*, 155–170.

Smith-Jentsch, K. A., Cannon-Bowers, J. A., Tannenbaum, S. I., & Salas, E. (2008). Guided team self-correction: Impacts on team mental models, behavior, and effectiveness. *Small Group Research, 39*, 303–327.

Stuster, J. (1998). Human and team performance in extreme environments: Antarctica. *Human Performance in Extreme Environments, 3*, 117–120.

Taggar, S., & Ellis, R. (2007). The role of leaders in shaping formal team norms. *The Leadership Quarterly, 18*, 105–120.

Tajfel, H., & Turner, J. C. (1979). An integrative theory of intergroup conflict. In W. G. Austin & S. Worchel (Eds.), *The social psychology of intergroup relations* (pp. 33–47). Monterey, CA: Brookes/Cole.

Tannenbaum, S. I., Smith-Jentsch, K. A., & Behson, S. J. (1998). Training team leaders to facilitate team learning and performance. In J. A. Cannon-Bowers & E. Salas (Eds.), *Decision making under stress: Implications for individual and team training* (pp. 247–270). Washington, DC: American Psychological Association.

Tjosvold, D., & Yu, Z. (2004). Goal interdependence and applying abilities for team in-role and extra-role performance in china. *Group Dynamics: Theory, Research, and Practice, 8*, 98–111.

Towler, A. J., & Dipboye, R. L. (2001). Effects of trainer expressiveness, organization, and trainee goal orientation on training outcomes. *Journal of Applied Psychology, 86*(4), 664–673.

Turner, J. C. (1984). Social identification and psychological group formation. In H. Tajfel (Ed.), *The social dimension: European developments in social psychology* (pp. 518–538). Cambridge, England: Cambridge University Press.

Van Mierlo, H., & Kleingeld, A. (2010). Goals, strategies, and group performance: Some limits of goal setting in groups. *Small Group Research, 41*(5), 524–555.

Vandewalle, D. (1997). Development and validation of a work domain goal orientation instrument. *Educational and Psychological Measurement, 57,* 995–1015.

VandeWalle, D., & Cummings, L. L. (1997). A test of the influence of goal orientation on the feedback-seeking process. *Journal of Applied Psychology, 82*(3), 390–400.

Wegge, J., Bipp, T., & Kleinbeck, U. (2007). Goal setting via videoconferencing. *European Journal of Work and Organizational Psychology, 16,* 169–194.

Wegge, J., & Haslam, S. A. (2005). Improving work motivation and performance in brainstorming groups: The effects of three group goal-setting strategies. *European Journal of Work and Organizational Psychology, 14,* 400–430.

Wong, A., Tjosvold, D., & Liu, C. (2009). Innovation by teams in Shanghai, China: Cooperative goals for group confidence and persistence. *British Journal of Management, 20,* 238–251.

Wu, J. B., Tsui, A. S., & Kinicki, A. J. (2010). Consequences of Differentiated Leadership in Groups. *Academy of Management Journal, 53*(1), 90–106.

Zaccaro, S. J., Rittman, A. L., & Marks, M. A. (2001). Team leadership. *The Leadership Quarterly, 12*(4), 451–483.

# 20  Units, Divisions, and Organizations
## Macro-Level Goal Setting

*Greg Young*  Poole College of Management,
North Carolina State University
*Ken G. Smith*  College of Business Administration,
University of Rhode Island

As the chapters in this volume indicate, goal setting theory is developed in over 1000 studies that provide multifaceted and robust insight into individual motivation. There have, however, been few studies of macro-level goal setting published in the 20 years since Locke and Latham's (1990) book. This is surprising given the prominence of macro-level goals in organizational processes including unit coordination, strategy, and resource allocation; and in strategic outcomes including organizational performance and stakeholder satisfaction.

Macro-level goals are the desirable objectives, aims, and standards of proficiency for activities connected in a structural hierarchy positioning them in units, divisions, and broad-based organizations. One study of macro-level goals, grounded in the self-reports of top managers, inductively identified alternative goal categories related to finances, customers, markets, operations, products, employees, culture, reputation, partnering, learning, and competitive dynamics (Bateman, O'Neill, & Kenworthy-U'ren, 2002).

Macro-level goals may have non-operational or operational content. Non-operational goals are communicated without specific measurable objectives and affect nonperformance attributes such as members' attitudes and commitment to the organization (Vancouver & Schmitt, 1991, p. 334) and serve to legitimize the organization. Non-operational goals "reflect the values and commitments of the founders, leaders, and employees who make up the organization …. [and] are a key issue in determining the fit of individuals and organizations [because] individuals are attracted to, selected by, and remain with organizations that have organizational goals to their liking" (Vancouver, Milsap, & Peters, 1994, p. 667). Operational goals, on the other hand, are communicated with specific measurable performance objectives (Vancouver & Schmitt, 1991) and thus are widely applied to assess organizational effectiveness. Goal setting theory, with the relationship between specific goals and performance at its core (Locke & Latham, 1990), calls attention to the processes, context, and performance consequences associated with macro-level operational goals.

This chapter focuses on operational macro-level goals. In this context, one of the primary objectives driving the formulation of goal setting theory is to deepen our understanding of performance on organizational tasks (Locke & Latham, 2002). Early macro-level goal setting research offered promising results by drawing on theory developed at the micro-level of analysis. For example, Smith, Locke, and Barry (1990) found that specific, challenging goals are significantly related to the performance of student teams managing simulated competing businesses. Smith and Locke (1990) extended this line of inquiry by drawing on a behavioral theory of the firm (e.g., Cyert & March, 1963; Mintzberg, 1983) to call attention to goal selection and prioritization challenges in the context of multiple goals and goal conflict (i.e., disagreement) among organizational members and units. However, early progress toward macro-level goal setting theory was promising but limited.

Smith et al. (1990) noted the lack of quantitative research on the relationship between goals and performance at the macro level. Similarly, Smith and Locke (1990), after surveying the empirical macro-level goal setting literature, called for researchers to accumulate evidence on specific topics on which there were substantial gaps in our understanding. This current chapter surveys the research that has responded in the more than two decades since their call. Our conclusion is that macro goal setting remains a relatively unexplored research area.

## Topics in Macro Goal Setting

This section summarizes and discusses the quantitative research published after 1990 that addresses macro-level goal setting topics. We begin according to the six topics identified by Smith and Locke (1990): multiple goals and goal mix, time horizon and causal ordering, goal commitment, goal conflict, strategy, and environmental uncertainty. The literature we review in these topics includes several calls (Baum & Locke, 2004; Baum, Locke, & Smith, 2001; Häsänen, Hellgren, & Hansson, 2011; Klein & Kim, 1998; Terpstra & Rozell, 1994) for more attention to the specific context surrounding the use of goals in organizations. In response, we add to the six topics identified by Smith and Locke (1990) one additional topic on situationally specific goal context. In this seventh topic, we discuss recent empirical research on macro goals in the separate domains of entrepreneurship and plant closure.

### Multiple Goals and Goal Mix

Business organizations typically are complex and have multiple operational goals to address different aspects of performance such as market share, profitability, customer satisfaction, and productivity (Ethiraj & Levinthal, 2009). Multiple operational goals are useful if they are correlated with an important common factor that is not directly measurable or, alternatively, if they measure important and distinct items that are not correlated (Ethiraj & Levinthal, 2009). On the other hand, the effort to accomplish multiple goals may exceed available resources or be logically incoherent so that progress on some hinders the achievement of others.

As Locke (2004, p. 132) noted, "[i]n any organization virtually everything that happens affects everything else, for better or for worse. Ideally, goals should be integrated across the entire organization, but this is usually impossible." An organization with multiple goals, therefore, may assign subsets, or intermediate goals, to separate divisions and units in order to focus local managerial attention and effort on efficient allocation of resources toward performance. For example, scorecard practices (e.g., Kaplan & Norton, 2001) are popular approaches to apply strategic coherence to multiple goals by focusing attention on the logic underlying goal mix, measurement, and organizational performance.

Despite the proliferation and utility of mechanisms such as scorecards, coordinating activity in an organization with multiple goals remains challenging if a single action may affect performance on many goals simultaneously and in different directions. Therefore, a trade-off often exists when attempting to achieve multiple goals simultaneously. Such trade-offs in performance consequences pose challenges to decision making for the prioritization and assignment of goals within the organization. Ethiraj and Levinthal (2009, p. 15) experimentally model these consequences for a baseline case in which "an organization is given multiple performance goals, each action is evaluated against all goals, and the actions that reduce performance are not adopted at all." Going beyond eight organizational goals in their baseline model does not improve overall organizational performance because additional action is more likely to reduce performance on at least one goal and thus reduce the probability of engaging in the additional effort. In this case, the baseline coordination strategy causes implementation to anchor on eight goals, and the bias to a status quo of eight macro-level goals is robust even for organizations that formulate more than eight goals. For organizations with more than four performance goals, however, their analyses show that three alternative goal coordination strategies— which they label *temporal differentiation, goal myopia,* and *spatial differentiation*—each improve overall organizational performance relative to the baseline model.

*Temporal differentiation* directs all units within the organization to allocate effort on the same performance goal; each unit and the overall organization evaluates its goal performance after each time period; in successive time periods, the entire organization switches all effort to the next goal until the organization has sequentially cycled through all of its performance goals. For example, an organization may choose a goal to build market share and thereafter pursue a goal of profitability, as gaining market share often comes at the expense of profits.

Ethiraj and Levinthal's (2009) *goal myopia* assignment strategy focuses on a single goal over all time periods. We relabel this strategy *single goal focus* to avoid any pejorative implication associated with conceptual myopia. An organization executing a *single goal focus* assignment strategy selects one goal from among its set of multiple performance goals; implements it across all organizational units and all time periods; evaluates unit and organization-wide performance after each time period, but across time periods it does not switch effort to any other performance goal. An example is an organizational focus on high product or service quality even if such high quality comes at the expense of increased costs, and perhaps tactical changes may be required to improve performance over time.

In the *spatial differentiation* assignment strategy, the organization assigns a subset of its performance goals to each of its units, and each unit makes decisions based only on its performance on its assigned goals. An example of this assignment strategy is illustrated by the Boston Consulting Group's growth share matrix portrayal of the different units of one organization that may be assigned different goals such as market share growth, profitability, and positive cash flows.

A multiplicity of goals is common in organizations (Locke, 2004) and poses a complex goal coordination problem for management (Ethiraj & Levinthal, 2009). We are reminded of James Thompson's observation long ago (1967, p. 158) that "in modern societies, it appears, we have passed ... into an era in which organizational rationality is the core of administration and the administration of multiorganization projects and activities the central challenge." However, we lack information on the management of goal setting principles in organizations. We suggest that future macro-level goal setting research investigate the dynamics of goal setting in actual organizations to advance our understanding, derived from Ethiraj and Levinthal (2009), of the likely performance outcomes from alternative coordination rules applied to multiple goals in the context of bounded rationality. It may be that a coordination strategy of evaluating all candidate actions against all performance goals ex ante implementation leads to a status quo bias in organization goals. Similarly, an organization may be able to improve its overall performance by applying a temporal differentiation, single goal focus, or spatial differentiation goal coordination strategy. It would be interesting to examine institutional effects of goal coordination strategies as "best practices" within a set of similar industries, and to examine the extent to which goal coordination strategies can provide an organization with a sustainable competitive advantage.

## Time Horizon and Causal Ordering

A coordination process view of goal setting in organizations suggests a sequence of goal formation and task implementation activities that are enacted over time as intermediate steps toward longer-term macro-level performance. As Baum noted earlier in this book, there have been a few studies of goal setting and the stages of entrepreneurship. For example, Hatfield and Pearce (1994) surveyed both partner companies in 30 different joint ventures. From their survey results, Hatfield and Pearce (1994) describe stages that start with goal formation by individual venture partners, then integration of venture partners' goals, followed by performance evaluation for individual venture partner goals, and finally overall assessment of venture partner satisfaction with the venture. The Hatfield and Pearce (1994) survey found that the number of goals pursued significantly influences goal formation and intermediate performance evaluation; the distinct components of the business model (i.e., operational scope, revenue, profitability, and cost) as well as knowledge and market power are separately pursued in intermediate goals; and the strongest influence on satisfaction with overall long-term outcome is achievement of the intermediate-stage goals.

We suggest that future research apply time-based designs to examine a macro-level goal setting coordination process generalized from the joint venture context described by Hatfield and Pearce (1994). The first stage in this generalized process is goal formation by key internal stakeholders; next is goal integration across organizational units, divisions, and boundaries; third is performance on intermediate activities; and finally is assessment of activity outcomes toward longer-term macro-level performance. Skill in managing the coordination of multiple goals is important in the goal formation and management of intermediate stages; in the intermediate stage, goals may consist of business model, knowledge, and/or market power content assigned to multiple tasks; and satisfaction with progress toward long-term macro-level goals is likely to be associated with achievement of intermediate stage goals in a causal chain.

The model of joint venture goal achievement developed by Hatfield and Pearce (1994) causally links the number of goals enabled in the early stage with the later evaluation of macro-level performance. The experimental modeling of Ethiraj and Levinthal (2009) we discussed earlier, however, causes us to expect that the coordination strategy that governs macro-level goals will significantly influence the number of goals enabled in the early formulation stage. If so, then the final stage of a macro-level goal setting process—satisfaction with progress toward long-term macro-level goals—is likely to be moderated by the choice of coordination strategy. In this moderation model, a coordination strategy of evaluating all candidate intermediate actions against all performance goals of internal stakeholders ex ante implementation should lead to the lowest level of satisfaction with progress toward long-term macro-level goals. Further, relative to a coordination strategy of evaluating all candidate intermediate actions against all performance goals of internal stakeholders ex ante implementation, the temporal differentiation, single goal focus, and spatial differentiation goal coordination strategies should each increase the level of satisfaction with progress toward long-term macro-level goals.

## Goal Commitment

Micro-level goal-setting research (Klein, Wesson, Hollenbeck, & Alge, 1999) shows that task performance is expected to be high when goal difficulty and goal commitment are both high, but task performance is expected to be unrelated to goal difficulty when goal commitment is low. Because of its important moderating role, "Locke and Latham (1990) recommended that goal commitment be measured in all goal-setting studies" (Klein et al., 1999, p. 892). Klein and Kim (1998), however, note that relatively few goal setting studies have examined goal commitment in a field setting.

Klein, Cooper, and Monahan (Chapter 6) conceptualize *goal commitment* as an attitudinal evaluation of binding motivational attachment to a course of action intended to reach a goal, and they recommend *goal commitment* be defined at the micro-level as "a volitional psychological bond reflecting dedication to, and responsibility for, a particular target." Their chapter surveys more than two decades of research on goal commitment and prompts their call for future research to conceptualize the construct with precision to avoid ex ante or ex post confounds.

Locke, Latham, and Erez (1988) suggested that goal commitment would be higher under conditions of formal authority and when there are high levels of organizational trust; and formal authority and high levels of trust will be greater when the organization's leaders have long tenured careers within the organization and have proven track records of success. Persistence in macro-level conduct may be one consequence of strong goal commitment because it "implies the extension of effort, over time, toward the accomplishment of an original goal and emphasizes an unwillingness to abandon or to lower the goal" (Wright, O'Leary-Kelly, Cortina, Klein, & Hollenbeck, 1994, p. 796).

Klein and Kim (1998) examined the influences of leader-member exchange (LMX, the perceived supportiveness of supervisors in relationships with employees) and situational constraints (such as lack of resources) on goal commitment and sales performance in four branches of a retail organization located in a Midwestern metropolitan area. They hypothesized that perceptions of situational constraints would be negatively related to goal commitment and (1998, p. 90) "a high level of performance is expected for those employees with a higher-quality [leader-member] exchange who are committed to a difficult performance goal. ... [but] for lower-LMX employees, goal commitment may not relate to performance at all. For these individuals, the motivation and intention to exert effort indicated by high commitment may not translate into high performance because of a lack of resources, support, and attention from their managers." Klein and Kim's (1998) analysis of employee surveys and store sales data found that pairwise correlation showed a significant positive correlation between goal commitment and LMX. However, regressing sales performance on LMX and situational constraints showed no significant direct effects from these two parameters. Results when LMX, situational constraints, and goal commitment were all included as independent variables showed significant positive direct influence on sales performance only from goal commitment; the direct effects from leader-member exchange and situational constraints on sales performance were not significant when goal commitment was included. Klein and Kim (1998) also reported that the interaction of leader-member exchange and goal commitment had a significant positive influence on sales performance, but we are not sure what insight to draw given the lack of a direct effect from leader-member exchange. Moreover, Klein and Kim (1998, p. 94) cautioned readers that their study had many limitations including "low questionnaire response rate and the resulting small sample ... the possibility cannot be ruled out that respondents differed from nonrespondents in some systematic manner ... common method variance could explain the relationships among these variables ... managers apparently undermined the store's incentive system... [and] the assigned performance standards were not the only available rewards." Nevertheless, Klein and Kim (1998) is one of the few empirical studies of goal commitment in the context of macro goal setting. We reiterate their recommendation that future research identify "the one or two constraints most prevalent in a particular context and [develop] multi-item scales to assess those specific constraints."

Smith and Locke (1990) pointed out that a "serious block to goal commitment in real organizations is the existence of different personal agendas ... where coalition making is a fact of life." Witt (1998) examined these personal agendas in organizational politics, framing them as (irrationally) selfish actions brought about by social exchanges without regard for harm to organizational goals. Applying survey research methods, he found that the perception of organizational politics harms the strength of organizational members' emotional attachment to and involvement with the organization, but this harm is attenuated by employee–supervisor goal congruence. (In the next section of this chapter, we discuss goal *conflict*, the inverse of goal *congruence*.) Witt's (1998) research model assumes that similarities in demographic profile—individual age, education, organizational tenure, and experience—are positively associated with congruence because they facilitate effective communication and mutual understanding of intended goal priorities. However, Witt (1998) did not aggregate to the macro-level nor attempt longitudinal analysis. We are not aware of empirical research demonstrating that demographic homogeneity of organizational personnel, either in leadership or employee–supervisor profiles, is an antecedent of macro-level goal commitment.

Management by Objectives (MBO) is a popular approach to increase employee–supervisor goal congruence and goal commitment in organizations by applying rewards and incentives, participatory decision making, and feedback. Research shows that MBO is significantly associated with higher performance (Smith & Locke, 1990; Rodgers & Hunter, 1991), but the relationship between MBO and performance is moderated by top management commitment to the implementation of MBO (Rodgers & Hunter, 1991). In their meta-analysis of 72 MBO studies, those authors (1991) found that the average gain in productivity was 56% when the level of top management commitment was high, but just 6% when commitment was low. Hunter and Schmidt (2004, p. 424) pointed out that earlier unpublished research erroneously found the effects of MBO on productivity are most observable if assessed over time horizons of more than two years, but "[m]ost of the long-term studies were studies with strong management commitment, while most of the short-term studies were studies with weak management commitment. Thus, the apparent impact of time horizon as a moderator variable was due to the fact that it was confounded with managerial commitment."

We reiterate the important role of goal commitment as a moderator of the relationship between goal difficulty and task performance in organizations. Macro-level goal setting research should examine the organizational context that may influence variation in goal commitment, including organizational leadership, size, politics, and employee–supervisor goal congruence. Baum and Locke (2004), for example, are explicit in their assumption that young entrepreneurial ventures managed by CEO founder-owners will have little variation in goal commitment. Also, Häsänen et al. (2011) discuss the likely reduction in goal commitment among employees experiencing the closedown of their organizational unit, and examine goal setting treatments to improve goal commitment in the specific situation of unit closedown. We discuss Baum and Locke (2004) and Häsänen et al. (2011) in more detail in a separate section later in this chapter that addresses recent research on situationally specific goal contexts.

## Goal Conflict

Earlier we noted that the management and coordination of multiple goals is critical in complex organization (Ethiraj & Levinthal (2009), but also can lead to conflict (i.e., disagreement) among organizational members required to select and prioritize goals whose performance outcomes are uncorrelated. Witt (1998, p. 669) points out that "the issue with regard to [goal conflict] … is that across the key goals of the organization, disagreement—whether explicitly recognized or not—may lead individuals to adopt and follow day-to-day priorities that are inconsistent with those of their peers and managers." In part to distinguish this form of goal conflict from those goal conflicts characterizing relationships between external principals and their agents, recent research (e.g., Vancouver et al., 1994; Vancouver & Schmitt, 1991; Witt, 1998) has examined the role of *goal congruence*, the inverse of goal conflict, as a moderator of the relationship between macro goals and performance.

Surveys of senior managers and employees in financial collection, production, and marketing sectors found that reducing goal conflict (i.e., increasing goal congruence) between individuals and their supervisors attenuates the negative influence that perceived political behavior has on supervisor ratings of performance (Witt, 1998). As we noted earlier, however, Witt (1998) did not attempt to aggregate responses to the organizational unit, and further research is needed at the macro level of analysis.

Goal theory proposes that task performance is expected to be high when goal difficulty and goal commitment are both high. This suggests that top management commitment to employee–supervisor goal congruence may be an important contingency for the relationship between macro-level goal difficulty and organizational performance. In organizations with difficult goals, for example, increasing the coverage of employee–supervisor goal congruence programs may increase organizational performance; and the contribution of employee–supervisor goal congruence programs to organizational performance may be stronger when top management commitment to these goal congruence programs is high.

Earlier in this chapter we discussed coordination challenges that may confront an organization when a single action may affect performance on many goals simultaneously and in different directions. In addition to the macro-level coordination strategies to improve performance in this situation (Ethiraj & Levinthal, 2009), organizations with such goal conflicts are likely to benefit from effective and efficient top management behaviors for goal selection and prioritization. Gupta, Govindarajan, and Malhotra (1999) hypothesized that feedback-seeking behavior is one such mechanism to reduce the uncertainty and ambiguity that is associated with goal conflict. Although their survey of subsidiary presidents in multinational corporations did not directly measure goal conflict, those authors found that executives facing high levels of goal conflict did report engaging in more frequent feedback-seeking behavior. It may be that, similar to the role of feedback in the learning processes of serial entrepreneurs (Chapter 28), executives in complex situations with conflicting goals also seek to learn how to strengthen their performance. In organizations with difficult goals and high levels of goal conflict facing top management, therefore, the contribution of employee–supervisor goal congruence programs to organizational performance should be stronger when top management engages in more frequent feedback-seeking behavior.

## Strategy

Baum et al. (2001, p. 295), in their study of entrepreneurial venture growth, found that "the greater the motivation of a venture's CEO with respect to vision, goals, and self-efficacy, the greater the likelihood that the venture will select a focus, low-cost, or differentiation strategy." They suggest, however, that this relationship may be specific to organizational contexts in which personal characteristics are strong determinants of organizational strategies. We discuss situationally specific goal contexts later in this chapter. In this section, we review empirical research that applies strategic concepts of governance structure, international scope, and industry characteristics to add to our understanding of macro goal setting.

In multi-unit organizations, also referred to as m-form corporations, subsidiary-level goals may conflict with one another and not readily coexist with or aggregate to the level of the entire organization. Such also may be the case in multinational corporations (MNCs) where each subsidiary faces potential goal conflict introduced by the multiplicity of stakeholders across organizational and national boundaries (Gupta et al., 1999). We expect, therefore, that in multi-unit or multi-division organizations (e.g., m-form or MNCs) the governance of organizational decision making will moderate the relationship between multiplicity of goals and goal conflict. For example, centralized decision making at the top of the organization may be necessary to ensure compliance with goal coordination strategies that cross unit or divisional boundaries, as is the case with the temporal differentiation and single goal focus coordination strategies that we discussed earlier. The unit- and division-level autonomy associated with decentralized decision making, on the other hand, is a stronger fit with the spatial differentiation goal coordination strategy in which each unit makes decisions based only on its performance on its assigned goals. However, we are not aware of any empirical research that has examined these relationships in the field with actual organizations.

Terpstra and Rozell (1994), motivated by propositions from micro-level goal setting theory, surveyed from a random sample of 1000 US companies with 200 or more employees. They received only about 200 surveys for analysis, but found no significant difference in industry type, sales volume, or number of employees between respondents and nonrespondents. Although they did not attempt to aggregate to the organizational level of analysis, they found a significant correlation between respondents' self-reported organizational profitability and use of goal setting practices across the six industries represented in their sample. Subsample analysis, however, showed this positive correlation between goal setting and profitability in just one of the six industries they surveyed: wholesale/retail. We note, however, that Terpstra and Rozell (1994) had about 32 respondents from this industry, but over 90 completed surveys from the manufacturing industry, about 25 respondents from the financial sector, and another 25 from service, and 15 or less in each of two other industries. Terpstra and Rozell (1994) suggest that the small sample size may account for the insignificant correlation in four industries they examine; the significant correlation between goal setting and profitability in the wholesale/retail industry reflects the prevalence and effectiveness of specific sales goals as a motivating device for sales personnel in that industry; and the insignificant correlation between goal setting and profitability in the manufacturing industry may be because the use of automated production technology limits variation in task execution and constrains the relationship between individual motivation and performance in that industry. We recommend that future research apply rigorous research designs to examine the influence of potential macro goal setting contingencies in specific situations; and avoid mixing situational contexts that might limit important variability or introduce spurious influence in critical relationships.

*Environmental Uncertainty*

Macro-level goal setting is an indicator of strategic planning activity in organizations (Boyd & Reuning-Elliott, 1998). In the context of environmental uncertainty, however, strategic options extend beyond the limits of bounded rationality so "establishing specific, difficult goals may be counterproductive because ambiguity concerning processes and outcomes makes the setting of specific goals difficult and sometimes inappropriate ... individuals [should be free] to do their best based on their knowledge, experience, and creativity to pursue, on a contingent basis, multiple alternative goals until the link between cause and effect is established" (Fried & Slowik, 2004, p. 416).

Greve (1998) conceptualized organizational goals as performance objectives and hypothesized that environmental uncertainty increases the likelihood that organizational change will be determined by historical organizational routines. Organizational decision makers, however, can reduce their uncertainty about likely performance outcomes by learning from the referent organizations taking action in the social environment of the marketplace. In this learning process, an organization's decision makers formulate appetites for organizational change and aspirational levels of performance by comparing their organization's performance to the performance of referent organizations in the marketplace. In his study of changing US radio station formats, Greve (1998) found that the likelihood of organizational change decreases as organizational performance increases relative to the social aspiration level, but a prior history of organizational change increases the probability of change even in the absence of performance feedback.

Audia, Locke, and Smith (2000, p. 841) explain that when uncertainty and change lead to anchoring on obsolete goals and strategies, then it may be that "higher future goals are linked with incorrect strategies, [or] this lethal combination can cause performance to drop more rapidly than it would have if high goals had not been set." In short, the relationship between macro-level goal difficulty and performance is likely to be mediated by the strategic alignment of the organization with an uncertain competitive environment. Thus, macro-goal setting research should consider this and other environmental contingencies that may hinder the efficacy of strategy in macro goal setting in actual organizations. For example, if high-performance goals are perceived to be difficult to achieve, then organization members may choose strategies with higher levels of risk (Knight, Durham, & Locke, 2001). We suggest that future research build on this insight to examine relationships between organizational risk appetites and macro goal setting in the context of environment uncertainty.

Examining how macro goals change in uncertain environments also may add to our understanding of the role of uncertainty as a moderator of the goal–performance relationship. For example, uncertainty may increase differences in goal content across participants in organizational goal formulation (Hatfield & Pearce, 1994). Differences in goal content across critical stakeholder groups may increase during periods of uncertainty caused by organizational change. Recently, however, Häsänen et al. (2011, p. 137) observed that "empirical research is somewhat limited when it comes to investigating the possible effects of goal setting during organizational changes."

## Situationally Specific Goal Contexts

Macro goal setting research emphasizes the importance of carefully considering the specific context surrounding the use of goals in organizations. In this chapter section, we discuss recent empirical research on macro goal setting during organizational unit closedown (Häsänen, Hellgren, & Hansson, 2011) and in entrepreneurial venture growth (Baum & Locke, 2004; Baum, Locke, & Smith, 2001).

**Unit Closedown.** Häsänen et al. (2011, p. 137) examined the "effects of goal setting on job performance, goal commitment, job satisfaction, organizational citizenship behaviour and perceived job-induced tension, during the process of a plant closure … of a large medical manufacturing company located in an urban environment in Sweden." They found, somewhat surprisingly, that the work motivation of employees actually increased during the closure. For this chapter, we focus on the macro-level dimensions of goal setting in their study, and we do not discuss their examination of micro-level behaviors and psychology.

Häsänen et al. (2011) argue that macro goal setting established in an ongoing organization must adapt to the announcement of a unit's closedown in order to continue to motivate employee performance. Adaptation to the closedown context is important because specific goals set before the closedown announcement may become obsolete after the announcement. Also, important processes established ex ante to administer performance feedback and rewards for goal achievement will lose motivational power if grounded in time horizons that exceed the expected life of the organizational unit to be closed. To continue to be effective, macro goal setting within the closing unit must manage risks including higher uncertainty introduced by organizational change, lower employee goal commitment because of imminent job loss, less time horizon for learning toward task improvement, and goal conflict between the closing unit and the ongoing organization.

Häsänen et al. (2011) argue that macro goal setting techniques that adapt to the closedown context can improve goal commitment, task learning, and performance outcomes. Accordingly, they hypothesize that outcomes will be higher if goals for a unit going through closedown are more short-term, if supervisors' appraisals of unit employees include evaluations of performance on short-term goals and tangible rewards for achieving these goals, if unit employees understand more of the rationale how their goal performance affects their performance evaluation, if unit goal conflicts are reduced, and if decision making in the unit is more participatory.

To test their hypotheses, Häsänen et al. (2011) conducted a goal setting intervention in a plant going through a 29 month closedown period (from announcement to closure). At the beginning of the intervention, plant employees were given goals for work-related behaviors and tasks; each employee received performance feedback on goals midway through the closedown period; and managers rated employees' goal attainment at the end of the period. In addition, Häsänen et al. (2011) surveyed all 450 plant employees and analyzed responses from 136 employees who each completed two rounds of surveys, the first eight months after announcement of the plant closure and the second survey one year after the first. Their results did not show significant improvement in managers' ratings of job performance during the closedown period; however, their regression analysis did show that survey respondents' performance rating was positively associated with the magnitude of his or her agreement that they clearly understood the goal rationale (including performance measurement and regular feedback on their performance). We note, however, that Häsänen et al. (2011) report low amount of variance explained by this regression model ($R^2$ adjusted $=.09$, $p <.05$), and our ability to interpret their result is confounded by the high multicollinearity they report between goal rationale and other independent variables in the model. Results of their regression on respondents' self-reported goal commitment was positively associated with the magnitude of agreement that tangible rewards (e.g., severance pay, re-employment, retirement, or education) are linked to goal attainment. Again, however, we note the high multicollinearity they report between tangible rewards and other independent variables in the model.

Despite these limitations, the significant relationships reported by Häsänen et al. (2011) suggest that the linkage between organizational goals and individual goals of critical stakeholder groups is an important contingency in goal setting. Further, the relevance of their field-based research design should encourage more research to examine macro-level goal setting in unique and dynamic organizational contexts.

**Entrepreneurial venture growth.** Baum, Locke, and Smith (2001) and Baum and Locke (2004) integrate entrepreneurship research with a variety of theoretical perspectives to develop multidimensional models of entrepreneurial venture growth in which macro goal setting is an important predictor. Baum and Locke (2004) extend and refine the model in Baum et al. (2001) by drawing on the domains of entrepreneurship research and goal, social-cognitive, and leadership theories. Both Baum et al. (2001) and Baum and Locke (2004) apply structural equation modeling to test hypotheses with survey data collected from young, small businesses run by owner-managers in the North American architectural woodwork industry. Although the statistical method in both studies is correlational and there may be reciprocal causal relationships among the variables in their models, both studies' results show significant relationships between micro-level psychology and macro goal setting in the specific context of entrepreneurship. Importantly, Baum and Locke (2004) "is the first to measure the independent effects of goals among entrepreneurs." We discuss both of these studies in more detail below; however, we leave outside the scope of this chapter the content of Baum et al. (2001) and Baum and Locke (2004) that does not specify goals.

Baum et al. (2001) draw on theories of organization, organizational behavior, and strategy to examine the simultaneous influence of competitive strategies, environment, and venture CEO characteristics of personality traits, competencies, and motivation on venture growth performance. They frame CEO goals, vision, and self-efficacy as latent components describing motivation, and find that motivation is a significant direct predictor of venture growth. Baum et al. (2001, p. 299, 301) also find that personality traits of entrepreneurs are "important predictors of venture growth … however, they worked primarily through competencies, motivation and strategy … and that industry-specific skill and relevant technical skill directly affect performance, as do vision, goals, and self-efficacy." As summarized by Baum and Locke (2004, p. 587), "Baum et al. (2001) found that motivation and organization factors have direct effects on new venture performance; however, the effects of the trait and skill composite factors were indirect through motivation and organizational factors." Thus, Baum et al. (2001) show that venture growth is more completely explained by models grounded in multiple theoretical perspectives, and macro-level goal setting is a significant direct path in such models.

Baum and Locke (2004, p. 590), reasoning from the substantial empirical support for goal theory's core proposition "that specific, challenging goals lead to higher performance than other types of goals, [hypothesized that] the higher the entrepreneur-CEO's goals for venture growth, the higher the subsequent venture growth will be." They also hypothesized direct effects on the magnitude of venture growth goals from the entrepreneur-CEO's communicated vision, self-efficacy about venture growth, skills to acquire and exploit new resources, and personality traits of passion and tenacity.

Baum and Locke (2004) test hypotheses with a sample composed of two-year longitudinal data collected in Baum et al. (2001) and another survey collected six years later from the same respondents. This sampling method gives substantial temporal scope to observe venture growth in sales and employment. Here we summarize Baum and Locke's (2004) results that specify the role of goals in venture growth. They found support for their hypotheses that "the higher the entrepreneur-CEO's goals for venture growth, the higher the subsequent venture growth … the more challenging the communicated venture growth content of the entrepreneur-CEO's vision, the more challenging the goals for subsequent venture growth … the higher the entrepreneur-CEO's self-efficacy about venture growth, the higher the goals for subsequent venture growth … the greater the entrepreneur-CEO's passion, the higher the goals for subsequent venture growth … [and] the greater the entrepreneur-CEO's tenacity, the higher the goals for subsequent venture growth." Further, they found that new resource skill is a "predictor of subsequent venture growth because of [its] significant indirect effects through vision, goals, and self-efficacy" (2004, 596).

Baum et al. (2001) and Baum and Locke (2004) significantly advance entrepreneurship research and our understanding of macro goal setting in that domain. However, Baum and Locke (2004) cautioned that their findings in the entrepreneurial context regarding CEO vision, traits, and goals may not be generalizable to larger and more complex organizations. The authors also note that their research did not examine the roles of goal commitment and performance feedback on venture growth, but rather assumed high levels of both in ventures created and managed by founders-owners. Thus, we reiterate a call for empirical research to develop and test multidimensional models of macro goal setting in specific contexts.

## Discussion

This chapter has used Smith and Locke (1990) as a starting point to survey recent quantitative research on macro goal setting. The literature we have reviewed addresses coordination strategies for multiple goals within one organization, the relationship between intermediate and long-term goals, organizational politics, organizational goal congruence, feedback-seeking behavior, stakeholder-driven goal conflict, actual performance–aspirational goals, the alignment of organizational goals with the internal and external environment, and the role of goals in specific situational contexts.

Given the complexity of today's modern organization and the environmental turbulence they face, there still remain substantial empirical gaps in our understanding of macro-level goal setting. Two noteworthy examples are the roles for impossible goals and for external stakeholder goal acceptance.

Impossible goals may motivate organizational creativity or hopelessness-driven inertia. Sitkin, See, Miller, Lawless, & Carton, (2011, p. 559), however, note that "scholars have placed little emphasis on understanding the specific underlying processes through which macro-level goals, particularly unattainable [or stretch] goals, can influence organizational outcomes" (but see Chapter 3).

Externally, an organization's goals are important attributes of its social character because "[a] legitimate organization … is one that is perceived [by its constituents] to be pursuing socially acceptable goals in a socially acceptable manner" (Ashforth & Gibbs, 1990, p. 177). Internally, goal commitment may lead to unethical behavior in organizations that assign performance goals and reward performance (Barsky, 2008). To deter such behavior, Latham (2004, p. 129) points out that "organizations require ethical climates as well as controls to detect and prevent cheating by employees." It may be that internal ethics and external social legitimacy moderate the relationship between macro-level goal setting and performance.

We note that much of the quantitative research surveyed in this chapter is based on surveys. We are mindful that research designs applying survey instruments to investigate macro-goal setting questions must overcome the problem of obtaining access to the top managers of large complex organizations. Further, a particular limitation of survey research is "the post hoc nature of the method of data collection" (Hatfield & Pearce, 1994, p. 446). Though individual behavior is at the core of macro-level phenomena, individual responses to direct questions about the attributes of organizational goals may be confounded by each individual's perception of their own ability, self-efficacy, and commitment (Smith & Locke, 1990). Thus, macro-level measures of goal attributes cannot be grounded in micro-level data collection instruments without first demonstrating construct validity of both the measure and the aggregation mechanism. In addition to validity issues, single method bias is likely to be introduced when one instrument investigates cross-level phenomena. We refer readers to Baum et al. (2001) and Baum and Locke (2004) as exemplars of excellent methodology to ensure reliability, validity, a longitudinal design, and the absence of single method bias in survey-based macro goal setting research.

Cross-level phenomena add to the richness expected in macro goal setting research. Within the organization is the *constituency*, a group of people with similar interests in and perceptions about the organization. This is an analytical level of aggregation between the individual and the overall organization. Vancouver et al. (1994) propose that "[u]sing the constituency to represent units of the organization ... provides a more fine-grained means of operationalizing the organization's goals than assuming the organization is a single entity." For example, in a hierarchical organizational structure, midlevel research questions typically examine *between*-constituency *goal congruence*, such as " ... the degree to which the subordinate constituency agrees with the supervisor constituency" (Vancouver et al., 1994, p. 666). *Within*-constituency goal congruence, however, also may influence goal conflict within an organization. Thus, these authors apply both between- and within-constituency goal congruence to describe a midlevel theoretical perspective on "organizational goal congruence [that] is the agreement between an individual and members of key constituencies within the individual's organization, namely peers and supervisors" (1994, p. 666). Future research can apply the constituency-level of analysis to examine the contingencies influencing employee–organizational goal alignment, the relationships between unit-level goals and employee performance outcomes, and the role of internal informal leadership groups as substitutes for formal organizational hierarchy in macro goal setting processes (Häsänen et al., 2011).

Macro-level research also must consider the implications of the external culture within which the organization is embedded. Over time, the dynamics of legitimacy may cause organizations to internalize the values of its external culture. Field research, for example, is more likely to observe variation in goal commitment with organizations in individualistic cultures than in either collectivistic cultures or laboratory experiments (Erez & Somech, 1996). Also, cultures may vary in their time orientation so that the role of time in macro goal setting may be culture-specific (Fried & Slowik, 2004).

Time is an important dimension in macro goal setting research (Fried & Slowik, 2004). Early studies of macro-level goal setting (e.g., Smith et al., 1990; Terpstra & Rozell, 1994) suggest the need for longitudinal studies to clearly identify the effects of organizational goal setting practices on performance. A more recent laboratory experiment using student teams in a business simulation found that high goals and high self-efficacy contribute to strategic persistence over time even when such persistence is maladaptive to environmental change (Audia et al., 2000). These interesting experimental results suggest a nuanced and dynamic perspective of macro-level goal setting that longitudinal field studies of actual organizations could reveal. The research effort associated with longitudinal studies with large samples, however, causes us to suggest the use of case studies in order to first identify in the field the important dimensions suggested by prior experimental research.

Because of the difficulty of obtaining access to organization managers to identify goals, one fruitful line of future research would be to infer unit, division, and organizational goals from archival documents such as filings with regulatory agencies, annual reports, corporate documents, and media accounts. However, researchers should be cautious about using corporate documents and media reports whose contents have not been independently verified. Agreement across multiple independent sources increases confidence in the reliability of these proxies for the underlying phenomena of interest. We expect that innovative search engine technology will continue to reduce the effort to collect converging archival material from multiple independent sources. Similarly, social media sources may support the observation of the dynamics of organizational goals over time.

While we have not uncovered an abundance of quantitative literature on macro goal setting, what we found is provocative. We expect future research will add to our understanding of macro goal setting by observing organizational action and performance that is influenced and mediated by individual behavior psychologically motivated and enabled, modified, and constrained by the organization and its specific context.

# References

Ashforth, B. E., & Gibbs, B. W. (1990). The double-edge of organizational legitimation. *Organization Science, 1*(2): 177–194.

Audia, P. G., Locke, E. A., & Smith, K. G. (*2000*). The paradox of success: An archival and a laboratory study of strategic persistence following a radical environmental change. *Academy of Management Journal, 43*: 837–853.

Bateman, T. S., O'Neill, H., & Kenworthy-U'Ren, A. (2002). A hierarchical taxonomy of top managers' goals. *Journal of Applied Psychology, 87*(6): 1134–1148.

Barsky, A. (2008). Understanding the ethical cost of organizational goal-setting: A review and theory development. *Journal of Business Ethics, 81*(1): 63–81.

Baum, J. R., & Locke, E. A. (2004). The relationship of entrepreneurial traits, skill, and motivation to subsequent venture growth. *Journal of Applied Psychology, 89*(4): 587–598.

Baum, J. R., Locke, E. A., & Smith, K. G. (2001). A multidimensional model of venture growth. *The Academy of Management Journal, 44*(2): 292–303.

Boyd, B. K., & Reuning-Elliott, E. (1998). A measurement model of strategic planning. *Strategic Management Journal, 19*(2): 181–192.

Cyert, R., & March, J. (1963). *A behavioral theory of the firm.* Englewood Cliffs, NJ: Prentice-Hall.

Ethiraj, S. K., & Levinthal, D. (2009). Hoping for A to Z while rewarding only A: Complex organizations and multiple goals. *Organization Science, 20*(1): 4–21.

Erez, M., & Somech, A. (1996). Is group productivity loss the rule or the exception? Effects of culture and group-based motivation. *The Academy of Management Journal, 39*(6): 1513–1537.

Fried, Y., & Slowik, L. H. (2004). Enriching goal-setting theory with time: An integrated approach. *The Academy of Management Review, 29*(3): 404–422.

Greve, H. R. (1998). Performance, aspirations, and risky organizational change. *Administrative Science Quarterly, 43*(1): 58–86.

Gupta, A. K., Govindarajan, V., & Malhotra, A. (1999). Feedback-seeking behavior within multinational corporations. *Strategic Management Journal, 20*(3): 205–222.

Häsänen, L., Hellgren, J., & Hansson, M. (2011). Goal setting and plant closure: When bad things turn good. *Economic and Industrial Democracy, 32*(1): 135–156.

Hatfield, L., & Pearce, J. A. II (1994). Goal achievement and satisfaction of joint venture partners. *Journal of Business Venturing, 9*: 423–449.

Hunter, J. E., & Schmidt, F. L. (2004). *Methods of meta-analysis: Correcting error and bias in research findings;* (2nd ed.). Thousand Oaks, CA: Sage.

Kaplan, R. S., & Norton, D. P. (2001). Transforming the balanced scorecard from performance measurement to strategic management: Part I. *Accounting Horizons, 15*(1): 87–104.

Klein, H. J., & Kim, J. S. (1998). A field study of the influence of situational constraints, leader-member exchange, and goal commitment on performance. *Academy of Management Journal, 41*(1): 88–95.

Klein, H. J., Wesson, M. J., Hollenbeck, J. R., & Alge, B. J. (1999). Goal commitment and the goal-setting process: Conceptual clarification and empirical synthesis. *Journal of Applied Psychology, 84*(6): 885–896.

Knight, D., Durham, C., & Locke, E. (2001). The relationship of team goals, incentives and efficacy to strategic risk, tactical implementation and performance. *Academy of Management Journal, 44*, 326–338.

Latham, G. P. (2004). The motivational benefits of goal-setting. *Academy of Management Executive, 18*(4): 126–129.

Locke, E. A. (2004). Linking goals to monetary incentives. *The Academy of Management Executive (1993–2005), 18*(4): 130–133.

Locke, E. A., & Latham, G. P. (2002). Building a practically useful theory of goal setting and task motivation: A 35-year Odyssey. *American Psychologist, 57*: 705–717.

Locke, E. A., Latham, G. P., & Erez, M. (1988). The determinants of goal commitment. *Academy of Management Review, 13*(1): 23–39.

Mintzberg, H. (1983). *Power in and around organizations.* Englewood Cliffs, NJ: Prentice-Hall.

Rodgers, R., & Hunter, J. (1991). Impact of management by objectives on organizational productivity. *Journal of Applied Psychology, 76*, 322–336.

Sitkin, S. B., See, K. E., Miller, C. C., Lawless, M. W., & Carton, A. M. (2011). The paradox of stretch goals: Organizations in pursuit of the seemingly impossible. *Academy of Management Review, 36*(3): 544–566.

Smith, K., & Locke, E. A. (1990). Macro vs. micro goal setting research: A call for convergence. In Locke, E. A., & Latham, G. P. 1990. *A theory of goal setting & task performance.* (pp. 320–336). Englewood Cliffs, NJ: Prentice Hall.

Smith, K., Locke, E. A., & Barry, D. (1990). Goal setting, planning and organizational performance: An experimental simulation. *Organizational Behavior and Human Decision Processes, 46*, 118–134.

Terpstra, D. E., & Rozell, E. J. (1994). The relationship of goal setting to organizational profitability. *Group and Organization Management, 19*, 285–294.

Thompson, J. (1967). *Organizations in action.* New York: McGraw-Hill.

Vancouver, J. B., Milsap, R. E., & Peters, P. A. (1994). Multilevel analysis of organizational goal congruence. *Journal of Applied Psychology, 79*, 666–679.

Vancouver, J. B., & Schmitt, N. (1991). An exploratory examination of person-organization fit: Organizational goal congruence. *Personnel Psychology, 44*, 333–352.

Witt, L. A. (1998). Enhancing organizational goal congruence: A solution to organizational politics. *Journal of Applied Psychology*, 83(4): 666–674.

Wright, P. M., O'Leary-Kelly, A. M., Cortina, J. M, Klein, H. J., & Hollenbeck, J. R. (1994). On the meaning and measurement of goal commitment. *Journal of Applied Psychology*, 79(6): 795–803.

Part VI

# Goal Setting in Specific Domains

# 21  The Relevance of Goal Setting Theory for Human Resource Management

*Gary P. Latham*  Rotman School of Management, University of Toronto

*Alana S. Arshoff*  Centre for Industrial Relations and Human Resources, University of Toronto

The practical significance of theories in the behavioral sciences is that they provide a framework for predicting, explaining, and influencing behavior (Latham, 2001). This is particularly true for the beneficial effect of Locke and Latham's theory of goal setting (2002, 2005; Latham & Locke, 2007) for the management of an organization's human resources. Evidence for this assertion can be found in two reviews of the literature where the central role that goal setting theory has played in human resource management is described (Latham, 1983, 1990). The purpose of this chapter is to update those two chapters with a review of the literature published subsequent to 1990. Specifically, the following topics relevant to human resource management are addressed: a super-ordinate goal; employee selection; performance appraisal/management; training, specifically training in self-management; motivation; and union management relations, particularly negotiations. Two topics have been excluded from this list, namely, learning goals and subconscious goals. These two topics are of sufficient importance that they deserve separate chapters devoted to them (see Chapters 13 and 33).

## Superordinate Goal

When the goals of one division, department, or team are viewed as competitive, employees in those respective groups are likely to withhold information. They may even obstruct the goal pursuit of others (Stanne, Johnson, & Johnson, 1999). If the goals among these groups are seen by employees as independent, they may withdraw from interacting with them and become indifferent to the interests of those in "outside" groups. This phenomenon is a frequent outcome in many large law firms as well as departments of psychology and business. The clinical, experimental, and industrial-organizational psychology faculty often display little or no interest in one another. Similarly, the HRM-OB faculty in business schools rarely interact with colleagues in Finance.

A solution to this issue is to set a superordinate goal or vision for the organization as a whole (Latham, 2004). Wong, Tjosvold, and Yu (2005) obtained empirical support for this practice. They found that doing so led to cooperative goal setting between a company and its suppliers. Once the different groups viewed their interests as positively and mutually beneficial, they were less likely to exploit the other, and more likely to work openly for the development of strategies of mutual benefit to both parties.

## Employee Selection

The most frequently used method for selecting employees continues to be the employment interview (Latham & Millman, 2002). Yet the use of the interview for this purpose has been problematic. Applicants are seldom asked the same questions, and when they are asked the same questions the questions typically are not job related; and when the questions are job related, the interviewers frequently are unable to agree among themselves as to what constitutes a good, adequate, or poor answer from an interviewee. Consequently, the reliability and validity of unstructured interviews for the selection of employees has historically been quite low (Wagner, 1949; Mayfield, 1964; Ulrich & Trumbo, 1965).

The situational interview was developed by Latham, Saari, Pursell, and Campion (1980) to minimize the above issues. The theoretical premise underlying the situational interview is that intentions or goals predict behavior. To minimize social desirability responses, a dilemma is presented in each interview question to "force" people to state what they would do in myriad job situations. These situational questions are developed from a systematic job analysis, namely, the critical incident technique (Flanagan, 1954). The situational interview is a structured interview in that the same questions are asked of each applicant. A panel of two or more interviewers evaluates an applicant's response. In order to facilitate objectivity in the scoring process, the situational interview is structured further by requiring subject matter experts, such as supervisors, job incumbents, and customers, to develop a scoring guide consisting of behavioral illustrations of good, acceptable, and poor responses to each SI question. A benefit of developing this scoring guide, in addition to facilitating inter-observer reliability, is that it requires organizational decision makers to articulate and agree on the organization's values. Thus, the SI questions, derived from the job analysis, and the scoring guide for assessing an interviewee's answers are customized to reflect an organization's culture.

With regard to the practicality of the situational interview, Latham and Finnegan (1993) found that managers rated the SI as most practical relative to the unstructured and patterned behavioral description interviews.[1] The same result was obtained from lawyers who defend clients in employment discrimination cases.

With regard to reliability and validity, meta-analyses have revealed that structured interviews, where all applicants are asked the same questions, are preferable to unstructured interviews where different applicants are asked different questions (McDaniel, Whetzel, Schmidt, & Maurer, 1994). Huffcutt and Arthur's (1994) meta-analysis revealed that the mean corrected validity was highest for the interview technique that has the highest degree of structure, namely, the SI (r = .57). This finding corroborates the conclusions of McDaniel et al. that the mean criterion-related validity of the situational interview is higher than that of other selection interviews. Another series of meta-analyses conducted by Cortina, Goldstein, Payne, Davison, and Gilliland (2000) revealed that highly structured interviews have incremental validity beyond measures of cognitive ability and conscientiousness combined.

A subsequent meta-analysis by Huffcutt, Weekley, Weisner, Degroot, and Jones (2001) showed that the validity of the situational interview, unlike the patterned behavior description interview (Janz, 1982), is limited to lower-level jobs. However, meta-analysis, similar to any other statistical technique, is affected by the axiom "garbage in–garbage out." This meta-analysis included data from several studies where the original authors (e.g., Latham & Saari, 1984) had stated that the SI had been misused (i.e., not using the scoring guide). In addition, the meta-analysis excluded the results obtained by Latham and Skarlicki (1995).

Latham and Skarlicki compared the criterion-related validity of the situational interview with the patterned behavior description interview regarding organizational citizenship behavior of university faculty, that is, behavior that typically is not assessed in a formal performance appraisal (Organ, 1988). It is unlikely that many people would consider this a low-level job. The results showed that only the situational interview correlated significantly with anonymous peer ratings of organizational citizenship behavior.

A meta-analysis conducted by Latham and Sue-Chan (1999) revealed that the situational interview is valid for a wide range of jobs, level of employees, performance criteria, and countries. This is likely due to the content validity of the situational interview and the minimization of interviewer biases. The meta-analysis revealed that the mean criterion-related validity is .35 and the mean corrected criterion-related validity is .47. These coefficients are consistent with those reported by Huffcutt and Arthur (1994), McDaniel et al. (1994), and Cortina et al. (2000).

Sue-Chan and Latham (2004) examined the situational interview as a predictor of academic and team performance of MBAs. They found that both the situational interview and cognitive ability had predictive validity for the academic performance of managers and professionals ($n = 75$) in an executive MBA course. Only the situational interview predicted team-playing behavior assessed by peers ($r = .32, p < .05$). The correlation between the situational interview and cognitive ability was not significant.

Similarly, Klehe and Latham (2005) examined the predictive and incremental validity of the situational interview and patterned behavior description interview for team-playing behavior in an MBA program. Both interview techniques were shown to be valid predictors, but only the situational interview, which measures intentions/goals, had incremental validity.

With regard to predicting typical versus maximum performance, Klehe and Latham (2006) conducted a predictive validation study to determine the extent to which the patterned behavior description interview and the situational interview predict typical versus maximum performance. Typical performance reflects choice/motivation; maximum performance assesses ability (Cronbach, 1960). Incoming MBA students were interviewed regarding their intentions/goals for team-playing behavior, as well as for where and how they had demonstrated team-playing behavior in the past. Both the situational interview and the patterned behavior description interview predicted typical performance in study groups. Only the situational interview predicted maximum team-playing performance on a simulation.

In conclusion, empirical research on the situational interview shows that intentions/goals correlate with performance on the job, organizational citizenship behavior, and team-playing behavior. Intentions/goals, as measured by the situational interview, also predict typical and maximum performance.

## Performance Appraisal/Performance Management

Once employees are hired, their performance needs to be assessed and managed. A primary purpose of performance appraisal/management is to coach employees in ways to instill in them the desire for continuous improvement. Two key variables of a performance appraisal are feedback on what an employee should start doing, stop doing, or be doing differently, and goal setting based on this information (Burke, Weitzel, & Weir, 1978; Meyer, Kay, & French, 1965). Goal setting is the mediating variable that explains the effectiveness of feedback for improving an employee's performance (Locke & Latham, 1990). This is because feedback is information that an employee can choose to act on or ignore. Feedback only improves performance when an employee chooses to set one or more goals based on the feedback. Goal setting theory also states that feedback moderates the goal–performance relationship. If employees do not know how they are doing in relation to goal pursuit, it is difficult, if not impossible, for them to adjust the level or direction of their effort, let along adjust their strategies to attain their goal (Locke & Latham, 2002).

Tziner, Joannis, & Murphy (2000) compared three appraisal instruments, namely, behavioral observation scales or BOS (Latham & Wexley, 1977), behavioral expectation scales or BES (Smith & Kendall, 1963), and trait scales to determine the extent to which they facilitate goal setting.[2] Goals set using behavioral observation scales were found to be more specific than those set using behavioral expectation scales or trait scales. This is because behavioral observation scales convey precisely what an employee must do to perform a job effectively.

Latham and Seijts (1997) examined whether the type of appraisal instrument— behavioral observation scales, trait scales, or using no formal appraisal instrument— affected satisfaction with a peer appraisal and perceptions of fairness. Ninety-one managers working in teams on a simulated task provided one another with feedback. Satisfaction with peer appraisals was higher when behavioral observation scales, trait scales, or no formal instrument was used to give feedback than was the case with a trait scale. The perceived fairness of one's appraisal was rated as higher when either the behavioral observation scales or no instrument was used to give a manager feedback than when the feedback was based on a trait scale.

Performance appraisals are discrete events in that they take place quarterly, bi-annually, or, in most instances, annually. A study of 400 companies, however, found that year-round performance management that emphasizes ongoing coaching in terms of feedback and goal setting in relation to the feedback improves organizational performance over that of discrete performance appraisals (Campbell, Garfinkel, & Moses, 1996). Another study examined the effect of coaching executives in a public sector municipal agency (Olivero, Bane, & Kopelman, 1997). The results showed that feedback, collaborative problem solving based on the feedback, and then setting goals improved their productivity. A study in the private sector revealed that senior managers who worked with an executive coach were more likely than other managers to set specific high goals, and to seek feedback on ways to improve their performance (Smither, London, Flautt, Vargas, & Kucine, 2003). This led to an improvement in their performance evaluations from both their supervisor and direct reports.

In addition to ability and feedback, goal setting theory states that goal commitment is a moderator variable of the goal–performance relationship (Locke & Latham, 2002, 2005; Latham & Locke, 2007). In a field study involving rehabilitation counselors in a state agency in the United States, Renn (2003) found that feedback has a positive relationship with job performance only for those employees who have high goal commitment.

It had a negative relationship with performance for those people with low goal commitment. This finding is consistent with the results of a previous meta-analysis that showed a strong relationship between goal commitment and performance, particularly when the goal is difficult (Klein, Wesson, Hollenbeck, & Alge, 1999).

A key variable for effective coaching/performance management is strengthening an employee's outcome expectancy for goal attainment (Bandura, 2001), that is, enabling a person to see the relationship between what he or she is doing and the outcomes the person can expect. Lee, Locke, and Phan (1997) showed that if people do not see how they can attain a high goal, offering a monetary incentive for goal attainment decreases their motivation. Similarly, Boswell and Boudreau (2002) reported that employees who do not see the link between improving their performance and an improvement in their appraisal show little or no motivation to change their behavior. Their findings replicated those obtained by Napier and Latham (1986) in a newsprint facility and bank. Of further relevance to the coaching/performance management process is Latham's (2001) finding that an understanding of an employee's outcome expectancies increases understanding of that person's behavior; changing an employee's outcome expectancies changes the person's behavior. The latter was done to effectively attain an organization's goal to minimize theft in a sawmill.

A controversy that raged throughout the 1970s and 1980s in the goal setting literature was the question as to whether goals should be assigned or set participatively (see Latham, 2007). Goal setting theory is silent on this issue. Empirical research by Latham, Winters, and Locke (1994) provided the answer. Participatively set goals are preferable to assigned goals only when two mediators are present: task strategies and self-efficacy. If participative decision making fails to lead to the development of appropriate task strategies as well as an employee's self-confidence that the strategies can be implemented, participative decision making does not have a beneficial effect on performance.

## Self-Management/Regulation

Even if a specific, high goal is set, even if an employee's outcome expectancy is high as to what must be done to attain the goal, performance will not improve if the self-efficacy for doing what is necessary to attain the goal is low. Self-efficacy is the belief in one's capacity to mobilize the physical, intellectual, and emotional resources necessary to master a task (Bandura, 1997). Thus, those individuals with high self-efficacy for goal attainment focus their attention and effort on the demands of the situation. Their colleagues with low self-efficacy for goal attainment typically focus on personal deficiencies and imagine potential difficulties as more pervasive than they are in reality (see Chapter 10).

Training in self-management/regulation has focused on ways to increase self-efficacy for goal attainment. Millman and Latham (2001) adapted Meichenbaum's (1971, 1977) methodology for shifting dysfunctional to functional self-talk. This training involves teaching people to systematically talk themselves through ways to overcome challenges to performing effectively. Specifically, this technique involves training people to change their negative, dysfunctional self-statements to positive, functional self-statements. The training involves a three-step process whereby a participant (1) observes a trainer model functional self-statements that guide the person through the actions needed to master a task, (2) performs the task while verbally instructing oneself, and (3) performs a task while verbally instructing oneself covertly. By training people in verbal self-guidance (VSG), unemployed managers increased their self-efficacy for finding, and they were more successful in attaining their goal for, re-employment than were the managers in the control group. Latham and Budworth (2006) used VSG to train native North American high school students in finding employment. Again, this technique increased their self-efficacy for, and actually performing well in, a mock selection interview conducted by Caucasian managers who were blind as to who was in the experimental versus the control group. Those in the experimental group also were more successful than their counterparts in the attainment of their goal to obtain employment meaningful to them. Similarly, Yanar, Budworth, and Latham (2009) found that Muslim women in Turkey over the age of 40 who were trained in VSG subsequently had significantly higher self-efficacy for attaining their goal of re-employment, and they persisted longer in job search behavior relative to those in the control group. Most importantly, they were also more likely to find a job in their area of interest within 6–12 months of training than those in the control group.

Brown and Latham (2006) examined the effect of VSG training and goal setting on the performance of students in an MBA program. The results revealed a main effect for VSG on performance effectiveness. Furthermore, there was an interaction effect such that participants who were trained in VSG and set goals had the highest level of performance effectiveness.

A meta-analysis showed an average standard deviation of .91 in the performance of teams with versus without a specific, high goal (O'Leary-Kelly, Martocchio, & Frink, 1994). Consequently, Brown (2003) applied VSG to teams. The results showed that VSG increased both collective efficacy as well as a team's performance.

Mental practice involves the symbolic guided rehearsal of a task in the absence of physical movements (Richardson, 1967). Morin and Latham (2000) used this technique, where goal setting was either implicit or explicit, as a transfer of training intervention to improve the communication skills of supervisors interacting with members of the union executive committee. Six months later, the supervisors who had received training in mental practice and set goals had higher self-efficacy than those in the control group. In addition, self-efficacy correlated significantly with goal commitment and communication skills on the job. Thus, training in VSG and in visualization appear to be effective ways of increasing the ability to attain one's goals.

Sitzman and Ely (2011) conducted a meta-analysis of self-regulated learning in work-related training and educational attainment. Self-regulation was defined as the ability to modulate affective, cognitive, and behavioral processes throughout a learning experience in order to attain a desired level of performance. The meta-analysis revealed that goal difficulty level and its mediators, effort and persistence along with self-efficacy, had the strongest effects on learning (see Chapter 11 for further information on self-management/regulation).

## Motivation

Maier (1955) was among the first to argue that an employee's performance = ability × motivation. Thus, once a person has been trained to do a job well, the person must be motivated to apply the requisite knowledge and skills. Knowledge in the absence of goals is useless to the extent that an employee has no desire to take action to make use of that knowledge (Latham, 2012). Goal setting is a motivational technique (see Chapter 1). Based on goal setting research and goal setting theory, which was inductively developed on the basis of this research, Locke and Latham (1990) proposed a comprehensive framework, the high performance cycle (HPC) for motivating employees. This framework states that (a) challenging, high goals on meaningful growth-facilitating tasks where people have high self-efficacy leads to (2) performance-contingent internal and external rewards that lead to (c) job satisfaction. The consequences of job satisfaction include (d) commitment to the organization. The HPC emphasizes reciprocal determinism in that commitment to the organization leads to (e) an employee's willingness to accept future challenging, high goals.

Latham, Locke, and Fassina (2002) reviewed the literature from 1990 through the spring of 2002 to determine the extent to which the individual pathways in the HPC have been supported, and Latham (2012) reviewed the literature from 2002 to 2007. The results showed that the HPC has withstood the test of time. However, only one study had examined the overall model quantitatively. Selden and Brewer (2000) adapted items from a survey conducted by the US Department of Labor to test the validity of the HPC. Their conclusion was that the model is a sound basis for formulating policies for motivating employees in the federal government.

Borgogni and Della Rousso have developed a scale specifically for assessing the validity of the HPC. In addition, they have applied the HPC in the private sector in Italy. Their scale and the results they obtained are reported in Chapter 18.

## Negotiations and Union–Management Relations

As noted above, Morin and Latham (2000) found that self-management through visualization and goal setting improved the communication skills of supervisors with union officials. That same year, Brown and Latham (2000) reported that unionized telecommunication employees had high performance and high satisfaction with the performance appraisal process when specific, high goals were set.

Both goal setting and self-efficacy are important to performing a negotiation task. Gist, Stevens, and Bavetta (1991) reported that people with high self-efficacy negotiated higher outcomes than those who reported moderate self-efficacy. Galinsky and Mussweiler (2001) found that pursuing a challenging goal in a distributive negotiation improved a negotiator's final outcome. A meta-analysis by Zetik and Stuhlmacher (2002) revealed that negotiators who have specific high, albeit conflicting, goals, attain higher profits than those with no goals.

In a union–management climate where the relationship between the two groups was considered good, Hasanen, Hellgren, and Hansson (2011) studied the effects of management increasing the goals for productivity during a 2-year factory closedown in Sweden. Goal setting was measured with a "back-translated" version of the questionnaire developed by Locke and Latham (1984). Hasanen et al. found, contrary to what might be expected, that (1) employees' job performance increased when the rationale for increasing productivity goals was explained, and feedback was provided regularly on goal attainment. This finding corroborates the laboratory finding obtained by Latham, Erez, and Locke (1988). When people understand the logic, an assigned goal is as effective as a participatively set goal for increasing performance. (2) Contrary to social determination theory (Deci & Ryan, 1990), Hasanen et al. found that tangible rewards predicted an increase in goal commitment and a decrease in job-induced tension. (3) Self-efficacy for goal attainment predicted organizational citizenship behavior, as defined by employees voluntarily assuming more responsibility for the functioning of the organization. (4) Supervisory support and participation in goal setting predicted job satisfaction. This finding is consistent with that obtained earlier by Ronan, Latham, and Kinne (1973) regarding the importance of supervisory supportiveness when setting goals in the logging industry.

## Concluding Comments

HR practices have been shown to be leading indicators of a firm's future financial performance (Watson Wyatt, 2002; Huselid & Becker, 1996). Lawler and Boudreau (2009) argued that the biggest challenge that currently confronts HR today is talent management, that is, how talent is managed in HR. This is because too often HR does not have the right talent, and too often it has talent that is inferior to the talent in other key parts of the organization. Goal setting theory provides a framework for action steps to remedy this situation. Goals can be set for cooperation with and across organizational units. Goals predict an employee's performance in sundry situations. Thus, they can be used to identify who should be hired to perform a job well. Goals and feedback on goal pursuit are the core of effective coaching practices that in turn are the keys to effective performance management and appraisals of employees. Goals and goal feedback are also the critical determinants of training in self-management and ongoing motivation in the workplace. Goals lie at the core of effective negotiations with others. They can even increase performance during the closing of a plant. In short, the setting of specific, high goals is a sound starting point for ensuring a high-performing HR department as well as an organization's human resources as a whole.

## Notes

1  A patterned behavior description interview asks job related questions pertaining to what a job applicant has done in the past.
2  The primary difference between BES and BOS is essentially the same as that which differentiates the Thurstone and Likert approaches to the development of attitude scales. The development of the BES is similar to the Thurstone approach in that judges numerically rate incidents obtained in the job analysis in terms of the extent to which each incident represents effective job behavior. The BOS is similar to the Likert method in that (1) a large number of behavioral statements related to the object in question (e.g., costs) are collected; (2) employees are observed and rated on a 5-point scale as to the frequency with which each of them engages in each of the behaviors; (3) a total score for each employee is determined by summing the observer's responses to all the behavioral items; and (4) a statistical analysis is conducted to identify those behaviors that more clearly differentiate effective from ineffective performers. It is the use of an item or factor analysis in the Likert and BOS methods to select items for building an appraisal instrument that most distinguishes it from the Thurstone/BES method.

# References

Bandura, A. (1997). *Self efficacy: The exercise of control*. New York: W. H. Freeman.

Bandura, A. (2001). Social cognitive theory: An agentic perspective. *Annual Review of Psychology, 52*, 1–26.

Boswell, W. R., & Boudreau, J. W. (2002). Separating the developmental and evaluative performance appraisal uses. *Journal of Business and Psychology, 16*, 391–412.

Brown, T. C. (2003). The effect of verbal self-guidance training on collective efficacy and team performance. *Personnel Psychology, 56*, 935–964.

Brown, T. C., & Latham, G. P. (2000). The effects of goal setting and self-instruction training on the performance of unionized employees. *Industrial Relations, 55*, 80–94.

Brown, T. C., & Latham, G. P. (2006). The effect of training in verbal self-guidance on performance effectiveness in a MBA program. *Canadian Journal of Behavioural Science, 38*, 1–11.

Burke, R. J., Weitzel, W., & Weir, T. (1978). Characteristics of effective performance review and development interviews: Replication and extension. *Personnel Psychology, 31*, 903–919.

Campbell, J. D., Garfinkel, R. B., & Moses, L. (1996). Strategies for success in measuring performance. *HR Magazine, 41*, 98.

Cortina, J. M., Goldstein, N. B., Payne, S. C., Davison, H. K., & Gilliland, S. W. (2000). The incremental validity of interview scores over and above cognitive ability and conscientiousness scores. *Personnel Psychology, 53*, 325–351.

Deci, E. L., & Ryan, R. M. (1990). A motivational approach to self: Integration in personality. In. R. Dienstbier (Ed.), *Nebraska symposium on motivation* (Vol. 38, pp. 237–288). Lincoln, NE: University of Nebraska Press.

Cronbach, L. J. (1960). *Essentials of psychological testing* (2nd ed.). Oxford, England: Harper.

Flanagan, J. C. (1954). The critical incident technique. *Psychological Bulletin, 51*, 327–358.

Galinsky, A. D., & Mussweiler, T. (2001). First offers as anchors: The role of perspective-taking and negotiator focus. *Journal of Personality and Social Psychology, 81*, 657–669.

Gist, M. E., Stevens, C. K., & Bavetta, A. G. (1991). Effects of self-efficacy and post-training intervention on the acquisition and maintenance of complex interpersonal skills. *Personnel Psychology, 44*, 837–861.

Hasanen, L. O., Hellgren, J., & Hansson (2011). Goal setting and plant closure: When bad things turn good. *Economic and Industrial Democracy, 32*, 135–156.

Huffcutt, A. I., & Arthur, W. (1994). Hunter and Hunter (1984) revisited: Interview validity for entry-level jobs. *Journal of Applied Psychology, 79*, 184–190.

Huffcutt, A. I., Weekley, A. I., Weisner, W. H., Degroot, T. G., & Jones, C. (2001). Comparison of situational and behavior description interview questions for higher-level positions. *Personnel Psychology, 54*, 619–644.

Huselid, M. A., & Becker, B. E. (1996). Methodological issues in cross-section and panel estimates of the Human Resource-firm. *Industrial Relations, 35*, 400–422.

Janz, T. (1982). Initial comparisons of patterned behavior description interviews versus unstructured interviews. *Journal of Applied Psychology, 67*, 577–80.

Klehe, U. C., & Latham, G. P. (2005). The predictive and incremental validity of the situational and patterned behavior description interviews for team playing behavior. *International Journal of Selection and Assessment, 13*, 108–115.

Klehe, U. C., & Latham, G. P. (2006). What would you do—really or ideally? Constraints underlying the behavior description interview and the situational interview in predicting typical vs. maximum performance. *Human Performance, 19,* 357–382.

Klein, H. J., Wesson, M. J., Hollenbeck, J. R., & Alge, B. J. (1999). Goal commitment and the goal-setting process: Conceptual clarification and empirical synthesis. *Journal of Applied Psychology, 84,* 885–896.

Latham, G. P. (1983). The central role of goal setting in human resource management. In K. N. Rowland & G. R. Ferris (Eds.), *Research in personnel and human resource* management (pp. 169–199). Greenwich, CT: JAI Press.

Latham, G. P. (1990). The role of goal setting in human resource management. In G. R. Ferris & K. M. Rowland (Eds.), *Performance evaluation, goal setting and feedback* (pp. 185–215). Greenwich, CT: JAI Press.

Latham, G. P. (2001). The importance of understanding and changing employee outcome expectancies for gaining commitment to an organizational goal. *Personnel Psychology, 54,* 707–716.

Latham, G. P. (2004). The motivational benefits of goal setting. *Academy of Management Executive, 18,* 126–129.

Latham, G. P. (2012). *Work motivation: History, theory, research and practice.* Thousand Oaks, CA: Sage.

Latham, G. P., & Budworth, M. H. (2006). The effect of training in verbal self-guidance on the self-efficacy and performance of Native North Americans in the selection interview. *Journal of Vocational Behavior, 68,* 516–523.

Latham, G. P., Erez, M., & Locke, E. A. (1988). Resolving scientific disputes by the joint design of crucial experiments by the antagonists: Application of the Erez-Latham dispute regarding participation in goal setting. *Journal of Applied Psychology Monograph, 73,* 753–772.

Latham, G. P., & Finnegan, B. (1993). Perceived practicality of unstructured, patterned, and situational interviews. In H. Schuler, J. Farr, & M. Smith (Eds.), *Personnel selection and assessment: Individual and organizational perspectives.* Hillsdale, NJ: Erlbaum.

Latham, G. P., & Locke, E. A. (2007). New developments in and directions for goal setting. *European Psychologist, 12,* 290–300.

Latham, G. P., Locke, E. A., & Fassina, N. E. (2002). The high performance cycle: Standing the test of time. In S. Sonnentag (Ed.), *The psychological management of individual performance: A handbook in the psychology of management in organizations* (pp. 201–228). Chichester: Wiley.

Latham, G. P., & Millman, Z. (2002). Context and the employment interview. In J. F. Gubrium & J. A. Holstein (Eds.), *Handbook of interview research: Context and method.* Thousand Oaks, CA: Sage.

Latham, G. P., & Saari, L. M. (1984). Do people do what they say? Further studies on the situational interview. *Journal of Applied Psychology, 69,* 569–573.

Latham, G. P., Saari, L. M., Pursell, E. D., & Campion, M. A. (1980). The situational interview. *Journal of Applied Psychology, 65,* 422–427.

Latham, G. P., & Seijts, G. H. (1997). The effect of appraisal instrument on managerial perceptions of fairness and satisfaction with appraisals from peers. *Canadian Journal of Behavioural Science, 29,* 275–282.

Latham, G. P., & Skarlicki, D. (1995). Criterion related validity of the situational and patterned behavior description interviews with organizational citizenship behavior. *Human Performance, 8,* 67–80.

Latham, G. P., & Sue-Chan, C. (1999). A meta-analysis of the situational interview: An enumerative review of reasons for its validity. *Canadian Psychology, 40,* 56–67.

Latham, G. P., & Wexley, K. N. (1977). Behavioral observation scales for performance appraisal purposes. *Personnel Psychology, 30,* 255–268.

Latham, G. P., Winters, D. C., & Locke, E. A. (1994). Cognitive and motivational effects of participation: A mediator study. *Journal of Organizational Behavior, 15,* 49–63.

Lawler, E. E., & Boudreau, J. W. (2009). *Achieving excellence in human resources management: An assessment of human resources functions.* Stanford, CA: Stanford University Press.

Lee, T. W., Locke, E. A., & Phan, S. H. (1997). Explaining the assigned goal-incentive interaction: The role of self-efficacy and personal goals. *Academy of Management Journal, 23,* 541–559.

Locke, E. A., & Latham, G. P. (1984). *Goal setting: A motivational technique that works.* Englewood Cliffs, NJ: Prentice Hall.

Locke, E. A., & Latham, G. P. (1990). *A theory of goal setting and task performance* (pp. 1–26). Englewood Cliffs, NJ: Prentice Hall.

Locke, E. A., & Latham, G. P. (2002). Building a practically useful theory of goal setting and task motivation: A 35-year odyssey. *American Psychologist, 57,* 705–717.

Locke, E. A., & Latham, G. P. (2005). Goal setting theory: Theory by induction. In K. Smith & M. Hitt (Eds.), *Great minds in management: The process of theory development* (pp. 128–150). Oxford Press.

Maier, N. R. F. (1955). *Psychology in industry* (2nd ed.). Boston: Houghton Mifflin.

Mayfield, E. C. (1964). The selection interview: A reevaluation of published research. *Personnel Psychology, 17,* 239–260.

McDaniel, M. A., Whetzel, D. L., Schmidt, F. L., & Maurer, S. D. (1994). The validity of employment interviews: A comprehensive review and meta-analysis. *Journal of Applied Psychology, 79,* 599–616.

Meichenbaum, D. H. (1971). Examination of model characteristics in reducing avoidance behavior. *Journal of Personality and Social Psychology, 17,* 298–307.

Meichenbaum, D. H. (1977). *Cognitive behavior modification. An integrative approach.* New York: Plenum Press.

Meyer, H. H., Kay, E., & French, J. R. P. (1965). Split roles in performance appraisal. *Harvard Business Review, 43,* 123–129.

Millman, Z., & Latham, G. P. (2001). Increasing re-employment through training in verbal self-guidance. In M. Erez, U. Kleinbeck, & H. K. Thierry (Eds.), *Work motivation in the context of a globalizing economy.* Mahwah, NJ: Lawrence Erlbaum.

Morin, L., & Latham, G. P. (2000). Effect of mental practice and goal setting as a transfer of training intervention on supervisors' self-efficacy and communication skills: An exploratory study. *Applied Psychology: An International Review, 49,* 566–578.

Napier, N. K., & Latham, G. P. (1986). Outcome expectancies of people who conduct performance appraisals. *Personnel Psychology, 39,* 827–837.

O'Leary-Kelly, A. M., Martocchio, J. J., & Frink, D. D. (1994). A review of the influence of group goals on performance. *Academy of Management Journal, 37,* 1285–1301.

Olivero, G., Bane, K. D., & Kopelman, R. E. (1997). Executive coaching as a transfer of training tool: Effects on productivity in a public agency. *Public Personnel Management, 26,* 461–469.

Organ, D. W. (1988). *Organizational citizenship behavior: The good soldier syndrome.* Lexington, MA: Lexington Books.

Selden, S. C., & Brewer, G. A. (2000). Work motivation in the senior executive service: Testing the high performance cycle theory. *Journal of Public Administration Research and Theory, 10,* 531–550.

Smith, P., & Kendall, L. M. (1963). Retranslation of expectations: An approach to the construction of unambiguous anchors for rating scales. *Journal of Applied Psychology, 47,* 149–155.

Smither, J. W., London, M., Flautt, R., Vargas, Y., & Kucine, I. (2003). Can working with an executive coach improve multisource feedback ratings over time? A quasi-experimental field study. *Personnel Psychology, 56,* 23–44.

Stanne, M. B., Johnson, D. W., & Johnson, R. T. (1999). Does competition enhance or inhibit motor performance: A meta-analysis. *Psychological Bulletin, 125,* 133–154.

Sue-Chan, C., & Latham, G. P. (2004). The situational interview as a predictor of academic and team performance: A study of the mediating effects of cognitive ability and emotional intelligence. *International Journal of Selection and Assessment, 12,* 312–320.

Renn, R. W. (2003). Moderation by goal commitment of the feedback-performance relationship: theoretical explanation and preliminary study. *Human Resource Management Review, 13,* 561–580.

Richardson, A. (1967). Mental practice: A review and discussion, Part I. *Research Quarterly, 38,* 95–97.

Ronan, W. W., Latham, G. P., & Kinne, S. B. (1973). The effects of goal setting and supervision on worker behavior in an industrial situation. *Journal of Applies Psychology, 58,* 302–307.

Tziner, A., Joannis, C., & Murphy, K. R. (2000). A comparison of three models of performance appraisal with regard to goal properties, goal perception and rate satisfaction. *Group & Organization Management, 25,* 175–190.

Ulrich, L., & Trumbo, D. (1965). The selection interview since 1949. *Psychological Bulletin, 63,* 100–116.

Wagner, R. (1949). The employment interview: A critical summary. *Personnel Psychology, 2,* 17–46.

Watson Wyatt Worldwide (2002). Human capital index: Human capital as a lead indicator of shareholder value. Washington, D.C.

Wong, A., Tjosvold, D., & Yu, Z. (2005). Organizational partnerships in China: Self-interest, goal interdependence, and opportunism. *Journal of Applied Psychology, 90,* 782–791.

Yanar, B., Budworth, M. H., & Latham, G. P. (2009). The effect of verbal self-guidance training for overcoming employment barriers: A study of Turkish women. *Applied Psychology: An International Review, 58,* 586–601.

Zetik, D. C., & Stuhlmacher, A. (2002). Goal setting and negotiation performance: A meta-analysis. *Group Process and Intergroup Relations, 5,* 35–52.

# 22    Goals and Creativity

*Christina E. Shalley and Gamze Koseoglu*    Scheller College of
Business, Georgia
Institute
of Technology

When the original *Theory of Goal Setting and Task Performance* was published in 1990, there was no research on goals and creativity. Since that time there have been a number of studies focused on this topic, as well as related work that has implications for the effect of goals on creativity. In this chapter, we briefly review all of the relevant empirical research published on goals and creativity, highlight gaps in the literature, and suggest potential areas for future work. First, we provide a brief general overview of the organizational creativity research area in order to provide a foundation for why it is important to examine the relationship between goals and creativity. Then we review the research conducted on goals and creativity by examining the mechanisms through which goals can impact creativity. Next, we discuss the influence of specific characteristics of goals on creativity, followed by a brief discussion of the effect of goal orientation on creativity. Finally, at the end of each section, gaps in our knowledge and areas for future research on goals and creativity are highlighted.

## General Overview of Organizational Creativity Research

Creativity is considered to be a critical success factor for organizations in today's rapidly changing business environment (Amabile, 1988; Ford, 1996; Shalley, Zhou, & Oldham, 2004; Woodman, Sawyer, & Griffin, 1993). Organizations depend on creative ideas from their employees, and creativity has been argued to be the key enabler for performance, growth, and competitiveness (Amabile, 1988; Oldham & Cummings, 1996; Woodman, Sawyer, & Griffin, 1993; Zhou & Shalley, 2008). Increasingly, managers have begun to focus their attention and resources on enhancing employee creativity in order to have their organizations respond in novel and useful ways to dynamic competitive conditions (Drazin, Glynn, & Kazanjian, 1999; Oldham & Cummings, 1996; Shalley, Gilson, & Blum, 2009). As a result, there has been an increase in research focusing on identifying contextual and personal factors that foster creativity (e.g., Grant & Berry, 2011; Madjar, Greenberg, & Chen, 2011; Zhang & Bartol, 2010).

Creativity is defined as the extent to which a product or process is both novel and appropriate (Amabile, Conti, Coon, Lazenby, & Herron, 1996; Shalley et al., 2004). In general, creativity has been conceptualized in two ways in the literature. First, the majority of research to date has treated creativity as an outcome (e.g., Amabile et al., 1996; Elsbach & Hargadon, 2006; Oldham & Cummings; 1996; Perry-Smith & Shalley, 2003; Tierney & Farmer, 2002; Zhou, 1998) that can range from minor adaptations to radical breakthroughs (Mumford & Gustafson, 1988). The second approach to creativity focuses on it as a process (e.g., Csikszentmihalyi, 1997; Drazin et al., 1999; Gilson, Mathieu, Shalley, & Ruddy, 2005; Gilson & Shalley, 2004; Mumford, 2000; Shalley & Perry-Smith, 2008; Shalley & Zhou, 2008), examining ways in which individuals develop creative ideas, including cognitive and behavioral processes. Within our overall organizing framework, we will be reviewing research on goals and creativity that focuses on creativity as both an outcome and a process, and within each section we will discuss research on creative outcomes followed by creative-process-based studies.

Until the 1980s, psychologists primarily studied creativity as an individual difference, such as a personality trait or a cognitive ability (e.g., Barron & Harrington, 1981; Gough, 1979; Runco & Chand, 1995). However, Amabile's componential model of creativity (1983) and Woodman, Sawyer, and Griffin's interactionist perspective (1993) moved the focus of creativity to the social psychological domain, and introduced the necessity of taking context into consideration. For example, according to the interactionist perspective, creativity is the product of the interaction between an individual and the situational context.

One of the first contextual factors examined with regard to creative performance was a "creativity goal." A number of other contextual factors have been studied in the organizational creativity literature (for more comprehensive reviews of this literature, see Anderson, De Dreu, & Nijstad, 2004; George, 2007; Shalley & Zhou, 2008; Shalley, Zhou, & Oldham, 2004; Zhou & Shalley, 2003, 2011). A creativity goal is a stated standard that an individual's output should be creative (i.e., novel and appropriate) or that individuals should engage in creative processes such as playing with ideas, scanning the environment, or being flexible in their thought processes (Shalley, 1991, 2008). Research on creativity goals shifted the efficiency focus of goals (e.g., productivity goals) from more quantitative aspects of performance toward more qualitative aspects of performance (i.e., creativity) (Carson & Carson, 1993). Creativity goals influence both creative outcomes (Carson & Carson, 1993; Shalley, 1991, 1995) and the creative process (Ford & Sullivan, 2004; Litchfield, 2008; Madjar & Shalley, 2008). Moreover, the relationship between creativity goals and creative performance has been investigated at the individual (Carson & Carson, 1993; Madjar & Shalley, 2008; Shalley, 1991, 1995) and team levels (Gilson & Shalley, 2004; Goncalo & Staw, 2006). There also have been a few studies that have looked at the effect of productivity goals on creative performance (Carson & Carson, 1993; Madjar & Shalley, 2008; Shalley, 1991).

## Mechanisms Through Which Goals Influence Creativity

In general, goals have been found to influence performance through four mechanisms: (1) directing attention and focus to the relevant activities; (2) increasing effort; (3) creating persistence, and (4) leading individuals to develop task-relevant cognitive strategies (Locke & Latham, 2002). The literature on goals and creativity is consistent with these four mechanisms. For example, there has been a strong emphasis on the need for individuals to focus their attention, given that the creative thought process is considered to be demanding cognitively. Also, individuals need to be motivated to work hard and persist in order to achieve breakthroughs that may at times require trying alternative cognitive strategies in problem solving.

Since goals are expected to direct individuals' attention toward important facets of the task, the presence of creativity goals should lead individuals to focus their attention and effort toward being creative by exploring possibilities and spending time on expanding potential solutions (Carson & Carson, 1993; Madjar & Shalley, 2008; Mainemelis, 2001; Shalley, 1995). Creativity goals stimulate an individual's thinking by increasing an individual's engagement with the task and increasing their focus on the novelty and usefulness of their ideas (Madjar & Shalley, 2008). Shalley (1995) found that individuals assigned a do-your-best creativity goal had higher creative performance than those with no creativity goal. This was because the presence of a creativity goal causes individuals to spend more time thinking about a task and trying to expand the range of potential solutions considered by searching a number of response pathways and generating a variety of possibilities before settling on a final response. Individuals who are not assigned a creativity goal may explore only a few potential solution pathways before coming up with a final solution.

On the other hand, productivity goals may help to improve quantitative aspects of performance, but inadvertently have a negative effect on creativity if a creativity goal is not present. Essentially, if a productivity goal is set, individuals would be expected to focus their attention and efforts on being as productive as possible. Research has found that goal setting causes aspects of a job for which no goals are set to be ignored (e.g., Bavelas & Lee, 1978; Locke & Bryan, 1969; Rothkopf & Billington, 1979). Shalley (1991) examined this possibility in a study looking at the effect of three levels of productivity goals (i.e., no goal, do-your-best, and specific difficult productivity goal) and three levels of creativity goals (i.e., no goal, do-your-best, and specific difficult creativity goal). Results indicated that individuals assigned both a do-your-best or specific difficult productivity goal had higher creativity if either a do-your-best or specific difficult creativity goal was also assigned. Therefore, the results of this study suggest that if creative performance is desired, setting a creativity goal is important. If goals are set on other performance dimensions, it is critical to also set them for creativity. As further evidence of the importance of a goal being set for desired types of performance, Shalley (1995) found that productivity suffered when a creativity goal was the only type of performance goal assigned. This result was expected both because goals are attentional controls that cause performance not directly addressed by the goal to be ignored, and also because a creativity goal encourages individuals to pursue a variety of solution pathways before generating a final solution. This may sometimes cause individuals to have lower productivity.

Carson and Carson (1993) also looked at both creativity and productivity when a specific, difficult creativity goal, a specific, difficult productivity goal, or both are assigned. They used a different measure of creativity than the other studies reviewed in this chapter. Specifically, they developed an index of statistically infrequent or rare responses for a divergent thinking task. Similar to Shalley (1991), they found that creativity was higher when a creativity goal was assigned alone or in combination with a productivity goal as compared to those assigned only a productivity goal. Also, in those conditions that had a productivity goal either alone or in combination with a creativity goal, individuals had higher productivity than those in the creativity-goal-only condition. Furthermore, there is less of a trade-off between productivity and creativity if multiple goals are assigned. Finally, performance feedback conditions were also included, along with the goal manipulations, and it was found that while multiple goal assignment can reduce the trade-off between productivity and creativity, feedback induces a positive relationship between productivity and creativity.

Besides having an effect on creative performance, how goals influence the creative process by affecting an individual's focus of attention has received some consideration. For instance, a study by Madjar & Shalley (2008) looked at both the creative process (i.e., incubation) and creative performance. Specifically, they examined whether an intervening task (i.e., noncreative task) distracts an individual's attention from the primary tasks (i.e., two creative tasks) and whether this varies by the presence of specific goals. Three conditions were compared in this study. In the first condition, individuals were only assigned a creativity goal for the two creative tasks. In the second condition, only a productivity goal for the intervening, noncreative task was assigned. Finally, in the third condition, both types of goals were assigned (i.e., creativity goal on the creative tasks and productivity goal on the intervening task). Madjar and Shalley found that when individuals had both a creativity goal for the creative tasks and a productivity goal on the intervening task, this causes them to keep a similar rhythm and pace on the intervening task as on the creative tasks and have higher creative performance compared to those not assigned a productivity goal for the intervening task. Results of this study also indicated that focus of attention mediated the effect of goals on creativity by shifting attention between one task and another. This study was the first to investigate how goal assignment on an intervening task can affect creative performance on creative tasks. It is not just having a goal on an intervening task that is important; the goal helps in refocusing attention for creativity. So, having multiple goals at the same time helps attention to be distributed across multiple tasks.

Finally, it should be mentioned that in the creativity literature, intrinsic motivation has been considered to be important for creative performance (Amabile, 1988; Oldham & Cummings, 1996) since it is one of the key components of creativity according to Amabile's (1983) componential model. Intrinsic motivation is inner-directed interest in or fascination with a problem or task. Intrinsic motivation has not been directly studied as a mechanism that explains the effect of goal setting on creativity. According to cognitive evaluation theory (Deci & Ryan, 1985), contextual factors influence the level of intrinsic motivation through two aspects: controlling and informational. The controlling aspect pressures the individuals to achieve a certain level of outcome or act in a specified way (Shalley & Perry-Smith, 2001). Therefore, this aspect is suggested to have a detrimental effect on intrinsic motivation since it reduces individuals' sense of autonomy (Deci & Ryan, 1985; Deci, Ryan, & Koestner, 1999). On the contrary, the informational aspect provides relevant information about the task without exerting performance pressure or dictating certain ways of acting (Shalley & Perry-Smith, 2001). Therefore, it is suggested that this aspect enhances intrinsic motivation by fulfilling individuals' need to feel competent (Deci & Ryan, 1985; Deci, Ryan, & Koestner, 1999). Using a cognitive evaluation framework, it could be argued both that the presence of goals may cause individuals to feel pressured to attain them (Amabile, Hadley, & Kramer, 2002) and that goals can provide a standard that can be used in order to gain information regarding competence on a task (Shalley, 1991). In other words, goals could potentially have both informational and controlling components. Since the empirical work that has examined goals and creativity has not used a cognitive evaluation framework, the relative effect of controlling or informational characteristics of goals for creativity has not been studied.

However, in the research conducted so far, there has been consistent empirical support for goals having a positive relationship with creativity. For example, in a study of customer service teams' engagement in creative processes, Gilson and Shalley (2004) found that the more creative teams were those that were higher on shared goals for task accomplishments. They suggested that if individuals believe that creativity is an important part of their job (e.g., a type of goal, objective or job requirement), they will have higher motivation to try new approaches and engage in creative processes. Relatedly, Amabile and Gryskiewicz (1987) found that R&D professionals cited management's setting clear, organizational goals as a critical factor for high creativity as opposed to when no clear goals are set.

In summary, it should be noted that more empirical research on creativity goals and their effect on creative performance is warranted. Research is needed to further examine how goals affect individuals or teams engagement in creative processes. Finally, the role of focus of attention as a mediator of the relationship between goals and creativity should be examined further.

## Characteristics of Goals and Creativity

The effect of specific characteristics of goals on quantitative aspects of performance (i.e., productivity) has long been studied in the literature. A number of these characteristics have also been examined for a qualitative aspect of performance, namely, creativity. In this section, we examine the influence of the specificity and difficulty of creativity goals on creative performance, the role of feedback, multiple goals, and research on creativity goals at the team level.

### *Goal Specificity and Goal Difficulty*

Goal specificity and goal difficulty are two key features of goal content (Locke and Latham, 1990). One of the core findings of goal setting theory is that specific, difficult goals lead to higher productivity compared with do-your-best goals or no goals (Latham & Locke, 1991). This has been examined within the context of creativity goals as well (Shalley, 1991). Specifically, it was found that in order to be creative, individuals need to have their attention and effort focused on either a do-your-best creativity goal or a specific, difficult creativity goal, with no improvement in creative performance for a specific, difficult creativity goal over the creative performance of those with a do-your-best creativity goal. Shalley offered two possibilities for why creativity goals act differently than productivity goals with regard to the importance of goal specificity. First, goal specificity may be important for quantitative aspects of performance, but not for creativity. Rather, it may be that the presence of a creativity goal facilitates creativity by causing individuals to focus their attention and effort on being as creative as possible. Second, since the task used in this study was a complex, heuristic task (i.e., open ended and ill structured), it may be that the goal setting effects found by previous research do not hold for tasks of this type but for more simple tasks requiring less cognitive demands on the individual (Campbell, 1984).

Future research should examine whether there are ways to phrase specific creativity goals that add value for creativity over and above a do-your-best creativity goal. Also, research should further examine the effect of creativity goal specificity on creative performance for different types of tasks. In addition, no study has examined the role of goal difficulty on creative performance for either productivity or creativity goals. Shalley's (1991) study could be taken as suggesting that creativity goal difficulty does not matter for creative performance, but there is no direct empirical examination of this. Also, we know nothing about the effect of varying the difficulty level of productivity goals on an individual's creative performance.

## Feedback

Carson and Carson (1993), drawing on work that has found that both goals and knowledge of results are needed to improve task performance (Locke & Latham, 1990), examined whether goal setting in combination with feedback has stronger positive effects, and if this varied by whether it is creative performance or quantity of performance. Specifically, all participants completed a practice trial, and those in the goal with feedback conditions were given feedback on their quantity and/or creative performance for that trial. They found that individuals value feedback on their creative performance more than on their quantity of performance. This is because individuals have an easier time evaluating the quantitative aspects of their performance than they do evaluating how they are doing in relation to qualitative aspects of their performance, such as creativity. Even though there is a growing literature on the effect of feedback and creativity (see Zhou, 2008, for a review), the interaction of creativity goals and feedback on a variety of dimensions (i.e., characteristics of feedback, the feedback seeker, and the feedback receiver) should be examined.

## Multiple Goals

In organizational settings, employees typically have to work on a number of different job assignments simultaneously. Therefore, it is important to understand the effect of multiple goals on creativity. Researchers have focused on the co-occurrence of productivity and creativity goals (Carson & Carson, 1993; Shalley, 1991), the effect of having multiple goals on different tasks, and their effect on each of the tasks (Madjar & Shalley, 2008), and goal conflict (James, 1995). Each of these pieces will be discussed in more detail.

As discussed earlier in this chapter, research (Carson & Carson, 1993; Shalley, 1991) has found that creativity and productivity goals assigned at the same time do not necessarily create conflict. This is because individuals have the ability to focus their attention on both of these goals. Thus, if there are two separate goals assigned for two separate performance dimensions (i.e., creativity and productivity), performance on each dimension should be high. On the other hand, a problem occurs when there is an assigned goal for one of the performance dimensions but not the other. For instance, having a difficult or do-your-best productivity goal in the absence of a creativity goal has been found to decrease creative performance (Carson & Carson, 1993; Shalley, 1991). Similarly, these studies found that individuals have lower productivity if they are assigned a creativity goal but not a corresponding productivity goal. Therefore, in order to maintain high levels of performance on both qualitative and quantitative performance dimensions, having multiple goals for each dimension is necessary.

Also, as discussed earlier in this chapter, Madjar and Shalley (2008) examined the independent and joint effects on creative performance of having a creativity goal on two creative tasks and a productivity goal on an intervening task, with the discretion to switch between these two tasks. They found that assignment of a creativity goal for the creative tasks had a positive, significant effect on their creativity, consistent with prior research (e.g., Shalley, 1995). Results also indicated that assigning a creativity goal for the creative tasks and a productivity goal for the intervening task had a positive effect on creative performance. Moreover, they found that the highest creative performance occurred when individuals were assigned a productivity goal for the intervening task and a creativity goal for the two creative tasks along with having the discretion to switch tasks. They suggested that this occurred because the goals focused individuals' attention on working hard on all three tasks, and they had the ability to take a break if needed to refresh themselves.

In a related study that looked at the originality of idea generation on an alternative uses task, James (1995) examined the interactive effect of individual's self-definitions (i.e., socially oriented versus instrumentally oriented) and goal conflict (i.e., conflict between career and family versus no conflict). In this study, he used instructions to activate self-definitions, and the participants read a passage concerning career and family where career and family goals were presented as either complementary or in conflict. He found a significant three-way interaction between self-definitions, goal conflict, and whether the tasks were congruent or incongruent with individuals' self-definitions. Specifically, if conflict was perceived by an individual, he or she had higher originality if the task was congruent rather than incongruent with this individual's self-definition. Partial support was found for the proposition that originality on tasks that are seen as less central to the individual's self-definition is highest in the absence of goal conflict.

Although the above findings provide consensus that multiple goals do not lead to performance loss, there is still much we do not know about the effects of multiple goals on creativity. For example, research could examine the potential effects of individual differences and multiple goals on creative performance. It may be worthwhile to examine the interactive role of self-efficacy, creative personality, or goal orientation. In addition, proximal and distal goals have played an important role in terms of achieving higher levels of productivity (Locke & Latham, 2002). However, the impact of the co-occurrence of such goals on creativity has not been investigated.

## Team Goals

Individual goals and team goals have been found to function in parallel ways, serving as a self-regulatory process at both levels (DeShon, Kozlowski, Schmidt, Milner, & Wiechmann, 2004). Therefore, creativity goals can be considered at the team level, in addition to the individual level. Creative or innovative tasks generally require a higher level of uncertainty and ambiguity compared to noninnovative tasks. Having creativity goals may serve to help teams deal with this uncertainty and maintain higher levels of effectiveness and efficiency in their innovative tasks to produce better solutions (Hoegl & Parboteeah, 2003). In the organizational creativity literature, historically there has been much less research on team creativity (Shalley, Zhou, & Oldham, 2004). However, recently there has been a significant increase in the number of studies that have focused on team creativity. Unfortunately, there has been little work directed at goals and creativity for teams. Two studies that have specifically examined goals and creativity are summarized below, along with a detailed discussion of areas that future research should consider. Additionally, there are two team studies that have examined goal orientation and creativity, and these are discussed in the next section on goal orientation.

Goncalo and Staw (2006) studied the interactive effect of team values (i.e., individualism versus collectivism) and team goals. Their manipulation of creative versus practical goals was in the form of instructions that stated that they were to work on a creative/practical decision-making task that involved brainstorming multiple solutions to a problem. They were asked to provide either creative or practical solutions. They found a significant interaction of culture and task goals. Specifically, individualistic teams were more creative than collectivist teams when they had a goal to be creative versus practical. Differences on the cultural variable were either nonsignificant or in the opposite direction when instructed to be practical on their different creative performance dimensions (i.e., fluency, flexibility, overall creativity, and most creative idea selected). These results led the researchers to conclude that individualist rather than collectivist team values are beneficial when creativity is the goal.

Using both quantitative and qualitative methods, Gilson and Shalley (2004) examined the engagement in creative processes of teams of service technicians who maintained large office equipment at customer sites. Teams that had stronger shared goals among team members engaged in more creative processes at work. Shared goals led to shared beliefs and understandings among team members concerning their priorities and desired outcomes for the team. Team goal congruence increased effort, efficiency, and effectiveness.

At the team level, there are a number of understudied areas on goals and creativity. First, teams' and team members' characteristics in relation to goals have been overlooked in the creativity literature. For example, team level personality and team level goal orientation have not been studied in relation to team creativity. Second, new directions should be taken by looking at different compositional factors, such as the influence of goal diversity in teams, the effect of faultlines in teams due to goal diversity, and the impact of goal conflict among team members. For example, at the team level, each individual may have the same type of goals, but the extent to which they are committed to these goals could be quite different. So, goal conflict and diversity can exist in teams due to the differences in goal content, or to different levels of goal commitment among team members. Third, team member's reward dependency on each other may influence the goal setting–creativity relationship, since extrinsic rewards have been found to influence creativity in different ways depending on the context and personality factors (Baer, Oldham, Cummings, 2003). Finally, characteristics of team goals (e.g., team creativity goal specificity, difficulty, and multiple team goals); interaction effects of team inputs (e.g., team composition, characteristics of teams and team members) and interaction effects of team processes (e.g., adaptation) have not been examined. Future research should focus on these areas to better understand the influence of team goals on team and individual creativity.

## Goal Orientation and Creativity

The impact of goal orientation on creative performance has recently received attention. In general, learning goal orientation (LGO) is thought to affect creative performance because it plays a major role in the acquisition of creativity relevant skills, domain relevant skills, and intrinsic motivation (Hirst, van Knippenberg, & Zhou, 2009). These are three key foundations for creativity according to Amabile's (1983) componential model of creativity. For example, individuals with higher LGO are motivated to work on acquiring new skills and understanding tasks (Janssen & van Yperen, 2004). Also, they are expected to have a higher intrinsic interest in working on challenging tasks, since they should have lower levels of fear of failure and be more likely to seek feedback to improve themselves. As for individuals high on performance orientation, they are not expected to be as creative as those high on LGO. However, some people are motivated by extrinsic factors such as rewards, competition, or receiving external recognition of their work. Performance goal orientation focuses on the demonstration of competence to others (VandeWalle, 1997). The two subdimensions of performance orientation, performance prove and performance avoid, would be expected to have different influences on creative performance. An individual with a performance-prove orientation would seek out favorable judgment from others, while an individual with a performance-avoid orientation would be concerned about avoiding unfavorable competence judgments. Therefore, performance-prove individuals may be more creative if creative performance is valued as a way to demonstrate competence (Hirst et al., 2009). On the other hand, those with a performance-avoid orientation would be less creative because they would want to avoid being seen as incompetent, which could occur since creativity involves working on challenging tasks and taking risks that potentially could lead to failure.

Gong, Huang, and Farh (2009) examined the direct and indirect effects of learning goal orientation on employee creativity since they viewed learning as an essential part of creativity. The mediating role of creative self-efficacy was examined in this study because when individuals believe their abilities are malleable (i.e., high on LGO), they tend to have relatively high self-efficacy. Also, those high on LGO use the negative feedback they receive to learn, keeping their self-efficacy high. They found that the indirect effect of LGO on creativity is mediated by creative self-efficacy. On the other hand, Simmons and Ren (2009) emphasized the moderation effect of LGO rather than its main effect. They argued that individuals have higher creativity under high- compared to low-risk situations. Consequently, they examined whether an individuals' goal orientation enhances (i.e., LGO) or diminishes (i.e., performance avoid and performance prove) the relationship of risk to creative performance. They found that the positive relationship between risk and creative performance became stronger if the individual had a low performance-avoid orientation. However, they found no significant moderation effects of LGO or a performance-prove orientation.

Two studies have considered the effect of goal orientation at multiple levels. Hirst et al. (2009) examined the cross-level influences of an individual's creative performance. Specifically, they examined the cross-level interaction between an individual's goal orientation and team learning behavior. They found that for teams with higher team learning behavior, there was an attenuated relationship between an individual's LGO and creative performance. Team learning behavior moderated the relationship between an individual's learning goal orientation and that person's creativity. Also, an individual's approach orientation was only positively related to creativity when team learning behavior was high. In another study, Hirst, van Knippenberg, Chen, and Sacramento (2011) examined the moderation effect of team bureaucratic practices on the goal orientation–creativity relationship. Centralization (i.e., distribution of power within the team) and formalization (i.e., extent to which specified rules and procedures exist) were the two contextual factors considered in this study. Specifically, they found that LGO was positively related to creativity only when there was low centralization, and a performance-prove orientation was positively related to creativity only when formalization was low. In addition, the negative relationship between performance-avoid orientation and creativity became stronger in contexts of low centralization. Together, their findings indicate that team bureaucratic practices may influence individuals' goal-directed behavior to activate or inhibit the creative expression of goal orientation.

Future research in this area should further examine the role of goal orientation for creativity. In particular, research has indicated that the three goal orientations can coexist differently within individuals. So future research could look at the different patterns of goal orientation, and how that affects an individual's and team's creativity. Also, more research related to Hirst and colleagues' (2011) piece on placing individuals within their context and seeing the potential positive or negative effects of context on creative performance depending on personal characteristics is warranted.

## Conclusion

Over the last 20 or so years, a body of research focusing on goals and creativity has developed. While this research has started to address important issues, there is still work that can be done in this area to better inform both literatures. In this chapter, we have reviewed all the relevant empirical research published to date, and pointed out important gaps in the literature for future research. The major research findings on goals and creativity are summarized in the following paragraph.

First, creativity goals are an important device in mobilizing attention and effort toward being creative on a task. Goal specificity does not seem to be important for creativity goals; rather, what is critical is for an individual to know that creativity is a desired outcome by having a do-your-best or specific, difficult creativity goal. Second, similar to past research with productivity goals, when goals are set solely for productivity rather than also setting a goal for creativity, creative performance will suffer. Third, performance feedback on prior performance in combination with creativity goals can improve performance over and above the performance of those only given creativity goals. Fourth, multiple goals can be set for different performance dimensions (i.e., creativity and productivity), and performance will be higher on these dimensions, since multiple goals have been found to help distribute attention across multiple tasks. Fifth, team goals can also be effective in enhancing team creativity. Finally, individuals' goal orientations (e.g., learning goal orientation) are typically studied as mediators or moderators in their relationship to creativity.

## References

Amabile, T. M. (1983). The social psychology of creativity: A componential conceptualization. *Journal of Personality and Social Psychology, 45*, 357–377.

Amabile, T. M. (1988). A model of creativity and innovation in organizations. In B. M. Staw & L. L. Cummings (Eds.), *Research in Organizational Behavior, 10*, 123–167.

Amabile, T. M., Conti, R., Coon, H., Lazenby, J., & Herron, M. (1996). Assessing the work environment for creativity. *Academy of Management Journal, 39*: 1154–1184.

Amabile, T. M., & Gryskiewicz, S. S. (1987). Creativity in the R&D laboratory. *Technical Report No. 30*, Greensboro, NC: Center for Creative Leadership.

Amabile, T. M., Hadley, C. N., & Kramer, S. J. (2002, August). Creativity under the gun. *Harvard Business Review, 80*, 52–61.

Anderson, N., De Dreu, C. K. W., & Nijstad, B. A. (2004). The routinization of innovation research: A constrictively critical review of the state-of-the-science. *Journal of Organizational Behavior, 25*, 147–153.

Baer, M., Oldham, G. R., & Cummings, A. (2003). Rewarding creativity: When does it really matter? *Leadership Quarterly, 14*, 569–586.

Barron, F., & Harrington, D. M. (1981). Creativity, intelligence, and personality. *Annual Review of Psychology, 32*, 439–476.

Bavelas, J., & Lee, E. S. (1978). Effect of focal level on performance: A trade-off of quantity and quality. *Canadian Journal of Psychology, 32*, 219–240.

Campbell, D. J. (1984). The effects of goal contingent payment on the performance of a complex task. *Personnel Psychology, 37*, 23–40.

Carson, P. P., & Carson, K. D. (1993). Managing creativity enhancement through goal setting and feedback. *Journal of Creative Behavior, 27*, 36–45.

Csikszentmihalyi, M. (1997). *Creativity*. HarperCollins: New York.

Deci, E. L., & Ryan, R. M. (1985). *Intrinsic motivation and self-determination in human behavior*. New York: Plenum.

Deci, E. L., Ryan, R. M., & Koestner, R. (1999). A Meta-analytical review of experiments examining the effect of extrinsic rewards on intrinsic motivation. *Psychological Bulletin, 125*, 627–668.

DeShon, R. P., Kozlowski, S. W. J., Schmidt, A. M., Milner, K. R., & Wiechmann, D. (2004). A multiple-goal, multilevel model of feedback effects on the regulation of individual and team performance. *Journal of Applied Psychology, 89*, 1035–1056.

Drazin, R., Glynn, M. A., & Kazanjian, R. K. (1999). Multilevel theorizing about creativity in organizations: A sensemaking perspective. *Academy of Management Review, 24*, 286–307.

Elsbach, K. D., & Hargadon, A. B. (2006). Enhancing creativity through "mindless" work: A framework of workday design. *Organization Science, 17*, 470–483.

Ford, C. M. (1996). A theory of individual creative action in multiple social domains. *Academy of Management Review, 21*, 1112–1142.

Ford, C. M., & Sullivan, D. M. (2004). A time for everything: How the timing of novel contributions influences project team outcomes. *Journal of Organizational Behavior, 20*, 1139–1155.

George, J. M. (2007). Creativity in organizations. In J. P. Walsh & A. P. Brief (Eds.), *Academy of management annals, 1*, 439–477. New York: Lawrence Erlbaum.

Gilson, L. L., & Shalley, C. E. (2004). A little creativity goes a long way: An examination of team's engagement in creative processes. *Journal of Management, 30*, 453–470.

Gilson, L.L., Mathieu, J. E., Shalley, C. E., & Ruddy, T. M. (2005). Creativity and standardization: Complementary or conflicting drivers of team effectiveness? *Academy of Management Journal, 48*, 521–531.

Goncalo, J. A., & Staw, B. M. (2006). Individualism-collectivism and group creativity. *Organizational Behavior and Human Decision Processes, 100*, 96–109.

Gong, Y., Huang, J. C., & Farh, J. L. (2009). Employee learning orientation, transformational leadership, and employee creativity: The mediating role of employee creative self-efficacy. *Academy of Management Journal*, 52: 765–778.

Gough, H. G. (1979). A creative personality scale for the adjective check list. *Journal of Personality and Social Psychology, 37,* 1398–1405.

Grant, A. M., & Berry, J. (2011). The necessity of others is the mother of invention: Intrinsic and prosocial motivations, perspective-taking, and creativity. *Academy of Management Journal, 54,* 73–96.

Hirst, G., van Knippenberg, D., & Zhou, J. (2009). A multi-level perspective on employee creativity: Goal orientation, team learning behavior, and individual creativity. *Academy of Management Journal, 52,* 280–93.

Hirst, G., van Knippenberg, D., Chen, C., & Sacramento, C. A. (2011). How does bureaucracy impact individual creativity? A cross-level investigation of team contextual influences on goal orientation–creativity relationships. *Academy of Management Journal, 54,* 624–641.

Hoegl, M., & Parboteeah, K. P. (2003). Goal setting and team performance in innovative projects: On the moderating role of teamwork quality. *Small Group Research, 34,* 3–19.

James, K. (1995). Goal conflict and originality of thinking. *Creativity Research Journal, 8,* 285–290.

Janssen, O., & Van Yperen, N. W. (2004). Employees' goal orientations, the quality of leader-member exchange, and the outcomes of job performance and job satisfaction. *Academy of Management Journal, 47,* 368–384.

Latham, G. P., & Locke, E. A. (1991). Self-regulation through goal setting. *Organizational Behavior and Human Decision Processes, 50,* 212–247.

Litchfield, R. C. (2008). Brainstorming reconsidered: A goal-based view. *Academy of Management Review, 33,* 649–668.

Locke, E. A., & Bryan, J. F. (1969). The directing function of goals in task performance. *Organizational Behavior and Human Resource Performance, 4,* 35–42.

Locke, E. A., & Latham, G. P. (1990). *A theory of goal-setting and task performance.* Englewood Cliffs, NJ: Prentice-Hall.

Locke, E. A., & Latham, G. P. (2002). Building a practically useful theory of goal setting and work motivation: A 35 year odyssey. *American Psychologist, 57,* 705–17.

Madjar, N., Greenberg, E., & Chen, Z. (2011). Factors for radical creativity, incremental creativity, and routine, noncreative performance. *Journal of Applied Psychology, 96,* 730–743.

Madjar, N., & Shalley, C. E. (2008). Multiple tasks' and multiple goals' effect on creativity: forced incubation or just a distraction? *Journal of Management, 34,* 786–805.

Mainemelis, C. (2001). When the muse takes it all: A model for the experience of timelessness in organizations. *Academy of Management Review, 26,* 548–565.

Mumford, M. D., & Gustafson, S. B. (1988). Creativity syndrome: Integration, application, and innovation. *Psychological Bulletin, 103,* 27–43.

Mumford, M. D. (2000). Managing creative people: Strategies and tactics for innovation. *Human Resources Management Review, 10,* 313–351.

Oldham, G. R., & Cummings, A. (1996). Employee creativity: Personal and contextual factors at work. *Academy of Management Journal, 39,* 607–634.

Perry-Smith, J. E., & Shalley, C. E. (2003). The social side of creativity: A static and dynamic social network perspective. *Academy of Management Review, 28,* 89–106.

Rothkopf, E. Z., & Billington, M. J. (1979). Goal-guided learning from text: Inferring a descriptive processing model from inspection times and eye movements. *Journal of Educational Psychology, 63*, 295–302.

Runco, M. A., & Chand, I. (1995). Cognition and creativity. *Educational Psychology Review, 7*, 243–267.

Shalley, C. E. (1991). Effects of productivity goals, creativity goals, and personal discretion on individual creativity. *Journal of Applied Psych*ology, *76*, 179–185.

Shalley, C. E. (1995). Effects of coaction, expected evaluation, and goal setting on creativity and productivity. *Academy of Management Journal, 38*, 483–503.

Shalley, C. E. (2008). Creating roles: What managers can do to establish expectations for creative performance. In J. Zhou, & C. E. Shalley (Eds.), *Handbook of organizational creativity* (pp. 147–164). Mahwah, NJ: Lawrence Erlbaum.

Shalley, C. E., Gilson, L., & Blum, T. C. (2009). Interactive effects of growth need strength, work context, and job complexity on self-reported creative performance. *Academy of Management Journal, 52*, 489–505.

Shalley, C. E., & Perry-Smith, J. E. (2001). Effects of social-psychological factors on creative performance: The role of informational and controlling expected evaluation and modeling exercise. *Organizational Behavior and Human Decision Processes, 84*, 1–22.

Shalley, C. E., & Perry-Smith, J. E. (2008). The emergence of team creative cognition: The role of diverse outside ties, socio-cognitive network centrality, and team evolution. *Strategic Entrepreneurship Journal, 2*, 23–41.

Shalley, C. E., & Zhou, J. (2008). Organizational creativity research: A historical overview. In J. Zhou and C. E. Shalley (Eds.), *Handbook of organizational creativity* (pp. 3–31). New York: Lawrence Erlbaum.

Shalley, C. E., Zhou, J., & Oldham, G. R. (2004). The effects of personal and contextual characteristics on creativity: Where should we go from here? *Journal of Management, 30*, 933–958.

Simmons, A. L., & Ren, R. (2009). The influence of goal orientation and risk on creativity. *Creativity Research Journal, 21*, 400–408.

Tierney, P., & Farmer, S. M. (2002). Creative self-efficacy: Potential antecedents and relationship to creative performance. *Academy of Management Journal, 45*, 1137–1148.

VandeWalle, D. (1997). Development and validation of a work domain goal orientation instrument. *Educational and Psychological Measurement, 57*, 995–1015.

Woodman, R. W., Sawyer, J. E., & Griffin, R. W. (1993). Toward a theory of organizational creativity. *Academy of Management Review, 18*, 293–321.

Zhang, X., & Bartol, K. M. (2010). Linking empowering leadership and employee creativity: The influence of psychological empowerment, intrinsic motivation, and creative process engagement. *Academy of Management Journal, 53*, 107–128.

Zhou, J. (1998). Feedback, valence, feedback style, task autonomy, and achievement orientation: Interactive effects on creative performance. *Journal of Applied Psychology, 88*, 413–422.

Zhou, J. (2008). Promoting creativity through feedback. In J. Zhou, & C. E. Shalley (Eds.), *Handbook of organizational creativity* (pp. 125–146). New York: Lawrence Erlbaum.

Zhou, J., & Shalley, C. E. (2003). Research on employee creativity: A critical review and directions for future research. In J. Martocchio & G. R. Ferris (Eds.), *Research in personnel and human resource management, 22*, 165–217. Greenwich, CT: JAI Press.

Zhou, J., & Shalley, C. E. (2008). Expanding the scope and impact of organizational creativity research. In J. Zhou, & C. E. Shalley (Eds.), *Handbook of organizational creativity* (pp. 347–368). New York: Lawrence Erlbaum.

Zhou, J., & Shalley, C. E. (2011). Deepening our understanding of creativity in the workplace: A review of different approaches to creativity research. In Sheldon Zedeck (Ed.), *APA handbook of industrial and organizational psychology, 1*, 275–302.

# 23    Leadership and Goal Setting

*Ronald F. Piccolo*  Rollins College
*Claudia Buengeler*  Jacobs University Bremen

The leadership literature is broad and includes a number of different theories and models of leader behavior. These theories and models tend to highlight specific aspects of leader activity that promote individual, team, and organizational functioning. Most often, models of leadership describe specific behavioral patterns that characterize a particular approach (e.g., transformational leadership; Bass, 1985). In the evolution of our field's pursuit of understanding and explaining leader effectiveness, scholars have defined leadership in terms of the individual traits that are present in exceptional leaders (e.g., Kirkpatrick & Locke, 1991), the behaviors that characterize effective leader interactions with followers (e.g., Stogdill, 1963), and finally, the process by which leaders inspire followers to achieve collective goals (e.g., House, 1971). In that way, goals and goal setting have become a central aspect of how leadership is defined in general, and effective leadership in particular.

The intersection of leadership theory and goal setting theory (Locke & Latham, 1990) is the focus of this chapter. The central elements of goal setting theory are pervasive in modern leadership research. Indeed, effective leaders set challenging and specific goals, encourage followers to participate in goal setting, demonstrate commitment to personal and organizational goals, and provide feedback on goal attainment (Bass, 1985; Bono & Judge, 2003). The very definition of leadership, as offered by the most popular leadership theories, draws extensively from the seminal work by Locke and Latham (1990).

In this chapter, a review of the extensive literature that has captured leadership and goal setting since Locke and Latham's book was published (1990) is provided. First, the ways various theories and definitions of leadership explicitly refer to goal setting and achievement is summarized. In doing so, how goal concepts are embedded in the most popular measures of leader behaviors and leader effectiveness is highlighted. Second, a summary of how the major tenets of goal setting theory and related concepts (e.g., goal orientation) have been treated in the leadership literature since 1990 is provided. Examples of how goal setting theory has been treated in the leadership literature are described in Table 23.1.

## Goal Setting and Leadership

Since the early stages of modern leadership research, the intersection of leadership and goal setting has been a central aspect of how leadership is defined and measured. In 1957, Hemphill and Coons described leadership as "the behavior of an individual ... directing the activities of a group toward *a shared goal*" (In Yukl, 2006, p. 7). Twenty-one years later, Burns (1978) integrated goal setting in his definition of leadership: "the reciprocal process of mobilizing, by persons with certain motives and values, various

*Table 23.1* Examples of How Goal Setting Theory Has Been Characterized in the Leadership Literature

| Goal concept | Empirical studies | Leadership concepts | Study type |
|---|---|---|---|
| Goal orientation | Janssen & Van Yperen (2004) | LMX | Field |
| | Whitford & Moss (2009) | Leader vision Leader personal recognition | Field |
| Goal commitment | Durham, Knight, and Locke (1997) | Coordinating versus commanding leader | Laboratory |
| | Klein & Kim (1998) | LMX | Field |
| | De Souza & Klein (1995) | Leadership emergence | Laboratory |
| | Piccolo & Colquitt (2006) | Transformational leadership; LMX | Field |
| | Klein, Wesson, Hollenbeck, & Alge (1999) | Leadership; supervisor supportiveness | Meta-analysis |
| Goal congruence | Colbert, Kristof-Brown, Bradley, and Barrick (2008) | Transformational leadership | Field |
| | Sapienza & Gupta (1994) | Frequency of leader–member interaction | Field |
| | Colbert & Witt (2009) | Goal-focused leadership | Field |
| Goal difficulty | Durham et al. (1997) | Coordinating versus commanding leader | Laboratory |
| | Bezuijen, van Dam, van den Berg, & Thierry (2010) | LMX | Field |
| Assigned goal level | Kane, Zaccaro, Tremble, & Masuda (2002) | Leadership behaviors: - Directing - Monitoring - Task - Motivating - Monitoring time - Demotivating - Requests direction | Laboratory |
| Self-set goal level | Kirkpatrick & Locke (1996) | Intellectual stimulation Inspiration Perceived charisma Leader communication style | Laboratory |
| | Frink & Ferris (1998) | Accountability | Lab & Field |
| Goal interdependence | Tjosvold, Andrews, & Struthers (1992) | Directive Influence Collaborative Influence | Field |
| | Chen & Tjosvold (2005) | Cross-cultural LMX - Chinese-American - Chinese-Asian - Chinese-Chinese | Field study |
| Goal feedback | Goodwin, Wofford, & Boyd (2000) | Transformational leadership Transactional leadership | Laboratory |

economic, political and other resources, in a context of competition and conflict, in order to realize *goals* independently or mutually held by both leaders and followers" (In Rost, 1991; p. 425). Yukl (2006) offers one of the most cited definitions of leadership. He described leadership as "the process of influencing others to understand and agree about what needs to be done and how to do it, and the process of facilitating individual and collective efforts to accomplish *shared objectives*" (p. 8). Similarly, Northouse (2009) defined leadership as "a process whereby an individual influences a group of individuals to achieve *a common goal*" (p. 3).

Clearly, both modern and classic definitions of leadership and leader effectiveness include specific reference to individual and collective goal accomplishment. Similarly, the most popular scales used to assess leadership often include items that tap a leader's willingness and ability to embed the central tenets of goal setting theory, along with its various facets (e.g., goal commitment), into standard leadership activity. A sample of leadership scale items that refer to goal setting concepts is provided in Table 23.2.

### Initiating Structure

Since its introduction as part of a broad investigation of leader behaviors (e.g., Fleishman, 1953; Korman, 1966; Stogdill, 1950), *Initiating Structure* is a set of behaviors that are oriented toward task and goal attainment. This style has been investigated in numerous studies and summarized in a meta-analytic review (Judge, Piccolo, & Ilies, 2004). Initiating Structure is the degree to which leaders define and organize their role and the roles of their followers. These leaders make a special effort to maintain standards for the manner in which work is to be accomplished (Fleishman, 1973). In the original (LBDQ; Hemphill & Coons, 1957) and revised (LBDQ-XII; Stogdill, 1963) forms of the *Leader Behavior Description Questionnaire*, goals are prominent in that respondents indicate the frequency with which their leaders "maintain definite standards of performance," "emphasize the meeting of deadlines," and "let group members know what is expected of them."

### Path-goal Leadership

Path-goal theory describes how leaders can motivate followers to pursue and accomplish organizationally relevant goals by influencing employees' satisfaction and expectancies (House, 1972; House & Dessler, 1974). Unlike the range of rather implicit versus explicit goal approaches of most leadership models, path goal theory treats leadership and goal attainment as its defining characteristic. This emphasis on goal attainment is also reflected in the measurement of two of the four path-goal leadership styles (e.g., Indvik, 1985, 1988; in Northouse, 2009). Items that capture the frequency with which leaders "set goals for subordinates' performance that are quite challenging" and "show that [they] have doubts about subordinates' ability to meet most objectives" (reverse-coded) are indicative of achievement-oriented leadership. Items representing directive leadership describe leaders who "inform subordinates about what needs to be done and how it needs to be done" as well as "explain the level of performance that is expected of subordinates."

Table 23.2 Sample of Leadership Scale Items That Refer to Goals and Goal Concepts

| Leadership concept | Measure | Sample items |
| --- | --- | --- |
| Transformational leadership | Multifactor Leadership Questionnaire (Bass & Avolio, 1995) | - Talks enthusiastically about what needs to be accomplished.<br>- Expresses confidence that goals will be achieved |
| | Transformational Leadership Inventory (Podsakoff, McKenzie, Moorman, & Fetter, 1990) | - Gets the group together to work for the same goal<br>- Inspires others with his or her plans for the future |
| Contingent reward | Multifactor Leadership Questionnaire (Bass & Avolio, 1995) | - Makes clear what one can expect to receive when goals are achieved |
| Empowering Leadership | Leadership Empowerment Behavior (Ahearne, Mathieu, & Rapp, 2005) | - My manager helps me understand how my objectives and goals relate to that of the company |
| | Empowering Leadership Questionnaire (Arnold, Sharon, Rhoades, & Drasgow, 2000) | - Helps my work group focus on our goals<br>- Explains company goals |
| Servant Leadership | Servant Leadership (Liden, Wayne, Zhao, & Henderson, 2008) | - My manager has an understanding of our organization and its goals<br>- My manager wants to know about my career goals |
| | Leadership Practices Inventory (Kouzes & Posner, 2007; 4th Ed.) | - Makes certain that goals, plans, and milestones are set |
| Initiating Structure | Leadership Behavior Description Questionnaire (Schriesheim & Stogdill, 1975) | - My leader maintains definite standards of performance<br>- My leader emphasizes the meeting of deadlines<br>- My leader lets group members know what is expected of them |
| | Directive Leadership (Sagie, Zaidman, Amichai-Hamburger, Te'eni, & Schwartz 2002) | Your manager provides inspiring strategic and organizational goals |
| | Path-Goal Leadership Questionnaire (e.g., achievement-oriented leadership, Indvik, 1985; in Northouse (2009), p. 143 | - I set goals for subordinates' performance that are quite challenging<br>- I consistently set challenging goals for subordinates to attain<br>- I give vague explanations of what is expected of subordinates on the job (r) |
| Team Leadership | Team Excellence and Collaborative Team Leader Questionnaire (adapted from LaFasto & Larson, 1987, and LaFasto & Larson, 1996; in Northouse, 2009) | - There is a clearly defined need—a goal to be achieved or a purpose to be served—that justifies the existence of our team<br>- Team members possess the essential skills and abilities to accomplish the team's objectives<br>- Achieving our team goal is a higher priority than achieving individual objectives—If it becomes necessary to adjust the team's goal, our team leader makes sure we understand why |

## Team Leadership

While the previously described leadership theories focus predominately on individual employees, the team leadership model takes into account the specific demands and challenges of leading teams. The underlying functional leadership rationale requests the team leader to "monitor the team and then take whatever action is necessary to ensure team effectiveness" (Northouse, 2009, p. 243). Among Larson and LaFasto's (1989) empirically derived characteristics of team excellence are "clear and elevating goals," "standards of excellence," as well as "principled leadership." Concordantly, a questionnaire on team leadership (adapted from the *Team Excellence Survey* by LaFasto & Larson, 1987 in Northouse, 2009) maps these goal concepts by asking team members to indicate their agreement with items such as, "There is a clearly defined need—a goal to be achieved or a purpose to be served—that justifies the existence of our team," "Team members possess the essential skills and abilities to accomplish the team's objectives," and "If it's necessary to adjust the team's goal, our team leader makes sure we understand why."

Beyond the leadership concepts, theories, and measures described above, additional management concepts have emerged since Locke and Latham's (1990) book that treat goal setting as an integral and defining characteristic of effective leadership. One such concept, *Goal-Focused Leadership* (Colbert & Witt, 2009), relies on a scale that assesses a leader's effectiveness in providing direction, and setting and clarifying goals. Sample items include "To what extent does [your leader] translate strategies into understandable objectives and plans?" "To what extent does he/she provide direction and define priorities?" and "To what extent does he/she link the unit's mission to the overall mission of the company?"

## Transformational Leadership

In the past two decades, transformational leadership has emerged as one of the most popular approaches to understanding leader effectiveness. Transformational leadership theory states that certain leader behaviors arouse followers to high levels of thinking (Bass, 1985; Burns, 1978). By appealing to followers' ideals and values, transformational leaders enhance commitment to a well-articulated vision and inspire followers to develop new ways of thinking about problems. A search of keywords in the PsycINFO database, 1990–2011, reveals that there have been more studies on transformational or charismatic leadership than all other theories of leadership (e.g., Least Preferred Coworker theory, path-goal theory, normative decision theory, substitutes for leadership) combined. Studies have been conducted in the laboratory (Jung & Avolio, 1999) and in the field (Yammarino, Dubinsky, Comer, & Jolson, 1997). There have been correlational (Hater & Bass, 1988) and experimental (Barling, Weber, & Kelloway, 1996) studies that have utilized both subjective perceptions of effective leaders (Judge & Bono, 2000) and "hard" economic criteria (Geyer & Steyrer, 1998). Judge and Piccolo (2004) have provided a comprehensive review.

Transformational leadership is most often measured with one of two scales designed to capture the multi-faceted nature of the concept. Explicit in the Multifactor Leadership

Questionnaire (MLQ; Bass & Avolio, 1995) are items that assess a leader's command of essential concepts in goal setting. Respondents to the MLQ indicate, for example, the extent to which they agree that their leaders "talk enthusiastically about what needs to be accomplished," "make clear what one can expect to receive when performance goals are achieved," and "express confidence that goals will be achieved." As it captures the "full range" of leader behaviors, the MLQ (Bass & Avolio, 1995) also measures contingent reward leadership and includes the item "My leader … makes clear what one can expect to receive when performance goals are achieved."

The Transformational Leadership Inventory (TLI; Podsakoff et al., 1990) includes items such as "My leader … gets the group together to work for the same goal" and "… inspires others with his/her plans for the future." As evidenced by items in these two scales, goal setting is a central component of how this theory of leadership is defined and measured.

## Empowering Leadership

By means of specific leader actions, such as sharing power and endowing followers with autonomy, empowering leadership intends to provoke favorable behaviors in followers (i.e., motivation, performance; Srivastava, Bartol, & Locke, 2006). One behavioral expression of empowering leadership is the extent to which a leader clarifies an individual's work goals and embeds them in the organization's mission. Sample items used to measure empowering leadership include "My leader helps me understand how my objectives and goals relate to that of the company" (Leadership Empowerment Behavior Measure; Ahearne, Mathieu, & Rapp, 2005), "My leader helps my work group focus on our goals," and "… explains the purpose of the company's policies to my work group" (Empowering Leadership Questionnaire; Arnold et al., 2000).

## Servant Leadership

Consistent with the revival of normative values and morality in today's increasingly unstable economic environment, the "servant" approach to leadership is characterized by a leader's personal integrity and serving behaviors with regards to employees, customers, and other parties (Liden et al., 2008). Servant leadership's conceptualization and measurement emphasizes goals in two important ways. From an organizational perspective, the concept captures the extent to which a manager "has a thorough understanding of an organization and its goals." As reflected by concern for an employee's welfare, the most common scale assesses the degree with which a leader "is interested in making sure that [followers] achieve their career goals" (Liden et al., 2008).

In sum, the very definitions and measurements of modern leadership include direct reference to goals and aspects of goal setting theory. Today's leaders are evaluated largely on their ability to set and accomplish specific, challenging goals.

## Leadership Research and Goal Setting

Despite goal setting's centrality in the definition and measurement of leadership and leader effectiveness, prior to Locke and Latham's (1990) book, only a handful of empirical studies captured the link between leadership and goals. In the 1990 book, for example, one paragraph citing six studies was all that was needed to summarize this literature. Since 1990, the literature on the intersection of leadership and goal setting has mushroomed. At least 70 published papers have measured leadership and various goal concepts, including a number of theoretical treatments of leadership and goal setting, influenced largely by Robert House's path-goal theory (1971). In the remainder of this chapter, several of these studies are highlighted to illustrate the broad and varied intersection of leadership and goal setting theory.

Empirical studies in this domain have examined leadership and goal setting at individual (e.g., Kirkpatrick & Locke, 1996; Klein & Kim, 1998) and team levels (e.g., Hu & Liden, 2011; Zohar, 2002) of analysis. Several studies manipulated both leadership behaviors and goal levels in laboratory settings (e.g., Goodwin et al., 2000; Hendricks & Payne, 2007). In general, they reported positive associations between socially desirable leadership behaviors (transformational leadership) and favorable work outcomes (e.g., goal pursuit; Bono & Judge, 2003).

Regarding the varied models of leadership examined, a number of studies focused on transformational leadership (e.g., Bono & Judge, 2003; Colbert et al., 2008; Gamble, 2010; Goodwin et al., 2000; Kark & van Dijk, 2007; Piccolo & Colquitt, 2006; Whittington et al., 2004; Xirasager et al., 2005; Zohar, 2002) and related styles (e.g., contingent reward, Schriesheim, 2006) in the framework of the "full range" model of leadership (Bass & Avolio, 1995). Similarly, a variety of studies illuminated the ties among goal-related concepts and Leader-Member Exchange (LMX). Other studies integrated goal concepts and leadership behaviors from the traditions of either task-oriented leadership, directive leadership, and initiating structure (e.g., Kane et al., 2002) or relations-oriented leadership, participative or supportive leadership, and consideration (e.g., Sarin & McDermott, 2003). Finally, Management by Objectives (MBO), arguably a central concept in leadership, also draws directly on goal setting theory (Conger et al., 1998; Rodgers & Hunter, 1992; Simons, 1991), specifically the concepts of challenge, feedback, and specificity. Lastly, several meta-analytic summaries of the leadership literature have estimated correspondence between leadership models (e.g., leader-member exchange) and goal concepts such as goal setting (DeChurch et al., 2010), goal orientation (Payne, Youngcourt, & Beaubien, 2007), and goal commitment (Klein et al., 1999; Rodgers & Hunter, 1992).

Whereas a large majority of these studies have appeared in the literature on organizational behavior and human resources management, the effects of goal setting theory on organizational effectiveness have extended knowledge beyond micro-oriented studies in applied psychology. Hence, we also present examples of how leadership and goal accomplishment have been examined in the strategic management and organizational literatures.

The first part of the following section is organized along the major tenets of goal setting theory, which are goal difficulty, goal commitment, and goal specificity. This is followed by group goals. Studies are then described that model goals as independent variables, mediators, and outcomes. The interaction between leadership and goal setting is complex; thus, researchers have modeled this relationship in various ways. Further, whereas numerous studies can be found on the interplay between leadership and goal commitment and goal difficulty, other goal concepts such as goal specificity and feedback are represented by only a few studies.

*Goal Difficulty*

In a field study on dyads from various organizations, Whittington, Goodwin, and Murray (2004) considered goal difficulty as a boundary condition on the relationship between transformational leadership and a number of desirable outcomes. Consistent with their hypotheses, challenging goals facilitated a positive relationship between a leader's transformational leadership style and a follower's affective organizational commitment. The relationship between transformational leadership and goal setting was positive at high levels of goal difficulty, but nonsignificant when goal difficulty was low. This suggests that the effectiveness of transformational leadership depends in part on the difficulty level of a goal.

Bezuijen et al. (2010) used a multi-level approach to examine the interaction between LMX and goal difficulty. They found that goal difficulty and feedback mediated the link between LMX and employee engagement. High-quality relationships, in the form of leader–member exchange, fostered goal-directed behavior (e.g., setting difficult, challenging goals, providing feedback). Further, LMX served as a boundary condition on the relationship between goal difficulty and employee engagement in learning, such that high-quality relationships between leaders and followers enhanced the effect of goal difficulty on employee behavior.

In an experimental setting with a student sample, de Souza and Klein (1995) investigated leadership emergence and its effect on goal setting and goal commitment. Groups were assigned group goals, individual goals, or both to determine if the nature of a group's goal was related to leader emergence. While the assigned goal type (e.g., group or individual goal) and difficulty were not associated with leader emergence, the emergent leader's personal goal for the group strongly influenced the group's chosen goal, highlighting the influence of leaders on goal choice, and the importance of an individual's participation in the goal setting process.

Drawing on results from experimental and field studies, Frink and Ferris (1998) found that followers' accountability to a team leader influenced the nature and difficulty of self-set goals. In a laboratory study, Frink and Ferris manipulated the participants' accountability for self-set goals. When participants were held accountable, self-set goals were used to impress managers, played by confederates. The authors labeled this phenomenon "context attentiveness." However, with no accountability, self-set goals were directed at enhancing performance on a particular task (i.e., task attentiveness). Goal levels were positively linked to performance under conditions of no or low accountability, but negatively linked when accountability to team leaders was high. These studies reveal the interaction between leadership, goal-setting, and accountability.

In an experiment manipulating leadership style and goal difficulty, Durham et al. (1997) assigned easy or difficult team-level goals to teams that were asked to perform a simulation task. Teams were led by either a commanding leader (selected based on personality) or a coordinating leader (selected by the team; involved sharing leadership responsibilities among team members). Compared to those with commanders, teams led by coordinators developed better team tactics that strongly enhanced team performance. In addition, the authors report an interaction between team tactics and goal difficulty, noting that the strength of the effect of team-set goal difficulty on performance was dependent upon the quality of team tactics. High-quality tactics combined with high team-set goal difficulty led to the highest level of team performance. These findings support the suggestion (Kirkpatrick & Locke, 1996) that leaders influence followers through numerous actions such as coordinating, communicating, training, and motivating (e.g., raising self-efficacy, setting goals).

Examining self-set goals as an intervening variable between leader behaviors and performance in a laboratory simulation, Kirkpatrick and Locke (1996) manipulated leader vision that focused on quality, vision implementation through task cues, and a charismatic communication style. They found that quality goals and quality self-efficacy mediated the relationship between quality vision and performance quality. Task cues affected quantity goals and thereby performance quantity. Charismatic style itself had no effects.

Taking a functional leadership perspective, Kane et al. (2002) examined leader goals and leader self-efficacy using different difficulty levels of a production task in a team experiment. Functional leadership was defined as behaviors that explained unique variance in the prediction of group outcomes. The authors found evidence that leader self-efficacy predicted the level of leader goals, which in turn affected important group outcomes (e.g., group profit, productivity, cohesion, collective efficacy, team members' evaluations of leaders). Both a leader's self-efficacy and goals were related to leader strategies, which were operationalized as the amount of strategy announcements that leaders declared to their groups. Leader strategies were directly linked to functional leader behaviors (e.g., directing, motivating task behavior) and also served as a mediator between leader goals and directing leader behavior. Moderator analysis on task complexity showed that high self-efficacy helped leaders to maintain challenging goals when facing a highly difficult production task, whereas leaders with low self-efficacy decreased their goal levels accordingly.

## Goal Commitment

Similar to the research attention that leadership and goal difficulty have provoked, goal commitment has been of major interest in a variety of leadership studies.

Piccolo and Colquitt (2006) linked transformational leadership with goal commitment, treating goal commitment as a means by which leaders ultimately achieve their intended outcomes. According to the authors, even though a number of other mediating processes had already been examined in the transformational leadership process (e.g., self-concept: Shamir, House, & Arthur, 1993; trust: Podsakoff et al., 1990), a critical step in fostering job performance lies in the leader's ability to encourage commitment to organizational goals. Goal commitment accounted for the relationship between leadership and both task and citizenship aspects of job performance.

Sagie (1996) investigated the effects of manipulating an assigned leader's directive communication style and the type of goal setting on a team's performance and attitudes in an experimental problem-solving task. Participative, but not assigned, goals enhanced personal attitudes, including goal commitment. As a moderator variable, participative goal setting also strengthened the positive link between leader directiveness and goal commitment. Although a directive communication style also positively affected performance, there was no main or interaction effect of goal setting with a leader's communication style on this outcome. Sagie concluded that joint application of a directive communication style and participative goal setting is most beneficial for improving positive work attitudes and performance.

In a meta-analysis of studies on management by objective (MBO) practices, Rodgers and Hunter (1992) estimated the relative impact of three essential MBO component processes: goal setting, participation in decision making, and objective feedback on organizational productivity. The authors further estimated the utility of MBO (goal setting) in both public and private sector organizations, finding MBO practices had a positive impact on productivity in all the public sector agencies studied. Sixty-eight of the 70 studies in the meta-analytic database reported productivity gains for organizations using MBO. The effectiveness of MBO in general, and goal setting in particular, was dependent in part on top management's commitment to the process.

Similarly, Antoni (2005) studied the effectiveness of MBO as an instrument for managing self-regulating teams, defining goal commitment as a proxy for MBO. Results showed positive predictions of this goal concept on job satisfaction and team productivity.

## Goal Specificity

In addition to its focus on goal difficulty, Bezuijen et al.'s (2010) study examined the role of goal specificity in an LMX framework. The authors identified goal specificity as a partial mediator of the association between LMX and the level of follower engagement in learning activities. Moreover, high goal specificity by leaders predicted learning activities regardless of LMX quality levels.

Ramus and Steger (2000) hypothesized a positive relationship between goal setting and sharing of responsibility for organizational goals to employee self-described environmental initiatives. The authors reasoned that a manager's role in setting specific, measurable goals can positively affect organizational learning and employee creativity. In a field study conducted in Europe, they found a strong positive link between supervisor support behaviors and goal *specificity* (i.e., delegates specific tasks, manages every detail) and *feedback* on goal pursuit (i.e., talks regularly with employees to assess progress toward explicit employee goals). The authors concluded, "… employees who perceived strong signals of organizational and supervisory encouragement were more likely to develop and implement creative ideas that positively affected the natural environment than employees who did not perceive such signals" (p. 622).

## Group Goals

Driven largely by organizational realities and analytical techniques that support multi-level analyses, the number of team- and organization-level studies has increased dramatically in the two decades since Locke and Latham's (1990) book. This phenomenon is reflected in the broad organizational behavior literature as well as in the goal setting literature (see Chapter 19 for an extensive review of the group goal literature).

Schriesheim et al. (2006), for example, investigated interactive effects of contingent reward and a goal-related subfacet of transformational leadership, namely, fostering the acceptance of group goals. This concept is specified in the Transformational Leadership

Inventory (Podsakoff et al., 1990). Contingent reward enhanced the positive effects of this transformational dimension on satisfaction, but not performance.

Contrary to their hypothesis, de Souza and Klein (1995) did not find evidence for a link between assigned type of goal setting (group goals, individual goals, or individual and group goals) and leadership emergence in a student team task. Nevertheless, the probability of emerging as a leader was higher for individuals who were committed to an assigned group goal. Moreover, this person's individual group goal in turn influenced the actual goal level set by the group.

Maner and Mead (2010) conducted five laboratory experiments to identify the conditions under which leaders exert their power for the attainment of group goals or for the attainment of self-interested goals. In general, leaders behaved in a manner that was consistent with group goals. However, in unstable situations where a leader's power and security were threatened, leaders who were high in power motivation prioritized their own goals over those of the group. These leaders were more likely to withhold important information from the group, discredited high-quality team members, and did not put a skilled team member in an influential position over a group task unless intergroup competition was high.

## Goal Effects on Leadership

Tjosvold et al. (1992) investigated the linkages among power, goal interdependence, and leadership style in terms of the leader's method of influence: collaborative or directive. When goals of supervisors with high power were cooperative, these leaders used a collaborative influence style. This facilitated employee commitment and work effectiveness. In the case of independent or competitive goals, organizational leaders relied on directive influence, which yielded nonsignificant effects on follower performance. These results suggest that the type of group goal shapes a leader's style of influence.

Similarly, Chen and Tjosvold (2005), in a cross-cultural setting, applied structural equation modeling to investigate the effects of goal interdependence on leaders' success. Cooperative goal interdependence enabled American, Asian, and Chinese managers to establish quality LMX relationships with their Chinese employees. This in turn fostered leader effectiveness, followers' organizational commitment, and the willingness for future collaboration with the leader. In other words, Chinese followers who perceived their own and their managers' goals to be cooperative were far more likely to establish high LMX relations with their supervisors than those who perceived competitive or independent goals.

## Other Goal and Leadership Studies

Hu and Liden (2011) examined the interrelations between self-goal regulation, "servant" leadership, and team outcomes in Chinese banks using structural equation modeling. Team potency fully mediated the link between goal clarity, process clarity, and team performance and organizational citizenship behaviors. The positive association between both goal concepts and team potency was increased when team leaders were high in servant leadership.

In a field study on product development teams, Sarin and McDermott (2003) contrasted facilitative leader behaviors (i.e., participation and consideration) with task-oriented behaviors (i.e., the initiation of goal and process structure) to estimate the relative impact of these distinct styles on team learning and knowledge application. While consideration and initiating process structure were unrelated to outcomes, participation and initiating goal structure fostered team learning, which in turn facilitated speed to market and innovation.

In an attempt to predict employees' ecological initiatives, a specific form of goals with signaling function, Ramus and Steger (2000) assessed supervisory support behaviors as well as employee-rated environmental policies in organizations in six European companies. Environmentally specific compared to general supervisory support behaviors were more likely to provoke eco-initiatives in employees (i.e., leadership style predicted goal setting). General supervisor support behaviors (e.g., competence building, communication, rewards and recognition) predicted eco-initiatives, but for only those employees who perceived that published environmental policies of their companies existed.

Using an experimental design examining real university and fictitious groups, Hoyt, Price, and Emrick (2010) focused on leadership as a potential cause for unethical behavior in pursuing group goals. Generally, individuals perceived their own group goals to be more important than other groups' goals. Being a leader strengthened these biased perceptions. In addition, leaders, compared to nonleading team members, were more likely to justify unethical behavior for securing group goal attainment than other groups. Leaders' justification bias was especially pronounced when group goal importance judgments were high.

Wooldridge and Floyd (1990) reported evidence on the importance of involving middle managers in strategy formation, a form of participative goal setting. Involvement of middle managers in the strategic process was linked to an organization's performance due to increasing goal understanding.

## Goals as Moderators

Many studies of leadership and goal setting have sought direct links between leader behavior and the accomplishment of organizational goals, or the extent to which the nature, clarity, or challenge of a goal fostered a particular leadership style. Alternatively, several studies have modeled goal concepts (e.g., feedback and commitment) as boundary conditions on the effect of leadership on performance-oriented outcomes (e.g., an organization's productivity and profitability; van Knippenberg et al., 2011). In the following paragraphs, these studies are introduced.

In a laboratory study (Goodwin et al., 2000), goal-related feedback on a subordinate's performance was found to moderate the link between self-rated leadership style and a leader's cognitions. Student participants assumed the role of a manufacturing manager and asked to respond to feedback on their subordinates' performance. Positive feedback on goal progress led to transformational leadership cognitions, whereas negative feedback led to transactional (exchange-oriented) cognitions. Further, the relationship between transformational leadership behaviors and transformational cognitions was strengthened when feedback received about subordinates was long term, vision-related as opposed to short-term, and goal-related. The relationship between transactional leadership behavior and transactional cognitions was strengthened when feedback was goal related, highlighting the effect of goal-related feedback on the leadership process.

Zohar (2002) found that safety goals (i.e., priorities) assigned by superiors moderated the effect of leadership style (transformational, transactional, or laissez faire) on minor injuries in work teams. The authors treated the establishment of safety priorities as a specific case of goal setting. Relationships between contingent reward and transformational leadership and low injury rate were strongest when assigned safety goals were high. Goals moderated the link between leadership and injury rate. In case of active and passive management by exception, injury rate was diminished when safety priority was high, but increased when it was low. Laissez faire leadership was positively related to minor injuries when safety goals were high but unrelated when they were low.

Gruenfeld, Inesi, Magee, and Galinsky (2008) examined the consequences of high power in six experiments using student and manager samples. The authors drew on the concept of *objectification*, or the process of subjugation whereby people, like objects, are treated as means to an end. Participants in a high-power condition, as compared to a low-power condition, were more likely to approach others based on their instrumental utility for fulfilling performance goals. This instrumental, utilitarian approach to others was enhanced by the salience of an active performance goal, illustrating the impact of performance goals on power dynamics in relationships.

### Goals as Mediators

Goals have not only been examined as moderators of the leadership–outcome relationship, they have also been studied as mediators that explain why leadership is effective.

Similar to the Piccolo and Colquitt (2006) study, Colbert et al. (2008) found that goal importance congruence, the extent to which members of the same team place similar levels of importance on shared goals, is a key step in the link between a CEO's leadership and the satisfaction, commitment, and performance of the top management team. On the team level (CEO and top management team), the CEO's transformational leadership increased goal importance congruence perceptions, which then affected an organization's performance.

Goal-focused leadership has been examined as a means that helps followers perceive their own goals to be consistent with an organization's priorities. In a mediated moderation model, Colbert and Witt (2009) found that this leadership style enhanced the positive link between conscientiousness and job performance, which was mediated by perceived person-organization goal congruence.

### Goals as Outcomes

A few studies have examined leadership as predictors of goal concepts. For example, Bono and Judge (2003) found that goal congruence is an important outcome of leadership. Transformational leaders were especially effective at getting followers to see the organization's goals as consistent with their own (goal congruence). The authors examined this phenomenon in an organizational context and again in an experimental simulation. In both settings, perceived goal congruence was higher for those employees whose supervisors used transformational leadership that emphasized participation in goal setting and feedback on progress toward goal attainment.

In a clinical setting, Xirasagar, Samuels, and Stoskopf (2005) related medical director's "full-range" leadership styles to the achievement of a center's clinical goals. Transformational leadership, as well as a conglomerate of contingent reward and active management-by-exception behaviors, was positively associated with the degree of goal achievement, whereas no such link could be observed for laissez faire behavior and passive management by exception.

Conducting four different experiments, Guinote (2007) studied the impact of leadership by manipulating a power- versus nonpower condition on the different stages of the goal setting process. Powerful, compared to powerless, individuals were more ready (in terms of speed and information taken into account) to make goal-related decisions, were more able to initiate goal-directed behaviors, persisted longer on the course of action, and were more flexible when facing hindrances. In addition, powerful individuals were more responsive to chances to pursue a goal.

## Conclusion

Since Locke and Latham's book was published in 1990, scholars in the leadership literature have actively integrated major tenets of goal setting theory in the definition, development, and examination of varied leadership models. Goal attainment is a central and explicit characteristic of most popular definitions of leadership. The scales used to assess leader effectiveness refer directly to major tenets of goal setting theory (e.g., participating, specificity, challenge). Indeed, effective leaders are those that set challenging goals (Indvik, 1985; Kouzes & Posner, 2007), make clear how goals are related to organizational performance (Ahearne et al., 2005), get groups to work together for goal accomplishment (Podsakoff et al., 1990), and express confidence that the goals will be achieved (Bass & Avolio, 1995). That said, as this burgeoning literature illustrates, the interaction between leadership and goal setting is complex. Leadership style affects the specificity and challenge of a team or individual goal, while the nature and difficulty of a goal appears to influence a leader's leader behavior. As such, leadership and goal setting appear to have a reciprocal relationship. Further, the strength of a leader's impact on followers is shaped in part by the salience of relevant goals. Future studies should attempt to clarify the causal relationship between leadership style and goals, which would lead to those conditions that alter the complex interaction between leadership and the major tenets of goal setting theory.

## References

Ahearne, M., Mathieu, J., & Rapp, A. (2005). To empower or not to empower your sales force? An empirical examination of the influence of leadership empowerment behavior on customer satisfaction and performance. *Journal of Applied Psychology, 90*(5), 945–955.

Antoni, C. (2005). Management by objectives—an effective tool for teamwork? *International Journal of Human Resource Management, 16*(2), 174–184.

Arnold, J. A., Sharon, A., Rhoades, J. A., & Drasgow, F. (2000). The empowering leadership questionnaire: The construction and validation of a new scale for measuring leader behaviors. *Journal of Organizational Behavior, 21*(3), 249–269.

Barling, J., Weber, T., & Kelloway, E. K. (1996). Effects of transformational leadership training on attitudinal and financial outcomes: A field experiment. *Journal of Applied Psychology, 81*(6), 827–832.

Bass, B. M. (1985). *Leadership and performance beyond expectations.* New York: Free press.

Bass, B. M., & Avolio, B. J. (1995). *Multifactor leadership questionnaire for research.* Menlo Park, CA: Mind Garden.

Bezuijen, X. M., van Dam, K., van den Berg, P. T., & Thierry, H. (2010). How leaders stimulate employee learning: A leader-member exchange approach. *Journal of Occupational & Organizational Psychology, 83*(3), 673–693.

Bono, J. E., & Judge, T. A. (2003). Self-concordance at work: toward understanding the motivational effects of transformational leaders. *Academy of Management Journal, 46*(5), 554–571.

Burns, J. M. (1978). *Leadership.* New York: Harper & Row.

Chen, Y. F., & Tjosvold, D. (2005). Cross-cultural leadership: Goal interdependence and leader–member relations in foreign ventures in China. *Journal of International Management, 11*(3), 417–439.

Colbert, A. E., Kristof-Brown, A. L., Bradley, B. H., & Barrick, M. R. (2008). CEO transformational leadership: The role of goal importance congruence in top management teams. *Academy of Management Journal, 51*(1), 81–96.

Colbert, A. E., & Witt, L. A. (2009). The role of goal-focused leadership in enabling the expression of conscientiousness. *Journal of Applied Psychology, 94*(3), 790–796.

de Souza, G., & Klein, H. J. (1995). Emergent leadership in the group goal-setting process. *Small Group Research, 26*(4), 475–496.

Durham, C. C., Knight, D., & Locke, E. A. (1997). Effects of leader role, team-set goal difficulty, efficacy, and tactics on team effectiveness. *Organizational Behavior and Human Decision Processes, 72*(2), 203–231.

Fleishman, E. A. (1953). The description of supervisory behavior. *Journal of Applied Psychology, 37*, 1–6.

Frink, D. D., & Ferris, G. R. (1998). Accountability, impression management, and goal setting in the performance evaluation process. *Human Relations, 51*(10), 1259–1283.

Geyer, A. L. J., & Steyrer, J. M. (1998). Transformational leadership and objective performance in banks. *Applied Psychology: An International Review, 47*(3), 397–420.

Goodwin, V. L., Wofford, J. C., & Boyd, N. G. (2000). A laboratory experiment testing the antecedents of leader cognitions. *Journal of Organizational Behavior, 21*(7), 769–788.

Gruenfeld, D. H., Inesi, M. E., Magee, J. C., & Galinsky, A. D. (2008). Power and the objectification of social targets. *Journal of Personality and Social Psychology, 95*(1), 111–127.

Guinote, A. (2007). Power and goal pursuit. *Personality and Social Psychology Bulletin, 33*(8), 1076–1087.

Hater, J. J., & Bass, B. M. (1988). Superiors' evaluations and subordinates' perceptions of transformational and transactional leadership. *Journal of Applied Psychology, 73*(4), 695–702.

Hemphill, J. K., & Coons, A. E. (1957). Development of the leader behavior description questionnaire. In R. M. Stogdill & A. E. Coons (Eds.), *Leader behavior: Its description and measurement*: Columbus: Ohio State University, Bureau of Business Research.

Hendricks, J. W., & Payne, S. C. (2007). Beyond the big five: Leader goal orientation as a predictor of leadership effectiveness. *Human Performance, 20*(4), 317–343.

House, R. J. (1971). A path goal theory of leader effectiveness. *Adminstrative Science Quarterly, 16*(3), 321–339.

House, R. J., & Dessler, G. (1974). The path-goal theory of leadership: Some post hoc and a priori tests. In J. G. Hunt & L. L. Larsons (Eds.), *Contingency approaches to leadership* (pp. 29–55). Carbondale: Southern Illinois University Press.

Hoyt, C. L., Price, T. L., & Emrick, A. E. (2010). Leadership and the more-important-than-average effect: Overestimation of group goals and the justification of unethical behavior. *Leadership, 6*(4), 391–407.

Hu, J., & Liden, R. C. (2011). Antecedents of team potency and team effectiveness: An examination of goal and process clarity and servant leadership. *Journal of Applied Psychology.*

Indvik, J. (1985). *A path-goal theory investigation of superior-subordinate relationships.* Unpublished doctoral dissertation, University of Wisconsin-Madison.

Indvik, J. (1988). *A more complete testing of path-goal theory.* Paper presented at the Paper presented at the Academy of Management Annual Meeting, Anaheim, CA.

Janssen, O., & Van Yperen, N. W. (2004). Employees' goal orientations, the quality of leader-member exchange, and the outcomes of job performance and job satisfaction. *Academy of Management Journal, 47*(3), 368–384.

Korman, A. K. (1966). "Consideration," "initiating structure," and organizational criteria—A review. *Personnel Psychology, 19,* 349–361.

Judge, T. A., & Bono, J. E. (2000). Five-factor model of personality and transformational leadership. *Journal of Applied Psychology, 85*(5), 751–765.

Judge, T. A., & Piccolo, R. F. (2004). Transformational and transactional leadership: A meta-analytic test of their relative validity. *Journal of Applied Psychology, 89*(5), 755–768.

Judge, T. A., Piccolo, R. F., & Ilies, R. (2004). The forgotten ones? The validity of consideration and initiating structure in leadership research. *Journal of Applied Psychology, 89*(1), 36–51.

Jung, D. I., & Avolio, B. J. (1999). Effects of leadership style and followers' cultural orientation on performance in group and individual task conditions. *The Academy of Management Journal, 42*(2), 208–218.

Kane, T. D., Zaccaro, S. J., Tremble, T. R., Jr., & Masuda, A. D. (2002). An examination of the leaders' regulation of groups. *Small Group Research, 33*(1), 65–120.

Kirkpatrick, S. A., & Locke, E. A. (1996). Direct and indirect effects of three core charismatic leadership components on performance and attitudes. *Journal of Applied Psychology, 81*(1), 36–51.

Kirkpatrick, S. A., & Locke, E. A. (1991). Leadership: Do traits matter? *Academy of Management Executive, 5*(2), 48–60.

Klein, H. J., & Kim, J. S. (1998). A field study of the influence of situational constraints, leader-member exchange, and goal commitment on performance. *The Academy of Management Journal, 41*(1), 88–95.

Klein, H. J., Wesson, M. J., Hollenbeck, J. R., & Alge, B. J. (1999). Goal commitment and the goal-setting process: Conceptual clarification and empirical synthesis. *Journal of Applied Psychology, 84*(6), 885–896.

Kouzes, J. M., & Posner, B. Z. (1995). *The leadership challenge: How to keep getting extraordinary things done in organizations* (2nd ed.). San Francisco, CA: Jossey-Bass.

LaFasto, F. M. J., & Larson, C. E. (1987). *Team excellence survey.* Denver, CO: Author.

LaFasto, F. M. J., & Larson, C. E. (1996). *Collaborative team leader survey.* Author.

Liden, R., Wayne, S., Zhao, H., & Henderson, D. (2008). Servant leadership: Development of a multidimensional measure and multi-level assessment. *The Leadership Quarterly, 19*(2), 161–177.

Locke, E. A., & Latham, G. P. (1990). *A theory of goal setting and task performance.* Englewood Cliffs, NJ: Prentice-Hall.

Maner, J. K., & Mead, N. L. (2010). The essential tension between leadership and power: When leaders sacrifice group goals for the sake of self-interest. *Journal of Personality and Social Psychology, 99*(3), 482–497.

Northouse, P. G. (2009). *Leadership: Theory and practice.* (5th ed.). Thousand Oaks, CA: Sage.

Payne, S. C., Youngcourt, S. S., & Beaubien, J. M. (2007). A meta-analytic examination of the goal orientation nomological net. *Journal of Applied Psychology, 92*, 128–150.

Perry, S. J., Witt, L. A., Penney, L. M., & Atwater, L. (2010). The downside of goal-focused leadership: The role of personality in subordinate exhaustion. *Journal of Applied Psychology, 95*(6), 1145–1153.

Piccolo, R. F., & Colquitt, J. A. (2006). Transformational leadership and job behaviors: The mediating role of core job characteristics. *Academy of Management Journal, 49*(2), 327–340.

Podsakoff, P. M., MacKenzie, S. B., Moorman, R. H., & Fetter, R. (1990). Transformational leader behaviors and their effects on followers' trust in leader, satisfaction, and organizational citizenship behaviors. *The Leadership Quarterly, 1*(2), 107–142.

Ramus, C. A., & Steger, U. (2000). The roles of supervisory support behaviors and environmental policy in employee "ecoinitiatives" at leading-edge european companies. *The Academy of Management Journal, 43*(4), 605–626.

Rodgers, R., & Hunter, J. E. (1992). A foundation of good management practice in government: Management by objectives. *Public Administration Review, 52*(1), 27–39.

Rost, J. C. (1991). *Leadership for the twenty-first century.* New York: Praeger.

Sagie, A. (1996). The effects of leader's communication style and participative goal setting on performance and attitudes. *Human Performance, 9*, 51–64.

Sagie, A., Zaidman, N., Amichai-Hamburger, Y., Te'eni, D., & Schwartz, D. G. (2002). An Empirical assessment of the loose-tight leadership model: Quantitative and qualitative analyses. *Journal of Organizational Behavior, 23*(3), 303–320.

Sapienza, H. J., & Gupta, A. K. (1994). Impact of agency risks and task uncertainty on venture capitalist-CEO interaction. *The Academy of Management Journal, 37*(6), 1618–1632.

Sarin, S., & McDermott, C. (2003). The effect of team leader characteristics on learning, knowledge application, and performance of cross-functional new product development teams. *Decision Sciences, 34*(4), 707–739.

Schriesheim, C. A., Castro, S. L., Zhou, X., & DeChurch, L. A. (2006). An investigation of path-goal and transformational leadership theory predictions at the individual level of analysis. *The Leadership Quarterly, 17*(1), 21–38.

Schriesheim, C. A., & Stogdill, R. M. (1975). Differences in factor structure across three versions of the Ohio State Leadership Scales. *Personnel Psychology, 28*(2), 189–206.

Srivastava, A., Bartol, K. M., & Locke, E. A. (2006). Empowering leadership in management teams: Effects on knowledge sharing, efficacy, and performance. *Academy of Management Journal, 49*(6), 1239–1251.

Stogdill, R. M. (1950). Leadership, membership and organization. *Psychological Bulletin, 47*, 1–14.

Stogdill, R. M. (1963). *Manual for the leader behavior description questionnaire form XII.* Columbus: Ohio State University, Bureau of Business Research.

Tjosvold, D., Andrews, I. R., & Struthers, J. T. (1992). Leadership influence: Goal interdependence and power. *Journal of Social Psychology, 132*(1), 39–50.

Whitford, T., & Moss, S. A. (2009). Transformational leadership in distributed work groups: The moderating role of follower regulatory focus and goal orientation [Article]. *Communication Research, 36*(6), 810–837.

Whittington, J. L., Goodwin, V. L., & Murray, B. (2004). Transformational leadership, goal difficulty, and job design: Independent and interactive effects on employee outcomes. *The Leadership Quarterly, 15*(5), 593–606.

Wooldridge, B., & Floyd, S. W. (1990). The strategy process, middle management involvement, and organizational performance. *Strategic Management Journal, 11*(3), 231–241.

Xirasagar, S., Samuels, M. E., & Stoskopf, C. H. (2005). Physician leadership styles and effectiveness: An empirical study. *Medical Care Research and Review, 62*(6), 720–740.

Yammarino, F. J., Dubinsky, A. J., Comer, L. B., & Jolson, M. A. (1997). Women and transformational and contingent reward leadership: A multiple-levels-of-analysis perspective. *The Academy of Management Journal, 40*(1), 205–222.

Yukl, G. (2006). *Leadership in organizations* (Pearson International Edition ed.). New Jersey: Pearson Prentice Hall.

Zohar, D. (2002). The effects of leadership dimensions, safety climate, and assigned priorities on minor injuries in work groups. *Journal of Organizational Behavior, 23*(1), 75–92.

# 24   Goal Setting in Sports

*Kevin J. Williams*   *Department of Psychology, University at Albany,*
*State University of New York*

## Goal Setting in Sports

Goals are universal in sports. Nearly all athletes set goals on a frequent basis to structure training and motivate performance (Munroe-Chandler, Hall, & Weinberg, 2004; Weinberg, Burton, Yukelson, & Weigand, 2000). Goals provide direction to athletic pursuits that vary in time from immediate (e.g., master a skill, win a competition) to long term (e.g., make the Olympic team in four years). In sports such as golf, tennis, and running, goals form the basis for the continuous process of growth and mastery, which sometimes spans much of one's adult life (Zimmerman & Kitsantas, 2007). Athletes also attach considerable importance to their goals, and as a result they experience a wide range of emotions in response to goal attainment and failure. Thus, sports provide an ideal context to test the propositions of goal setting theory (Locke & Latham, 1990) and to explore new directions for research on goal effectiveness (cf., Locke & Latham, 2006).

This chapter has three general purposes. First, empirical tests of the propositions of goal setting theory will be reviewed. Research on goal setting in sports has proliferated since the publication of Locke and Latham's (1990) volume on goal setting theory, and the current review provides a summary of the extant research in this area. Second, the different types of goals used by athletes and their effects on goal processes and outcomes will be examined. Research on goal setting in sports has the potential to inform several new developments in goal setting theory, particularly those related to goal choice, affect, stress, and learning (Latham & Locke, 2007; Locke & Latham, 2006). Third, the centrality of goals for ongoing self-regulation of performance will be examined. Studies show that athletes structure goals hierarchically and use them to monitor and optimize performance.

## Tests of Goal Setting Theory

### Goal Characteristics

Given the ubiquity of goals in sports, it is surprising that research on goal setting in sports did not gain momentum until several years after goal setting theory was introduced in the organizational psychology literature. Interest among sports psychologists in the effects of goal setting was sparked by the publication of Locke and Latham's (1985) article on the application of goal setting to sports. Locke and Latham (1985) suggested that goal setting could have stronger effects in sports than other settings because performance measurement—a precondition for the positive effects of goal setting—is typically easier and more objective in sports. Many sports have clear measures of performance (e.g., race time, distance jumped or thrown, batting average, points scored), which makes it easy for athletes both to set goals and judge goal–performance discrepancies. Surprisingly, early reviews of the research on goal setting in sports indicated that the effect of goals on performance was weaker than in other settings. Kyllo and Landers (1995) conducted a meta-analysis of 36 studies that examined goal setting in sport and physical activity and reported an overall effect size of .34. Although statistically significant, the effect size was smaller than the .50 to .80 range reported in the organizational psychology literature (Locke & Latham, 2002; Tubbs, 1986). Burton (1992) published a qualitative review of goal setting studies and reported that about two-thirds of the studies supported the propositions of goal-setting theory, a value that was lower than the 90% support reported by Locke and Latham (1990) for all performance contexts.

Based on these early results, researchers such as Weinberg (1994) questioned whether goal setting, a motivational intervention, would have incremental effects on performance in sports because performers are likely to be highly motivated already. However, Locke (1991) identified several methodological flaws in the early studies that may have accounted for the muted effect of goals, particularly the failure to control for spontaneous goal setting and competition effects, and the absence of measures of personal goals. Many of the early goal setting studies in sports involved physical activity tasks such as sit-ups and juggling that provided intrinsic task feedback to participants, allowing those in the "do-your-best" or no-goal conditions to set and monitor their own personal goals. In addition, assigned goals affect performance indirectly through personal goals (Locke & Latham, 2002), and thus measuring personal goals is essential for assessing the true effects of goal specificity and difficulty. Another limitation noted by Locke (1991) was that "difficult" goals were not all that difficult. Success rates sometimes exceeded 50%, much higher than the 10% rate suggested by Locke and Latham (1990) for difficult goal manipulations.

The field was generally receptive of Locke's (1991) critique, and studies published since then provide stronger support for the goal difficulty and specificity hypotheses. Bar-Eli, Tenenbaum, Pie, Btesh, and Almong (1997), for example, controlled for social comparison effects and found that specific and difficult but attainable goals resulted in better performance on an endurance task than easy, do-best, and no-goal conditions. This effect was observed across three different training periods (4, 6, and 8 weeks). Burton and Weiss (2008) reviewed 88 goal setting studies in sports and physical activity and concluded that 70 demonstrated moderate to strong goal setting effects, an 80% effectiveness rate that approaches the 90% rate found in non-sports settings. It should be noted, however, that Burton and Weiss (2008) included all of the early goal setting studies in their review, which may result in a downwardly biased estimate of goal effects. Nonetheless, the motivational effects of goals are widely recognized in the sports psychology literature (Filby, Maynard, & Graydon, 1999; Gould, 2006; Zimmerman & Kitsantas, 2007).

Despite the improved support for goal setting theory, the sports goal setting literature still has limitations. The number of studies that have used sports populations and sports tasks is remarkably small. Only about one-fourth of the published studies involve sports populations, with the vast majority using non-athlete (e.g., student) or recreational samples (Burton, Pickering, Weinberg, Yukelson, & Weigand, 2010). Further, most of the tasks involved in the studies involve motor skills or physical fitness tasks, such as sit-ups and juggling. Relatively few studies have used sports-specific tasks in simulated or actual competitions or training environments. Finally, no direct tests of goal setting theory have been conducted with elite athletes, despite the fact that goals may be most beneficial for them, given their high levels of ability and commitment (Burton et al., 2010). Laboratory methods are critical for establishing control over variables and identifying causal relationships, but the ecological validity of research findings also needs to be addressed. It is uncertain whether the conclusions of studies based on non-athletes performing general physical activity tasks will generalize to experienced and elite athletes performing sports-specific tasks. The results may generalize better to physical exercise in general than to sports specifically.

There have been some recent field studies that provide correlational evidence of goal setting effects in competition. Donovan and Williams (2003) examined the relation between goal setting and performance among college track and field athletes over the course of a competitive season. Controlling for differences in ability, competition goals were strongly related to performance in competition ($r = .67$). Kane, Baltes, and Moss (2001) found in a sample of 216 high school wrestlers that goals that athletes self-set prior to a season predicted season performance over and above the athlete's prior performance. Stoeber, Uphill, and Hotham (2009) found that personal goal difficulty predicted race performance in triathletes beyond the athletes' personal best prior to competition. These studies increase confidence in the generalizability of the earlier studies. In sum, there is ample evidence that goal setting improves performance on sports and exercise tasks, although the effect of goals on performance of experienced and elite athletes is understudied.

## Mediators

In the organizational literature, the effects of assigned goals are mediated by personal goals and by self-efficacy judgments, and the effects of personal goals are mediated by effort, attention, persistence, and knowledge (Locke & Latham, 2002). There have been relatively few tests of mediators of assigned goals in the sports psychology literature, perhaps due to the greater emphasis that sports psychologists place on personal or self-set goals than assigned goals (Weinberg & Weigand, 1993). Studies that have been conducted confirm the mediating roles of both personal goals and self-efficacy (e.g., Lerner & Locke, 1995; Theodorakis, 1996). Lerner and Locke (1995), for example, found that personal goals and self-efficacy fully mediated the effect of goal difficulty on performance on a physical activity task. Research also indicates that the effects of personal goals are mediated by effort, attention, and strategy development (Zimmerman & Kitsantas, 1996, 2007).

Self-efficacy is a robust predictor of performance in sports, with an estimated effect size of .38 across 45 studies (Moritz, Feltz, Fahrbach, & Mack, 2000). Further, studies suggest that a recursive relationship exists between self-efficacy, personal goals, and performance. Past performance is a strong predictor of self-efficacy (Feltz & Lirgg, 2001) and personal goals (Kane, Marks, Zaccaro, & Blair, 1996; Williams, Donovan, & Dodge, 2000). Personal goals and self-efficacy, in turn, have direct and independent effects on performance (Kane et al., 1996, 2001; Lerner & Locke, 1995). In additional, self-efficacy has been found to have both direct and indirect effects on performance through personal goals (Kane et al., 1996) and enhanced goal commitment (see Chapter 6).

## Moderators

There have also been several tests of moderators of the goal-performance effect in the sports psychology literature. Research confirms that the relationship between goal characteristics and performance is strongest when people are highly committed to their goals and feedback is provided (Burton & Weiss, 2008; Filby et al., 1999; Kyllo & Landers, 1995). By the same token, commitment is most important when goals are difficult (see Chapter 6). The sports goal setting literature diverges from the organizational literature regarding the effects of participation in goal setting. Reviews of goal setting theory (Locke & Latham, 1990, 2002) indicate no difference in the effectiveness of assigned, participatively set, and self-set goals, once differences in goal difficulty are controlled. However, in the sports literature, participation in goal setting has been associated with stronger goal effects. Kyllo and Landers' (1995) meta-analysis revealed that participatively set goals were associated with a stronger effect size (.62) than assigned goals (.30). However, it is unclear if these studies adequately controlled for effects of goal difficulty.

## Types of Goals in Sports

### Outcome, Performance, and Process

Researchers in sports psychology stress the importance of distinguishing between three types of goals: outcome, performance, and process (Filby et al., 1999; Hardy, 1997). *Outcome goals* refer to the "end points" of activities, such as results of competition (e.g., winning versus losing; finishing place in a race; making the varsity team). The focus of outcome goals is often a normative comparison, and thus goal attainment depends on the performance of competitors. *Performance goals* refer to an athlete's personal achievement, such as the number of points scored in a game or finishing time for a 5K race. These goals are often related to personal standards of success; for example, a distance runner may want to improve her time by 15 seconds in a 5k race. *Process goals* refer to the specific skills, technique, and strategies used to perform satisfactorily (Hardy, 1997). For example, a process goal related to rebounding in basketball would be to box out an opponent. Outcome, performance, and process goals are interrelated, and each contributes to success in sports. To win the 100 m freestyle in the Olympics (an outcome goal), a male swimmer has to be able to swim as fast as 46.9 seconds (a performance goal), a time that is faster than the current champion. To attain that performance goal, he may set a series of process goals that focus on improved technique, strength, and reaction time.

In the organizational psychology literature, goal setting researchers have used the term *learning goal* to refer to goals that focus on acquiring the skills, knowledge, or strategies needed to perform a task successfully (Seijts & Latham, 2001; Winters & Latham, 1996). Learning goals are similar to process goals in that they emphasize the building blocks for attaining performance goals. However, learning/process and performance goals should not be confused with the types of goal orientation studied by achievement motivation researchers. In the achievement motivation literature, goal researchers make the distinction between mastery goals, which focus on development of competence and task mastery, and performance goals, which focus on demonstrating competence relative to others (Dweck & Leggett, 1988; Elliot, 1999). It is important to note that this conceptualization of a performance goal emphasizes social comparison and competition, whereas goal setting theory research virtually never involved the use of competitive goals but only goals as a standard to be met. According to achievement goal theories, the notion of goal refers to a global purpose for involvement in an activity and can be seen as a trait or dispositional variable as opposed to a state variable. The effect of goal disposition on goal setting and performance in sports will be discussed in a later section; for now it is useful to note that performance goal orientation is aligned with outcome goals in sports, whereas mastery goal orientation is aligned with process and performance goals (Hardy, 1997).

Most tests of goal setting in sports employed performance goals, so less is known about the effectiveness of process and outcome goals. There has been a debate in the sports and exercise psychology literature about the effectiveness and appropriateness of outcome goals. Some researchers have argued that athletes should avoid outcome goals and set performance and process goals only. To support this position, they point to studies linking outcome goals to low levels of personal control, increased dropout rate among young athletes, and impaired performance under stressful conditions (Burton & Weiss, 2008; Duda, 1992). They also argue that outcome goals create a climate that places too much emphasis on winning, which may result in maladaptive motivation patterns and unhealthy attitudes toward sports. Burton's fundamental goal concept epitomizes this position: "the fundamental goal concept that emphasizes process and performance over outcome goals plays the biggest role in determining goal-setting effectiveness in sports" (Burton & Weiss, 2008; p. 340). Other researchers argue that there is insufficient evidence to support the superiority of process and performance goals (Hardy, 1997), and hold that outcome goals are essential to sports, if not defining it. In addition, studies have found that successful athletes use a combination of process, performance, and outcome goals (Filby et al., 1999; Kingston & Hardy, 1997). As will be suggested in the sections that follow, outcome goals play an important motivational role in helping athletes organize their training and competitive activities. They may also be important for building commitment to process and performance goals. The challenge for coaches and athletes is to identify the correct goal or combination of goals for different situations.

*Training versus Competition Goals*

Locke and Latham (1985) stressed the importance of distinguishing between training and competition when studying the effects of goals. In training, athletes spend considerable time improving their skills, developing strategies, and preparing for competition. Too few studies exist to allow reliable conclusions regarding the relative strength of the goal difficulty and goal specificity in competition versus training settings. In fact, no studies were found that compared directly the relative strength of practice and competition goals. Kyllo and Landers (1995) reported that the meta-analytic effect size for goal setting was higher in competition settings than noncompetition settings. Their analysis, however, was based on a small set of studies.

Other studies have examined the frequency, type, and function of self-set goals in competition and training. Survey studies confirm that athletes of all ability levels, from novice to elite, set goals for both competition and practice. It seems intuitive that process goals would be more common in practice, where the athlete's focus may be on learning and execution, and that performance and outcome goals would be more common in competition, where the athlete's focus is on performing optimally or winning (Burton et al., 2010). However, research suggests that practice and competition goals may be more similar than dissimilar. Munroe-Chandler et al. (2004) performed a qualitative analysis of goals reported by 249 athletes representing 18 sports. They found that athletes set more outcome goals in competition than practice, but found surprising similarity in the frequency and nature of process goals in both practice and competition. Specifically, athletes reported setting goals for mastering skills and improving execution equally in competition and training settings. Competition is viewed not only as a venue for determining relative rank versus opponents, but also an opportunity for improving skills, execution, and strategy. These findings indicate that although outcome goals may be more salient in competitions than training, athletes perceive utility in all three types of goals in both settings.

Although all athletes may set similar types of goals, the characteristics of personal goals differ between experts and nonexperts. Olympic athletes reported setting more competition goals than practice goals (Weinberg et al., 2000), which may reflect the importance of competition to elite athletes. Cleary and Zimmerman (2001) found that during practice sessions, varsity basketball players who excelled at making free throws during games ("experts") set more specific performance ("make 10 of 10 free throws") and process ("keep my elbow in as I shoot") goals than their less proficient peers ("non-experts") and novice basketball players. Skilled athletes may have stronger meta-cognitive and motivational skills that allow them to set more effective goals than less skilled athletes. These findings also imply that goal setting interventions during training may be especially helpful for novices because the goals they set may lack the specificity and difficulty needed to produce results.

## Goal Hierarchies

Athletes typically pursue goals within specific cycles, reflecting seasons of competition, playoff and championship tournaments, Olympic cycles, and school or professional careers. Within a specific cycle, athletes are likely to set multiple goals and may partition long-term (distal) goals into short-term (proximal) goals. Distal goals represent one's ultimate or ideal level of performance, and typically represent a significant challenge to the actor. Proximal goals are subgoals that serve as stepping stones or building blocks to one's ideal goal (Donovan & Williams, 2003). Proximal goals serve important motivational functions by providing short-term incentives and direction for behavior, boosting self-efficacy, and reducing frustration stemming from failure to meet challenging goals (Bandura, 1986).

Proximal goals may simply represent intermediate steps leading to a distal goal, as when a distance runner looking to improve her time by 30 seconds over 6 months may set a proximal goal of a 5 second improvement per month. Goal hierarchies may also be organized more complexly, with one proximal goal serving multiple distal goals, or distal outcome goals used to organize proximal process and performance goals. Athletes often set challenging goals that require significant development of skill and strategy. As Hardy (1997) suggested, a combination of multiple goals, organized hierarchically but employed in a flexible manner, may facilitate skill acquisition and provide the motivation to sustain the training needed to attain the distal goal.

Unfortunately, research on the effectiveness of goal hierarchies in sports is virtually nonexistent, except for descriptive studies that confirm that athletes hold multiple goals simultaneously. Research has been stymied by the lack of reliable and valid measures of athletes' goal hierarchies (Burton & Weiss, 2008). Measurement methods are needed that capture both goal priorities and temporal considerations. In addition, longitudinal research designs are needed that look at goal attainment and goal adjustment among temporally organized goals (cf., Donovan & Williams, 2003).

## Team Goals

The effectiveness of team goals in sports was demonstrated by Anderson, Crowell, Doman, and Howard (1988), who examined the effect of three interventions—individual feedback, team goal setting, and praise—on the rate of legal body checking by members of a university ice hockey team. The three interventions were staggered in an ABCD design (baseline, feedback, goal setting, praise) for two consecutive seasons. The goal setting manipulation involved establishing a team objective for increased checking, followed by individualized goal setting plans for each player on the team. Although group goal setting was introduced after a successful feedback intervention, it had a significant incremental effect on checking behavior in each season. The goal setting intervention used by Anderson et al. (1988) created individual goals that were highly compatible with the team goal. This is consistent with Seijts and Latham's (2000) finding that compatibility between individual and team goals moderated the effects of team goals on team effectiveness. When individual goals were compatible with team goals, team goal difficulty predicted team success. When individual and team goals were in conflict, team goals were ineffective.

Lee (1988) examined the relationship between perceived characteristics of team goals and performance in a sample of female field hockey players from nine college teams. Results revealed that perceived team goal clarity was a significant predictor of a team's winning percentage. Further, perceived goal specificity and difficulty mediated the effect of self-efficacy on winning percentage. Team goals may also affect group processes and dynamics. In a study of 145 adult athletes representing 13 community-based teams, Brawley, Carron, and Widmeyer (1993) found team goals were positively related to team satisfaction, cohesion, and perceived performance. They also reported that perceived participation in team goal setting was related to cohesion and satisfaction with team goals.

## Processes and Outcomes

### Skill Acquisition

Studies in a variety of settings have shown that specific, difficult performance goals may be detrimental to performance when people have yet to acquire the requisite knowledge, skills, or abilities for a task (Kanfer & Ackerman, 1989; Petersen, 2009; Seijts & Latham, 2005). Recent advances in goal setting theory incorporate these findings by suggesting that learning goals should substitute for performance goals when learning rather than just performance motivation is required (Latham & Locke, 2007; Locke & Latham, 2006—see also Chapter 13). Similar recommendations have been made in the sports literature, where process goals are recommended over performance and outcome goals during early phases of learning.

Zimmerman and Kitsantas (1996) examined self-regulated learning of dart throwing in a sample of adolescent girls. Participants were assigned either a process goal that emphasized proper execution of motor actions or a performance goal (score as many points as possible by hitting the center of the dartboard). After the practice period, skill mastery was assessed on a series of 6 test trials, and perceived self-efficacy was measured on a survey. Results showed that compared to performance goals, process goals increased dart-throwing mastery and self-efficacy perceptions. One explanation for these findings is that the self-evaluative requirements of performance goals place additional processing demands on novices, depleting their cognitive and attentional resources and delaying learning.

However, once skills have been mastered, athletes may benefit from shifting from process to performance or outcome goals. As a function of practice, motor behaviors are routinized and performed automatically, at which point attention is no longer needed to execute subactions correctly. In fact, the conscious processing of automatized behavior may be disruptive because it slows down the execution of motor skills and produces inefficient organization of subactions. Results of a second study by Zimmerman and Kitsantas (1997) support the shifting goal model of skill acquisition. Participants were assigned a performance goal, one of two process goals, or a shifting goal, and then practiced throwing darts for 20 minutes. In the shifting goal condition, participants were given a process goal for 12 minutes, the point at which strategic proficiency was assumed to be routinized, and then switched to a performance goal for the final 8 minutes of the practice period. Results showed that participants in the shifting goal condition outperformed those in the process goal conditions, who in turn outperformed those in the outcome goal condition. Based on these results, Zimmerman (2008) developed a model of self-regulated learning that emphasizes sequencing of process, performance, and outcome goals. According to this model, effective self-regulators set multiple goals and use them to monitor and evaluate performance. They must be able to shift adaptively between goals, employing controlled processes when learning a skill, but relying on automatic processes when performing well-learned skills.

The timing of the shift from process to performance or outcome goals may also be important. Petersen (2009) had novice adolescent tennis players practice a forehand tennis stroke in one of four goal conditions: performance, intermediate process, extended process, or self-shifting goal. All participants practiced the stroke 60 times. In the performance goal condition, participants were told to focus on where the ball landed and count the number of times they hit the target. In the other three conditions, participants were given a process goal of hitting the ball with the "sweet spot" of the racket each time. In the intermediate process condition, participants used the process goal for 20 attempts and then shifted to the performance goal for the final 40 attempts. In the extended process condition, participants used the process goal for 40 attempts and then shifted to the performance goal for 20 attempts. Participants in the self-shifting condition shifted from process to performance goal when they felt that they had mastered the skill.

Participants in the extended process condition displayed greater service shot accuracy during the test phase of the experiment than those given performance goals only, those who shifted after intermediate process practice, and those who shifted on their own. Participants in the extended process condition were also more successful at hitting the "sweet spot." These results suggest that prolonging attention to processes provides a learning advantage that translates to better performance. The findings also highlight the advantage of "overlearning" sports-specific skills.

More generally, goals influence what a performer chooses to attend to while performing a task (Zimmerman, 2008). By concentrating on process goals during learning, athletes deliberately attend to important behaviors that facilitate skill acquisition and obtain feedback on effectiveness at a critical development stage. This helps facilitate learning. Once skills are learned, performance and outcome goals should be introduced in order to focus attention on exerting effort, identifying strategies, and adjusting to competitive situations.

### Deliberate Practice

Studies on expertise emphasize the importance of practicing deliberately for years before reaching elite status. According to Ericsson (2006), the type of training that is required to become an expert is not simply training of any type, but a highly regimented, goal-oriented practice that requires high effort and sustained attention. This type of training is defined as "deliberate practice" and has the explicit goal of improving performance (Ericsson, Krampe, & Tesch-Römer, 1993). Deliberate practice has specific characteristics: (1) it presents an appropriate level of difficulty, one that is challenging but not frustrating; (2) it provides informative feedback to performers; (3) it involves a fair amount of repetition; and (4) it provides performers with opportunities to correct errors. Deliberate practice is not mindless repetition of activities, but, rather, careful attention to the processes involved in performance. Goal setting lies at the heart of this type of training: "performers and their teacher's identify specific goals for improving particular aspects of performance and design training activities that allow the performer to gradually refine performance with feedback and opportunities for repetition" (Ericsson, 2006; p. 696).

Although deliberate practice is defined as a goal-driven activity, there has been limited research on the characteristics of goals that best motivate athletes to commit to it. The research on deliberate practice in sports has focused on Ericsson's 10-year rule, which states that a minimum of 10 years of specific preparation is necessary to reach expert level in a field (Baker, Côté, & Abernethy, 2003; Hodges & Starkes, 1996). As a result, there has been more focus on the number of hours and years athletes practice than on the content of practice, including the nature of one's goals. Research is needed that examines the characteristics of goals that increase an athlete's motivation to engage in deliberate practice. Given Ericsson's (2006) emphasis on the processes involved in performance, it seems intuitive to focus on process goals when practicing deliberately. Process goals serve an attentional cueing function, keeping athletes focused on what needs to be done to improve performance. However, it seems reasonable to suggest that outcome and performance goals are most likely the driving force behind the athlete's willingness to put in so many hours of highly structured, repetitive training. The anticipated tangible and intangible outcomes associated with attaining performance and outcome goals, and strong commitment to these goals, are likely to sustain deliberate practice. Athletes with clearly specified goal hierarchies organized around challenging distal goals may be more willing to put in the hours of training needed to reach elite level than athletes with less well-specified goal hierarchies. There are no empirical tests of this assertion, but future research should investigate the relationship between goal structures and the motivation to practice deliberately.

### Goals and Stress

Beggs (1990) suggested that outcome and performance goals are "double-edged swords" in that they have the motivational potential to improve performance but may also generate high levels of stress in performers. Performance and outcome goals in competition may be particularly problematic because athletes are highly invested in these goals and the possibility of not reaching them can be ego threatening. High levels of stress may impair sports performance through several mechanisms. First, stress and anxiety may induce excessive muscular tension, resulting in reduced efficiency and coordination. Second, anxiety may divert attentional resources from the task at hand and direct them toward controlling the anxiety. Persistent anxiety may deplete the cognitive resources needed to sustain performance (Mullen & Hardy, 2010). Third, high anxiety may also disrupt automatic task control processes that typically are associated with skilled performance. As a result, athletes may attempt to exert conscious control over the execution of critical skills, creating slow, deliberate movements characteristic of earlier, less proficient stages of skill acquisition (Masters, 1992).

Research in the achievement motivation literature provides evidence of stress-mediated detrimental effects of goals. Senko and Harackiewicz (2005) found that difficult performance goals increased perceived pressure to perform, which impaired performance when perceived competence was low. High perceived competence buffered the negative effects of pressure on performance. Perceived competence and self-efficacy are closely related, so these findings suggest that self-efficacy may help people cope with competitive pressure. Bueno, Weinberg, Fernández-Castro, & Capdevila (2008) proposed that perceived threat mediates the effects of goals on performance during competition. Their coping model suggests that during competition athletes assess the extent to which an important outcome goal will be reached. The perception that one's goal will not be reached creates feelings of threat and helplessness. These negative emotions, in turn, may reduce goal commitment, self-efficacy, and performance. Bueno et al. (2008) tested this model with a sample of distance runners by experimentally manipulating goal attainability and competitive success. Participants completed three five-minute repetitions on an inclined treadmill and were randomly assigned attainable or unattainable goals and were provided with normative success or failure feedback. Results showed that threat perceptions indirectly influenced performance through decreased self-efficacy and personal goals.

Based partly on these findings, some researchers and consultants advocate using process goals during competition rather than performance and outcome goals. Process goals may reduce the negative effects of competitive anxiety by shifting the athlete's focus away from the outcomes of performance to salient aspects of the task.

Although some studies support this hypothesis (e.g., Kingston, Hardy, & Markland, 1992), focusing on the task-related components of a skill may also disrupt automatic task processing and create performance deficits (Mullen & Hardy, 2010). Jackson, Ashford, and Norsworthy (2006) found that process goals that focus on the specific movements involved in dribbling a soccer ball (i.e., "part" process goals) impaired performance under pressure conditions. These findings regarding the effect of process goals on anxious performance have produced a paradox: process goals may reduce susceptibility to anxiety by serving an attentional cueing function, but they may also lead to performance decrements by increasing the conscious processing of specific aspects of a sports-related skill.

Mullen and Hardy (2010) have recently suggested a resolution to the process goal paradox. They distinguished between part process goals that break a task down into its subactions, and holistic process goals that emphasize whole movement or action. Part process goals draw attention to different components of an integrated set of movements. For example, a golfer may be cued to "keep the wrists firm" and "keep the hands if front of the putter blade." Holistic process goals such as "smooth swing" encourage chunking of the components of a skill, allowing for fluid and automatic execution of the skill. As a result, holistic process goals may promote the automatic control of behavior, whereas part process goals may replace automaticity with controlled processing. Mullen and Hardy (2010) tested the effects of part versus holistic oriented process goals on performance in a series of studies involving long jumpers, basketball players shooting free throws, and golfers performing a putting task. Athletes performed their tasks under low and high anxiety conditions and were instructed to use a part or holistic process goal. An example of a part process goal for the long jumpers was "thrust hips forward after take-off"; a corresponding holistic process goal was "reach." Results showed that in the high-anxiety condition across all three studies, athletes using holistic process goals performed significantly better than athletes using part process goals. Performance improved from low- to high-anxiety conditions for those using holistic goals, but remained constant or decreased slightly for those using part process goals. These results suggest that anxious performers may benefit from holistic process goals compared with single part-focused process goals. Mullen and Hardy (2010) found that a single-cue part process goal did not impair anxious performance. However, studies using multiple cues have demonstrated negative effects of part process goals (Jackson et al., 2006). This suggests that the likelihood of conscious control of behavior increases with the number of cues associated with a part process goal. For example, a process goal with the cues "make full foot contact on the penultimate step" and "thrust the hip forward after takeoff" may be more disruptive of an anxious long jumper's performance than a process goal with a single cue. Alternatively, multiple cues may create cognitive overload and distract attention from critical aspects of the task.

In sum, goals have the potential to create stress that impairs performance, particularly in competition. This may occur when performance and outcome goals divert attention from task execution to concerns about goal progress and performance evaluation. Process goals may reduce performance decrements associated with ego threat, but paradoxically may impair performance by disrupting automatic execution of skills. Process goals that focus on holistic movements may reduce performance and outcome-related stress while preserving automaticity.

## Goals and Personality

Over the past decade, research interest in the effects of personality traits on goal setting has increased (Latham & Locke, 2007). In the sports psychology literature, two traits that have implications for goal setting are achievement goal orientation and perfectionism.

### Achievement Goal Orientation

Goal orientations capture the purposes for engaging in achievement activities and the standards by which competence and successful performance are judged (Duda, 2007). Two distinct but parallel frameworks exist in the achievement goal literature that identify two goal dispositions, one reflecting task involvement and one reflecting ego involvement. Nicholls (1984) labeled these dispositions task and ego orientation, respectively, whereas Dweck and Leggett (1988) labeled them mastery and performance orientation, respectively. People with task-mastery dispositional goals focus on developing skills in achievement settings and evaluate their performance using self-referenced criteria. They feel successful when they show improvement on a task or master a skill. People with ego-performance dispositional goals focus on outperforming others in achievement settings and rely on normative standards to evaluate their performance. They feel successful when they perform better than others. Elliot (1999) further distinguished between two types of ego-performance goals, reflecting approach and avoidance tendencies in achievement situations. "Performance-approach" goals focus on attaining normative competence (i.e., doing better than others), whereas "performance-avoidance" goals focus on not demonstrating normative incompetence (i.e., not doing worse than others). The achievement goal literature provides evidence that these goal orientations generate the meaning that individuals attach to achievement settings and provide the lens through which goal pursuits are experienced and interpreted (Duda, 2007).

The vast majority of studies on achievement goals in sports have examined affective consequences of goal dispositions. Findings show that task-mastery goals relate positively to intrinsic motivation, enjoyment, and performance satisfaction (see Duda, 2007, for a review). Ego-performance goals do not show a consistent relationship with affective outcomes of sports. Surprisingly, there are only a handful of studies that examine the relationship between goal dispositions and performance in sports. Stoeber et al. (2009) measured goal disposition in triathletes prior to a major competition. They found that performance-approach goals were positively related to race times, indicating that triathletes with a strong motivation to do better than others (i.e., an outcome goal) raced faster than those low on this motivation. Conversely, performance-avoidance goals were negatively related to race times, indicating that athletes strongly motivated to avoid doing worse than others raced slower than those low in this motivation. Stoeber et al. (2009) also found that the effect of performance-approach goals on performance was fully mediated by self-set performance (time) and outcome (rank) goals. Individuals motivated to do better than others set more difficult time and rank goals, which were fully responsible for better race times. This supports Latham and Locke's (2007) suggestion that goal setting mediates the effects of goal disposition on performance.

Based on the evidence of positive relationships between task-mastery goal orientation and affective outcomes, many sports psychologists advocate the use of task-mastery goals over ego-performance goals (Burton & Weiss, 2008; Weinberg, 2002). This conclusion seems premature. There is insufficient evidence regarding the effect of goal dispositions on performance, and that which exists supports the superiority of ego-performance (outcome) goals, as long as they are accompanied by approach rather than avoidance motivation. Further, evidence indicates that the motivation to do better than others (outcome goal) leads to more effective goals setting, which results in superior performance (Senko & Harackiewicz, 2005; Stoeber et al., 2009). Obviously, more research is needed that examines the relationships among goal disposition, goal setting, and performance, but recent evidence presents a more sanguine view of ego-performance and outcome goals than earlier reviews of the literature.

## Perfectionism

Perfectionism is a multidimensional trait that is characterized by striving for flawlessness, setting of excessively high standards for performance, and critical evaluation of one's performance (Frost, Marten, Lahart, & Rosenblate, 1990; Stoll, Lau, & Stoeber, 2008). Stoeber, Stoll, Pescheck, and Otto (2008) identified two facets of perfectionism that have important implications for goal setting: striving for perfection (perfectionistic standards) and negative reactions to imperfection. Striving for perfection involves holding oneself to high standards of performance, and hence should be positively correlated with the level of challenge in one's personal goals. Indeed, Stoeber and colleagues found that, for both elite and non-elite athletes, perfectionistic standards were positively related to both mastery and performance-approach goals (Stoeber et al., 2008; Stoeber, Stoll, Salmi, & Tiikkaja, 2009). On the other hand, negative reaction to imperfection was related to performance-avoidance goals.

Stoll et al. (2008) examined the relationship between perfectionism and performance on a novel basketball training task. They found that perfectionistic standards were positively related to performance across several trials of learning. They also found an interesting interaction between perfectionistic standards and negative reactions to imperfection when predicting increments in performance from trial to trial. Performance increased the most for participants who were high on both perfectionistic standards and negative reactions to imperfection. One explanation for this finding is that high perfectionistic standards created challenging improvement goals for each trial, while high negative reactions to imperfection created sensitivity to goal-performance discrepancies and motivation to reduce perceived discrepancies (cf., Williams, Donovan, & Dodge, 2000). Unfortunately, Stoll et al. (2008) did not include measures of goal setting or reactions to discrepancies in their study, and thus this explanation remains speculative.

Perfectionistic standards were associated with personal goals and performance in Stoeber et al.'s (2009) study of triathletes. These researchers examined the joint effects of perfectionism, achievement goals, and personal goal setting on race performance. They found that the positive relationship between perfectionistic standards and race performance was mediated by goal orientation, such that high perfectionistic standards were related to a stronger emphasis on performance-approach than performance-avoidance goals, which in turn predicted race performance. In other words, high perfectionists set outcome goals for competition, and these outcome goals predicted race times. This provides further evidence that goals mediate the effect of individual differences on performance.

## Dynamic Self-Regulation of Performance

Researchers interested in the self-regulation of performance seek to explain how self-set goals affect performance trajectories over the course of performance cycles (Donovan & Williams, 2003; Zimmerman & Kitsantas, 2007). In contrast to traditional goal setting research, these studies do not focus on the effects of a discrete goal, but rather focus how athletes set, pursue, and revise goals over time. Social cognitive theories distinguish three phases of self-regulation: forethought, performance, and self-reflection (Bandura, 1986; Zimmerman & Campillo, 2003). Figure 24.1 presents a model developed by Zimmerman and Campillo (2003) that is useful for investigating self-regulation processes in athletes. During the forethought phase, athletes set goals for upcoming cycles of training and competition. Key decisions during this phase relate to the choice of goals—what type and combination of goals (distal versus proximal; process versus performance versus outcome, etc.), level of difficulty, and time frame for goal attainment. Athletes (and their coaches) also plan strategies for reaching these goals during this phase. Goal setting and planning processes will be influenced by self-motivation beliefs, such as self-efficacy and goal orientation. During the performance phase, athletes pursue goals using task-execution and attention-focusing strategies. A critical task during the performance phase is self-observation and monitoring of performance and goal progress. The self-reflection phase is characterized by self-evaluations and self-reactions.

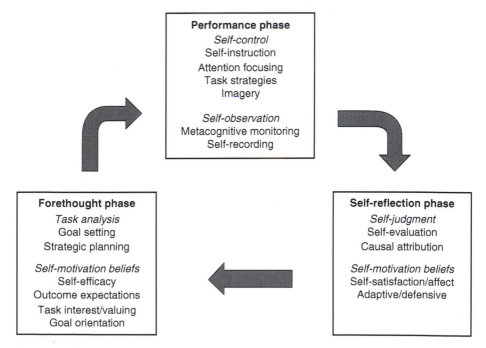

*Figure 24.1*  Phases and processes involved in self-regulation of performance. (From Zimmerman, B. J., & Campillo, M. (2003). Motivating self-regulated problem solvers. In J. E. Davidson & R. J. Sternberg (Eds.), *The nature of problem solving* (p. 239). New York: Cambridge University Press.)

Self-evaluation is based primarily on the size of the goal-performance discrepancy; attempts that fall short of the goal produce self-dissatisfaction, whereas attempts that match or exceed the goal produce self-satisfaction (Bandura, 1986; Williams et al., 2000). These self-reactions influence subsequent goal choice and planning decisions.

Two mechanisms operate during the cyclic process depicted in Figure 24.1: discrepancy production and discrepancy reduction (Bandura, 1986). Discrepancy production refers to feedforward control, whereby athletes motivate themselves initially by setting performance goals above current levels of performance and mobilizing effort on the basis of anticipated outcomes. Discrepancy reduction, or feedback control, refers to the subsequent adjustments of effort and strategies to achieve the desired level of performance (Williams et al., 2000). During self-reflection, people compare performance against their goal and use discrepancy information to evaluate the effectiveness of performance. Positive discrepancies (performance > goal) are likely to prompt individuals to raise their goal for subsequent performance attempts. Negative discrepancies (performance < goal) create self-dissatisfaction, which serves as an incentive for increased effort, better strategic planning, or revised goals (Bandura, 1986). The regulation of performance in this model centers on one's personal goals. Goals stimulate planning and initiate action during the forethought phase; they provide direction and guide attentional processes during the performance phase; and they provide the standards against which performance is judged in the reflection phase.

My colleagues and I conducted research with track and field athletes that sheds light on discrepancy production and reduction mechanisms and supports the model depicted in Figure 24.1. In two studies, we measured athletes' performance goals prior to the beginning of a competitive season and assessed performance, goal-performance discrepancies (GPDs), attributions for performance, self-reactions to performance, and goal revision using weekly post-competition diaries (Donovan & Williams, 2003; Williams, Donovan, & Dodge, 2000). The first study (Williams et al., 2000) examined goal pursuit and goal revision processes related to season goals (distal goals). In the second study (Donovan & Williams, 2003), weekly competition goals (proximal goals) were measured in addition to distal season goals. By measuring proximal and distal goals and weekly GPDs, we were able to provide some preliminary evidence regarding structure and function of goal hierarchies.

## Goal Choice

Strong support for discrepancy production was found in both studies. The vast majority of athletes set their season goals significantly higher than their personal best performance heading into the season. Throughout the season, for each competition and each event they competed in, athletes set goals that were higher than their best performance at that point of the season. There was also a clear hierarchical structure to their goals: competition goals were set at a level between their current best performance for the season and their distal season goal.

## GPD and Goal Revision

Satisfaction was positively correlated with goal attainment. The closer athletes were to competition and season goals, the greater their satisfaction with performance. GPD was a strong predictor of goal revision; the farther athletes were below their goal, the greater the downward goal revision. This relationship held for both competition (proximal) and season (distal) goals, but was stronger for proximal goals. Consistent with the model in Figure 24.1, the GPD–goal revision relationship was moderated by causal attributions (see also Chapter 4). Williams et al. (2000) found that controllability attributions moderated the effects of GPD on goal revision. When athletes perceived low personal control over the causes of their performance, goals were revised downward according to the magnitude of goal failure. However, when athletes perceived high personal control over the causes of performance, the GPD–goal revision relationship was nonsignificant. Donovan and Williams (2003) reported a similar interaction, but with stability attributions rather than controllability attributions. When the causes of performance were seen as stable, GPD was strongly related to goal revision, but when perceived causes were unstable, GPD and goal revision were unrelated. Outcomes that are attributed to uncontrollable and stable causes are likely to be seen as repeatable, and thus athletes experiencing goal failure under these conditions are likely to have reduced expectancies for success in the future. As a result, they may choose to lower their goal.

Several other interesting findings emerged. First, when athletes revised their goal downward, they did not eliminate the goal-performance discrepancy but rather reduced it to what was perhaps perceived as a more manageable level. They typically reduced the observed discrepancy by about 30%, leaving a discrepancy that was still substantial. Second, very few athletes attained their competition or season goals, but did not wait to reach their goals before raising them. As athletes approached their goals, they were likely to make them even more challenging for the next competition. Third, the phase of the season moderated the GPD–goal revision relationship in both studies: GPD and goal revision were weakly related during the first half of the season, but were strongly related in the second half of the season. As the season wound down, athletes may have lowered their goals in hopes of reaching them and finishing the season with a sense of accomplishment. The results of these studies indicate that GPD produces dissatisfaction; whether dissatisfaction is followed by downward goal revision (cognitive adjustment) or goal persistence (reactance) depends on the attributions that athletes make for performance and contextual factors such as phase of the performance cycle.

## Performance Trajectories

Although it may be tempting to view goal attainment as a meta-goal of performers and the primary source of self-satisfaction (Bandura, 1986), the findings of Donovan and Williams (2003) and Williams et al. (2000) suggest that athletes prioritize performance improvement over goal attainment. As noted above, athletes raised competition and season goals before reaching them, and when they lowered them in response to goal failure, they still left a substantial discrepancy between current and goal performance. They also used proximal goals to keep performance improving toward distal season goals. In fact, Donovan and Williams (2003) found that when distal goal-performance discrepancy was large, athletes raised the difficulty of their upcoming competition (proximal) goal, seemingly in an attempt to "get performance back on track." Figure 24.2 presents the trajectories of performance and proximal goals in relation to distal goals in the Donovan and Williams (2003) study. Proximal goals can be seen as leading performance

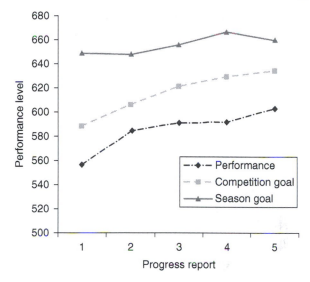

*Figure 24.2* Mean performance, competition goals, and season goals by progress report. (From Donovan, J. J., & Williams, K. J. (2003). *Journal of Applied Psychology, 88*, 379–390.).

toward distal goals. These data imply that eliminating discrepancies may not be the primary concern of individuals in achievement settings. Rather, self-regulation seems to be centered on making progress toward one's goals (cf. Carver & Scheier, 1990). Ultimately, athletes may feel self-satisfied and rewarded if their performance improves substantially, even if their goals have not been met (Bandura & Cervone, 1986).

## Conclusions

Nearly all athletes set goals for training and competition, and the empirical literature confirms the effectiveness of goal setting for increasing performance on sports-related tasks. There are surprising few studies that test goal setting propositions with sports populations in training or competitive environments; however, those that exist confirm the beneficial effects of specific and difficult goals. Athletes set and use different types of goals in both training and competitions, with successful athletes employing a combination of process, performance, and outcome goals. Contrary to speculation by some researchers, recent evidence suggests that outcome goals that focus on normative comparisons (e.g., winning) are not necessarily ineffective or demotivating. In fact, research suggests that challenging outcome goals are associated with effective goal setting and performance during competition. Focusing on outcome goals only may be ill-advised, but there are potential benefits to having outcome goals in one's motivational tool kit.

Goal hierarchies are an important area for future research on goal setting in sports. Research shows that possessing multiple goals is associated with positive outcomes in training and competition, but little is known about how best to structure and organize one's goals. Process goals offer several advantages for mastering skills during practice, and for directing attention and controlling stress during competition. However, outcome and performance goals provide the objectives for process goals and strengthen commitment to them. Highly structured goal hierarchies may be particularly important for providing the motivation to put in the many hours of highly structured, repetitive training needed to reach the elite level of one's sport. A better understanding of goal hierarchies seems essential for advancing research on deliberate practice, skill acquisition, and self-regulation of performance.

Goals may also lose their effectiveness when they disrupt automatic task control processes that are associated with skilled performance. This may occur when athletes attempt to control stress by exerting conscious control over the execution of critical skills or when they attend to multiple cues while performing a task. The process goals that athletes bring to competitions should emphasize holistic movements that support automatic execution of skills. The stress-mediated detrimental effects of goals are particularly likely to occur for athletes low in self-efficacy or perceived competence. During competition, if athletes sense that an outcome goal may not be met, feelings of ego threat and helplessness may emerge, which reduce goal commitment and performance. Efficacy boosting interventions may be the most effective way to prevent stress-induced effects of goals.

Finally, research on self-regulation of performance indicates that athletes use goals as tools for improving performance. They set distal and proximal performance goals to develop skills and improve performance over the course of performance cycles. Notably, athletes appear to prioritize performance improvement over goal attainment. They set challenging goals and manage their goals so as to maintain sizeable discrepancies between current and intended performance. Our studies suggest that athletes may not be bothered too much by goal-performance discrepancies but use discrepancy information to provide the motivation for continuous improvement.

# References

Anderson, D. C., Crowell, C. R., Doman, M., & Howard, G. S. (1988). Performance posting, goal setting, and activity-contingent praise as applied to a university hockey team. *Journal of Applied Psychology, 73,* 87–95.

Baker, J., Côté, J., & Abernethy, B. (2003). Sport-specific practice and the development of expert decision-making in team ball sports. *Journal of Applied Sport Psychology, 15,* 12–25.

Bandura, A. (1986). *Social foundations of thought and action: A social cognitive theory.* Englewood Cliffs, NJ: Prentice Hall.

Bandura, A., & Cervone, D. (1986). Differential engagement of self-reactive influences in cognitive motivation. *Organizational Behavior and Human Decision Processes, 38,* 92–113.

Bar-Eli, M., Tenenbaum, G., Pie, J., Btesh, Y., & Almong, A. (1997). Effect of goal difficulty, goal specificity and duration of practice time intervals on muscular endurance performance. *Journal of Sport Sciences, 15,* 125–135.

Beggs, A. (1990). Goal setting in sport. In J. G. Jones and L. Hardy (Eds.), *Stress and performance in sport* (pp. 135–170). Chichester, UK: Wiley.

Brawley, L. R., Carron, A. V., & Widmeyer, W. N. (1993). The influence of the group and its cohesiveness on perceptions of group goal-related variables. *Journal of Sport and Exercise Psychology, 15,* 245–260.

Bueno, J., Weinberg, R. S., Fernández-Castro, J., & Capdevila, L. (2008). Emotional and motivational mechanisms mediating the influence of goal setting on endurance athletes' performance. *Psychology of Sport and Exercise, 9,* 786–799.

Burton, D. (1992). The Jekyll/Hyde nature of goals: Reconceptualizing goal setting in sport. In T. Horn (Ed.), *Advances in sport psychology* (pp. 267–297). Champaign, IL: Human Kinectics.

Burton, D., Pickering, M., Weinberg, R., Yukelson, D., & Weigand, D. (2010). The competitive goal effectiveness paradox revisited: Examining the goal practices of prospective Olympic Athletes. *Journal of Applied Sport Psychology, 22,* 72–86.

Burton, D., & Weiss, C. (2008). The fundamental goal concept: The path to process and performance success. In T. S. Horn (Ed.), *Advances in sport psychology* (3rd ed., pp. 340–375). Champaign, IL: Human Kinetics.

Carver, C. S., & Scheier, M. F. (1990). Origins and functions of positive and negative affect: a control-process view. *Psychological Review, 97,* 19–35.

Cleary, T. J., & Zimmerman, B. J. (2001). Self-regulation differences during athletic practice by experts, non-experts, and novices. *Journal of Applied Sport Psychology, 13,* 185–206.

Donovan, J. J., & Williams, K. J. (2003). Missing the mark: effects of time and causal attributions on goal revision in response to goal-performance discrepancies. *Journal of Applied Psychology, 88,* 379–390.

Duda, J. L. (1992). Sport and exercise motivation: A goal perspective analysis. In G. Roberts (Ed.), *Motivation in sport and exercise* (pp. 57–91). Champaign, IL: Human Kinetics.

Duda, J. L. (2007). Motivation in sport: The relevance of competence and achievement goals. In A. J. Elliot and C. S. Dweck (Eds.), *Handbook of competence and motivation* (pp. 318–335). New York: Guilford.

Dweck, C. S., & Leggett, E. L. (1988). A social-cognitive approach to motivation and personality. *Psychological Review, 95,* 256–273.

Elliot, A. J. (1999). Approach and avoidance motivation and achievement goals. *Educational Psychology, 34,* 169–189.

Ericsson, K. A. (2006). The influence of experience and deliberate practice on the development of superior expert performance. In K. A. Ericsson, N. Charness, R. R. Hoffman, & P. J. Feltovich (Eds.), *The Cambridge handbook of expertise and expert performance* (pp. 685–705). New York: Cambridge University Press.

Ericsson, K. A., Krampe, R. T., & Tesch-Römer, C. (1993). The role of deliberate practice in the acquisition of expert performance. *Psychological Review, 100,* 363–406.

Feltz, D. L., & Lirgg, C. D. (2001). Self-efficacy beliefs of athletes, teams, and coaches. In R. Singer, H. Hausenblas, & C. Janelle (Eds.), *Handbook of sport psychology* (2nd ed., pp. 340–361). New York: Wiley.

Filby, W. C. D., Maynard, I. W., & Graydon, J. K. (1999). The effect of multiple-goal strategies on performance outcomes in training and competition. *Journal of Applied Sport Psychology, 11,* 230–246.

Frost, R. O., Marten, P., Lahart, C., & Rosenblate, R. (1990). The dimensions of perfectionism. *Cognitive Therapy and Research, 14,* 449–468.

Gould, D. (2006). Goal setting for peak performance. In J. M. Williams (Ed.), *Applied psychology: Personal growth to peak performance* (5th ed., pp. 240–259). Mountain View, CA: Mayfield.

Hardy, L. (1997). The Coleman Roberts Griffith address: Three myths about applied consultancy work. *Journal of Applied Sport Psychology, 9,* 277–294.

Hodges, N. J., & Starkes, J. L. (1996). Wrestling with the nature of expertise: A sport-specific test of Ericsson, Krampe and Tesch-Römer's (1993) theory of deliberate practice. *International Journal of Sport Psychology, 27*, 400–424.

Jackson, R. C., Ashford, K. J., & Norsworthy, G. (2006). Attentional focus, dispositional reinvestment, and skilled motor performance under pressure. *Journal of Sport and Exercise Psychology, 28*, 29–48.

Kane, T. D., Baltes, T. R., & Moss, M. C. (2001). Causes and consequences of free-set goals: An investigation of athletic self-regulation. *Journal of Sport and Exercise Psychology, 23*, 55–75.

Kane, T. D., Marks, M. A., Zaccaro, S. J., & Blair, V. (1996). Self-efficacy, personal goals, and wrestlers' self-regulation. *Journal of Sport and Exercise Psychology, 18*, 36–48.

Kanfer, R., & Ackerman, P. L. (1989). Motivation and cognitive abilities: An integrative/aptitude-treatment interaction approach to skill acquisition. *Journal of Applied Psychology, 74*, 657–690.

Kingston, K. M., & Hardy, L. (1997). Effects of different types of goals on processes that support performance. *The Sport Psychologist, 11*, 277–293.

Kingston, K. M., Hardy, L., & Markland, D. (1992). Study to compare the effect of two different goal orientations and stress levels on a number of situationally relevant performance subcomponents. *Journal of Sport Sciences, 10*, 610–611.

Kyllo, L. B., & Landers, D. M. (1995). Goal-setting in sport and exercise: A research synthesis to resolve the controversy. *Journal of Sport and Exercise Psychology, 17*, 117–137.

Latham, G. P., & Locke, E. A. (2007). New developments in and directions for goal-setting research. *European Psychologist, 12*, 290–300.

Lee, C. (1988). The relationship between goal setting, self-efficacy, and female hockey team performance. *International Journal of Sport Psychology, 20*, 147–161.

Lerner, B. S., & Locke, E. A. (1995). The effects of goal setting, self-efficacy, competition, and personal traits on the performance of an endurance task. *Journal of Sport and Exercise Psychology, 17*, 138–152.

Locke, E. A. (1991). Problems with goal-setting research in sports—and their solution. *Journal of Sport and Exercise Psychology, 8*, 311–316.

Locke, E. A., & Latham, G. P. (1985). The application of goal setting to sports. *Journal of Sports Psychology, 7*, 205–222.

Locke, E. A., & Latham, G. P. (1990). *A theory of goal setting and task performance.* Englewood Cliffs, NJ: Prentice Hall.

Locke, E. A., & Latham, G. P. (2002). Building a practically useful theory of goal setting and task motivation: A 35-year odyssey. *American Psychologist, 57*, 705–717.

Locke, E. A., & Latham, G. P. (2006). New directions in goal-setting theory. *Current Directions in Psychological Science, 15*, 265–268.

Masters, R. S. W. (1992). Knowledge, nerves, and know-how: The role of explicit versus implicit knowledge in the breakdown of a complex motor skill under pressure. *British Journal of Psychology, 83*, 343–358.

Moritz, S. E., Feltz, D. L., Fahrbach, K. R., & Mack, D. E. (2000). The relation of self-efficacy measures to sport performance: A meta-analytic review. *Research Quarterly for Exercise and Sport, 71*, 280–294.

Mullen, R., & Hardy, L. (2010). Conscious processing and the process goal paradox. *Journal of Sport and Exercise Psychology, 32*, 275–297.

Munroe-Chandler, K. J., Hall, C. R., & Weinberg, R. S. (2004). A qualitative analysis of the types of goals athletes set in training and competition. *Journal of Sport Behavior, 27*, 58–74.

Nicholls, J. G. (1984). Achievement motivation: Conceptions of ability, subjective experience, task choice, and performance. *Psychological Review, 91*, 328–246.

Petersen, S. (2009). *The role of goal setting and automaticity in novice athletes' development and performance of a tennis skill: A coaching intervention* (Doctoral dissertation). City University of New York (CUNY), New York.

Senko, C., & Harackiewicz, J. M. (2005). Achievement goals, task performance, and interest: Why perceived goal difficulty matters. *Personality and Social Psychology Bulletin, 31*, 1739–1753.

Seijts, G. H., & Latham, G. P. (2000). The effects of goal setting and group size on performance in a social dilemma. *Canadian Journal of Behavioral Science, 32*, 104–116.

Seijts, G. H., & Latham, G. P. (2001). The effect of learning, outcome, and proximal goals on a moderately complex task. *Journal of Organizational Behavior, 22*, 291–307.

Seijts, G. H., & Latham, G. P. (2005). Learning versus performance goals: When should each be used? *Academy of Management Executive, 19*, 124–131.

Stoeber, J., Stoll, O., Pescheck, E., & Otto, K. (2008). Perfectionism and goal orientations in athletes: Relations with approach and avoidance orientations in mastery and performance goals. *Psychology of Sport and Exercise, 9*, 102–121.

Stoeber, J., Stoll, O., Salmi, O., & Tiikkaja, J. (2009). Perfectionism and achievement goals in young Finnish ice-hockey players aspiring to make the Under-16 national team. *Journal of Sports Sciences, 27*, 85–94.

Stoeber, J., Uphill, M. A., & Hotham, S. (2009). Predicting race performance in triathlon: The role of perfectionism, achievement goals, and personal goal setting. *Journal of Sport & Exercise Psychology, 31*, 211–245.

Stoll, O., Lau, A., & Stoeber, J. (2008). Perfectionism and performance in a new basketball training task: Does striving for perfection enhance or undermine performance? *Psychology of Sport and Exercise, 9*, 620–629.

Theodorakis, Y. (1996). The influence of goals, commitment, self-efficacy and self-satisfaction on motor performance. *Journal of Applied Sport Psychology, 8*, 171–182.

Tubbs, M. E. (1986). Goal setting: a meta-analytic examination of the empirical evidence. *Journal of Applied Psychology, 71*, 474–483.

Weinberg, R. S. (1994). Goal setting and performance in sport and exercise settings: A synthesis and critique. *Medicine and Science in Sports and Exercise, 26*, 269–277.

Weinberg, R. S. (2002). Goal setting in sport and exercise: Research to practice. In J. Van Raalte and B. W. Brewer (Eds.), *Exploring sport and exercise psychology* (2nd ed., pp. 25–48). Washington, DC: American Psychological Association.

Weinberg, R. S., Burton, D., Yukelson, D., & Weigand, D. (2000). Perceived goal setting practices of Olympic athletes: An exploratory investigation. *The Sport Psychologist, 14*, 279–295.

Weinberg, R., & Weigand, D. (1993). Goal setting in sport and exercise: A reaction to Locke. *Journal of Sport and Exercise Psychology, 15*, 88–96.

Winters, D., & Latham, G. P. (1996). The effect of learning versus outcome goals on a simple versus a complex task. *Group and Organization Management, 21*, 236–250.

Williams, K. J., Donovan, J. J., & Dodge, T. L. (2000). Self-regulation of performance: Goal establishment and goal revision processes in athletes. *Human Performance, 13*, 159–180.

Zimmerman, B. J. (2008). Goal setting: A key proactive source of academic self-regulation. In D. H. Schunk & B. J. Zimmerman (Eds.), *Motivation and self-regulated learning: Theory, research and applications* (pp. 267–297). New York: Taylor & Francis.

Zimmerman, B. J., & Campillo, M. (2003). Motivating self-regulated problem solvers. In J. E. Davidson & R. J. Sternberg (Eds.), *The nature of problem solving* (pp. 233–262). New York: Cambridge University Press.

Zimmerman, B. J., & Kitsantas, A. (1996). Self-regulatory learning of a motoric skill: The role of goal setting and self-monitoring. *Journal of Applied Sport Psychology, 8,* 69–84.

Zimmerman, B. J., & Kitsantas, A. (1997). Developmental phases in self-regulation: Shifting from process goals to outcome goals. *Journal of Educational Psychology, 89,* 29–36.

Zimmerman, B. J., & Kitsantas, A. (2007). The hidden dimension of personal competence: Self-regulated learning and practice. In A. J. Elliot and C. S. Dweck (Eds.), *Handbook of competence and motivation* (pp. 509–526). New York: Guilford.

# 25   Goals and Negotiation

*Kevin Tasa*   Schulich School of Business, York University

*Glen Whyte*   Rotman School of Management, University of Toronto

*Geoffrey J. Leonardelli*   Rotman School of Management,
University of Toronto

Negotiation is a ubiquitous social activity that for years has been recognized as an important skill in a wide range of organizational domains (e.g., Lax & Sebenius, 1986). Negotiation is ubiquitous, because it is used to accomplish many important tasks including making deals, resolving disputes, allocating resources, making decisions, and solving problems. Using a number of different tasks, designs, and contexts, researchers have consistently found that people often fail to recognize the potential for reaching agreements that offer gains for both parties. In other words, people often attain outcomes that are not as beneficial as they could have been (Thompson & Hrebec, 1996; Thompson, 1990; Ritov & Moran, 2008). Explanations for these problems are numerous, and tend to focus on intrapersonal characteristics such as power and gender, and interpersonal characteristics such as trust, tactics, and situational constraints (Thompson, Wang, & Gunia, 2010).

All of these factors relate to negotiation behavior and outcomes in certain circumstances, but for the most part they are difficult to control. In this chapter, we focus, or rather re-focus, attention on something that every negotiator potentially has control over: the goals they set prior to negotiation. Specifically, we examine the extant literature relevant to the effects of goal setting on negotiation. We explore the effects of goal setting on the processes and outcomes of negotiation, as well as on the behavior of negotiators. We also aim ultimately to provide guidance to negotiators who strive to determine their goals, objectives, and aspirations in what are frequently complex and ambiguous situations.

We define the term *goal* conventionally to mean "what an individual is trying to accomplish; it is the object or aim of an action" (Locke, Shaw, Saari, & Latham, 1981). There is no question that goal setting is frequently prescribed in negotiation. It is a topic that has a long history in the negotiations literature (e.g., Pruitt & Rubin, 1986; Siegel, 1957; Siegel & Fouraker, 1960). Negotiators are often counseled to determine their goals in advance of meeting with counterparts, because such goals are considered to provide the focus that powers a negotiation strategy. Consider, for example, the following advice: "The first step in developing and executing a negotiation strategy is to determine one's goals. Negotiators must anticipate what goals they want to achieve in the negotiation and focus on how to achieve those goals. Negotiators must consider substantive goals (e.g., money or a specific outcome), intangible goals (e.g., winning, beating the other party, or getting a settlement at any cost), and procedural goals (e.g., shaping the agenda or simply having a voice at the table). Effective preparation requires a thorough, thoughtful approach to these goals; negotiators should specify their goals and objectives clearly. This includes listing all goals they wish to achieve in the negotiation, determining the priority among these goals, identifying potential multigoal packages, and evaluating possible trade-offs among multiple goals" (Lewicki, Saunders, & Barry, 2011, p. 89).

At the outset, it is important to note a fundamental distinction in the negotiation literature between distributive and integrative bargaining. Distributive bargaining involves the allocation of limited resources between parties with conflicting interests. In these situations, each negotiator is usually attempting to claim as much value as possible, which comes at the expense of the other side. Integrative negotiation, on the other hand, involves the search for mutually beneficial outcomes. This type of negotiation also involves both the creation and the allocation of limited resources, often by adding and trading off issues between parties with conflicting yet sometimes compatible interests (Bazerman & Neale, 1992; Pruitt, 1981). In integrative situations, negotiators can create value, as well as claim it, and one party's gain is not necessarily at the other's expense (Thompson et al., 2010). Distributive and integrative approaches to negotiation are, in fact, not entirely separable because efforts to create value can facilitate value claiming by resulting in more value to claim, and efforts to create value can affect how it is divided or allocated. Lax and Sebenius (1986) noted the tension between value creation and value claiming when they stated: "No matter how much creative problem solving enlarges the pie, it must still be divided; value that has been created must be claimed" (p. 33).

To examine the research that has explored empirically the relationship between goals and negotiation, we searched the literature across a variety of types of goals, including, for example, outcome, learning, and stretch goals. The specific focus of this search was to examine how goals of all types have been found to influence the processes and outcomes that are characteristic of negotiation. An example of a negotiation process might be how trust evolves or how information is exchanged between or among counterparts. Negotiation outcomes include the amount of value or benefit created, how this value or benefit is distributed, changes in the quality of the relationship between or among counterparts, satisfaction with the outcome, impasse rates, and frequency or volume of negotiated agreements attained within a specific amount of time.

We also examined in this context empirical findings on reference-level effects in negotiation. Reference levels or points are a type of goal that is at the core of prospect theory (Kahneman & Tversky, 1979). This research may not necessarily be considered mainstream with respect to work in the domain of negotiation and goal setting, but in our view it is germane to any comprehensive discussion focused on the confluence of these topics.

Relatedly, we also examine in this paper the empirical research concerning aspects of regulatory focus theory and outcomes in negotiation. This research also involves goal-directed behavior, albeit behavior that is promotion versus prevention focused. We begin with a review of the empirical literature examining the effects of goals in negotiation.

## Goal Effects in Negotiation

Most research on goal effects in negotiation was conducted during the 1980s and 1990s. Scholars then were primarily concerned with whether goals of different types and levels of difficulty had an influence on the outcomes of negotiated agreements. For example,

Neale and Bazerman (1985) assigned participants to four goal conditions—no goal, compromise goal, challenging goal, and difficult goal—and had them participate in a competitive, multi-transaction market simulation. The market was designed such that participants could complete several negotiated transactions during a 25 minute period, and each negotiation had integrative potential. Results showed that different goal conditions created differences in performance. Most significantly, participants with challenging goals and difficult goals had significantly higher average individual profit per transaction than those with compromise goals or no goals. There was, however, an inverse relationship between the difficulty of the assigned goal and the number of transactions completed. Finally, when considering joint profit between dyads as a performance outcome, negotiators with the most difficult goal had the lowest level of performance.

A subsequent study using the same market simulation (Huber & Neale, 1986) also manipulated goal difficulty, this time creating easy, moderate, and difficult levels based on outcomes of prior uses of the simulation. Consistent with the earlier study, negotiators assigned difficult goals averaged greater individual profit per transaction than negotiators assigned easy or moderate goals. Participants in this study were also asked to revise their goals and choose a goal level for subsequent hypothetical rounds of the simulation. Participants initially assigned easy goals raised their goal level, participants assigned moderate goals set similar goals, and participants with initial difficult goals slightly lowered their future goal level. The goal level of those assigned difficult goals, however, remained significantly higher than those originally assigned easy goals.

In a follow-up study, Huber and Neale (1987) extended the focus on goals to include the goals of a negotiation counterpart. They argued that because negotiation is an interdependent task, it is important to examine the influence of differing aspiration levels between participants. Using the same market simulation as the two earlier studies, they replicated the finding that specific and difficult goals led to higher individual profit than when goals were easy or nonspecific. When examining whether agreements were efficient with respect to value creation, Huber and Neale (1987) found that negotiating dyads with moderate goals, or a moderate-difficult disparity, created the most mutually beneficial deals. However, they also found that when negotiating dyads had participants who both had difficult goals, performance did not approach pareto optimality, the most mutually beneficial result.

White and Neale (1994) used a simulated house purchase negotiation to study the effects of goal asymmetry on negotiated outcomes. A noteworthy aspect of the structure of the task was the existence of a positive zone of possible agreement (ZOPA) in which the buyer was willing to pay $10,000 more than the minimum the seller would accept. Each negotiator was assigned a goal (or aspiration) that was either $5000 or $25,000 away from their minimum acceptable settlement. Structurally, negotiators were then either in a symmetrical situation with their counterpart (either both close to or far away from their minimum) or in an asymmetrical situation (one far away and one close to their minimum). Results showed that in the asymmetrical condition, the party with the aspiration that was farther away from their minimum claimed more value than their counterpart. However, the asymmetrical conditions also had significantly more impasses than did the symmetrical conditions.

Brett, Pinkley, and Jackofsky (1996) further examined the relationship between goals, performance, and impasse rates. Using a simulated scorable negotiation between a job candidate and a recruiter, they found that negotiators assigned a specific and challenging goal, and negotiators given the same goal combined with an attractive alternative offer, attained higher individual scores and thus claimed more value than those in a control condition. Negotiators who were assigned a specific and ambitious goal combined with an attractive alternative also, however, had significantly higher impasse rates.

Polzer and Neale (1995) expanded the boundary of research on goal effects in negotiation by examining additional factors in two separate studies. First, they examined whether negotiators with specific goals could adapt to new information acquired during the course of negotiations better than negotiators with no goals. Second, they examined the impact of goal scope on negotiation performance. Goal scope in multi-issue negotiation refers to the difference between having one overarching goal versus having subgoals on each issue. In study one, subjects participated in an eight-issue negotiation, but each participant was given only six of the eight negotiation issues prior to the start of bargaining. Using a cover story, the experimenters distributed information concerning the remaining two issues to participants shortly after the start of the discussion. Results showed that negotiators with specific and challenging goals achieved in this case poorer outcomes than negotiators with do-your-best goals, suggesting they did not revise their goals adequately in the face of new information.

In study two, using the same negotiation exercise as the first study, Polzer and Neale (1995) found that negotiation dyads in which both negotiators had one single overarching goal with respect to quality of the agreement had higher joint gains than dyads in which both negotiators had subordinate goals (or goals with respect to each of the eight issues). However, they also found that when results were examined at the individual rather than dyadic level, individuals with subordinate goals outperformed their counterparts who had a superordinate or overarching goal. Analysis revealed that this finding was attributable to the success of those in the subordinate condition on the two distributive (win-lose) issues embedded in the simulation. The authors also observed that the assignment of overarching superordinate goals created a dilemma for negotiators. Whereas dyadic superordinate goals led to more value being created than when goals are mixed, a negotiator is never certain what type of goal their counterpart has. This makes the setting of an appropriate goal problematic.

Zetik and Stuhlmacher (2002) used meta-analysis to synthesize research on the relationship between negotiator goals and negotiated outcomes in the time period 1966 to 1997. Their sample included 22 studies, and strong support was found for the hypothesis that negotiators with specific and challenging goals achieve higher individual profits than counterparts with vague and less challenging goals. This main effect for goals and negotiated outcomes in terms of value claimed was found regardless whether the goal was coded as optimal versus suboptimal or whether the goal was coded as a goal versus a no-goal comparison.

The sample size was also large enough to examine the impact of three important moderators: goal difficulty, participation in goal setting, and the goal difficulty of the negotiation counterpart (called goal symmetry). Results for goal difficulty were consistent with goal setting theory, such that goals of higher levels of difficulty were more significantly related to negotiated outcomes than when goals were less difficult. Goal symmetry was also a significant moderator, in that negotiators attained higher profits when their counterpart had relatively lower goals than when their counterpart had equal or higher goals. Finally, participation in the goal setting process did not moderate the goal–negotiated outcome relationship.

These results are in general consistent with the predictions of goal setting theory (Locke & Latham, 1990). Zetik and Stuhlmacher (2002) also noted, however, that caution was warranted before generalizing these results to all negotiations, for several reasons. One concern stems from the interdependent nature of negotiation (Walton & McKersie, 1965). In most goal setting research, a participant is performing a task individually against a predetermined benchmark or objective. In contrast, a negotiator must consider the perspective of their counterpart as well as their own, and this introduces an element of contextual complexity and interdependence that is missing from most goal setting research.

An important theoretical distinction is made in the negotiation literature between a negotiator's position and his or her interests. Interests as defined by Fisher, Ury, and Patton (1991) underlie and motivate positions. Interests refer to or explain the reasons why a negotiator aspires to achieve a particular goal or outcome. In contrast, a position taken by a negotiator is a publicly stated request or demand that often describes the desired outcome or goal. For example, a request for a $10,000 raise is conceptually distinct from the reasons behind the request. This distinction is significant in terms of effective negotiation, because although it is not always possible to reconcile competing positions (e.g., no raise versus $10,000), reconciling interests between the parties may still be possible and is a hallmark of successful negotiation (e.g., Pruitt, 1981; Thompson & Hrebec, 1996). It is currently unclear how goal setting influences whether or not negotiators successfully reconcile interests or merely accommodate competing positions with those with whom they are interdependently linked.

It is also unclear how goals relate to perceptions of fairness in negotiation. In one study, Ganegoda, Latham, and Folger (2011) primed negotiators to focus on either creating a fair and equitable resolution or doing their best. Results showed that negotiators primed to focus on a justice goal formulated agreements with less profit inequality. More work in this area is warranted.

Another concern stems from the limited dependent variables used in prior research on goals in negotiation, most notably the variable of profit. Zetik and Stuhlmacher (2002) argued that we need to know more about the relationship between goals and additional outcomes relevant to the field of negotiation, such as how long negotiations take, whether negotiators agree upon a deal or reach an impasse, and whether goals influence problem solving or flexibility. In the rest of this chapter, we elaborate on these and other concerns, discuss research conducted after the publication of the meta-analysis, and provide suggestions for future research on the relationship between goals and negotiation behavior and outcomes.

## Goal Type

Focusing on one's goals or target points has been shown to reduce the effects that typically arise when one's counterpart makes the opening offer (Galinsky & Mussweiler, 2001). Such effects include the tendency to anchor on a counterpart's opening offer when making a counteroffer, often to the detriment of the anchored party in terms of value claimed. Thus, in distributive bargaining at least, goals appear to focus attention on one's own perspective, reduce the likelihood that information favoring one's counterpart will be considered, and increase the amount of value claimed.

Galinsky, Mussweiler, and Medvec (2002) also found that negotiators who focused on their target price (or goal) outperformed negotiators who focused on what was minimally acceptable to them. The former negotiators, however, despite having attained superior outcomes, were less satisfied with their results than the latter negotiators. As the discussion up to this point illustrates, goal setting in negotiation has been associated with both positive and negative consequences. We suggest that part of the reason for these mixed results is that prior research has focused almost exclusively on narrow types of goals: specifically, the dichotomous comparison of specific and challenging outcome goals versus a do-your-best condition.

*Outcome versus Learning Goals.* Most prior research on goals in negotiation has focused on goals that are explicit and known before task performance. Examples include trying to attain a certain measurable target or attempting to sell a piece of property for a certain price. These types of goals, called outcome goals (or performance goals), focus on the achievement of specific tasks according to certain standards of proficiency (Locke & Latham, 1990). More recently, Winters and Latham (1996) introduced the notion of learning goals, which focus more on the context-specific strategies that lead to successful performance by drawing attention to the task-specific behaviors, information, and strategies needed to perform well. They stated: "A learning goal gives individuals the specific assignment to develop strategies to accomplish a task …" (p. 237). The purpose of a learning goal, in short, is to direct attention to task processes in terms of strategy development and away from task outcome achievement. To illustrate this distinction, Seijts , Latham, Tasa, and Latham, (2004) instructed participants in a complex business simulation to either adopt a performance goal (achieve 21% market share) or adopt a learning goal (identify and implement six or more strategies to achieve market share). Participants in the learning goal condition attained significantly more market share than participants in the performance goal condition and those told to simply "do their best." Thus, in complex situations, learning goals can improve outcomes, whereas in straightforward tasks performance goals will suffice (Seijts & Latham, 2005).

Because the purpose of a learning goal in the goal setting tradition is to draw attention to task-specific strategies and behaviors, this type of goal might be most useful when negotiators are inexperienced and have yet to master the fundamental skills required to perform well. Bereby-Meyer, Moran, and Unger-Aviram (2004) experimentally created two types of three-person negotiation teams. High learning teams were assigned learning goals, induced to hold high learning values, and were encouraged to focus on continuous learning. Low learning teams were assigned performance goals, induced to hold low learning values, and were not encouraged to focus on continuous learning. Results showed that high learning teams outperformed low learning teams when the task changed from a free-market negotiation task to an integrative negotiation task. The effect of learning goals, however, is unfortunately impossible to isolate in this case because the learning goal manipulation was embedded in instructions that also included information on learning values and continuous learning.

Tasa, Celani, and Bell (forthcoming) conducted two experiments to examine whether learning goals affect negotiator behavior and outcomes differently from outcome goals. The first study used a negotiation exercise that required creative problem solving to arrive at a negotiated outcome that satisfied the interests of both parties. Participants in one role (i.e., the buyer) were given experimental manipulations (learning goal, outcome goal, do-your-best). Their counterparts (i.e., the seller) were not given any instructions beyond their normal role instructions. Results showed that negotiators with learning goals created more integrative deals, had lower rates of impasse, and were judged by their counterparts to be more cooperative than negotiators given an outcome goal. Study two replicated these results using a more traditional simulation (i.e., job candidate versus recruiter) and also found that the learning goal manipulation interacted with negotiator's dispositional goal orientation. Results also showed that negotiators with learning goals developed a more complete understanding of their counterpart's interests.

Despite recognition by negotiation scholars that impasses are a common and often functional occurrence in negotiation, questions about the causes and effects of impasses have surprisingly received only limited empirical attention (White & Neale, 1994; O'Connor & Arnold, 2001). Although research shows that a negotiator's prior impasses increase the likelihood of future impasses (O'Connor, Arnold, & Burris, 2005), it remains unknown whether different types of goals affect impasse rates. White and Neale (1994) found that extreme goals led to higher impasse rates, but their goal condition was compared with a do-your-best condition and not a learning goal condition.

Freshman and Guthrie (2009) recently described the "goal setting paradox," which reflects the empirical observation that negotiators who set higher goals tend to perform objectively well but experience lower levels of satisfaction with the outcome and on other subjective measures. According to this discussion, negotiators may face a second goal setting paradox. The adoption and pursuit of performance goals increase the likelihood of value claiming in zero-sum or distributive situations, whereas the adoption and pursuit of learning goals increase the likelihood of value claiming and creating when the situation has integrative potential. Whether the assignment of learning goals also leads to both enhanced performance but diminished satisfaction would appear to be a question worth exploring. At the very least, the standard advice to negotiators that they should set high goals early on likely needs to be more nuanced to reflect the context in which it is offered. Performance goals have benefits for value claiming in purely distributive situations (e.g., Galinsky et al., 2002). When the issues to be negotiated are vague and uncertain, however, and require more information, learning goals may be more functional. Whether such advice should be tempered in contexts where satisfaction with the result, rather than the objective quality of the outcomes, is paramount is in need of further exploration.

*Achievement goals.* Another type of goal that has received attention in the negotiation literature is rooted in educational psychology (e.g., Dweck & Leggett, 1988). This topic deserves attention here because the labels used to describe phenomena in this literature appear similar, but in fact are different from those used by traditional goal setting theorists. In this research, goals are not assigned in advance but instead refer to one's dispositional goal orientation. Research in the goal orientation tradition has its origins in the work of Dweck and Leggett (1988), who found that children have two different primary orientations toward demonstrating their abilities. Those who believe ability is fixed are described as "entity theorists" and have a performance goal orientation. Those who believe ability is malleable are described as "incremental theorists" and have a learning goal orientation (VandeWalle & Cummings, 1997).

Kray and Haselhuhn (2007) examined the impact of these beliefs, which they called implicit negotiation beliefs, on negotiator performance. In a series of studies, they found that incremental theorists tended to claim more value and behave in a more integrative manner than those with entity beliefs. Although implicit negotiation beliefs have been shown to influence negotiated outcomes, it should be emphasized that these beliefs are not synonymous with the setting of specific and challenging goals. To illustrate, Seijts et al. (2004) examined the joint effect of dispositional goal orientation and goal setting by assigning both learning and performance goals to individuals engaged in a complex decision making task. In addition to the positive impact of assigned learning goals, they found that one's dispositional goal orientation interacted with the type of goal that was set. When a performance goal was set, there was no relationship between goal orientation and task performance. However, when a learning goal was set, there was a significant positive correlation between learning goal orientation and task performance. These results point to an interaction between goal type and goal orientation.

Tasa et al. (forthcoming) examined the interaction between goal type and implicit negotiation beliefs in a multi-issue negotiation simulation. Replicating the pattern found by Seijts et al. (2004), results showed that a negotiator's implicit beliefs interacted with goal type. When the negotiator had a performance goal, the relationship between implicit negotiation beliefs and outcomes was attenuated. However, when a negotiator had a learning goal, the relationship between implicit negotiation beliefs and outcomes was highly significant, suggesting that learning goals affect outcomes more strongly when a negotiator believes their negotiation skills are malleable.

## Regulatory Focus and Negotiation Goal Setting

A central theme in the goal setting literature is that a goal's properties, such as whether they are challenging or difficult, influence what negotiators can achieve. Additional research reveals that *how* individuals approach such goals also influences the process of goal setting, which in turn affects what they can achieve. Even though negotiators could have the same desired end, such as claiming maximum value, for example, people can still approach that goal in different ways.

Regulatory focus theory (Higgins, 1997, 2005) provides a framework for how individuals may approach the same desired end, but could do so in two different ways. A promotion focus refers to the individual tendency to approach a desired end by defining that end as a hope, wish, or aspiration. Such objectives are then pursued by focusing on the achievement of positive outcomes. In contrast, a prevention focus refers to the individual tendency to approach a desired end by defining that end as a duty, obligation, or responsibility. Such individuals tend to pursue these objectives by focusing on the prevention of negative outcomes. Regulatory focus has been shown to affect a wide range of goal-related outcomes (e.g., Förster, Grant, Idson, & Higgins, 2001; Leonardelli, Lakin, & Arkin, 2007; Leonardelli & Lakin, 2010; Shah, Higgins, & Friedman, 1998), and specifically, behaviors and outcomes in negotiations (Appelt & Higgins, 2010; Appelt, Zou, Arora, & Higgins, 2009; Galinsky, Leonardelli, Okhuysen, & Mussweiler, 2005; Gu, Bohns, & Leonardelli, 2011; Piasentin, Shultz, Willness, Fassina, & Uggerslev, 2005; Ten Velden, Beersma, & De Dreu, 2009, 2011; Werth, Mayer, & Mussweiler, 2006).

Most relevant for the present discussion is that regulatory focus affects the negotiator's goal setting process. Even if negotiators may want to accomplish the same outcome, those with a promotion focus tend to set their target price, the outcome they hope to achieve, higher than those with a prevention focus (Galinsky et al., 2005, Study 1). In exploring the consequences of this effect further, Galinsky et al. examined whether regulatory focus would affect the behaviors of negotiators. Past research has revealed that individuals with higher target prices capture more value in negotiated agreements because they tend to make more aggressive first offers (Galinsky et al., 2002). In two studies and consistent with this past research, negotiators with a promotion focus attained more value in final agreements than those with a prevention focus, and additional data revealed that this greater value was a function of more aggressive first offers. Individuals with a promotion focus claimed more value because their first offers reflected aggressive targets.

Promotion focus thus led to more successful distributive negotiating strategies relative to a prevention focus. By logical extension, one may be tempted to conclude that the promotion-focused negotiator's more aggressive approach may lead to worse integrative outcomes, especially when both parties share the same regulatory focus. With two aggressive parties striving for the best outcome, it is easy to expect that these parties may be more rigid and less accommodating in the process of reaching an agreement. On the contrary, when both parties shared a regulatory focus, those with a promotion focus were *more likely* to achieve optimal integrative agreements than those with prevention focus (Galinsky et al., 2005). The authors argue that those negotiators with a promotion focus care most about reaching their ideal solution and with that ideal in mind are motivated to flexibly consider different ways of achieving it. This argument is similar to the idea that by focusing on a superordinate goal (Polzer & Neale, 1995), negotiators can more flexibly achieve mutually beneficial outcomes. Moreover, this may also be a function of the efforts by promotion-focused negotiators to perceive value in terms of gains or non-gains (Idson, Liberman, & Higgins, 2000; see also Shah et al., 1998; Liberman, Idson, & Higgins, 2005).

One puzzling question in this research is why individuals with a prevention focus set less difficult goals (Galinsky et al., 2005, Study 1). After all, presumably regardless of regulatory focus, individuals still want the same end in terms of claiming value for themselves and thus making themselves better off than they were in the absence of a negotiated agreement. Why, then, does the prevention of negative outcomes lead to the setting of less difficult goals than the promotion of positive outcomes? Gu, Bohns, and Leonardelli (2011) shed some light on this puzzle. Critically, they found that differences in regulatory focus on goal setting were not due to social orientation (i.e., intention to be pro-social or pro-self). Individuals with a prevention focus were just as motivated to cooperate as those with a promotion focus. Rather, across three studies, they found that negotiators with a prevention focus are concerned with multiple outcomes—claiming what they themselves can claim, and also preventing the other party from claiming more than they themselves receive. Juggling the prevention of these multiple negative outcomes may have weakened their ability as negotiators to more strongly commit to simply one outcome (Kruglanski, Shah, Fishbach, Friedman, Chun, & Sleeth-Keppler, 2002; Soman & Zhao, 2011).

## Prospect Theory

Another stream of research relevant to the topic of goals in negotiation is prospect theory (Kahneman & Tversky, 1979, 1984; Tversky & Kahneman, 1992). Prospect theory is a highly influential descriptive model of individual decision making under risk. It describes individual decision making more accurately than normative models of choice, including expected utility theory, because it was built to account for several anomalies of choice that are inconsistent with models of rational choice.

Three aspects of prospect theory are relevant to the present discussion (Heath, Larrick, & Wu, 1999). First, outcomes including those from negotiation are normally evaluated as changes from a reference point, which may reflect the status quo but which can also reflect goals, expectations, or aspirations. Outcomes that are superior to the reference point are gains, and outcomes that are inferior are losses. This is consistent with goal theory, which describes goals as both the object of an action and a benchmark from which to determine satisfaction (Locke & Latham, 1990). Goal theory, in contrast, is more explicit in assuming that goals as reference points (or otherwise) reflect self-efficacy, past performance, affect, modeling, feedback, incentives, personality, and other factors (see Chapter 9).

Second, deviations from the reference point or goal are felt most intensely the closer they occur to it. For example, the subjective difference between receiving $900 or $1000 is greater than the subjective difference between receiving $9900 or $10,000. One implication of this diminishing sensitivity is that individuals will display risk aversion when making choices in the domain of gains above the reference point, but will display risk-seeking behavior when making choices in the domain of losses below it. Individuals, according to prospect theory, are considered to be risk averse if they prefer a sure thing over a gamble of equal or greater expected value.

A third relevant feature of prospect theory is loss aversion, which implies that losses are more unpleasant than comparable gains are pleasing. In other words, losses are more salient or psychologically potent than gains of the same magnitude. Loss aversion thus means that the desire to avoid a loss will be stronger than the desire to either achieve an equally large gain or avoid an equally large foregone gain. Another consequence of loss aversion is the willingness to take on increased risk to prevent or restore otherwise certain losses. Interestingly, only one goal study has compared the effect of degree of positive or negative deviation from the goal on satisfaction, and found the effect to be linear (Locke, 1967). Further, success tended to have a stronger influence on affect than failure.

The world of professional golf provides a surprising example of a context involving high stakes in which individuals have been observed to work harder to avoid a loss than to achieve a gain relative to a goal. Pope and Schweitzer (2011) deduced from loss aversion that players would work harder to avoid a bogey (one stroke over par) then to achieve a birdie (one stroke under). Evidence indeed suggests that players, all things being equal, were 3.6% more successful when putting for par than for birdie. The aversion to a bogey or loss on any given hole appears to have induced extra effort to avoid a negative outcome.

When goals act as reference points in negotiation, most people are likely to perceive or frame a situation in which they are falling short of a goal as a loss even if they are still doing better than they would do in the absence of a negotiated agreement. Loss aversion may thus be induced, as well as the desire to seek risk in the domain of losses. The perception of loss may make the act of granting concessions painful, and the decision to accept a viable agreement extremely difficult. In contrast, positively framed negotiators who are therefore operating above the reference point will be more inclined to offer concessions and are more likely to be successful (Neale & Bazerman, 1985). For example, an offer of a $10,000 increase in salary when one's goal was a $20,000 increase can legitimately be perceived either positively relative to the status quo or negatively relative to the goal. Such perceptions have consequences for behavior and outcomes in negotiation.

Previous work has speculated (e.g., Neale & Bazerman, 1985; Knight, Durham, & Locke, 2001), and recent research demonstrates (Larrick, Heath, & Wu, 2009), that goal setting may affect risk preferences in negotiation. For example, Larrick et al. (2009) found in three negotiation experiments that, when compared to a "do-your-best" condition, a "specific, challenging goal" condition consistently led to the pursuit of greater risk. In short, negotiators motivated by specific and challenging goals chose riskier strategies and preferred riskier gambles than those with less ambitious or more vague goals. Knight, Durham, and Locke (2001) previously obtained similar results.

These findings are consistent with the view that goals motivate partly because they provide a basis for performance evaluation (Lewin, Dembo, Festinger, & Sears, 1944; Locke & Latham, 1990). More precisely, a goal in negotiation imbues an outcome with a positive or negative taint depending on where it resides in relation to the goal. Loss aversion can thus be induced according to prospect theory, as can the tendency for people to manifest risk-seeking behavior when choosing between losses versus risk aversion when choosing between gains. These processes may encourage individuals to take excessive risks in the face of a negotiation that is falling short of important goals.

Beyond evidence from both the lab and the field that negative framing relative to a negotiation goal induces a propensity for risk, negotiators bargaining over losses tend to make fewer concessions, find fewer integrative agreements, and more often fail to reach agreement than negotiators operating in the domain of gains (Bazerman, Magliozzi, & Neale, 1985: Neale & Bazerman, 1985: Neale & Northcraft, 1986: Neale, Huber, & Northcraft, 1987). Negotiator strategy, efficiency, and performance all appear to some extent to be dependent on reference points and framing effects. (Bazerman et al., 1985; Bottom, 1991; Bottom & Studt, 1993; De Dreu, Carnevale, Emans, & Van de Vliert, 1995; Neale & Bazerman, 1985; Neale, Huber, & Northcraft, 1987; Olekalns, 1994). When using a high reference point and thus likely a negative or loss frame with respect to an evaluation of the outcomes, negotiators concede less, use more contentious but risky moves such as threats, and are in general less inclined to agree than those negotiators who are using a lower reference point that may induce the perception of a positive or gain frame with respect to the outcomes.

These effects are attributable to variable risk preferences that exist above and below the negotiator's reference point, and to loss aversion (Kahneman, 1992). Kahneman and Tversky (1995) have also referred to the impact of loss aversion in negotiation as concession aversion. If concessions that increase a negotiator's perceived losses (or distance below the goal) are more painful to make than concessions that reduce a negotiator's perceived gains (distance above the goal), it seems likely that a negatively framed negotiator will be particularly reluctant to make concessions.

In contrast to the findings above, Bottom (1998) found something different in two experiments. These studies examined the impact of reference points on negotiator tactics, concessions, and settlements in the context of uncertainty with respect to the final outcomes of negotiated agreements. In these studies, negotiators reaching an agreement would have to gamble to determine how much money they would receive or pay as a result of the agreement. Consequently, reaching a settlement created risk for negotiators. If negotiators are in the domain of losses, they should be risk seeking and thus eager to settle with this type of outcome. Negotiators in the domain of gains, in contrast, should be risk averse and thus reluctant to settle. In the context of risky outcomes, negatively framed negotiators were found to be more cooperative and more likely to settle, and negotiated more integrative agreements than positively framed negotiators. When negotiation involves large uncertainties with respect to the ultimate consequences of agreement, which is often the case in complex negotiations, then according to Bottom (1998) the risk-seeking propensity associated with below-goal performance actually leads to more cooperative negotiation and an increased chance of agreement.

Northcraft, Brodt, and Neale (1995) found that a negotiator will value an opponent's concessions more heavily when they occur in the vicinity of the negotiator's reference point or goal. In addition, according to loss aversion, a negotiation opponent's concessions will likely mean more to a negotiator when they reduce a negotiator's losses or distance below the goal than when they increase his or her gains or distance above the goal (Northcraft et al., 1995).

In the section to follow, we provide suggestions about possible future research directions for goal setting as it relates to negotiation. We also describe some of the implications of the research we have discussed in this chapter for negotiation and negotiators.

## Future Research Directions and Implications for Practice

The research conducted to date supports the conclusion that a negotiator with a specific and challenging goal attains greater profit than a negotiator with vague or easy goals when the negotiation is a distributive or zero-sum situation. Beyond this type of situation, however, the result of setting a goal prior to negotiation becomes less straightforward. Although goals have been positively associated with individual gain, researchers have also found that goals can hinder value creation and adaptability. There are thus pitfalls that need to be considered as negotiators consider their goals. Our review of the literature on goal setting in negotiation highlights many unanswered questions that unfortunately limit our ability to provide practical advice to negotiators. Many of these questions deserve greater scholarly attention.

A number of future research directions are implied by our discussion of empirical findings concerning the effects of goal setting on the processes and outcomes of negotiation. A reasonable first step would be for researchers to consider the impact of goals on outcomes beyond simple profit. We encourage a broadening of negotiation outcomes to include such factors as willingness to engage in future negotiations with a counterpart, perceptions of competitive and cooperative behavior, and whether a deal or an impasse is reached. Negotiation scholars also recognize that reputations influence subsequent interactions (e.g., O'Connor & Arnold, 2001). Research is therefore also warranted on the degree to which the types of goals a negotiator adopts relate to how a negotiator is perceived by his or her counterparts.

One obvious concern associated with the setting of ambitious performance goals in negotiation is that this may exacerbate the mythical fixed pie bias. In other words, the natural tendency to approach a negotiation as a situation in which you achieve your objectives by frustrating your counterpart from achieving theirs may be heightened when negotiators are instructed to attain specific and ambitious outcomes in terms of value claimed. In the context of distributive bargaining, where a future relationship with one's counterpart is not desired, such an effect may well have functional consequences for performance. In contrast, in a situation that has integrative potential and involves interaction with those whom we desire to interact productively in the future, such an effect may facilitate the souring of relationships and the capturing of a large piece of a very small value pie.

One way to potentially mitigate this effect in the context of integrative bargaining with esteemed counterparts is to ensure that specific and difficult goals are set with respect to multiple determinants of negotiation effectiveness. For example, instead of simply setting a goal with respect to price in a negotiation, negotiators should also set specific and difficult goals with respect to value created, their counterpart's satisfaction with the final result, and the impact of the process of negotiation on the bargaining relationship. If a truly successful negotiation requires the attainment of all these objectives simultaneously, then to be effective, goal setting should reflect this reality.

At the same time, however, a commitment to too many goals may increase the difficulty of reaching an agreement. Requiring that a deal be reached only when it achieves goals on price, value creation, and counterpart satisfaction may prove difficult—if not impossible—and increase the likelihood that negotiators walk away from an agreement that would be better than their alternatives. To reduce the potential difficulty of reaching agreement with multiple goals, it may make more sense according to regulatory focus theory for the negotiators to adopt a promotion focus, and thus to perceive the negotiation as an opportunity to search for ways to reach an agreement and gain value. Evidence that negotiators both claim and create more value with a promotion relative to a prevention focus suggests that a promotion focus may be most effective in assisting negotiators to achieve agreement that benefit themselves and others. Framing the failure to achieve the goal as a loss may be quite aversive and provoke risky behavior, but this interpretation is also more characteristic of a negotiator with a prevention rather than a promotion focus. Individuals with a promotion focus are more likely to interpret failure to reach a goal as a non-gain versus a loss.

Another topic for future research might be the extent to which risk seeking in the domain of losses and loss aversion exacerbate the tendency to use unethical or illegal tactics in negotiation. If desperate situations require desperate measures, then such behaviors during negotiation may well be the product primarily of situational forces rather than individual determinants. Whether the tendency to display questionable ethics and use dubious tactics is a product of overly ambitious goal setting in negotiation and the potential resulting perception of having to accept certain losses unless drastic steps are taken is a question worth exploring.

The advice for negotiators that flows from prospect theory is not that goal setting should be avoided in advance of an important negotiation. We continue to subscribe to the view that goal setting is an integral part of successful negotiation planning and preparation. Moreover, it is relatively easy to set goals for oneself or for others in negotiation. The overarching goals of an important and complex negotiation might be best described briefly as follows: create a large amount of mutual benefit; claim or capture a great deal of this value that you have helped to create; ensure that your counterpart also believes he or she has won or done well; and finally, do all of this in such a way that your relationship with your counterpart has been improved as a result.

Where things get difficult is in providing negotiation-specific content to these goals. For example, it is of no use in negotiation to set a goal that cannot possibly be attained. Whether a goal in negotiation is attainable depends on whether there is an overlap in terms of acceptability between oneself and one's counterpart. What is minimally acceptable to one's counterpart is frequently unknown in advance of meeting with him or her, and may still be uncertain even after. Therefore, to mitigate the risks of setting goals where they cannot possibly be reached, and of producing a result such as an impasse that would be worse than if no goals were set, perhaps the setting of specific and ambitious goals should await the development of an understanding of one's counterpart's interests, and priorities, and alternatives. Only then will one be in a position as a negotiator to set goals that are both specific and difficult, as opposed to specific and modest or specific and outrageous.

Another suggestion that flows from our discussion of setting goals in negotiation is to do this in such a way that allows for and legitimizes recalibration in response to new information, in much the same way that goal theory suggests failure to achieve goals will lead eventually to a change downward depending on self-efficacy and commitment (Locke & Latham, 1990).

The economically rational benchmark with which to evaluate the outcomes of negotiation, after all, is not the goals that one sets prior to negotiating. Rather, it is the consequences of no agreement. In some respects, the entire point of negotiating is to do better than you would do without negotiating. If so, then how much better did you do? Anything in excess of this, commonly referred to in the negotiation literature as one's best alternative to a negotiated agreement (BATNA), or by economists as one's opportunity cost, is in essence what one has gained as a result of negotiation. Setting goals in negotiation may thus be entirely functional for performance, but such goals should not be used to evaluate performance. The quality of performance in negotiation is best determined in relation to what has been gained relative to the consequences of no agreement, not relative to some goal that may or may not have been arbitrarily set and which one does not attain in any case in the event of no agreement. When goals, both learning and outcome, are used to motivate performance in negotiation, but not to evaluate it, we believe that the main benefits of goal setting in negotiation are most likely to be realized and the liabilities minimized.

## Conclusion

Our review points to the inescapable conclusion that goals are potentially highly influential in negotiation. Whether goals have positive or negative effects on negotiator behavior and outcomes, in turn, depends on the type of negotiation, the type of goal, and how goals are formulated and perceived. Therefore, we believe the evidence extant supports the advice that determining one's goals is an important first step in the process of effectively preparing for a negotiation (e.g., Lewicki et al., 2011). Our review, however, also highlights areas where this advice needs to be better nuanced, such as when new information arises in the process of negotiating or when the current situation is framed with respect to an unrealistic reference point. Additional research is clearly warranted if we hope to provide further constructive advice to negotiators about how to set goals while struggling to navigate their way through uncertain and unpredictable negotiations.

# References

Appelt, K. C., & Higgins, E. T. (2010). My way: How strategic preferences vary by negotiator role and regulatory focus. *Journal of Experimental Social Psychology, 46*(6), 1138–1142.

Appelt, K. C., Zou, X., Arora, P., & Higgins, E. T. (2009). Regulatory fit in negotiation: Effects of "prevention-buyer" and "promotion-seller" fit. *Social Cognition, 27*(3), 365–384.

Bazerman, M. H., Magliozzi, T., & Neale, M. (1985). Integrative bargaining in a competitive market. Organizational Behavior and Human Decision Processes, 35, 294–313.

Bazerman, M. H., & Neale, M. A. (1992). *Negotiating rationally.* New York: Free Press.

Bereby-Meyer, Y., Moran, S., & Unger-Aviram, E. (2004). When performance goals deter performance: Transfer of skills in integrative negotiations. *Organizational Behavior and Human Decision Processes, 93,* 142–154.

Bottom, W. P. (1991). Adaptive reference points in integrative bargaining. In Borcherding, K. M., Messick, D. M., & Larichev, O. I. (Eds.), *Contemporary issues in decision-making,* pp. 429–447. Amsterdam: North Holland.

Bottom, W. P. (1998). Negotiator risk: Sources of uncertainty and the impact of reference points on negotiated agreements. *Organizational Behavior and Human Decision Processes, 76,* 89–112.

Bottom, W. P., & Studt, A. (1993). Framing effects and the distributive aspect of integrative bargaining. *Organizational Behavior and Human Decision Processes, 56,* 459–474.

Brett, J. F., Pinkley, R. L., & Jackofsky, E. F. (1996). Alternatives to having a BATNA in dyadic negotiation: The influence of goals, self-efficacy, and alternatives on negotiated outcomes. *Journal of Conflict Management, 7,* 121–138.

De Dreu, C. K. W., Carnevale, P. J. D., Emans, P. J. M., & Van de Vliert, E. (1995). Effects of gain loss frames in negotiation: loss aversion, mismatching, and frame adoption. *Organizational Behavior and Human Decision Processes, 60,* 90–107.

Dweck, C. S., & Leggett, E. L. (1988). A social-cognitive approach to motivation and personality. *Psychological Review, 95,* 256–273.

Fisher, R., Ury, W., & Patton, B. (1991). *Getting to yes: Negotiating agreement without giving in.* New York: Penguin.

Förster, J., Grant, H., Idson, L. C., & Higgins, E. (2001). Success/failure feedback, expectancies, and approach/avoidance motivation: how regulatory focus moderates classic relations. *Journal of Experimental Social Psychology, 37*(3), 253–260.

Freshman, C., & Guthrie, C. (2009). Managing the goal-setting paradox: How to get better results from high goals and be happy. *Negotiation Journal, 25,* 217–231.

Galinsky, A. D., & Mussweiler, T. (2001). First offers as anchors: The role of perspective-taking and negotiator focus. *Journal of Personality and Social Psychology, 81,* 657–669.

Galinsky, A. D., Mussweiler, T., & Medvec, V. H. (2002). Disconnecting outcomes and evaluations: The role of negotiator focus. *Journal of Personality and Social Psychology, 83,* 1131–1140.

Galinsky, A. D., Leonardelli, G. J., Okhuysen, G. A., & Mussweiler, T. (2005). The role of regulatory focus in negotiation: Promoting distributive and integrative success. *Personality and Social Psychology Bulletin,* 31(8), 1087–1098.

Ganegoda, D. B., Latham, G. P., & Folger, R. (2011). Motivating people to act fairly: A study of subconscious goal setting in organizational justice. *Paper presented at the Society of industrial and organizational psychology conference*, Chicago, IL.

Gu, J., Bohns, V., & Leonardelli, G.J. (2011). Regulatory focus and social decision-making: Securing interdependence through a relative orientation. Revision submitted for review.

Heath, C., Larrick, R. P., & Wu, G. (1999). Goals as reference points. *Cognitive Psychology, 38,* 79–109.

Higgins, E. T. (1997). Beyond pleasure and pain. *American Psychologist, 52,* 1280–1300.

Higgins, E. T. (2005). Value from regulatory fit. *Current Directions in Psychological Science, 14,* 209–213.

Huber, V. L., & Neale, M. A. (1986). Effects of cognitive heuristics and goals on negotiator performance and subsequent goal-setting. *Organizational Behavior and Human Decision Processes, 38,* 342–365.

Huber, V. L., & Neale, M. A. (1987). Effects of self-goals and competitor goals on performance in an interdependent bargaining task. *Journal of Applied Psychology, 72,* 197–203.

Idson, L. C., Liberman, N., & Higgins, E. T. (2000). Distinguishing gains from nonlosses and losses from nongains: A regulatory focus perspective on hedonic intensity. *Journal of Experimental Social Psychology, 36,* 252–274.

Kahneman, D. (1992). Reference points, anchors, norms, and mixed feelings. *Organizational Behavior and Human Decision Processes, 51,* 296–312.

Kahneman, D., & Tversky, A. (1979). Prospect theory: An analysis of decisions under risk. *Econometrica, 47,* 263–291.

Kahneman, D., & Tversky, A. (1984). Choices, values, and frames. *American Psychologist, 39,* 341–350.

Kahneman, D., & Tversky, A. (1995). Conflict resolution: A cognitive perspective. In K. Arrow et al. (Eds.), *Barriers to conflict resolution*. Stanford, CA: Stanford Center on Conflict and Negotiation.

Knight, D., Durham, C., & Locke, E. (2001). The relationship of team goals, incentives and efficacy to strategic risk, tactical implementation, and performance. *Academy of Management Journal, 44,* 326–338.

Kray, L. J., & Haselhuhn, M. P. (2007). Implicit negotiation beliefs and performance: Experimental and longitudinal evidence. *Journal of Personality and Social Psychology, 93,* 49–64.

Kruglanski, A. W., Shah, J. Y., Fishbach, A., Friedman, R., Chun, W., & Sleeth-Keppler, D. (2002). A theory of goal-systems. In Zanna, M. P. (Ed.), *Advances in experimental social psychology* (Vol. 34). New York: Academic Press.

Larrick, R. P., Heath, C., & Wu, G. (2009). Goal-induced risk taking in negotiation and decision making. *Social Cognition, 27,* 342–364.

Lax, D. A., & Sebenius, J. K. (1986). *The manager as negotiator*. New York: Free Press.

Leonardelli, G. J., & Lakin, J. L. (2010). The new adventures of regulatory focus: Self-uncertainty and the quest for a diagnostic self-evaluation. In R. M. Arkin, K. C. Oleson, & P. J. Carroll (Eds.), *The uncertain self: A handbook of perspectives from social and personality psychology*. Mahwah, NJ: Lawrence Erlbaum.

Leonardelli, G. J., Lakin, J. L., & Arkin, R. M. (2007). A regulatory focus model of self-evaluation. *Journal of Experimental Social Psychology, 43(6),* 1002–1009.

Lewicki, R. J., Saunders, D. J., & Barry, B. (2011) *Essentials of negotiation* (5th ed.). New York: McGraw-Hill Irwin.

Lewin, K., Dembo, T., Festinger, L., & Sears, P. S. (1944). Level of aspiration. In Mevhunt, J. (Ed.), *Personality and the Behavior Disorders* (Vol. 1, pp. 333–378). New York: Ronald Press.

Liberman, N., Idson, L. C., & Higgins, E. T. (2005). Predicting the intensity of losses vs. non-gains and non-losses vs. gains in judging fairness and value: A test of the loss aversion explanation. *Journal of Experimental Social Psychology, 41*, 527–534.

Locke, E. A. (1967). Relationship of success and expectations to affect on goal-seeking tasks. *Journal of Personality and Social Psychology, 7(2)*, 125–134.

Locke, E. A., & Latham, G. P. (1990). *A theory of goal setting and task performance.* Englewood Cliffs, NJ: Prentice-Hall.

Locke, E. A., Shaw, K. N., Saari, L. M., & Latham, G. P. (1981). Goal setting and task performance: 1969–1980. *Psychological Bulletin, 90*, 125–152.

Neale, M. A., & Bazerman, M. H. (1985). The effect of externally set goals on reaching integrative agreements in competitive markets. *Journal of Occupational Behaviour, 6*, 19–32.

Neale, M. A., Huber, V. L., & Northcraft, G. B. (1987). The framing of negotiations: Context versus task frames. *Organizational Behavior and Human Decision Processes, 38*, 305–317.

Neale, M. A., & Northcraft, G. B. (1986). Experts, amateurs, and refrigerators: Comparing expert and amateur negotiators in a novel task. *Organizational Behavior and Human Decision Processes, 38*, 305–317.

Northcraft, G. B., Brodt, S. A., & Neale, M. A. (1995). Negotiating with nonlinear subjective utilities: Why some concessions are more equal than others. *Organizational Behavior and Human Decision Processes, 63*, 298–310.

O'Connor, K. M., & Arnold, J. A. (2001). Distributive spirals: Negotiation impasses and the moderating role of disputant self-efficacy. *Organizational Behavior and Human Decision Processes, 84*, 148–176.

O'Connor, K. M., Arnold, J. A., & Burris, E. R. (2005). Negotiators' bargaining histories and their effects on future negotiation performance. *Journal of Applied Psychology, 90*, 350–362.

Olekalns, M. (1994). Context, issues, and frame as determinants of negotiated outcomes. *British Journal of Social Psychology, 33*, 197–210.

Piasentin, K. A., Shultz, J. W., Willness, C. R., Fassina, N. E., & Uggerslev, K. L. (2005, June). *Recasting goal setting in negotiation: A regulatory focus perspective.* Presented at the 18th annual meeting of the International Association for Conflict Management, Seville, Spain.

Polzer, J. T., & Neale, M. A. (1995). Constraints or catalysts—reexamining goal-setting within the context of negotiation. *Human Performance, 8*, 3–26.

Pope, D. G., & Schweitzer, M. E. (2011). Is Tiger Woods loss averse? Persistent bias in the face of experience, competition, and high-stakes. *American Economic Review, 101*, 129–157.

Pruitt, D. G. (1981). *Negotiation behavior.* New York: Academic Press.

Pruitt, D., & Rubin, J. (1986). *Social conflict: Escalation, stalemate, and settlement.* New York: Random House.

Ritov, I., & Moran, S. (2008). Missed opportunity for creating value in negotiations: Reluctance to making integrative gambit offers. *Journal of Behavioral Decision Making, 21*, 337–351.

Seijts, G. H., & Latham, G. P. (2005). Learning versus performance goals: When should each be used? *Academy of Management Executive, 19*, 124–131.

Seijts, G. H., Latham, G. P., Tasa, K., & Latham, B. W. (2004). Goal setting and goal orientation: An integration of two different yet related literatures. *Academy of Management Journal, 47*, 227–239.

Shah, J. Y., Higgins, E. T., & Friedman, R. (1998). Performance incentives and means: How regulatory focus influences goal attainment. *Journal of Personality and Social Psychology, 74,* 285–293.

Siegel, S. (1957). Level of aspiration and decision making. *Psychological Review, 64,* 253–262.

Siegel, S., & Fouraker, L. E. (1960). *Bargaining and group decision-making: Experiments in bilateral monopoly.* New York: McGraw-Hill.

Soman, D., & Zhao, M. (2011). The Fewer the Better: Number of Goals and Savings Behavior. *Journal of Marketing Research, 48*(6), 944–957.

Tasa, K., Celani, A., & Bell, C. (forthcoming). Goals in negotiation revisited: The impact of goal setting and implicit negotiation beliefs. *Negotiation and Conflict Management Research.*

Ten Velden, F. S., Beersma, B., & De Dreu, C. K. W. (2009). Goal expectations meet regulatory focus: How appetitive and aversive competition influence negotiation. *Social Cognition, 27,* 437–454.

Ten Velden, F. S., Beersma, B., & De Dreu, C. K. W. (2011). When competition breeds equality: Effects of appetitive versus aversive competition in negotiation. *Journal of Experimental Social Psychology, 47,* 1127–1133.

Thompson, L. (1990). An examination of naive and experienced negotiators. *Journal of Personality and Social Psychology, 59,* 82–90.

Thompson, L., & Hrebec, D. (1996). Lose-lose agreements in interdependent decision making. *Psychological Bulletin, 120,* 396–409.

Thompson, L. L., Wang, J. W., & Gunia, B. C. (2010). Negotiation. *Annual Review of Psychology, 61,* 491–515.

Tversky, A., & Kahneman, D. (1992). Advances in prospect theory: Cumulative representation of uncertainty. *Journal of Risk and Uncertainty, 5,* 297–323.

VandeWalle, D., & Cummings, L. L. (1997). A test of the influence of goal orientation on the feedback seeking process. *Journal of Applied Psychology, 82,* 390–400.

Walton, R. E., & McKersie, R. B. (1965). *A behavioral theory of labor negotiations: An analysis of a social interaction system.* New York: McGraw-Hill.

Werth, L., Mayer, J., & Mussweiler, T. (2006). How regulatory focus influences integrative negotiations. *Zeitschrift für Sozialpsychologie, 37,* 19–25. doi:10.1024/0044-3514.37.1.19.

White, S. B., & Neale, M. A. (1994). The role of negotiator aspirations and settlement expectancies in bargaining outcomes. *Organizational Behavior and Human Decision Processes, 57,* 303–317.

Winters, D., & Latham, G. P. (1996). The effect of learning versus outcome goals on a simple versus a complex task. *Group & Organization Management, 21,* 236–250.

Zetik, D. C., & Stuhlmacher, A. F. (2002). Goal setting and negotiation performance: A meta-analysis. *Group Processes & Intergroup Relations, 5,* 35–52.

# 26 Using Goal Setting to Promote Health Behavior Change

## Diet and Physical Activity

*Mical K. Shilts* Department of Family and Consumer Sciences, California State University, Sacramento

*Marilyn S. Townsend* Department of Nutrition, University of California – Davis

*Rod K. Dishman* Department of Kinesiology, University of Georgia

Physical activity and dietary behaviors can have independent, additive, and interactive benefits on public health (Physical Activity Guidelines Advisory Committee, 2008; U.S. Department of Health and Human Services, 2010), but their prevalence rates in the United States are far below current recommendations. Community interventions to increase physical activity and dietary behaviors have had modest success (Ammerman et al., 2002; Kahn et al., 2002). In 2005, only 32.6% and 27.2% of adults consumed at least 1 cup of fruit and 1.5 cups of vegetables per day (CDC, 2007). Similarly, nearly 65% report not meeting minimal recommendations for sufficient physical activity, and 36% say they get no leisure-time physical activity (U.S. Department of Health and Human Services, 2010). In 2009, just 11% of adolescent girls, and 25% of boys, said they were active enough to meet the new guideline of an hour or more of moderate-to-vigorous physical activity every day (CDC, 2010). When an objective measure (i.e., not self-report) of physical activity is used, physical activity rates in the United States are even lower (Troiano et al., 2008; Tucker et al., 2011).

## Goal Setting Review

Although goal setting research in workplace settings has been proliferating for decades, it is only recently that nutrition and physical activity interventionists have begun to systematically test its effects in community health promotion. A recent meta-analysis found that goal setting was one of two promising behavioral intervention components to help modify dietary fat, fruit, and vegetable intake (Ammerman et al., 2002). Four goal setting reviews applicable to health promotion interventions focusing on nutrition and physical activity behavior have been published in the last 15 years (Bodenheimer & Handley, 2009; Cullen et al., 2001; Shilts et al., 2004a; Strecher et al., 1995). Strecher et al. (1995) extended goal setting research from the workplace literature to health behaviors. Cullen et al. (2001) targeted nutrition interventions, and Shilts et al. (2004a) reviewed both nutrition and physical activity interventions. And most recently, Bodenheimer and Handley (2009) focused on health promotion interventions in primary care/clinic settings. Each of these reviews is summarized with important and relevant findings highlighted.

The seminal goal setting review by Strecher et al. (1995) focused on applying what was already known from organizational and laboratory settings to health behaviors. Findings were applied into practical recommendations that have informed many health behavior goal setting interventions and research studies. The recommendations focused on the premise that carefully constructed goal setting procedures are necessary. When using goal setting to promote health behavior change, interventionists are recommended to (1) assess client commitment to change a specific behavior; (2) assess if desired behavior change is complex and needs to be organized into subgoals or an action plan; (3) determine individuals' level of self-efficacy and focus on skills development to increase self-efficacy; (5) ensure goals set are difficult enough to elicit significant effort and yet are realistic; and (6) provide goal feedback regularly through a graphical approach such as charting individual performance.

In a 2001 review, a four-step goal setting process was delineated, based on Locke and Latham's (1990) goal setting theory (Cullen et al., 2001). The purpose of this four-step process was to help dietitians use goal setting strategies in nutrition counseling in clinical settings by (1) recognizing a need for change initiated by external or internal sources, (2) establishing a goal that should be specific and challenging, (3) adopting a goal-directed activity such as mobilizing resources and self-monitoring it, and (4) self-rewarding goal attainment that can motivate continued goal setting and effort. The four-step process was then applied to published nutrition interventions. Of the 13 adult intervention studies included in the analyses, one intervention included each of the four steps identified (Berry et al., 1989). Six interventions included both steps 2 and 3, which appeared to enhance outcomes. Many nutrition interventions with a youth focus reported the use of goal setting, but only three studies reported enough details to be evaluated. Positive results were observed, but none of the studies systematically varied components of the intervention with and without goal setting, so teasing out the effect of goal setting was not feasible. Cullen et al. (2001) also found that the goal setting literature for nutrition interventions were lacking sufficient details on how the goal was set and other goal setting procedures. Studies did not vary goal setting components and did not evaluate developmental, ethnic, age, and SES differences.

The Shilts et al. (2004a) review examined the effectiveness of goal setting as a strategy for changing nutrition and physical activity behaviors. Three broad research objectives were identified among the studies. The first objective was assessing goal setting effectiveness. Thirteen of the 23 adult studies used the relevant study design to assess this research objective; 8 of the 13 studies reported positive results supporting goal setting. No adolescent or child studies used this study design for the analyses.

The second research objective identified was assessment of the contribution of a goal setting characteristic. These characteristics pertained to goal type, goal components, and goal properties (see Tables 26.1 and 26.2). To test this objective, a study design must compare a goal setting intervention featuring one goal setting characteristic with an identical goal setting intervention without the characteristic. Shilts et al. (2004a) found six adult and one adolescent studies meeting the requirements of this design. These results provide inconclusive evidence to suggest superior characteristics to include in an intervention.

The third research objective identified was evaluation of the effectiveness of a diet and/or physical activity behavior intervention featuring goal setting. The research design for this objective required the comparison group to be usual care or no intervention.

Eight studies (four adult, zero adolescent, and four child) were found with this design, and all reported positive outcomes. Each study was rated by the reviewers for level of goal setting support. Minimal support was defined as a goal was set, but no other support was provided. Full support required application of goal setting theory, including extensive goal attainment support (i.e., feedback, contracting, barriers counseling, goal attainment, and skills development). Only 32% of the studies included full support. Shilts et al. (2004a) concluded that moderate evidence was found to support inclusion of goal setting as a strategy to promote dietary and physical activity behavior change among adults, and those interventions fully supporting goal setting were more likely to produce positive results. Methodological issues remain unresolved. The literature with adolescents and children is limited.

Bodenheimer and Handley (2009) explored the use of goal setting to promote health behavior change in primary care/clinic settings for patients, adults, and adolescents, with chronic conditions. Of the eight studies meeting inclusion criteria, all set goals in a collaborative manner where goals were negotiated rather than patients being told what their goals would be. Goals set were proximal and specific and often included follow-up feedback. Clinicians were found to be minimally involved in goal setting discussions with patients; the additional time required to conduct goal setting during the clinical visit was a barrier. Nonclinical staff to assist in patient goal setting and interactive computer programs were used in several studies. Both of these represent appropriate strategies to reduce clinician time spent on goal setting. Bodenheimer and Handley (2009) concluded that there was not enough evidence to support that goal setting is superior to other change techniques, although it is often used in a primary care setting. They specified that controlled trials were needed to investigate whether goal setting actually improves patient outcomes.

In the last two decades, a significant increase in breadth and depth of goal setting research to promote health behavior change has occurred. Several reviews documented that goal setting is frequently used to facilitate adoption of healthful eating and physical activity behaviors to reduce chronic disease risk. (Bodenheimer & Handley, 2009; Cullen et al., 2001; Shilts et al., 2004a; Strecher et al., 1995). The reviews provide evidence that goal setting is an appropriate strategy to facilitate health behavior change. What is not evident from the current research is how to most effectively implement goal setting targeting health behaviors, and whether the methods need to change according to setting and target audience. In this chapter, we will present information on goal type, computer tailoring, rehabilitation and mediators/moderators highlighting recent research in diet and physical activity interventions focusing on specific target audiences and settings.

## Goal Setting Types

Borrowing from the workplace literature on goal setting, researchers have identified goal properties (proximity, specificity, difficulty) and goal setting components (feedback, rewards, commitment, knowledge) that are important in promoting motivation, self-efficacy and, ultimately, behavior change (Locke & Latham, 1990; Locke & Latham, 2002; Bandura & Simon, 1977; Neubert, 1998; Strecher et al., 1995). These properties and components are shown in Table 26.1 with application to diet and physical activity interventions.

An important issue to be addressed when developing a goal setting strategy to promote health behavior change is how the goal will be set, that is, selection of goal type. Three types

*Table 26.1* Goal Properties and Components Important for Effective Goal Setting in Workplace Literature with Applications to Diet & Physical Activity Interventions (Reprinted from Shilts et al., 2004a with permission from *American Journal of Health Promotion*)

| Goal properties | Description from workplace literature | Practical application for diet & physical activity interventions |
|---|---|---|
| **Difficulty & attainable** | To induce effort, a goal should be difficult yet attainable. Difficult goals require more effort to achieve than easy goals. As goal difficulty increases, so does the required effort and consequently performance, assuming the goal is reasonable to achieve. | Eating 4 servings of dairy a day could constitute a difficult but appropriate goal, if the individual is currently consuming 2 servings daily. |
| **Specificity** | A specific goal provides a clear and narrow target and designates the type and amount of effort necessary to accomplish the goal; general goals provide little basis for regulating one's effort. | A specific goal would be, "Walk 1 mile, during lunch, 3 times this week with Anne", compared to the general goal, "Exercise more often". |
| **Proximity** | Goals can be set at a proximal (short-term) or distal (long-term) level. Proximal goals mobilize effort now. In contrast, distal goals make it is easy to postpone efforts. | A proximal goal would be, "Eat 5 servings of fruit and vegetables today: 1 at breakfast, 1 at lunch, 2 at dinner and 1 for snack", compared to the distal goal, "Eat more fruits and vegetables this month". |

| Goal setting components | Description from workplace literature | Practical application for diet & physical activity interventions |
|---|---|---|
| **Feedback** | Feedback can be described as knowledge of personal status about one's selected goal. Feedback enhances goal achievement and should be provided regularly. | Having participants track their goal progress can function as feedback. An educator can review participant's goal progress and provide individual feedback. |
| **Rewards** | Rewards function as a motivator to continue goal progress. They can be *internal* that is, pride in accomplishment or *external* that is, recognition. | For goal progress, provide participants with raffle tickets to be drawn for prizes. For goal achievement, present the participant with a certificate of achievement. |
| **Knowledge, plans, & strategies** | Application of skills and knowledge (either newly acquired or prior knowledge) are used to develop relevant goal strategies that will facilitate goal attainment. | Have participants design a personal action plan with customized strategies for meeting goals. |
| **Commitment** | If a person is not committed to (i.e., trying for) the goal, there will be no goal effect and, consequently no behavior change. | Participants complete a contract by indicating the goal selected, signing the contract and having a peer sign. |

of goal setting have been investigated extensively targeting adults in a workplace setting: self-set, assigned/prescribed, and participatory/collaborative (see Table 26.2). Research results do not provide clear evidence to suggest that one goal type is more effective; varying type of goal did not change work performance (Locke & Latham, 1990). It does seem logical that many factors (age, readiness to change, type of behavior being targeted, respect for the educator/clinician, setting) can influence appropriateness of goal type in health behavior interventions.

### Self-Set, Assigned, and Participative (Collaborative)

Shilts et al. (2004a) reported in a review that assigned/prescribed goal setting was the most common type of goal setting used among the adult studies (e.g., Baron & Watters, 1982; Dubbert & Wilson, 1984; Duncan & Pozehl, 2002; Lutz et al., 1999; Schnoll & Zimmerman, 2001). Participatory or collaborative goal setting was used in three studies (Mann & Sullivan, 1987; Schultz, 1993; Stenstrom, 1994), and self-set goal setting was used in four studies (Annesi, 2002; Cobb et al., 2000; Mazzeo-Caputo et al., 1985; McKay et al., 2001). Goal type could not be determined in one study (Burke et al., 2002). Only two studies compared the effect of different goal types on goal attainment (Alexy, 1985; Mazzeo-Caputo et al., 1985). On the basis of the results of these studies, a single type of goal setting cannot be determined as superior for changing diet or physical activity behaviors (Shilts et al., 2004a).

On the other hand, all studies reviewed by Bodenheimer and Handley (2009) targeting health promotion in a primary care setting were found to use collaborative/participatory goal setting. This goal setting type may be better suited for the clinical setting, where the

*Table 26.2* Goal-Setting Types, Description, and Examples in the Nutrition and Physical Activity Behavior Change Literature (Reprinted from Shilts et al., 2004a with permission from *American Journal of Health Promotion*)

| | | |
|---|---|---|
| Self-set | Goals are designed and chosen by the participant. | Annesi (Annesi, 2002) Mazzeo-Caputo et al. (Mazzeo-Caputo, et al., 1985) |
| Assigned/ prescribed | Goals are designed and chosen by the practitioner without input from participant. | Schnoll and Zimmerman (Schnoll & Zimmerman, 2001) Duncan and Pozehl (Duncan & Pozehl, 2002) Alexy(Alexy, 1985)Lutz et al. (Lutz et al., 1999)Baron and Watters (Baron & Watters, 1982) |
| Collaborative/ participatory | Goals are designed and chosen jointly by practitioner and participant. | Alexy (Alexy, 1985) Schultz (Schultz, 1993) Stenstrom (Stenstrom, 1994) |
| Guided | The practitioner designs multiple goal choices and the participant chooses one goal. | Shilts, Horowitz, & Townsend (Shilts et al., 2009) Contento (Contento et al., 2007) Block (Block et al., 2008) |
| Group-set | Goals are designed and chosen either by practitioner or group and goal attainment is contingent on the performance of the group. | — |

clinician and patient can have a one-on-one discussion to set the goal/goals during the medical appointment. This collaborative approach is different from the health care provider telling the patient what he should do and assigning the clinician-preferred goal. Bodenheimer and Handley (2009) suggested that this collaborative, as opposed to assigned, goal setting could foster improved goal commitment and motivation. This is in contrast with goal setting in the workplace, where performance is not shown to be contingent upon whether the goal is assigned, self-set, or set participatively. A possible explanation is the inherent difference between an employer assigning a goal to an employee where job performance is compensation-based and a clinician assigning a goal to a patient who must be intrinsically motivated.

Although collaborative goal setting may lend itself to the clinical setting where one-on-one interaction is the norm and patient autonomy and goal commitment is fostered, this type of goal setting is often time intensive. This can be a barrier in the clinical setting. It is definitely a barrier in a community setting where group classes are the norm. One educator usually does not have the luxury of time to collaboratively set a goal with each individual in the class. This is a possible explanation as to why assigned goal setting was found to be more frequently used in community-based diet and physical activity interventions.

## Guided

Using a "guided" approach to goal setting could be an alternative to the time- and educator-intensive collaborative goal setting where the practitioner develops major and minor goals with attributes necessary for optimal goal effectiveness such as specificity, proximity, difficulty, and attainability (Table 26.1) (Locke & Latham, 2002; Shilts et al., 2004b). The participant makes an independent decision in selecting a major goal based on a personal assessment, a key element in this strategy, and then couples the choice of major goal with specific minor goal. This approach allows for the element of autonomy for the participant without requiring individual educator or teacher assistance. An example of a major goal is "increase fruit and vegetable intake" and a minor goal, "add fruit to your cereal three mornings a week." Each broad major goal is coupled with a collection of minor goals that are specific in terms of what, when, and how often.

Guided goal setting was developed initially to meet the challenges of implementing a goal setting behavioral intervention for adolescents in a school setting (Shilts et al., 2004a). Formative evaluation revealed that of the three types of goal setting identified in the workplace literature, (i.e., self-set, participatory, or assigned), each presented limitations for the adolescent audience and for a school setting with the classroom teacher implementing the intervention (Shilts, 2003). Setting a goal requires abstract reasoning, a process noted by Piaget to begin during adolescence (Piaget, 1972). Some adolescents may not yet have the cognitive ability to "self-set" an appropriate goal. Focus group interviews revealed that adolescents could identify when goal setting was being used and could explain its purpose, but they did not have the ability to formulate specific goals for themselves (Shilts, 2003). Collaborative goal setting is not an option for most school settings because of the time commitment needed from the teacher with each individual adolescent. Desiring autonomy, that is, a separation from adults, is a well-known developmental characteristic of adolescents (Berk, 2006). Thus, assigned goal setting may limit adolescent autonomy and ignore the adolescent's quest for independence, thereby decreasing goal commitment. Consequently, a fourth type of goal setting, guided, was developed specifically to meet these challenges. This new type was informed by focus group and individual interviews (Shilts, 2003), previous goal setting research (Locke & Latham, 1990; Shilts et al., 2004a), and cognitive development theory (Piaget, 1972). Guided goal setting eliminates the possibility of inappropriate goal selection (i.e., goals that are too general or unrealistic) that could occur when goals are self-set. Guided goal setting ensures that the goal choices contain attributes necessary for optimal goal effectiveness as shown in the workplace literature.

Two examples of how guided goal setting has been implemented in diet and physical activity behavior change interventions are detailed, both targeting adolescents in a school setting. Guided goal setting is an integral part of the EatFit intervention, which was designed to improve the dietary and physical activity behaviors of middle school students living in low-income communities (Horowitz et al., 2004; Shilts et al., 2004b). Step-by-step guidelines are included for targeting practitioners wishing to implement this type of goal setting strategy (see Table 26.3). Students are guided to set one diet and one physical activity goal for the duration of the nine-week school-based obesity prevention intervention. There are six specific major dietary goal options (increase calcium, fruit, vegetable, and iron intake; improve eating habits; decrease fat or added sugar

*Table 26.3* Practitioner Step-by-Step Guide for Implementing Guided Goal Setting in a Diet and/or Physical Activity Intervention (Reprinted from Shilts et al., 2004b with permission from Elsevier)

| Practitioner steps | Examples from the EatFit intervention |
| --- | --- |
| 1. Choose main concept(s) to be improved. | Improve diet and physical activity behaviors. |
| 2. Research target audience motivators for desired behaviors to incorporate into goal construction using qualitative research methods. | Increase energy or improved appearance for the adolescent audience. |
| 3. Develop predetermined major goals based on main concepts selected. | Increase fruit and vegetable intake. |
| 4. Develop at least three minor goal options for each major goal. Goals should be constructed with the following attributes: proximity, specificity, difficulty, and attainability. | Add 1 serving of fruit to your cereal three mornings a week. |
| 5. Choose or develop a self-assessment tool. | 24-hour diet record, physical activity diary |
| 6. Choose or develop a method for scoring the assessment tool and generating goals. | EatFit eating analysis, www.eatfit.net |
| 7. Develop a contract to include the selected major and minor goals for participants and a peer or practitioner to sign. | A computer generated contract is tailored for each student and includes selected diet and fitness goals, personalized motivators for change, and a space for signatures from student, parent and friend. |
| 8. Develop a method for participants to track goal progress. | A graphing system, designed like a thermometer to easily show progress from "cold" to "hot". |
| 9. Develop a reward system for goal attainment. | Raffle tickets to be drawn for a prize. |

intake) and four specific physical activity goal options (flexibility, aerobic, strength, and lifestyle). Students complete self-assessment activities for dietary and physical activity behaviors. Based on the results of the assessments, students are presented with two areas for improvement and one for positive recognition (Horowitz et al., 2005). The student selects his goal area, for example, "decrease added sugar intake." This would be his major goal. The student then chooses from three minor goals, for example, "eat a breakfast cereal with less than 10 g of sugar per serving three mornings a week." This process is repeated for physical activity. The goals were designed to employ appropriate adolescent motivators: increased energy, improved appearance, and independence. The major and minor goals selected are written into a contract. The contract is signed by the student, a peer, and a parent or guardian. Peer and parent signatures on the contract are meant to facilitate social support at school and at home. Students track goal progress and are rewarded with raffle tickets and prizes. The EatFit intervention specifically supports goal attainment through skill-building activities, social support, barrier counseling, and cue management (Horowitz, et al., 2004).

In another low-income middle school setting, the Choice, Control, and Change (CCC) curriculum (24 lessons) employed the Shilts et al. guided goal setting procedure as one of the behavioral approaches to fostering healthy eating and physical activity behaviors (Contento et al., 2007). Students collect and analyze personal food and activity behaviors and compare their data to preformatted goals from which the students choose one and develop an action plan. The goal choices are based on behaviors under the control of middle school students (getting enough fruits, vegetables, water, and physical activity and not getting too many sweetened beverages, packaged snacks, and fast food). The curriculum provides opportunities to learn skills to attain diet and physical activity goals as well as understand the scientific evidence for why the goals are important. Middle school students (n = 562) who received the CCC intervention compared to the delayed intervention controls (n = 574) were shown to decrease sweetened beverage intake, packaged snacks, screen time and fast food serving sizes, and increased intention to walk for exercise (Contento et al., 2010). No changes were found for water or fruit and vegetable intake. Improvements were seen in several psychosocial mediating variables: outcome expectations, goal intentions, competence, autonomy, and self-efficacy for drinking fewer sweetened beverages, eating less at fast-food restaurants, eating fewer packaged snacks, drinking lots of water, walking, and taking the stairs. These improvements were attributed to the "increased sense of autonomy to take control and make good decisions about food and physical activity choices, and in their sense of competence in being able to set goals and carry through with them" (Contento et al., 2010, p. 1837).

Although the above results would suggest that the collaborative and/or guided approach to goal setting would have advantages over prescribed or self-set goals in clinical and group class settings targeting diet and physical activity behavior change, more research is needed. This research question, although fairly rudimentary, should be studied to maximize participant impact and reduce barriers for educators and clinicians. Computer technology may facilitate tailoring goal options to participant preferences in the "guided" process while saving clinicians' time. Research should focus on comparing goal types with various age, cultural, and socioeconomic groups in different settings.

## Computer Managed

Use of computer technology is an innovative way to engage youth and adults in goal setting to improve dietary and physical activity behaviors (Lytle & Achterberg, 1995; Baranowski et al., 2003; Kroeze et al., 2006). Computer programs and games can create a fun and interactive experience that allows for tailoring of goals for a personalized health education approach. For example, goals can be tailored to baseline dietary and physical activity behaviors; individual motivators and preferences; or demographic profiles such as age, ethnicity, and gender characteristics. Constructing personalized goal options without the aid of a computer program would be time intensive for the educator or clinician in addition to the individualized time necessary for goal selection and action planning. In addition to computer tailoring for personalized goal generation, tailoring could also be used to facilitate goal attainment through individualized goal tracking, and feedback on performance, motivation, and skill building to change behaviors. Web-based applications could also provide a source of social support (Kroeze et al., 2006).

More than half of the primary care goal setting studies aimed at chronic disease risk reduction reviewed by Bodenheimer and Handley (2009) used interactive computerized systems to aid in goal selection. The use of the computer programs reduced time spent by clinic staff, a major barrier to implementing goal setting in that setting. A potential benefit of using computer tailoring to facilitate goal setting with patients is that patients can self-select goals via the computer, leaving time for follow-up with staff for motivation, barriers counseling, and education (Bodenheimer & Handley, 2009).

Alive! is an example of a primary prevention intervention completely delivered via the computer, which uses "guided" goal setting to facilitate diet and physical activity behavior change in adults (Block et al., 2008). A behavior change model was developed to provide details on how goal setting and achievement were facilitated in Alive! (see Figure 26.1). The intervention guides participants to choose one of three major goals (paths): increase physical activity, decrease fats/sugars, or increase fruit/vegetables. Participants choose preformulated minor (small step) goals (4-6) for each week of the intervention. The preformulated goals included attributes known to enhance goal effectiveness from the workplace literature: specific, proximal, attainable, and relevant. For example, participants who select the fruit and vegetable major goal (path) could choose from the following minor (small step) goals to work on for the week:

(1) I will add vegetables to pizza or other carry-out this week.
(2) I will increase my vegetables 3 days this week by having a second portion (any vegetable except potatoes).
(3) I will have tomato juice or V-8 juice as a snack 4 days this week.
(4) I will have vegetable soup at lunch or dinner two days this week.
(5) I will include a serving of fresh fruit every day.

Alive! goal were tailored based on stage of change, lifestyle constraints (e.g., whether children are at home, whether most meals are home-cooked or eaten out), and physical activity preferences (group or individual activities, structured exercise, or lifestyle activities). Goal commitment and attainment were facilitated by goal specific tips, additional information, simulation tools, goal tracking, tips for overcoming barriers and,

---

**The *Alive!* Behavior Change Model**

**1. *Elicit* small-step behaviors that are relevant and achievable**

- **Build the *intention* to achieve the overall health goal (fruit and vegetables, fats and sugars, or physical activity)**
  - Provide personal feedback on behavioral health status, including areas needing improvement, through Health Risk Assessments for dietary intake and PA.
  - Develop knowledge of the impact of physical activity and nutrition on specific disease prevention, through Health Notes and Health Headlines.

- **Suggest *personally appropriate and achievable small-step goals***
  - Tailor suggested goals to each person's current practices, practical life constraints, and Stage of Change

- **Provide for continued *goal-setting***
  - Induce commitment to a small-step goal each week
  - Provide for individual choice of that weekly goal

**2. Enhance the probability of *achieving* a small-step goal**

- **Increase behavior-specific *self-efficacy***
  - Provide tips on how to achieve the goal
  - Provide tips on overcoming barriers

- **Provide *reminders of commitments* to each weekly goal**

- **Encourage social support**

**3. *Sustain* the new behaviors**

- **Provide *reinforcement* for achieving goals**
  - Provide messages acknowledging progress
  - Track goal achievement, through the Goal Tracker

- **Encourage *repetition* of previously achieved goals, to make them habitual**

- **Keep the *intention* to achieve the overall health goal *salient,* through**
  - Continued Health Notes on the link between nutrition/PA and health outcomes
  - Use of the Health Habits Simulator, to see that small changes will build toward the overall goal

- **Steadily *increase self-efficacy* for behaviors supporting the overall intention**
  - Have participants achieve success in a series of small-step behavioral goals
  - Reduce concerns about future barriers, through tips for overcoming them
  - Build a growing repertoire of behavioral strategies and tips for achieving them
  - End with an HRA showing the effect of changes achieved on health standards

---

*Figure 26.1* The Alive! Behavior Change Model (From © Block et al., 2008. Originally published in the *Journal of Medical Internet Research* (http://www.jmir.org).

mid-week minor goal reminder messages all delivered via e-mail. A randomized controlled trial was conducted to investigate the efficacy of the 16-week computer tailored, goal setting intervention, Alive!, with employees (n = 787) of a large healthcare organization. The intervention group made significant improvements in physical activity levels and fruit and vegetable intake. Saturated and trans fat intake also decreased significantly. Differences between intervention and control groups were evident four months post intervention (Sternfeld et al., 2009).

Lytle and Achterberg (1995) identified key components to behavior change for youth interventions: (1) self-assessment of eating patterns, (2) personalized and targeted messages, and (3) use of interactive computer technology. The Squire's Quest! intervention uses each of these strategies to target fourth grade students and increase fruit, juice, and vegetable servings via a multimedia computer game (Baranowski et al., 2003). The entire intervention is delivered via the computer, and each of the 10 game sessions, lasting approximately 25 minutes, begins with goal setting activities. Goal attainment is rewarded with game points. Problem-solving strategies are integrated into the game to increase likelihood of goal attainment. Students' goals focus on making a fruit or vegetable recipe demonstrated in the game, eating another fruit, juice, or vegetable serving at a meal or as a snack, or asking for more of their favorite fruit, juice, or vegetable to be stocked at home. The intervention was found to increase students' fruit, juice, and vegetable intake by 1.0 servings. Students reported the game was fun, and kept their attention with preference for tailoring of goal setting (Baranowski et al., 2003).

## Goal Setting in Managing Rehabilitation

Rehabilitation treatments for heart disease and diabetes often include promotion of physical activity and diet behavior change. Goal setting can be an important component of this rehabilitation process. Recently, a systematic review of controlled trials was conducted to examine the effectiveness of psycho-education on health behavior change in adults participating in cardiac rehabilitation (Aldcroft et al., 2011). Seven randomized controlled trials were included in the meta-analysis, showing that the interventions produced significant positive effects, over a medium term, for the promotion of physical activity. The authors noted that strategies, such as goal setting, problem solving, self-monitoring, and role modeling, appeared to be influential in the promotion of health behavior change. Goal setting was a common behavior change strategy, and was identified in five of the seven interventions reviewed. Based on the review, further recommended research included the need to confirm the behavior change strategies or combinations that are the most effective at producing health behavior change in cardiac rehabilitation patients (Aldcroft et al., 2011).

Scobbie et al. (2011) affirmed that goal setting is a fundamental component of the rehabilitation process, but stated that there is a lack of a usable theory-driven goal setting framework to guide rehabilitation interventionists. Causal modeling was used to determine a goal setting–action planning framework based on social cognitive theory, goal setting theory, and health action process with the objective to "guide healthcare professionals systematically through the process of setting and achieving goals in a general rehabilitation setting" (Scobbie et al., 2011, p. 478). Based on the modeling, four components of a goal-setting and action-planning practice framework were identified: (1) negotiating rehabilitation goals between clinicians and patients, (2) setting specific goals, (3) breaking specific goals into steps for an action plan, and (4) appraising goal performance and providing feedback. Including coping plans to address action plan barriers was also noted as important (see Figure 26.2). Two variables were identified by Scobbie et al. (2011) as mediators, namely, self-efficacy and action-plan attainment. Pilot testing of the four-component framework provided initial support for its usability. Interventionists found that the framework facilitated setting and attaining goals, improved structure and focus in the goal setting process, and made it more patient centered. The need for training all team members prior to implementation of the framework was identified as a barrier, as well the additional time and effort required to implement

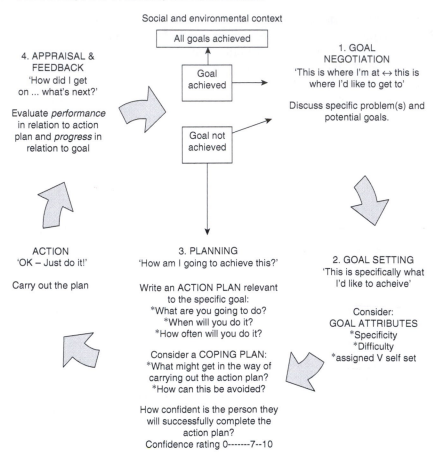

Social and environmental context

*Figure 26.2* Goal-setting and action-planning practice framework (Reprinted from Scobbie et al., 2011 with permission from Sage Publications).

the framework. A potential strength of the newly established framework is that it combines a "theoretical and clinical approach" so interventionists know "what they are doing and why they are doing it in a particular way" (Scobbie et al., 2011, p. 479).

Recent studies demonstrate that goal setting can be used to promote health behavior change in cardiac rehabilitation and diabetes management settings (Butler et al., 2009; Estabrooks et al., 2005; Furber et al., 2010; Redfern et al., 2008; West et al., 2010). A description of how the goal setting behavior change strategy was implemented and results of the interventions are discussed below.

To promote physical activity after attending cardiac rehabilitation, a pedometer-based telephone intervention that includes goal setting was evaluated for effectiveness (Butler et al., 2009). Key intervention components included individualized goal setting (pedometer step count or walking minutes), verbal reinforcement, feedback, outcome expectations of goal attainment, and barriers counseling via four phone calls. Patients set their own goals with guidance from the researcher, aiming for 30 minutes of moderate intensity physical activity on all or most days of the week. The pedometer-based intervention with goal setting improved physical activity levels, psychosocial health, and cardiorespiratory fitness in cardiac patients relative to control patients who only received two exercise brochures (Butler et al., 2009). Similar results were found implementing the same pedometer-based goal setting intervention with cardiac patients not attending cardiac rehabilitation (Furber et al., 2010).

In another group of cardiac patients not attending cardiac rehabilitation, a patient-centered, collaborative goal setting intervention delivered via modules was tested (Redfern et al., 2008). A risk-factor assessment provided the basis for collaborative goal setting. The patient completed an action plan for the specific risk factor they selected to modify, selected relevant education modules (blood pressure, smoking cessation, or physical activity), and were referred to relevant community resources. Four follow-up phone calls were conducted focusing on risk factors and personal goals. Compared to the usual care control group, treatment patients receiving the collaborative goal setting intervention reduced total cholesterol, blood pressure, BMI, physical activity, and smoking rates. Patient choice in goal setting and education modules significantly improved cardiac risk factor profiles compared with controls.

As with cardiac rehabilitation, goal setting can also be used in interventions targeting other patient groups such as those suffering from diabetes. To improve diabetes management, rural elderly patients were targeted in a telemedicine, home-based intervention that included goal setting (West et al., 2010). The televisits were scheduled every 4–6 weeks, with the key component being collaborative goal setting. The patient and the certified diabetes educator (CDE) collaboratively set at least one goal with up to six at each televisit. Frequently the patient selected a general goal, and with help from the CDE, specific, measurable, attainable, relevant goals with a time frame would be chosen. Sixty-eight percent of the collaboratively set goals were met or improved upon. Nutrition-related goals were set more often than physical activity goals, and no differences were found for goal setting and achievement between male and female patients. The telemedicine intervention with goal setting spanned over five years, resulting in 18,355 televisits with an average of 33 goal setting televisits per patient. Telemedicine was found to be a feasible way to promote health behavior change through collaborative goal setting in rural diabetes patients. In a randomized controlled trial, comparing this type of goal setting intervention to the usual care, improvements were found in glycemic control, blood pressure, and LDL levels (Shea et al., 2009).

Diabetes self-management was also the focus of Estabrooks et al.'s (2005) evaluation of a computer-assisted, patient-directed goal setting intervention. The clinic-based, goal selection process began with a brief physical activity and dietary assessment where results were compared to recommended guidelines. Participants self-selected a behavior change goal related to diet, physical activity, or smoking. The computer program facilitated patient selection of activities, barriers, and barrier strategies, which were all used to generate a hard copy of an action plan, goal, barriers, and strategies to overcome them (see Figure 26.3). After the computer session, a brief counseling session was conducted by a medical assistant to review goals selected. A follow-up call was conducted two weeks later to review goal progress and provide feedback. Results from the RCT found that patients selected personally relevant goals (e.g., selecting a goal from the area that could use the most improvement), which resulted in significant changes in physical activity, fruit, vegetable, and fat intake (Estabrooks et al., 2005).

```
DIABETES PRIORITY PROGRAM
──────────────────────────────────────────────────────────────────────────
Personalized Action Plan for: [Participant's Name]                    6/21/04

MY MEDICAL ACTION PLAN (tests you may be due for)

HEMOGLOBIN A1C TEST      Scheduled for Date: _____  Time: _____  Date completed: _____
DILATED EYE EXAM         Scheduled for Date: _____  Time: _____  Date completed: _____
FOOT EXAM/RISK ASSESS    Scheduled for Date: _____  Time: _____  Date completed: _____
ALBUMIN, MICRO-ALBUMIN   Scheduled for Date: _____  Time: _____  Date completed: _____
FLU SHOT                 Scheduled for Date: _____  Time: _____  Date completed: _____
──────────────────────────────────────────────────────────────────────────
MY SELF CARE ACTION PLAN (between now and my next doctor's appointment, I will):
1) I will reduce my intake of saturated fats
In order to reach the above goal, I will do the following activities:
  *Broil or grill meats and fish, boil or poach eggs, and not fry them.
  *Snack on vegetables, fruits, air-popped popcorn  (no butter!), baked crackers, baked pretzels.
I will begin these activities on: 07/01/2004
──────────────────────────────────────────────────────────────────────────
BARRIERS that get in my way    How I will overcome these barriers
*I have no self-discipline      1) Find a partner to support you.
                                2) Join a support group such as TOPS or Weight Watchers.
*I eat out a lot.               1) When eating out, order food that is baked, broiled, grilled,  lean,
                                   roasted, skinless, or steamed.
                                2) When eating out, choose condiments such as chili peppers, mustard,
                                   soy sauce (low sodium), Tabasco sauce, lemon juice, vinegar, salsa, or
                                   horseradish.
```

*Figure 26.3* Example of a participant's action plan with reduced dietary fat as the goal (Reprinted from Estabrooks et al., 2005 with permission from Sage Publications).

There is evidence to support the use of goal setting for rehabilitation focusing on the promotion of healthful nutrition and physical activity behaviors (Butler et al., 2009; Estabrooks et al., 2005; Furber et al., 2010; Redfern et al., 2008; West et al., 2010). The establishment of a theoretical framework for rehabilitation interventionist could provide a systematic way to develop and compare interventions (Scobbie et al., 2011). Similar to primary prevention goal setting interventions, questions about optimal numbers of goals, goal type, and who will benefit most still need to be addressed.

## Youth Interventions

Goal setting research is limited with few studies focusing on child (<12 years) and adolescent (12–19 years) nutrition and physical activity (Shilts et al., 2004a). Four goal setting intervention effectiveness studies targeting children (Coates et al., 1981; Howison et al., 1988; Ma & Contento, 1997; Sallis et al., 1997) were reported and none for adolescents (Shilts et al., 2004a); no goal setting effectiveness studies and only one goal setting characteristic study for adolescents was found (White & Skinner, 1988). More recently, three goal setting intervention effectiveness studies (Contento et al., 2010; Patrick et al., 2006; Singh et al., 2009) and one goal setting effectiveness study (Shilts et al., 2009) were reported in the literature targeting adolescents, with each showing positive results.

Although goal setting is frequently used as a behavior change strategy in youth interventions, there is a lack of youth studies determining its effectiveness. Most youth goal setting studies compare the impact of a goal setting intervention to usual care or no intervention (Coates et al., 1981; Contento et al., 2010; Howison et al., 1988; Ma & Contento, 1997; Patrick et al., 2006; Sallis et al., 1997; Singh et al., 2009). This focus will determine if the particular intervention containing goal setting is effective, but not if the goal setting component is responsible for the impact. There are many challenges to investigating the effect of goal setting. For example, it is difficult to strip an intervention of the goal setting components (e.g., goal selection, contracting, and tracking), particularly if goal setting is one of the primary change techniques. Another challenge is detecting change attributable to one single behavioral strategy among many, necessitating a large sample size and sensitive measures. Shilts et al. (2009) used this focus to assess guided goal setting effectiveness. The results and challenges are summarized below.

The effect of goal setting on obesity risk reduction was studied with low-income, middle school adolescents (n = 136). Each student was randomly assigned to one of two groups: (1) intervention with guided goal setting [treatment group] or (2) the identical intervention but without goal setting component [control group]. This research indicated that participants in the treatment group (goal setting) who were not committed to their goals (e.g., making goal effort) confounded the results of goal setting. In addition, participants in the control group (no goal setting) who spontaneously set goals also confounded the results. In addition to assessing dietary and physical activity self-efficacy and behaviors, goal commitment questions were asked to ascertain treatment group dedication to the goal. Spontaneous goal setting items with a yes/no response determined if participants in the control group individually set a goal during the course of the study. To further support the inclusion of questions to determine adherence to the designated protocol, Gross and Fogg (2004) suggested in prevention trials, such as this one, that non-adherence is often not associated with the dependent variables. Thus, there is value in finding out how much benefit could be expected with full adherence. This is in contrast to the intent-to-treat (ITT) principle that included all participants in the analysis regardless of adherence.

After the 10-week intervention period, no significant differences were found between groups using the full sample. In order to more clearly evaluate the effect of goal setting, the control participants who "spontaneously" set goals and the treatment participants who did not make goal effort were excluded from analyses. Using this subsample, treatment participants (who made goal effort) scored significantly higher than control participants (who did not spontaneously set goals) on dietary behavior ($p < .05$), physical activity behavior ($p < .05$), and physical activity self-efficacy ($p < .05$) variables. No significant difference was found between groups for the dietary self-efficacy variable. Change in physical activity behaviors was mediated by self-efficacy.

This study demonstrated the effectiveness of goal setting, specifically guided goal setting, for changing dietary and physical activity behaviors using a subsample of treatment participants who made goal effort, and control participants who did not spontaneously set goals. The primary purpose of the study was to explore the effect of guided goal setting as part of an intervention compared to a no-goal setting intervention; therefore, accounting for spontaneous goal setting and goal commitment was important to the research question. In the full sample, non-adherence may be the cause of the nonstatistically significant differences as described by Gross and Fogg (2004) in their commentary on intention to treat (ITT). Including all participants, regardless of adherence to the protocol, does not clarify whether the guided goal setting was more effective than the no-goal setting. When adherence was accounted for, and the control participants who did not spontaneously set goals were compared to those implementing guided goal setting, significant differences in physical activity self-efficacy and dietary and physical activity behaviors were revealed. Including measures of goal commitment and spontaneous goal setting in future health-related goal setting effectiveness studies is strongly recommended.

To help alleviate spontaneous goal setting among control participants, Locke recommends eliminating or reducing the amount of feedback given to the control participants (Locke, 1991). In order to keep the intervention similar for treatment and control groups, except for the goal setting component, dietary and physical activity self-assessment was included for all participants. Providing this personal feedback to participants could have unintentionally motivated the control participants to set personal goals (Locke, 1991; Weinberg, 1994). This also could explain why there were fewer females in the subsample. Of the 26 girls originally in the control group, 19 reported spontaneously setting goals, resulting in more females being excluded than anticipated in the subsample. The self-assessment activity experienced by the control participants may have been sufficient motivation for females to spontaneously set their own goals. The self-assessment activity may not have been as motivating to the boys. Examining gender as a moderating variable is an area for future research.

## Mediated and Moderated Effects in Goal Setting Interventions

With rare exceptions (Shilts et al., 2009), previous interventions that used goal setting to increase physical activity or dietary behaviors (Shilts et al., 2004a) did not directly examine whether goal setting mediated the influences of environmental or social-cognitive variables on physical activity, or whether the effects of goal setting were related to theoretical moderators of goal setting, which might explain their mixed positive and null effects. Moderators and mediators of physical activity that can guide successful interventions to increase physical activity are poorly understood. Mediators of outcomes (i.e., mechanisms) are variables in a causal sequence that transmit all or part of the relation or effect of an independent variable on a dependent variable (MacKinnon et al., 2007). Goal setting works to increase behavior by enhancing the direction, self-regulation (e.g., use of tactics), and persistence of task-directed effort, which are the mediators of its effects (Bandura, 1997, 2004; Locke & Latham, 2002). Moderators of outcomes are variables not in a causal sequence but which modify the relation or effect between independent and dependent variables (Kraemer et al., 2001). Moderators of goal setting include satisfaction levels about current goal status, people's efficacy beliefs about their ability to carry out goal setting, as well as their commitment to the goal setting process (Locke & Latham, 2002) and their intention to act. If the link between goals and goal outcomes is stronger in people with high goal commitment and self-efficacy, those factors moderate the influence of goals. Hence, moderation occurs when goals are related to goal outcomes only, or more strongly, in one level of an extraneous variable that is otherwise unrelated to either goals or goal outcomes.

Goal setting theory (Locke & Latham, 2002) suggests that people who are not satisfied with their current level of physical activity are more likely to set goals to increase activity and are more satisfied when they are successful. Hence, changes in satisfaction should be related to changes in goals and physical activity. Similarly, goals are most related to performance outcomes when people are committed to the goals and are confident that they can attain them (Locke & Latham, 2002). People with high self-efficacy set higher goals, are more committed to the goals, are more likely to act on the goals, and are more likely to develop tactics to reach the goals (Locke & Latham, 2002; see Chapter 10). Hence, goal commitment and self-efficacy moderate the influence of goals on physical activity. The act of goal setting motivates the development and use of self-regulation skills (i.e., tactics) that increase the likelihood of goal attainment (Locke & Latham, 1990; see Chapter 10), so moderators of goal setting must be taken into account.

Self-efficacy conceptualizes a belief in personal capabilities to organize and execute the courses of action required to attain a behavioral goal (see Chapter 10). Like self-efficacy, perceived behavioral control includes efficacy beliefs about internal factors (e.g., skills, abilities, and willpower) and external factors (e.g., time, opportunity, obstacles, and dependence on other people) that are imposed on behavior (Ajzen, 2002). Although both constructs represent personal efficacy judgments about the ease or difficulty of performing a behavior, perceived behavioral control also emphasizes beliefs about personal control over performance of the behavior. Although people are more likely to form an intention to behave when they value an expected outcome of the behavior, that likelihood is increased when a proximal goal is set (Ajzen, 2001). Past studies of physical activity had not examined whether their effects on intentions and behavior are mediated by goal setting, so those ideas were tested while observing naturally occurring change during high school in a cohort of 443 black and white girls from the LEAP trial (Dishman et al., 2004; Pate et al., 2005). Structural equation modeling and panel analysis were used to determine whether changes in goal setting and satisfaction would mediate relations of perceived behavioral control and self-efficacy with changes in intention and physical activity. That is, indirect effects of perceived behavioral control and self-efficacy, operating through goal setting, were tested. As hypothesized, goal setting and intention accounted for the indirect relation between self-efficacy and change in physical activity. Perceived behavioral control and physical activity change were related directly and also indirectly by a path mediated through satisfaction and intention (Dishman et al., 2006).

Those longitudinal results were consistent with theoretical ideas that girls who set goals to be more physically active are likely to form intentions to be active and to carry out those intentions, especially if they believe they are capable of overcoming barriers and controlling their activity level. Experimental studies are needed to confirm that positive manipulation of goal setting can mitigate the decline of physical activity among girls during high school.

Goal setting interventions used to increase physical activity at the workplace have often yielded modest results, but they seldom employed theory-based goal setting (Dishman et al., 1998). A group-randomized 12-week intervention consisting of organizational action and personal and team goal setting was implemented with a multiracial/ethnic sample of 1442 employees at 16 worksites of a national retail company. The intervention focused on setting and attaining primary and secondary personal goals, as well as team goals that were self-set, specific regarding performance and time, challenging yet realistic and attainable (Dishman et al., 2009). The primary personal goals involved graduated increases in the accumulation of 10-minute blocks of exercise and pedometer steps per week during the 12weeks of the intervention (Figure 26.4). Personal

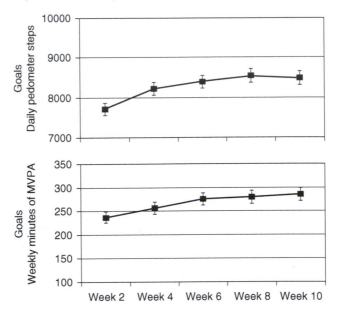

*Figure* 26.4 Growth in physical activity goals during a 12-week workplace goal-setting intervention. Source: (Dishman et al., 2010).

goals were targeted toward meeting or exceeding established public health recommendations accumulating 150 or more minutes each week of moderate-to-vigorous physical activity and/or 10,000 or more pedometer steps each day.

Participants in the intervention had greater increases in moderate and vigorous physical activity and walking compared to participants in a health education control condition (Figure 26.5). The proportion of participants that met the US public health recommendation for regular participation in either moderate or vigorous physical activity remained near 25% at control sites during the study but increased to 50% at intervention sites. During the last 6 weeks of the study, intervention participants exceeded 300 weekly minutes of moderate to vigorous physical activity and 9000 daily pedometer steps. Consistent with Locke & Latham's (1994, 2002) goal setting theory, it was hypothesized that increases in goal-related physical activity would be directly related to goal setting and indirectly through putative moderators of goal setting, specifically self-efficacy and commitment to attain new goals. It was also hypothesized that increased goal setting would mediate the relationship between change in satisfaction with current physical activity and subsequent change in goal-related physical activity. The cohort of participants (N = 664) from the 8 worksites randomized to the intervention were asked at baseline and subsequently every two weeks to provide self-ratings of their satisfaction with their current physical activity levels (1 = not at all, 2 = somewhat, 3 = moderately, 4 = very) and self-set goals to [1] increase the weekly number of 10-minute blocks of MVPA and daily pedometer steps accumulated during the subsequent 2-week period. Participants also were asked to provide biweekly self-ratings (1 = not at all, 2 = somewhat, 3 = moderately, 4 = very) of moderators of goal-setting: confidence (i.e., self-efficacy)

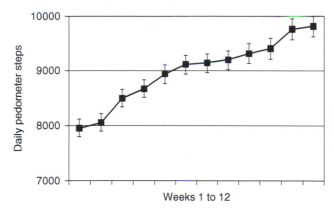

*Figure 26.5* Growth in physical activity during a 12-week workplace goal-setting intervention. Source: (Dishman et al., 2010).

and commitment to carry out the new goal. Participants who sustained higher levels of self-efficacy and commitment about attaining their goals also had greater increases in pedometer steps and greater increases and less leveling off in MVPA. Change in satisfaction with current activity levels was related to change in MVPA indirectly through change in goal setting. The results showed a dose relation of increased physical activity with changes in goal setting, satisfaction, self-efficacy, and commitment, consistent with goal setting theory (Dishman et al., 2010).

The results confirmed theory-derived hypotheses (Locke & Latham, 2002) that (1) participants' self-efficacy and commitment about their goals were related to changes in physical activity and (2) goal setting mediated the relationship between changes in satisfaction with current physical activity and subsequent changes in weekly minutes of MVPA, also consistent with goal setting theory.

## Conclusion

Whether diet and physical activity interventions are delivered one on one, via the Internet, or in a group class, goal setting provides a viable health behavior change strategy (Bodenheimer & Handley, 2009; Cullen et al., 2001; Shilts et al., 2004a; Strecher et al., 1995). However, there is still a need for systematic evaluation to determine optimal implementation and how implementation may change with different audiences and settings. As an intervention strategy, goal setting should be referenced often and fully supported throughout intervention implementation.

When reporting goal setting research targeting health behaviors, it is necessary to provide complete details on how goal setting was implemented, not merely that goal setting was used (Cullen et al., 2001; Shilts et al., 2004a). This detailed reporting will allow for better comparisons among studies and determination of optimal methods. Michie et al. (2009) recently identified 26 theory-driven behavioral "component techniques" from 122 physical activity and healthy eating interventions focusing on five behavioral theories/models so researchers and program developers could better describe intervention content suitable for comparison with other interventions (Abraham & Michie, 2008). Of the 26 techniques, 7 have direct application to goal setting theory: prompt self-monitoring, prompt intention formation, prompt specific goal setting, agreement on behavioral contract, feedback on performance, contingent rewards, and prompt review of behavioral goals. The research of Michie et al. (2009) affirms that goal setting is an important behavior change technique, and methods used need to be described in detail to permit close scrutiny by other researchers.

### Recommended Future Diet and Physical Activity Goal Setting Research

- Conduct randomized controlled trials comparing a diet and/or physical activity intervention with goal setting compared to same intervention without goal setting.
- Vary goal attributes such as type, proximity, or level of feedback to determine the optimal implementation of goal setting for various target audiences and settings.
- Use standard tests of mediation effects in goal setting trials and test of putative moderators of goal setting such as self-efficacy and goal commitment.
- Use process evaluation to confirm the adoption, fidelity, reach, and sustainability of goal setting trials implemented in community and rehabilitation settings.
- Investigate at what age goal setting is developmentally appropriate and which types may be better suited for different developmental stages.
- Determine the optimal number of goals for an intervention period.
- Investigate if goal commitment is enhanced by the tailoring goal options to baseline characteristics (SES, ethnicity, gender, preferences).
- Investigate which audiences and health behaviors are best suited for goal setting interventions.

## References

Abraham, C., & Michie, S. (2008). A taxonomy of behavior change techniques used in interventions. *Health Psychology, 27*(3), 379–387.

Ajzen, I. (2001). Nature and operation of attitudes. *Annual Review of Psychology, 52*, 27–58.

Ajzen, I. (2002). Perceived behavioral control, self-efficacy, locus of control, and the theory of planned behavior. *Journal of Applied Social Psychology, 32*, 665–683.

Aldcroft, S. A., Taylor, N. F., Blackstock, F. C., & O'Halloran, P. D. (2011). Psychoeducational rehabilitation for health behavior change in coronary artery disease: A systematic review of controlled trials. *Journal of Cardiopulmonolgy Rehabilitation and Prevention, 31*, 1–9.

Alexy, B. (1985). Goal setting and health risk reduction. *Nursing Research, 34*(September/October), 283–288.

Ammerman, A. S., Lindquist, C. H., Lohr, K. N., & Hersey, J. (2002). The efficacy of behavioral interventions to modify dietary fat and fruit and vegetable intake: A review of the evidence. *Preventive Medicine, 35*(1), 25–41.

Annesi, J. J. (2002). Goal-setting protocol in adherence to exercise by Italian adults. *Perceptual and Motor Skills, 94*(2), 453–458.

Bandura, A. (2004). Health promotion by social cognitive means. *Health Education and Behavior, 31*(2), 143–164.

Bandura, A. (1997). *Self-efficacy: The excercise of control.* New York: W.H. Freeman & Company.

Bandura, A., & Simon, K. M. (1977). The role of proximal intentions in self-regulation of refractory behavior. *Cognitive Therapy and Research, 1*: 177–193.

Baranowski, T., Baranowski, J., Cullen, K. W., Marsh, T., Islam, N., Zakeri, I., Honess-Morreale, L., & deMoor, C. (2003). Squire's Quest! Dietary outcome evaluation of a multimedia game. *American Journal of Preventive Medicine, 24*(1), 52–61.

Baron, P., & Watters, R. G. (1982). Effects of goal setting and of goal levels on weight loss induced by self monitoring. *International Review of Applied Psychology, 31*, 369–382.

Berk, L. E. (2006). *Development through the life span* (4th ed.). Allyn & Bacon.

Berry, M. W., Danish, S. J., Rinke, W. J., & Smiciklas-Wright, H. (1989). Work-site health promotion: The effects of a goal-setting program on nutrition-related behaviors. *Journal of the American Dietetic Association, 89*, 914–920, 923.

Block, G., Sternfeld, B., Block, C. H., Block, T. J., Norris, J., Hopkins, D., Husson, G., Quesenberry Jr, C. P., & Clancy, H. A. (2008). Development of alive! (A Lifestyle Intervention Via Email), and its effect on health-related quality of life, presenteeism, and other behavioral outcomes: randomized controlled trial. *Journal of Medical Internet Research, 10*(4), e43.

Bodenheimer, T., & Handley, M. A. (2009). Goal-setting for behavior change in primary care: an exploration and status report. *Patient Education and Counseling, 76*(2), 174–180.

Burke, V., Mori, T. A., Giangiulio, N., Gillam, H. F., Beilin, L. J., Houghton, S., Cutt, H. E., Mansour, J., & Wilson, A. (2002). An innovative program for changing health behaviours. *Asia Pacifici Journal of Clinical Nutrition, 11*(Suppl 3), S586–597.

Butler, L., Furber, S., Phongsavan, P., Mark, A., & Bauman, A. (2009). Effects of a pedometer-based intervention on physical activity levels after cardiac rehabilitation: A randomized controlled trial. *Journal of Cardiopulmonary Rehabilitation and Prevention, 29*(2), 105–114.

Centers for Disease Control and Prevention (CDC). (2007). Fruit and vegetable consumption among adults—United States, 2005. *Morbidity and Mortality Weekly Report, 56*(10), 213–217.

Centers for Disease Control and Prevention (CDC). (2010). Youth risk behavior surveillance—United States, 2009. *Morbidity and Mortality Weekly, Surveillance Summaries, 59*(5), 117–126.

Coates, T. J, Jeffery, R., & Slinkard, L. A. (1981). Heart healthy eating and exercise: Introducing and maintaining changes in health behaviors. *American Journal of Public Health, 71*(1), 15–23.

Cobb, L., Stone, W., Anonsen, L., & Klein, D. (2000). The influence of goal setting on exercise adherence. *Journal of Health Education, 31*(5), 277–281.

Contento, I. R., Koch, P. A., Lee, H., & Calabrese-Barton, A. (2010). Adolescents demonstrate improvement in obesity risk behaviors after completion of choice, control & change, a curriculum addressing personal agency and autonomous motivation. *Journal of the American Dietetic Association, 110*(12), 1830–1839.

Contento, I. R., Koch, P. A., Lee, H., Sauberli, W., & Calabrese-Barton, A. (2007). Enhancing personal agency and competence in eating and moving: formative evaluation of a middle school curriculum—choice, control, and change. *Journal of Nutrition Education and Behavior, 39*(5 Suppl), S179–186.

Cullen, K. W., Baranowski, T., & Smith, S. P. (2001). Using goal setting as a strategy for dietary behavior change. *Journal of the American Dietetic Association, 101*(5), 562–566.

Dishman, R. K., DeJoy, D. M., Wilson, M. G., & Vandenberg, R. J. (2009). Move to Improve: a randomized workplace trial to increase physical activity. *American Journal of Preventive Medicine, 36*(2), 133–141.

Dishman, R. K., Motl, R. W., Saunders, R., Felton, G., Ward, D. S., Dowda, M., & Pate, R. R. (2004). Self-efficacy partially mediates the effect of a school-based physical-activity intervention among adolescent girls. *Preventive Medicine, 38*(5), 628–636.

Dishman, R. K., Oldenburg, B., O'Neal, H., & Shephard, R. J. (1998). Worksite physical activity interventions. *American Journal of Preventive Medicine, 15*(4), 344–361.

Dishman, R. K., Saunders, R. P., Felton, G., Ward, D. S., Dowda, M., & Pate, R. R. (2006). Goals and intentions mediate efficacy beliefs and declining physical activity in high school girls. *American Journal of Preventive Medicine, 31*(6), 475–483.

Dishman, R. K., Vandenberg, R. J., Motl, R. W., Wilson, M. G., & DeJoy, D. M. (2010). Dose relations between goal setting, theory-based correlates of goal setting and increases in physical activity during a workplace trial. *Health Education Research, 25*(4), 620–631.

Dubbert, P., & Wilson, G. (1984). Goal-setting and spouse involvement in the treatment of obesity. *Behaviour, Research & Therapy, 22*(3), 227–242.

Duncan, K., & Pozehl, B. (2002). Staying on course: the effects of an adherence facilitation intervention on home exercise participation. *Progress in Cardiovascular Nursing, 17*, 59–65.

Estabrooks, P. A., Nelson, C. C., Xu, S., King, D., Bayliss, E. A., Gaglio, B., Nutting, P. A., & Glasgow, R. E. (2005). The frequency and behavioral outcomes of goal choices in the self-management of diabetes. *The Diabetes Educator, 31*(3), 391–400.

Furber, S., Butler, L., Phongsavan, P., Mark, A., & Bauman, A. (2010). Randomised controlled trial of a pedometer-based telephone intervention to increase physical activity among cardiac patients not attending cardiac rehabilitation. *Patient Education and Counseling, 80*(2), 212–218.

Gross, D, & Fogg, L. (2004). A critical analysis of intent-to-treat principle in prevention research. *Journal of Primary Prevention, 25*(4), 475–489.

Horowitz, M, Shilts, M. K., & Townsend, M. S. (2004). EatFit: a goal oriented intervention that challenges middle school adolescents to improve their eating and fitness choices. *Journal of Nutrition Education and Behavior, 36*(1), 43–44.

Horowitz, M., Shilts, M. K., & Townsend, M. S. (2005). Adapting a diet analysis program for an adolescent audience. *Journal of Nutrition Education and Behavior, 37*, 43–44.

Howison, D., Niedermyer, F., & Shortridge, R. (1988). Field testing a fifth-grade nutrition education program designed to change food-selection behavior. *Journal of Nutrition Education, 20*(2), 82–86.

Kahn, E. B., Ramsey, L. T., Brownson, R. C., Heath, G. W., Howze, E. H., Powell, K. E.,... Corso, P. (2002). The effectiveness of interventions to increase physical activity. A systematic review. *American Journal of Preventive Medicine, 22*(4 Suppl), 73–107.

Kraemer, H. C., Stice, E., Kazdin, A., Offord, D., & Kupfer, D. (2001). How do risk factors work together? Mediators, moderators, and independent, overlapping, and proxy risk factors. *American Journal of Psychiatry, 158*(6), 848–856.

Kroeze, W., Werkman, A., & Brug, J. (2006). A systematic review of randomized trials on the effectiveness of computer-tailored education on physical activity and dietary behaviors. *Annals of Behavioral Medicine, 31*(3), 205–223.

Locke, E. A. (1991). Problems with goal-setting research in sports and their solution. *Journal of Sport and Exercise Psychology, 8*, 311–316.

Locke, E. A., & Latham, G. P. (1994). Goal setting theory. In H. F. O'Neil & M. E. Drillings (Eds.), *Motivation: Theory and research*. Hillsdale, NJ: Lawrence Erlbaum.

Locke, E. A., & Latham, G. P. (2002). Building a practically useful theory of goal setting and task motivation. A 35-year odyssey. *American Psychologist, 57*(9), 705–717.

Locke, E. A., & Latham, G.P. (1990). *A theory of goal setting and performance.* Englewood Cliffs, NJ: Prentice-Hall.

Lutz, S. F., Ammerman, A. S., Atwood, J. R., Campbell, M. K., DeVellis, R. F., & Rosamond, W. D. (1999). Innovative newsletter interventions improve fruit and vegetable consumption in healthy adults. *Journal of the American Dietetic Association, 99*(6), 705–709.

Lytle, L., & Achterberg, C. (1995). Changing the diet of America's children: What works and why? *Journal of Nutrition Education, 27*(5), 250–260.

Ma, F. C., & Contento, I. R. (1997). Development and formative evaluation of a nutrition education curriculum aimed at reducing fat intake in Taiwan elementary students. *Journal of Nutrition Education, 29*(5), 237–243.

MacKinnon, D. P., Fairchild, A. J., & Fritz, M. S. (2007). Mediation analysis. *Annual Review of Psychology, 58,* 593–614.

Mann, K. V., & Sullivan, P. L. (1987). Effect of task-centered instructional programs on hypertensives' ability to achieve and maintain reduced dietary sodium intake. *Patient Education and Counseling, 19,* 53–72.

Mazzeo-Caputo, S. E., Danish, S. J., & Kris-Etherton, P.M. (1985). Dietary change: Prescription vs. goal setting. *Journal of the American Dietetic Association, 85*(5), 553–556.

McKay, H., King, D., Eakin, E., Seeley, J., & Glasgow, R. (2001). The diabetes network internet-based physical activity intervention. *Diabetes Care, 24*(8), 1328–1334.

Michie, S., Abraham, C., Whittington, C., McAteer, J., & Gupta, S. (2009). Effective techniques in healthy eating and physical activity interventions: a meta-regression. *Health Psychology, 28*(6), 690–701.

Neubert, M. J. (1998). The value of feedback and goal setting over goal setting alone and potential moderators of this effect: a meta-analysis. *Human Performance,* 11, 321–335.

Pate, R. R., Ward, D. S., Saunders, R. P., Felton, G., Dishman, R. K., & Dowda, M. (2005). Promotion of physical activity among high-school girls: A randomized controlled trial. *American Journal of Public Health, 95*(9), 1582–1587.

Patrick, K., Calfas, K. J., Norman, G. J., Zabinski, M. F., Sallis, J. A., Rupp, J., Covin, J., & Cella, J. (2006). Randomized controlled trial of a primary care and home-based intervention for physical activity and nutrition behaviors. *Archives of Pediatric and Adolescent Medicine, 160,* 128–136.

Physical Activity Guidelines Advisory Committee. (2008). Physical activity guidelines advisory committee report, 2008. Washington, DC: Department of Health and Human Services.

Piaget, J. (1972). Intellectual evolution from adolescence to adulthood. *Human Development, 15,* 1–12.

Redfern, J., Briffa, T., Ellis, E., & Freedman, S. B. (2008). Patient-centered modular secondary prevention following acute coronary syndrome: a randomized controlled trial. *Journal of Cardiopulmonary Rehabilitation and Prevention, 28*(2), 107–115; quiz 116-107.

Sallis, J. F., McKenzie, T. L., Alcaraz, J. E., Kolody, B., Faucette, N., & Hovell, M. F. (1997). The effects of a 2-year physical education program (SPARK) on physical activity and fitness in elementary school students. *American Journal of Public Health, 87*(8), 1328–1334.

Schnoll, R., & Zimmerman, B. J. (2001). Self-regulation training enhances dietary self-efficacy and dietary fiber consumption. *Journal of the American Dietetic Association, 101*(9), 1006–1011.

Schultz, S. (1993). Educational and behavioral strategies related to knowledge of and participation in an exercise program after cardiac positron emission tomography. *Patient Education and Counseling, 22*(1), 47–57.

Scobbie, L., Dixon, D., & Wyke, S. (2011). Goal setting and action planning in the rehabilitation setting: development of a theoretically informed practice framework. *Clinical Rehabililitation, 25*(5), 468–482.

Shea, S., Weinstock, R. S., Teresi, J. A., Palmas, W., Starren, J., Cimino, J. J., Lai, A. M., Field, L., Morin, P. C., Goland, R., Izquierdo, R., Ebner, S., Silver, S., Petkova, E., Kong, J., & Eimicke, J. P. (2009). A Randomized Trial Comparing Telemedicine Case Management with Usual Care in Older, Ethnically Diverse, Medically Underserved Patients with Diabetes Mellitus: 5 Year Results of the IDEATel Study. *Journal of the Medical Informatics Association, 16*(4), 446–456.

Shilts, M. K. (2003). *The effectiveness of guided goal setting on dietary and physical activity self-efficacy and behaviors of middle school adolescents.* Dissertation, University of California, Davis, Davis.

Shilts, M. K., Horowitz, M., & Townsend, M. S. (2004a). Goal setting as a strategy for dietary and physical activity behavior change: a review. *American Journal of Health Promotion, 19*(2), 81–93.

Shilts, M. K., Horowitz, M., & Townsend, M. S. (2004b). An innovative approach to goal setting for adolescents: guided goal setting. *Journal of Nutrition Education and Behavior, 36*(3), 155–156.

Shilts, M. K., Horowitz, M., & Townsend, M. S. (2009). Guided goal setting: Effectiveness in a dietary and physical activity intervention with low-income adolescents. *Internation Journal of Adolescent Medicine and Health, 20*(1), 111–122.

Singh, A. S., Chin, A. Paw, M. J. M., Brug, J., & Van Mechelen, W. (2009). Dutch obesity intervention in teenagers. *Archives of Pediatric and Adolescent Medicine, 163*(4), 309–317.

Stenstrom, C. H. (1994). Home exercise in rheumatoid arthritis functional class II: Goal setting versus pain attention. *Journal of Rheumatology, 21*(4), 627–634.

Sternfeld, B., Block, C., Quesenberry, C. P., Jr., Block, T. J., Husson, G., Norris, J. C., & Block, G. (2009). Improving diet and physical activity with ALIVE: A worksite randomized trial. *American Journal of Preventive Medicine, 36*(6), 475–483.

Strecher, V. J., Seijts, G. H., Kok, Gerjo J., Glasgow, R., DeVillis, B., Meertens, R. M., & Bulger, D. W. (1995). Goal setting as a strategy for health behavior change. *Health Education Quarterly, 22*(2), 190–200.

Troiano, R. P., Berrigan, D., Dodd, K. W., Masse, L. C., Tilert, T., & McDowell, M. (2008). Physical activity in the United States measured by accelerometer. *Medicine and Science in Sports and Exercise, 40*(1), 181–188.

Tucker, J. M., Welk, G. J., & Beyler, N. K. (2011). Physical activity in U.S.: Adults compliance with the Physical Activity Guidelines for Americans. *American Journal of Preventive Medicine, 40*(4), 454–461.

U.S. Department of Health and Human Services. (2010). Healthy people 2020: National health promotion and disease prevention objectives. Washington, DC: Office of Disease Prevetnion and Health Promotion.

Weinberg, R. S. (1994). Goal setting and performance in sport and exercise settings: A synthesis and critique. *Medicine and Science in Sports and Exercise, 26*(4), 469–477.

West, S. P., Lagua, C., Trief, P. M., Izquierdo, R., & Weinstock, R. S. (2010). Goal setting using telemedicine in rural underserved older adults with diabetes: Experiences from the informatics for diabetes education and telemedicine project. *Telemedicine Journal and E-Health, 16*(4), 405–416.

White, A. A., & Skinner, J. D. (1988). Can goal setting as a component of nutrition education effect behavior change among adolescents? *Journal of Nutrition Education, 20*(6), 327–335.

# 27    Linking Goals and Aging

## Experimental and Lifespan Approaches

*Robin L. West and Natalie C. Ebner*   Department of Psychology,
University of Florida

*Erin C. Hastings*   Department of Neurology, University of Florida

## Introduction

By nature, human beings are goal-oriented. Goals and goal-related processes motivate, organize, and direct behavior at all ages (Chapman & Skinner, 1985; Heckhausen, 1999). Across the lifespan, goals provide the individual with standards and ideal outcomes to consider in evaluating personal functioning in a variety of different domains (Carver & Scheier, 1990). Nevertheless, the majority of work conducted on goal theory has focused on educational (Schunk & Zimmerman, 1996) and work (Locke & Latham, 2002) settings, settings that rarely include older adults. In the 1990 book by Locke and Latham that laid out a theory of goal setting and task performance, for example, there was no mention of older adults as a special case for study. Since then, scholars have begun to consider how goals might apply to older adults, particularly in the context of cognition (especially memory), a life domain that is highly relevant to older individuals. The purpose of this chapter is to review the literature considering how goals may be related to cognition as people age. In linking goals and aging, this chapter will seek to understand how cognitive task performance is affected by specific "task goals" (i.e., situational "desire to do …" goals) at different ages. However, it will also consider goals in the more general context of everyday life, to consider ways in which such "life goals," (i.e., continuing "desire to be …" goals) may interact with specific situational task goals in their impact on cognitive activities across the lifespan.

## Situation-Specific Task Goals

Considerable work on cognition has been done in relation to Locke and Latham's goal setting theory. For instance, goals for reading or subtraction lessons can enhance school performance (e.g., Schunk, 1990) and goals for decision making or problem solving in the workplace can enhance job performance (Bandura & Wood, 1989). Almost every cognitive task situation poses a set of requirements for those who seek to successfully complete the task. In a very broad sense, one could conceptualize task requirements ("remember the list," "go as fast as you can," "avoid making errors") as goals and consider all cognitive research in a review such as this one. But that would be neither feasible nor constructive. Instead, this review will focus on two types of studies. First, we consider research in which participants of differing ages were given explicit targets or goals for their cognitive performance in a controlled laboratory situation. Second, we consider research that examines cognition in the context of more general life goals. In both cases, the linkage between goals and aging is central.

Before 2000, almost no laboratory work on memory had been done to test goal theory, and almost no studies on goal theory had been conducted to examine age differences. Yet as we shall see, the results of early work on goals in memory aging often dovetailed nicely with the dominant findings of goal setting research (Locke & Latham, 2002). Testing goal theory in this new context, studies had two objectives: (1) to confirm that the basic tenets of goal theory also applied to laboratory memory, and (2) to show that older adults responded to cognitive goals in the same way as younger adults do. Beginning with the first objective, we now consider the evidence from this experimental research that supports these traditional tenets of goal theory:

- Goals are motivational
- People work harder for more challenging goals
- Variations in ability impact goal-related performance gains
- Self-efficacy and related belief systems influence goal achievement
- Feedback interacts with goal success
- Goal commitment moderates the impact of goal setting
- Goals direct attention and affect activity selection

## Goals are Motivational

Not only in real life but also in the laboratory context, when there is a cognitive challenge handed to people, they will typically work to meet that challenge (Locke & Latham, 2002). Across a number of studies on memory, specific goals have raised performance levels, and individuals with specific goals have shown higher performance than those without goals. For example, using briefly presented sets of five letters, a self-set goal raised performance by 17% (Stadtlander & Coyne, 1990). With more meaningful stimuli—partially categorizable shopping lists—performance showed strong and consistent goal-directed gains across trials in both younger and older adults, in some cases showing more than 25% improvement in memory test scores (West, Dark-Freudeman, & Bagwell, 2009). In contrast to conditions with no goals, memory gains across time in goal setting conditions were significant even when lists were increasing in difficulty over trials (West, Bagwell, & Dark-Freudeman, 2005; West, Thorn, & Bagwell, 2003). The motivational effect of having specific goals was stronger, and better maintained over trials, when the same list was used repeatedly for testing. Perhaps both younger and older participants were then able to easily observe the gains they were making, which enhanced the motivational impact (e.g., West et al., 2009).

## People Work Harder for More Challenging Goals

Although this notion was once viewed as counterintuitive, there is a substantial body of research showing that individuals will strive to meet even very challenging goals (Locke & Latham, 2002). A good example of the positive impact of challenging goals on laboratory cognition is a study that directly compared low-challenge and high-challenge memory goals given to adults of differing ages. Participants were asked to recall shopping lists, beginning with a 15-item list that they studied for one minute. It was assumed, given the brevity of the list, that most individuals knew how they had performed on that first baseline trial, even without feedback. Participants were then assigned randomly to either a low-challenge (i.e., recall 5 more items on the list) or a high-challenge (i.e., recall 15 more items on the list) goal for the next trial. The list length of every subsequent trial was set in relation to the participant's level of performance on the preceding trial. That is, on each trial they were assigned to recall the shopping items remembered on the previous trial plus 5 or 15 additional shopping list items, depending on a low- or high-challenge goal assignment. In this way, the list length systematically increased as the goals were met, providing more and more challenge, especially in the high-challenge condition. At the same time, the goals were achievable, because they were tied directly to individual performance levels. The investigators found improvements from Trial 1 to Trial 2 for the low-challenge group, and continuing improvements from Trial 2 to 3, and from Trial 3 to 4, for the high-challenge group. Younger and older individuals in the goal condition responded with increased performance, regardless of goal type. This result reflected the greater motivation to persist in cognitive effort for the high-challenge group, even as the task became increasingly demanding (West et al., 2003).

In the domain of text memory, researchers have compared comprehension goals and recall goals, considering the latter as more challenging. Adults of all ages were able to allocate additional attention to that more challenging goal and successfully recall assigned texts (Stine-Morrow, Milinder, Pullara, & Herman, 2001). In line with these findings, individuals instructed to set personal goals will set goals higher if they are performing well, and will continue to increase memory performance when engaged in these more challenging goals (West, Welch, & Thorn, 2001). In addition, high-performing adults will often set goals that are 10–15% higher, once their initial goal is met (West & Thorn, 2001). These results again suggest that challenging cognitive goals are effective motivators.

### Variations in Ability Impact Goal-Related Performance Gains

The second objective of the early studies that linked goals and aging was to show that goals would have comparable effects on younger and older adults, namely, leading to significant improvements in performance under goal setting conditions (relative to no-goal conditions), and higher performance gains with more challenging as opposed to less challenging goals. Individual differences in ability have long been recognized as important factors in goal achievement: "… If the goals set are not within the ability of the person to attain, they will not be attained" (Locke & Latham, 1990, p. 223). Studies on aging provide a unique context for examining the impact of cognitive ability variations because decades of research have revealed age-related declines in various cognitive abilities (Anderson & Craik, 2000). As one would expect, empirical evidence indeed shows that age-related cognitive limitations sometimes affect how much gain is achieved as a function of goal setting.

Over several studies, West and colleagues have established that, compared to younger adults, older adults are less reliably influenced by goals to improve their test scores (West & Thorn, 2001; West & Yassuda, 2004). If the demands appear to surpass older adults' skill levels, they may flounder, withdrawing effort from a challenging goal, resulting in weak goal-related performance gains (West & Thorn, 2001; West et al., 2001). At the same time, under relatively ideal conditions, older adults can be successful when striving for cognitive performance improvements. For instance, older adults can be successful when task difficulty is set in relation to individual levels of performance (West et al., 2005, 2009). Older adults also tend to set their own personal test score goals lower than younger adults, supporting the notion that goal choice is affected by ability (Locke, Frederick, Lee, & Bobko, 1984; Riediger, Li, & Lindenberger, 2006).

It is also important to consider strategic processing when considering age variations in ability that could affect goal achievement, as identification and implementation of effective strategies is often a key factor in goal attainment (Locke & Latham, 1990). Evidence for age declines in the effectiveness of strategy usage is substantial (e.g., Dunlosky, Hertzog, & Powell-Moman, 2005). At the same time, research on goals and aging has been somewhat mixed with respect to strategy use. West and Thorn (2001), for example, found that self-set recall goals, combined with performance feedback, had no impact on categorization as a cognitive strategy during recall of a highly categorizable shopping list. In a recent study using a more challenging list, individual categorization predicted goal-related score gains for both younger and older adults. Older adults who were given experimenter-set performance goals and feedback on their progress toward those goals used more category clustering than an older control group with no goals and no feedback (West et al., 2009). Also, greater goal-directed memory improvement was evident for individuals who utilized more category grouping strategies.

In the domain of text memory, Stine-Morrow and colleagues (2001) were able to eliminate the typical age differences found on laboratory-based memory tasks through goal manipulation. The researchers found that younger and older adults performed similarly on both a recall and a comprehension task. The recall task was identified by the authors as the more difficult of the two tasks, so it is notable that both age groups performed similarly on this task. The authors concluded that older adults were able to compensate for age-related declines in information processing skills by successfully reallocating attentional resources to meet the more challenging recall goal. In a later study, however, age differences in working memory were shown to limit the effect of goals on performance for older learners (Stine-Morrow, Shake, Miles, & Noh, 2006a). Clearly, more work is needed to understand these variations in strategic outcomes with respect to aging.

Varying cognitive abilities are only one of the possible explanations for older adults' lesser ability to respond effectively to performance goals for cognition. Belief systems are also relevant to goal attainment (Locke & Latham, 1990). The most researched belief in this respect is self-efficacy.

## Self-Efficacy and Related Belief Systems Influence Goal Achievement

Self-efficacy is one's assessment of individual capability in a defined task domain, for example, the belief that your memory is pretty good most of the time. Not surprisingly, goals are most motivating when self-efficacy is higher (Maddux, 1995) because those with higher self-efficacy have an expectation that additional effort will lead to a positive outcome (Bandura, 1989; Pervin, 1989). There is considerable evidence that such beliefs, particularly in the domain of cognition, decline over the lifespan (Berry, 1999), and one might assume that such a change would result in older adults not being motivated by cognitive goals. However, research shows that older adults are motivated by cognitive goals and that self-efficacy is an important factor in how goals influence cognitive performance in older adults (West et al., 2009).

For example, levels of memory self-efficacy predicted self-set memory goals, with younger adults showing higher memory self-efficacy and setting their goals much higher than older adults (West & Thorn, 2001; West et al., 2001). It is often the case that repeated memory testing is associated with declines in memory self-efficacy (Dittmann-Kohli, Lachman, Kliegl, & Baltes, 1991; West, Dennehy-Basile, & Norris, 1996). However, those participants who were showing performance gains due to goal setting (as opposed to no gains) reported no declines in self-efficacy (West & Thorn, 2001) and sometimes even showed increases in self-efficacy over trials (West et al., 2001, 2003, 2005). Also, those with goals and those receiving positive feedback about goal progress showed increases in self-efficacy (Miller & West, 2010; West et al., 2005) compared with those having no goals (West et al., 2003).

Theoretically, self-efficacy is related to performance in a reciprocal fashion (Bandura, 1997). That is, initial levels of self-efficacy should affect initial performance. Subsequent evaluations of that performance, in light of one's beliefs, should raise or lower self-efficacy, which will in turn affect future performance (Berry, 1999; Valentijn et al., 2006). Researchers have examined this reciprocal relationship from both directions. In addition to the studies above showing that goal condition predicted self-efficacy over trials, Stine-Morrow and colleagues have shown that, along with working memory, self-efficacy beliefs predicted significant variance in the differential allocation of attentional resources to meet cognitive goals (e.g., to read for high comprehension, or to read quickly). Specifically, participants with high self-efficacy were better than participants with low self-efficacy at adjusting their reading times to meet their assigned reading goal (Stine-Morrow et al., 2006a). In this kind of test situation, it is likely that an ongoing personal assessment of performance ("I'm struggling with this reading," "I need to try a different strategy," "I'm not very good at this"), related to beliefs about abilities, as well as explicit experimenter feedback, informs subsequent on-task behavior such as the setting of goals, the degree of invested effort, the activation of attention, and the employment of strategies (Stine-Morrow, Miller, & Hertzog, 2006b). In this way, belief systems may mediate goal setting effects. In line with this notion, individuals who reported a high degree of control over their memory scores also selected higher goals for themselves (West et al., 2001), and improved their memory scores over trials with or without goals (West & Yassuda, 2004). In contrast, when those reporting low control had no goal, they showed no improvement in scores over trials, and only showed performance gains when given a goal (West & Yassuda, 2004).

### Feedback Interacts with Goal Success

Given the beliefs of older adults, and in particular, the degree to which they doubt their own capability to perform well and to control cognitive performance outcomes, it is not surprising that feedback would influence goal progress for older adults even more so than for younger adults. There are a number of ways for participants in cognitive studies to obtain feedback: (1) with relatively easy tasks and/or obvious performance indicators, adults can directly observe their own score gains (internal feedback), (2) experimenters can provide neutral or objective feedback by pointing out scores in relation to self-set or experimenter-set goals, (3) experimenters can provide encouraging or positive feedback ("that's good," "you are improving") based on performance, and (4) false feedback ("bogus feedback") can be utilized, which might be negative or positive.

With younger adults, evidence revealed that goals and feedback together led to better performance than goals alone (e.g., Bandura & Cervone, 1983), that memory performance improved under most goals and goals-feedback conditions (West et al., 2009), and that feedback showing goal achievement encouraged younger individuals to set even more challenging goals for themselves (West & Thorn, 2001). Younger adults appear to have little difficulty improving memory scores over trials, once motivated to do so, and thus they are likely to receive positive feedback. Studies of false feedback have shown that positive feedback was more motivating than negative feedback (e.g., Thompson & Perlini, 1998). However, older adults, who experience more memory difficulties, may not always obtain positive feedback in a goals-feedback condition. Thus, it is not surprising that a critical variable affecting goal progress for older learners appears to be the type of feedback.

Performance feedback, by itself, shows mixed and partly counterintuitive effects in aging research, in that older adults often do not benefit from feedback (Ellis, Palmer, & Reeves, 1988; Fristoe, Salthouse, & Woodard, 1997; Rebok & Balcerak, 1989). Interestingly, in situations where performance gains were possible, older adults often performed better with goals alone, rather than goals plus feedback (cf. West et al., 2001, 2005). Older adults appeared to become discouraged by objective or neutral feedback that did not highlight performance gains (West & Thorn, 2001; West et al., 2001, 2005). For example, in one study, two-thirds of the older participants did not even gain one point from baseline to final trial in a goals-feedback condition, and they performed more poorly in the goals-feedback condition than in the control condition (West et al., 2001). In contrast, with a relatively simple task (recalling five letters), for which feedback was mostly positive, goals-feedback conditions showed the expected motivational effects for older adults (Stadtlander & Coyne, 1990). This was also found in a task situation in which progressive gains were easily observed by the participants (West et al., 2005). Taken together, these studies provided evidence that objective or negative feedback can be discouraging, resulting in disengagement by older adults. In contrast, positive feedback that emphasizes performance gains as a result of goal setting can lead to higher self-set goals (West & Thorn, 2001; West et al., 2001), greater performance gain (West & Thorn, 2001; West et al., 2001, 2005, 2009), and increased use of strategic categorization (West & Thorn, 2001; West et al., 2009) for both younger and older adults.

## Goal Commitment Moderates the Impact of Goal Setting

In research on aging and goal setting, relatively little is known about goal commitment effects on cognitive tasks. Locke and Latham (1990) reported that goal commitment is often quite high, with minimal variation. In addition, commitment shows a relationship to performance only when task circumstances lead to more variability in goal commitment. In the only published report on age-related goal commitment, this variation was achieved by manipulating feedback for assigned goals. The task was constructed so that goals were not attainable but that each individual would show at least minor score gains on each trial. After scores were provided for each trial, the goal for the next trial was given, and a "tell and sell" approach (Latham, Erez, & Locke, 1988) was used for the positive feedback condition, by saying phrases such as *You are improving, Go for it!*

In the objective feedback condition, only the scores were provided. Both age groups showed the highest performance and greatest goal commitment in the positive feedback condition (West et al., 2005). Interestingly, older adults showed significantly higher goal commitment than younger adults, and this effect was primarily due to older adults' very high commitment scores in the positive feedback condition. (As will be shown below, older adults are more sensitive to the valence of the feedback than younger adults.)

Although reliable multi-item scales of goal commitment have not typically been administered in aging studies, investigators have often asked participants, at the conclusion of a session, about degree of effort and willingness to *work more* on the task. Such items may represent commitment. In the study described above, the *work more* measure was significantly higher in the positive feedback condition. It was also higher for older than younger adults, mirroring the findings for performance and the more extensive goal commitment scale (West et al., 2005; also see West et al., 2003). In a later study, using regression to predict performance after three goal trials, subjective effort (but not the *work more* item) was a significant predictor of gain scores, along with age and goal condition (West et al., 2009). More laboratory work on this issue would definitely be valuable.

Although there is relatively little laboratory work on goal commitment, the research on life goals is clearly driven by the issue of commitment (e.g., *What life goals are people invested in achieving? Do people vary in their commitment to particular life goals as age changes occur?*) and how it affects goal choice and activity selection.

## Goals Direct Attention and Affect Activity Selection

Goals may influence the focus of cognitive operations (Chartrand & Bargh, 1996), with resource allocation being driven by goal or task priorities (Hess, 2005; Miller & Gagne, 2005; Stine-Morrow et al., 2006b). Further, "… when cognitive resources (e.g., attention) are allocated to one task, they must, in part, be withdrawn from other tasks." (Locke & Latham, 1990, p. 53). For instance, in text-based processing, readers seek to minimize the discrepancy between what is currently known (the "input function") and the standard established by the reader for adequate comprehension (the "reference value"). The level of the reference value may differ from person to person because it is based on each reader's motivations and goals (Stine-Morrow et al., 2006b). As a result, the amount of effort allocated to reducing the discrepancy (i.e., learning the information) should differ depending on the reader's standard. Stine-Morrow and colleagues (2001) found that both younger and older adults adjusted study time based on task goals such that they spent more time attending to a text when the goal was to recall the text later than when the goal was to comprehend it. Stine-Morrow and colleagues (2006a) have also shown that younger adults, more so than older adults, adjusted their cognitive behavior while reading text in line with experimenter-set goals: when asked to read with the goal of accuracy, they took more time to really learn the material, but when asked to read with the goal of efficiency (i.e., finishing the task quickly), they took less time to learn the information.

Up to now, our focus has been to establish that goals given to younger and older adults in a cognitive laboratory context confirm many established goal theory principles. We have also noted that age differences in memory skills, beliefs, and reactions to feedback sometimes lead to differential outcomes for younger and older adults in goal setting research.

To draw a more complete picture of how goals and their effects on performance may or may not change with age, it is necessary to consider broader, everyday contexts in which self-selected goals may affect cognition. There are several models designed to understand how life goals, that is the "desire to be" goals, might change over the lifespan. These approaches largely focus on how life goals are framed and modified to help individuals, and in particular aging individuals, manage and cope with changes in cognitive skills and other losses in capability that accompany the aging process. These models focus on selection and pursuit of self-selected goals and the way in which these personal goals guide behavior, outside as well as in the laboratory. As we shall see, this work also shows that goals direct attention and affect the activities that people choose to do, but this represents, in the case of life goals, a much broader influence on behavior than is true for those specific goals that people work to achieve in laboratory contexts.

## General Life Goals

A useful framework for understanding the impact of goals on everyday functioning is to consider goals in a lifespan developmental context (Ebner & Freund, 2007; Freund & Riediger, 2003). Lifespan psychology (Baltes, 1997) describes development as a lifelong process of flexible, individual adaptation to changes in opportunities and constraints on social, biological, and psychological levels (Baltes, Lindenberger, & Staudinger, 2005; Boesch, 1991; Brandtstädter & Lerner, 1999; Freund & Baltes, 2000). From this perspective, goals that are challenging, but attainable, represent important self-regulatory processes positively related to well-being (Omodei & Wearing, 1990; Sheldon & Elliot, 1999) and conducive to successful aging (Brandtstädter & Renner, 1990; Freund & Baltes, 2000).

The self-regulatory theories that focus on goal-related processes in development converge on the assumption of a dynamic person–context interaction (see Boerner & Jopp, 2007; Riediger & Ebner, 2007). They largely agree that goal-related resources change over the lifespan, and become more limited in old age, and that successful development requires suitable mechanisms for allocation of these limited resources.

Table 27.1 lists three prominent goal-related theories on development and aging: the model of Selection, Optimization, and Compensation (SOC; e.g., Baltes, 1997; Baltes & Baltes, 1990; Baltes, Freund, & Li, 2005), the model of Optimization in Primary and Secondary Control (OPS; Heckhausen, 1997, 1999; Heckhausen & Schulz, 1995), and Socioemotional Selectivity Theory (SST; Carstensen, Gross, & Fung, 1997; Carstensen, Isaacowitz, & Charles, 1999). Each of these models proposes specific goal-related strategies as briefly summarized in Table 27.1. Evidence suggests an age-related change in the use and benefit of these goal-related strategies. For example, self-report studies on SOC confirm that the three strategies of selection, optimization, and compensation are represented in younger and older adults' knowledge about what is pragmatic and beneficial for goal pursuit in everyday life (Freund & Baltes, 2002a). Middle-aged adults reported higher use of all three strategies than younger and older adults, and endorsement of these strategies was related to global and domain-specific well-being and goal success (Freund & Baltes, 2002b; see also Wiese, Freund, & Baltes, 2002). Focusing on age differences in the process of selection, Riediger, Freund, and Baltes (2005) found that older, compared with younger, adults selected more coherent, nonconflicting goals and that

*Table 27.1* Three Prominent Goal-Related Theories on Development and Aging: Proposed Goal-Related Strategies and Examples

| Theory | Goal-related strategy | Example |
|---|---|---|
| *Model of selection, optimization, and compensation* | *Elective selection*: Developing and choosing a subset of goals out of multiple options | *Play the piano as a musical instrument* |
| | *Loss-based selection*: Adapting existing or developing new goals to fit losses in resources | *Focus on the piano and quit playing the guitar* |
| | *Optimization*: Adapting means for achieving desired outcomes and new skills | *Increase hours of practicing the piano* |
| | *Compensation*: Counteracting losses by changing goal-relevant means to maintain a given goal | *Play simple pieces on the piano when difficult ones become unmanageable* |
| *Model of optimization in primary and secondary control* | *Selective primary control*: Actions that are directly aimed at goal achievement through the focused investment of internal resources | *Invest more time in learning how to program to improve one's analysis skills* |
| | *Compensatory primary control*: Use of external resources for goal achievement, typically when internal resources are depleted | *Attend a programming class to improve one's analysis skills* |
| | *Selective secondary control*: Increased personal commitment to a selected goal | *Further emphasize the role of knowing how to program for improving one's analysis skills* |
| | *Compensatory secondary control*: Cognitive reframing of goals when goals become unachievable | *Decide that knowledge about programming is not useful for improving one's analysis skills* |
| *Socioemotional selectivity theory* | *Knowledge acquisition*: Directing goals toward learning new information and preparing for the future | *Learn the cultural norms of a foreign country* |
| | *Emotion regulation*: Directing goals toward the satisfaction of emotional needs | *Discuss difficult life decisions with a close friend* |

inter-goal coherence was associated with greater goal success. In addition, older adults considered a more restricted range of goals than did younger adults (Riediger & Freund, 2006; see also Staudinger, Freund, Linden, & Maas, 1999), possibly due to increased resource limitations (Baltes & Smith, 2003; Freund & Riediger, 2001). Arguing along similar lines, Ebner, Freund, and Baltes (2006; see also Ebner, Riediger, & Lindenberger, 2009; Freund, 2006; Freund & Ebner, 2005) showed that younger adults adopted, and profited more from, goals that aimed at increasing levels of performance, whereas older adults were more motivated to pursue goals geared toward compensation of losses and maintenance of levels of functioning.

Similarly, evidence related to the OPS model suggests that maximization of primary control characterizes the most adaptive functioning for most adults, but that this control strategy becomes particularly difficult in older ages when declines in goal-relevant resources make the achievement of goals increasingly difficult (Schulz, 1986). As a consequence, with advancing age and when opportunities for goal attainment are unfavorable, compensatory control strategies become more prevalent and adaptive (Wrosch & Heckhausen, 1999; also see Brandtstädter & Wentura, 1995; Rothermund & Brandtstädter, 2003).

SST, finally, has proved particularly useful in predicting age differences in emotion, motivation, and cognition (see Carstensen & Mikels, 2005; Mather & Carstensen, 2005, for overviews). Due to a greater focus on the present and a more limited future time perspective (Fingerman & Perlmutter, 1995; Lang & Carstensen, 2002), older adults prefer goals associated with positive emotional experiences over goals targeted at acquisition of new information (see also Table 27.1). This shift reflects older adults' increased motivation for gratifying experiences "in the moment" rather than maximization of future rewards (Carstensen, 2006) and was shown to be accompanied by a selective engagement in smaller but more emotionally meaningful social networks (Carstensen et al., 1999; see also Fung, Carstensen, & Lutz, 1999).

## Life Goals, Cognition, and Aging

Clearly, there is substantial evidence that life goals show systematic shifts in aging. The important issue to consider next is whether and how those life goal shifts impact cognition. Freund (2006), for instance, used a sensorimotor task. In one condition ("optimization") participants were instructed to try to get as good as possible at the task, and in the other condition ("compensation") participants were instructed to try to match their best performance after being confronted with a "loss" (the task was manipulated to be more challenging). In line with SOC theory, both age groups showed goal pursuit behavior that matched expected age-associated shifts in motivational orientation: the older adult group spent more time persisting in the compensation condition, whereas the younger adult group spent more time persisting in the optimization condition.

Other work has used dual-task paradigms to examine whether and how older adults prioritize compensatory goals over goals related to task improvement (Kemper, Herman, & Lian, 2003; Krampe, Rapp, Bondar, & Baltes, 2003; Li, Lindenberger, Freund, & Baltes, 2001; Lindenberger, Marsiske & Baltes, 2000; Rapp, Krampe, & Baltes, 2006). Dual-task situations are characterized by the necessity to manage two goals simultaneously. Scholars refer to the "cost" associated with adding a second goal, because it reduces the resources available for meeting one's first goal. Two notable studies have focused on simultaneous goals—to walk and to remember (Li et al., 2001; Lindenberger et al., 2000). These studies suggested that older adults tend to direct their goal-related resources to those domains of functioning that have high priority for their survival, such as walking carefully to avoid falls. Lindenberger and colleagues (2000) found that, as age increased, participants showed greater decreases in memory performance when walking as opposed to sitting or standing. In a subsequent study by Li and colleagues (2001), older adults showed greater costs than younger adults when performing both a cognitive and a memory behavior concurrently. Because the greater cost occurred for memory, it could be surmised that older adults prioritized walking performance over memory performance. At the same time, older adults showed more compensatory strategies for walking (i.e., using a handrail) to keep their balance while maintaining memory performance. Younger adults, in contrast, showed more compensatory strategies (i.e., slowing down the speed of presentation for to-be-remembered words) in the domain of memory. Taken together, these studies examining simultaneous walking and recall suggested that older adults compensated for declining control over postural stability by shifting attentional resources from memory to walking (Li et al., 2001; Lindenberger et al., 2000).

Another life goal shift that has been shown to affect cognition is an increased tendency to focus on emotion regulation goals with advancing age, as postulated by SST. As outlined above, the theory suggests that older adults respond to a decreased perception of time left to live by maximizing social and emotional well-being within this limited future time frame (see Carstensen, Fung, & Charles, 2003). Mather and Knight (2005) found evidence that this change in life goals could affect older adults when faced with a memory task. The researchers showed participants a slideshow of pictures comprising positive, negative, and neutral images. In line with the theory, older adults recalled proportionally more positive images than younger adults, and younger adults recalled proportionally more negative images. Interestingly, this effect was only found for older adults with high scores on cognitive control measures, and disappeared when older adults were given a simultaneous task that required them to divide their attention (but see Allard & Isaacowitz, 2008).

Some scholars have argued that age differences in memory may be partly (not completely) explained by the fact that most studies comparing younger and older adults' memory do not control for individual differences in goals and motivation to learn the material. However, it is likely that such goals do influence the effort allocated by the learner (Adams, Smith, Pasupathi, & Vitolo, 2002; Hess, 2005). In line with this notion, memory for emotional as opposed to non-emotional information was relatively greater in older as compared to younger adults (Carstensen & Turk-Charles, 1994). In other research on the impact of goals on task effort, younger and older women encoded a story under two different conditions: to retell the story to a young child or to an experimenter (Adams et al., 2002). In the latter condition, younger women outperformed older women in the amount of material recalled. However, this age difference was eliminated when retelling the story to a child. The results were interpreted as evidence that life goals (specifically, the prioritization of social well-being) played a role in memory performance.

SST proposes that older adults prioritize emotion regulation over information acquisition (Carstensen, 2006). This shift in prioritization may explain why older adult readers allocate more attentional resources to text related to social and emotional motives than they do to factual text (Stine-Morrow et al., 2006b). In the problem-solving domain, Blanchard-Fields, Mienaltowski, and Seay (2007) examined how younger and older adults approached interpersonal everyday problems (complications associated with other people) versus instrumental problems (trying to achieve a desired task outcome). They found that older adults reported using more emotion-focused strategies to deal with interpersonal problems and more problem-focused strategies to deal with instrumental problems. In contrast, younger adults used similar amounts of problem-focused strategies regardless of the problem type, showing a reduced proclivity to consider emotion-focused problem solutions (Blanchard-Fields et al., 2007).

These studies represent a variety of experimental contexts in which investigators have examined the impact of broader life goals on more specific on-task behavior. Together these findings suggest that older adults allocate cognitive resources toward tasks that are in line with their life goals, namely, the goal of maximizing social and emotional well-being (see also Carstensen & Mikels, 2005; Mather & Carstensen, 2005, for overviews), and the goal of optimizing control and task success in the face of dual task requirements or resource losses (Freund, 2006; Lindenberger et al., 2000; Rapp et al., 2006). However, the extant research is still quite limited in its scope, and much more could be done to link on-task information processing to age-related variations in life goals.

## Future Directions

To advance our understanding of the impact of goals on cognition across the adult lifespan, more work is needed, both to identify underlying mechanisms for goal responsiveness (e.g., declines in strategy effectiveness, changes in neural networks) and to expand our investigations into different domains of function. The following section discusses some promising future directions.

### New Experimental Contexts for Linking Goals and Aging

To date, research on goals and aging has focused primarily on list memory and text recall, with very little exploration of alternative domains of cognition. It would be fruitful, for example, to increase investigation into problem solving, perceptual speed, reasoning, and decision making, and to gain a broader understanding of the processing trade-offs that are implemented to emphasize one task goal and de-emphasize another. Even within the domain of memory, there is much more to be learned, including how goal setting might affect memory for faces, names, numbers, or prospective memory. Using a broader range of cognitive tasks, it would be interesting to continue to explore emotion-focused processing and compensatory processing. To shed further light on the underlying processes governing the link between goals and performance in younger and older adults, future studies will also need to integrate concepts such as goal-related mindsets and implementation intentions (see Gollwitzer & Oettingen, 2011). This will, for example, clarify whether the beneficial effect of goal setting is mediated by increases in concreteness of the situation, the strategies used, and or the task requirements.

More importantly, a number of tenets of goal setting theory have not yet been explored fully in aging. For instance, we still know relatively little about the best way to time goals (i.e., immediate versus longer-term such as over an hour, a day, or a week), so that adults of all ages can achieve beneficial effects of goals on performance, and there are only a couple of studies addressing varying levels of goal difficulty. There are few systematic studies of goal-directed changes in persistence with adults of different ages on cognitive tasks (but see Freund, 2006), and we know very little about goal commitment. We also have only a few studies of how goal setting affects strategic processing, resulting in many unresolved questions. For example, what are the characteristics of the strategic changes that people of varying ages implement to attain their cognitive goals? Is more effort applied to known, as opposed to novel, strategies, and how is this different for younger and older adults? Do goals lead to an increased investment of resources in service of applying multiple strategies rather than just one or two? And are strategic changes comparable for younger and older adults when faced with goal challenges? These and other questions need to be addressed in future research to gain a more complete picture of the mechanisms driving goal-directed changes in cognition across the adult lifespan.

## Linking Goals and Aging for Achievement Goal Orientation

Another broad framework for thinking about goals, achievement goal orientation, may be an area for interesting future aging research. According to Dweck (1986), people may adopt one of two types of goals when confronted with a task: learning goals or performance goals. Learning goals focus on the development of competence and progress, whereas performance goals focus on external evaluations of ability (e.g., test scores or grades). In younger samples, learning goals have generally been linked with good performance, and performance goals have been linked with poorer performance in the achievement goal literature (Button, Mathieu, & Zajac, 1996; Elliott & Dweck, 1988; Utman, 1997).

From a goal theory perspective, the term *performance goals* takes on a different meaning, to refer to meeting a particular criterion of achievement on a certain task. From this perspective (as discussed by Seijts and colleagues in Chapter 13), learning goals are most important when tasks are new and complex. When developing a new skill, goals of expanding knowledge are crucial (learning goals), but when a skill is already mastered, goals of achieving a certain level of attainment (performance goals) may be just as motivating, particularly in academic settings (also see Morisano & Locke, in press). Thus, once an individual has gained a certain level of mastery, the person may be motivated by continually striving to meet a higher level of achievement. None of these findings, however, have been confirmed with older adults (Hastings, 2011; Hastings & West, 2011).

Learning and performance goals have also been considered as general achievement goal orientations that may be somewhat trait-like (Button et al., 1996). In a general cognitive task context, participants' mindset is probably focused either on personal improvement and growth (essentially, adopting a learning goal orientation) or on earning positive appraisals from others (a performance goal orientation). Elliott and Lachman (1989) hypothesized that older adults may be at risk for adopting a performance goal mindset, due to concerns about being perceived as "senile" or experiencing dementia. When tested empirically, however, older adults were more likely than younger adults to focus on process goals—similar to learning goals. In contrast, younger adults were more likely to focus on outcome goals—similar to performance goals (Freund, Hennecke, & Riediger, 2010). Further complicating hypothesized relationships between achievement goal orientation and age, questionnaire measures of these two types of goals showed no relationship between age and goal orientation (Hastings, 2011; Hastings & West, 2011). Clearly, associations between achievement goal orientation and age need further study.

More broadly, it would be interesting to examine how adults of all ages behave when disposed to view cognitive activities through a learning goal lens or a performance goal lens. As a trait-like disposition, goal orientation could have a general impact on cognition, affecting the interpretation of occasional failures, confidence for success, strategy use and, ultimately, performance. For instance, the impact of goal orientation, as a disposition, was examined across age in a recent study. The positive impact of learning goals and negative impact of performance goals on recall were confirmed in adults of all ages (Hastings & West, 2011). However, these effects occurred indirectly, via their relationship to memory self-efficacy. This mediating effect of self-efficacy, as well as other self-regulatory variables, has also been supported by Seijts and colleagues (see Chapter 13). More work is needed to explore how varying goal orientations might be related to other beliefs and to cognitive outcomes on a range of tasks.

## Exploration of Mechanisms Linking Goals and Aging

Two promising avenues for research would consider possible mechanisms that may underlie goal-related changes in cognition, including attentional processes and motivational processes. Eye-tracking constitutes a direct measure of attention that might have heuristic value in studies of attentional mechanisms. To date, no study has explored how younger and older adults' visual attention may change as a function of age-associated shifts in goals, and how this may be linked to (i.e., benefit or hinder) subsequent task performance. However, one recent eye-tracking study examined the effects of visual attention on mood regulation in young and older adults (Isaacowitz, Toner, Goren, & Wilson, 2008) and found that older, but not younger, adults' looking patterns helped to regulate mood. Even though this study did not examine attention and goals, it nicely demonstrated age differences in the relation between attention and mood. Thus, the eye-tracking approach offers a promising starting point for research on the attentional processes underlying the link between goals and behavior in younger and older adults.

Studies of brain activity in relation to motivational processes may also increase our understanding of underlying mechanisms for the impact of goals on cognition across the adult lifespan. For example, a recent study by Mitchell, Raye, Ebner, Tubridy, Frankel, and Johnson (2009) suggested that younger and older adults focus on different information when thinking about goals geared toward optimization versus goals focused on compensation. These differences in the content of goal-related thought are reflected in differences in brain activity in the medial cortex, a brain region associated with self- and motivationally relevant thinking (for reviews, see Cavanna & Trimble, 2006; Northoff et al., 2006; Ochsner et al., 2005). In particular, using functional magnetic resonance imaging, younger and older adults' brain activity was measured while thinking about personally relevant agendas related to optimization versus compensation. In younger adults, an area of the anterior medial cortex was more active when thinking about optimization, whereas an area of the posterior medial cortex was more active during reflection about compensation (see also Johnson et al., 2006). However, this double dissociation did not hold for older adults. Interestingly, this pattern of brain activation was in line with behavioral evidence showing that even though older adults have a relatively greater orientation toward, and are more motivated by, compensation than optimization goals, they differentiate less between these two types of goals than younger adults (Ebner et al., 2006; Lockwood, Chasteen, & Wong, 2005). It would be interesting to extend this finding in neural studies of optimization versus compensation goals in relation to cognitive performance.

## Conclusions

Goals and goal-related processes have been shown to motivate behavior across adult-hood both in terms of isolated cognitive tasks (such as word list and text memory) and general life desires (such as the pursuit of positive emotional experiences). In light of the research evidence outlined here, we now revisit the tenets of goal theory presented earlier in this chapter. Goal theory is clearly relevant in aging, both for cognitive tasks as well as life goals. Specifically, it has been shown that goals are motivational, in that they impact task performance and memory behavior for older adults similar to younger adults, and that both age groups seem to work harder for more challenging cognitive goals. Ability impacts goal-directed performance gains, with older adults showing more variation than younger adults in response to task goals both in the lab and in life, most likely due to their cognitive limitations. The role of ability is also evident in older adults' increased likelihood to engage in compensatory behavior. Moreover, self-efficacy and related beliefs have been shown to affect goal achievement and behavior across adult-hood; to some extent, goal setting even seems to boost self-efficacy and buffer the nega-tive effects of lower confidence levels found in older adults. Feedback also appears to influence goal achievement at all ages, but its effects can be complicated by whether the feedback is positive or negative (which is influenced partly by ability). Negative feedback may have more deleterious effects on cognition for older adults. Finally, as outlined in theories of general life goals (i.e., SOC, OPS, and SST), goals direct behavior and activity selection toward particular domains and tasks—for example, emotionally satisfying experiences rather than information-gathering experiences in late life—whether the goals are experimentally assigned or personally meaningful. Goals are clearly relevant at all ages, with a demonstrated impact on cognition across the lifespan. Research linking goals and aging is relatively new and offers an exciting new frontier for extending existing research on goal theory.

## References

Adams, C., Smith, M. C., Pasupathi, M., & Vitolo, L. (2002). Social context effects on story recall in older and younger women: Does the listener make a difference? *Journal of Gerontology: Psychological Sciences, 57B*, P28–P40.

Allard, E. S., & Isaacowitz, D. M. (2008). Are preferences in emotional processing affected by distraction? Examining the age-related positivity effect in visual fixation within a dual-task paradigm. *Aging, Neuropsychology, and Cognition, 15*, 725–743.

Anderson, N. D., & Craik, F. I. M. (2000). Memory in the aging brain. In E. Tulving & F. I. M. Craik (Eds.), *The Oxford handbook of memory* (411–425). New York: Oxford University Press.

Baltes, P. B. (1997). On the incomplete architecture of human ontogeny: Selection, optimization, and compensation as foundation of developmental theory. *American Psychologist, 52*, 366–380.

Baltes, P. B., & Baltes, M. M. (1990). Psychological perspectives on successful aging: The model of selective optimization with compensation. In P. B. Baltes & M. M. Baltes (Eds.), *Successful aging: Perspectives from the behavioral sciences* (pp. 1–34). New York: Cambridge University Press.

Baltes, P. B., Freund, A. M., & Li, S.-C. (2005). The psychological science of human aging. In M. Johnson, V. L. Bengtson, P. Coleman, & T. Kirkwood (Eds.), *The Cambridge handbook of age and aging* (pp. 47–71). New York: Cambridge University Press.

Baltes, P. B., Lindenberger, U., & Staudinger, U. M. (2005). Life-span theory in developmental psychology. In R. M. Lerner (Ed.), *Handbook of child psychology: Vol. 1. Theoretical models of human development* (6th ed.). New York: Wiley.

Baltes, P. B., & Smith, J. (2003). New frontiers in the future of aging: From successful aging of the young old to the dilemmas of the fourth age. *Gerontology, 49*, 123–135.

Bandura, A. (1997). *Self-efficacy: The exercise of control.* New York: Freeman and Co.

Bandura, A. (1989). Self-regulation of motivation and action through internal standards and goal systems. In L. A. Pervin (Ed.), *Goal concepts in personality and social psychology.* Hillsdale, NJ: Lawrence Erlbaum.

Bandura, A., & Cervone, D. (1983). Self-evaluative and self-efficacy mechanisms governing the motivational effects of goal systems. *Journal of Personality and Social Psychology, 45*, 1017–1028.

Bandura, A., & Wood, R. (1989). Effect of perceived controllability and performance standards on self-regulation of complex decision-making. *Journal of Personality and Social Psychology, 56*, 805–814.

Berry, J. M. (1999). Memory self-efficacy in its social cognitive context. In T. M. Hess & F. Blanchard-Fields (Eds.), *Social cognition and aging* (pp. 70–98). San Diego, CA: Academic Press.

Blanchard-Fields, F., Mienaltowski, A., & Seay, R. B. (2007). Age differences in everyday problem-solving effectiveness: Older adults select more effective strategies for interpersonal problems. *Journals of Gerontology: Psychological Sciences and Social Sciences, 62B*, P61–P64.

Boerner, K., & Jopp, D. (2007). Improvement/maintenance and reorientation as central features of coping with major life change and loss: Contribution of three lifespan theories. *Human Development, 50*, 171–195.

Boesch, E. E. (1991). *Symbolic action theory and cultural psychology.* Berlin: Springer.

Brandtstädter, J., & Lerner, R. M. (Eds.). (1999). *Action and self-development: Theory and research through the life span.* Thousand Oaks, CA: Sage.

Brandtstädter, J., & Renner, G. (1990). Tenacious goal pursuit and flexible goal adjustment: Explication and age-related analysis of assimilative and accommodative strategies of coping. *Psychology & Aging, 5*, 58–67.

Brandtstädter, J., & Wentura, D. (1995). Adjustment to shifting possibility frontiers in later life: Complementary adaptive modes. In R. A. Dixon & L. Bäckman (Eds.), *Compensating for psychological deficits and declines: Managing losses and promoting gains* (pp. 83–106). Hillsdale, NJ: Erlbaum.

Button, S. B., Mathieu, J. E., & Zajac, D. M. (1996). Goal orientation in organizational research: A conceptual and empirical foundation. *Organizational Behavior and Human Decision Processes, 67*, 26–48.

Carstensen, L. L. (2006). The influence of a sense of time on human development. *Science, 312*, 1913–1915.

Carstensen, L. L., Fung, H. H., & Charles, S. T. (2003). Socioemotional selectivity theory and the regulation of emotion in the second half of life. *Motivation and Emotion, 27*, 103–123.

Carstensen, L. L., Gross, J. J., & Fung, H. H. (1997). The social context of emotional experience. In K. W. Schaie & M. P. Lawtons (Eds.), *Annual review of gerontology and geriatrics, Vol. 17: Focus on emotion and adult development* (pp. 325–352). New York: Springer.

Carstensen, L. L., Isaacowitz, D. M., & Charles, S. T. (1999). Taking time seriously: A theory of socioemotional selectivity. *American Psychologist, 54*, 165–181.

Carstensen, L. L., & Mikels, J. A. (2005). At the intersection of emotion and cognition: Aging and the positivity effect. *Current Directions in Psychological Science, 14,* 117–121.

Carstensen, L. L., & Turk-Charles, S. (1994). The salience of emotion across the adult lifespan. *Psychology and Aging, 9,* 259–264.

Carver, C. S., & Scheier, M. F. (1990). Origins and functions of positive and negative affect: A control-process view. *Psychological Review, 97,* 19–35.

Cavanna, A. E., & Trimble, M.R. (2006). The precuneus: A review of its functional anatomy and behavioral correlates. *Brain: A Journal of Neurology, 129,* 564–583.

Chapman, M., & Skinner, E. A. (1985). Action in development—development in action. In M. Frese & J. Sabini (Eds.), *Goal directed behavior: The concept of action in psychology* (pp. 200–213). Hillsdale, NJ: Erlbaum.

Chartrand, T. L., & Bargh, J. A. (1996). Automatic activation of impression formation and memorization goals: Nonconscious goal priming reproduces effects of explicit task instructions. *Journal of Personality and Social Psychology, 71,* 464–478.

Dittmann-Kohli, F., Lachman, M. E., Kliegl, R., & Baltes, P. B. (1991). Effects of cognitive training and testing on intellectual efficacy beliefs in elderly adults. *Journals of Gerontology, 46,* P162–P164.

Dunlosky, J., Hertzog, C., & Powell-Moman, A. (2005). The contribution of mediator-based deficiencies to age differences in associated learning. *Developmental Psychology, 41,* 389–400.

Dweck, C. S. (1986). Motivational processes affecting learning. *American Psychologist, 41,* 1040–1048.

Ebner, N. C., & Freund, A. M. (2007). Personality theories of successful aging. In Blackburn, J. A. & Dulmus, C. N. (Eds.), *Handbook of gerontology: Evidence-based approaches to theory, practice, and policy* (87–116). Hoboken, NJ: John Wiley & Sons.

Ebner, N. C., Freund, A. M., & Baltes, P. B. (2006). Developmental changes in personal goal orientation from young to late adulthood: From striving for gains to maintenance and prevention of losses. *Psychology and Aging, 21,* 664–678.

Ebner, N. C., Riediger, M., & Lindenberger, U. (2009). Schema reliance for developmental goals increases from early to late adulthood: Improvement for the young, loss prevention for the old. *Psychology and Aging, 24,* 310–323.

Elliott, E. S., & Dweck, C. S. (1988). Goals: An approach to motivation and achievement. *Journal of Personality and Social Psychology, 54,* 5–12.

Elliott, E. S., & Lachman, M. E. (1989). Enhancing memory by modifying control beliefs, attributions, and performance goals in the elderly. In P. S. Fry (Ed.), *Psychological perspectives of helplessness and control in the elderly* (pp. 339–367). North Holland: Elsevier Science Publishers B.V.

Ellis, N. R., Palmer, R. L., & Reeves, C. L. (1988). Developmental and intellectual differences in frequency processing. *Developmental Psychology, 24,* 38–45.

Fingerman, K. L., & Perlmutter, M. (1995). Future time perspective and life events across adulthood. *Journal of General Psychology, 122,* 95–111.

Freund, A. M. (2006). Age-Differential motivational consequences of optimization versus compensation focus in younger and older adults. *Psychology and Aging, 21,* 240–252. DOI: 10.1037/0882-7974.21.2.240.

Freund, A. M., & Baltes, P. B. (2000). The orchestration of selection, optimization and compensation: An action-theoretical conceptualization of a theory of developmental regulation. In W. J. Perrig

& A. Grob (Eds.), *Control of human behavior, mental processes, and consciousness* (pp. 35–58). Mahwah, NJ: Erlbaum.

Freund, A. M., & Baltes, P. B. (2002a). Life management strategies of selection, optimization and compensation: Measurement by self-report and construct validity. *Journal of Personality & Social Psychology, 82,* 642–662.

Freund, A. M., & Baltes, P. B. (2002b). The adaptiveness of selection, optimization, and compensation as strategies of life management: Evidence from a preference study on proverbs. *Journal of Gerontology: Psychological Sciences, 57B,* 426–434.

Freund, A. M., & Ebner, N. C. (2005). The aging self: Shifting from promoting gains to balancing losses. In W. Greve, K. Rothermund, & D. Wentura (Eds.), *The adaptive self: Personal continuity and intentional self-development* (pp. 185–202). Ashland, OH: Hogrefe & Huber.

Freund, A. M., & Riediger, M. (2001). What I have and what I do: The role of resource loss and gain throughout life. *Applied Psychology: An International Review, 50,* 370–380.

Freund, A. M., & Riediger, M. (2003). Successful aging. In R. M Lerner, M. A. Easterbrooks, & J. Mistry (Eds.), *Comprehensive handbook of psychology: Vol. 6. Developmental psychology* (pp. 601–628). New York: Wiley.

Freund, A. M., Hennecke, M., & Riediger, M. (2010). Age-related differences in outcome and process goal focus. *European Journal of Developmental Psychology, 7,* 198–222.

Fristoe, N. M., Salthouse, T. A., & Woodard, J. L. (1997). Examination of age-related deficits on the Wisconsin card sorting test. *Neuropsychology, 11,* 428–436.

Fung, H. H., Carstensen, L. L., & Lutz, A. M. (1999). Influence of time on social preferences: Implications for life-span development. *Psychology and Aging, 14,* 595–604.

Gollwitzer, P. M. & Oettingen, G. (2011). Planning promotes goal striving. In K. D. Vohs & R. F. Baumeister (Eds.), *Handbook of self-regulation: Research, theory, and applications (2nd ed.)* (pp. 162–185). New York: Guilford Press.

Hastings, E. C., & West, R. L. (2011). Goal orientation and self-efficacy in relation to memory in adulthood. *Aging, Neuropsychology, and Cognition, 18,* 471–493.

Hastings, E. C. (2011). *The achievement goal framework and learning in adulthood.* (Doctoral dissertation). University of Florida, Gainesville, FL.

Heckhausen, J. (1997). Developmental regulation across adulthood: Primary and secondary control of age-related changes. *Developmental Psychology, 33,* 176–187.

Heckhausen, J. (1999). *Developmental regulation in adulthood: Age-normative and sociostructural constraints as adaptive challenges.* New York: Cambridge University Press.

Heckhausen, J., & Schulz, R. (1995). A life-span theory of control. *Psychological Review, 102,* 284–304.

Hess, T. M. (2005). Memory and aging in context. *Psychological Bulletin, 131,* 383–406.

Isaacowitz, D. M., Toner, K., Goren, D., & Wilson, H. R. (2008). Looking while unhappy: Mood congruent gaze in young adults, positive gaze in older adults. *Psychological Science, 19,* 848–853.

Johnson, M. K., Raye, C. L., Mitchell, K. J., Touryan, S. R., Greene, E. J., & Nolen-Hoeksema, S. (2006). Dissociating medial frontal and posterior cingulate activity during self-reflection. *Social Cognitive and Affective Neuroscience, 1,* 56–64.

Kemper, S., Herman, R. E., & Lian, C. H. T. (2003). The costs of doing two things at once for young and older adults: Talking while walking, finger tapping, and ignoring speech of noise. *Psychology & Aging, 18,* 181–192.

Krampe, R. T., Rapp, M. A., Bondar, A., & Baltes, P. B. (2003). Selektion, Optimierung und Kompensation in Doppelaufgaben. *Der Nervenarzt, 74,* 211–218.

Lang, F. R., & Carstensen, L. L. (2002). Time counts: Future time perspective, goals, and social relationships. *Psychology and Aging, 17,* 125–139.

Latham, G. P., Erez, M., & Locke, E. A. (1988). Resolving scientific disputes by the joint design of crucial experiments by the antagonists: Application to the Erez–Latham dispute regarding participation in goal setting. *Journal of Applied Psychology, 73(4),* 753–772.

Li, K. Z. H., Lindenberger, U., Freund, A. M., & Baltes, P. B. (2001). Walking while memorizing: Age-related differences in compensatory behavior. *Psychological Science, 12,* 230–237.

Lindenberger, U., Marsiske, M., & Baltes, P. B. (2000). Memorizing while walking: Increase in dual-task costs from young adulthood to old age. *Psychology & Aging, 3,* 417–436.

Locke, E. A., Frederick, E., Lee, C., & Bobko, P. (1984). Effect of self-efficacy, goals, and task strategies on task performance. *Journal of Applied Psychology, 69(2),* 241–251.

Locke, E. A., & Latham, G. P. (Eds.) (1990). *A theory of goal setting and task performance.* Englewood Cliffs, NJ: Prentice Hall.

Locke, E. A., & Latham, G. P. (2002). Building a practically useful theory of goal setting and task motivation: A 35-year odyssey. *American Psychologist, 57,* 705–717.

Lockwood, P., Chasteen, A. L., & Wong, C. (2005). Age and regulatory focus determine preferences for health-related role models. *Psychology and Aging, 20,* 376–389.

Maddux, J. E. (Ed.). (1995). *Self-efficacy, adaptation, and adjustment: Theory, research, and application.* New York: Plenum Press.

Mather, M., & Knight, M. (2005). Goal-directed memory: The role of cognitive control in older adults' emotional memory. *Psychology and Aging, 20,* 554–570.

Mather, M., & Carstensen, L. L. (2005). Aging and motivated cognition: The positivity effect in attention and memory. *Trends in Cognitive Sciences, 10,* 496–502.

Miller, L. M. S., & Gagne, D. D. (2005). Effects of age and control beliefs on resource allocation during reading. *Aging, Neuropsychology, and Cognition, 12,* 129–148.

Miller, L. M. S., & West, R. L. (2010). The effects of age, control beliefs, and feedback on self-regulation of reading and problem solving. *Experimental Aging Research, 36,* 40–63.

Mitchell, K. J., Raye, C. L., Ebner, N. C., Tubridy, S. M., Frankel, H., & Johnson, M. K. (2009). Age group differences in medial cortex activity associated with thinking about self-relevant agendas. *Psychology and Aging, 24,* 438–449.

Morisano, D., & Locke, E. A. (2012, in press). Goal setting and academic achievement. In J. A. C. Hattie & E. M. Anderman (Eds.), *International handbook of student achievement.* New York: Routledge.

Northoff, G., Heinzel, A., de Greck, M., Bermpohl, F., Dobrowolny, H., & Panksepp, J. (2006). Self-referential processing in our brain: A meta-analysis of imaging studies on the self. *NeuroImage, 31,* 440–457.

Ochsner, K. N., Beer, J. S., Robertson, E. R., Cooper, J. C., Gabrieli, J. D. E., Kihlstrom, J. F., & D'Esposito, M. (2005). The neural correlates of direct and reflected self-knowledge. *NeuroImage, 28,* 797–814.

Omodei, M. M., & Wearing, A. J. (1990). Need satisfaction and involvement in personal projects: Toward an integrative model of subjective well-being. *Journal of Personality & Social Psychology, 59,* 762–769.

Pervin, L. A. (Ed.). (1989). *Goal concepts in personality and social psychology.* Hillsdale, NJ: Lawrence Erlbaum.

Rapp, M. A., Krampe, R. T., & Baltes, P. B. (2006). Adaptive task prioritization in aging: Selective resource allocation to postural control is preserved in Alzheimer disease. *The American Journal of Geriatric Psychiatry, 14,* 52–61.

Rebok, G. W., & Balcerak, L. J. (1989). Memory self-efficacy and performance differences in young and old adults: The effect of mnemonic training. *Developmental Psychology, 25*, 714–721.

Riediger, M., & Ebner, N. C. (2007). A broader perspective on three lifespan theories: Comment on Boerner and Jopp. *Human Development, 50*, 196–200.

Riediger, M., & Freund, A. M. (2006). Focusing and restricting: Two aspects of motivational selectivity in adulthood. *Psychology and Aging, 21*, 173–185.

Riediger, M., Freund, A. M., & Baltes, P. B. (2005). Managing life through personal goals: Intergoal facilitation and intensity of goal pursuit in younger and older adulthood. *Journal of Gerontology, 60B*, P84–P91.

Riediger, M., Li, S. C., & Lindenberger, U. (2006). Selection, optimization, and compensation (SOC) as developmental mechanisms of adaptive resource allocation: Review and preview. In J. E. Birren & K. W. Schaie (Eds.), *Handbook of the psychology of aging (6th ed.)* (pp. 289–313). Amsterdam: Elsevier.

Rothermund, K., & Brandtstädter, J. (2003). Depression in later life: Cross-sequential patterns and possible determinants. *Psychology and Aging, 18*, 80–90.

Schulz, R. (1986). Successful aging: Balancing primary and secondary control. *Adult Development & Aging News, 13*, 2–4.

Schunk, D. H. (1990). Goal setting and self-efficacy during self-regulated learning. *Educational Psychologist, 25*, 71–86.

Schunk, D. H., & Zimmerman, B. J. (1996). Modeling and self-efficacy influences on children's development of self-regulation. In J. Juvonen, & K. R. Wentzel (Eds.), *Social motivation: Understanding children's school adjustment* (pp. 154–180). Cambridge, UK: Cambridge University Press.

Sheldon, K. M., & Elliot, A. J. (1999). Goal striving, need satisfaction, and longitudinal well-being: The self-concordance model. *Journal of Personality & Social Psychology, 76*, 482–497.

Stadtlander, L. M., & Coyne, A. C. (1990). The effect of goal-setting and feedback on age differences in secondary memory. *Experimental Aging Research (16)*, 91–94.

Staudinger, U. M., Freund, A. M., Linden, M., & Maas, I. (1999). Self, personality, and life regulation: Facets of psychological resilience in old age. In P. B. Baltes & K. U. Mayer (Eds.), *The Berlin Aging Study: Aging from 70 to 100 (302–328)*. New York: Cambridge University Press.

Stine-Morrow, E. A. L., Shake, M. C., Miles, J. R., & Noh, R. S. (2006a). Adult age differences in the effects of goals on self-regulated sentence processing. *Psychology and Aging (21)*, 790–203.

Stine-Morrow, E. A. L., Milinder, L., Pullara, O., & Herman, B. (2001). Patterns of resource allocation are reliable among younger and older readers. *Psychology and Aging, 16*, 69–84.

Stine-Morrow, E. A. L., Miller, L. M., & Hertzog, C. (2006b). Aging and self-regulated language processing. *Psychological Bulletin, 132*, 582–606.

Thompson, R. F., & Perlini, A. H. (1998). Feedback and self-efficacy, arousal, and performance of introverts and extroverts. *Psychological Reports, 82*, 707–716.

Utman, C. H. (1997). Performance effects of motivational state: A meta-analysis. *Personality and Social Psychology Review, 1*, 170–182.

Valentijn, S. A. M., Hill, R. D., Van Hooren, S. A. H., Bosma, H., Van Boxtel, M. P. J. et al. (2006). Memory self efficacy predicts memory performance: Results from a six-year follow-up study. *Psychology and Aging, 21*(1), 165–172.

West, R. L., Bagwell, D. K., & Dark-Freudeman, A. (2005). Memory and goal-setting: The response of younger and older adults to positive and objective feedback. *Psychology and Aging*, 20(2), 195–201.

West, R. L., Dark-Freudeman, A., & Bagwell, D. K. (2009). Goals-feedback conditions and episodic memory: Mechanisms for memory gains in older and younger adults. *Memory, 17(2)*, 233–244.

West, R. L., Dennehy-Basile, D., & Norris, M. P. (1996). Memory self-evaluation: The effects of age and experience. *Aging, Neuropsychology, and Cognition, 3*, 67–83.

West, R. L., & Thorn, R. M. (2001). Goal-setting, self-efficacy, and memory performance in older and younger adults. *Experimental Aging Research, 27*, 41–65.

West, R. L., Thorn, R. M., & Bagwell, D. K. (2003). Memory performance and beliefs as a function of goal setting and aging. *Psychology and Aging, 18*, 111–125.

West, R. L., Welch, D. C., & Thorn, R. M. (2001). Effects of goal-setting and feedback on memory performance and beliefs among older and younger adults. *Psychology and Aging, 16*, 240–250.

West, R. L., & Yassuda, M. S. (2004). Aging and memory control beliefs: Performance in relation to goal setting and memory self-evaluation. *Journal of Gerontology: Psychological Sciences*, 59B(2), P56–P65.

Wiese, B. S., Freund, A. M., & Baltes, P. B. (2002). Subjective career success and emotional well-being: Longitudinal predictive power of selection, optimization and compensation. *Journal of Vocational Behavior, 60*, 321–335.

Wrosch, C., & Heckhausen, J. (1999). Control processes before and after passing a developmental deadline: Activation and deactivation of intimate relationship goals. *Journal of Personality & Social Psychology, 77*, 415–427.

# 28    Goals and Entreprenuership

*J. Robert Baum*   R.H. Smith School of Business, University of Maryland

In this chapter, the central role of goals in entrepreneurship is described. Entrepreneurship research about goals and related concepts is reviewed, and research opportunities are identified. Fortunately, the explanatory power of goal theory is not isolated to individual entrepreneur behavior. Goal theory applies even as ventures grow beyond the dreams of the founding entrepreneur (Locke & Latham, 2006; Olson, Morris, & Terpstra, 1993).

Successful entrepreneurs set goals as they explore markets for product and business model opportunities. They also use goals to exploit their opportunities through activities such as human and financial resource gathering, business start-up planning and organizing, and market entry. High-potential early-stage entrepreneurs draw upon goals for technical development, proof of concept, and external financing (Shane, Locke, & Collins, 2001). For example, Mark Zuckerberg, founder of Facebook, has repeatedly explained the specific growth and financing goals he set for his company (Grossman, 2010). Larry Page, the successful cofounder of Google, explained specific social and business unit goals for 2012, as he retook the role of CEO in 2011 (Hardawar, 2011), and both Zuckerberg and Page presented goal-laden business plans to angel and private equity financiers as they grew their businesses.

Understanding the value of goals for successful entrepreneurship is important because entrepreneurs make essential contributions to international social and economic well-being. Indeed, entrepreneurs' new ventures are the dominant source of international job creation, market innovation, and economic growth (Aldrich, 1999). Entrepreneurship is the economic mechanism through which inefficiencies in economies are identified and mitigated. For example, entrepreneurs' technological and organizational innovation motivates established competitors to improve products and processes and streamline supply chains (Schumpeter, 1934).

According to venture financiers, entrepreneurs' personal behaviors, such as goal setting, are the most important factors for business success—even more important than the business idea or industry setting (Shepherd, 1999; Zopounidis, 1994). Entrepreneurs themselves claim that their decisions, goals, and actions are the most important reasons for their company's survival—even as they complain about external challenges and resource shortages (Smith & Smith, 2000).

This chapter begins with a brief history of entrepreneurship psychology research and draws upon entrepreneurship motivation research to summarize findings about the role of entrepreneurs' goals in terms of goal theory's core findings plus goal mediators and moderators. Finally, entrepreneurship research about three concepts that are related to entrepreneurs' goals (entrepreneurs' vision, self-efficacy, and intentions) is discussed.

## Entrepreneurship Research

Entrepreneurship is fundamentally personal. Although entrepreneurship research has shown that there are multiple personal, organizational, and external causes of successful new venture creation (Baum, Locke, & Smith, 2001; Rauch, & Frese, 2000), it takes *human* vision, intention, and work to conceive and convert business ideas to successful products and services. Goal setting processes tap new venture founder's self-regulatory and metacognitive processes that mediate cognitive and affective functioning for the purpose of attaining goals. Through their thinking and action, entrepreneurs integrate human and financial resources to organize, produce, and market products and services that yield value for customers and workers.

In the 1960s, early entrepreneurship researchers tried to find the answer to the question, "why do some people start and grow successful companies and others do not?" Personality research by David McClelland (1961) and others focused on traits and motives such as nAch (the need for achievement trait). Achievement-related concepts were the only personal traits that were consistent predictors of new venture success. Indeed, in a meta analysis, Collins, Hanges, and Locke (2004) found that subconscious and conscious achievement motivation both predicted 20% of variance in entrepreneurship success. Other psychological-based studies explored the effects of locus of control, risk propensity, tolerance of ambiguity, and a variety of knowledge and skill concepts. The studies gained some traction, but even the most successful studies explained less than 7% of performance variance (Johnson, 1990).

Thus, entrepreneurship researchers shifted attention to economic variables of the macro strategic management variety (e.g., entry strategies, environmental effects). Improved, but theoretically incomplete, explanations of performance variance were gained. During the 1990s, and in search of integrated explanations of venture performance, researchers returned to study entrepreneurs' personal characteristics, but concentrated on motivation and other cognitive variables in mediating and moderating configurations that are close to performance outcomes (Baron, 2002; Baum & Locke, 2004; Busenitz & Barney, 1997). Explained performance variance improved in these studies as motivating factors such as (1) vision/purpose, (2) self-efficacy, and (3) goals were included in performance models. It was apparent that when entrepreneurs were high in these factors, their focused direction, effort, and persistence amplified the effects of more distant personal factors such as traits.

## Entrepreneurship Motivation Research: The Beginnings of Entrepreneurship Goal Research

The study of the effects of entrepreneurs' goal setting emerged from the study of entrepreneurs' motivation (Baum, Frese, & Baron, 2006). Personal motivation is important for understanding entrepreneurship because it bears upon venture planning and entrepreneurs' behavior. For example, motivation controls an important and difficult issue for entrepreneurs: Do I make this company grow or not? The issue forces the entrepreneur to value current versus future compensation and lifestyle.

Motivation is based on the individual's needs, values, desires, and intentions, as well as incentives and rewards that affect those internal mechanisms (Steers & Porter, 1991). Entrepreneurship motivation is an inner drive toward entrepreneurship goals. It directs, energizes, and sustains new venture creation and growth. For example, C.C. Chialastri, founder of American Orthopedic Devices, LLC., invented a surgical device to reduce back pain. His dream of a significant and financially successful company, passion for surgical tools, fierce energy, and confidence drove him through multiple legal and financial challenges to his publically stated goal to create a premier orthopedic devices company. A person may have a brilliant idea, sufficient technical skill, and money to start a business, but without motivation nothing happens. However, motivation, in the absence of knowledge and belief, leads to random or unproductive action (Locke, 2000).

Entrepreneurship motivation researchers, Gartner, Bird, and Starr (1992), reviewed Landy and Becker's (1987) categories of motivation theory, namely, needs, reinforcement, equity, expectancy, social cognitive, and goal theory. They concluded that social cognitive theory (Bandura, 1982, 1986; Earley, 1985) and goal theory (Locke & Latham, 2002) offered useful structures for understanding entrepreneurs' motivation. Gartner et al. (1992) suggested that expectancy theory (Vroom, 1964) may also provide a framework for understanding entrepreneurship, but he concluded that self-efficacy, a broader conception of expectancy than that which is included in valence—instrumentality— "expectations" theory, is a more useful motivation concept for understanding an entrepreneur's varied situations. Subsequently, Naffziger, Hornsby, and Kuratko (1994) proposed a theoretical model of entrepreneurial motivation that included goal and equity theory comparisons, as proposed by Adams (1965) and others, but goal theory's explanatory power stood out. Several entrepreneurship researchers focused on quantitative research about entrepreneurs' motivation (Baum et al., 2001; Mitchell, Busenitz, Bird, Gaglio, McMullen, Morse, & Smith, (2007); Mitchell, Smith, Seawright, & Morse, 2000; Noel & Latham, 2006), and this effort produced growing support for inclusion of motivation in entrepreneurship performance models.

Goals have played an important role in entrepreneurship motivation studies. Baum et al. (2001) conducted a study that included multiple personal and organizational factors as predictors of venture growth. The study found strong relationships between goals, self-efficacy, and performance. The results indicated that goal setting was far more successful at predicting behavior than general value theories because goals are more immediate regulators of human action. Indeed, goal theory had demonstrated more scientific validity than any other motivation theory (Pinder, 1984) and had the greatest scope (Landy & Becker, 1987). Ultimately, only goals and self-efficacy have stimulated much research interest about motivation among entrepreneurship researchers. I now focus on goal theory research in entrepreneurship.

## Goal Theory and Entrepreneurship: Opportunities for Future Research

Goal theory is well suited for studying entrepreneurship because it covers self-set goals and involves explicit, consciously chosen targets that are usually focused on performance. To explain, venture founders typically choose their own goals and state them explicitly in terms of product volumes and financial performance, consistent with the performance focus of goal theory. Furthermore, goal theory is a direct, close to the action, theory of motivation—more direct than expectancy theory, and direct theories are particularly appropriate in the entrepreneurship setting because early stage entrepreneurs are closely involved with their products and customers. Many experience their business success and failure personally with great emotion in terms of their personal goals (Timmons, 2000).

Goal theory points to the benefits of challenging goals, and most founders are "big dreamers" who set their own challenging goals to include tight timelines (Gartner &

Carter, 2003). Indeed, early-stage financiers report that most successful entrepreneurs begin with goals that are beyond normal conceptions of the possible (Smith & Smith, 2000). Goal setting theory states that given goal commitment, the higher the goal the higher the performance.

Goal theory is also attractive for entrepreneurship research because it applies at the individual, group, and organization level. The prototypical new venture begins small and is intimately managed by the founder/entrepreneur. But successful ventures usually grow beyond the personal control of the entrepreneur. Taken together, the goal theory explanation that the causal chain begins with a desired end and leads to performance-focused action makes sense to entrepreneurs and entrepreneurship scholars.

Goal theory's prediction that challenging goals associate with high performance was supported in the entrepreneurship setting studied by Baum et al. (2001). Their study found that three-year goals, along with self-efficacy, had a direct affect on growth of firm level employment and sales. A six-year follow-up study (Baum & Locke, 2004) confirmed the results. In another study, Tracy, Locke, and Renard (1999) found significant relationships between venture growth and innovation goals of printing industry entrepreneurs. Importantly, the performance measures were obtained two years after the goal measurements. Finally, Segal, Borgia, and Schoenfeld (2009) found a significant relationship between business plan goals (product, impact, and sales growth) and early-stage venture growth.

While the strategic growth process is well researched by entrepreneurship scholars in terms of the founder's entry strategy and financing, goal setting across venture stages has not received much attention. Olson et al. (1993) surveyed the "INC 500 fastest growing new ventures" (Stanton, 1987). They found that entrepreneurs set the same goal types across stages (sales growth, profitability, and innovation). However, entrepreneurs tended to rank the importance of the goal types differently as their ventures aged. Start-up firms ranked sales growth #1, innovation #2, and profitability #3. In contrast, second-stage (early growth) firms ranked profitability #1, sales growth #2, and innovation #3. Thus, it may be productive for entrepreneurship researchers to compare the levels of goal challenge, specificity, and performance across stages.

To date, entrepreneurship research has focused on single industries. Doing so has obvious advantages in terms of clarity of findings, but it does not address important decisions for nascent entrepreneurs. That is, nascent entrepreneurs must face decisions that cross industry and product domains. Entry strategy research across industries has yielded interesting information that guides classroom prescriptions (Chandon, Morwitz, & Reinartz, 2005), so entrepreneurship goal researchers may identify important industry effects to enlighten theory and practice. Indeed, entrepreneurship studies that compare features of high-technology businesses, and businesses that profit from efficiency alone, have yielded useful information for financiers. Thus, benefits may be gained through the study of goal effects across industry and product type.

Much research about the relation of goal theory and entrepreneurship performance is incomplete (Shane, 2008). Studies of specific process goals (e.g., the first sale, acquisition of venture capital, development of the prototype) set by entrepreneurs, as well as studies of the goals entrepreneurs establish for other individuals involved in the emerging organization, may reveal best practices for new venture management (Baum et al., 2006). For example, organizing (start-up deadlines) goals have received little attention

(Gartner & Carter, 2003), and, as explained below, the potential damaging effects of impossibly challenging goals have not been studied in the venture setting (Liao & Welsch, 2004).

## Characteristics of Entrepreneurship Goals: Self-Set Goals, Goal Difficulty, and Learning Goals

Entrepreneurship scholars have explored the effects of several goal characteristics and types that have been addressed in goal theory. First, most venture founders set their own goals. Of course, if their venture grows beyond their financial capability, financiers may become involved in venture goal setting. Second, I explain current entrepreneurship research interest in the relationship between self-set goals and goal difficulty. Some theorists have suggested that the relationship fits an inverted U-shaped curve (goal difficulty up, performance up at first, and then down. Finally, I offer comments about entrepreneurs' learning goals and point to interest by those who study serial (repeat) entrepreneurs.

*Self-Set Goals.* Importantly for entrepreneurs, self-set goals work to motivate high performance in the same manner as externally set goals (Locke & Latham, 1990). Thus, goal theory about self-set goals has been a useful guide for entrepreneurship researchers because entrepreneurs typically start their companies alone or with a small team. Indeed, most field studies of new ventures collect self-reports from founders about their own start-up. Multiple entrepreneurship studies support the view that entrepreneurs who set their own goals are motivated to attain higher performance than if they had no goals (Miner, 2002). Baum and Locke (2004) found that high-challenge, self-set growth goals yielded the highest venture growth.

Entrepreneurs may not be alone in setting their goals if their venture grows and requires external financing. Although most new ventures reflect their founder's personal characteristics, including a passion for the product, some entrepreneurs with high-potential/high-investment ideas require venture capital financing from the outset (other entrepreneurs can draw upon personal resources). Venture-capital-financed new businesses are deeply imprinted with the financiers' extreme profit-making goals (1000% return in 6 years), which can cause a shift in business goals and create much pain for the founder. This need not be the case. For example, changes in Google's initial social mission goal, driven by founders Sergy Brin and Larry Page, were dramatic over 10 years. The 2004 IPO replaced the 1994 "do no evil" goals with short-term financial goals (30% annual growth in cash returns) (Vise & Malseed, 2008). Interestingly, the firm continues to be remarkably innovative and profitable; however, acquisition is now favored over internal research and development. The effect of goal change in rapidly growing companies presents an interesting research question for entrepreneurship scholars: What is the impact upon performance of a shift from self-set founder goals to financier-oriented goals? What conditions or strategies may moderate or mediate the rate of goal change— if any—in a growing venture?

*Goal Difficulty.* Financiers hold that entrepreneurs should accept their challenging financial and market penetration goals (Smith & Smith, 2000). Complaints have followed from failed entrepreneurs (entrepreneurship failure rates are high) that expecting too much too soon yields excess operational and financial risk and, thus, high failure rates.

This conflict attracted research on entrepreneurship and goal difficulty. In a study that involved external financing, Kuratko, Hornsby, and Naffizer (1997) found a significant direct effect between goal difficulty and venture start-up success. They had expected an inverted U relationship. That is, they expected performance to increase until goals became "out of reach" with falling performance thereafter. Nevertheless, their data supported goal theory, namely, that difficult goals inspire higher performance than easy goals (Locke & Latham, 1990). The inverted U relationship explanation of goal effects occurs when goal difficulty exceeds ability. Ability is a moderator variable in goal theory (Locke & Latham, 1990, 2002).

*Learning Goals.* Interest in learning goals has emerged in the entrepreneurship literature based on a simulation study by Noel and Latham (2006). Results suggest that entrepreneurs who focus on learning goals [e.g., learning from experimental (small step) product introduction in a new market], rather than ultimate firm financial performance goals, achieve higher rates of firm survival. The study suggests that it is useful to generate learning at all stages of the entrepreneurship process by setting process goals for idea generating, resource aggregation, organization building, market entry, and product and sales experimentation.

Further interest in the goals and learning styles of serial entrepreneurs has emerged among those who study their behavior and performance (Alsos & Kolvereid, 1998; Westhead & Wright, 1998). Their research on the interaction of learning styles and goal setting indicates that serial entrepreneurs who set performance goals *and get feedback* are more successful than those who just set goals. Feedback is another moderator variable in goal theory. The more successful group had higher levels of search for more successful task strategies. Indeed, Seijts, Latham, Tasa, and Latham (2004) explained that when faced with new complex tasks, it may be best to strive not for performance outcome goals but rather for learning goals.

The entrepreneurship literature about serial (repeat) entrepreneurs supports use of learning goals, since the entrepreneurship culture does not present permanent penalties for failure. Rather, multiple successful repeat entrepreneurs point to the learning benefits of high goals followed by failure—particularly when their failed businesses were low-stakes enterprises compared with later high-potential start-ups. Some financiers are even attracted to investing with entrepreneurs who have failure in their past because they have presumably learned the importance of creating options for their ventures.

## Mediators: Entrepreneurs' Goals as Mediators of the Trait–Venture Performance Relationship

The focus here is on entrepreneurs' goals as situationally specific mediators of their traits. Of course, goals are also mediated by personal characteristics (direction, choice, effort, and persistence). Goal theory's propositions that certain traits are mediated by goals in performance relationships were attractive to entrepreneurship researchers because entrepreneurship research had a deep history of studying the effects of type A personality, need for achievement, focus, effort (energy), and tenacity/persistence (Begley & Boyd, 1987; Brockhaus & Horwitz, 1986; McClelland, 1961; Vesper, 1996) on venture performance. Researchers hypothesized that including goals as mediators of traits in their performance models would clarify previously inconsistent results.

The initial research examined both general and situationally specific motivators of entrepreneurship performance. How should they be combined to best predict success? There are at least two possibilities: (1) they could be used as simultaneous predictors, or (2) the situationally specific motivators could mediate (or partially mediate) the effects of the general traits. The latter model makes the most sense logically in that general variables would be "applied" through their effects on specific variables.

The mediation model has generally been supported. The Baum et al. (2001) study included two general variables: traits (composed of tenacity, proactivity, and passion for the work) and a cognitive variable: general competencies (composed of organization skill and opportunity skill). Neither traits nor competencies had any direct effect on venture growth. They operated through their effects on specific variables, namely, situationally specific motivation (vision, goals, and efficacy), specific competencies (industry and technical skills), and competitive strategies [focus (negative), low cost (negative), and differentiation]. Motivational traits were strongly related to specific motivation and strategies, and even to general competencies. This suggests that traits can motivate the development of business skills, as well as the direct motivation to perform.

The mediation model was also supported by Baum and Locke (2004). Passion, tenacity, and new resource skill (a general cognitive variable) affected six-year venture growth solely through their effects on communication vision, self-efficacy, and growth goals. All three general variables were significantly related to each of the three specific variables. Observe, also, that growth goals partly mediated the effects of vision and self-efficacy.

These results help explain why entrepreneurship researchers and commentators have often been disappointed by the results of trait studies (e.g., Low & MacMillan, 1988). If general traits have only indirect effects, then their relationship to performance outcomes would not show up, or not show up strongly, unless the mediating variables were also included in the studies. Future studies of entrepreneurs that include trait measures would do well to include both general and situationally specific variables in their research models. Skills such as being able to find capital, organizing the enterprise, selling and marketing the product, and developing teamwork should be included as well.

## Moderation of Entrepreneurship Goals in Performance Relationships

Locke and Lathams' (1990) theory states that ability and situational variables moderate goals, and that several personality variables may also have moderating effects (Type A, nAch, etc.). As explained above, entrepreneurship researchers had initially studied traits as direct predictors of performance and have now included traits in quantitative tests of models with motivation mediators. However, entrepreneurship researchers have not conducted quantitative tests of feedback, goal commitment, goal choice (self-set difficulty), task strategies, and task complexity as moderators of the goal–performance relationship. Research opportunities exist here.

*Feedback.* Feedback cues individuals about when to alter strategies (Locke & Latham, 2002) and increase their efforts (Matsui, Okada, & Inoshita, 1983) in small and large companies (McDonald, Khanna, & Westphal, 2008). Entrepreneurship researchers support the view that feedback moderates the effects of goals, and they point to the ease with which early-stage entrepreneurs can gain feedback because of their proximity to their customers. However, they note that entrepreneurs who rely on performance feedback from continuing customers and suppliers are disadvantaged since these sources are apparently satisfied (Baron & Shane, 2007). It is far better to draw on feedback from investors (angels, venture capitalists, and bankers) who monitor quantitative goals such as sales volume, revenues, and profits, and this feedback is quickly available (Gartner, Shaver, Carter, & Reynolds, 2004). Despite sufficient theory about the effects of feedback in the entrepreneurship domain, there is little quantitative entrepreneurship research. An opportunity exists here.

*Goal Commitment.* Goal setting works most effectively when people are committed to their goals. Also, goal commitment is affected by external factors such as legitimate authority, peer group influence, models, and external rewards and internal factors such as performance–reward expectancy, and self-efficacy (Locke, Latham, & Erez, 1988). Unfortunately, there are no known quantitative studies of the moderation of the entrepreneurship goal–venture performance relation that included goal commitment.

In contrast to the absence of entrepreneurship-performance-based research on goal commitment, DeClercq, Menzies, Diochon, and Gasse (2009) studied the factors that inspire nascent entrepreneurs' goal commitment. Drawing upon a set of 81 nascent entrepreneurs, they found that among multiple factors, self-efficacy and financial support related positively with goal commitment. This is not surprising, in light of the strong effects of self-efficacy on multiple factors that lead to venture success (Baum et al., 2006). Perhaps the authors will follow the nascent entrepreneurs, measure successful start-ups, and test a model of goal commitment as a moderator of the goal–venture performance relationship.

*Goal Choice.* Goal choice is related to goal commitment, and one would expect goal commitment to be high when one chooses their own goals. Of course, choice of the goal involves the choice of goal difficulty, which raises the interesting research question: Does the ability to choose your own goal lead to choice of a less difficult goal? This has not been addressed in the entrepreneurship setting, where entrepreneurs typically set their own goals in the midst of high uncertainty about outcomes or rewards. However, entrepreneurs do follow peer behavior that may impact the choice of goal difficulty level. Of course, their self-efficacy impacts the choice of goal and associated difficulty. As noted earlier, Olson et al. (1993) found that early-stage entrepreneurs chose and ranked three types of goals as important (#1: growth, #2: profit, and #3: innovation), but the degree of commitment, self-set difficulty, and performance relationship was not explored.

*Task Strategies.* Goal studies on task strategies at the firm level in newer smaller companies may expose stronger effects because the founder/CEO often has relatively direct control over the plans and actions that lead to goal accomplishment. This direct control is a rarely achieved goal in large firms, where more layers exist and most of the work is delegated.

Task strategies in the entrepreneurship setting may involve speed and experimentation. A study of goals, self-efficacy, and exploitation strategies in the printing industry revealed the importance of task strategies as moderators of entrepreneur's goals and venture performance (Baum & Bird, 2010). Other entrepreneurship researchers could study the relationships between goals, task strategies, and performance. Interesting entrepreneurship task strategy subjects might include "make" versus "buy" decisions (outsourcing) or "fixed" versus "custom" product line design.

*Task Complexity.* The effects of the entrepreneur's personal goals diminish as the firm grows (growth implies increased complexity) (Shane, 2008). High uncertainty, a characteristic of the new venture situation, increases task complexity because it increases the options that must be available to deal with barriers to entry. In the unresolved and messy entrepreneurship setting, task complexity is a reflection of market dynamism (a correlate of uncertainty), firm size (revenue and employee counts), and market size (product line size and customer counts). Entrepreneurship researchers have not yet addressed the moderating effects of task complexity on the goal–performance relationship.

## Concepts Related to Goals and Entrepreneurship: Vision, Self-Efficacy, and Intentions

Concepts related to goals have received attention in the entrepreneurship literature. They include vision, self-efficacy, and intentions.

*Vision.* A business vision is the projected image of the products, services, and organization that a business leader wants to achieve. It is a bold, audacious, overarching goal (Collins & Lazier, 1992). There appears to be some confusion among practitioners about the difference among vision, purpose, values, and strategic intent. The essence of vision is that it is the idea of the business. Specifically, it is the leader's concept of what the business will be and what will make it attractive to customers and make it profitable—the products, services, technologies markets, strategy, etc. Vision should not be confused with vision statements. The vision statement is a shorthand summary, usually formulated for the purpose of inspiring others (e.g., we will make the best-quality cars in the world). The full vision, however, is inside the entrepreneur's head and is much more detailed than any one statement or slogan (Baum, Locke, & Kirkpatrick, 1998).

Entrepreneurship starts with a business idea. This core idea is often referred to as the entrepreneur's vision (Timmons, 2000). Successful entrepreneurs hold and communicate visions of desirable futures that are general distant venture goals (Baum et al., 1998). The entrepreneur defines the nature of the business, sees the parts, sees the whole, and sees how each part relates to the whole. Formulating successful business principles requires inductive reasoning ability. The entrepreneur must look at hundreds or thousands of concrete facts, decide which ones are important, observe how they are connected, and integrate these observations into a small number of key ideas. Successful entrepreneurs bring order out of seeming chaos. They do not get overwhelmed by minutiae, and they think in terms of principles (Locke, 2000).

Vision, of course, is primarily cognitive, although it has motivating aspects too. Entrepreneurs must make inferences from their observations and integrations. The key element in being visionary is having foresight (Locke, 2000). Foresight is the ability to see beyond the immediate moment, to see past what is working now, to see what will work in the future. It's the ability to see not just actuality but potentiality. Steve Jobs saw the potential of the PC when no one else did and started a whole new industry.

Bird (1989) suggested that entrepreneurs use vision as an end point in the emotional distance that she refers to as "temporal tension." She explained that the stretch between current conditions and the entrepreneur's vision causes a motivating force. She suggested that the degree of temporal tension maintained by an entrepreneur is affected by personality and ability and that those who focus more on the future and present and less on the past are more successful.

In pursuit of understanding the roots of entrepreneurs' business visions, Filian (1991) interviewed 59 entrepreneurs and rated their responses along multiple dimensions. He suggested that entrepreneurs' values, energy level, and relations with family and peers imprinted the vision that was produced. No attempt was made to relate the existence or characteristics of the vision with firm performance.

Bull and Willard (1993) recommended that entrepreneurship research investigate the importance of vision for achievement of entrepreneurship success. A subsequent study found that entrepreneurs' vision content and attributes (brevity, clarity, abstractness, challenge, future orientation, stability, and desirability) affect subsequent venture growth directly and through verbal and written communication (Baum et al., 1998).

*Self-Efficacy.* Self-efficacy has an important place in goal theory and entrepreneurship research because of its direct effects on performance and self-set goals—and its effect on goal choice and goal commitment (Bandura, 1986; Bandura & Cervone, 1986). Baum et al. (2001) found that entrepreneur's self-efficacy was significantly related to the growth of early-stage ventures within the same industry for the two years following measurement. In a follow-up study of the same entrepreneurs, CEO self-efficacy was used as a single variable and was significantly related to a firm's growth over the subsequent six years (Baum & Locke, 2004). Segal et al. (2009) also found a significant relationship between self-efficacy and early-stage growth.

Situationally specific self-efficacy can be measured more generally than specifying a graduated series of performance levels (e.g., "how confident are you that you can successfully expand your business?"). Sometimes this is necessary because no relevant quantitative outcomes can be specified, though one would expect that the validities of these less precise measures would be somewhat lower than those using quantitative outcome levels.

There can be a downside to setting high goals and having high self-efficacy from goal attainment. In an experimental simulation, Audia, Locke, and Smith (2000) found that people with high self-efficacy (along with high goals and satisfaction) based on past success were less likely to change strategies in the face of a radical environmental change than those with lower efficacy who in addition had lower past success. This led to lower subsequent performance for those with high self-efficacy. This result stresses the need to pay attention to feedback from the environment to ensure that efficacy levels are appropriate. Furthermore, people with very high efficacy may work less hard than people with low efficacy, if the task is not seen as highly challenging.

*Intentions.* Shepherd and Krueger (2002) and Krueger (2000, 2003) advanced the study of entrepreneurship motivation through application of the theory of intentional behavior (Ryan, 1970). They pointed to entrepreneurial intentions, and perceptions of desirability and feasibility, to explain new venture (and corporate entrepreneurship) behaviors. In particular, Krueger (2000) translated intentions theory to the entrepreneurship domain to explain opportunity recognition. He suggested that the antecedents of intentions to start a new venture were opportunity desirability, business and personal feasibility (efficacy), and positive exogenous and precipitating factors.

The relationship between intentions to start a company and actual start-up has been studied, but I am not aware of any large sample quantitative studies of the relationship between intentions and venture performance. This is not surprising because intentions are closely held cognitive concepts that are difficult to measure. Nevertheless, marketers have measured customers' intentions to purchase using indicators of the amount of effort that customers would expend to buy a product (Chandon, Morwitz, & Reinartz, 2005). Thus, it may be possible to measure the strength of venture intentions to test Ryan's (1970) proposition that the stronger the intentions, the stronger the effort.

## Discussion

Goal theory has demonstrated its practical value for understanding entrepreneurs' motivation, behavior, and firm level results [new venture creation (start-up) and growth]. Knowledge gained has impacted financiers' evaluations of venture teams (Sheppard, 1999) and helped entrepreneurship teachers explain the practices and strategies that work with new venture teams. Importantly, goal theory's principles apply across venture stages to guide understanding about how to motivate a growing workforce in a setting of novelty and uncertainty.

The importance of specific, high goals within the highly uncertain entrepreneurship domain has been supported in multiple entrepreneurship studies. However, entrepreneurship researchers have just begun to explore the moderation effects of feedback, task complexity, and goal choice. Industry and product domain (technology versus efficiency) effects have not been studied, and studies of goal theory concepts across venture stages and within venture teams deserve attention.

Nevertheless, goal theory has added much to knowledge of entrepreneurs' behavior and venture outcomes. The results have already impacted classroom cases and themes and, hopefully, will guide entrepreneurs as they create new useful products, additional jobs, and inspire existing companies to innovate and improve products.

## References

Adams, J. S. (1965). Injustice in social exchange. In L. Berkowitz (Ed.), *Advances in experimental social psychology* (Vol. 2). New York: Academic Press.

Aldrich, H. E. (1999). *Organizations evolving*. London: Sage.

Alsos, G. A., & Kolvereid, L. (1998). The business gestation process of novice, serial, and parallel business founders. *Entrepreneurship Theory and Practice, 22*, 101–114.

Audia, P., Locke, E. A., & Smith, K. G. (2000). The paradox of success: An archival and a laboratory study of strategic persistence following a radical environmental change. *Academy of Management Journal, 43*, 837–853.

Bandura, A. (1982). Self-efficacy mechanism in human agency. *American Psychologist, 37*, 747–755.

Bandura, A. (1986). *Social foundations of thought and action: A social cognitive view*. Englewood Cliffs, NJ: Prentice Hall.

Bandura, A., & Cervone, D. (1986). Differential engagement of self-reactive influences in cognitive motivation. *Organizational Behavior and Human Decision Processes, 38*, 92–113.

Baron, R. A. (2002). OB and entrepreneurship: The reciprocal benefits of closer conceptual links. *Research in Organizational Behavior, 24*, 225–269.

Baron, R. A., & Shane, S. A. (2007). *Entrepreneurship: A process perspective*. Mason, OH: Thomson.

Baum, J. R., & Bird, B. J. (2010). The successful intelligence of high growth entrepreneurs: Links to new venture growth. *Organization Science, 21*(2), 397–412.

Baum, J. R., & Locke, E. A. (2004). The relationship of entrepreneurial traits, skill and motivation to subsequent venture growth. *Journal of Applied Psychology, 89*(4), 587–598.

Baum, J. R., Frese, M., & Baron, R. (2006). *The psychology of entrepreneurship.* New York: Erlbaum.

Baum, J. R., Locke, E. A., & Kirkpatrick, S. (1998). A longitudinal study of the relation of vision and vision communication to venture growth in entrepreneurial firms. *Journal of Applied Psychology, 83,* 43–54.

Baum, J. R., Locke, E. A., & Smith, K.G. (2001). A multidimensional model of venture growth. *Academy of Management Journal, 44,* 292–303.

Begley, T. M., & Boyd, D. P. (1987). Psychological characteristics associated with performance in entrepreneurial firms and smaller businesses. *Journal of Business Venturing, 2,* 79–93.

Bird, B. J. (1989). *Entrepreneurial behavior.* Glenview, IL: Scott Foresman.

Brockhaus, R. H., & Horwitz, P. S. (1986). The psychology of the entrepreneur. In D. L. Sexton & R. W. Smilor (Eds.), *The art and science of entrepreneurship* (pp. 25–48). Cambridge, MA: Ballinger Publishing.

Bull, I., & Willard, G. E. (1993). Toward a theory of entrepreneurship. *Journal of Business Venturing, 8,* 183–195.

Busenitz, L. W., & Barney, J. B. (1997). Differences between entrepreneurs and managers in large organizations: Biases and heuristics in strategic decision-making. *Journal of Business Venturing, 12,* 9–30.

Chandon, P., Morwitz, V. G., & Reinartz, W. J. (2005). Do intentions really predict behavior? Self generated validity. *Journal of Marketing, 69*(April), 1–14.

Collins, C. J., & Lazier, W. C. (1992). *Beyond entrepreneurship.* Englewood Cliffs, NJ: Prentice Hall.

Collins, C. J., Hanges, P., & Locke, E.A. (2004). The relationship of achievement motivation to entrepreneurial behavior: A meta-analysis. *Human Performance, 17,* 95–177.

DeClercq, D. D., Menzies, T. V., Diochon, M., & Gasse, Y. (2009). Explaining nascent entrepreneurs' goal commitment: An exploratory study. *Journal of Small Business and Entrepreneurship, 22*(Spring), 2–7.

Earley, P. C. (1985). Influence of information, choice and task complexity upon goal acceptance, performance, and personal goals. *Journal of Applied Psychology, 70,* 481–491.

Filian, L. J. (1991). Vision and relations: Elements for an entrepreneurial metamodel. *International Small Business Journal, 9,* 112–131.

Gartner, W. B., Bird, B. J., & Starr, J. A. (1992). Acting as if: Differentiating entrepreneurial from organizational behavior. *Entrepreneurship Theory and Practice,* Spring, 13–31.

Gartner, W. B., & Carter, N. M. (2003). Entrepreneurial behavior and firm organizing processes. In ACS, Z. J., & Audretsch, D. B. (Eds.), *Handbook of entrepreneurship research* (pp. 195–221). Boston: Lower.

Gartner, W. B., Shaver, K. G., Carter, N. M., & Reynolds, P. D. (2004). *Handbook of Entrepreneurial dynamics: The process of business creation.* Thousand Oaks, CA: Sage.

Grossman, L. (2010, January 3). Mark Zuckerberg: Person of the year 2010. *Time Magazine,* 42–46.

Hardawar, D. (2011, April 8). Larry page reorganizes Google: Tied bonuses to social success. *VentureBeat.com* (p. 2). Retrieved online April 9, 2011.

Johnson, B. R. (1990). Toward a multidimensional model of entrepreneurship: The case of achievement motivation and the entrepreneur. *Entrepreneurship Theory and Practice, 14,* 39–54.

Krueger, N. F. Jr. (2000). The cognitive infrastructure of opportunity emergence. *Entrepreneurship Theory and Practice, 24*(3), 5–15.

Krueger, N. F., Jr. (2003). The cognitive psychology of entrepreneurship. In Z. Acs & D. B. Audretsch (Eds.), *Handbook of entrepreneurial research.* London: Kluwer Law International.

Kuratko, D. F., Hornsby, J. S., & Naffziger, D. W. (1997). An examination of owner's goals in sustaining entrepreneurship. *Journal of Small Business Management, 35*, 24–35.

Landy, F. J., & Becker, W. S. (1987). Motivation theory reconsidered. In L. L. Cummings & B. M. Staw (Eds.), *Research in organizational behavior* (Vol. 9, pp. 1–38). New York: Elsevier.

Liao, J., & Welsch, H. (2004). Entrepreneurial intensity. In W. B. Gartner, K. G. Shaver, N. M. Carter, & P. D. Reynolds (Eds.). *Handbook of entrepreneurial dynamics: The process of business creation* (pp. 186–204). Thousand Oaks, CA: Sage.

Locke, E. A. (2000). *The prime movers: Traits of the great wealth creators.* New York: AMACOM.

Locke, E. A., & Latham, G. P. (1990). *A theory of goal-setting and task performance.* Englewood Cliffs, NJ: Prentice Hall.

Locke, E. A., & Latham, G. P. (2002). Building a practically useful theory of goal setting and task motivation: A 35-year odyssey. *American Psychologist, 57*, 705–717.

Locke, E. A., & Latham, G. P. (2006). New directions in goal-setting theory. *Current Directions in Psychological Science, 15*, 265–268.

Locke, E. A., Latham, G. P., & Erez, M. (1988). The determinants of goal commitment. *Academy of Management Review, 13*, 23–39.

Locke, E. A., Frederick, E., Buckner, E., & Bobko, P. (1984). Effects of previously assigned goals on self-set goals and performance. *Journal of Applied Psychology, 69*, 694–699.

Low, M. B., & MacMillan, I. C. (1988). Entrepreneurship: Past research and future challenges. *Journal of Management, 14*, 139–151.

Matsui, T., Okada, A., & Inoshita, O. (1983). Mechanism of feedback affecting task performance. *Organizational Behavior and Human Performance, 31*, 114–122.

McClelland, D. (1961). *The achieving society.* New York: Free Press.

McDonald, M. L., Khanna, P., & Westphal, J. D. (2008). Getting them to think outside the circle: corporate governance, CEOs' external advice networks, and firm performance, *Academy of Management Journal, 51*, 453–475.

Miner, J. B. (2002). Goal-setting theory. In J.B. Miner (Ed.), *Organizational behavior: Foundations, theories, and analyses* (pp. 233–253). New York: Oxford University Press.

Mitchell, R. K., Busenitz, L. W., Bird, B. J., Gaglio, C., McMullen, J. S., Morse, E. A., & Smith, J. B. (2007). The central question in entrepreneurial cognition research. *Entrepreneurship Theory and Practice, 31*(1), 1–22.

Mitchell, R. K., Smith, L. W., Seawright, E. A., & Morse, E. A. (2000). Cross-cultural cognitions and the venture creation decision. *Academy of Management Journal, 43*(5), 974–993.

Naffziger, D. W., Hornsby, J. S., & Kuratko, D. F. (1994). A proposed research model of entrepreneurial motivation. *Entrepreneurship Theory and Practice, 18*(3), 29–42.

Noel, T. W., & Latham, G. P. (2006). The importance of learning goals versus outcome goals for entrepreneurs. *The International Journal of Entrepreneurship and Innovation, 7*, 213–220.

Olson, P. D., Morris, J. S., & Terpstra, D. E. (1993). Small growing firms: Goals and factors related to goal choices. *Journal of Business and Entrepreneurship, 5*(2), 63–77.

Pinder, C. C. (1984). *Work motivation.* Glenview, IL: Scott Foresman.

Rauch, A., & Frese, M. (2000). Psychological approaches to entrepreneurial success: A general model and overview of findings. In C. L. Cooper & I. T. Robertson (Eds.), *International review of industrial and organizational psychology* (Vol. 15, pp. 101–142). New York: John Wiley & Sons.

Ryan, T. A. (1970). *Intentional behavior.* New York: Ronald Press.

Schumpeter, J. A. (1934). *The theory of economic development.* Cambridge, MA: Harvard University Press.

Segal, G., Borgia, D., & Schoenfeld, J. (2009). Founder human capital and small firm performance: an empirical study of founder-managed natural food stores. *Journal of Management and Marketing Research, 4*, 1–10.

Seijts, G. H., Latham, G. P., Tasa, K., & Latham, B. W. (2004). Goal setting and goal orientation: An integration of two different yet related literatures. *Academy of Management Journal, 47* (2), 227–240.

Shane, S. (2008). *The illusions of entrepreneurship.* New Haven, CT: Yale University Press.

Shane, S., Locke, E. A., & Collins, C. J. (2003). Entrepreneurial motivation. *Human Resources Management Review, 13*, 257–279.

Shepherd, D. A. (1999). Venture capitalists' assessment of new venture survival. *Management Science, 45*(5), 621–632.

Shepherd, D. A., & Krueger, N. F. (2002). An intentions-based model of entrepreneurial teams' social cognition. *Entrepreneurship Theory and Practice*, Winter, 167–185.

Smith, K. S., & Smith, R.L. (2000). *Entrepreneurial finance.* New York: Wiley.

Stanton, R. (1987, December 1). The 1987 Inc. 500. *INC Magazine*, pp. 136–153.

Steers, R. M., & Porter, L. W. (1991). *Motivation and work behavior.* New York: McGraw-Hill.

Timmons, J. A. (2000). *New* venture creation: Entrepreneurship 2000 (5th edition). Homewood, IL: Irwin.

Tracy, K., Locke, E. A., & Renard, M. (1999). Conscious goal setting vs. subconscious motives: Longitudinal and concurrent effects on the performance of entrepreneurial firms. Paper present at the annual meeting of the Academy of Management, Chicago, IL.

Vesper, K. H. (1996). *New venture experience.* Midland, MI: Vector Publishing.

Vise, D. A., & Malseed, M. (2008). *The Google story (updated): Inside the hottest business, media, and technology success story of our time.* New York, Random House.

Vroom, V. (1964). *Work and motivation.* New York: McGraw-Hill.

Westhead, P., & Wright, M. (1998). Novice, serial and portfolio founders: Are they different? *Journal of Business Venturing, 13*, 173–204.

Zopounidis, C. (1994). Venture capital modeling: Evaluation criteria for the appraisal of investments. *The Financier, 1*(2), 54–64.

# 29    Working with Goals in Therapy

*Per Jostein Matre*   Centre for Cognitive Practice, Norway

*Kitty Dahl*   Centre for Child and Adolescent Mental Health, Norway

*Robert Jensen*   Centre for Cognitive Practice, Norway

*Hans M. Nordahl*   Department of Psychology, Norwegian University of Science and Technology

## Introduction

This chapter will present the role and purpose of goals and goal setting in cognitive behavior treatments of psychological disorders. Cognitive behavior therapy (CBT) is essentially a goal-directed approach, and the work carried out in therapy is goal driven (J. S. Beck, 1995). The process of setting goals and the significance of working with specific goals based on the clients' own situations, and their suffering and strengths as well as their personal values, play a central role in achieving success in therapy (Orlinsky, Rønnestad, & Willutzki, 2004). This will be highlighted by introducing some key principles when working with goals in CBT.

We will focus on the role of goal setting by showing how to use CBT techniques as a method to (1) establish; (2) facilitate; (3) achieve; and (4) maintain desired goals. We want to address clinical important components of goals by describing procedures of goal setting, and how to ask key questions through demonstrations of cases and vignettes from therapies in our clinics.

An overarching goal in all treatments is to increase the person's sense of control; both feedforward as well as feedback control (Bandura, 1992; Locke & Latham, 1990). The therapeutic relationship is based on collaboration and negotiation as key factors for developing goals that will increase engagement, hope, optimism, and self-efficacy. By increasing people's sense of hope and self-efficacy, one will also strengthen further therapeutic goal processes. Likewise, collaborative empiricism through goal setting is essential when evaluating the process and outcome of therapy (looking back to see ahead).

In cognitive behavioral approaches to therapy, we start out with the fact that all human beings have basic values, goals, and assumptions about ourselves, other people, and the world. These basic values, goals, and assumptions guide our decisions and actions (A. T. Beck & Mahoney, 1979). However, people suffering from emotional distress, psychiatric disorders, or negative life events often experience breakdown of their plans and goal-directed behaviors, which may result in ineffective cognitive processing (Matthews, Davies, Westerman, & Stammers, 2000; Wells, 2008; Wells & Matthews, 1994). To put it simply, one often loses sight of goals that are positive, future-oriented, and adaptive.

Clients with emotional problems need to develop a variety of goals such as reducing fight-flight response, excessive worrying, threat monitoring, or ineffective cognitive and behavioral control strategies. CBT can, for example, help a person to be more active when suffering from depression and facing difficulties in dealing with the challenges in daily life. Similarly, CBT can help people create images of new ways of being, and increase peoples use of adaptive self-regulating skills and enhance behavioral skills (J. S. Beck & Beck, 2011; Carr, 2009; Kendall, 2006; Kuyken, Padesky, & Dudley, 2009; Weisz & Kazdin, 2010).

## Importance of Goals in Therapy

In CBT there is an underlying assumption that all people have a set of basic values and goals that guide their decisions and actions (A. T. Beck & Mahoney, 1979). Goals are defined as human cognitive capacities of forethoughts that enable us to imagine future states and our capacities of foreseeing future consequences and committing to them (Bandura, 1986; Bandura & Cervone, 1983; Locke & Latham, 1990). Goals represent an important part of the therapeutic process in CBT and influence both directly and indirectly the therapeutic contract, operations, and alliance throughout the therapy (Orlinsky et al., 2004).

Even though the process of goal setting is important across different forms of therapies, it is often not addressed or is underestimated as a basic element in the therapeutic process of change. In many therapies, goals are implicit, meaning that goals are inherent in the context and evidence-based knowledge of each and every specific disorder.

There is also growing empirical data derived from neuroscience and cognitive science, applied most of all in sports psychology, that generating positive images has a positive influence on emotions and performance (Hackmann, Bennett-Levy, & Holmes, 2011). This can be illustrated by three models of positive imagining and goal setting that are rapidly growing in the field of CBT: (1) Gilbert's model of Compassionate Mind Training (CMT), which is used mostly when people struggle with self-criticism and shame (Gilbert, 2005, 2010); (2) The model of Competitive Memory Training (COMET), which is used to help clients feel at an emotional level what they know at an intellectual level (Korrelboom, Marissen, & van Assendelft, 2011); and (3) the model of changing dysfunctional assumptions and beliefs that focus on people's poor adaptation to circumstances here and now (Hackmann et al., 2011; Padesky & Mooney, 2005). These principles are also strongly emphasized in the field of Positive Psychology (PP) (Lyubomirsky, 2007; Snyder & Lopez, 2005).

This is in line with what Bandura stated in 1986:

> Having people visualize themselves executing activities skillfully raises their perceived self-efficacy that they will be able to perform better. Such boosts of self-efficacy are likely to improve performance by reducing impeding self-doubts and by enlisting the effort needed to do well.

The field of CBT is evolving. Metacognitive therapy (MCT) will be introduced as this approach emphasizes the person's self-regulatory goals and maladaptive self-regulatory strategies in the person's efforts to solve problems. Coping strategies such as worrying, doubt, and dwelling on past failures are examples of ineffective problem solving and maladaptive strategies. Research shows that these ineffective strategies for most of us serve as escalating and maintaining mechanisms that increase psychological pain and emotional distress (Najmi & Wegner, 2009; Nordahl, 2009; Wells, 2009).

## Procedures of Goal Setting in Therapy: Case 1

### *The Starting Point*

When clients come to therapy, one of the early questions to be answered is which goals to (1) prioritize, (2) develop and work with throughout the therapy process, and (3) what goals to achieve in the therapy (Kuyken et al., 2009). This starting point in therapy is a highly individualized process and holds the possibility of defining a myriad of individualized goals. The early stage of working with goals often starts by establishing a step-by-step procedure established from the first session. Examples of typical questions to be asked are as follows: *What do you want to achieve in the therapy? Which goals are the most important ones for you to achieve first? Can you describe how your future would look like if your symptoms or problems vanished tomorrow?*

For example, when a depressed client can't imagine what is attainable in therapy, one might ask them to trigger the imagery process; *Can you first imagine (1) in a detailed way how you came into the office, (2) walked up the stairs, and (3) came through the door? And second, can you reverse what you just saw and now imagine (1) walking out the door, (2) walking down the stairs, and (3) going out of the building.* Most clients can do this easy exercise, which can be understood as goals, and can serve as a starting metaphor in the step-by-step goal setting procedure. To help the imagery process, we sometimes physically go through the imagined route by going out of the office, walking down the stairs, and out through the main door. The same procedure can be used to illustrate the bridge from imagery goals to actions. These steps can emphasize the starting point of goal setting in therapy.

### *Assessment and Conceptualization*

Assessments in CBT are usually carried out by applying individualized and disorder-specific tests in addition to a therapeutic interview. Through collaborative empiricism based on Socratic dialog, we reassess and conceptualize as a way of continuing evaluation during therapy. This discovery process enables us to

(1) Describe the link between thoughts, feelings, behavior, and bodily sensations.
(2) Identify triggering and maintaining factors.
(3) Identify crucial contextual information about the person's history, automatic assumptions, and biological and socioeconomic background.
(4) Identify personal strengths.

The process of conceptualization in CBT is essential for developing individual goals as well as to facilitate a shared goal setting process based on collaborative work. This mutual effort of identifying specific goals and related tasks strengthens the therapeutic alliance throughout therapy. This process of negotiating goals based on shared knowledge will be illustrated through the following case.

### *Case example*

*Kate, a 43-year-old woman, came to therapy referred by her GP. She had been suffering for several months from a moderate to severe depression, and she was also struggling with moderate anxiety. Kate had been on sick leave for three months, and her plan was to get back to work in some weeks' time. She was a mother of two girls (aged 7 and 14) and was living by her own. She had a relatively stable relationship with her boyfriend. She worked in a department store selling clothes. She had been in therapy over a period of one year, four years ago. The initializing assessment showed that she scored 28 on Beck's Depression Inventory (BDI) and 21 on the Beck's Anxiety Inventory (BAI), which indicates moderate to severe depression and moderate level of anxiety. The background information gave a picture of Kate as a person who worked hard to keep up with both her own as well as other people's standards and demands in addition to her vulnerability to relational stress. This was based on growing up with a heavy-drinking, violent father and a mother who suffered from severe depression. Her stability and back up, as she described it, was her supportive older sister and her sports activities; over many years she had joined a positive and stable group of supportive friends.*

### Forming Individual Goals through Collaboration and Negotiation

The two first therapy sessions with Kate were used to assess the actual problem and start out building a CBT case conceptualization. In addition to assessments, a history taking was created based on a translated version of "The history taking form" (Kuyken et al., 2009) and a short form of the Early Trauma Inventory–Adult version. The aim of the collaborative work in the third session was to use these data to increase Kate's awareness of the connection between stressful events and her thoughts, feelings, behaviors, and bodily sensations. Kate agreed that the first task for her homework was to identify shifts in mood as a result of her tendency to worry. In the next therapy session, we explored how she had experienced the homework. Kate had identified several episodes of worrying, but did not quite know which one to focus on. She decided to pick the most challenging episode, which was according to Kate *"the emotion that really turned her off!"* The stressful situation described by Kate was when she was sitting alone at home, waiting for her youngest daughter to return from school. Earlier that day she had been thinking several negative thoughts about the future. The thoughts were mostly worries about potential difficulties returning to work, such as what her colleagues might ask her, what her boss would say, what if she didn't manage to return to work, etc. During the collaborative case conceptualization, we used and shared the four-level conceptualization model described by exploring the stressful situation by using the "cognitive diamond" as a technique to obtain a descriptive conceptualization by establish the connections between the four modalities (Figure 29.1). This made sense to Kate. She saw for the first time the link between her thoughts, feelings, behavior, and bodily sensations.

At the end of the session, Kate was assigned new homework. She was asked to monitor "mood shifts" and write these down in detail, focusing on what happened before and after the actual mood change occurred. The therapeutic goal in this session was to help Kate establish a link between the activating events (A), her beliefs (B), and the emotional, behavioral, and bodily sensations (C) illustrated in Table 29.1. The therapist asked Kate to summarize and evaluate the session. She was very surprised to see the connection between her thoughts, negative emotions, and her tendency to become passive and pointed to the fact that she had got a better and clearer understanding of her own thoughts and feelings.

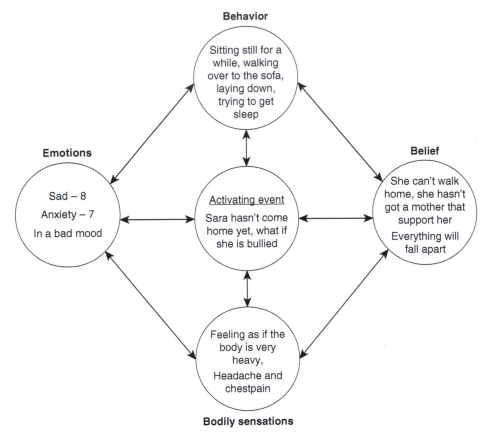

*Figure 29.1* Descriptive conceptualization: establishing the link between activating event, beliefs, emotions, behavior, and bodily sensations.

The development of a *cross-sectional conceptualization* in the fourth session made Kate aware of how the triggers (*sitting down, worrying about future*) and the functional maintaining factors (*her bodily sensations and feelings, her effort to reduce feelings of anxiety and depression, the act of lying down on the sofa*) reinforced her tendency to be passive. Kate used a three-column form to establish the link between these factors more clearly.

*Table 29.1* Functional Conceptualization: Describing Activating Event (Trigger) and Maintaining Factors

| A (Activating event) | B (Belief) | C (Consequences) |
| --- | --- | --- |
| Sitting down by the kitchen table<br>Worrying about future events in a very negative way | Everything will fall apart<br>I am a bad mother for my two daughters<br>I can't make it<br>Nothing works | Lying down on the sofa<br>Reduced anxiety<br>Reduction of body sensation of heaviness |

The goal was to establish a connection between activating events, her beliefs, and the maintaining consequences as shown in Table 29.1.

In the following sessions, we tried to establish a clearer picture of how the two first levels of conceptualization were linked with Kate's history and earlier experiences using guided discovery. The guided discovery gave her an understanding that early-established assumptions combined with her vulnerability based on relational insecurity over a long time in her childhood gave rise to beliefs and behavior patterns that were reactivated by current stressful situations. She also realized that it was her past experiences and her interpretations of them that were the main reason why she often fell into the negative tendency to stay passive in the dark ditch, unable to see any positive consequences in the near future.

## Establishing SMART Goals Using Visualization

As we worked through the full conceptualization, Kate identified specific areas to change. We discussed time frames and the possible impact working on specific areas could have on her mental distress. Kate was given the rationale of how to work with positive images as a way of creating new specific goals, which would be a way of working on her new being. Kate wanted to start out with changing her passive behavior and distressing worry. She wanted to become more active and worry less about the future. In short, she wanted to get more goal directed and reestablish everyday plans and activities for herself, her two daughters, and her boyfriend. Kate summarized for herself that she, like her mother, had been a worrier as long as she could remember. As a metaphor, we introduced an image of her as a worry warrior effectively fighting to win back positive everyday life for herself and her daughters. Kate was highly committed to the ongoing work. We agreed upon a working model combining CMT (Gilbert & Irons, 2005) with the model of Padesky and Mooney. Step by step, we used Socratic dialog, relaxation, and visual techniques to establish SMART goals (Specific, Measurable, Attainable, Relevant, Timely) Kate visualized during this process: (1) her new way of life, (2) the effort needed for the new strategies, and (3) how she could support herself. The therapist carefully monitored the pitfalls of ending up in dwelling on past failures, unrealistic fantasies and the challenge of having good intentions but no performance strategies connected to them (Gollwitzer & Brandstatter, 1997; Gollwitzer & Schaal, 1998; Heckhausen, 2003).

In order to increase her motivation and effort, we worked with goals that were all (1) positive, (2) challenging (stretch goals), (3) shared (with her daughters and boyfriend), and (4) future oriented. The whole procedure was carried out by going through a cycle of six levels described in Figure 29.2. The three first levels of the cycle, starting from the top, focus on specific and measurable dimensions, while the next four levels focus on the dimensions of attainability, where we explore whether the goals are realistic and where they are on a time-framing and time horizon dimension. An additional intensity dimension was also incorporated through the session.

The process of working on these dimensions went on for six sessions. Kate had to become convinced that she could manage to actually perform what she had visualized, before she was ready to test it out in real-life situations. The criteria to be met were that Kate scored her level of confidence as 60 or higher on a scale from 0 to 100, and that she actually would manage to carry out the imagined performance in a natural setting.

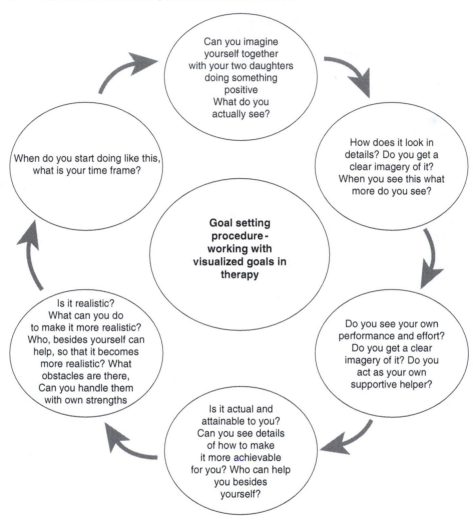

*Figure 29.2* Specifying visualized goals in therapy, starting at the top going all around the circle.

We developed different experiments where she should test out her performance. Kate had her own workbook or treatment diary where she wrote down her SMART goals and collected various photos that she used for her visualization exercises.

### Facilitating Goals by Using Images of New Positive Self

Throughout the procedure, Kate was asked whether she could imagine details such as the following:

*When you imagine the situation, do you see how you will carry it out? Do you have images of yourself doing it? Is this the way you actually see it or is this the way you want it to be? How convinced are you on a scale from 0 to 100 that you will carry it out? Would you exert effort toward attaining the goal? Is the time frame realistic? And who can help you and support your effort toward seeking the goal? Can you imagine yourself being your own good and supportive helper?*

Kate used photos of herself as well as other people to illustrate both *her new way of life and her new strategies to achieve the visualized goal*. By doing this exercise, she built up (1) new scenarios for her performance, (2) new ways of interpreting situations, and (3) new ways of supporting herself. She worked with her new plans and goals at home and mailed these as PowerPoint presentations to her therapist before the next session. As homework, Kate made new scenarios, new interpretations, and developed ways to support herself in addition to testing one or two scenarios in real-life experiments. Experiences from these experiments were then implemented in the process of visualization in the next session, thus serving as a feedback loop for Kate and the therapist.

We explored how she could apply the goals and tasks in natural settings by asking questions such as the following: *Do you now see how to act outside the therapeutic room? Who can support you? How would the person give you the support? Are there any barriers or obstacles that could stop you from working on the task? Can you now imagine yourself being your own good and supportive helper?*

The aim throughout these sessions was to facilitate SMART goals, explorer the transfer process, and to work with possible obstacles and barriers and go through alternative helpful strategies. As a therapist, it is considered important that one uses positive coaching procedures and state that this collaboration and shared work will help increase self-efficacy, hope, and optimisms. It is also important to use enough time, letting the images evolve naturally without too much interference from the therapist during the sessions.

During the last two sessions (13 and 14), we returned to the cognitive diamond and discussed the benefits of continued work with her goals. Kate came up with an idea that she could use a tree as a metaphor were she could hang up her new strategies and alternative ways of imagining herself. The branches on the tree would symbolize (1) herself, (2) herself together with her two daughters, and (3) herself together with her boyfriend. She also made similar trees for different life domains, with branches representing different situations at work, such as communicating with her boss and relating to colleagues, in addition to branches for her health and leisure time activities (e.g., workout lessons). In this way, Kate was able to maintain focus on the two main domains of visualized goals: (1) new alternative thoughts about herself and (2) new strategies based on new assumptions.

This became a natural point for ending the therapy, except for agreeing on two booster sessions at three and six months after the last session. We made a short blueprint of the whole procedure, and Kate stated that she was convinced that she would continue using the techniques by herself.

### Booster Sessions and Follow-Up

Kate came to the first booster session reporting that she had continued on the positive development. She was back in her job, worried less about her daughters, and was planning to live together with her boyfriend. Reassessment showed that she scored very low on both anxiety and depression. She needed a short repetition of the model and said that she would continue working with the techniques.

In the second follow-up session, Kate reported that she had experienced a setback and had felt very bad for two days. She had, however, put effort into freeing herself, done her own analyses of the situation, and used the techniques to *get herself going* as she expressed it. The most effective technique for her was to return to her imagined goals and reinforce these by using visualization to imagine herself performing and being self-supportive and kind to herself.

## Procedures of Goal Setting in Therapy: Case 2

### The Starting Point

The principles of goal setting and collaborative empiricism in CBT will be illustrated through a description of a time-limited exposure and response-prevention treatment (ERP) of obsessive compulsive disorder (Kozak & Coles, 2005). When a person over a long period of time has suffered from breakdown in goal-directed behavior, working with symptom hierarchies and exposure can be an efficient method of reestablishing new functional plans and goals (Solem, Haland, Vogel, Hansen, & Wells, 2009). Obsessive-compulsive disorder (OCD) is a disorder in which the person suffers from recurrent unwanted and frightening thoughts (obsessions) that provoke a high level of anxiety. In order to reduce anxiety or catastrophic thoughts, the person develops repeating rituals (compulsions). The anxiety reduction is usually very short-lived, and the OCD patient will either repeat the rituals or avoid the anxiety-provoking situation, which will rather increase than reduce the anxiety over time (Foa & Franklin, 1998; Franklin & Foa, 2011). CBT is recommended as the first treatment of choice for OCD (March, 1997; National Institute of Clinical Excellence, 2011).

### Assessment and Conceptualization

The procedures of working with goals in exposure and response prevention treatment of OCD will be described by a case example of an OCD patient in his mid-twenties. This patient made some revealing drawings prior to entering therapy that better than any words show his level of suffering. Three of John's drawings are presented to illustrate his case since they give us such a good idea of the disorder and how heavily John felt burdened by his OCD (drawing 1, Figure 29.3), as well as how paralyzed and locked in he felt (drawing 2, Figure 29.4). Finally, the last of the three drawings show how difficult or impossible he saw the road toward attaining his goal of getting rid of the disorder (drawing 3, Figure 29.5).

### Case Example

*John is a young man who had suffered from OCD for several years. He was quite depressed at the time he came to therapy and expressed strong feelings of hopelessness since he had almost given up the thought of getting rid of his OCD symptoms. His quality of life was strongly influenced by his OCD. He was not able to work, and his daily functioning was markedly reduced in spite of having been in psychodynamic therapy for the last year.*

*Figure 29.3* The Burden of OCD: The drawing pictures how depressed John feels by the heaviness and all-consuming feelings of the disorder.

*John came from a stable, well-educated middle class family; he was happily married and had one young child. The foundation for a happy life was all there; he was, however, tormented by recurrent thoughts of being responsible for hurting other people or causing serious accidents. He was unable to drive a car or ride a bicycle. He could only walk outside the house if his wife walked behind him to assure him that he had not caused an accident. He was very dependent on his wife, who had to frequently reassure him that he had not caused any harm. John was unable to leave the house last. He had to check all the electrical equipment as well as water fuses, locks, and windows endless times to be sure they were turned off every time he was planning to leave the house. He did not trust himself and had to repeat the checking again and again since he was never convinced that he had checked well enough. This endless doubt and inability to trust his own judgment made him very depressed and helpless. The problems accelerated when John was the last person leaving his workplace with the responsibility of locking the doors and turning off electrical equipment. John addressed his fear by avoiding being the last person to leave the office or any other place, including his home. In spite of his efforts to avoid these anxiety-provoking situations, his fear of causing accidents increased. He stopped driving automobiles entirely and started to bike instead. However, his recurrent thoughts of causing injuries continued, which made him also stop biking and even walking alone without his wife, since he needed her reassurance that he had not accidentally hit a child and left her bleeding to death. He was unable to go away for a weekend with the family leaving their house unattended.*

John scored very high on the severity scale for OCD as well as for major depression, which is quite common for patients with a primary OCD diagnosis. When the depression

*Figure 29.4* Stuck with OCD: The drawing illustrates how John is paralyzed by his own fear. He wants to get out of the door but is stopped by his OCD symptoms, which force him to do endless checking, with the result that he is unable him to leave the house.

is secondary or a consequence of the OCD disorder, the depressive symptoms usually drop when the patients starts to experience success and personal mastery from the exposure therapy.

### Working with Specific Goals through a Collaborative Relationship

The main goal of a patient seeking therapy is to reduce suffering and improve life quality. For persons suffering from OCD, this goal means having a life without recurrent obsessive thoughts and without having to indulge in compulsive behavior. This reestablishing of new goals and plans and new behavioral strategies seems, however, almost impossible for most OCD patients. It is therefore important for the therapist to establish a setting where the patient feels validated and can get hope and motivation for therapy by forming realistic expectations and goals.

The first goal for the therapist is to build trust and establish a collaborative relationship with the patients. Second, the therapist should describe the disorder and the therapy to be used. The therapist and patient need to develop a shared understanding of the presenting problem and what they want to achieve from therapy. The following questions should to be addressed to the patient: (1) Does he have any well-defined goals? (2) Is he willing to put in effort to change his behavior in order to achieve the specific goals? (3) Are there any motivating factors that will reinforce achieving these goals? (4) Are there any barriers that could come in the way of him reaching these goals? (5) What are his expectations of the therapy or the therapist? (6) Does he have any

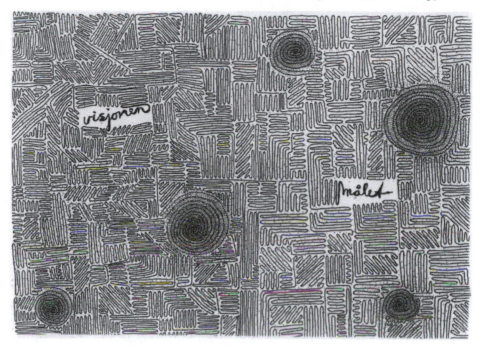

*Figure 29.5* The unattainable goal: The vision of a life without OCD. This drawing illustrates an almost impossible road to get to the desired goal. The road to follow in the drawings is one single line that starts out from the word *Visjonen*, which is the Norwegian word for "the vision," and ends in the word *Målet*, which is the Norwegian word for "the goal."

specific expectations of himself? Finally, (7) how motivated is he to put personal effort into the therapy?

Through an analysis of the presenting problem, the therapist conceptualizes the individual case, which forms the basis for discussing expectations and realistic therapeutic outcomes and negotiating individual goals.

Most OCD patients are embarrassed about their symptoms since they usually know very well that the perceived threat is unlikely and that their anxiety-reducing rituals are unnecessary. This may make them hold back information. By enhancing trust, and being sensitive to the patient's needs and suffering, the therapist is in a better position to collect detailed information about underlying anxiety-producing fear and the link to the rituals that are the maintaining factors in the OCD. In CBT, the patients provides the basic information about the problem, while the therapist often acts as the expert, like the coach in sports who knows the techniques and the procedures of coaching necessary to achieve the specific goals. By putting it this way, it is the coach rather than the patient who is responsible if the exercises are made too difficult.

### Establishing Goals Through Negotiation and Commitment to Therapy

In order to fulfill the goals of treatment, one needs to specify the time frame and the main criteria's for the therapy. Both the therapist and the patient should also be aware of limiting and maintaining factors that can undermine treatment outcome.

In order to form an individual treatment plan and discuss goals for treatment outcome and necessary exposure targets, it is important to make a symptom hierarchy based on a thorough understanding of the patient's obsessions or level of anxiety in different situations when they are not engaged in any anxiety-reducing rituals. The triggering situations are established and placed in the hierarchy by asking what situations trigger the obsessions and how strong the level of anxiety is (on a scale from 0 to 100) if the patient can resist compulsive actions.

Through the collaborative relations they should explore (1) why the patient feels such an urge to perform the rituals in order to reduce anxiety, (2) the catastrophic assumptions about what could happen if he is unable to perform the rituals, and (3) why the rituals have to be done in a certain way or order. By understanding the way the patient reasons, the therapist will be able to follow the patient's own logic and thus be able to find the link between the obsessions and compulsion, which are rarely based on logic. Since the link between the obsessions and compulsion is the maintaining reinforcing factor of the disorder, the therapeutic goal is to break this link in order to achieve a successful result. Thus, the purpose of the exposure and response prevention therapy is to have the patients expose themselves to the obsessive fears without engaging in any anxiety-reducing rituals. The patient needs to experience anxiety reduction without engaging in any anxiety-reducing behavior in order to weaken the bond between the obsessive thoughts and the compulsive actions. By identifying the patient's logic of why compulsions produce anxiety reduction, the therapist is in a position to help the patient find specific exposure targets and help with developing and picking appropriate exposure exercises as well as guiding in performing the exercises without performing any rituals.

### Facilitate Functional Goals and Forming an Individual Treatment Plan

John expressed strong doubts that the therapy would work, but was willing to give it a chance since a life with OCD symptoms seemed intolerable. He had great support from his wife and close family, and was highly motivated to put time and effort into therapy. We therefore decided to go for an intensive exposure and response prevention approach that consisted of several hours of therapy five days a week for a month's time, rather than the more commonly used once-a-week approach.

John got thorough information about the therapy and what was expected of him. He realized that he had to put in a high degree of personal effort into this type of therapy, which essentially required full-time involvement. By committing to therapy, he agreed to trust the therapist as an expert and a guiding coach. The therapist described the premises for the intensive therapy as follows: (1) engage in no rituals from the first day of therapy (as far as possible), (2) do the exposure exercises at the top of the symptom hierarchy from day six of exposure, (3) commit to 2 hours of exposure five days with the therapist, (4) commit to 2–4 hours of homework every day at home, and (5) family members should only assist in accordance with therapeutic guidelines.

In order to form the necessary targets for the exposure exercises, we formed a detailed symptom hierarchy, from 0 to 100, on a so-called subjective unit of discomfort scale (SUD). The placement on the scale was based on the anxiety level John believed he would experience in different situations when not allowed to do any of his rituals, including getting reassurance from his wife.

*Table 29.2* John's Symptom Hierarchy

| | |
|---|---|
| **100** | • Driving a car |
| **90–99** | • Biking<br>• Leaving the home for a weekend<br>• Do shopping alone<br>• Leave the house with the top of the stove on |
| **80–89** | • Leave the house without checking or reassurance from his wife<br>• Leaving electrical equipment on like PC, radio, TV.<br>• Leaving water fuses running<br>• Leaving the door unlocked<br>• Leaving windows open |
| **70–79** | • Walk on sidewalks on the side closest to thick bushes or trees<br>• Leave the train without looking behind |
| **60–69** | • Walk on the sidewalk on the side closest to the traffic |
| **50–59** | • Leave the house with electrical lamps on<br>• Walk across an open field (grass) alone without checking/turning |
| **40–49** | • Leave the water fuse on in the bathroom |
| **30–39** | • Throw something in the garbage that is not garbage |
| **20–29** | • Pick up the mail from the mailbox once without checking for mail left behind |
| **10–19** | • Watch TV |
| **0** | • Be home with his family |

It is advisable to be thorough in filling out the details of the system hierarchy, which will give a solid understanding of the symptoms in addition to providing several target areas for the exposure exercises.

Working with symptom hierarchy and exposure serves as a method of reestablishing more functional plans and goals at the same time as it serves the purpose of reducing rituals and the sense of anxiety. Table 29.2 shows a shortened version of John's symptom hierarchy based on SUD with some of the targets used during therapy.

Several colleagues thought it was far too optimistic that John should make driving a car as one of the outcome goals of the therapy. We believe, however, that it is crucial to get to the top of the hierarchy for OCD patients if they are going to get rid of their OCD problem. Since driving a car was at the top of John's hierarchy and the reason that he had quit driving was such a direct result of his obsessional fear, we discussed the importance of choosing *driving a car* as the main exposure target to be reached (though it was not where we started; see below). He could not imagine how this was possible. In spite of the doubt, he was highly motivated to follow the treatment plan and made a commitment to put in his best effort to achieve this specific goal.

After trying out some easy exposures as a part of developing his symptom hierarchy, John was instructed to select exposure targets from the symptom hierarchy with a difficulty level at the middle of the scale. A subjective unit of discomfort at around 50 would indicate situations in which he had prior experiences of being able to withstand his need to do rituals approximately half the time. John used various mental techniques, such as pep talks and positive imageries, in order to mitigate the anxiety without doing any rituals.

He also learned how to reward himself as well as how to ask for praise from his wife or other close family members for staying in anxious situations rather than giving in to OCD and the urge to do rituals. As a part of the psychoeducation and preparation for the treatment, John and his wife made a contract with each other that she should not give him any reassurance to reduce his anxiety. John realized that this commitment from his wife was a sign of her love and great support in his effort to fight OCD, and began instead to praise her for not giving him reassurance.

When John returned to therapy after having done exposure exercises at home, he was asked if he had managed to (1) put himself in a situation that elicited enough anxiety, (2) stay in the anxiety-provoking situation over time, and (3) continue to stay in the situation until the anxiety decreased.

This way of addressing these targets made him understand the purpose of exposure exercises. Most anxiety disorder patients would initially answer that the homework had gone well if they did not get anxious. Anxiety disorder patients have to learn that the target of exposure therapy is to learn to be afraid and thus change their interpretation of possible threats (Franklin & Foa, 2011). Similarly, by learning to give up their endless effort to control possible danger, they will paradoxically develop a sense of control.

John approached the exposure exercises in two different ways during therapy: mental exposure (in vitro) and in real-life settings (in vivo). After having selected an exposure target, John and the therapist came up with a five-minute story based on the fearful target situation. The story was then audiotaped. John was listening with eyes closed and had to rate his anxiety levels at one-minute intervals. The therapist read the story, first making sure to include possible negative factors such as hearing ambulance sirens, etc. Second, John read the same story having to still rate his anxiety every minute. Finally, the therapist read the story for the last time. John listened to the audiotape every night at home as part of his daily homework exercises.

After the mental exposure training, John had to engage in real-life exposure. During the exposure, he still had to rate his anxiety every minute in order to be sure he had reached the intended level of anxiety as well as to evaluate a possible change in anxiety level. The first exposure exercise John tried out was to walk alone on the sidewalk without looking back or getting any reassurance either from his wife or the therapist. John experienced a high level of anxiety, both during the mental and real life exposures. The therapist reminded him both before and during the exposure that the anxiety was both required and expected. It was also necessary that he continue with the exposure until he experienced reduced anxiety without leaving the situation or performing any mental or active rituals intended to convince him that he had not caused any harm.

John moved quite fast up the symptom hierarchy and was able to drive a car on the seventh day of therapy, which was one of his main goals. Every day, John and the therapist evaluated the success or failures of the exposure exercises. Had the exercises gone according to the treatment plan? Were the selected targets appropriate? Where the exercises more or less difficult than expected? Did he reach the expected anxiety levels and did the anxiety fall to a desired level? John and the therapist discussed what adjustments to the treatment plan were necessary for further success. It was a huge success to reach the top of the hierarchy early in the therapy, making it possible to spend much time with continuing practice on high-anxiety-provoking situations. When John had reached the top of the hierarchy, his sense of mastery was highly strengthened, and he was quite motivated to continue in his effort to put time into further training.

The entire therapy was very time consuming for both John, his wife, and the therapist. John spent between four and six hours with exposure exercises every day. Most of the exposure with the therapist took place in the therapy office or in environments close to the clinic, but the therapist also went to John's house to guide him with exposure exercises in his house. John spent much time exposing himself to the fear of leaving the house with electrical equipment turned on and water fuses running, etc. As John experienced success by coping with the exposure tasks, his self-esteem increased. The earlier feelings of depression and hopelessness disappeared, and he began to believe that his vision of a life without OCD could be achieved.

## Maintaining Achieved Goals Through Relapse Prevention

As therapy evolved, we spent more time evaluating the factors involved in his success and discussed how he best should keep up the good work in order to maintain the positive result and avoid possible setbacks. It is important to spend time on relapse prevention (Franklin, Ledley, & Foa, 2009; Marlatt & Gordon, 1985), since patients have a tendency to undermine their own success and forget the hard work behind the attainment of each and every goal they set. They need to be told that it is expected that they will have setbacks during time of stress and to use the techniques they have learned in order to withstand the urge to engage in rituals. The patients need to be reminded of what has been learned in order to ensure future success. They cannot allow themselves to perform rituals, but must at the same time expect to have relapses. They also need to be reminded of the ineffectiveness of avoidance behavior as a strategy for fear reduction.

John got strong support from his wife and managed to continue the exposure training after the intensive therapy ended. He continued with weekly booster sessions for a couple of months. Approximately seven years later, John called the therapist and asked whether he could have a session since he had experienced some recurrence of his OCD symptoms and was afraid of relapsing. He said that he had gotten about 5% of the symptoms back, which was not much compared to the seriousness of his disorder seven years earlier. After just a few therapy sessions in which we discussed his situation and how he best could use the techniques he already knew quite well, John believed he could continue without any further help. John managed to do well. He has three children with his wife and is doing very well in his creative profession, where he has to drive a car by himself around the country promoting his work. The thoughts of causing harm are still there in certain situations, particularly when he has to leave the house by himself, but he has learned to ignore the thoughts that nagged him without giving way to ritual behavior (Najmi & Wegner, 2009).

The success of John's therapy was based on a strong collaborative relationship in which we invested much time in developing a solid treatment plan by discussing and negotiating the important specific goals to be achieved. John's level of distress over an extended period and the unrelenting support he got from his wife made him highly motivated to put in time and effort into the therapy. The opportunity to follow an intensive approach over a limited time frame probably increased the likelihood of a successful outcome.

The intensive treatment made it easy for the therapist to follow and guide John in his effort without too many factors interfering with the treatment. John's problem was well suited for exposure therapy. Even though John initially did have enough depressive symptoms that could have qualified for a major depressive diagnosis, he did not suffer from any other psychiatric diagnosis than OCD, or other factors that could indicate that an ERP approach was inappropriate or had to be postponed.

## From Content-Based to Metacognitive Goals

There are different ways to conceptualize goals within cognitive behavioral approaches. A common theme is that they all emphasize developing a collaborative approach in exploring methods for change, therapeutic targets, and homework. The therapeutic goals can be negotiated with the client from session to session (session goals), and they can range from changing biased thinking to learning a new coping technique to master a situation in a desirable manner.

In metacognitive therapy (Wells, 2000, 2009), the concept of goals goes beyond what is usually the case in most CBTs. As in CBT, there are session and treatment goals that overlap with those in CBT. In addition, goals are explicitly part of the self-regulatory system (S-REF model; Wells & Matthews, 1994) in the metacognitive model of disorder. Metacognitive therapy focuses on the cognitive attentional syndrome (CAS) and meta-cognitions that are involved in the control of cognitive and affective processes. Thus, in metacognitive therapy, a distinction can be made between the patients' internal self-regulatory goals and therapeutic goals. In essence, part of this therapy has the goal of changing the patients' unhelpful self-regulatory goals.

### Integrating Metacognitions in Human Goal Processes

Metacognition refers to cognition about cognition and involves cognitive processes that are involved in appraisal, monitoring, or control of cognition. This implies that meta-cognition is knowledge of one's cognitive and affective processes, and involves the process of monitoring and regulating these processes and states in reference to a goal (Flavell, 1979).

In metacognitive therapy developed by Wells (2000, 2009), the distinction between meta-level and object level is important in psychological disorders. The model proposes that patients suffering from psychological disorders are predominantly in an "object mode" of cognition and do not have the resources, cognitive flexibility, or the knowl-edge to process information in a "meta-cognitive mode." In an object mode, patients experience their thoughts as the reality, whereas in the metacognitive mode they experi-ence their thoughts as cognitive constructions and interpretations of the experienced reality. In the metacognitive model, a psychological disorder is linked to the persistence of thinking and an inability to disengage perseverative thinking processes. Persistent thinking occurs as the Cognitive Attentional Syndrome (CAS), which is a pattern of thinking involving worry/rumination, threat monitoring, and unhelpful coping behav-iors such as thought suppression that have harmful effects (Najmi & Wegner, 2009; Wegner, Schneider, Carter, & White, 1987). This pattern is activated in response to negative thoughts and emotions and is caused by the individual's metacognitive beliefs.

Wells (2000) has specified two broad categories of metacognitive beliefs: (1) positive beliefs about the value of engaging in features of the CAS, for example, "I must worry in order to be safe" or "if I scrutinize my depressed feelings I can understand why I feel so bad." The second group of metacognitions are the negative metacognitions, which are negative beliefs about cognition, for example, "I have no control over my mind" or "I could go crazy if I think too much."

The therapeutic goals of metacognitive therapy are to help the client to acquire metacognitive processing skills, which involve (1) developing a metacognitive perspective on their worry and rumination, (2) removing the CAS, and (3) modifying metacognitive beliefs about worry and rumination as uncontrollable and dangerous.

A common goal for self-regulation is often to suppress or avoid worry and rumination. Paradoxically, these strategies often lead to failures of ineffective mental control and coping. For example, clients will worry in order to attain a goal of safety in foreseeing what may occur. The rumination can be formulated as a coping strategy to deal with a negative mood by analyzing why they feel depressed. This easily results in preservation of worry and rumination and heightens negative emotions. Clients have to develop personal goals to reduce negative affect by developing new strategies that decrease thought suppression (not to think about upsetting things), threat monitoring (being vigilant of potential danger), and avoidance (to escape potential problems). From a therapeutic viewpoint, these maladaptive coping strategies have a tendency to backfire and to be ineffective in reducing the level of worry and rumination. When patients use worry and rumination as a strategy, most of them develop a vicious circle of sustained worry and rumination, which worsen their symptoms of anxiety and depression.

The goal in MCT is to reduce the worry and rumination process. Instead, patients need to deal with their worries from a metacognitive perspective, that is, to see the worries and ruminations as thoughts (metacognitive mode) and not as imminent real-life problems (object mode).

Two central techniques will be described. Patients have to learn new techniques that are designed to achieve, first, Detached Mindfulness (Wells, 2000), which is a technique that helps clients to disengage from the thinking or worry process by being aware of the thoughts without acting or engaging in them. Clients are asked to observe the inner processes of thoughts and experiences and to leave them alone. Instead, clients can redirect their focus of attention to external events. Second, worry postponement is a useful strategy to dismiss worry and postpone it. It works as clients contract with themselves to postpone issues of worry and rumination to a time later on the day. Any worry is postponed, but can be revisited at a certain time of the day where clients decide to take a 15-minute "worry time." In this way, clients spend less time on worry during the daytime and can focus better on work or other tasks during the day. The emotional distress will then be alleviated.

Another important goal in MCT is to modify the positive and negative metacognitive beliefs of clients. Most clients believe they are incapable of reducing their worrying, and also believe that worries can be harmful to their mental and physical health. Behavioral experiments are a helpful strategy to overcome beliefs about uncontrollability. By setting up tests to lose control of worries and also to postpone worrying, clients can learn that the worry process is controllable, and not damaging. To help clients explore worry and increase the level of worry is a useful way to modify beliefs about worry leading to insanity.

To change the patients' metacognitive assumptions about their thinking style—that worry and rumination is uncontrollable and damaging—is necessary in order to help them reduce these ineffective strategies. In MCT, it is therefore crucial to explore and modify the clients' unrealistic or biased goals for self-regulation and to help them use more adaptive strategies when dealing with negative thoughts and emotions.

## Chapter Summary

In CBT and MCT, the role of goal setting is emphasized. These therapies are directed by goals. In therapy, goals are both established for each session as well as for the therapy outcome. We have demonstrated which questions should be addressed and shown some of the most central cognitive behavioral techniques used in order to facilitate goals and new plans when working to reduce emotional distress and psychological problems.

The various vignettes illustrate the important domain of goals and goal setting in therapy as part of working with self-regulation applied to patients with various psychological problems.

Through collaboration and Socratic questioning, the therapist and the patient develop in-session and between-session goals, and as such the process of goal setting is a trademark in both CBT and metacognitive therapy.

## References

Bandura, A. (1986). *Social foundations of thought and action: A social cognitive theory.* Englewood Cliffs, NJ: Prentice-Hall.

Bandura, A. (1992). Self-efficacy mechanism in psychobiologic functioning *Self-efficacy: Thought control of action* (pp. 355–394). Washington, DC: Hemisphere Publishing Corp.

Bandura, A., & Cervone, D. (1983). Self-evaluative and self-efficacy mechanisms governing the motivational effects of goal systems. *Journal of Personality and Social Psychology, 45*(5), 1017–1028.

Beck, A. T., & Mahoney, M. J. (1979). Schools of "thought". [Comment/Reply]. *American Psychologist, 34*(1), 93–98.

Beck, J. S. (1995). *Cognitive therapy: basics and beyond.* New York: Guilford Press.

Beck, J. S., & Beck, A. T. (2011). *Cognitive behavior therapy: basics and beyond.* New York: Guilford Press.

Carr, A. (2009). *What works with children, adolescents, and adults?: A review of research on the effectiveness of psychotherapy.* New York: Routledge.

Flavell, J. H. (1979). Metacognition and cognitive monitoring: A new area of cognitive-developmental inquiry. *American Psychologist, 34*(10), 906–911.

Foa, E. B., & Franklin, M. E. (1998). Cognitive-behavioral treatment of obsessive-compulsive disorder. *The science of clinical psychology: Accomplishments and future directions* (pp. 235–263). Washington, DC: American Psychological Association.

Franklin, M. E., & Foa, E. B. (2011). Treatment of obsessive compulsive disorder. *Annual Review of Clinical Psychology, 7,* 229–243.

Franklin, M. E., Ledley, D. A., & Foa, E. B. (2009). Response prevention. *General principles and empirically supported techniques of cognitive behavior therapy* (pp. 543–549). Hoboken, NJ: John Wiley & Sons.

Gilbert, P. (2005). *Compassion: conceptualisations, research and use in psychotherapy.* London: Routledge.

Gilbert, P. (2010). *Compassion focused therapy: Distinctive features.* New York: Routledge/Taylor & Francis.

Gilbert, P., & Irons, C. (2005). Focused therapies and compassionate mind training for shame and self-attacking *Compassion: Conceptualisations, research and use in psychotherapy* (pp. 263–325). New York: Routledge.

Gollwitzer, P. M., & Brandstatter, V. (1997). Implementation intentions and effective goal pursuit. *Journal of Personality and Social Psychology, 73*(1), 186–199.

Gollwitzer, P. M., & Schaal, B. (1998). Metacognition in action: The importance of implementation intentions. *Personality and Social Psychology Review, 2*(2), 124–136.

Hackmann, A., Bennett-Levy, J., & Holmes, E. A. (2011). *Oxford guide to imagery in cognitive therapy.* Oxford, UK: Oxford University Plass.

Heckhausen, J. (2003). The future of lifespan psychology: Perspectives from control theory. *Understanding human development: Dialogues with lifespan psychology* (pp. 383–400). Dordrecht, Netherlands: Kluwer Academic Publishers; Netherlands.

Kendall, P. C. (2006). *Child and adolescent therapy: Cognitive-behavioral procedures* (3rd ed., pp. xvi, 528). New York: Guilford Press.

Korrelboom, K., Marissen, M., & van Assendelft, T. (2011). Competitive memory training (COMET) for low self-esteem in patients with personality disorders: A randomized effectiveness study. *Behavioural and Cognitive Psychotherapy, 39*(1), 1–19.

Kozak, M. J., & Coles, M. E. (2005). Treatment for OCD: Unleashing the power of exposure. *Concepts and controversies in obsessive-compulsive disorder* (pp. 283–304). New York: Springer Science + Business Media.

Kuyken, W., Padesky, C. A., & Dudley, R. (2009). *Collaborative case conceptualization: Working effectively with clients in cognitive-behavioral therapy.* New York: Guilford Press.

Locke, E. A., & Latham, G. P. (1990). *A theory of goal setting & task performance.* Englewood Cliffs, NJ: Prentice-Hall.

Lyubomirsky, S. (2007). *The how of happiness: A scientific approach to getting the life you want.* New York: Penguin Press.

March, J. S. (1997). Treatment of obsessive-compulsive disorder. The Expert Consensus Panel for obsessive-compulsive disorder. *Journal of Clinical Psychiatry, 58*(Suppl. 4), 2–72.

Marlatt, G. A., & Gordon, J. R. (Writer). (1985). Relapse prevention: Maintenance strategies in the treatment of addictive behaviors. New York: Guilford Press.

Matthews, G., Davies, D. R., Westerman, S. J., & Stammers, R. B. (2000). *Human perfomance: Cognition, stress and individual differences.* Hove, England: Psychology Press/Taylor & Francis (UK).

Najmi, S., & Wegner, D. M. (2009). Hidden complications of thought suppression. *International Journal of Cognitive Therapy, 2*(3), 210–223.

National Institute of Clinical Excellence. (2011). Obsessive compulsive disorder (OCD) and body dysmorphic disorder (BDD): Core interventions in the treatment of obsessive-compulsive disorder and body dysmorphic disorder. Retrieved from http://guidance.nice.org.uk/CG31.

Nordahl, H. M. (2009). Effectiveness of brief metacognitive therapy versus cognitive-behavioral therapy in a general outpatient setting. *International Journal of Cognitive Therapy, 2*(2), 152–159.

Orlinsky, D. E., Rønnestad, M. H., & Willutzki, U. (2004). Fifty years of pschotherapy. Process—outcome research: Continuity and change. In M. J. Lambert, F. J. Bergin, & S. L. Garfield (Eds.), *Begin and Garfield's handbook of psychotherapy and behavior change.* New York: Wiley.

Padesky, C. A., & Mooney, K. (2005). *Cognitive therapy for personality disorders: Constructing a new personality. Workshop.* Paper presented at the The 5th International Congress of Cognitive Therapy.

Snyder, C. R., & Lopez, S. J. (2005). *Handbook of positive psychology*. New York: Oxford University Press.

Solem, S., Haland, A. T., Vogel, P. A., Hansen, B., & Wells, A. (2009). Change in metacognitions predicts outcome in obsessive-compulsive disorder patients undergoing treatment with exposure and response prevention. *Behaviour Research and Therapy, 47*(4), 301–307.

Wegner, D. M., Schneider, D. J., Carter, S. R., & White, T. L. (1987). Paradoxical effects of thought suppression. *Journal of Personality and Social Psychology, 53*(1), 5–13.

Weisz, J. R., & Kazdin, A. E. (2010). *Evidence-based psychotherapies for children and adolescents* (2nd ed., pp. xx, 602). New York: Guilford Press.

Wells, A. (2000). *Emotional disorders and metacognition: Innovative cognitive therapy*. New York: John Wiley & Sons.

Wells, A. (2008). Metacognitive therapy: Cognition applied to regulating cognition. *Behavioural and Cognitive Psychotherapy, 36*(6), 651–658.

Wells, A. (2009). *Metacognitive therapy for anxiety and depression*. New York: Guilford Press.

Wells, A., & Matthews, G. (1994). *Attention and emotion: A clinical perspective*. Hillsdale, NJ, England: Lawrence Erlbaum.

# 30   Goal Setting in the Academic Arena[1]

*Dominique Morisano*   Centre for Addiction and Mental Health (CAMH); Dalla Lana School of Public Health, University of Toronto

## Grades and Goals

Over 1000 studies have shown that the effects of goals on performance are both meaningful and reliable. They have the strongest effects on behavior or performance outcomes when the goals are both challenging and specific (Locke & Latham, 1990, 2002). These outcomes include academic performance indicators such as course grades (e.g., Locke & Bryan, 1968; Locke & Kristof, 1996; Wood & Locke, 1987). Zimmerman and Bandura (1994) found that grade goals were not only associated with students' actual attained grades, but also that perceived self-efficacy affected goals (a topic to be addressed later). In a review of three decades of research on university students, Pascarella and Terenzini (2005) concluded that course grades are the best predictor of student persistence and degree completion.

Many of these correlational studies raise the question of causality, but goal intervention programs have also been found to improve student performance (e.g., Morisano et al., 2010), thus providing strong evidence of the causal effect of goals and supporting Locke and Latham (2002). In the Morisano et al. study, which was based on the first author's dissertation, recruitment was aimed at self-nominated "academically struggling" students from McGill University (Montreal, Canada) who had grade point averages (GPAs) of B– or lower. Recruitment efforts were extensive, and notifications indicated that the study was designed to investigate the effects of two brief interventions for improving academic performance. Participants (sophomores to seniors) were randomized to one of two groups; ultimately, 45 students (goal group) completed a single-session (2.5-hour), online, and narrative personal goal-setting program (adapted by Morisano from Peterson & Mar, 2004), while 40 (control group) completed a 2.5-hour face-valid placebo online "intervention" (matched for time and use of writing). Goal-group students were not restricted in the goals that were set; they were encouraged to write about their personal goals over a series of eight steps that included (1) free-writing about multiple aspects of their ideal future self and life; (2) extracting from the first step, labeling, and providing brief descriptions for seven or eight of their top personal goals; (3) evaluating and ranking their goals as well as goal attainability; (4) considering the consequences of goal achievement (both for themselves and others in their lives); (5) determining subgoals and detailed goal-achievement strategies; (6) describing ways to overcome obstacles to achievement of each outlined goal; (7) setting specific benchmarks for goal attainment; and (8) evaluating commitment levels for the completion of each goal. It was hypothesized that students who articulated both their personal goals and a pathway to their attainment would, over the course of a year, (a) earn better grades than students in the control group, (b) maintain a full-time course load, and (c) demonstrate improved psychological well-being. Results from baseline to post-intervention assessment indicated that only goal-group students demonstrated statistically significant grade improvements. Although students' grades did not differ by group at the study's start, those who completed goal setting had semester GPAs that shot up 30% post goal-setting intervention.

Furthermore, the numbers of students in both groups who continued carrying a full course load post-intervention were examined. Even though all students in the study were taking three or more classes in the semester before they completed the intervention, things changed for those who did not do the goal-setting exercises. Out of the 40 students in the control group, 8 (20%) either dropped out of school or dropped to a part-time course load in the semester following the intervention; yet all students in the goal group maintained a full course load. Notably, maintaining a full-time course load is highly related to eventual degree attainment. Adelman (1999) provided evidence that the ratio of a university student's number of dropped, withdrawn, and repeated courses to their overall number of attempted courses had a significant and negative influence on ultimate degree attainment.

With regard to well-being, goal-group students reported significantly greater reduced negative affect than control-group students, and they directly attributed their mood changes to the goal-setting process. Their reduced negative-affect scores were also correlated with observed grade improvements, although it was not clear from the analyses whether the improved well-being was a cause or consequence of students' better academic performance. In sum, the Morisano et al. study demonstrated that the process of brief but intensive personal goal setting could produce significant and differential improvements in academic success among young adults.

Furthermore, as Holahan (1988) stated, "the ability to establish and maintain appropriate goals and commitments appears to be integral to development throughout adulthood" (p. 286). Humans have both the ability and fortitude to actively regulate their lives through purposeful thought (Bandura, 1997).

In educational-psychology studies focusing specifically on the setting of academic ("grade") goals, a number of grade-goal measures have been used (Locke & Bryan, 1968) including a grade that one tries for, hopes for, expects, or the minimum grade that would provide satisfaction. "Try for" and "hope for" grade-goal measures have tended to be overoptimistic, and "expected grades" do not accurately reflect a goal per se; the most accurate and valid measure of a grade goal is the minimum grade that one would be satisfied with (or alternatively, the minimum one would not be dissatisfied with; Locke & Latham, 1990).

## Mechanisms of Action

Goals affect performance through specific mediators, that is, causal mechanisms (Locke & Latham, 1990; Smith et al., 1990). They direct *attention* toward goal-relevant activities while influencing the avoidance of goal-irrelevant actions. They arouse *effort* in accordance with how difficult they are. They also affect *persistence*, because if one is committed to a goal, one keeps working until it is attained. Finally, in the cognitive realm, goals motivate people to recall or discover task *strategies* that facilitate goal achievement.

Goals do not always lead to the result desired, however. There are moderating factors that can get in the way, one of which is *goal commitment*. People might not be committed to actually achieving their goals; goals might simply represent fantasy or an abstract wish. High commitment (see Chapter 6) is based on two core factors: (a) perceiving the goal as important or desirable, and (b) having task-specific confidence that it is attainable (Locke & Latham, 1990). Bandura (1997) calls this latter confidence "self-efficacy": the belief that one can bring about a certain performance result on one's own.

A second moderating factor is *feedback*. Some people might not get enough progress information from their goal-related efforts to allow them to track goal headway; in this case, they could end up in a situation where they are unsure whether to increase effort or to switch strategies if things are not going well.

Third, people might not possess the knowledge or skills required to perform well in a chosen pursuit. With regard to the latter scenario, when people lack necessary task knowledge, specific, difficult goals might conceivably harm performance in comparison with "do-your-best" goals. When people are too outcome-focused, they might not take the time to focus on the best way to attain their goals on the task. Seijts, Latham, and Woodwark (Chapter 13) have noted, accordingly, that when people are faced with new, complex tasks, setting specific learning goals rather than outcome-based goals is preferable. Once people have developed and established some level of skill and strategy knowledge, outcome goals should be set.

As alluded to above, Zimmerman and Bandura (1994) suggested that goals operate largely through self-processes (e.g., perceived self-efficacy, effort) rather than directly regulating motivation and behavioral attainments. The higher the self-efficacy, the higher the goals, and the greater the goal commitment. Self-efficacy (Bandura, 1997) has many other benefits aside from affecting goal commitment, however. It is not only a predictor of self-set goals, but also often has a direct effect on performance and retention along with goal effects (e.g., Caprara et al., 2008; Locke & Latham, 1990). Self-efficacy affects one's chosen goal level (if goals are self-set), as well as the effectiveness of one's strategies and response to failure (Erez & Judge, 2001). Failure can lower self-efficacy and lead to goal abandonment or the lowering of goals, but those whose levels of self-efficacy are resilient will respond to setbacks with increased effort and dedication. Indeed, it has been shown that self-efficacy affects both effort and persistence, mediators themselves of performance-approach goals (see definition and discussion below), and exam performance (Elliot et al., 1999). Self-efficacy thereby mediates the effect of other variables on achievement, such as acquisition of skills and self-regulatory practices (e.g., goal-setting), which can in turn impact self-efficacy and thereby influence academic performance (Pajares, 1996). Additionally, both goals and self-efficacy have been determined to be mediators of feedback effects (Locke & Latham, 2002).

Student achievement, of course, is not the result of just one factor such as goal setting, but rather stems from a myriad of interconnected causal factors, including cognitive ability (Rohde & Thompson, 2007), knowledge and skill (e.g., study skills), self-efficacy, self-protective mechanisms (e.g., defensive pessimism), and emotions (e.g., pride, hopelessness; cf. Pekrun et al., 2009) that change dynamically as different milestones are reached (see Covington, 2000, for a broad review). In an important illustration of this, Locke and Kristof (1996) found that over and above students' "minimum-grade" goals correlating with both their GPAs and course grades (consistent with Locke & Bryan, 1968), grades were also positively related to many student choices. These included (a) using specific study methods, (b) doing all the work assigned, (c) programming the material into memory, (d) paying full attention in class, (e) tying lecture points together, and (f) linking lecture notes to assigned readings. The authors also found that certain ways of dealing with setbacks or frustrations were associated with higher GPAs, for example, seeking information, putting in extra effort, and trying new strategies instead of wallowing in negative emotions and avoiding class or homework. Grades were negatively related to both making goal choices based on parental expectations and low effort in the face of failure, and positively related to tying grades to one's self-concept. Furthermore, students' goal choices fully mediated the effects of their grade goals on exam performance.

An earlier study by Wood and Locke (1987) demonstrated that both grade goals and self-efficacy were significantly related to overall GPA and course grades in three college student samples. The self-efficacy scales required students to rate their confidence in being able to concentrate, memorize, understand course concepts, and take good notes, among other abilities. This study showed that beyond making proper study choices, students also needed to believe they could skillfully execute necessary study methods in order to perform well. This adds to the body of evidence that "goals alone" do not affect grades, but rather goals in concert with specific behavior choices and beliefs.

## General Mastery and Performance Goals

Both goals and self-efficacy are state variables; they are task and situationally specific. In most conditions, specific, challenging goals lead to better results than general goals (e.g., "do-your-best" goals; Locke & Latham, 2002). However, within the field of education, general goals, such as achievement goals, have also been studied. An "achievement goal," as originally defined, involves the desire to improve one's performance on some task or develop some skill (Dweck, 1986). More recently, as will be discussed below, some researchers have modified this definition to include qualifiers; for example, Hulleman et al. (2010) defined an achievement goal as "a future-focused cognitive representation that guides behavior to a competence-related end state that the individual is committed to either approach or avoid" (p. 423). In either case, as with quantitative goals, people differ in the strength of their levels of achievement motivation. Achievement motivation in this context should not be confused with McClelland's subconscious need for achievement motive (McClelland et al., 1976), which was focused more narrowly; he argued that it was mainly applicable to entrepreneurial work. Achievement goals in the educational realm are measured consciously, through self-reports. The common element in both views, however, is the desire to do well or improve.

Two major types of achievement goals have been identified in the literature (Ames, 1992; Dweck & Leggett, 1988): Mastery goals (sometimes called learning goals; Grant & Dweck, 2003) and performance goals (also called ego- or ego-involved goals, ability goals, self-enhancing goals; Nicholls, 1984). There has been considerable confusion and disagreement as to the meaning of performance goals in the education literature (cf. Hulleman et al., 2010, for a critical meta-analysis of achievement goal constructs and measures). Whereas in goal theory, "having a performance goal" simply means trying to beat a standard without any explicit motive being implied, in the achievement-goal literature, performance goals can imply many different things, for example, trying to impress others or prove oneself by succeeding, gaining rewards (or awards), or competing with others without knowing how others performed. Occasionally, performance goals in this realm have referred to self-set goals, which may or may not be quantitative. When self-set goals are too easy or too vague, or when the reasons behind them serve to increase anxiety, they can diminish in value as effective motivators. Variations in construct definition can thus make it difficult to determine what to conclude from studies that used performance goals. For example, Linnenbrink-Garcia and colleagues (2008) addressed the mastery/performance[2] goal distinction with a review of over 90 articles, and found that 40% of reported effects showed a positive relationship between both mastery and performance goals with academic achievement, and less than 5% showed a negative relation. However, they did not provide explicit details about the manner in which performance goals (or orientation) were assessed in the reviewed studies, and it is unclear whether they should have been lumped together. The authors noted this limitation generally in their conclusions by calling for a more careful consideration of how achievement goals are defined or assessed in the literature (moving forward); they also suggested that meta-analysis might provide a more systematic approach to reviewing the existing literature. Although they concluded that they found no support for the idea that either a mastery or performance-approach goal orientation was better than the other, they stated that the method of defining either type of goal is still an "unresolved" issue in the literature. In a more recent meta-analysis of 243 correlational studies on achievement goals, Hulleman et al. (2010) attempted to break down and define goals more explicitly; they found that performance-approach goal scales coded as having mainly normatively referenced items (e.g., "my goal this semester is to get a better grade than other students") were positively correlated with performance outcomes, while scales with largely appearance (e.g., "it is important to me that my peers think I am good at math") and evaluative items (e.g., "I want to show my teacher that I'm smarter than other students") were negatively correlated with performance outcomes. The authors concluded from their meta-analysis what many researchers had either alluded to or plainly suggested in previous research-study discussion sections: "achievement goal researchers have been using the same label for conceptually different constructs" (p. 422).

Mastery goals, which have been more generally and singularly defined as focusing on the acquisition of new knowledge or skills, are usually not connected to potentially debilitating motives (but see the discussion on the avoidance-type below). Furthermore, with the exception of some studies yielding null academic-achievement effects (i.e., no perceivable impact; see Daniels et al., 2008), they have routinely been associated with achievement-related positive outcomes, such as (a) deeper and more organized processing of information and classroom work (see Brdar et al., 2006; Covington, 2000; Elliot et al., 1999; Rozendaal et al., 2001); (b) effort and tenacity in the face of challenges (see below); and (c) motivation and interest in the educational material (cf. Urdan, 1997). Although studies on the achievement effects of mastery goals have not always demonstrated significant direct positive impact on grades (e.g., Harackiewicz et al., 2000), there have been many notable exceptions. For example, when a course involves sustained difficulty and complexity, or when the task is personally inspiring, mastery goals have been shown to positively influence achievement despite setbacks and even poor self-efficacy (Grant & Dweck, 2003). Differences in outcomes might further depend, as with performance goals, on construct definitions and measures used. In the same meta-analysis referenced previously, Hulleman and colleagues (2010) argued that there is sometimes variability in the components of mastery goals as defined by various researchers, ranging from curiosity to improvement or even from interest to the fulfillment of one's potential.

Classroom context might be a contributing factor to the development of a particular achievement-goal orientation. Harackiewicz et al. (1997) found that in large introductory psychology classes, students who had mastery goals had more interest in the class, but those with performance goals (defined by the authors as aiming to demonstrate competence relative to others in class) ultimately attained higher grades. In Harackiewizc's study, interest as such does not guarantee high performance; rather, interest suggests the liking of something, in this case course material, and does not imply any particular standard of excellence. In an ideal scenario, of course, interest and goals could operate in concert—doing something enjoyable and doing it well.

## Approach and Avoidance Mastery and Performance Goals

Many researchers in the academic goal-setting literature have further subdivided mastery and performance achievement goals into approach- and avoidance-goal subtypes, that is, pursuing something you want versus avoiding something you do not want. Early literature on this topic utilized a trichotomous framework, applying the approach/avoidance distinction to performance goals only and leaving mastery goals undivided (cf. Elliot & Church, 1997; Elliot & Harackiewicz, 1996). Later, the subtyping was extended to mastery goals ("2 × 2 perspective;" cf. Elliot, 1999; Elliot & McGregor, 2001; Hulleman et al., 2010; Pintrich, 2000a,b), though not all researchers who utilize the avoidance/approach label have followed suit. In any case, approach goals of either type tend to be more effective at motivating performance than avoidance goals (cf. Anderman et al., 2002; Daniels et al., 2008). While general performance-approach goals such as "do well in school" can lead to high grades, frequent rehearsal of the material, and the setting of additional performance-approach goals, little to no deep processing of content occurs (e.g., Elliot & McGregor, 2001; Zusho et al., 2005). Harackiewicz's group (2008) showed that performance-approach goals in a single course predicted overall long-term GPA. Performance-avoidance goals, which aim to prevent revealing lack of ability (Grant & Dweck, 2003), ultimately have been found to produce a negative string of results including unproductive study methods, disorganization, anxiety, low grades, more frequent health-center visits, and the setting of more performance-avoidance goals (Elliot & McGregor, 2001; Okun et al., 2006).

Mastery-approach goals have been associated with mainly positive outcomes (Elliot & McGregor, 2001). These goals have most frequently been defined in the literature as focusing on mastering or improving on a task, learning, or understanding the material; seeking challenge; or utilizing self-improvement, progress, or deep processing standards (Pintrich, 2000a; see Hulleman et al., 2010, for a critique of the construct definitions across studies). Positive outcomes (Daniels et al., 2008; Elliot & McGregor, 2001; Elliot et al., 1999; Pekrun et al., 2006) have been found to include deep processing of material, the subsequent setting of more mastery-approach goals and fewer performance-avoidance goals, higher grades (although some have found this outcome to be moderated by students' perceptions of the social desirability and social utility of mastery goals;

Dompnier et al., 2009), fewer health-center visits, perceived success, higher well-being, and negative correlations with anxiety levels.

Mastery-avoidance goals (e.g., focusing on avoiding negative outcomes such as misunderstanding, not learning, or not mastering a task; striving to avoid doing worse than one has done before; utilizing standards of "not being wrong," or not doing something incorrectly with regard to the task at hand; see Hulleman et al., 2010; Pintrich, 2000a; Van Yperen et al., 2009) do not lead to positive results (e.g., Elliot & McGregor, 2001; Van Yperen et al.). They have been found to predict negative outcomes including disorganized studying, anticipatory test anxiety (state test anxiety, worry, and emotionality), and the subsequent choosing of more mastery-avoidance goals (see Elliot & McGregor), and have been generally negatively associated with motivational processes (Moller & Elliot, 2006). According to Hulleman et al. (2010), Elliot and colleagues (Cury et al., 2006; Elliot & McGregor, 2001; Elliot & Murayama, 2008) are the only ones to have published scales that include mastery-avoidance goals thus far, with the exception of dissertation research and unpublished conference presentations. Similarly, few researchers have yet applied the approach-avoidance framework to mastery goals, or have chosen to leave out mastery-avoidance goals altogether from their analyses (e.g., Diseth & Kobbeltvedt, 2010; Dompnier et al., 2009; Durik et al., 2009).

In an illustration of the contrasting outcomes of approach versus avoidance goals, Durik et al. (2009) used a semi-trichotomous framework (mastery-approach goals versus performance-avoidance/approach goals) to demonstrate among 214 first-semester undergraduate students that (a) performance-approach goals for college in general positively predicted overall GPAs for the subsequent two years ($p < .01$), and (b) performance-avoidance goals predicted poor performance ($p < .05$). These predictions held even when high school ability and levels of achievement motivation were controlled for. Mastery-approach goals were not found to be predictive of GPA, and mastery-avoidance goals were not mentioned.

In keeping with these subcategories, some have endorsed a "multiple-goals" model (e.g., Pintrich et al., 2003) in which students would pursue both performance-approach and mastery-approach goals. This is a refinement of the idea noted above that learning and performance goals (of the right type) together would be more beneficial than either one alone. Consistent with this concept, Diseth and Kobbeltvedt (2010) conducted a mediation analysis of achievement motives, goals, learning strategies (deep, surface, and strategic), and exam grades among 229 undergrads in Norway, and found that grades were positively correlated with both performance-approach and mastery-approach goals (though the correlation with mastery-approach goals was via strategic learning strategies), and negatively correlated with performance-avoidance goals. Furthermore, Daniels and colleagues (2008), who focused on differences between either combined or separated mastery- and performance-approach goals, showed that individuals with multiple (high mastery-approach/performance-approach), performance-approach-alone, or mastery-approach-alone goals had similar levels of achievement (measured by a single course grade and overall GPA), but students in the performance-approach-alone group reported more emotional vulnerability related to academic achievement (i.e., less enjoyment, more boredom, and more anxiety) than either the multiple-goal or mastery-approach-goal groups. Avoidance goals of either type were not measured. The results implied that for straight achievement, approach goals, regardless of type, are better than no goals. The authors suggested that for overall success, however, a multiple-goal perspective is required, as performance-approach goals seemed to undermine positive affect unless coupled with mastery goals.

## Discussion and Recommendations

Many higher-education institutions offer new students options for easing the transition to university, by way of freshman-interest groups, seminars or learning communities, service-learning programs, or opportunities for receiving formal mentorship. It is often proclaimed that these kinds of programs serve to generally heighten the student experience; however, very little hard evidence is offered for their success. Few rigorous, randomized, or controlled experimental trials have been conducted in the field to assess whether these kinds of initiatives improve even general student outcomes, let alone academic achievement (grades). The majority of those in existence have also focused on particular subgroups of at-risk students, such as particular subgroups of minority students in community college; this has made the generalization of any successful intervention results exceedingly difficult.

Thus, it is imperative that achievement-goal research continues to focus on gathering rigorous evidence for what works. As described above, there is solid experimental evidence accruing that helping students to set personal or academic goals while in school improves their academic outcomes (e.g., Morisano et al., 2010). Additional causal evidence is needed, however, and the mechanisms by which these changes occur have to be further investigated and disseminated. Most, if not all, of the studies that have honed in on the dichotomous (mastery, performance), trichotomous (mastery, performance-approach, and performance-avoidance), or 2 × 2 (mastery approach/avoidance and performance approach/avoidance) frameworks have utilized a correlational approach to highlight relationships. Measurement issues abound when studying goal definitions, goal distinctions, and the role of contextual factors, as previously discussed (see Hulleman et al., 2010; Pintrich et al., 2003).

It has also been suggested (Harackiewicz et al., 1997) that people themselves might vary in the types of goals that they adopt; for instance, students who are keenly engaged in a topic might be more likely to opt for a mastery approach to that topic, while students who have experienced academic success might have a tendency to adopt performance-type goals. Classroom and teacher approach might also influence the types of goals that students adopt. Okun and colleagues (2006) discussed the idea that the shallower type of information processing often associated with performance goals (versus mastery goals) might be better aligned with particular exam formats such as multiple-choice, due to the emphasis of these formats on rote-learning. These kinds of exams are often used for assessing knowledge in large classes. Mastery goals (associated with deeper information processing strategies such as relating, structuring, and critical thinking; Rozendaal et al., 2001) might be elicited more frequently among students if assessments required students to do more than memorize details. The relationship between goals, strategies, and classroom assessment needs further exploration.

More research is also needed on goal combinations. Are future investigators better off utilizing dichotomous, trichotomous, or 2 × 2 goal models? Beyond this, Pintrich and colleagues (2003) also posed an important question when they asked whether students tend to operate according to their one most salient goal or according to multiple goals (see Chapter 12 for a related discussion). Diseth and Kobbeltvedt (2010) recommended that practically, there might already be enough evidence to both encourage the use of both performance- and mastery-approach goals among university students, and to discourage the use of performance-avoidance goals altogether. Pintrich et al. (2003) similarly endorsed a multiple-goal approach, made within the contextual background of teachers' diverse instructional practices and classroom motivational climates.

Similarly, we need to consider how culture operates and exerts influence in achievement goal research. In this volume, Erez (see Chapter 31) discusses differences in the ways that individualistic and collectivistic cultures approach goal setting. The need for a better approach to addressing cultural considerations has been discussed in the educational goal literature as well (see Covington, 2000); there is room to grow.

As discussed in the first part of this chapter, a number of factors can contribute to substandard academic achievement. Poor goal clarity and low goals and lack of achievement motivation can pave a pathway to poor grades. Evidence-based interventions are needed to ensure that small academic failures (e.g., a D on one test) do not lead to demotivation, which can lead to even lower grades, then course failures, then probation, then in the worst of scenarios, school departure or even expulsion. The cycle of academic failure can be vicious. Irrespective of when or why an academic performance drop occurs (i.e., first, second, third year, or beyond), intervention is crucial, and teaching our students how to set goals is a simple and reasonable solution. Zimmerman and Bandura (1994) also advised that due to the interconnectedness of self-efficacy, goal-setting, and academic achievement, teachers should consider conducting diagnostic assessments of students' self-regulatory efficacy at the beginning of a course, in order to reveal any areas in which each student feels inadequate (e.g., time management) and to highlight appropriate solutions. Secondary-school teachers, classroom aids, guidance counselors, and parents should then consider promoting the setting of specific, challenging goals by students, and asking them to choose and reflect on personally important short- and long-term goals at the same time that they prepare for college, or trade school, or a career. Universities might greatly benefit from the inclusion of pre-matriculation writing assignments that ask students to clarify their personal goals (e.g., Morisano et al., 2010); professors or instructors might include writing about short- or long-term life goals as an assignment.

At every step, there is the potential for learning environments to be shaped in ways that enhance achievement. And, notwithstanding the importance of outstanding teaching and institutional support, there is an upshot to the above discussion: High academic performance coupled with positive well-being is best achieved with a combination of cognitive ability, high self-efficacy, high grade goals, good study and coping strategies, specific and challenging approach goals focused on self-set outcomes, clear feedback, and high levels of goal commitment.

## Notes

1 This chapter is based in part on the chapter "Goal Setting and Academic Achievement in College Students" written by Dominique Morisano and Edwin Locke for the 2012 *International Handbook of Academic Achievement*, edited by J. A. C. Hattie & E. M. Anderman (Routledge).

2 Performance-approach goals only; performance-avoidance goals were excluded from the review (see discussion in text).

# References

Adelman, C. (1999). *Answers in the toolbox: Academic intensity, attendance patterns, and bachelor's degree attainment.* Washington, DC: Office of Educational Research and Improvement, U.S. Department of Education.

Ames, C. (1992). Classrooms: Goals, structures, and student motivation. *Journal of Educational Psychology, 84,* 261–271.

Anderman, E. M., Austin, C. C., & Johnson, D. M. (2002). The development of goal orientation. In A. Wigfield & J. S. Eccles (Eds.), *Development of achievement motivation* (pp. 197–220). San Diego, CA: Academic Press.

Bandura, A. (1997). *Self-efficacy: The exercise of control.* New York: Freeman.

Brdar, I., Rijavec, M., & Loncaric, D. (2006). Goal orientations, coping with school failure and school achievement. *European Journal of Psychology of Education, 21*(1), 53–70.

Caprara, G. V., Fida, R., Vecchione, M., Del Bove, G., Vecchio, G. M., Barbaranelli, C., & Bandura, A. (2008). Longitudinal analysis of the role of perceived self-efficacy for self-regulated learning in academic continuance and achievement. *Journal of Educational Psychology, 100,* 525–534.

Covington, M. V. (2000). Goal theory, motivation, and school achievement: An integrative review. *Annual Review of Psychology, 51,* 171–200.

Cury, F., Elliot, A. J., Da Fonseca, D., & Moller, A. C. (2006). The social-cognitive model of achievement motivation and the 2 × 2 achievement goal framework. *Journal of Personality and Social Psychology, 90,* 666–679.

Daniels, L. M., Haynes, T. L., Stupnisky, R. H., Perry, R. P., Newall, N., & Pekrun, R. (2008). Individual differences in achievement goals: A longitudinal study of cognitive, emotional, and achievement outcomes. *Contemporary Educational Psychology, 33,* 584–608.

Diseth, A., & Kobbeltvedt, T. (2010). A mediation analysis of achievement motives, goals, learning strategies, and academic achievement. *British Journal of Educational Psychology, 80,* 671–687.

Dompnier, B., Darnon, C., & Butera, F. (2009). Faking the desire to learn: A clarification of the link between mastery goals and academic achievement. *Psychological Science, 20,* 939–943.

Durik, A. M., Lovejoy, C. M., & Johnson, S. J. (2009). A longitudinal study of achievement goals for college in general: Predicting cumulative GPA and diversity in course selection. *Contemporary Educational Psychology, 34,* 113–119.

Dweck, C. S. (1986). Motivational processes affecting learning. *American Psychologist, 41,* 1040–1048.

Dweck, C. S., & Leggett, E. L. (1988). A social-cognitive approach to motivation and personality. *Psychological Review, 95,* 256–273.

Elliot, A. J. (1999). Approach and avoidance motivation and achievement goals. *Educational Psychologist, 34,* 169–189.

Elliot, A. J., & Church, M. (1997). A hierarchical model of approach and avoidance achievement motivation. *Journal of Personality and Social Psychology, 72,* 218–232.

Elliot, A. J., & Harackiewicz, J. M. (1996). Approach and avoidance achievement goals and intrinsic motivation: A mediational analysis. *Journal of Personality and Social Psychology, 70,* 461–475.

Elliot, A. J., & McGregor, H. A. (2001). A 2×2 achievement goal framework. *Journal of Personality and Social Psychology, 80,* 501–519.

Elliot, A. J., McGregor, H. A., & Gable, S. (1999). Achievement goals, study strategies, and exam performance: A mediational analysis. *Journal of Educational Psychology, 91,* 549–563.

Elliot, A. J., & Murayama, K. (2008). On the measurement of achievement goals: Critique, illustration, and application. *Journal of Educational Psychology, 100,* 613–628.

Erez, A., & Judge, T. A. (2001). Relationship of core self-evaluations to goal setting, motivation, and performance. *Journal of Applied Psychology, 86,* 1270–1279.

Grant, H., & Dweck, C. S. (2003). Clarifying achievement goals and their impact. *Journal of Personality and Social Psychology, 85,* 541–553.

Harackiewicz, J. M., Barron, K. E., Carter, S. M., Lehto, A. T., & Elliot, A. J. (1997). Predictors and consequences of achievement goals in the college classroom: Maintaining interest and making the grade. *Journal of Personality and Social Psychology, 73,* 1284–1295.

Harackiewicz, J. M., Barron, K. E., Tauer, J. M., Carter, S. M., & Elliot, A. J. (2000). Short-term and long-term consequences of achievement goals: Predicting interest and performance over time. *Journal of Educational Psychology, 92,* 316–330.

Harackiewicz, J. M., Durik, A. M., Barron, K. E., Linnenbrink-Garcia, L., & Tauer, J. M. (2008). The role of achievement goals in the development of interest: Reciprocal relations between achievement goals, interest and performance. *Journal of Educational Psychology, 100,* 105–122.

Holahan, C. K. (1988). Relation of life goals at age 70 to activity participation and health and psychological well-being among Terman's gifted men and women. *Psychology and Aging, 3,* 286–291.

Hulleman, C. S., Schrager, S. M., Bodmann, S. M., & Harackiewicz, J. M. (2010). A meta-analytic review of achievement goal measures: Different labels for the same constructs or different constructs with similar labels? *Psychological Bulletin, 136,* 422–449.

Linnenbrink-Garcia, L., Tyson, D. E., & Patall, E. A. (2008). When are achievement goal orientations beneficial for academic achievement? A closer look at main effects and moderating factors. *International Review of Social Psychology, 21,* 19–70.

Locke, E. A., & Bryan, J. F. (1968). Grade goals as determinants of academic achievement. *Journal of General Psychology, 79,* 217–228.

Locke, E. A., & Kristof, A. L. (1996). Volitional choices in the goal achievement process. In P. M. Gollwitzer & J. A. Bargh (Eds.), *The Psychology of action: Linking cognition and motivation to behavior* (pp. 365–384). New York, NY: Guilford.

Locke, E. A., & Latham, G. P. (1990). *A theory of goal setting and task performance.* Englewood Cliffs, NJ: Prentice Hall.

Locke, E. A., & Latham, G. P. (2002). Building a practically useful theory of goal setting and task motivation: A 35-year odyssey. *American Psychologist, 57,* 705–717.

McClelland, D. C., Atkinson, J. W., Clark, R. A., & Lowell, E. L. (1976). *The achievement motive.* Oxford, England: Irvington.

Moller, A. C., & Elliot, A. J. (2006). The 2 × 2 achievement goal framework: An overview of empirical research. In A. Mittel (Ed.), *Focus on educational psychology* (pp. 307–326). New York: Nova Science.

Morisano, D., Hirsh, J. B., Peterson, J. B., Pihl, R. O., & Shore, B. M. (2010). Setting, elaborating, and reflecting on personal goals improves academic performance. *Journal of Applied Psychology, 95,* 255–264.

Nicholls, J. G. (1984). Achievement motivation: conceptions of ability, subjective experience, task choice, and performance. *Psychological Review, 91,* 328–346.

Okun, M. A., Fairholme, C., Karoly, P., Ruehlman, L. S., & Newton, C. (2006). Academic goals, goal process cognition, and exam performance among college students. *Learning and Individual Differences, 16*, 255–265.

Pajares, F. (1996). Self-efficacy beliefs in academic settings. *Review of Educational Research, 66*, 543–578.

Pascarella, E. T., & Terenzini, P. T. (2005). *How college affects students: A third decade of research.* San Francisco, CA: Jossey-Bass.

Pekrun, R., Elliot, A. J., & Maier, M. A. (2006). Achievement goals and discrete achievement emotions: A theoretical model and prospective test. *Journal of Educational Psychology, 98*, 583–597.

Pekrun, R., Elliot, A. J., & Maier, M. A. (2009). Achievement goals and achievement emotions: Testing of a model of their joint relations to academic performance. *Journal of Educational Psychology, 101*, 115–135.

Peterson, J. B., & Mar, R. A. (2004). *Goal-setting program: The ideal future.* University of Toronto, ON, Canada.

Pintrich, P. R. (2000a). An achievement goal theory perspective on issues in motivation terminology, theory, and research. *Contemporary Educational Psychology, 25*, 92–104.

Pintrich, P. R. (2000b). The role of goal orientation in self-regulated learning. In M. Boekaerts, P. R. Pintrich, & M. Zeidner (Eds.), *Handbook of self-regulation: Theory, research and applications* (pp. 451–502). San Diego, CA: Academic Press.

Pintrich, P. R., Conley, A. M., & Kempler, T. M. (2003). Current issues in achievement goal theory and research. *International Journal of Educational Research, 39*, 319–338.

Rohde, T. E., & Thompson, L. A. (2007). Predicting academic achievement with cognitive ability. *Intelligence, 35*, 83–92.

Rozendaal, J. S., Minnaert, A., & Boekaerts, M. (2001). Motivation and self-regulated learning in secondary vocational education: Information-processing type and gender differences. *Learning and Individual Differences, 13*, 273–289.

Smith, K. G., Locke, E. A., & Barry, D. (1990). Goal setting, planning and organizational performance: An experimental simulation. *Organizational Behavior and Human Decision Processes, 46*, 118–134.

Urdan, T. (1997). Achievement goal theory: Past results, future directions. In P. R. Pintrich & M. L. Maehr (Eds.), *Advances in Motivation and Achievement* (Vol. 10, pp. 99–142). Greenwich, CN: JAI.

Van Yperen, N. W., Elliot, A. J., & Anseel, F. (2009). The influence of mastery-avoidance goals on performance improvement. *European Journal of Social Psychology, 39*, 932–943.

Wood, R. E., & Locke, E. A. (1987). The relation of self-efficacy and grade goals to academic performance. *Educational and Psychological Measurement, 47*, 1013–1024.

Zimmerman, B. J., & Bandura, A. (1994). Impact of self-regulatory influences on writing course attainment. *American Educational Research Journal, 31*, 845–862.

Zusho, A., Pintrich, P. R., & Cortina, K. S. (2005). Motives, goals, and adaptive patterns of performance in Asian American and Anglo American students. *Learning and Individual Differences, 15*, 141–158.

# Part VII

# Cross Cultural Issues in Goal Setting

# 31   Cross-Cultural Issues in Goal Setting

*Miriam Erez*   Faculty of Industrial Engineering and Management,
Technion—Israel Institute of Technology

This chapter examines the effect of cultural values at the national level on individuals' perceptions of the meaning of goals, on their goal choice and goal commitment, on the relationship between goals and life satisfaction, and on the effects of different types of feedback on the goal–performance relationship. In particular, the effects of the cultural values of collectivism versus individualism, power distance, and uncertainty avoidance on goal setting and its performance outcomes will be examined.

## Culture, Goal Importance, and Goal Choice

Goals are considered to be the mechanism by which values lead to action (Latham & Pinder, 2005). Values can be seen as trans-situational goals that serve as guiding principles for goal choice (Latham & Pinder 2005). As such, values represent distal goals that influence proximal goals, which are the immediate regulators of behaviors (Kanfer, 1990).

The importance of values differs across cultures. For example, the importance of cultural values such as collectivism–individualism, power distance, uncertainty avoidance, and masculinity–femininity differ across cultures (Hofstede, 2001; House, Hanges, Javidan, Dorfman, & Gupta, 2004). Therefore, there are also differences in goal preferences. The same goal can be of high importance in one culture and of low importance in another culture. A meta-analysis conducted by Taras, Kirkman, and Steel (2010) revealed that cultural values have a stronger effect than personality traits on work-related outcomes of feedback seeking, team-related attitudes, organizational commitment, and organizational identification. Power distance has a significant negative effect on feedback seeking, which is relevant for the goal–performance relationship and a positive effect on organizational commitment, which has implications for commitment to organizational goals.

The overarching definition of culture is a shared meaning system that represents similar patterns of perceptions, basic assumptions, values, thoughts, emotions, and behaviors in response to external stimuli (Erez & Earley, 1993). These shared values and norms are transmitted from one generation to the next through the social learning processes of modeling, observation, and a person's own actions (Bandura, 1986). Societies differ in the strength of their social norms and in the strength of sanctioning, or tolerance for deviance from norms within societies (Gelfand, Niishi, & Raver, 2006). Cultures with strong norms and lack of tolerance to deviations from the norms are considered to be tight cultures, whereas loose cultures are more tolerant to deviations from the norm (Gelfand, Raver, Nishii, Leslie, Lun, Lim et al., 2011). Individuals in tight cultures tend to conform to the norms more than individuals in loose cultures.

Therefore, they are more strongly motivated by goals that are aligned with the norms than by goals that deviate from the social norms. We therefore expect a higher level of group goal commitment in tight cultures when the goal adheres to the cultural values than in loose cultures, where individuals follow their personal rather than their group goals (Gelfand et al., 2011).

A recent study on the structure of goal content across 15 countries shows a high similarity in the structure of goals across cultures (Grouzet, Kasser, Ahuvia, Dols, Kim, Lau et al., 2005). Goals were found to be universally organized according to two primary dimensions: intrinsic (e.g., self-acceptance, affiliation) versus extrinsic (e.g., financial success, image) and self-transcendent (e.g., spirituality) versus physical (e.g., hedonism, pleasure) (Grouzet et al., 2005). The similarity in the circumflex structure means that across the 15 countries, in most cases similar goals, for example, goals that represent intrinsic motivation, appear close to each other on the circumflex, and opposite to the extrinsic goals. However, there were some deviations from the universal structure of the circumflex, in particular, between wealthy and poor countries concerning the meaning of financial success. Financial success more strongly relates to hedonism, which conveys pleasure seeking in wealthy countries and to security in poor countries (Grouzet et al., 2005). Financial aspirations more closely relate to affiliation in poor rather than in wealthier countries, suggesting that in poor countries fiscal ambitions are associated with the duty to help others.

National wealth positively correlates with individualism (Hofstede, 1980, 2001). This correlation is supported by the example of China: after changing the incentive system and dismantling central control, China has been enjoying an economic boom and a growth in entrepreneurship, demonstrating that less collectivism and lower power distance enables economic growth (Keister & Zhang, 2009). It also suggests that economic growth enables individuals to be less dependent on others and more individualistic. Therefore, differences in goal choice between poor and wealthy countries can also be explained by differences in individualistic versus collectivistic values.

Most Western cultures, for example, advocate individualistic values, which emphasize individual autonomy, self-fulfillment, uniqueness, and concern for oneself over others. In contrast, most Far East and South Asian cultures emphasize the importance of collectivistic values, emphasizing social embeddedness, interdependence, and concern for the group over the self (e.g., Hofstede, 1980; Triandis, 1995; Brewer & Chen, 2007). Therefore, financial success seems to be universally important in different cultures but for different reasons that reflect the cultural values in the society (Erez & Earley, 1993; Erez, 2010). This finding supports of DeShon and Gillespie (2005)'s model, which shows that the same action goal can be activated by different higher-order goals that satisfy the self-driven goals, which conform to cultural values and norms. Financial success enhances the self-worth and well-being of collectivists via the appreciation that they receive from their in-group, and often because it involves giving to others. Yet, for individualists, financial success contributes to a person's self-worth and well-being because they fulfill their personal aspiration to be successful.

Chinese philosophy, representative of Far Eastern culture, reflects a relational mindset, which views all entities as existing within the context of one another, seeking integration, balance, and harmony, rather than distinction and comparison (Chen & Miller 2011). The Chinese relational mindset has a different worldview from the

Western mindset in that it endorses a holistic, dialectic view, as opposed to an analytic and syllogistic logic (Nisbett, Peng, Choi, & Norenzayan, 2001). This should explain why for Chinese, lack of consistency in their perceived social roles did not strongly influence their subjective well-being. In contrast, for Americans, lack of consistency in their social roles significantly correlated with low subjective well-being (Boucher, 2011). Hence, members of collectivistic cultures who view contradictions as interrelated to each other (i.e., yin & yang) may be able to hold two seemingly competing goals without having a negative impact on their subjective well-being.

Individuals strive to maintain a positive self-view, and to experience a sense of self-worth and well-being (Bandura, 2001). Yet, the meaning of a positive self-view depends on cultural values and hence differs when serving the independent versus the interdependent self, or the relational versus the personal self or the collective self (Brewer & Gardner, 1996; Kitayama, Markus, Matsumoto, & Norasakkunkit, 1997). Such differences in cultural values and in self-construal—the independent and the interdependent self—explain differences in preferences for influence goals as opposed to adjustment goals (Tsai, Sepalla, Miao, Seppala, Fung, & Yeung, 2007). Influence goals denote asserting the self and changing others. Adjustment goals denote suppressing the self and conforming to others. Indeed, four studies reveal that Euro-Americans value influence goals more than adjustment goals. Furthermore, they value a high arousal positive state, which accompanies the goals of asserting the self and changing others, more than the low arousal positive state, which accompanies the goal of suppressing the self and conforming to others. The opposite effect was shown for individuals from Hong Kong (Tsai et al., 2007). Yet, results also showed that when the situation required the dominance of influence goals, both Euro-Americans and members of Far East cultures valued high arousal more than low arousal.

Oishi and Diener (2001) examined the role of independent goal pursuit for fun and enjoyment and interdependent goal pursuit to make friends and family happy, in the subjective well-being of Asian and Euro-American college students. They found that the two groups expressed similar levels of goal pursuits for fun and enjoyment, and for making their family and friends happy. Furthermore, the degree of goal progress over time was similar to both groups, and goal progress was significantly related to the subjective well-being of both groups. Yet, there were significant differences between Euro-Americans and Asian Americans regarding the goals that contributed to their subjective well-being. Independent goal pursuit, aimed at satisfying personal desires for fun and enjoyment, increased the benefit of goal attainment on subjective well-being among Euro-Americans but not among Asian Americans. In contrast, interdependent goal pursuit, aimed to satisfy the needs of the in-group, to please parents and friends, increased the benefit of goal attainment on the subjective well-being of Asian Americans, but not of Euro-Americans. Similar findings were obtained for Japanese. These findings reveal that independent and interdependent goal pursuits result in different effects on subjective well-being across cultures. The difference between Euro-Americans and AsianAmericans suggests that even when Asian Americans become similar to Euro-Americans in their level of expression of independent or interdependent goal pursuits, they are also influenced by their cultural heritage. Interdependent goal pursuit that is consistent with their collectivistic cultural heritage positively influenced the subjective well-being of Asian Americans, whereas independent goal pursuit did not influence their subjective well-being.

Culture influences the regulatory focus of promotion versus prevention (Elliot, Chirkov, Kim, & Sheldon, 2001; Förster, Higgins, & Taylor-Bianco, 2003). Individuals in collectivistic cultures, such as Korea and Russia, were driven by prevention goals more than Americans (Elliot et al., 2001). Furthermore, priming the self as independent resulted in being more persuaded by promotion statements, whereas priming the self as interdependent resulted in being more persuaded by prevention statements (Aaker & Lee, 2001). Setting prevention goals of avoiding errors motivates individuals with a prevention focus, whereas setting promotion goals of "go get it" motivates individuals with a promotion focus. Thus, collectivists reach higher performance levels in the face of prevention goals, whereas individualists reach higher performance levels in the face of promotion goals.

The effect of collectivism on goal choice and goal pursuit can also be seen at the individual level, indicating within-culture variation. Psychological collectivism at the individual level, consisting of preference, reliance, and concern for in-groups; acceptance of in-group norms; and prioritization of in-group goals, were found to predict group members' performance. Results showed that collectivistic members performed their group tasks better, demonstrated more citizenship behaviors, and were less engaged in counter-productive or withdrawal behaviors (Jackson, Colquitt, Wesson, & Zapata-Phelan, 2006).

## Goal Difficulty

The meaning of goal difficulty to a person's sense of self-worth and well-being varies across cultures. Specific, difficult goals motivate people in Western, individualistic societies to exert effort and be persistent until goals are accomplished (Locke & Latham, 2002). Difficult goals catalyze a differentiation between the minority who reach the difficult goal and the majority who do not. Challenging goals serve as a strong motivator for Westerners, because they offer an opportunity to distinguish oneself from others. This is not the case in collectivistic countries, where people define themselves in relational terms and as being part of a collective. In these cultures, individuals prefer moderate goals that do not differentiate themselves from others and attenuate the risk of failing the group they represent (Kurman, 2001). However, once the goals are set in line with the preference, they motivate individuals to reach the goal, whether it is a moderate or difficult goal. This has implications for persistence in face of failure. Individuals who believe that effort influences performance continue to exert effort even in face of failure in order to reach the goal (Hong, Chiu, Dweck, Lin, & Wan, 1999).

## Goal Specificity

Goal specificity increases clarity, reduces misinterpretation of the goal, and improves performance. Goal specificity is more important in tight rather than loose cultures (Gelfand et al., 2011). Tightness–looseness correlates with collectivism/individualism and with power distance. There is more tolerance for deviation from the norms in individualistic and low-power-distance cultures, as in most Western cultures (i.e., the United States, Australia, New Zealand, The Netherlands, Israel), than in collectivistic and high-power-distance cultures, where there is low tolerance for deviation from the norm (i.e., Korea, China, India, Malaysia, and Singapore).

Goal specificity is of particular importance in the context of culturally diverse work teams. In this context, clear goals will enable the culturally diverse team members to interpret goals in a similar way. However, when goals are not specific and clear, cultural values and norms will serve as criteria for interpreting the goals, causing inconsistency across team members in their goal understanding and consequently will harm performance (Erez & Nouri, 2010). Hence, clear and specific team performance goals, can override cultural variation.

## Goal Assignment: Assigned versus Participative Goals

Very little research has been done on assigned versus participatively set goals in relation to culture. Erez and Earley (1987) demonstrated that participatively set goals by group members had a positive effect on performance in low-power-distance cultures such as the United States and Israel. Yet, while assigned goals had a similar effect on participation in the United States, they had a negative effect on the performance of Israelis, who represent low power distance but moderate collectivistic values. For Israelis, goal commitment was significantly higher under participation than no participation and, consequently, they performed better when allowed to participate in setting the goal. Furthermore, a within-country variance in collectivistic values of three sectors—kibbutz, public (the general federation of labor), and private—explained the effectiveness of three goal setting strategies: assigned, participation by representation, and group participation. In the private sector, the most effective strategy was assigned goals; in the public sector, participation by representation; and in the kibbutz, group participation (Erez, 1986). A series of studies by Latham, Erez, and Locke (1988) showed that for Americans, goal commitment was similar under participative goals and "tell-and-sell" assigned goals, but it was significantly lower under "tell"-style assigned goals. Furthermore, Erez and Somech (1996) demonstrated that differences in collectivistic values between subcultures consisting of individuals who are members of the kibbutz, which is highly collectivistic, and ones who live in a more individualistic urban setting, had implications for social loafing. In the absence of specific goals, social loafing occurred for individualists in the urban setting, who were less committed to the group task performance. Yet, social loafing did not occur for kibbutz members who were more highly committed to the group task performance. However, this social loafing effect disappeared in the presence of specific, difficult group goals in both subcultures. A more recent study was conducted on a heterogeneous sample consisting of Australians, Singaporeans, and Malaysians who differed in their level of power distance, with a lower power distance for Australians than for the two other groups. The results showed that participative goals had a significantly stronger effect on goal commitment and on performance than assigned goals for individuals with low rather than high power distance (Sue-Chan & Ong, 2002).

## Feedback on Performance

The effect of feedback on performance has different implications in collectivistic, high-power-distance cultures as compared with individualistic, low-power-distance cultures. In low-power-distance cultures such as the United States, positive feedback resulted in upward goal revision, whereas negative feedback resulted in downward goal revision. Similarly, internal attribution resulted in upward goal revision, but external attribution resulted in downward goal revision over time. Self-efficacy mediated the effect of feedback and attribution on goal revision (see Chapters 4, 5, and 10 for more details). Furthermore, internal attribution was associated with self-efficacy following success, but decreased self-efficacy following failure (Tolli & Schmidt, 2008). For individualists, personal feedback self-directs individuals toward goal accomplishment. For example, employees in Germany and the Netherlands, two individualistic cultures, better attained companies' goals in an organizational culture that enabled open discussions of errors and treatment of errors than when no such culture existed (van Dyck, Frese, Baer, & Sonnentag, 2005). The effectiveness of individual versus collective feedback depends on the cultural values of the recipients (Van de Vliert, She, Sanders Wang, & Huang, 2004). The organizational design in collectivistic cultures is built on teamwork. For this reason, collectivists are more open to accepting feedback on collective performance than on individual performance (Van de Vliert, Shi, Sanders, Wang, & Huang, 2004). In contrast, individual feedback seeking is higher in individualistic, low-power-distance cultures such as the United States than in collectivistic, high-power-distance cultures such as Hong Kong (Morrison, Chen, & Salgado, 2004).

Members of collectivistic and high-power-distance cultures, more than members from individualist and low-power-distance cultures, seek feedback from peers rather than from superiors, because they feel uncomfortable about approaching their superiors. They also seek more feedback from peers than from subordinates, because they do not expect their subordinates to criticize their boss (Luque & Sommer, 2000; Taras, Kirkman, & Steel, 2010).

Collectivists and individualists differ in their response to negative feedback. Collectivists are more open to recognizing negative feedback than individualists (Heine, Kitayama, Lehman, Takata, Leung, & Matsumoto, 2001). Canadians, for example, unlike Japanese, discounted the task they performed when receiving negative feedback. Furthermore, they continued to rank themselves high on positive personal characteristics, regardless of whether their performance feedback was positive or negative. In contrast, Japanese were more responsive to the negative feedback and attempted to improve their performance (Heine et al., 2001). Similar findings were shown by Zhang and Cross (2011), who found that Euro-Americans were less persistent on a task in face of receiving negative feedback on performance (but see Chapters 5 and 10). In contrast, East Asians were found to be more persistent on a task after negative than positive feedback (Zhang & Cross, 2011). Furthermore, Euro-American remembered success experiences more than failure experiences, whereas East Asians remembered positive and negative experiences at the same rate. Far East participants, more than Euro-Americans, interpreted success events, as bringing more pride to their significant others, including their families. Moreover, Americans reported a higher level of self-esteem in response to success than Far Easterners. Americans had a propensity to interpret a negative event as intolerable and as unfair more than did Chinese individuals (Zhang & Cross, 2011). Finally, Americans were more willing to try again after success than Chinese, whereas the Chinese were more willing to try again after failure than Americans. These differences can be explained by differences in the regular focus between collectivists and individualists, with the formers being more regulated by a prevention focus, whereas the latter regulate behaviors by a promotion focus (Elliott et al., 2001). Furthermore, differences in goal orientations across cultures also explain cultural variation in response to positive versus negative feedback as shown below (Lee, Tinsley, & Bobko, 2003).

## Performance versus Learning Goal Orientation

Dweck and Leggett (1988) distinguished between a learning goal orientation—the belief that a person aims to gain mastery of knowledge, skills, and behaviors that improve over time—and a performance goal orientation—the belief that a person has a fixed level of ability that determines performance. A comparison between Hong Kong and the United States revealed that the distinction between performance and learning goal orientation as two independent factors is a characteristic of Western culture (VandeWalle, Cron, & Slocum, 2001). In contrast, in Hong Kong, the two goal orientations positively relate to each other, meaning that Hong Kong people had difficulties differentiating between these two goal orientations. Indeed, Confucianism strongly stresses learning as the most important value (Lee et al., 2003), which also explains the high importance given to effort, rather than to a fixed level of ability.

Persistence in goal striving after failure depends on whether failure is attributed to ability or to effort (Chapter 4). Research has demonstrated that Hong Kong students attributed failure to effort more than to ability, as compared to Americans (Chang, Arkin, Leong, Chan, & Leung, 2004; Yan & Gaier, 1994), and they took more remedial actions than students who attributed failure to ability (Hong et al., 1999).

## Goals and Cultural Adaptation

Goals play an important role in facilitating cultural adaptation (Earley & Ang, 2003; Ang, Van Dyne, Koh, Ng, Templer, Tay, & Chandrasekar, 2007). Gong and Chang (2007) demonstrated that sojourning students who set for themselves an academic goal earned higher grades than others. In addition, sojourners who set themselves social interaction goals were better adjusted than others. Furthermore, goal orientation also influenced expatriates' adjustment to foreign countries. Learning goal orientation and proving goal orientation facilitated work adjustment and interpersonal adjustment, whereas avoidance goal orientation resulted in premature return intentions (Wang & Takeuchi, 2007). These last studies suggest that goals play an important role in adaptation to the global context, which is culturally diverse and geographically dispersed. Indeed, the motivation to adjust explained the success of expatriates adaptation to their host culture (Chen, Kirkman Kim, Farh, & Tangirala, 2010).

## Discussion

The goal setting theory of motivation focuses on the goal–performance relationship (Locke & Latham, 1990). The theory proposes that specific, difficult goals yield high performance levels. This seems to be universal given the boundary conditions of feedback, goal commitment, and task complexity, which also seem to be universal (Locke & Latham, 2002). Even the structure of goals along the two dimensions of intrinsic versus extrinsic motivation, and self-transcendence versus physical, has been shown to be universal (Chang et al., 2004; Grouzet et al., 2005). However, higher-order goals that pertain to the self seem to differ across cultures, because the value criteria that serve to evaluate the contribution of goal attainment to a person's self-worth and well-being vary across cultures. Different values serve for evaluating the contribution of specific and difficult personal goals to a person's self-worth and well-being than the values that serve to evaluate the contribution of moderately difficult group goals to the self. These differences are embedded in their self-construal: the independent or the personal self, versus the interdependent or the relational self, which are shaped by different cultural values (Chen & Miller, 2011; Diener & Oishi, 2001). Therefore, culture serves to answer the question of why people in collectivistic cultures may choose different goals than people in individualistic cultures, and why the same goal is some-time chosen, but for different reasons, by people in different cultures. Cultural values explain why individual feedback is more highly preferred in individualistic than collectivistic cultures (Luque & Sommer, 2000; Tarras et al., 2010). They explain why individuals in collectivistic cultures prefer to use implicit feedback: to avoid losing face, maintain good interpersonal relationship, and preserve group harmony.

The value of collectivism versus individualism explains most of the cross-cultural variance. Yet, other values may also be relevant for understanding the effect of goals on performance, such as power distance and uncertainty avoidance. Power distance explains why participatively set goals enhance goal commitment and performance in low- rather than high-power-distance cultures (Erez & Earley, 1993; Sue-Chan & Ong 2002). Uncertainty avoidance explains why specific goals are more highly valued in low- rather than high-uncertainty-avoidance cultures and why loose cultures that allow deviations from the norm generate more creativity than tight cultures (Gelfand et al., 2006). Future research should further examine the influence of uncertainty avoidance and tightness–looseness on the effect of specific versus do-your-best goals on performance and on creativity.

Finally, in a global work environment that is culturally diverse and geographically dispersed, other goal dimensions such as shared goals are likely to be relevant for understanding the goal–performance relationship. Individuals working in a culturally diverse global context may more easily agree on action plan goals than on goals that activate their culturally diverse selves. Therefore, goal setting theory, which activates action plan goals, has important implications for motivating global employees, who have to overcome cultural and geographical distances.

## References

Aaker, J., & Lee, A. (2001). I seek pleasures, we avoid pains: the role of self regulatory goals in information processing of persuasion. *Journal of Consumer Research*, *28*, 33–49.

Ang, S., Van Dyne, L., Koh, C. K. S, Ng, K. Y., Templer, K. J., Tay, C., & Chandrasekar, N. A. (2007). Cultural intelligence: Its measurement and effects on cultural judgment and decision making, cultural adaptation and task performance. *Management and Organization Review, 3*(3), 335–371.

Bandura, A. (2001). Social cognitive theory: An agentic perspective. *Annual Review of Psychology, 52*(1), 1–26.

Bandura, A. (1986). *Social foundations of thought and action: A social cognitive theory.* Englewood Cliffs, NJ: Prentice-Hall.

Boucher, H. C. (2011). The dialectic self-concept II: Cross-role and within-role consistency, well-being, self-certainty and authenticity. *Journal of Cross-Cultural Psychology, 42*(7), 1251–1271.

Brewer, M. B., & Chen, Y. R. (2007). Where (who) are collectives in collectivism? toward conceptual clarification of individualism and collectivism. *Psychological Review, 114*(1), 133–151.

Brewer, M. B., & Gardner, W. (1996). Who is this "we"? levels of collective identity and self representations. *Journal of Personality and Social Psychology, 71*(1), 83–93.

Chang, L. C., Arkin, R. M., Leong, F. T., Chan, D. K. S., & Leung, K. (2004). Subjective overachievement in American and Chinese college students. *Journal of Cross-Cultural Psychology, 35*(2), 152–173.

Chen, G., Kirkman, B. L., Kim, K., Farh, C. I. C., & Tangirala, S. (2010). When does cross-cultural motivation enhance expatriate effectiveness? A multilevel investigation of the moderating roles of subsidiary support and cultural distance. *The Academy of Management Journal (AMJ), 53*(5), 1110–1130.

Chen, M. J., & Miller, D. (2011). The relational perspective as a business mindset. *The Academy of Management Perspectives, 25,* 6–18.

DeShon, R. P., & Gillespie, J. Z. (2005). A motivated action theory account of goal orientation. *Journal of Applied Psychology, 90*(6), 1096–1127.

Diener, E., & Oishi, S. (2001). Goals, culture, and subjective well-being. *Personality and Social Psychology Bulletin, 27*(12), 1674–1679.

Dweck, C. S., & Leggett, E. L. (1988). A social-cognitive approach to motivation and personality. *Psychological Review, 95*(2), 256–273.

Earley, P. C., & Ang, S. (2003). *Cultural intelligence: Individual interactions across cultures.* CA: Stanford Business Books.

Elliot, A. J., Chirkov, V., Kim, Y., & Sheldon, K. M. (2001). A cross-cultural analysis of avoidance (relative to approach) personal goals. *Psychological Science, 12,* 505–510.

Erez, M. (1977). Feedback: A necessary condition for the goal setting - performance relationships. *Journal of Applied Psychology, 62,* 624–627.

Erez, M. (1986). The congruence of goal-setting strategies with socio-cultural values, and its effect on performance. *Journal of Management, 12,* 83–90.

Erez, M. (2010). Cross cultural and global issues in organizational psychology. In S. Zedeck. (Ed.), *Handbook of industrial and organizational psychology,* V13, 1138–54. Washington, D.C.: The American Psychological Association.

Erez, M., & Earley, P. C. (1993). *Culture, self-identity and work.* New York: Oxford University Press.

Erez, M., & Earley, P. C. (1987). Comparative analysis of goal-setting strategies across cultures. *Journal of Applied Psychology, 72*(4), 658–665.

Erez, M., & Nouri, R. (2010). Creativity: The influence of cultural, social, and work contexts. *Management and Organization Review, 6*(3), 351–370.

Erez, M., & Somech, A. (1996). Is group productivity loss the rule or the exception? effects of culture and group-based motivation. *The Academy of Management Journal, 39*(6), 1513–1537.

Förster, J., Higgins, E. T., & Taylor-Bianco, A. (2003). Speed/accuracy in task performance: Build-in trade-off or separate strategic concerns? *Organizational Behavior and Human Decision Processes, 90(1),* 148–164.

Gelfand, M. J., Nishii, L. H., & Raver, J. L. (2006). On the nature and importance of cultural tightness-looseness. *Journal of Applied Psychology, 91*(6), 1225–1244.

Gelfand, M. J., Raver, J. L., Nishii, L., Leslie, L. M., Lun, J., Lim, B. C. et al. (2011). Differences between tight and loose cultures: A 33-nation study. *Science, 332*(6033), 1100–1104.

Gong, Y., & Chang, S. (2007). The relationships of cross-cultural adjustment with dispositional learning orientation and goal setting: A longitudinal analysis. *Journal of Cross-Cultural Psychology, 38,* 19–25.

Grouzet, F. M. E., Kasser, T., Ahuvia, A., Dols, J. M. F., Kim, Y., Lau, S. et al. (2005). The structure of goal contents across 15 cultures. *Journal of Personality and Social Psychology, 89,* 800–816.

Heine, S. J., Kitayama, S., Lehman, D. R., Takata, T., Ide, E., Leung, C., & Matsumoto, H. (2001). Divergent consequences of success and failure in Japan and North America: An investigation of self-improving motivations and malleable selves. *Journal of Personality and Social Psychology, 81*(4), 599–615.

Hofstede, G. (2001). *Culture's consequences: Comparing values, behaviors, institutions and organizations across nations.* Thousand Oaks, CA: Sage.

Hofstede, G. (1980). *Culture's consequences: International differences in work-related values.* Newbury Park, CA: Sage.

Hong, Y-Y., Chiu, C. Y., Dweck, C. S., Lin, D. M.-S., & Wan, D. (1999). Implicit theories, attributions, and coping: A meaning system approach. *Journal of Personality and Social Psychology, 77*(3), 588–599.

House, R. J., Hanges, P. J., Javidan, M., Dorfman, P. W., & Gupta, V. (Eds.) (2004). *Culture, leadership, and organizations: The GLOBE study of 62 societies.* Thousand Oaks, CA: Sage.

Jackson, C. L., Colquitt, J. A., Wesson, M. J., & Zapata-Phelan, C. P. (2006). Psychological collectivism: A measurement validation and linkage to group member performance. *Journal of Applied Psychology, 91*(4), 884–899.

Kanfer, R. (1990). Motivation theory and industrial and organizational psychology. In M. D. Dunnette, & L. M. Hough (Eds.), *Handbook of industrial and organizational psychology* (2nd ed., pp. 75–170). Palo Alto, CA: Consulting Psychologists Press.

Keister, L. A., & Zhang, Y. (2009). Organization and management in China. *Academy of Management Annals, 3* (1), 377–420.

Kitayama, S., Markus, H. R., Matsumoto, H., & Norasakkunkit, V. (1997). Individual and collective processes in the construction of the self: Self-enhancement in the United States and self-criticism in Japan. *Journal of Personality and Social Psychology, 72,* 1245–1267.

Kurman, J. (2001). Self-regulation strategies in achievement settings. *Journal of Cross-Cultural Psychology, 32,* 491–503.

Latham, G. P., Erez, M., & Locke, E. A. (1988). Resolving scientific disputes by the joint design of crucial experiments by the antagonists: Application to the Erez–Latham dispute regarding participation in goal setting. *Journal of Applied Psychology, 73*(4), 753–772.

Latham, G. P., & Pinder, C. C. (2005). Work motivation theory and research at the dawn of the twenty-first century. *Annual Review of Psychology, 56,* 485–516.

Lee, C., Tinsley, C., & Bobko, P. (2003). Cross-cultural variance in goal orientations and their effects. *Applied Psychology, 52*, 272–297.

Locke, E. A., & Latham, G. P. (1990). A theory of goal—setting and task performance. New York: Prentice-Hall.

Locke, E. A., & Latham, G. P. (2002). Building a practically useful theory of goal setting and task motivation: A 35-year odyssey. *American Psychologist, 57*, 705–717.

Luque, M. F. S. D., & Sommer, S. M. (2000). The impact of culture on feedback-seeking behavior: An integrated model and propositions. *The Academy of Management Review, 25*, 829–849.

Morrison, E. W., Chen, Y., & Salgado, S. R. (2004). Cultural differences in newcomer feedback seeking: A comparison of the United States and Hong Kong. *Applied Psychology, 53*, 1–22.

Nisbett, R. E., Peng, K., Choi, I., & Norenzayan, A. (2001). Culture and systems of thought: Holistic vs. analytic cognition. *Psychological Review, 108*, 291–310.

Oishi, S., & Diener, E. (2001). Goals, culture, and subjective well-being. *Personality and Social Psychology Bulletin, 27*, 1674–1682.

Sue-Chan, C., & Ong, M. (2002). Goal assignment and performance: Assessing the mediating roles of goal commitment and self-efficacy and the moderating role of power distance. *Organizational Behavior and Human Decision Processes, 89*, 1140–1161.

Taras, V., Kirkman, B. L., & Steel, P. (2010). Examining the impact of culture's consequences: A three-decade, multilevel, meta-analytic review of Hofstede's cultural value dimensions. *Journal of Applied Psychology, 95*, 405–439.

Tolli, A. P., & Schmidt, A. M. (2008). The role of feedback, causal attributions, and self-efficacy in goal revision. *Journal of Applied Psychology, 93*, 692–701.

Triandis, H. C. (1995). *Individualism and collectivism.* Boulder, CO: Westview Press.

Tsai, J. L., Miao, F. F., Seppala, E., Fung, H. H., & Yeung, D. Y. (2007). Influence and adjustment goals: Sources of cultural differences in ideal affect. *Journal of Personality and Social Psychology, 92*, 1102–1117.

Van de Vliert, E., Shi, K., Sanders, K., Wang, Y., & Huang, X. (2004). Chinese and Dutch Interpretations of supervisory feedback. *Journal of Cross-Cultural Psychology, 35*, 417–434.

VandeWalle, D., Cron., W. L., & Slocum, J. W. (2001). The role of goal orientation following performance feedback. *Journal of Applied Psychology, 86*, 629–640.

Van Dyck, C., Frese, M., Baer, M., & Sonnentag, S. (2005). Organizational error management culture and its impact on performance: A two-study replication. *Journal of Applied Psychology, 90*, 1228–1240.

Wang, M., & Takeuchi, R. (2007). The role of goal orientation during expatriation: A cross sectional longitudinal investigation. *Journal of Applied Psychology, 92*(5), 1437–1445.

Yan, W., & Gaier E. L. (1994). Causal Attribution for college success and failure. An Asian-American comparison. *Journal of Cross Cultural Psychology, 25*, 146–158.

Zhang, M., & Cross, S. E. (2011). Emotions in memories of success and failure: A cultural perspective. *Emotion, 11*, 866–880.

# Part VIII

# Goals and the Subconscious

# 32 Regulating Goal Pursuit Through Mental Contrasting with Implementation Intentions

*Gabriele Oettingen*  Psychology Department New York University
and University of Hamburg

*Marion Wittchen*  Psychology Department New York University

*Peter M. Gollwitzer*  Psychology Department New York University
and University of Konstanz

Research on goals has employed a variety of approaches (Bargh, Gollwitzer, & Oettingen, 2010). Some approaches focus on the determinants of goal content and goal structure (e.g., the determinants of setting specific, challenging goals), whereas others investigate the consequences that the adoption of goals with certain content or structure has for goal striving and goal attainment. Still other approaches investigate which contextual variables affect the selection of certain types of goals and their subsequent implementation (e.g., affective states, competing action tendencies, power positions). More recent research analyzes how people promote goal pursuit by engaging in self-regulation strategies. Here, goal pursuit is said to consist of two different subsequent tasks (Oettingen & Gollwitzer, 2001): first, firmly committing to certain goals, and second, effectively implementing them. For each of these tasks, different self-regulation strategies have been found to be effective. Mental contrasting of a desired future with obstacles of present reality (Oettingen, 2000, 2012; Oettingen, Pak, & Schnetter, 2001) was identified as an effective self-regulation strategy for wisely pursuing goals, that is, committing and actively striving for goals. We define wise goal pursuit as strong commitment to and striving for goals that are perceived as feasible (high expectations of success) and abstinence or disengagement from goals that are perceived as unfeasible (low expectations of success; Oettingen, 2012). Forming implementation intentions (Gollwitzer, 1999; Gollwitzer & Sheeran, 2006) has turned out to be a self-regulation strategy of effective goal attainment as it helps planning out in advance the various challenges that arise during goal pursuit.

In the present chapter, we discuss research showing how the self-regulation strategies of mental contrasting and forming implementation intentions unfold their effects across various life domains, and we point to implications of the findings for facilitating goal pursuit in the context of organizations. We start with a review of research on the effects and processes of mental contrasting and implementation intentions in individuals. We then describe how the two strategies complement each other in facilitating wise goal pursuit, and point out how they may foster goal attainment in organizations beyond the effects of formulating challenging, specific goals. Finally, we exemplify the contributions of the combined strategy of mental contrasting with implementation intentions (MCII) for managerial leadership in two domains: self-leadership and health management.

## Regulating Goal Pursuit

According to classic approaches, effective self-regulation involves the basic subfunctions of self-monitoring, self-evaluation, and self-reaction (Bandura, 1991). While self-monitoring refers to accurately, consistently, and frequently collecting valid information about one's progress toward a goal (e.g., by using diary methods or by requesting regular peer feedback), self-evaluation refers to evaluating the information about one's progress using personal or social standards. Finally, intentional self-reactions in terms of self-rewards (e.g., a coffee break after completing a difficult problem) or unintentional self-reactions (e.g., emotions such as pride/embarrassment after success/failure) further promote goal attainment. While self-monitoring, self-evaluation, and self-reactions are trainable through mid-term to long-term interventions (e.g., Frayne & Latham, 1987), recent research demonstrates that goal pursuit can be improved almost instantly through the introduction of self-regulation strategies in terms of mental contrasting, implementation intentions, and a combination of both strategies.

### The Self-Regulation Strategy of Mental Contrasting

The model of fantasy realization (Oettingen, 2000, 2012; Oettingen et al, 2001) proposes that mentally contrasting a desired future with the reality that impedes its realization will create selective, that is, expectancy-dependent goal commitments with subsequent goal striving and goal attainment. Specifically, in mental contrasting, people imagine the attainment of a desired future (e.g., becoming a clinical psychologist; giving a great talk) and then reflect on the present reality that stands in the way of attaining the desired future (e.g., the GRE exam yet to be taken; evaluation anxiety). When expectations (perceived chances) of success are high, people will actively commit to and strive toward reaching the desired future; when expectations of success are low, people will refrain from doing so.

The model of fantasy realization specifies two other ways of thinking about the future, both of which fail to produce expectancy-dependent goal pursuit (commitment and goal striving; for a review of the determinants and consequences of goal commitment, see Chapter 6). People may either solely envision the attainment of the wished-for future (i.e., indulging) or solely reflect on the impeding reality (i.e., dwelling). The level of goal commitment and subsequent goal striving is determined by the a priori commitment that the person has with respect to attaining the desired future. In other words, it is only mental contrasting, but not indulging and dwelling, that succeeds in strengthening goal pursuit when expectations of success are high, and in weakening it when expectations of success are low. Indulging and dwelling should thus protect a person's resources less than mental contrasting; the former strategies lead to a medium level of engagement even when no engagement (in the case of low expectations of success) or full engagement (in the case of high expectations of success) would be the resource-efficient way to act.

*Empirical evidence.* A multitude of studies have tested the effects of mental contrasting versus indulging and dwelling on goal commitment and goal striving (Oettingen, 2000; Oettingen, Hönig, & Gollwitzer, 2000; Oettingen, Mayer, Thorpe, Janetzke, & Lorenz, 2005; Oettingen et al., 2001; summary by Oettingen, 2012). For example, in one study, freshmen enrolled in a vocational school for computer programming (Oettingen et al., 2001, Study 4) first indicated their expectations of excelling in mathematics. Then they named aspects that they associated with excelling in mathematics (participants named, e.g., feelings of pride, increasing job prospects) and aspects of present reality that may hinder such excelling (participants named, e.g., being distracted by peers, feeling lazy). Subsequently, three experimental conditions were established: In the mental contrasting condition, participants had to elaborate in writing two aspects of the desired future and two aspects of present reality, in alternating order, beginning with an aspect of the desired future. Participants in the indulging condition were asked to mentally elaborate four aspects of the desired future; in the dwelling condition, they instead elaborated on four aspects of present reality. As a dependent variable, participants indicated how energized they felt with respect to excelling in mathematics (e.g., how active, eventful, energetic). Two weeks after the experiment, participants' teachers reported how much effort each student had invested for the last two weeks and provided each student with a grade for that time period. As predicted, only in the mental contrasting condition did the students feel energized, exert effort, and earn grades in line with their expectations of success: Participants in the mental contrasting condition with high expectations of success felt the most energized, invested the most effort, and received the highest grades. Conversely, participants in the mental contrasting condition with low expectations of success felt the least energized, invested the least effort, and received the lowest course grades. Participants in the indulging and dwelling conditions felt moderately energized, exerted moderate effort, and received moderate grades independent of their expectations of success.

A variety of studies covering different life domains replicated these results. For example, experiments pertained to studying abroad (Oettingen et al., 2001, Study 2), acquiring a second language (Oettingen et al., 2000, Study 1), getting to know an attractive stranger (Oettingen, 2000, Study 1), finding a balance between work and family life (Oettingen, 2000, Study 2), reducing cigarette consumption (Oettingen, Mayer, & Thorpe, 2010), and idiosyncratic interpersonal wishes of great importance (e.g., establishing a good relationship with one's mother; Oettingen et al., 2001, Studies 1 and 3). Further, strength of goal pursuit was assessed by cognitive (e.g., making plans), affective (e.g., feeling responsible for the wished-for ending), motivational (e.g., feelings of energization), and behavioral indicators (e.g., invested effort and achievements). Indicators were measured via self-report or observations and either directly after the experiment or weeks later. In all of these studies, the same pattern of results emerged: Given high expectations of success, participants in the mental contrasting group showed the strongest goal commitment and goal striving; given low expectations, people showed the least goal commitment and goal striving. Participants who indulged in a desired future or dwelled on present reality showed moderate goal pursuit independent of their expectations of success. In sum, it was only mental contrasting that regulated goal pursuit in a way that protects a person's resources: high investment in goals where attainment is likely, and low or no investment where attainment is unlikely.

It is important to mention that the effects of mental contrasting depend on perceiving the present reality as standing in the way of the desired future. When engaging in mental contrasting, individuals first elaborate a desired future, establishing the positive future as their reference point, and only thereafter elaborate the present reality, thereby potentially perceiving the reality as an obstacle standing in the way of attaining the future. Reversing this order (i.e., reverse contrasting), by first elaborating the present reality followed by elaboration of the desired future, thwarts the expectancy-dependent construal of the present reality as standing in the way of the future and thus fails to elicit goal commitments congruent with high expectations of success (e.g., Oettingen et al., 2001, Study 3).

*Mediators of mental contrasting effects.* Locke and Latham (2002) identify *feelings of energization* as paramount to promoting goal-directed behavior. They contend that commitment to realizing a desired future is linked to an "energizing function" (i.e., activity incitement; Brunstein & Gollwitzer, 1996; subjective vitality; Ryan & Frederick, 1997). Thus, energization may qualify as a mediator of the effects of mental contrasting on expectation-dependent goal commitment and goal striving (Oettingen et al., 2009, Studies 1 and 2). This mediation hypothesis was tested in a study using an acute stress paradigm (i.e., videotaped public speaking), where goal pursuit was measured by the quantity and quality of performance in the laboratory. Economics students participating in this study were informed that they were to deliver a speech in front of a video camera to help with the development of a measure of professional skills for a human resource department. Participants were randomly assigned to either a mental contrasting or an indulging condition. As dependent variables, participants indicated their initial feelings of energization by a self-report measure (e.g., how energized do you feel when you think about giving your talk). To assess participants' subjective performance, we asked them to rate their actual performance; persistence was measured by the length of each participant's presentation, and objective performance by independent raters evaluating the quality of the videotaped presentations (Oettingen et al., 2009, Study 2).

Consistent with previous mental contrasting studies, individuals in the mental contrasting condition, but not those in the indulging condition, evidenced a strong link between expectations of success and successful performance as measured by subjective self-evaluations of task performance and objective ratings of the videotaped presentations. Moreover, feelings of energization showed the same pattern of results as these performance variables. Additionally, when considering the mental contrasting condition by itself, the relationship between expectations of success and performance was fully mediated by feelings of energization. Physiological data as measured by systolic blood pressure also showed the just-described pattern of results (Oettingen et al., 2009, Study 1). Cardiovascular responses, such as systolic blood pressure, are considered reliable indicators of effort mobilization (i.e., energization; Gendolla & Wright, 2005; Wright & Kirby, 2001).

As to potential cognitive mediators of mental contrasting effects, changes in perceived feasibility (expectation) and desirability (incentive value) were never found to be affected by mental contrasting (summary by Oettingen, 2012). Rather, mental contrasting was observed to produce changes in implicit cognition, which in turn strengthened goal pursuit. For instance, mental contrasting of a desired and feasible future with an obstacle of present reality strengthened the mental association between the desired future (e.g., obtaining a good grade in an impending exam) and the respective obstacle (e.g., being invited to a close friend's party), and between the obstacle and the required instrumental behavior to overcome it (e.g., making an appointment with the friend after the exam; A. Kappes & Oettingen, 2012; A. Kappes, Singmann, & Oettingen, 2012).

Mental contrasting also produces changes in higher-level cognition. For instance, in adolescents, mental contrasting improved performance on tasks that require perspective taking and it facilitated the willingness to tolerate and integrate immigrants (Oettingen et al., 2005); it also helped with meeting the goal of getting to know an attractive stranger (Oettingen, 2000, Study 1). Recent research employing a dyadic negotiation paradigm in which pairs of participants take the role of a car seller and a car buyer (Kirk, Oettingen, & Gollwitzer, 2011) suggests an increase in perspective taking. Mentally contrasting the desired outcome of a high gain of the dyad with obstacles of reality (i.e., anticipated difficulties in the upcoming negotiation) led to more conjoint gains than mere indulging in an imagined high gain or dwelling on the obstacles to reaching such a positive outcome.

*Moderators of mental contrasting.* There exists an important moderator variable of mental contrasting effects on expectancy-dependent goal commitment and goal striving: incentive value. Early on, Oettingen (2000) has shown that mental contrasting effects can only be observed when people's future is at least minimally desired. For example, in an experiment on mental contrasting and its role in creating commitment to integrative goals, female doctoral students had to think about their future ten years ahead. Those who in their future thoughts had mentioned combining an academic career and having children were responsive to mental contrasting: two weeks after the experiment, they showed the anticipated expectancy-dependent goal commitment. In the indulging and dwelling conditions, no expectancy-related commitment was observed. On the contrary, female doctoral students who in their future thoughts failed to mention both an academic career and having children showed no relationship between expectations of success and commitment to integrate these two life-tasks, regardless of which of the three conditions they were in. This and more recent research points out that wise (expectancy-dependent) goal selection through mental contrasting can only be achieved if people are able to generate positive fantasies about realizing the thought of future.

*Origins of mental contrasting.* Another important question is, which variables determine the spontaneous use of mental contrasting. Next to assignments of elaborations of future and reality (see the reported experiments), context variables should influence whether people spontaneously use mental contrasting—rather than indulging, dwelling, and reverse contrasting. H. B. Kappes, Oettingen, Mayer, and Maglio (2011) reasoned that mental contrasting, because it is a problem-solving procedure, should be triggered by sad mood. Sad mood has been found to facilitate problem solving and signals a need for changing the status quo. Indeed, sad mood fostered mental contrasting more than happy or neutral mood: In six studies, H. B. Kappes et al. (2011) showed that across various mood inductions, sad mood facilitated self-initiated mental contrasting more than neutral mood or happy mood. Importantly, mood did not affect the relation between mental contrasting and selective formation of goal commitment. These studies imply that sad mood supports the generation of self-regulation strategies that lead to wise commitment to potential goals.

Recent research points to other contextual variables influencing the spontaneous generation and use of mental contrasting. Sevincer and Oettingen (2012), applying content analysis of spontaneous thoughts, observed that people were more likely to mentally contrast when goal-relevant action was imminent. Next to context variables (such as mood or imminent action), person variables can also work as determinants of the spontaneous use of mental contrasting: People who were high (versus low) in self-control skills (Tangney, Baumeister, & Boone, 2004) and need for cognition (Cacioppo, Petty, & Kao, 1984) were more likely to spontaneously use mental contrasting. The results illuminate how context and person characteristics shape the self-regulation of goal commitments and goal striving during everyday life.

*Mental contrasting and behavior change.* As noted above, mental contrasting promotes pursuits of feasible goals, whereas it helps people to refrain from pursuing infeasible goals. A recent study involving health care professionals directly speaks to such wise goal selection as a product of mental contrasting (Oettingen, Mayer, & Brinkmann, 2010). Participants in one condition were taught to use mental contrasting regarding their everyday concerns, while participants in the other condition were taught to indulge. Two weeks later, participants in the mental contrasting condition reported to have fared better in managing their time and decision making during everyday life than those in the indulging condition. More specifically, mental contrasting participants reported a better use of their time, completing promising and relinquishing unpromising projects, and finding it easy to decide between projects. Recent studies targeted the choice of suitable means in terms of seeking and giving help (Oettingen, Stephens, Mayer, & Brinkmann, 2010). In the first study, mental contrasting students with the goal to seek academic help managed to discriminate between people who might or might not help them, and behaved accordingly. In the second study, pediatric nurses with the goal of improving communication with patients' relatives successfully discriminated between opportunities where they were confident that the families will respond well and opportunities where the families might be less responsive.

The negotiation study described above also speaks to the issue of successfully selecting adaptive means (Kirk et al., 2011). The negotiation task implied a multi-issue negotiation where logrolling (i.e., finding trade-offs) improves joint profits. In logrolling, the best means to the desired goal (i.e., maximizing profit) is expressing demands that benefit oneself, but do not hurt the other person as well as making concessions that benefit the other person but do not hurt oneself. Mental contrasting, as it promotes discrimination among possible means to goal attainment, should help negotiators to make such reasonable demands and concessions. In line with this reasoning, mental contrasting did not only enhance the amount of joint profits achieved, it also produced heightened equity of achieved profits.

But mental contrasting may not only be used as a powerful self-regulation tool when it comes to choosing between appropriate goals and means; rather, it can also be applied for the purpose of enhancing one's commitment to a focal goal with subsequent goal striving and goal attainment. In this instance, one needs to keep in mind that mental contrasting creates goal pursuit in line with a person's expectations of success. Accordingly, it is important that high expectations of success are in place before people are asked to engage in mental contrasting. To ensure this prerequisite, one recent study simply induced high expectations of success by giving positive feedback in the critical performance domain (i.e., solving creative insight problems; Oettingen, Marquardt, & Gollwitzer, 2012). A further line of research targeting the learning of foreign language vocabulary words in schoolchildren (A. Gollwitzer, Oettingen, Kirby, Duckworth, & Mayer, 2011) took a more indirect approach. First, learning tasks were chosen that were new to the children (i.e., learning foreign language vocabulary where no prior efficacy expectations existed), and second, these tasks were then introduced in ways that ensured that the students were confident of mastering them. In the two studies (one with elementary schoolchildren and the other with middle schoolchildren), teaching students to mentally contrast the desired future of being successful in the task of learning foreign language vocabulary with obstacles of present reality (e.g., being easily distracted) resulted in better vocabulary task performance than teaching students to only think about the desired future of successfully solving the vocabulary tasks.

Whereas in the study described above participants were asked to practice their mental contrasting with regard to those outcomes they later were tested on, other studies investigated whether mental contrasting can also be taught and practiced as a meta-cognitive strategy that people then apply to all kinds of their desired outcomes. In the study reported above (Oettingen, Mayer, & Brinkmann, 2010), where mental contrasting was used to promote adaptive goal choices, this meta-cognitive approach was taken. Participants practiced mental contrasting with respect to a variety of their current daily problems; they were then told to use the learned self-regulation strategy to deal with the same or other of their daily problems in the upcoming two weeks. A recent study in the health domain suggests that the meta-cognitive intervention approach can be used not only to help people make more adaptive goal and means choices in one domain, but also to help people to more effectively commit to and strive for goals in other domains (Johannessen, Oettingen, & Mayer, 2012). In this study, participants were taught to use mental contrasting on their dieting wishes. Two weeks later, it was found that mental contrasting participants succeeded in reducing their calorie intake; importantly, they also succeeded in engaging in more physical activity. In other words, mental contrasting improved health behavior not only in the original domain that was targeted by the mental contrasting technique, but also in another related domain. Assuming that participants had applied the mental contrasting technique (they had acquired with respect to their dieting wishes) to their exercise concerns implies that teaching people the self-regulation technique of mental contrasting in one domain facilitates successful goal pursuit in general or at least with different goals of the same domain (e.g., the health domain).

## The Self-Regulation Strategy of Forming Implementation Intentions

So far we have dealt with the issue of how people arrive at wise goal commitments with subsequent goal striving. And although mental contrasting instigates goal commitment that is strong enough to imply strong effort and successful performance, to guarantee successful goal attainment, strategies of effective planning are often needed (Gollwitzer & Moskowitz, 1996; Lewin, Dembo, Festinger, & Sears, 1944; Oettingen & Gollwitzer, 2001). In other words, strongly committing to and striving for a goal is a necessary but often not sufficient step toward goal attainment as the way to the goal may be lined with hindrances, temptations, and setbacks (Bargh et al., 2010). The four challenges of goal implementation that people are confronted with most frequently are the following: people may fail to get started with goal striving, fail to stay on track, overextend with one goal thus losing sight of other equally important goals, and, finally, they may fail to disengage from an unattainable goal or futile means (Gollwitzer & Sheeran, 2006). In fact, meta-analytic findings suggest that goals (also referred to as goal intentions because goals can be understood as self-instructions to perform a certain behavior or to achieve a certain outcome; Triandis, 1980) account for no more than 28% of the variance in goal-directed behavior (Sheeran, 2002). Next to selecting only feasible goals which is promoted by mental contrasting, one remedy to such impaired goal striving is planning out in advance how one wants to deal with the four challenges described above. Planning out in advance is promoted by adding implementation intentions to one's goal intentions.

*Strategic automaticity in goal striving.* Gollwitzer (1993, 1999) highlighted the importance of furnishing goal intentions with implementation intentions. While goal intentions (goals) have the structure of "I intend to reach Z!" with Z relating to a desired future behavior or outcome, implementation intentions have the structure of "If situation X is encountered, then I will perform the goal-directed response Y!" Thus, implementation intentions define as to when, where, and how one wants to act on one's goal intentions. In order to form an implementation intention, individuals need to identify a goal-relevant situational cue (such as an obstacle to goal attainment or a good opportunity to act) and link it to an instrumental goal-directed response. Whereas goal intentions merely specify a desired future behavior or outcome, the if-component of an implementation intention specifies when and where one wants to act on this goal, and the then-component of the implementation intention specifies how this will be done. For instance, an employee with the goal of making more constructive contributions in the weekly team meetings (goal intention) might form the following implementation intention to support the attainment of her goal: "And whenever a colleague is desperately trying to answer an awkward question, then I'll immediately jump to her rescue!" Research supports the assumption that implementation intentions help close the gap between holding goal intentions and attaining them, and this is true for all of the four challenges of effective goal attainment listed above. A meta-analysis based on close to a hundred studies shows a medium to large effect on increased rate of goal attainment ($d =.61$; Gollwitzer & Sheeran, 2006).

*Mediators of implementation intention effects.* Research on the underlying mechanisms of implementation intention effects has discovered that implementation intentions facilitate goal attainment on the basis of psychological mechanisms that relate to the anticipated situation (specified in the if-part of the plan), and the associative link forged between the if-part and the then-part of the plan. Because forming an implementation intention implies the selection of a critical future situation, the mental representation of this situation becomes highly activated and hence more accessible (Gollwitzer, 1999). This heightened accessibility of the if-part of the plan has been observed in several studies using different experimental paradigms. For instance, Webb and Sheeran (2004, Studies 2 and 3), using a cue detection task, observed that implementation intentions improve cue detection (fewer misses and more hits), without stimulating erroneous responses to similar cues (false alarms and correct rejections). Using a dichotic listening task paradigm, Achtziger, Bayer, and Gollwitzer (2012) found that words describing the anticipated critical situation were highly disruptive to focused attention in implementation-intention participants compared to mere goal-intention participants (i.e., participants in the implementation intention condition were less able than control participants to repeat aloud words that were read to them). Moreover, in a cued recall experiment, they observed that participants more effectively recalled the available situational opportunities to attain a set goal given that these opportunities had been specified in if–then links (i.e., in implementation intentions). Furthermore, in a study by Parks-Stamm, Gollwitzer, and Oettingen (2007) using a lexical decision task paradigm, it was observed that implementation intentions did not only increase the activation level of the specified critical cues but also diminished the activation level of nonspecified competing situational cues. And finally, Wieber and Sassenberg (2006), using a flanker task paradigm (i.e., distracting stimuli are presented as flankers next to the stimuli relevant to performing a focal task), observed that those flanker stimuli that had been specified in implementation intentions attracted more attention; this observation is in line with the findings of the dichotic listening study reported above (Achtziger et al., 2012).

There are even studies that explicitly tested whether the heightened accessibility of the mental representation of critical cues that are specified in an implementation intention mediates the attainment of the respective goal intention. For instance, Aarts, Dijksterhuis, and Midden (1999), using a lexical decision task, found that the formation of implementation intentions led to faster lexical decision times for those words that described the specified critical situation. Furthermore, the heightened accessibility of the critical situation (as measured by faster lexical decision responses) mediated the beneficial effects of implementation intentions on goal attainment.

Recent studies indicate that forming implementation intentions not only heightens the activation (and thus the accessibility) of the mental representation of the situational cues specified in the if-component but it also forges a strong associative link between the mental representation of the specified opportunity and the mental representation of the specified response (Webb & Sheeran, 2007, 2008). These associative links seem to be quite stable over time (Papies, Aarts, & de Vries, 2009), and they allow for the activation of the mental representation of the specified response (the plan's then-component) by subliminal presentation of the specified critical situational cue (if-component) (Webb & Sheeran, 2007). Moreover, mediation analyses suggest that cue accessibility and the strength of the cue–response link together mediate the impact of implementation intention formation on goal attainment (Webb & Sheeran, 2007, 2008).

Gollwitzer (1999) suggested that the upshot of the strong associative (critical situation with goal-directed response) links created by forming implementation intentions is that—once the critical cue is encountered—the initiation of the goal-directed response specified in the then-component of the implementation intention exhibits features of automaticity, including immediacy, efficiency, and redundancy of conscious intent. Having formed an implementation intention, individuals can act in situ without having to deliberate on whether to act or not. There is vast empirical evidence that if–then planners act more quickly (e.g., Gollwitzer & Brandstätter, 1997, Experiment 3), deal more effectively with cognitive demands (e.g., such speed-up effects are still evidenced under high cognitive load; Brandstätter, Lengfelder, & Gollwitzer, 2001), and do not need to consciously intend to act at the critical moment. Consistent with this last assumption, implementation intention effects are observed even when the critical cue is presented subliminally (e.g., Bayer, Achtziger, Gollwitzer, & Moskowitz, 2009) or when the respective goal is activated outside of awareness (Sheeran, Webb, & Gollwitzer, 2005, Study 2).

The processes underlying implementation intention effects (enhanced cue accessibility, strong cue–response associative links, automation of responding) mean that if–then planning allows people to see and to seize good opportunities to move toward their goal intentions. Fashioning an if–then plan thus *strategically automates* goal striving; people intentionally make if–then plans that delegate control of goal-directed behavior to preselected situational cues, with the explicit purpose of reaching their goals. This delegation hypothesis has recently been tested by studies that collected brain data using electroencephalography (EEG) and functional magnetic resonance imaging (fMRI). A study by Schweiger Gallo, Keil, McCulloch, Rockstroh, and Gollwitzer (2009, Study 3) using dense-array EEG, behavioral data indicated that implementation intentions specifying an ignore-response in the then-component of an implementation intention helped control fear in response to pictures of spiders in participants with spider phobia. Importantly, the obtained electro-cortical correlates revealed that those participants who bolstered their goal intention to stay calm with an ignore-implementation intention showed significantly reduced early activity in the visual cortex in response to spider pictures, as reflected in a smaller P1 (assessed at 120 ms after a spider picture had been presented). This EEG finding suggests that implementation intentions indeed lead to strategic automation of the specified goal-directed response (an ignore response) when the critical cue (a spider picture) is encountered, as conscious effortful action initiation is known to last longer than 120 ms (at least 300 ms; see Bargh & Chartrand, 2000).

Further support for the delegation hypothesis was obtained in an fMRI study reported by Gilbert, Gollwitzer, Cohen, Oettingen, and Burgess (2009), in which participants had to perform a prospective memory task on the basis of either goal or implementation intention instructions. Acting on the basis of goal intentions was associated with brain activity in the lateral rostral prefrontal cortex, whereas acting on the basis of implementation intentions was associated with brain activity in the medial rostral prefrontal cortex. Brain activity in the latter area is known to be associated with bottom-up (stimulus) control of action, whereas brain activity in the former area is known to be related to top-down (goal) control of action (Burgess, Dumontheil, & Gilbert, 2007).

In sum, heightened cue accessibility and increased strength of the cue–response association together mediate implementation intention effects on goal attainment (Gollwitzer & Oettingen, 2011; Webb & Sheeran, 2007, 2008). The search for further mediating variables was quite unsuccessful (meta-analysis by Webb & Sheeran, 2008). Numerous studies showed that neither an increase in goal commitment nor an increase in self-efficacy qualify as potential alternative mediators of implementation intention effects (e.g., Brandstätter et al., 2001; Oettingen et al., 2000, Study 2).

*Implementation intentions as a means to overcome typical problems of goal striving.* The effects of implementation intentions have been demonstrated with respect to the four challenges of goal attainment listed above: getting started, staying on track, avoiding resource depletion, and disengaging from futile goal intentions. Implementation intentions were found to help individuals to get started with goal striving in terms of remembering to act (e.g., with respect to taking vitamin pills; Sheeran & Orbell, 1999), not missing opportunities to act (e.g., with respect to obtaining a mammography; Rutter, Steadman, & Quine, 2006), and overcoming an initial reluctance to act (e.g., with respect to undertaking a testicular self-examination; Sheeran, Milne, Webb, & Gollwitzer, 2005). Moreover, goals to perform regular breast examinations (Orbell, Hodgkins, & Sheeran, 1997) or cervical cancer screening (Sheeran & Orbell, 2000), to resume activity after joint replacement surgery (Orbell & Sheeran, 2000), to eat a low-fat diet (Armitage, 2004), to recycle (Holland, Aarts, & Langendam, 2006), and to engage in physical exercise (Milne, Orbell, & Sheeran, 2002) were all found to be more readily acted upon by individuals who previously had formed implementation intentions (Gollwitzer & Oettingen, 2011).

However, many goals cannot be accomplished by a simple, discrete, one-shot action because they require that people keep striving over an extended period of time. Staying on track may then become very difficult when certain internal stimuli (e.g., being anxious, tired, overburdened) or external stimuli (e.g., temptations, distractions) interfere with the ongoing goal pursuit. Implementation intentions can be used to protect an ongoing goal striving from the negative influence of interferences from both inside (e.g., Achtziger, Gollwitzer, & Sheeran, 2008) and outside the person (e.g., Gollwitzer & Schaal, 1998). Such implementation intentions may use very different formats. For instance, if a person wants to stay friendly to a colleague who is known to makes outrageous requests, she can form suppression-oriented implementation intentions, such as "And if my colleague approaches me with an outrageous request, then I will not get upset!" The then-component of such suppression-oriented implementation intentions does not have to be worded in terms of not showing (i.e., negating) the critical behavior (in the present example getting upset); it may alternatively specify a replacement behavior ("..., then I will respond in a friendly manner!"), or focus on ignoring the critical cue ("..., then I'll ignore her request!"). Recent research (Adriaanse, Van Oosten, De Ridder, De Wit, & Evers, 2011) suggests that mere negation implementation intentions are less effective than the latter two types of implementation intentions (i.e., replacement and ignore implementation intentions).

An important alternative way of using implementation intentions to protect ongoing goal striving from derailment is to form implementation intentions geared toward stabilizing the ongoing goal pursuit (Bayer, Gollwitzer, & Achtziger, 2010). Using, again, the example of a person who has to cope with an outrageous request of a colleague, let us assume that the recipient of the request has stipulated in advance in an implementation intention about what she will converse about with her colleague when she runs into her. The interaction with the colleague may then come off as planned even if the colleague expresses her outrageous request. Bayer et al. (2010) demonstrated the effectiveness of this strategy in a series of studies analyzing whether making if-then plans that stabilize an ongoing goal pursuit effectively blocked the disruptive effects of self-definitional incompleteness, inappropriate mood, and ego-depletion.

Forming implementation intentions can also help prevent resource depletion as it enables individuals to engage in automated goal striving and behavior control that does not require high levels of deliberate effort. As a consequence, the self should not become depleted (Muraven & Baumeister, 2000) when goal striving is regulated by implementation intentions. Indeed, in studies using different ego-depletion paradigms, research participants who used implementation intentions to self-regulate in one task did not show reduced self-regulatory capacity in a subsequent task (e.g., Webb & Sheeran, 2003).

Finally, goals that are no longer feasible and/or desirable in their current form may require individuals to adjust goal striving and to disengage from a goal or a chosen means. Such disengagement from unattainable goals or dysfunctional means can free up resources and minimize negative affect and health issues resulting from repeated negative feedback (Carver & Scheier, 1998; Locke & Latham, 1990, 2006). However, individuals often stick to a chosen goal or means too long, thus hurting themselves (i.e., escalation of commitment; Brockner, 1992). Implementation intentions can be used to promote functional disengagement by (1) specifying negative feedback as a critical cue, and (2) linking this cue to switching to a functional alternative goal or means. Indeed, when research participants were asked to form implementation intentions that linked negative feedback on the ongoing goal striving to immediately switching to a different goal or means, or to reflecting on the quality of the received failure feedback on the ongoing goal striving, functional disengagement from goals and means was found to occur more frequently than for participants who had only formed respective goal intentions or had formed no intentions at all (Henderson, Gollwitzer, & Oettingen, 2007).

*How much willpower is afforded by forming implementation intentions?* Any self-regulation strategy that claims to facilitate goal striving has to prove itself under conditions in which people commonly fail to demonstrate willpower. Such conditions are manifold, but the following three situations stick out: (1) situations in which a person's knowledge and skills constrain performance, such as taking academic tests; (2) situations in which an opponent's behavior limits one's performance, such as is true for negotiation settings; and (3) situations in which the desired behavior (e.g., no littering) conflicts with habits favoring an antagonistic response. For all three of these situations, implementation intentions, however, stood their test.

As to situations where knowledge and skills constrain performance, very simply, implementation intentions were found to enhance participants' performance on a standardized intelligence test (Bayer & Gollwitzer, 2007). Participants only had to form the following simple implementation intention: "Whenever I start a new problem on this test, then I will tell myself: I can solve this problem!" As to situations where an opponent limits one's performance, studies in which pairs of negotiators had to distribute a common resource were conducted (Trötschel & Gollwitzer, 2007). In these studies, negotiators played the roles of representatives of two neighboring countries and negotiate the distribution of the regions, villages, and towns of a disputed island. When the participants formed implementation intentions to make cooperative counterproposals whenever a proposal from the counterpart was received, the pairs of negotiators managed to be more cooperative even when the negotiation had to take place under a loss frame (i.e., participants are told how many points they lose rather than win during each round of negotiation and are thus reluctant to make concessions; e.g., Bottom & Studt, 1993). Apparently, implementation intentions managed to break the competiveness-enhancing effect of loss framing. Recent research using the ultimatum game (Kirk, Gollwitzer, & Carnevale, 2011) also shows that implementation intentions can help performance in the face of opponents. Angry impulsive responses to ultimatums, which are known to cause the rejection of unfair offers at a cost to oneself, were successfully curbed by making if-then plans geared toward downregulating anger.

Finally, as to situations where a desired behavior is in conflict with an antagonistic habitual response, a host of research has been conducted as well. The self-regulation of goal striving becomes difficult when habitual responses are in conflict with initiating and executing the needed goal-directed responses that are instrumental to goal attainment (e.g., Wood & Neal, 2007). Can the self-regulation strategy of forming if–then plans help people to let their goals win out over their habitual responses? By assuming that action control by implementation intentions is immediate and efficient, and adopting a simple horserace model of action control (i.e., the stronger action tendency will win out over the weaker one; Adriaanse, Gollwitzer, De Ridder, De Wit, & Kroese, 2011), people might be in a position to break habitual responses by forming strong implementation intentions (e.g., if–then plans that spell out a response contrary to the habitual response to the critical situation; Holland et al., 2006). Cohen, Bayer, Jaudas, and Gollwitzer (2008, Study 2; see also Miles & Proctor, 2008) demonstrated that implementation intentions helped suppressing habitual behavioral responses in a Simon task. In this task paradigm, participants are asked to respond to a nonspatial aspect of a stimulus (i.e., whether a presented tone is high or low) by pressing a left or right key, and to ignore the location of the stimulus (i.e., whether it is presented on one's left or right side). The difficulty of responding is high when the location of the tone (e.g., right) and the required key press (e.g., left) are incongruent, as people habitually respond to stimuli presented at the right or left side with the corresponding hand. Automatic cognitive biases, such as stereotyping, represent another type of habitual response that can be in opposition to one's goals. Extending earlier work (Gollwitzer & Schaal, 1998), Stewart and Payne (2008) found that implementation intentions designed to counter automatic stereotypes (e.g., "When I see a black face, I will then think 'safe'") could indeed reduce automatic stereotyping. Recent research by Mendoza, Gollwitzer, and Amodio (2010) has added to these findings that implementation intentions can also be used to suppress the behavioral expression of implicit stereotypes.

Still, forming implementation intentions may not always block habitual responses. Whether the habitual response or the if–then guided response will "win the race" depends on the relative strength of the two behavioral orientations. If the habitual response is based on strong habits (Webb, Sheeran, & Luszczynska, 2009), and the if-then guided response is based on weak implementation intentions, the habitual response should win over the if-then planned response; and the reverse should be true when weak habits are in conflict with strong implementation intentions. This implies that controlling behavior based on strong habits requires the formation of strong implementation intentions. Such enhancement of if-then plans can be achieved by various measures. One pertains to creating particularly strong mental links between situational cues (if component) and goal-directed responses (then component), for instance, by asking participants to use mental imagery (Knäuper, Roseman, Johnson, & Krantz, 2009; see also Papies et al., 2009). Alternatively, Adriaanse, De Ridder, and De Wit (2009) suggested tailoring the critical cue specified in the if part of an implementation intention to personally relevant reasons for the habitual behavior one wants to overcome, and then link this cue to an antagonistic response. Also, certain formats of implementation intentions (i.e., replacement and ignore implementation intentions) seem to be more effective in fighting habits than others (i.e., negation implementation intentions). Pertaining to the discussion of whether strong habits can be broken by implementation intentions, one should however always keep in mind that behavior change is possible without changing old habits; one can focus as well on the building of new habits in new situational contexts. The "delegation of control to situational cues principle," on which implementation intention effects are based, can unfold its facilitative effects in the new situational context undisturbed by the old habits.

*Moderators of implementation intention effects.* Recent research has identified a number of moderators of implementation intention effects on goal striving and goal attainment. First, implementation intentions only benefit goal attainment when goal commitment is high (Sheeran et al., 2005); the same is true with respect to people's commitment to executing the formed implementation intention (Achtziger et al., 2012, Study 2). In addition, self-efficacy was also found to moderate implementation intention effects. Prompting participants to form an implementation intention as to when, where, and how to pursue their most important New Year's resolution, and in addition reflect on past mastery experiences (i.e., situations in which they achieved a similar goal) led to significantly higher levels of self-reported goal progress compared to control conditions and a mere implementation-intention condition (Koestner, Horberg, Gaudreau, Powers, Di Dio, Bryan, 2006). In a recent study (Wieber, Odenthal, & Gollwitzer, 2010), high versus low self-efficacy was manipulated by asking participants to solve low- or high-difficulty goal-relevant tasks. It was observed that high-self-efficacy participants showed stronger implementation intention effects than low-self-efficacy participants, especially when the tasks to be solved were difficult rather than easy.

Finally, person attributes have been found to moderate implementation intention effects as well. For instance, Powers, Koestner, and Topciu (2005) report that socially prescribed perfectionists who try to conform to standards and expectations by others show weaker implementation intention effects. Possibly social perfectionists may fail to commit to implementation intentions because they feel social expectations and standards to change quickly and unpredictably which may be impeded by strong commitments to the preplanned course of action as defined in implementation intentions. Moreover, in an experimental study using undergraduate students (Webb, Christian, & Armitage, 2007), attendance in class was studied as a function of conscientiousness, openness to experience, goal intentions, and implementation intentions. Implementation intention effects were found to be moderated by conscientiousness, such that increased class attendance due to planning occurred only for low/moderately conscientious students as high conscientious students showed a perfect class attendance to begin with. This observation is in line with the finding (Gollwitzer & Sheeran, 2006) that implementation intention effects are generally stronger for difficult than for easy goals.

## Combining Mental Contrasting with Implementation Intentions: MCII

Knowledge about strategies of both effectively committing to and striving for goals allows for interventions that teach people how to effectively pursue goals on their own. One such intervention (Adriaanse, Oettingen, Gollwitzer, Hennes, De Ridder, & De Wit, 2010;

Christiansen, Oettingen, Dahme, & Klinger, 2010; Stadler, Oettingen, & Gollwitzer, 2009, 2010; review by Oettingen, 2012; Oettingen & Gollwitzer, 2010) combines mental contrasting with forming implementation intentions (i.e., MCII). To unfold their beneficial effects, implementation intentions require that strong goal commitments are in place (Sheeran et al., 2005, Study 1), and mental contrasting creates such strong commitments (Oettingen et al., 2001, review by Oettingen, 2012). Implementation intentions are also found to show enhanced benefits when the specification of the if-component is personalized (Adriaanse et al., 2009). Mental contrasting guarantees the identification of personally relevant obstacles that can be specified as the critical cue in the if-component of an implementation intention. Finally, mental contrasting has been found to create a readiness for making plans that link anticipated obstacles of reality to instrumental behaviors (A. Kappes, Singmann, & Oettingen, 2012; Oettingen et al., 2001). And although these plans instigated by mental contrasting have been shown to be strong enough to lead to respective effort and successful performance, complementing them by explicit instructions of forming implementation intentions has yielded additional benefits for promoting successful goal attainment (Adriaanse et al., 2010; Kirk, Oettingen, & Gollwitzer, in press).

For example, in a recent intervention study with middle-aged women (Stadler et al., 2009), participants were taught the cognitive principles and individual steps of the MCII technique. This intervention allowed participants to apply MCII by themselves to their idiosyncratic everyday wishes and concerns; hence, MCII qualifies as a *metacognitive* self-regulation strategy. Specifically, in the Stadler et al. (2009) study participants were taught how to use MCII for their idiosyncratic wishes of exercising more. Participants were free to choose whatever form of exercising they wished to mentally contrast on, and they were encouraged to anticipate exactly those obstacles that were personally most relevant and to link them to exactly those goal-directed responses that personally appeared to be most instrumental. As dependent measures, participants maintained daily behavioral diaries to keep track of the amount of time they exercised every day. Overall, teaching the MCII technique enhanced exercise more than only providing relevant health-related information (i.e., information-only control intervention). Participants in the MCII group exercised nearly twice as much as before the intervention and an average of 1 hour more per week than participants in the information-only control group. This effect showed up immediately after the intervention and it stayed stable throughout the entire period of the study (16 weeks after the intervention).

Conducting the same MCII intervention was also effective for promoting healthy eating in middle-aged women (i.e., eating more fruits and vegetables). The achieved behavior change persisted even over the extensive time period of 2 years (Stadler et al., 2010). In another study, Adriaanse et al. (2010) targeted the negative eating habit of unhealthy snacking in college students. MCII worked for both students with weak and strong such habits, and it was more effective than either mental contrasting or forming implementation intentions alone. Moreover, MCII was observed to benefit chronic back pain patients in increasing their mobility (Christiansen et al., 2010). Over a period of both 3 weeks and then 3 months patients learning MCII for altogether just one hour, increased their exercise more as compared to a standard treatment control group. Physical mobility was measured by objective (i.e., bicycle ergometer test and number of weight lifts achieved in 2 minutes) and subjective indicators (reported physical functioning).

Finally, MCII has shown beneficial effects outside of the health area as well. For example, it benefited study efforts in adolescents preparing for standardized tests (Duckworth, Grant, Loew, Oettingen, & Gollwitzer, 2011). Moreover, MCII was found to promote integrative bargaining (Kirk et al., in press). Before negotiating in dyads over the sale of a car, participants in the MCII condition were to mentally contrast achieving success in this bargaining task with obstacles standing in the way of this success (e.g., being too competitive) and to subsequently form respective if-then plans on how to overcome these obstacles. Participants in the mental contrasting only condition did not form if-then plans, whereas participants in the if-then plan only condition did not engage in mental contrasting. Results showed that MCII led to higher joint gains than either mental contrasting or if-then plans alone. Importantly, MCII participants arrived at significantly more cooperative implementation intentions than participants who formed their if-then plans without mental contrasting. The number of cooperative implementation intentions also mediated the effects of MCII on joint gains. These findings suggest that MCII helps people form cooperative plans and thus reach high-quality agreements in negotiations.

In sum, the reported MCII research suggests that MCII qualifies as a self-regulation strategy that people can apply to their own idiosyncratic wishes and concerns and that can be taught in a cost- and time-effective way. When it comes to the effective self-regulation of goal pursuit, starting with committing to and striving for goals and ending with their successful attainment, MCII seems to facilitate solving all of these tasks of successful goal pursuit. Not surprisingly, then, combining mental contrasting with implementation intentions offers additional advantages compared to each strategy alone.

## MCII and the Goal Setting Framework

### Theoretical Aspects

While research based on goal setting theory focuses on outcome-specific, challenging goals in work settings, MCII-related research focuses on how to promote goal commitment and goal striving in various settings. Subsequently, we discuss the potential contributions of MCII for task performance and behavioral change beyond the effects of specific, challenging goals (for a review of using goal setting theory to promote health behavior change, see Chapter 26). In short, MCII should promote goal pursuit beyond goal setting effects especially when (a) self-regulatory demands are high and (b) current self-regulatory effectiveness is low.

First, when it comes to meeting heightened self-regulatory demands, people can turn to MCII when the desired outcomes themselves and/or the ways to achieve these outcomes are unclear, when conflicting goals or habits have to be dealt with, and when the current workload is high. Though sometimes challenging tasks are assigned or predetermined and thus allow for a clear definition of the goal (e.g., in terms of specific outcomes), at other times a clear definition of the goal is not provided. In MCII then, by naming a particular wish, people can specify the desired future. Finding clarity about the desired future is further facilitated by MCII's instructions to name and imagine the best outcome of the desired future, and to then immediately turn to name and imagine the reality that stands in the way of reaching the desired outcome (i.e., obstacle). This naming and imagining of the obstacle juxtaposed to the desired future facilitates ideas of how to reach these goals (i.e., when and how to initiate goal-directed action, how to keep up goal striving over time). For personal goals related to behavioral change, defining the obstacles as specific cues to goal-directed actions will render subsequent goal striving an automatic process thus promoting goal attainment.

Heightened self-regulatory demand also results from conflicts between goals and habits. In fact, many personal, academic, or job-related goals involve breaking counter-productive habits, such as procrastination (Wieber & Gollwitzer, 2010). Forming implementation intentions provides a strategy for breaking interfering habits (e.g., Adriaanse et al., 2009; Owens, Bowman, & Dill, 2008; Webb et al., 2009), as they lead to automatic initiation of wanted responses to the critical situational cues inhibiting the dominant habitual response (Adriaanse, Gollwitzer et al., 2011; Gollwitzer & Sheeran, 2006). Breaking habits by implementation intentions has been observed to be particularly effective when the latter are backed up by mental contrasting (Adriaanse et al., 2010). As a consequence, even though conflicting habits do handicap the effects of goal striving on outcome variables, MCII provides a reliable means for tackling such conflicts.

Finally, in industrial/organizational settings, high overall workload may create challenging self-regulatory demands. When workload is high, goal conflicts due to limited resources such as time, energy, or budget are more likely, and this even when job goals are not directly in conflict with other goals or with existing habits. In addition, high job demands increase the necessity to negotiate job engagement with other goals, such as health goals and family-related goals. As work-life balance requires a sufficient amount of off-job time and detachment from job demands, highly demanding jobs are particularly likely to increase self-regulatory demands. To live up to such heightened self-regulation demands, people may turn to mental contrasting as it has been found to promote both the prioritizing of conflicting goal pursuits (Oettingen, Mayer, & Brinkmann, 2010; Oettingen, Mayer, & Thorpe, 2010), and the finding of integrative solutions to conflicting goal pursuits in the short-term (e.g., in negotiations; Kirk et al., 2011; in press) and in the long-term (e.g., combining career and child rearing, Oettingen, 2000; Study 2); adding implementation intentions as is done in MCII, guarantees that people will stick to striving for the chosen goal, as striving for it becomes automated.

Second, when it comes to facilitating goal striving in organizations, people can again turn to MCII. Even when a goal has been clearly defined, low and moderate goal commitment may lead individuals to not exert maximum effort to achieve that goal. Mental contrasting helps individuals to identify personally desirable and feasible goals and to strongly commit to them. Moreover, mental contrasting has been found to promote self-regulation by helping individuals to effectively cope with critical performance feedback. While adequately processing negative feedback is a core element of reaching one's goals, staying on track requires individuals to maintain their competence beliefs. In fact, individuals using mental contrasting were found to not only process negative feedback accurately, they also attributed negative feedback to low effort rather than low competence (A. Kappes, Oettingen, & Pak, 2012). In addition, research suggests that implementation intentions can be used to directly increase self-efficacy beliefs (Bayer & Gollwitzer, 2007; Yanar, Budworth, & Latham, 2009) by specifying self-assuring inner speech in the then-component (e.g., "..., then I will tell myself that I can do this!") and linking it to a respective critical situation specified in the if-component (e.g., "And if I should start feeling self-doubts, then ...!").

## Practical Managerial Implications: Remote Work Settings and Employee Health Management

While remote work settings provide various strategic advantages, physical and psychological distance makes it harder for individuals to evaluate fellow team members' reliability and to build and maintain interpersonal trust (Kirkman, Rosen, Tesluk, & Gibson, 2004; Latham & Saari, 1979; O'Hara-Devereaux & Johansen, 1994; Ronan, Latham, & Kinne, 1973). Accordingly, new forms of leadership have evolved that demand an increasing degree of self-regulation by employees (Barry, 1991; Carte, Chidambaram, & Becker, 2006; Manz, 1986; Tyran, Tyran, & Sheperd, 2003). In self-managing teams an official supervisor does not exist, or is hardly involved in the team's daily decisions and work processes; electronic tools are used for communicating, coordinating, and executing team processes (Kirkman & Mathieu, 2005) as team members are often located in different geographic locations and/or time zones (Foster & Coovert, 2006). In such "virtual" teams (Kirkman et al., 2004), team members are responsible for team performance and team process quality (O'Connell, Doverspike, & Cober, 2002).

While goal setting has proved to be highly effective especially in virtual teams, these teams also benefit from self-regulation strategies. Empowerment was found to increase team members' engagement and affective commitment, which mediates the effects of leadership on team members' innovative and teamwork behaviors and turnover intentions (Chen, Sharma, Edinger, Shapiro, & Farh, 2011). As part of team development interventions, MCII could contribute to selecting a group's goals, recognizing the main obstacles to the group's success, identifying the actions that are required for overcoming the obstacles to attaining the goals, and to explicitly forming "if-then" plans to overcome, circumvent, or prevent the specified obstacles (Oettingen & Gollwitzer, 2010). On the individual level, MCII could also help aligning individual goals both within and outside the team, thereby avoiding or minimizing goal conflict. Initial findings demonstrate that asking trainees reflective questions to stimulate self-regulatory engagement reduces attrition and promotes learning (Sitzmann & Ely, 2010).

In addition, MCII might aid people to deal effectively with team diversity regarding goal orientation (e.g., learning versus performance goals). Team diversity regarding learning versus performance goal orientation was found to harm team performance (Nederveen Pieterese, van Knippenberg, & van Ginkel, 2011), provided team reflexivity was low (i.e., the extent to which team members engage in meta-communication about the team's objectives and strategies; De Dreu, 2002; van Knippenberg & Schippers, 2007). When team reflexivity was high, work group diversity was even found to increase team performance (Bantel & Jackson, 1989). As virtual teams may be particularly vulnerable to diversity effects because of reduced opportunities for interaction and discussion, MCII may be used to increase reflexivity in these teams. Formal interventions that are known to foster team member interactions in terms of information sharing, questioning others, and managing time (Okhuysen & Eisenhardt, 2002) might be supplemented by MCII to promote reflexivity in virtual teams.

*Employee health management* (EHM) is another managerial problem that could benefit from MCII interventions. Accidents and chronic illnesses such as cardiovascular diseases, cancer, and chronic obstructive pulmonary diseases have become the most important causes of premature death in Western countries (Maes & Gebhardt, 2000). As these factors are largely caused or exacerbated by behavior such as smoking, alcohol abuse, lack of physical activity, lack of sleep, or unhealthy diet, many of them may be prevented or attenuated by interventions aiming at improving health behavior. Fortunately, a number of organizations have been making systematic efforts to improve employee health. Aside from employers' obligation to observe and care for employee well-being (De Simone & Harris, 1998), EHM also has implications for organizational effectiveness regarding outcomes such as job satisfaction, fluctuation, and absenteeism. Meta-analytical findings suggest that determined participation in EHM programs is the key to the success of these programs, as their effects disappear when individuals' participation is not voluntary (de Groot & Kiker, 2003). Moreover, while assigned and self-set goals lead to similar levels of goal commitment and task performance (provided goal difficulty is held constant; Strecher, Seijts, Kok, Latham, Glasgow, DeVellis, Meertens, & Bulger, 1995), assigned health goals may trigger reactance (Brehm, 1966; Wicklund, Slattum, & Solomon, 1970) and lead to poor goal commitment if they are presented in a work context but not directly linked to individual job role demands.

Individuals may thus be unwilling to respond to EHM programs unless measures are taken to develop health goals people feel they can commit to. Moreover, health-relevant behaviors may not be easily changed due to conflicts with existing habits. Taking healthy eating as an example, effective behavior change requires a number of behavioral sub-changes for which various specific goals and plans need to be developed in order to effectively overcome habitual responses (Adriaanse et al., 2009, 2010, 2011; Stadler et al., 2009, 2010). Committing to and attaining health goals should therefore benefit from using self-regulation strategies. MCII could help people to identify and commit to personally meaningful and relevant health goals without triggering reactance, and to promote goal striving by specifying respective action plans. MCII could also help employees to effectively shield off-job time from job demands, which is known to predict exhaustion, disengagement, and psychosomatic problems especially in case of high job demands (Sonnentag, Binnewies, & Mojza, 2010). In summary, MCII might improve health management by increasing commitment to health goals, by preventing reactance toward EHM interventions, by providing an effective tool to block habits from impeding health goal attainment, and by resolving role conflicts.

## Conclusion

Locke and Latham (2006) assert that goal setting theory allows for the integration of other theories. Therefore, the present contribution aimed at integrating research on self-regulation into goal setting theory and exemplified this integration in the area of managerial leadership. First, we introduced two corroborative self-regulation strategies of goal pursuit, mental contrasting fostering goal commitment and goal striving, and implementation intentions fostering effective goal implementation, and discussed research attesting to their processes, moderators, and effects on behavioral change. Second, complementing each other in creating a powerful self-regulatory strategy of goal pursuit, mental contrasting with implementation intentions (MCII), has been shown to be especially beneficial when self-regulatory problems are unclear and/or demands are high. For example, these benefits should particularly unfold when the tasks are complex, the workload is high, goals or habits are in conflict, or critical feedback is impending. Regarding applied implications, two areas were highlighted. MCII may benefit teams burdened by diverse goal orientations or lack of team reflexivity. As part of employee health management programs, MCII can promote commitment to health goals, prevent reactance toward health management interventions, and help overcome conflicts between and among habits and goals.

# References

Aarts, H., Dijksterhuis, A., & Midden, C. (1999). To plan or not to plan? Goal achievement or interrupting the performance of mundane behaviors. *European Journal of Social Psychology, 29,* 971–979.

Achtziger, A., Bayer, U. C., & Gollwitzer, P. M. (2012). Committing to implementation intentions: Attention and memory effects for selected situational cues. *Motivation and Emotion, 36,* 287–300.

Achtziger, A., Gollwitzer, P. M., & Sheeran, P. (2008). Implementation intentions and shielding goal striving from unwanted thoughts and feelings. *Personality and Social Psychology Bulletin, 34,* 381–393.

Adriaanse, M. A., De Ridder, D. T. D., & De Wit, J. B. F. (2009). Finding the critical cue: Implementation intentions to change one's diet work best when tailored to personally relevant reasons for unhealthy eating. *Personality and Social Psychology Bulletin, 35,* 60–71.

Adriaanse, M. A., Gollwitzer, P. M., De Ridder, D. T. D., De Wit, J. B. F., & Kroese, F. M. (2011). Breaking habits with implementation intentions: A test of underlying processes. *Personality and Social Psychology Bulletin, 37,* 502–513.

Adriaanse, M. A., Oettingen, G., Gollwitzer, P. M., Hennes, E. P., De Ridder, D. T. D., & De Wit, J. B. F. (2010). When planning is not enough: Fighting unhealthy snacking habits by mental contrasting with implementation intentions (MCII). *European Journal of Social Psychology, 40,* 1277–1293.

Adriaanse, M. A., Van Oosten, J. M. F., De Ridder, D. T. D., De Wit, J. B. F., & Evers, C. (2011). Planning what not to eat: Ironic effects of implementation intentions negating unhealthy habits. *Personality and Social Psychology Bulletin, 37,* 69–81.

Armitage, C. J. (2004). Evidence that implementation intentions reduce dietary fat intake: A randomized trial. *Health Psychology, 23,* 319–323.

Bandura, A. (1991). Social cognitive theory of self-regulation. *Organizational Behavior and Human Decision Processes, 50,* 248–287.

Bantel, K., & Jackson, S. (1989). Top management and innovations in banking: Does the composition of the top team make a difference? *Strategic Management Journal, 10,* 107–124.

Bargh, J. A., & Chartrand, T. L. (2000). The mind in the middle: A practical guide to priming and automaticity research. In H. T. Reis & C. M. Judd (Eds.), *Handbook of research methods in social and personality psychology* (pp. 253–285). New York: Cambridge University Press.

Bargh, J. A., Gollwitzer, P. M., & Oettingen, G. (2010). Motivation. In S. T. Fiske, D. T. Gilbert, & G. Lindzey (Eds.), *Handbook of Social Psychology* (5th ed.). New York: Wiley.

Barry, D. (1991). Managing the bossless team: Lessons in distributed leadership. *Organizational Dynamics, 21,* 31–47.

Bayer, U. C., Achtziger, A., Gollwitzer, P. M., & Moskowitz, G. (2009). Responding to subliminal cues: Do if-then plans cause action preparation and initiation without conscious intent? *Social Cognition, 27,* 183–201.

Bayer, U. C., & Gollwitzer, P. M. (2007). Boosting scholastic test scores by willpower: The role of implementation intentions. *Self and Identity, 6,* 1–19.

Bayer, U. C., Gollwitzer, P. M., & Achtziger, A. (2010). Staying on track: Planned goal striving is protected from disruptive internal states. *Journal of Experimental Social Psychology, 146,* 505–514.

Bottom, W. P., & Studt, A. (1993). Framing effects and the distributive aspect of integrative bargaining. *Organizational Behavior and Human Decision Processes, 56,* 459–474.

Brandstätter, V., Lengfelder, A., & Gollwitzer, P. M. (2001). Implementation intentions and efficient action initiation. *Journal of Personality and Social Psychology, 81,* 946–960.

Brehm, J. W. (1966). *A theory of psychological reactance.* New York: Academic Press.

Brockner, J. (1992). The escalation of commitment to a failing course of action: Toward theoretical progress. *Academy of Management Review, 17,* 39–61.

Brunstein, J. C., & Gollwitzer, P. M. (1996). Effects of failure on subsequent performance: The importance of self-defining goals. *Journal of Personality and Social Psychology, 70,* 395–407.

Burgess, P. W., Dumontheil, I., & Gilbert, S. J. (2007). The gateway hypothesis of rostral PFC (Area 10) function. *Trends in Cognitive Sciences, 11,* 290–298.

Cacioppo, J. T., Petty, R. E., & Kao, C. F. (1984). The efficient assessment of need for cognition. *Journal of Personality Assessment, 48,* 306–307.

Carte, T., Chidambaram, L., & Becker, A. (2006). Emergent leadership in self-managed virtual teams: A longitudinal study of concentrated and shared leadership behaviors. *Group Decision and Negotiation, 15,* 323–343.

Carver, C., & Scheier, M. (1998). *On the self-regulation of behavior.* New York: Cambridge University Press.

Chen, G., Sharma, P. N., Edinger, S. K., Shapiro, D. L., & Farh, J.-L. (2011). Motivating and demotivating forces in teams: Cross-level influences of empowering leadership and relationship conflict. *Journal of Applied Psychology, 96,* 541–557.

Christiansen, S., Oettingen, G., Dahme, B., & Klinger, R. (2010). A short goal-pursuit intervention to improve physical capacity: A randomized clinical trial in chronic back pain patients. *Pain, 149,* 444–452.

Cohen, A-L., Bayer, U. C., Jaudas, A., & Gollwitzer, P. M. (2008). Self-regulatory strategy and executive control: Implementation intentions modulate task switching and Simon task performance. *Psychological Research, 72,* 12–26.

De Dreu, C. K. W. (2002). Team innovation and team effectiveness: The importance of minority dissent and reflexivity. *European Journal of Work and Occupational and Organizational Psychology, 70,* 285–298.

De Groot, T., & Kiker, D. S. (2003). A meta-analysis of the non-monetary effects of employee health management programs. *Human Resource Management, 42,* 53–69.

De Simone, R. L., & Harris, D. M. (1998). *Human resource development* (2nd ed.). Orlando, FL: Dryden Press.

Duckworth, A. L., Grant, H., Loew, B., Oettingen, G., & Gollwitzer, P. M. (2011). Self-regulation strategies improve self-discipline in adolescents: Benefits of mental contrasting and implementation intentions. *Educational Psychology, 31,* 17–26.

Foster, L. F., & Coovert, M. D. (2006). Understanding and developing virtual computer-supported cooperative work teams. In C. Bowers, E. Salas, and F. Jentsch (Eds.), *Creating high-tech teams: Practical guidance on work performance and technology* (pp. 213–241). Washington: APA.

Frayne, C. A., & Latham, G. P. (1987). Application of social learning theory to employee self-management of attendance. *Journal of Applied Psychology, 72,* 387–392.

Gilbert, S. J., Gollwitzer, P. M., Cohen, A.-L., Oettingen, G., & Burgess, P. W. (2009). Separable brain systems supporting cued versus self-initiated realization of delayed intentions. *Journal of Experimental Psychology: Learning Memory and Cognition, 35,* 905–915.

Gendolla, G. H. E., & Wright, R. A. (2005). Motivation in social settings studies of effort-related cardiovascular arousal. In J. P. Forgas, K. D. Williams, & S. M. Laham (Eds.), *Social motivation: Conscious and unconscious processes* (pp. 71–90). New York: Cambridge University Press.

Gollwitzer, A., Oettingen, G., Kirby, T., Duckworth, A., & Mayer, D. (2011). Mental contrasting facilitates academic performance in school children. *Motivation and Emotion, 35,* 403–412.

Gollwitzer, P. M. (1993). Goal achievement: The role of intentions. *European Review of Social Psychology, 4,* 141–185.

Gollwitzer, P. M. (1999). Implementation intentions: Strong effects of simple plans. *American Psvchologist, 54,* 493–503.

Gollwitzer, P. M., & Brandstätter, V. (1997). Implementation intentions and effective goal striving. *Journal of Personality and Social Psychology, 73,* 186–199.

Gollwitzer, P. M., & Moskowitz, G. B. (1996). Goal effects on action and cognition. In E. T. Higgins and A. W. Kruglanski (Eds.), *Social psychology: Handbook of basic principles* (pp. 361–399). New York: Guilford.

Gollwitzer, P. M., & Oettingen, G. (2011). Planning promotes goal striving. In K. D. Vohs and R. F. Baumeister (Eds.), *Handbook of self-regulation: Research, theory, and applications* (2nd ed., pp. 162–185). New York: Guilford.

Gollwitzer, P. M., & Schaal, B. (1998). Metacognition in action: The importance of implementation intentions. *Personality and Social Psychology Review, 2,* 124–136.

Gollwitzer, P. M., & Sheeran, P. (2006). Implementation intentions and goal achievement: A meta-analysis of effects and processes. *Advances in Experimental Social Psychology, 38,* 69–119.

Henderson, M. D., Gollwitzer, P. M., & Oettingen, G. (2007). Implementation intentions and disengagement from a failing course of action. *Journal of Behavioral Decision Making, 20,* 81–102.

Holland, R. W., Aarts, H., & Langendam, D. (2006). Breaking and creating habits on the working floor: A field-experiment on the power of implementation intentions. *Journal of Experimental Social Psychology, 42,* 776–783.

Johannessen, K. B., Oettingen, G., & Mayer, D. (2012). Mental contrasting of a dieting wish improves self-reported health behavior. *Psychology and Health, 27,* 43–58.

Kappes, A., Oettingen, G., & Pak, H. (2012). Mental contrasting and the self-regulation of responding to negative feedback. *Personality and Social Psychology Bulletin, 38,* 845–856.

Kappes, A., & Oettingen, G. (2012). *The emergence of goal commitment: Mental contrasting connects future and reality.* Manuscript submitted for publication.

Kappes, A., Singmann, H., & Oettingen, G. (2012). Mental contrasting instigates behavior by linking reality with instrumental behavior. *Journal of Experimental Social Psychology, 48,* 811–818.

Kappes, H. B., Oettingen, G., Mayer, D., & Maglio, S. (2011). Sad mood promotes self-initiated mental contrasting of future and reality. *Emotion, 11,* 1206–1222.

Kirk, D., Gollwitzer, P. M., & Carnevale, P. J. (2011). Self-regulation in ultimatum bargaining: Goals and plans help accepting unfair but profitable offers. *Social Cognition, 29,* 528–546.

Kirk, D., Oettingen, G., & Gollwitzer, P. M. (2011). Mental contrasting promotes integrative bargaining. *International Journal of Conflict Management, 22,* 324–341.

Kirk, D., Oettingen, G., & Gollwitzer, P. M. (in press). Promoting integrative bargaining: Mental contrasting with implementation intentions. *International Journal of Conflict Management.*

Kirkman, B. L., & Mathieu, J. E. (2005). The dimensions and antecedents of team virtuality. *Journal of Management, 31,* 700–718.

Kirkman, B. L., Rosen, B., Tesluk, P. E., & Gibson, C. B. (2004). The impact of team empowerment on virtual team performance: The moderating role of face-to-face interaction. *Academy of Management Journal, 47,* 175–192.

Knäuper, B., Roseman, M., Johnson, P., & Krantz, L. (2009). Using mental imagery to enhance the effectiveness of implementation intentions. *Current Psychology, 28,* 181–186.

Koestner, R., Horberg, E. J., Gaudreau, P., Powers, T. A., Di Dio, P., Bryan, C. et al. (2006). Bolstering implementation plans for the long haul: The benefits of simultaneously boosting self-concordance or self-efficacy. *Personality and Social Psychology Bulletin, 32,* 1547–1558.

Latham, G. P., & Saari, L. M. (1979). The effects of holding goal difficulty constant on assigned and participatively set goals. *Academy of Management Journal, 22,* 63–168.

Lewin, K., Dembo, T., Festinger, L., & Sears, P. S. (1944). Level of aspiration. In J. McHunt (Ed.), *Personality and the behaviour disorders* (Vol. 1, pp. 333–378). New York: Ronald.

Locke, E. A., & Latham, G. P. (1990). *A theory of goal setting and task performance.* Englewood Cliffs, NJ: Prentice-Hall.

Locke, E. A., & Latham, G. P. (2002). Building a practically useful theory of goal setting and task motivation: A 35-year odyssey. *American Psychologist, 57,* 705–717.

Locke, E. A., & Latham, G. P. (2006). New directions in goal-setting theory. *Current Direction in Psychological Science, 15,* 265–268.

Maes, S., & Gebhardt, W. A. (2000). Self-regulation and health behavior: The Health Behavior Goal model. In: M. Boekaerts, P. R. Pintrich, & M. Zeidner (Eds.), *Handbook of self-regulation* (pp. 343–368). San Diego, CA: Academic Press.

Manz, C. C. (1986). Self-leadership: Toward an expanded theory of self-influence processes in organizations. *Academy of Management Review, 11,* 585–600.

Mendoza, S. A., Gollwitzer, P. M., & Amodio, D. M. (2010). Reducing the expression of implicit stereotypes: Reflexive control through implementation intentions. *Personality and Social Psychology Bulletin, 36,* 512–523.

Miles, J. D., & Proctor, R. W. (2008). Improving performance through implementation intentions: Are preexisting response biases replaced? *Psychonomic Bulletin and Review, 15,* 1105–1110.

Milne, S., Orbell, S., & Sheeran, P. (2002). Combining motivational and volitional interventions to promote exercise participation: Protection motivation theory and implementation intentions. *British Journal of Health Psychology, 7,* 163–184.

Muraven, M., & Baumeister, R. F. (2000). Self-regulation and depletion of limited resources: Does self-control resemble a muscle? *Psychological Bulletin, 126,* 247–259.

Nederveen Pieterese, A., van Knippenberg, D., & van Ginkel, W. P. (2011). Diversity in goal orientation, team reflexivity, and team performance. *Organizational Behavior and Human Decision Processes, 114*, 153–164.

O'Connell, M. S., Doverspike, D., & Cober, A. B. (2002). Leadership and semiautonomous work team performance: A field study. *Group and Organization Management, 27*, 50–65.

Oettingen, G. (2000). Expectancy effects on behavior depend on self-regulatory thought. *Social Cognition, 18*, 101–129.

Oettingen, G. (2012). Future thought and behavior change. In W. Stroebe & M. Hewstone (Eds.), *European Review of Social Psychology, 23*, 1–63.

Oettingen, G., & Gollwitzer, P. M. (2001). Goal setting and goal striving. In A. Tesser and N. Schwarz (Eds.), *The Blackwell handbook of social psychology* (pp. 329–347). Oxford, England: Blackwell.

Oettingen, G., & Gollwitzer, P. M. (2010). Strategies of setting and implementing goals: Mental contrasting and implementation intentions. In J. E. Maddux & J. P. Tangney (Eds.), *Social psychological foundations of clinical psychology* (pp. 114–135). New York: Guilford.

Oettingen, G., Hönig, G., & Gollwitzer, P. M. (2000). Effective self-regulation of goal attainment. *International Journal of Educational Research, 33*, 705–732.

Oettingen, G., Marquardt, M. K., & Gollwitzer, P. M. (2012). Mental contrasting turns positive feedback on creative potential into successful performance. *Journal of Experimental Social Psychology, 48*, 990–996.

Oettingen, G., Mayer, D., & Brinkmann, B. (2010). Mental contrasting of future and reality: Managing the demands of everyday life in health care professionals. *Journal of Personnel Psychology, 9*, 138–144.

Oettingen, G., Mayer, D., Sevincer, T. A., Stephens, E. J., Pak, H., & Hagenah, M. (2009). Mental contrasting and goal commitment: The mediating role of energization. *Personality and Social Psychology Bulletin, 35*, 498–512.

Oettingen, G., Mayer, D., & Thorpe, J. S. (2010). Self-regulation of commitment to reduce cigarette consumption: Mental contrasting of future with reality. *Psychology and Health, 25*, 961–977.

Oettingen, G., Mayer, D., Thorpe, J. S., Janetzke, H., & Lorenz, S. (2005). Turning fantasies about positive and negative futures into self-improvement goals. *Motivation and Emotion, 29*, 237–267.

Oettingen, G., Pak, H., & Schnetter, K. (2001). Self-regulation of goal-setting: Turning free fantasies about the future into binding goals. *Journal of Personality and Social Psychology, 80*, 736–753.

Oettingen, G., Stephens, E. J., Mayer, D., & Brinkmann, B. (2010). Mental contrasting and the self-regulation of helping relations. *Social Cognition, 28*, 490–508.

O'Hara-Devereaux, M., & Johansen, R. (1994). *Global work: bridging distance, culture, and time.* San Francisco, CA: Jossey-Bass.

Okhuysen, G. A., & Eisenhardt, K. M. (2002). Integrating knowledge in groups: How simple formal interventions help. *Organization Science, 13*, 370–386.

Orbell, S., Hodgkins, S., & Sheeran, P. (1997). Implementation intentions and the theory of planned behavior. *Personality and Social Psychology Bulletin, 23*, 953–962.

Orbell, S., & Sheeran, P. (2000). Motivational and volitional processes in action initiation: A field study of the role of implementation intentions. *Journal of Applied Social Psychology, 30*, 780–797.

Owens, S. G., Bowman, C. G., & Dill, C. A. (2008). Overcoming procrastination: The effect of implementation intentions. *Journal of Applied Social Psychology, 38*, 366–384.

Papies, E., Aarts, H., & de Vries, N. K. (2009). Grounding your plans: Implementation intentions go beyond the mere creation of goal-directed associations. *Journal of Experimental Social Psychology, 45*, 1148–1151.

Parks-Stamm, E. J., Gollwitzer, P. M., & Oettingen, G. (2007). Action control by implementation intentions: Effective cue detection and efficient response initiation. *Social Cognition, 25*, 248–266.

Powers, T. A., Koestner, R., & Topciu, R. A. (2005). Implementation intentions, perfectionism, and goal progress: Perhaps the road to hell is paved with good intentions. *Personality and Social Psychology Bulletin, 31*, 902–912.

Ronan, W. W., Latham, G. P., & Kinne, S. B. (1973). Effects of goal setting and supervision of worker behavior in an industrial setting. *Journal of Applied Psychology, 58*, 302–307.

Rutter, D. R., Steadman, L., & Quine, L. (2006). An implementation intentions intervention to increase uptake of mammography. *Annals of Behavioral Medicine, 32,* 127–134.

Ryan, R. M., and Frederick, C. M. (1997). On energy, personality, and health: Subjective vitality as a dynamic reflection of well-being. *Journal of Personality, 65*, 529–565.

Schweiger Gallo, I., Keil, A., McCulloch, K. C., Rockstroh, B., & Gollwitzer, P. M. (2009). Strategic automation of emotion regulation. *Journal of Personality and Social Psychology, 96*, 11–31.

Sevincer, A. T., & Oettingen, G. (2012). *Mental contrasting of future and reality: Prevalence, predictive validity, and determinants.* Under revision.

Sheeran, P. (2002). Intention-behavior relations: A conceptual and empirical review. In W. Stroebe & M. Hewstone (Eds.), *European Review of Social Psychology* (Vol. 12, pp. 1–30). Chichester: Wiley.

Sheeran, P., & Orbell, S. (1999). Implementation intentions and repeated behavior: Augmenting the predictive validity of the theory of planned behavior. *European Journal of Social Psychology, 29*, 349–369.

Sheeran, P., & Orbell, S. (2000). Using implementation intentions to increase attendance for cervical cancer screening. *Health Psychology, 19*, 283–289.

Sheeran, P., Webb, T. L., & Gollwitzer, P. M. (2005). The interplay between goal intentions and implementation intentions. *Personality and Social Psychology Bulletin, 31*, 87–98.

Sheeran, P., Milne, S. E., Webb, T. L., & Gollwitzer, P. M. (2005). Implementation intentions. In M. Conner & P. Norman (Eds.), *Predicting health behavior* (2nd ed., pp. 276–323). Buckingham: Open University Press.

Sitzmann, T., & Ely, K. (2010). Sometimes you need a reminder: The effects of prompting self-regulation on regulatory processes, learning, and attrition. *Journal of Applied Psychology, 95,* 132–144.

Sonnentag, S., Binnewies, C., & Mojza, E. J. (2010). Staying well and engaged when demands are high: The role of psychological detachment. *Journal of Applied Psychology, 95*, 965–997.

Stadler, G., Oettingen, G., & Gollwitzer, P. M. (2009). Physical activity in women. Effects of a self-regulation intervention. *American Journal of Preventive Medicine, 36*, 29–34.

Stadler, G., Oettingen, G., & Gollwitzer, P. M. (2010). Intervention effects of information and self-regulation on eating fruits and vegetables over two years. *Health Psychology, 29*, 274–283.

Stewart, B. D., & Payne, B. K. (2008). Bringing automatic stereotyping under control: Implementation intentions as efficient means of thought control. *Personality and Social Psychology Bulletin, 34*, 1332–1345.

Strecher, V. J., Seijts, G. H., Kok, G. J., Latham, G. P., Glasgow, R. DeVellis, B., Meertens R. M., & Bulger, D. W. (1995). Goal setting as a strategy for health behavior change. *Health Education Quarterly, 22,* 190–200.

Tangney, J. P., Baumeister, R. F., & Boone, A. L. (2004). High self-control predicts good adjustment, less pathology, better grades, and interpersonal success. *Journal of Personality, 72,* 271–322.

Triandis, H. C. (1980). Values, attitudes, and interpersonal behavior. In H. Howe & M. Page (Eds.), *Nebraska symposium on motivation* (Vol. 27, pp. 195–259). Lincoln, NB: University of Nebraska Press.

Trötschel, R., & Gollwitzer, P. M. (2007). Implementation intentions and the willful pursuit of prosocial goals in negotiations. *Journal of Experimental Social Psychology, 43,* 579–589.

Tyran, K. L., Tyran, C. K., & Sheperd, M. (2003). Exploring emerging leadership in virtual teams. In C. B. Gibson & S. G. Cohen (Eds.), *Virtual teams that work: Creating conditions for virtual team effectiveness* (pp. 187 ff.). San Francisco, CA: Jossey-Bass.

van Knippenberg, D., & Schippers, M. C. (2007). Work group diversity. *Annual Review of Psychology, 58,* 515–541.

Webb, T. L., Christian, J., & Armitage, C. J. (2007). Helping students turn up for class: Does personality moderate the effectiveness of an implementation intention intervention? *Learning and Individual Differences, 17,* 316–327.

Webb, T. L., & Sheeran, P. (2003). Can implementation intentions help to overcome ego-depletion. *Journal of Experimental Social Psychology 39,* 279–286.

Webb, T. L., & Sheeran, P. (2004). Identifying good opportunities to act: Implementation intentions and cue discrimination. *European Journal of Social Psychology, 34,* 407–419.

Webb, T. L., & Sheeran, P. (2007). How do implementation intentions promote goal attainment? A test of component processes. *Journal of Experimental Social Psychology, 43,* 295–302.

Webb, T. L., & Sheeran, P. (2008). Mechanisms of implementation intention effects: The role of goal intentions, self-efficacy, and accessibility of plan components. *British Journal of Social Psychology, 47,* 373–395.

Webb, T. L., Sheeran, P., & Luszczynska, A. (2009). Planning to break unwanted habits: Habit strength moderates implementation intention effects on behaviour change. *British Journal of Social Psychology, 48,* 507–523.

Wicklund, R. A., Slattum, V., & Solomon, E. (1970). Effects of implied pressure toward commitment on ratings of choice alternatives. *Journal of Experimental Social Psychology, 6,* 449–457.

Wieber, F., & Gollwitzer, P. M. (2010). Overcoming procrastination through planning. In C. Andreou & M. D. White (Eds.), *The thief of time: Philosophical essays on procrastination* (pp. 185–205). New York: Oxford University Press.

Wieber, F., Odenthal, G., & Gollwitzer, P. M. (2010). Self-efficacy feelings moderate implementation intention effects. *Self and Identity, 9,* 177–194.

Wieber, F., & Sassenberg, K. (2006). I can't take my eyes off of it—attention attraction of implementation intentions. *Social Cognition, 24,* 723–752.

Wright, R. A., & Kirby, L. D. (2001). Effort determination of cardiovascular response: An integrative analysis with applications in social psychology. In M. P. Zanna (Ed.), *Advances in experimental social psychology* (Vol. 33, pp. 255–307). San Diego, CA: Academic Press.

Wood, W., & Neal, D. T. (2007). A new look at habits and the habit–goal interface. *Psychological Review, 114,* 842–862.

Yanar, B., Budworth, M., & Latham, G. P. (2009). The effect of training in verbal self guidance on self-efficacy and reemployment of Turkish women. *Applied Psychology: An International Review, 58,* 586–601.

# 33  Priming Subconscious Goals

*Shlomit Friedman*  Department of Organizational Behavior,
Faculty of Management, Tel Aviv University

Goal setting theory is based on decades of findings that show that conscious goals affect actions (Locke & Latham, 1990, 2002). Accumulating evidence shows that primed goals may have similar effects on behavior as well. Bargh (2006), for example, has argued that priming affects individuals' motivation in general and goal pursuit in particular. "Priming" refers to the passive, subtle, and unobtrusive activation of relevant mental representations by external stimuli, such that people are not aware of their influence (Bargh & Huang, 2009).

The goal-priming literature has shown that goals can be primed through a wide variety of "environmental triggers": verbal stimuli semantically related to a goal (e.g., Chartrand & Bargh, 1996), material objects such as backpacks and briefcases (e.g., Kay, Wheeler, Bargh, & Ross, 2004), scents such as cleaning fluids (e.g., Holland Hendriks, & Aarts, 2005), and the names of an individual's significant others (e.g., Fitzsimons & Bargh, 2003).

Bargh (1990) has argued that the motive–goal–plan structure becomes activated whenever a relevant triggering situational feature is present in the environment, and that once activated, a primed goal operates like a conscious goal (Bargh, Gollwitzer, & Oettingen, 2010). The only difference is that it does so outside of awareness. A primed goal leads to the same outcomes, operates on relevant information in the environment, and, once attained, is deactivated. In short, a conscious goal is chosen or assigned explicitly, while a primed goal is triggered implicitly. A conscious goal motivates an individual to choose to exert effort and persist in goal-directed behavior intentionally. A primed goal has the same effect, only it operates autonomously from the conscious control of an individual.

The purpose of this chapter is twofold. First, a literature review describes the effects of a primed goal from both a social-psychology and an organizational psychology perspective. Second, the chapter explores possible explanations for the mechanisms through which a primed goal affects behavior.

## Social Psychology Research on Primed Goals

Priming any construct linked in an individual's mind to a goal may activate that goal (Kruglanski & Kopetz, 2009). Supraliminal priming techniques present priming stimuli to participants' conscious awareness, but the participants are unaware of the potential influence of the prime on their subsequent goal-directed behavior (Chartrand & Bargh, 1996). Subliminal priming refers to the presentation of stimuli with an intensity that is below the threshold of awareness. That is, people cannot consciously detect these stimuli, yet they are nevertheless influenced by them (Custers & Aarts, 2010). In both supraliminal and subliminal priming, participants are unaware that their goal-directed behavior is activated by a means other than conscious choice (Chartrand & Bargh, 1996). The dependent variables in social psychology experiments on primed goals include mimicry (e.g., Bargh & Chartrand, 1999), norm activation (e.g., Aarts & Dijksterhuis, 2003), a trait (e.g., aggression; Bargh, Chen, & Burrows, 1996, experiment 1; Srull & Wyer, 1979), a stereotype (e.g., the elderly; Bargh et al., 1996, experiment 2), or a behavior (e.g., shaking one's foot; Chartrand & Bargh, 1999). This section describes the common means of priming goal directed behavior in social psychology research.

### Semantic Priming

Typically, this supraliminal priming technique requires participants to construct grammatically correct sentences out of sets of four or five words (a certain percentage of which are primed words such as "achieve") presented in a scrambled order, or to find a list of words embedded in a $10 \times 10$ matrix of letters (e.g., Bargh, Gollwitzer, Lee-Chai, Barndollar, & Troetschel, 2001). Subliminal priming exposes participants to stimuli that are flashed outside participants' foveal visual field (e.g., Chartrand & Bargh, 1996).

Bargh, Gollwitzer, Lee-Chai, Barndollar, and Troetschel (2001) conducted five experiments in which participants were supraliminally primed with either a goal to perform well or a goal to cooperate with others. The priming of the goal to perform well caused participants to perform comparatively better on an intellectual task, and the priming of the goal to cooperate caused participants to replenish a commonly held resource more readily than those in the respective control groups. In addition, the results showed that the perceptual effects of priming vanished after a five minute delay, but the motivational effects of priming for performing the task increased significantly.

Hassin, Bargh, and Zimerman (2009) conducted two experiments to examine whether a primed goal can increase open-mindedness, when the latter improves the likelihood of goal achievement. In the first experiment, participants were primed with an achievement goal, and then performed the Wisconsin Card Sorting Test (WCST) to examine their adaptation to changing environmental conditions. The primed participants made fewer perseverative errors than those in the control group. The second experiment used a variation of the Iowa Gambling Task. On a different task and under different circumstances, participants primed with an achievement goal performed better than those in the control condition because they altered their choice of card-deck behavior; those in the control group failed to do so. Although goals can lead to tunnel vision, and *automatic* goal pursuit may be by implication inflexible, Hassin et al. argued that it is not necessarily so. Moreover, they argued that in order to be beneficial, automatic goal pursuit needs to be flexible. They explained that because goal priming enhances the use of proper means, when flexibility is a means for attaining a goal (i.e., successful performance in WCST), priming increases the probability of using it.

Shah and Kruglanski (2003) found that a goal can be activated by implicit perception of the means used to attain it. The perceived instrumentality of the means for attaining the goal was the crucial determinant of this priming effect. For example, participants who were subliminally primed with the name of a strategy to solve an anagram recognized goal-relevant words in a lexical decision task faster than nonprimed participants; participants in the strong means priming condition demonstrated greater goal accessibility, as assessed by their average latency in responding to goal-related stimuli. In short, priming the means to a given goal, or opportunity to pursue a goal, activated that goal and increased goal accessibility as well as goal persistence, and the quality of task performance.

## Interpersonal Relationships Priming

Shah (2003) found that "significant others" play an implicit role in determining how people perceive the difficulty, value, and regulatory focus (i.e., promotion–prevention) of their goals. Specifically, asking participants to provide the first name of the significant other (e.g., a friend or a family member) who would have the strongest belief about either how difficult the upcoming task will be for them (study 1), or about how important the upcoming task would be for the participant (study 2), affected their rating of the likelihood of goal attainment, and their own appraisal of the value of attaining the anagram task goal. Furthermore, the significant other influenced a participant's task persistence and performance. Priming participants with father-related words affected the regulatory focus (promotion–prevention) participants adopted while pursuing a task goal, as well as their emotional reaction to performance feedback (study 3).

Fitzsimons and Bargh (2003) found that relationship representations activate (prime) interpersonal goals that influence behavior in the absence of awareness. In their first experiment, participants in a friend-priming condition were more likely to subsequently volunteer to help the researcher, and to participate in an additional, longer study than participants in the co-worker-priming condition. In other words, the primed goal of maintaining interpersonal relationships activated goal-directed behavior.

Chartrand, Dalton, and Fitzsimons (2007) tested the boundary conditions under which individuals nonconsciously reject goals they associate with relationship partners, and instead pursue opposing goals. They found that participants subliminally primed with the name of a "controlling" significant other who wanted them to work hard answered fewer anagrams correctly compared to those primed with a controlling significant other who wanted them to have fun. A second experiment showed that chronic reactance (i.e., the motivation to behave in opposition to social influences when the latter are perceived as threats to autonomy) moderated this effect: Low-reactant individuals adopted a subliminally primed significant other's goal, whereas high-reactant individuals pursued an opposing goal. Chartrand et al. concluded that for chronically reactant individuals, the prime automatically elicited oppositional goal pursuits, and led to a "backlash."

Aarts, Gollwitzer, and Hassin (2004) found that goal contagion—a process by which people infer goals from others' behavior without conscious intent, and consequently act on these goals unaware of the fact they are doing so—is moderated by the value of the goal to the person. In a series of six experiments, participants automatically pursued a goal implied by another person's behavior. However, this goal contagion was dependent on goal attractiveness for that individual. For example, in the first experiment, goal pursuit only occurred for those who had a high need for making money, and thus were sensitive to the incentive value of attaining the monetary goal. In the second experiment, males who were exposed to another male's "wooing (of a female) efforts" were subsequently more inclined to help a female, but not a male. Furthermore, they found that goal contagion is unlikely to occur when others' goal pursuits unfold in a socially unacceptable way. For example, in the fourth experiment, when goal pursuit was performed in a socially unacceptable manner (i.e., seeking casual sex while being engaged), the goal failed to be contagious. Similarly, when negative affect is associated with a primed goal, its effect on behavior decreases (Custers, 2009).

Dik and Aarts (2007) found that perceiving effort in the movements of an agent affects goal contagion, and that the goal inferences occur spontaneously without awareness of doing so. An animated film showed a tree with a kite stuck in the branches. After a few seconds, participants saw a large ball "behave" in different ways to try to open a room with a ladder. Performance (i.e., finding six-letter words beginning with the letter H) was higher for participants when the ball's goal-directed movements increased in effort. In a follow up experiment, participants' willingness to help fill out an additional questionnaire for free increased in a linear relationship to the amount of effort on the part of the ball in the animated film.

Kawada, Oettingen, Gollwitzer, and Bargh (2004, studies 2 and 3) showed that participants supraliminally primed with the goal to compete, and those explicitly instructed to compete equally projected significantly more competitive behavioral intentions onto fictional characters shown in a prisoner's dilemma game than did those in the control group. Furthermore, the two goal groups did not differ from each other, suggesting that goal projection effects are equally strong when the person is aware and unaware of possessing the projected goal.

## Conceptual Priming

Abstract constructs such as stereotypes and commercial logos may also activate non-conscious goals.

### Social Norms

Oettingen, Grant, Smith, Skinner, and Gollwitzer (2006) examined the affective consequences of primed and conscious goal pursuit that either violates or maintains a prevailing social norm. They asked participants to work together on a joint task (writing stories) that typically leads to the social norm of cooperation. Then, they either subliminally primed or consciously set a goal to be either accommodating or combative. Control groups were created by using neutral words in the priming procedure, or by not setting a goal, respectively. Participants in the primed norm-violating goal condition reported more negative affect than those in the conscious norm-violating goal condition, because, unlike those in the conscious condition, they were not able to explain and justify their behavior. This difference was only in the affective responses, but not in the behavioral responses of participants. In other words, both nonconscious and conscious goals conditions had similar goal-directed behavior effects.

Zhong and Liljenquist's (2006) "Macbeth effect" provides an illustration of the goal-completion effect. In four experiments, they showed that a threat to moral purity activates a need for physical cleansing, and that physical cleansing helps people cope with moral threats. For example, their fourth experiment showed that participants who were asked to describe an unethical deed from their past and subsequently cleansed their hands with an antiseptic wipe, were less willing to volunteer to help a desperate graduate student than those who were not given the opportunity to wash their hands. Bargh et al. (2010) interpreted these findings as a de-activation process: Once a primed goal (moral purity) is satisfied (by physical washing of the hands), its influence on behavior disappears.

Holland, Hendriks, and Aarts (2005) found that compared with participants in the control group, those who were primed with a cleanliness goal by exposure to the citrus scent of an all-purpose cleaner responded faster to cleaning-related words in a word detection task (study 1), responded to cleaning words faster than to control words (study 1), listed cleaning activities in greater frequency (study 2), and kept their sitting area substantially cleaner when eating a biscuit that produces crumbs (study 3). Thus, exposing participants to that scent primed a cleanliness goal that subsequently led to these goal-relevant behaviors.

## Stereotypes

Aarts, Chartrand, Custers, Danner, Dik, Jefferis, & Cheng, (2005) contended that only goals that have previously existed for an individual can be primed. The results of their first experiment showed that participants who were subliminally primed with social groups who stereotypically have the goal of helping others (i.e., nurses) are more willing to exert effort in helping another person. But this behavioral effect was more pronounced for those with a pre-existing conscious goal of helping others. In the second experiment, participants who were subliminally primed with social groups associated with the goal of making money (i.e., stockbrokers) accelerated their performance on an unrelated mouse-click task that enabled them to then pursue the task that was instrumental in attaining the goal to make money. But this occurred only when they were confronted with a potential time constraint on achieving the goal-relevant task. This suggests that goal-primed participants speeded up their behavior to ensure they had enough time to engage in the primed goal-related task.

Sassenberg and Moskowitz (2005) found that priming creativity as a goal caused participants to generate more unusual uses for a given object compared with those in the control condition.

Huang, Sedlovskaya, and Bargh (2011) found that priming participants with a mating goal (i.e., reproduction) led to age-related prejudice. Participants who were primed by reading a 184-word passage describing a romantic date, subsequently made an inferior evaluation of older female university professors, compared with those who read a passage about two friends at the cinema. In three additional experiments, Huang, Sedlovskaya, Ackerman, and Bargh (2011) found that priming participants with a goal to avoid contamination (i.e., protecting oneself against the threat of contagious disease) increased their prejudice against members of an out-group.

## Logos, Brand Names, and Consumer Concepts

In a series of three experiments, Zhong and DeVoe (2010) found that priming participants with the goal of saving time by exposing them to fast-food-related concepts automatically increases speed- and time-related preferences. Specifically, compared with participants in the control group, those who were subliminally exposed to fast food logos read significantly faster, even though there was no time pressure to do so (study 1); desired time-saving products, while their preference for control products did not differ (study 2); and exhibited impatience in financial decisions, as they were more likely to accept a smaller payment now rather than wait for a bigger payment in a week (study 3).

Fitzsimons, Chartrand, and Fitzsimons (2008) found that priming goals of creativity and honesty by using brand logos affected participants' behavior. In their first experiment, participants were subliminally primed with the goal of creativity by Apple logos outperformed those who were subliminally exposed to IBM logos on a standard creativity measure of unusual uses test. In a second experiment, participants were primed with the goal of honesty by the Disney logo behaved more honestly than participants exposed to the E! logo (E! Entertainment Television is a 24-hour network of NBCUniversal Cable Entertainment, a division of NBCUniversal. Its programs are dedicated to the world of entertainment news, fashion, movie reviews, and celebrity gossip (source: http://www.eonline.com/about/index.jsp)). A third experiment showed that participants who did not value the goal "to be a creative person" were unaffected by the brand stimuli. In short, to have an effect on behavior, it appears that a prime must activate a goal that is important to a participant.

In a series of four studies that used supraliminal (a scrambled-sentence task) and subliminal priming, Chartrand, Huber, Shiv, and Tanner (2008) showed that priming of the goal to spend money (prestige) versus the goal to save money (thrift) had an effect on hypothetical and real consumer choices. These effects initially increased with a greater time interval (i.e., it was higher for the eight minute time interval than for the three minute interval) between the priming and the choice task, and declined when satisfied by a real (but not by a hypothetical) choice. For example, in the first experiment, participants made a hypothetical choice between two sock options. Results indicated that a greater proportion of participants chose the higher-priced Nike socks in the prestige condition than in the thrift condition. In another experiment, where participants had to make two real choices after which they received the product they chose, the difference in the second choice between the prestige and the thrift prime conditions vanished. Chartrand et al. explained that this is because participants satiated their primed goals when they made the first choice (i.e., when they chose and received a product), and the goal-priming manipulation did not carry over to the subsequent choice (i.e., a second choice participants were asked to make). In sum, Chartrand et al. concluded that primed goals have motivational properties consistent with conscious goal pursuit, that the effects are greater with a longer time interval between the priming task and the choice, and are less pronounced when the primed goal is attained by an actual choice (i.e., people who are primed to spend money get to choose and receive an expensive brand). Hypothetical choices do not satiate a primed goal, and therefore an increase in the time interval between the priming task and the choice task augments the effect of the prime. In contrast, a real choice attenuates the effect of a primed goal, so that when participants had previously made a real choice, the effect of priming (i.e., the difference in choice between the prestige and the thrift prime conditions) vanished.

Harris, Bargh, and Brownell (2009) found that priming a short-term hedonic enjoyment goal through the exposure to food advertising while watching TV caused participants to eat the food that was available. For both children and adults, food advertising increased automatic eating behavior even though the food (i.e., cheddar cheese "goldfish" crackers, carrots, and celery with dip, mini chocolate chip cookies, trail mix, and multigrain tortilla chips) was not presented in the advertisements. Moreover, this consumption was not related to reported hunger or other conscious influences.

In summary, the activation of a goal does not require conscious awareness or regulation. People can pursue a primed goal unaware that they are doing so (Chartrand & Bargh, 1996; Bargh et al., 1996; Bargh et al., 2001). Regardless of whether a goal is activated consciously or in the absence of awareness, it operates effectively to guide a person's goal-relevant cognition, affect, and behavior (Bargh et al., 2001). The social psychology research in this domain provides strong evidence that primed goals in diverse contexts motivate people to initiate and exhibit behaviors available in their repertoire when the goals are desired outcomes.

## Organizational Psychology Research on Primed Goals

In their review of this literature, Latham, Stajkovic, and Locke (2010) observed that many of the dependent variables used in social psychology experiments are of questionable relevance to an employee's performance in an organizational setting. Moreover, the time length between the manipulation of the primed goal and subsequent performance is typically only a few minutes. In addition, the dependent variable is typically a discrete event (e.g., choice of food) rather than ongoing behavior that is required in the workplace (e.g., job performance). Consequently, a small number of organizational psychologists have conducted empirical research to determine whether goals that are primed affect behavior in typically strong situations (Mischel, 1977), namely, a work setting.

Stajkovic, Locke, and Blair (2006) used Bargh's methodology of scrambled words to make sentences to prime achievement motivation. Unlike social psychologists who use general, vague conscious goals (e.g., behave cooperatively), they compared a specific conscious with an unconscious goal on a brainstorming task for uses of a coat hanger. Both types of goals significantly increased performance relative to a control condition. This corresponds to previous studies, in which the behavioral responses of participants were the same when the goals were either primed or consciously set (e.g., Kawada et al., 2004; Oettingen et al., 2006). The primed goal significantly enhanced the effect of the do-best general goal, and a specific, high goal. However, the performance effect of the specific, high conscious goal was stronger than that of a primed goal. These findings were replicated in a follow-up experiment the next day where the participants were asked to recall the sentences they unscrambled, and the goal they were given the day before. Subsequently, participants worked on a brainstorming task for uses of a wooden ruler for the same time duration. All effects from the study the previous day were obtained.

Eitam, Hassin, and Schul (2008) examined different implicit learning paradigms. In a simulation of a dynamic system that was presented to the participants as a "sugar factory," priming an achievement goal supraliminally (i.e., using a word-search puzzle) affected performance on the implicit learning tasks, namely, "the sugar factory" simulation, and the serial reaction time (SRT) task in which learning is incidental. For both tasks, those in the priming condition learned more than participants in the control condition. In the "sugar factory" task, primed participants attained their goal, the target production level, a significantly greater number of times than did participants in the control group. In the SRT task, those in the priming condition had a larger difference between the average response time in the two random blocks and the average response time in the fixed-sequence block, indicating additional learning. These results demonstrate the facilitation of implicit learning in a novel task by priming an achievement goal. Goal priming led to improved implicit learning without a concomitant increase in participants' explicit motivation or explicit knowledge.

Shantz and Latham (2009) conducted the first field experiment to test the effectiveness of a primed goal alone and in conjunction with a specific, difficult, consciously set goal on employee performance in a call center during a three-hour work shift. Employees' goal was either primed, using a photograph of a woman winning a race, or made specific. Performance was assessed in dollars raised from donors. There was a significant main effect for both the primed and the specific, high conscious goal. However, the conscious goal had a stronger effect on the amount of money raised than did the primed goal.

The results of this first field experiment on priming were replicated in two additional field experiments (Shantz & Latham, 2011). The results from these three field experiments provided further evidence that a primed goal has a positive effect on job performance. In all three work settings, employees in the primed condition raised more money than those in the control condition. The average $d$-statistic across the three field experiments was .56 (Shantz & Latham, 2011).

Social psychologists to date use the terms prime, nonconscious, and unconscious goals synonymously, and infer that a subconscious motive was aroused by a primed goal from a subsequent increase or change in performance. To determine whether a primed goal actually affects the subconscious, Shantz and Latham (2009) used a picture story exercise (TAT) to determine whether the prime (e.g., the image of the woman winning the race) influences a person's implicit motive for achievement. After manipulating the prime, participants were asked to write three imaginative stories based on pictures that were shown to them. Each story was analyzed using a computer software program, namely, the Linguistic Inquiry and Word Count (Pennebaker, Francis, & Booth, 2001), which calculates the extent to which people use different categories of words in texts. Individuals who were primed with the photograph wrote stories using significantly more achievement-related words than those in the control condition, indicating that this prime influences the implicit motive for achievement. Thus, the term *subconscious goal* is used throughout the remainder of this chapter.

Latham and Piccolo (2012) conducted a field experiment to test whether a subconscious goal that is context specific to the work that is to be performed leads to a significant increase in job performance relative to a primed general achievement goal. The prime for the context-specific condition was a color photograph of three call center employees. The prime for the general achievement condition was the same color photograph of a woman winning a race used by Shantz and Latham (2009, 2011). Employees' performance was measured in terms of the number of donors who pledged dollars to an organization. Latham and Piccolo found that both subconscious context-specific goals and subconscious general achievement goals led to significant increases in job performance over a no-goal control group, but the employees in the context-specific prime obtained significantly more pledges than did those employees in the general prime or the control group.

Whereas Shantz and Latham (2009) had administered the TAT to college students in a laboratory experiment, Latham and Piccolo administered the TAT to the employees in the call center. They replicated the previous results. Both photographs aroused the subconscious need for achievement.

Ganegoda, Latham, and Folger (2011) found that participants who were supraliminally primed in a laboratory experiment for a fairness goal (i.e., were asked to evaluate company mission statements for fairness, equality, justice, and respect for others) displayed lower levels of profit inequality with their negotiation partner, higher levels of perceived fairness regarding the offer, and higher levels of offer acceptance compared with those who had not been primed to behave fairly. The same results were obtained for participants who were given a conscious, specific, self-set goal for a fair and equitable deal for both parties, compared with those who were given a general do-your-best goal to negotiate a deal that is acceptable to both parties. Furthermore, the subconscious goal significantly improved fair behavior for participants in the conscious-goal and the do-best conditions, the effect being greater for those in the conscious-goal condition compared to those in the do-your-best condition.

In a laboratory experiment, Stajkovic, Locke, Blair, and Piccolo (2009) examined what occurs when a subconscious and a specific, conscious goal are in conflict, namely, speed versus accuracy. They found that when a conscious goal for speed was paired with a primed goal for accuracy (or vice versa) on a proofreading task, each undermined the other. In another laboratory experiment, Stajkovic, Locke, Bandura, and Greenwald (2009) found that a primed achievement goal affected goals that are self-set and subsequent performance. The effect of primed goals on performance was fully mediated by self-set specific goals, but not by conscious self-efficacy. These findings suggest that subconscious concepts may, at times, work through their conscious counterparts to affect performance.

## Theoretical Explanations of Subconscious Goals

Priming appears to activate goals in the subconscious that are representations of desired end states, thereby eliciting action consistent with conscious goal attainment (Forster, Liberman, & Friedman, 2007). There are at least five theoretical explanations for why a subconscious goal affects behavior.

### Auto-Motive Theory

Bargh's (1990) auto-motive theory states that although many of the goals an individual pursues are the result of conscious deliberation and choice, conscious choice is not necessary for goal activation and operation. The theory states that goals are represented in memory in the same way as social attitudes, stereotypes, and schemas. Because social attitudes and stereotypes can be automatically activated by environmental stimuli, goal representations should have this capacity as well. Therefore, repeated and consistent choice of a particular goal in a specific situation over time renders the representation of that goal directly and automatically linked in memory to the representation of that situation.

As a result, exposure to a particular situational feature in the environment can automatically trigger goals chronically associated with those features. Auto-motive theory further states that the automatically activated goal, in turn, activates plans to attain the goal and that these plans then operate interactively with the available goal-relevant information in the environment. The entire sequence of goal activation and operation occurs without an individual's conscious intention or awareness (Bargh & Barndollar, 1996).

## Priming by Association

Priming, it is claimed, activates a discrepancy between an existing and a desired state, followed by a tension that the individual seeks to resolve (Moskowitz, 2009). The course of action the individual chooses to resolve this tension depends on the person's previous experience. If a goal is repeatedly pursued in a specific manner and in a specific setting, the goal may become associated with this behavior and setting. The stronger the association, the higher is the likelihood that on encountering that specific setting, the person automatically pursues the goal without awareness (Shah, 2005). The environmental cues activate (i.e., prime) the goal in a way that is similar to the establishment of cognitive associations through conditioning, which develops and maintains coactivation of different stimuli (e.g., *bell* and *food*) over repeated occasions (Shah & Kruglanski, 2003). But what appears to be an automatic pathway between the environmental cue and a behavior is in fact an environmental cue activating a particular goal that produces the behavior.

## Priming as Interplay of External Cues and Internal Motivation

Moskowitz and Gesundheit (2009) argued that mental representations of goals vary in their accessibility. "Priming" a goal means retrieving that goal from a person's long-term memory to short-term memory in the absence of a person's awareness. Once priming has occurred, that goal is ready to be used in interpreting and responding to environmental cues. What becomes accessible is partly determined by what the individual has been exposed to in the environment. The person does not need to consciously activate the goal; this is done by environmental cues that act as primes. Once the cue is detected by the perceptual system (whether supraliminally or subliminally), it will lead to attempts to categorize it, thus retrieving associated representations (such as goals) from long-term memory to a state of heightened accessibility in short-term memory. A given environment may contain many cues that are capable of pushing a wide range of goals to heightened accessibility. Which cues grab an individual's attention will also depend on how the opportunities for various goal pursuits in a given context relate to the value, strength, and commitment an individual has to each of the potentially activated goals. Thus, accompanying the push of the environment is the pull of an individual's motivational system. There is an interaction between the needs of the person, the strength of the goals associated with those needs, and environmental opportunities available for the person to pursue those goals. The association between environmental cues and goals can be created consciously or triggered implicitly.

Moskowitz and Gesundheit (2009) listed three ways in which a subconscious goal can attain a heightened state of accessibility. The first is "implicit priming of a goal without awareness of the mediating processes that give rise to the goal accessibility" (p. 207). In other words, the person is not only unaware of the fact that a goal has been triggered, but is also unaware of the stimulus that is relevant to the goal. This includes subliminal priming and implicit inference of goals. The second way is "implicit priming of a goal despite awareness of some component(s) of the process that give rise to the goal accessibility" (p. 207). In other words, a goal becomes accessible through consciously detected cues in the environment. The accessibility of the goal persists after the cue (priming stimulus) has been removed, and the individual is no longer aware of its influence at the time of goal-relevant responses. The third is "a conscious decision to pursue a goal followed by subsequent lack of awareness that the goal is accessible" (p. 207). This is analogous to forming implementation intentions, discussed in Chapter 32.

### Priming as Pre-Programming of the Mind

Custers and Aarts (2010) argued that the mind is designed for action, and continuously and, mostly subconsciously, processes behaviorally relevant information in order to direct behavior, and deal with the opportunities and challenges presented by the environment. Thus, setting, pursuing, and attaining a goal often occurs in the absence of conscious choice. The subconscious activation of goals follows the same ideomotor principle by which the mere activation of the idea of a behavior or an outcome moves the pre-programmed human body to act without making a conscious decision. People are able to initiate action by thinking about the outcomes when action and outcomes are associated on a perceptual, sensory, and motor level. Through prior learning, certain patterns of muscle contraction and relaxation become associated with their observable outcomes. Custers and Aarts argued that the ideomotor principle holds not only for the preparation and execution of a simple goal directed response such as getting a cup of coffee, it also holds for cognitive control of complex social behavior. Furthermore, Custers and Aarts argued that the pursuit of goals depends on the value of the goal for an individual, and is therefore characterized by flexibility and persistence.

Dijksterhuis and Aarts (2010) argued that "goals guide attention and thereby often behavior, and both goals and attention are largely independent from consciousness" (p. 469). When a representation of a behavior is primed with positive affect, it becomes a goal that motivates attainment. Attention is the selective information processing of incoming stimuli. Because information-processing capacity is limited, attention facilitates which stimuli get access to these capacity-limited cognition and behavioral processes. Dijksterhuis and Aarts argued further that both the amount and duration of attention devoted to incoming information is determined by active goals, and that incoming information that is relevant for goal attainment is attended to much more than information that is irrelevant. Goals direct attention in the service of goal pursuit. By modulating attention processes, goals guide behavior in the absence of awareness.

## McClelland's Theory of Implicit Motives

McClelland (1965) argued that all motives are learned. Biological discomforts or pleasures are linked to cues that can signify their presence or absence, and become "drives" or "urges." "Motives" are clusters of such associations that grow around affective experiences, not necessarily connected with biological needs.

McClelland (e.g., McClelland, Koestner, & Weinberger, 1989) distinguished between self-reported measures of achievement, which he termed "self attributed need of achievement," and implicit motives as measured by the Thematic Appreciation Test (TAT). Because measures of self-attributed needs and implicit motives seldom correlate in empirical studies, McClelland concluded that they tap two qualitatively different kinds of human motivation. Unlike questionnaire measures of self-attributed motivations, which tap an individual's cognition-based self-concept, implicit motives tap an individual's emotional–motivational dispositions, and can predict spontaneous behavioral trends over time. McClelland et al. (1989) demonstrated that a motivational disposition (e.g., n Achievement) energizes, directs, and selects behavior. McClelland termed these motivational dispositions "implicit motives," and argued that they are based on incentives involved in doing or experiencing certain things, built on association with innately triggered affective experiences, called *natural incentives* or *primes* (McClelland, 1985). McClelland et al. (1989) suggested that implicit motives are like a semantic memory, in that they automatically influence behavior without conscious effort, whereas conscious goal setting is analogous to episodic recall, which involves a voluntary act (pp. 698–699). In other words, implicit motives are based on emotional (not cognitive) learning, that a specific behavior is instrumental in attaining an incentive (McClelland, 1989). Implicit motives are aroused by affective experiences intrinsic to an activity, not by explicit reference to an unmet goal.

A motive (for McClelland) is implicit in the sense that it functions outside of awareness, and is not correlated with self-attributed questionnaire-based measures (Koestner et al., 1991). It affects an individual's fantasies and behavior if aroused by relevant stimuli in the individual's environment. Therefore, the strength of a person's motive can be determined by analyzing the content of fantasies reported in response to picture cues thematically related to that motive (Schultheiss, Campbell, & McClelland, 1999).

McClelland's (1985) intervention to increase the strength of n Achievement, a subconscious motive, was done explicitly at the conscious level, including writing n Achievement relevant goals and plans for the next two years, and sending trainees reminders of their conscious goals every six months. However, McClelland stated that implicit motives should be measured not explicitly (i.e., by self-report) but by counting the number of associations belonging to a given motive cluster as compared to others that an individual produces in a given number of opportunities. An implicit motive is measured by a content analysis of associative thought streams produced in response to the Thematic Apperception Test. The coding of the stories assesses the frequency with which a person who wrote the story tends to think spontaneously in those terms, even though it was not required (McClelland, 1962). Stories written to pictures are successful in reflecting implicit motives because they provide a direct read-out of motivational and emotional experiences. The imaginative stories from which implicit motives are coded reflect motivational and emotional themes in a person's life, evaluated as to their appropriateness in terms of concepts of the self, others, and what is important to this individual (McClelland et al., 1989). The fantasy-derived motives are considered *implicit* needs in the sense that the person is not explicitly describing him or herself as having the motive (Koestner, Weinberger, & McClelland, 1991). McClelland's methodology for building a subconscious motive focuses on conscious goals, associative networks, and environmental cues (Latham & Locke, 2012).

In summary, there are at least five explanations for the way subconscious goal affects behavior. These explanations share the following understandings: (a) Conscious choice is not necessary for goal activation and operation; (b) exposure to an environmental stimulus can automatically activate a goal that is associated with it; (c) this automatic activation is learned, in the sense that the environmental stimulus is repeatedly associated with an affect, a behavior, or a goal; (d) when an environmental stimulus primes a goal, it retrieves the goal from memory, and renders it accessible to the individual; and (e) the individual's value and motivation impact retrieval and accessibility.

## Relevance to Organizational Settings

Although organizations are unlikely to use scrambled sentences or word puzzles as primes, other stimuli such as photographs, music, artifacts, and scents are more relevant to, and easier to use, in an organizational setting as primes promoting adaptive goal pursuit. Priming keeps an individual tied to the present, freeing conscious processing to contemplate the past or plan for the future. In this sense, the subconscious goal ensures effective goal pursuit even under new, complex, or difficult circumstances (assuming people possess the needed knowledge and skills). It is an effective means of ensuring goal attainment, because it does not depend on the additional, and often uncertain, steps of conscious decision making and attentional guidance at the moment of truth (Bargh et al., 2001).Thus, organizations may promote desired behaviors that are aligned with organizational strategy. In addition, subconscious goal pursuit is efficient as it does not consume cognitive resources (Parks-Stamm & Gollwitzer, 2009).

Shantz and Latham's field experiments (2009, 2011) revealed that the beneficial effect of a primed goal on job performance endures beyond a few seconds, to an actual work shift of four hours; Latham and Piccolo (2012) found that it affected job performance for a four-day work week. Furthermore, because a conscious goal and a subconscious goal are not necessarily correlated, their effect on job performance has been found to be additive. The two goals together have a greater effect on performance than either one alone. The practical implication of this finding is that the subconscious can be harnessed to an employee's and employer's advantage, using environmental cues in the workplace, such as photographs relevant to appraising, coaching, and training employees, allowing employees to apply what has been learned during training to their job. Employees can self-manage themselves, and increase their performance, without direct supervision.

Given the powerful influence subconscious goals have on behavior, one might question the ethics and morality of using them in organizational settings. However, only goals that preexist in the mind can be primed (Aarts et al., 2005). Goals that become negatively represented or morally questioned lose their attractiveness (Aarts et al., 2004). This suggests that goals can be primed without posing a threat to *organizational* ethics and policies. This assumes, of course, that the organization itself insists on honest practices.

## Conclusion

Goals are conceptualized as mental representations of a desirable end state, and as such they provide a reference point for almost all behavior (Dijksterhuis & Aarts, 2010). Recent studies in the fields of social psychology and human resource management show that goals can be activated outside of awareness by features of the environment. However, the fact that priming works does not mean it controls every aspect of our lives. Conscious goals chosen by the individual affect behavior as well. In fact, a subconscious goal affects behavior only when it is aligned with the person's values and pre-existing goals. In an organizational setting, the greatest impact on employees' behavior would be the result of a specific, challenging, conscious goal, complemented by a congruent subconsciously primed goal. The effects of the two types of goals on performance are additive (Latham & Locke, 2012).

## References

Aarts, H., Chartrand, T. L., Custers, R., Danner, U., Dik, G., Jefferis, V. E., & Cheng, C. M. (2005). Social stereotypes and automatic goal pursuit. *Social Cognition, 6*, 465–490.

Aarts, H., & Dijksterhuis, A. (2003). The silence of the library: Environment, situational norm, and social behavior. *Journal of Personality and Social Psychology, 84*, 18–28.

Aarts. H. Gollwitzer, P. M., & Hassin R. R. (2004). Goal contagion: Perceiving is for pursuing. *Journal of Personality and Social Psychology, 87*, 23–37.

Bargh, J. A. (1990). Auto-motives: Preconscious determinants of thought and behaviour. Multiple affects from multiple stages. In E. T. Higgins & R. M. Sorrentino (Eds.), *Handbook of motivation and cognition: Foundations of social behavior* (Vol. 2, pp. 93–130). New York: Guilford Press.

Bargh, J. A. (2006). What have we been priming all these years? On the development, mechanisms, and ecology of nonconscious social behavior. *European Journal of Social Psychology, 36*, 147–168.

Bargh, J. A., & Barndollar, K. (1996). Automaticity in action: The unconscious as repository of chronic goals and motives. In P. M. Gollwitzer, & J. A. Bargh (Eds.), *The psychology of action: Linking cognition and motivation to behavior* (pp. 457–481). New York, NY: Guilford Press.

Bargh, J. A., & Chartrand, T. L. (1999). The unbearable automaticity of being. *American Psychologist, 54*, 462–479.

Bargh, J. A., Chen, M., & Burrows, L. (1996). Automaticity of social behavior: Direct effects of trait construct and stereotype activation on action. *Journal of Personality and Social Psychology, 71*, 230–244.

Bargh, J. A., Gollwitzer, P. M., Lee-Chai, A., Barndollar, K., & Troetschel, R. (2001). The automated will: Nonconscious activation and pursuit of behavioral goals. *Journal of Personality and Social Psychology, 81*, 1014–1027.

Bargh, J. A., Gollwitzer, P. M., & Oettingen, G. (2010). Motivation. In S. T. Fiske, D. T. Gilbert, & G. Lindzey (Eds.), *Handbook of social psychology* (5th ed.). New York: Wiley.

Bargh, J. A., & Huang, J. Y. (2009). The selfish goal. In G. B. Moskowitz & H. Grant (Eds.), *The psychology of goals* (pp. 127–150). New York: Guilford Press.

Chartrand, T. L., & Bargh, J. A. (1996). Automatic activation of impression formation and memorization goals: Nonconscious goal priming reproduces effects of explicit task instructions. *Journal of Personality and Social Psychology, 71*, 464–478.

Chartrand, T. L., & Bargh, J. A. (1999). The chameleon effect: The perception—Behavior link and social interaction. *Journal of Personality and Social Psychology, 76*, 893–910.

Chartrand, T. L., Dalton, A. N., & Fitzsimons, G. J. (2007). Nonconscious relationship reactance: When significant others prime opposing goals. *Journal of Experimental Social Psychology, 43*, 719–726.

Chartrand, T. L., Huber, J., Shiv, B., & Tanner, R. J. (2008). Nonconscious goals and consumer choice. *Journal of Consumer Research, 35*, 189–201.

Custers, R. (2009). How does our unconscious know what we want? The role of affecting goal representation. In G. B. Moskowitz & H. Grant (Eds.), *The psychology of goals* (pp. 179–202). New York: Guilford Press.

Custers, R., & Aarts, H. (2010). The unconscious will: How the pursuit of goals operates outside of conscious awareness. *Science, 329*, 47–50.

Dijksterhuis, A., & Aarts, H. (2010). Goals, attention, and (un)consciousness. *Annual Review of Psychology, 61*, 467–490.

Dik, G., & Aarts, H. (2007). Behavioral cues to others' motivation and goal pursuits: The perception of effort facilitates goal inference and contagion. *Journal of Experimental Social Psychology, 43*, 727–737.

Eitam, B., Hassin, R. R., & Schul, Y. (2008). Nonconscious goal pursuit in novel environments: The case of implicit learning. *Psychological Science, 19*, 261–267.

Fitzsimons, G. M., & Bargh, J. A. (2003). Thinking of you: Nonconscious pursuit of interpersonal goals associated with relationship partners. *Journal of Personality and Social Psychology, 84*, 148–164.

Fitzsimons, G. M., Chartrand, T. L., & Fitzsimons, G. J. (2008). Automatic effects of brand exposure on motivated behavior: How Apple makes you think different. *Journal of Consumer Research, 35*, 21–34.

Forster, J., Liberman, N., & Friedman, R. S. (2007). Seven principles of goal activation: A systematic approach to distinguishing goal priming from priming of non-goal constructs. *Personality and Social Psychology Review, 11*, 211–233.

Ganegoda, D. B., Latham, G. P., & Folger, R. (2011). The effect of subconscious and conscious goal setting on organizational justice in negotiations. Manuscript submitted for publication.

Harris, J. L., Bargh, J. A., & Brownell, K. D. (2009). Priming effects of television food advertising on eating behavior. *Health Psychology, 28*, 404–413.

Hassin, R. R., Bargh, J. A., & Zimerman, S. (2009). Automatic and flexible: The case of nonconscious goal pursuit. *Social Cognition, 27*, 20–36.

Holland, R. W., Hendriks, M., & Aarts, H. (2005). Smells like clean spirits: Non-conscious effects of scent on cognition and behaviour. *Psychological Science, 16*, 689–693.

Huang, J. H., Sedlovskaya, A., Ackerman, J. M., & Bargh J. (2011). Immunizing against prejudice: Effects of disease protection on attitudes toward out-groups. *Psychological Science, 22*, 1550–1556.

Huang, J. Y., Sedlovskaya, A., & Bargh, J. A. (2011). The mating goal and professorial evaluations. Paper presented at the meeting of Marketing and OBHRM Departments, Rotman School of Management, University of Toronto.

Kawada, C. L. K., Oettingen, G., Gollwitzer, P. M., & Bargh, J. A. (2004). The projection of implicit and explicit goals. *Journal of Personality and Social Psychology, 86*, 545–559. DOI: 10.1037/0022-3514.86.4.545.

Kay, A. C., Wheeler, C. S., Bargh, J. A., & Ross, L. D. (2004). Material priming: The influence of mundane physical objects on situational construal and competitive behavioural choice. *Organizational Behavior and Human Decision Processes, 95*, 83–96.

Koestner, R., Weinberger, J., & McClelland, D. C. (1991). Task-intrinsic and social-extrinsic sources of arousal for motives assessed in fantasy and self-report. *Journal of Personality, 59,* 57–82.

Kruglanski, A. W., & Kopetz, C. (2009). What is so special (and nonspecial) about goals? In G. B. Moskowitz & H. Grant (Eds.), *The psychology of goals* (pp. 27–55). New York: Guilford Press.

Latham, G. P., & Locke, E. A. (2012). The effect of subconscious goals on organizational behavior. *International Review of Industrial-Organizational Psychology* (pp. 39–63). Chichester, England: Wiley.

Latham, G. P., & Piccolo, R. F. (2012). The effect of a specific versus and nonspecific subconscious goal on employee performance. *Human Resource Management, 51,* 535–548.

Latham, G. P., Stajkovic, A. D., & Locke, E. A. (2010). The relevance and viability of subconscious goals in the workplace. *Journal of Management, 36,* 234–255.

Locke, E. A., & Latham, G. P. (1990). *A theory of goal setting and task performance.* Upper Saddle River, NJ: Prentice Hall.

Locke, E. A., & Latham, G. P. (2002). Building a practically useful theory of goal setting and work motivation: A 35 year odyssey. *American Psychologist, 57,* 705–717.

McClelland, D. C. (1962). Business drive and national achievement. *Harvard Business Review, 40,* 99–112.

McClelland, D. C. (1965). Toward a theory of motive acquisition. *American Psychologist, 20,* 321–333.

McClelland, D. C. (1985). *Human motivation.* Glenview, IL: Scott, Foresman.

McClelland, D. C. (1989). Motivational factors in health and disease. *American Psychologist, 44,* 675–683.

McClelland, D. C., Koestner, R., & Weinberger, J. (1989). How do self-attributed and implicit motives differ? *Psychology Review, 96,* 690–702.

Mischel, W. (1977). The interaction of person and situation. In D. Magnusson & N. S. Endler (Eds.), *Personality at the crossroads: Current issues in interactional psychology.* Hillsdale, N.J.: Erlbaum.

Moskowitz, G. B. (2009). The compensatory nature of goal pursuit: From explicit action to implicit cognition. In G. B. Moskowitz & H. Grant (Eds.), *The psychology of goals* (pp. 304–336). New York: Guilford Press.

Moskowitz, G. B., & Gesundheit, Y. (2009). Goal priming. In G. B. Moskowitz & H. Grant (Eds.), *The psychology of goals* (pp. 203–233). New York: Guilford Press.

Oettingen, G., Grant, H., Smith, P. K., Skinner, M., & Gollwitzer, P. M. (2006). Nonconscious goal pursuit: Acting in an explanatory vacuum. *Journal of Experimental Social Psychology, 42,* 668–675.

Parks-Stamm, E., & Gollwitzer, P. M. (2009). Goal Implementation: The benefits and costs of if-then planning. In G. B. Moskowitz & H. Grant (Eds.), *The psychology of goals* (pp. 362–391). New York: Guilford Press.

Pennebaker, J. W., Francis, M. E., & Booth, R. J. (2001). *Linguistic inquiry word count,* Mahwah, NJ: Erlbaum.

Sassenberg, K., & Moskowitz, G. B. (2005). Do not stereotype, think different! Overcoming automatic stereotype activation by mindset priming. *Journal of Experimental Social Psychology, 41,* 317–413.

Schultheiss, O. C., Campbell, K. L., & McClelland, D. C. (1999). Implicit power motivation moderates men's testosterone responses to imagined and real dominance success. *Hormones and Behavior, 36,* 234–241. DOI: 10.1006/hbeh.1999.1542.

Shah, J. (2003). The motivational looking glass: how significant others implicitly affect goal appraisals. *Journal of Personality and Social Psychology, 85*, 424–439.

Shah, J. Y. (2005). The automatic pursuit and management of goals. *Current Directions in Psychological Science, 14*, 10–13.

Shah, J., and Kruglanski, A. (2003). When opportunity knocks: Bottom-up priming of goals by means and its effects on self-regulation. *Journal of Personality and Social Psychology, 84*, 1109–1122.

Shantz, A., & Latham, G. P. (2009). An exploratory field experiment on the effect of subconscious and conscious goals on employee performance. *Organizational Behavior and Human Decision Making Processes, 109*, 9–17.

Shantz, A., & Latham, G. P. (2011). The effect of primed goals on employee performance: Implications for human resource management. *Human Resource Management, 50*, 289–299.

Srull, T., & Wyer, R. (1979). The role of category accessibility in the interpretation of information about persons: Some determinants and implications. *Journal of Personality and Social Psychology, 37*, 1660–1672.

Stajkovic, A. D., Locke, E. A., & Blair, E. S. (2006). A first examination of the relationships between primed subconscious goals, assigned conscious goals, and task performance. *Journal of Applied Psychology, 91*, 1172–1180.

Stajkovic, A. D., Locke, E. A., Bandura, A., & Greenwald, J. (2009). The effects of subconscious self-efficacy on performance and mediation of conscious self-efficacy and conscious self-set goals. In A. D. Stajkovic (Chair), *Subconscious goals, self efficacy, need for achievement: The latest priming research.* Symposium at the annual meeting of the Society of Industrial-Organizational Psychology, New Orleans.

Stajkovic, A. D., Locke, E. A., Blair, E., & Piccolo, R. (2009). The effects of pitting assigned conscious goals against primed subconscious goals. Unpublished manuscript. [The earlier version of this manuscript was presented at the Academy of Management, *Human Resources, and Managerial and Organizational Cognition* divisions. Philadelphia, 2007.]

Zhong, C. B., & DeVoe, S. E. (2010). You are how you eat: Fast food and impatience. *Psychological Science, 21*, 619–622.

Zhong, C. B., & Liljenquist, K. (2006). Washing away your sins: Threatened morality and physical cleansing. *Science, 313*, 1451–1452.

# Part IX

# Problems and Pitfalls

# 34 Potential Pitfalls in Goal Setting and How to Avoid Them

*Gary P. Latham*   Rotman School of Management, University of Toronto
*Edwin A. Locke*   Robert H. Smith School of Business, University of Maryland

There are pitfalls to be avoided when using virtually any method or technique. The potential dangers to be avoided when setting specific, high goals have been enumerated repeatedly by us, starting over 25 years ago (Latham, 2012; Latham & Locke 2006; Locke & Latham, 1984). These concerns include: risk taking, fear of failure, goals as a threat, stress and anxiety, ability, skill, and self efficacy, non-goal areas ignored, choosing what goals to set, stretch goals, multiple goals, short versus long range thinking, conflict, success, dishonesty and cheating, and tying monetary incentives to goals. The purpose of this chapter is to provide an update of what we recommend regarding these issues. In some instances, the potential pitfalls are in reality advantages of setting a specific, high goal.

## Risk taking

A laboratory experiment by Larrick, Heath, and Wu (2009) showed that goals increased risk taking. But this fact alone is not the issue. Risk taking can lead to positive (Knight, Durham, & Locke, 2001) as well as negative outcomes. All decisions, within business and without, entail risk because no one is omniscient. The issue is to limit unnecessary risk and not take risks that are irrational. BB&T, an eastern seaboard banking company, was one of the few major banks that did not buy subprime mortgages. Why didn't they? They looked at their past experience and found that people who take out mortgages they cannot really afford make poor risks, which means securities based on such mortgages are also poor risks. BBT's goals did not involve maximizing short-term gains but in making sound long-term investments. Two factors are critical in limiting risk, over and above effort and persistence. The first is to look at all the relevant facts objectively divorced from emotion, if relevant facts are available. The second is to develop needed skills in whatever you are doing. Steve Jobs did not do market surveys to invent Apple's stunning products because it is hard to figure out if people would like something they have never imagined, but he was very good at creating dynamite products. (Goals can even be set for creativity—see Chapter 22).

## Fear of failure

Nobody likes to fail, so they may fear hard goals. People may fear the errors that are inevitably made in pursuing such goals. However, Frese and colleagues' research (e.g., Keith & Frese, 2005) shows that errors can be framed positively by enlightened managers and executives. In fact, when errors are accepted and people are given the opportunity to make them, performance ultimately improves if there is error management training that induces both emotion control and metacognitive activity (e.g., thinking, problem solving) when errors are made. The errors typically enhance an individual's mental model of a task by leading to new insights and creative solutions. (Obviously there must be good control systems to prevent catastrophic errors such as large, irrational investments).

People may also fear failure because their bosses react to failure in a punitive manner without taking account of context factors such as uncompetitive products or poor market conditions. It is not irrational to fear bad management, and it may stimulate looking for a better job.

People also may fear not having the needed knowledge and skill to succeed—they may lack self-efficacy (confidence in being able to do the job—see Chapter 10). It is management's job to hire the right people and give them the needed training and experience so that they will be able to succeed. Some skills, of course, need to be acquired on one's own.

Finally, people may also make attaining particular targets an issue of self-esteem as opposed to something that is desirable. This is unwise because it can lead to feelings of desperation and thereby foolish risk taking or even dishonesty. It is more psychologically sound to base self-esteem on how you go about pursuing the goal (e.g., did you look at all the facts, do your homework, get needed advice, talk to customers, put forth effort, try different strategies? etc.) More often than not this leads to success, but there can always be factors outside your control. If you never succeed, perhaps you are in the wrong job or career.

## Goals as a threat

Whether people view a specific, difficult goal as a threat or a challenge affects their performance. With goal difficulty held constant, individuals who perceive the goal as a threat to them have been shown to have significantly lower performance than people who appraise their goal as a challenge (Drach-Zahavy & Erez, 2002). The solution lies in the way a goal is framed in terms of striving to attain a positive versus striving to avoid a negative outcome. For example, telling people to "try to answer 12 of these 15 questions correctly" leads to significantly higher performance than telling people to "try not to get more than three of these 15 questions wrong." Anticipated shame and anxiety for not attaining the goal explains the detrimental effect on performance of negatively framed goals (Roney & Lehman, 2008; Roney & O'Connor, 2008).

As noted earlier, goal striving can be objectively threatening if the managers or executives set unrealistic goals or react punitively to failure that was unavoidable. To illustrate this point with a real-life example, Teresa worked for a large telecommunications firm and spent incredibly long hours working to make customers happy. At the end of the year she got an outstanding performance appraisal and a promised bonus in line with her goal achievement. The next year management raised the goal 400% (the business environment had not changed). This was perceived by her and the other customer service representatives as a punishment and a signal that the company did not want to pay any more bonuses. Teresa eventually quit her job.

## Stress and anxiety

Stress is closely related to threat. When people perceive threats to their values, including to themselves, and are not sure they can deal with them, they experience anxiety. Goals are standards by which performance is evaluated. Goals can increase stress and anxiety for the reasons noted earlier. But goals, used intelligently, can also reduce stress because they remove the ambiguity surrounding how performance will be assessed. They reduce uncertainty. To cite another example, The Child and Family Institute, St. Luke's-Roosevelt Hospital in New York, found that 25% of students who enroll in four-year university programs typically do not graduate. An online goal setting intervention (1) increased grades, (2) resulted in students maintaining a full course load, and (3) led to a decrease in "dropouts." Morisano, Hirsh, Peterson, Shore, and Pihl (2010) found that this was due to these students having clearly defined goals and strategies for attaining them. Not only did the goals give the students purpose, the researchers found that they lowered anxiety (see Chapter 30). The caveat is that the goals must be few enough in number so that people can "focus" and prioritize (see Chapter 12). Too many goals that exceed a person's ability to process and attain them will likely lead to stress and anxiety as well as low to zero goal commitment.

## Ability, skill, and self-efficacy

Ability (a precursor to skill learning) is a moderator variable in goal setting theory (Locke & Latham, 2002). This is because the choice to exert effort and to persist until a specific high goal is attained is all but useless unless an individual has the requisite knowledge and skill to attain it. Self-efficacy, as noted, is one's belief in one's ability to attain certain ends but is not identical to it. Self-efficacy can be higher or lower than one might think from ability measures because people draw their own conclusions about what they can do from past accomplishments and how they did what they did. They might think they succeeded by luck and were not actually that skilled (see Chapter 4). Or they might think failure was due to a bad day (e.g., lack of sleep, illness) and not an indicator of actual competence.

How can efficacy be increased aside from providing training? One way is to assign specific, challenging, learning goals rather than performance outcome goals so that people can acquire knowledge of how to do their jobs (Seijts & Latham 2005; see also Chapter 13). Learning goals draw attention away from, and hence lower stress/anxiety, from the pursuit, of what is for those who lack ability, an impossible performance target. A learning goal focuses attention on discovering and mastering strategies, processes, or procedures for performing the requisite task effectively. And as is the case with a goal for performance, the higher the learning goal, the higher an individual's performance (Latham, Seijts, & Crim, 2008). A specific, high-performance goal should only be set when an individual or team already has the knowledge and ability to attain it.

Research shows that people who are given a specific learning goal for strategies to be discovered (i.e., learned) have significantly higher performance than those who either had a specific performance goal to attain or were urged to do their best (Drach-Zahavy & Erez, 2002). MBA students who set a specific high learning goal for discovering ways to make their education meaningful had significantly higher grade point averages at the end of the academic year than those who only had a distal performance outcome goal or were exhorted by the dean to do their best. Further, their satisfaction with their experience in the MBA program was significantly higher than for those in the other two conditions (Latham & Brown, 2006). The beneficial effects of learning goals on performance when ability is lacking has been shown to occur regardless of an individual's personality, specifically, a person's learning versus performance goal orientation (Seijts, Latham, Tasa, & Latham, B., 2004).

In summary, a learning goal facilitates planning, monitoring, and evaluating solutions to an impasse, and implementing them and monitoring their effectiveness for desired behavior. A learning goal should be set when an employee currently lacks the skill to attain a desired performance outcome.

## Non-goals areas ignored

This "problem" has a certain irony. When goals are pursued, *non-goal areas are supposed to be ignored*. That is the whole point. Goals direct attention and action toward A at the expense of B, C, and D. A primary benefit of setting a specific, high goal is "focus." Full attention is given to the focal goal while alternative pursuits are ignored, from which arises the concept of goal shielding (Shah, Friedman, & Kruglanski, 2002). The greater the degree of goal commitment, the greater an individual's ability to inhibit the pursuit of alternative tasks. Hence, the self-regulatory benefit of setting and committing to a specific, high goal: goal setting results in a singleness of purpose. People cognitively inhibit goal distractions that compete for their attentional resources.

Given this, it becomes very important to set goals for the right things. Goal theory does not specify what the right thing is, that is, what goals should be set for. This issue is important enough to devote a separate section to it.

## How to choose what goals to set

If it is a fairly routine job, the solution is to conduct a job analysis to identify the critical dimensions of effective performance (Flanagan, 1954; Latham & Mann, 2006), and then set performance, behavioral, or learning goals as needed for each of these performance dimensions. In this way, important aspects of job performance are not overlooked.

At the managerial or executive level, things are not so simple. All private organizations need to make a profit, but profits are caused by numerous factors. If one sets only a profit goal, this ignores focusing attention on all the factors that make it possible (e.g., innovation, customer service, speed, cost control, quality, skilled employees, teamwork). These factors, in turn are affected by other factors. Thus a great deal of thought needs to be given as to what goals to set. Ram Charan, arguably among the world's leading consultants, wrote, "the quality of any leader's goals [is based on]... the quality and rigor of thinking that underlies them" (2007, p. 184). What should one think about? First, thinking about how the goals might be achieved, that is, having a plan. GE CEO Jeff Immelt "established aggressive goals only after he assessed how the organization might go after them" (Charan, 2007, p. 188). This was an issue of strategy. Second, it is thinking about "the opportunities that lie ahead and what is possible *for your business*" (p. 189). This involves assessing your capabilities and projecting into the future (i.e., vision).

Setting the wrong goals can be very destructive. Consider everyone working very hard to make a product that won't sell. In such a case it would be better, ironically, to have everyone not work hard so there would not be so many product returns! Charan (2007) cited the real-world example of former GM's CEO Rick Wagoner who set a goal for the company to attain a substantial increase in market share. However, GM did not have the capability of doing this, because it had too many models to start with and, even so, did not have enough models that were competitive. Market share actually fell, and Wagoner lost his job. Charan wrote "You need to assess whether the goals are do-able" (2007, p. 193). He added, "when people are held accountable for goals that cannot be accomplished, the emotional toll is very high, and the business suffers" (Charan, 2007, p. 195).

## Stretch goals

Stretch goals were popularized by GE under Jack Welch (see Chapter 3). Stretch goals were distinguished from minimum or operative goals that had to be made on pain of risking the wrath of Welch (though he strove to make the goal for the divisions fair and tied to the industry context). Stretch goals were designed to stretch thinking, to get people thinking "outside the box". To make up an example, Welch might ask the division that made MRI machines to halve the cost or double the speed. Now such goals might not be possible to attain, but they might get the executives in that division to develop creative ideas for improvements. Charan (2007) wrote, "... stretch goals are strategic. They require leaders to think about what they're doing in a radically different way, not just to work harder or be more alert" (p. 198).

Recently Sitkin, See, Miller, Lawless, and Carton (2011) in a purely theoretical article concluded that organizations that would most benefit from stretch goals are least likely to use them, whereas those that would benefit least are most likely to use them. Companies such as GE, exemplars of stretch goals that violated the authors' theory, were simply dismissed as outliers. This is not our view of how theory building should proceed (see the Introduction to this volume and Chapter 37. The authors also failed to distinguish stretch goals designed to stimulate thinking, as explained above, from challenging performance goals that are supposed to be reached—GE's actual policy.

## Multiple goals

Most organizations have multiple goals. Goal theory has nothing to say about how many goals any one person or organization should have (for more, see Chapter 12). Locke and Latham (1990) listed eight contingency factors that could affect how many different goals an individual can handle, for example, cognitive capacity, time, the ability to delegate. Obviously goals should be consistent with one another or at least not in conflict. It is useful to develop causal models to lay out how profitability is to be attained, for example (to oversimplify), competent employees produce quality products that enhance sales which lead to profits. Then goals can be set for each. It is also important that goal priorities be clear. The late Roberto Goizueta, CEO of Coca Cola, was pressured to make community service a major company priority. But he rejected that in favor of focusing on profits. He concluded that if the stock price appreciated, those holding the stock would be in the best position to undertake community projects. And that is just what happened. One of BB&T's major projects has been to promote university programs (now numbering over 60) focused around the moral basis of capitalism.

## Short-range versus long-range thinking

Just as goal theory has nothing to say about what specific goals to set, as each organization has its own context, it has nothing to say about the proper time span for a goal. We know, of course, that all viable businesses have to think both short range and long range, but how to integrate or balance the two, again, takes a lot of hard thinking. A goal can be too far removed in time to provide an effective incentive for and guide to action (Bandura, 1997). Moreover, in a dynamic environment, a goal that is appropriate at one point in time may be inappropriate at another. Research shows that distal (more distant) goals are more effective if supported by proximal goals. In a turbulent environment, setting only a distal goal has been shown to lead to worse performance than urging people to do their best (Latham & Seijts, 1999). This is because in turbulent environments it is critical for effective performance that an individual or team search for feedback and react quickly to it (Frese & Zapf, 1994). Performance errors in dynamic situations are often due to deficient decomposition of a distal goal into subgoals (Domer, 1991). Subgoals or proximal goals facilitate error management. Errors yield information as to whether what an employee is doing is likely to lead to goal attainment. There is more informative feedback when subgoals are set relative to setting a distal goal only (Frese & Zapf, 1994). Finally, subgoals have been found to increase the number of effective strategies people discover (Seijts & Latham, 2001). In this way, the time frame for the goals that are set can be made appropriate.

## Conflict

Conflict can fall into two broad classes: within individuals and between individuals. If an individual has two conflicting goals, action toward one undermines the other. This can lead to anxiety and paralysis. Or the individual may "resolve" the conflict by simply ignoring one of the two goals to the detriment of the organization. Between-person conflict can be due to nonproductive competition. When two or more employees perceive one another's goals as competitively rather than cooperatively related, they are likely to pursue their goal at the expense of others (Seijts & Latham, 2000). Knowing that others on their team may subsequently conclude that they have been taken advantage of, an employee who does so may even engage in subtle forms of deception to hide the pursuit of a self-enhancing goal (Wathne & Heide, 2000) while looking for ways to obstruct the goal attainment of others (Stanne, Johnson, & Johnson, 1999).

A solution to these issues is to set a superordinate goal or vision (Latham, 2004). A superordinate goal unites employees within and across teams by giving them a cause to rally around (e.g., Jack Welch's "boundaryless organization"). A superordinate goal minimizes opportunistic behavior and increases the probability of cooperative interdependence.

For example, working with two companies and their supplier in China, Wong, Tjosvold, and Zi-Ya (2005) found that the relationship between a high level of a shared vision and a low level of dysfunctional opportunism among employees was due to cooperative goal setting. The superordinate goal and the resulting cooperatively set goals led people to draw boundary lines around one "in-group," that is, the companies and suppliers. The outcome was employees setting and pursuing goals for mutual benefit.

As Erez notes in Chapter 31, the setting of specific goals can be invaluable for culturally diverse teams. This is because such goals increase the likelihood that the employee will interpret the priorities similarly and act upon them. When goals are not specific, cultural values and norms may determine what employees perceive is important for them to get done. This can make teamwork difficult and hurt a team's performance.

As Saari notes (Chapter 17) regarding the transformation of IBM through goal setting, teams and team members need to see the relationship between what they are doing and both an individual's and a team's success. From the standpoint of employee selection, employers can facilitate the effectiveness of these steps by hiring people whose values are consistent with the organization's (Schneider, Smith, Taylor, & Fleenor, 1998).

## Success

It seems paradoxical that success in attaining goals can pose a threat to subsequent performance. Nevertheless, it can happen. Audia, Locke, and Smith (2000) found that previous success in attaining high goals, not surprisingly, increased the satisfaction of strategic decision makers. Consequently, they continued to use the same strategies. Their high satisfaction was associated with high self-efficacy for attaining subsequent high-performance goals. But doing so became dysfunctional when radical changes in the environment occurred and strategies needed to be changed. In the real world of business, change is the norm. Overconfidence is always a danger. Effective leaders are visionary enough to figure when the company needs to go in a new direction (Locke, 2008).

As noted earlier, it helps to have proximal goals in order to see right away that something is going wrong. The feedback derived from failing to meet subtargets may signal the need for re-examining what one must start doing, stop doing, or be doing differently to attain the goal. A distal goal alone, as noted earlier, may be too far off in the future to allow executives to discern whether they have discovered and implemented an effective strategy for goal attainment. The most visionary leaders will even see the need to change before the bottom line is affected. John Watson, Jr., pushed IBM into electronic computers even when sales of mechanical calculators were quite profitable.

## Dishonesty and cheating

As we said in the opening to this chapter, virtually any intervention, whether in medicine or the behavioral sciences, is subject to misuse. And as we said elsewhere, the fault lies not in the goals, but in our values (Latham & Locke, 2009). BB&T, the banking company mentioned above, is well known for its strong value system, which is not just preached but practiced. Two of the company's key values are honesty and integrity. Unlike the other large banks, BB&T, to the authors' knowledge has never had a scandal.

In addition, to ensure ethical behavior, all organizations need control systems. Unethical leaders may set unethical goals or support unethical means because they fail to set up or enforce appropriate control systems. The necessity for doing so was explained by Jensen (2001). He believes that there is substantial cheating in the workplace to earn bonuses for goal attainment. For example, salespeople may ship unfinished products to customers in order to reach their sales goals. We believe that this should not happen if there is a strong value system backed up by control systems.

There is scant research on the issue of cheating of this type. In a laboratory experiment, Schweitzer, Ordóñez, and Douma (2004) found that students who came close to, but failed to attain their goal, were more prone to overstating their performance than peers who were not close to attaining their goal, or those who were urged to do their best. Yet the students, even though they were anonymous to the researchers, did not take a monetary bonus they did not earn even though they could have done so. Moreover, the mean performance overstatement was 0.11, a very low score given that the means in the three goal setting conditions (money, no money, do your best) ranged from 5.46 to 6.17. Barsky (2008), in his doctoral dissertation, presented a model that explains why he believes goal setting may lead to unethical behavior. However, his empirical research failed to support his model. Nevertheless, as we have said repeatedly, goal setting can be misused (Latham, 2012; Latham & Locke, 2006; Locke & Latham, 1984).

In a turbulent environment, when revenue streams are drying up while costs are also going up, senior management may set performance outcome goals that are perceived by the managers who report to them as excessively high. This has been shown to be related to perceived abuse of subordinates by these managers (Bardes, Folger, & Latham, 2010). Over and above value systems and control systems, executives can set specific, high learning rather than performance goals. Setting specific learning goals in a turbulent environment by managers who are trusted by their subordinates correlates positively with high departmental performance (Porter & Latham, in press).

## Tying monetary incentives to goal setting

Goal setting theory does not specify how best to tie a monetary reward to goal attainment. The issue is problematic in that monetary rewards, when used correctly, can be powerful motivators (Locke, Feren, McCaleb, Shaw, & Denny, 1980). Yet money tied to an easy goal will reward people for not working hard. On the other hand, goals that are so hard they simply cannot be reached can hurt rather than help increase performance when a monetary bonus is only paid for goal attainment (Lee, Locke, & Phan, 1997). This is called an all-or-none bonus system, because you get nothing if you fail to reach the goal.

In addition to the above method for tying money to performance, Locke (2004) described three others. The second way is to link multiple goal levels (e.g., five tiers) with a higher bonus attached to each higher level. This circumvents the problem of employees getting all or none of the bonus. The downside is that employees may decide they are happy with attaining a moderately difficult goal and receiving a moderate payoff because this is seen by them as less stressful. Furthermore, there is still a range within each level. An employee who gets a 20% bonus for a 25% improvement will not get that bonus if he or she achieves 24.5%. A third alternative is a piece-rate system: a linear function relating pay with goal progress (e.g., or the increments may be very small such as 1% or 2%). This guarantees that everyone receives approximately what they earned using the chosen metric. With ongoing progress toward the goal, and concomitant monetary rewards, employees may safely pursue higher and higher goals. A drawback is that it is dependent on having exact quantitative performance goals and monetary inducements toward high goal attainment. This is relatively easy through time and motion studies in the logging industry (Latham & Kinne, 1974; Latham & Locke, 1975); this may be very difficult for many other jobs. Further, like the 5-tier system, people may be content with average performance. A fourth method is to assign goals and pay for performance but with performance being measured, at least partly, through judgment calls by superiors. An advantage of this method is its flexibility (Kerr & Landauer, 2004). For example, there can be stretch goals to motivate innovation combined with minimum profit goals to be attained. Such a system can include multiple goals, including goals that are qualitative or hard to quantify (e.g., teamwork) and allow people to be judged on "the whole package." The disadvantage is the judgmental factor that some employees may perceive as biased.

If there ever was an area begging for empirical research, the issue of goal-contingent bonuses is it.

In summary, with careful thought and planning pitfalls in setting goals in the workplace can be prevented or overcome. Some have argued that goals in organizations should be used only in very special circumstances. This is not possible; a goal-less organization is a contradiction in terms. In reality, all organizations need goals if they are to function at all. It is not a question of if but how.

# References

Audia, P. G., Locke, E. A., & Smith, K. G. (2000). The paradox of success: An archival and a laboratory study of strategic persistence following radical environmental change. *Academy of Management Journal, 43*, 837–853.

Bandura, A. (1997). *Self-efficacy: The exercise of control.* Stanford, NY: W. H. Freeman.

Bardes, M., Folger, R., & Latham, G. P. (2010). *Exceedingly difficult goals and abusive* supervision. Symposium: Society for Industrial-Organizational Psychology. Atlanta, April.

Barsky, A. (2008). Understanding the ethical cost of organizational goal setting: A review and theory development. *Journal of Business Ethics, 81*, 63–81.

Charan, R. (2007) *Know-how: The 8 skills that separate people who perform from those who don't.* New York: Crown.

Domer, D. (1991). The investigation of action regulation in uncertain and complex situations. In J. Rasmussen & B. Brehmer (Eds.), *Distributed decision making: Cognitive models for cooperative work* (pp. 349–354). Chichester, UK: John Wiley & Sons.

Drach-Zahavy, A., & Erez, M. (2002). Challenge versus threat effects on the goal-performance relationship. *Organizational Behavior and Human Performance, 88*, 667–682.

Flanagan, J. C. (1954). The critical incident technique. *Psychological Bulletin, 51*, 327–358.

Frese, M., & Zapf, D. (1994). Action as the core of work psychology: A German approach. In H. C. Triandis, M. D. Dunnette, & L. Hough (Eds.), *Handbook of industrial and organizational psychology* (vol. 4, pp. 271–340). Palo Alto, CA: Consulting Psychologists Press.

Jensen, M. C. (2001). Corporate budgeting is broken—let's fix it. *Harvard Business Review, 79*, 94–101.

Keith, N., & Frese, M. (2005). Self-regulation in error management training: Emotion control and metacognition as mediators of performance effects. *Journal of Applied Psychology, 90*, 677–691.

Kerr, S., & Landauer, S. (2004). Using stretch goals to promote organizational effectiveness and personal growth: General Electric and Goldman Sachs. *Academy of Management Executive, 18*, 134–138.

Knight, D., Durham, C. C., & Locke, E. A. (2001). The relationship of team goals, incentives, and efficacy to strategic risk, tactical implementation, and performance. *Academy of Management Journal, 44*, 326–338.

Larrick, R. P., Heath, C., & Wu, G. (2009). Goal-induced risk taking in negotiation and decision making. *Social Cognition, 27*, 342–364.

Latham, G. P. (2004). The motivational benefits of goal setting. *Academy of Management Executive, 18*, 126–129.

Latham, G. P. (2012). *Work motivation: History, theory, research and practice*. Thousand Oaks, CA: Sage.

Latham, G. P., & Brown, T. C. (2006). The effect of learning vs. outcome goals on self-efficacy, satisfaction and performance in an MBA Program. *Applied Psychology: An International Review, 55*, 606–623.

Latham, G. P., & Kinne, S. B. (1974). Improving job performance through training in goal setting. *Journal of Applied Psychology, 59*, 187–191.

Latham, G. P., & Locke, E. A. (1975). Increasing productivity with decreasing time limits: A field replication of Parkinson's law. *Journal of Applied Psychology, 60*, 524–526.

Latham, G. P., & Locke, E. A. (2006). Enhancing the benefits and overcoming the pitfalls of goal setting. *Organizational Dynamics, 35*(4), 332–340.

Latham, G. P., & Locke, E. A. (2009). Science and ethics: What should count as evidence against the use of goal setting? *Academy of Management Perspectives, 23*, 88–91.

Latham, G. P., & Mann, S. (2006). Advances in the science of performance appraisal: Implications for practice. In G. P. Hodgkinson & J. K. Ford (Eds.), *International Review of Organizational and Industrial Psychology, 21*, 295–337.

Latham, G. P., & Seijts, G. H. (1999). The effects of proximal and distal goals on performance on a moderately complex task. *Journal of Organizational Behavior, 20*, 421–429.

Latham, G. P., Seijts, G., & Crim, D. (2008). The effects of learning goal difficulty level and cognitive ability on performance. *Canadian Journal of Behavioural Science, 40*, 220–229.

Lee, T. W., Locke, E. A., & Phan, S. H. (1997). Explaining the assigned goal-incentive interaction: The role of self-efficacy and personal goals. *Journal of Management, 23*, 541–559.

Locke, E. A. (2004). Linking goals to monetary incentives. *Academy of Management Executive, 18*, 130–133.

Locke, E. A. (2008). *The prime movers: Traits of the great wealth creators*. Irvine, CA: Ayn Rand Bookstore.

Locke, E. A., & Latham, G. P. (1984). *Goal setting: A motivational technique that works.* Englewood Cliffs, NJ: Prentice Hall.

Locke, E. A., & Latham, G. P. (1990). *A theory of goal setting and task performance.* Englewood Cliffs, NJ: Prentice-Hall.

Locke, E. A., & Latham, G. P. (2002). Building a practically useful theory of goal setting and task motivation: A 35-year odyssey. *American Psychologist, 57,* 705–717.

Locke, E. A., Feren, D. B., McCaleb, V. M., Shaw, K. N., & Denny, A. T. (1980). The relative effectiveness of four methods of motivating employee performance. In K. D. Duncan, M. M. Greenberg, & D. Wallis (Eds.), *Changes in working life* (pp. 363–388). London: John Wiley & Sons.

Morisano, D., Hirsh, J. B., Peterson, J. B., Shore, B., & Pihl, R. O. (2010). Setting, elaborating, and reflecting on personal goals improves academic performance. *Journal of Applied Psychology, 95,* 255–264.

Porter, R. L., & Latham, G. P. (in press). The effect of employee learning goals and goal commitment on departmental performance. *Journal of Leadership and Organizational Studies.*

Roney, C. J., & Lehman, D. R. (2008). Self-regulation in goal striving: Individual differences and situational moderators of the goal-framing/performance link. *Journal of Applied Social Psychology, 38,* 2691–2709.

Roney, C. J., & O'Connor, M. C. (2008). The interplay between achievement goals and specific target goals in determining performance. *Journal of Research in Personality, 42,* 482–489.

Schneider, B., Smith, D. B., Taylor, S., & Fleenor, J. (1998). Personality and organization: A test of the homogeneity of the personality hypothesis. *Journal of Applied Psychology, 83,* 462–470.

Schweitzer, M. E., Ordóñez, L., & Douma, B. (2004). The role of goal setting in motivating unethical behavior. *Academy of Management Journal, 47,* 422–432.

Seijts, G. H., & Latham, G. P. (2000). The effects of goal setting and group size on performance in a social dilemma. *Canadian Journal of Behavioural Science, 32,* 104–116.

Seijts, G. H., & Latham, G. P. (2001). The effect of learning, outcome, and proximal goals on a moderately complex task. *Journal of Organizational Behavior, 22,* 291–307.

Seijts, G. H., & Latham, G. P. (2005). Learning versus performance goals: When should each be used? *Academy of Management Executive, 19,* 124–131.

Seijts, G. H., Latham, G. P., Tasa, K., & Latham, B. W. (2004). Goal setting and goal orientation: An integration of two different yet related literatures. *Academy of Management Journal, 47,* 227–239.

Shah, J. Y., Friedman, R., & Kruglanski, A. W. (2002). Forgetting all else: On the antecedents and consequences of goal shielding. *Journal of Personality and Social Psychology, 83,* 1261–1280.

Sitkin, S. B., See, K. E., Miller, C. C., Lawless, M. W., & Carton, A. M. (2011) The paradox of stretch goals: Organizations in pursuit of the seemingly impossible. *Academy of Management Review, 36,* 544–566.

Stajkovic, A. D., Locke, E. A., & Blair, E. S. (2006). A first examination of the relationships between primed subconscious goals, assigned conscious goals, and task performance. *Journal of Applied Psychology, 91,* 1172–1180.

Stanne, M. B., Johnson, D. W., & Johnson, R. T. (1999). Does competition enhance or inhibit motor performance: A meta-analysis. *Psychological Bulletin, 125,* 133–154.

Wathne, K. H., & Heide, J. B. (2000). Opportunism in interfirm relationships: Forms, outcomes, and solution. *Journal of Marketing, 64,* 35–51.

Wong, A., Tjosvold, D., & Zi-Ya. (2005). Organizational partnerships in China: Self-interest, goal interdependence, and opportunism. *Journal of Applied Psychology, 90,* 782–791.

# Part X

# The Goal Setting Questionnaire

# 35 Re-Examining the Goal-Setting Questionnaire

*Ho Kwong Kwan*  School of International Business Administration,
Shanghai University of Finance and Economics

*Cynthia Lee*  College of Business Administration, Northeastern University
and Department of Management and Marketing,
Hong Kong Polytechnic University

*Phyllis L. Wright*  Gary Cook School of Leadership,
Dallas Baptist University

*Chun Hui*  School of Business, University of Hong Kong

## Introduction

The theory of goal setting is generalizable across more than 100 different tasks in various occupations (Latham, 2009) and across numerous countries, including Australia, Canada, China, Europe, Israel, and the United States (Locke & Latham, 1990), suggesting that goal setting is one of the most valid and practical theories of motivation (Lee & Earley, 1992). Despite such robust findings, field and laboratory studies on goal setting have typically measured goal setting attributes of *specificity* or clarity (the degree of quantitative precision with which the aim is specified) and *difficulty* (the degree of proficiency or level of performance sought) in different ways (cf. Austin & Vancouver, 1996; Lee & Bobko, 1992) with psychometrically untested items, scales, or manipulation checks (Lee, Bobko, Earley, & Locke, 1991). One reason for this may be that the systematic development of goal setting measures has been rather limited. For example, the most complete measure of goal setting was proposed and developed by Locke and Latham (1984). The scale was designed to capture the core goal attributes of specificity and difficulty, as well as support elements such as supervisor support and worker participation, and providing rationales for the goals set and feedback on goal progress. Support elements ensure that the goals set will be channeled into successful actions (Lee et al., 1991). Goals, however, can be dysfunctional when achieving a goal is seen as a way to avoid negative outcomes, or to please one's boss. Additionally, too many and too difficult goals can lead to elevated stress and conflict (Latham & Locke, 2006).

A limitation of Locke and Latham's (1984) 53-item goal setting measure is that it did not contain information on psychometric properties or a priori structure. This resulted in Lee et al.'s (1991) study to examine the factor structure and psychometric properties of this goal setting questionnaire. Using principal component analysis, Lee et al. (1991) found 10 meaningful factors, including goal attributes, support elements of goal rationales, goal efficacy, supervisory support and feedback, organizational facilitation of goal achievement, tangible rewards, and performance review as well as avoiding the negative effects of goal stress, goal conflict, and other dysfunctional behavior that result from the goal setting process.

Lee et al. (1991) noted that the core goal attributes of specificity and difficulty were underrepresented. More importantly, there was no emergent factor of goal difficulty, a core dimension of goal setting that has been demonstrated to be predictive of employee reactions and performance. To further explore goal difficulty, Lee and Bobko (1992) conducted a review of the goal difficulty measures. They found that some studies adopted a single-item measure of goal difficulty, whereas other studies adopted multiple items of goal difficulty. Moreover, the items included in different studies differ in their content and are inconsistent in the definition of goal difficulty (Wright, 1990). Consequently, Lee and Bobko developed three operationalizations of the goal difficulty construct: the assigned goal level is (1) objective and (2) quantifiable, and (3) self-referenced. Externally referenced goal difficulty measures are subjective, reflecting an individual's perception of goal difficulty.

The self-referenced goal difficulty factor, Lee and Bobko (1992) argued, is a typical way of measuring perceived goal difficulty in field settings. It is also used as a manipulation check in many experimental studies. Respondents were frequently asked to rate how difficult a particular goal is for them, or to rate their intention to perform well (Wright, 1990). Lee and Bobko (1992) noted that perception of self-referenced goal difficulty is often contaminated by an individual's initial ability since individuals with high initial ability may see a goal as relatively easy. On the other hand, those with lower initial ability may perceive the same goal as being relatively difficult. In order to control for initial ability, Lee and Bobko (1992) developed and validated an externally referenced goal difficulty measure by asking respondents to assess the difficulty of particular goals for someone of "average ability on the task or job." They found that, over two experimental trials, externally referenced goal difficulty was correlated with personal goals and performance quantity. On the contrary, self-referenced goal difficulty did not correlate with personal goals and performance quantity. Instead, it was negatively related to self-efficacy. Their results support Wright's (1990) finding that the operationalization of goal difficulty has profound implications for the observed effect sizes.

Despite the work of Lee et al. (1991) and Lee and Bobko (1992), there have been very few empirical tests of the goal setting questionnaire, and there has been no empirical test of the externally referenced goal difficulty measure. The most comprehensive study examining the goal setting questionnaire was conducted by Nel, Crafford, and Roodt (2004). Using 80 management consultants from South African consulting firms, they found the reliabilities for the ten goal setting dimensions, as well as goal specificity and goal difficulty, range from 0.64 to 0.94. However, because of the small sample size, they did not report the factor structure. Recently, Häsänen, Hellgren, and Hansson (2011) collected data from 136 employees in a subsidiary production unit of a large medical manufacturing company in Sweden. Results of their exploratory factor analyses showed ten meaningful factors with reliabilities ranging from from 0.68 to 0.88. These findings were consistent with that of Lee et al. (1991). However, the use of goal setting in performance appraisal, tangible rewards, and goal clarity had factor loadings below 0.40, and no confirmatory factor analyses were conducted to further examine the factor structure.

Another consideration is that, to date, very few field studies have fully applied the goal setting constructs to predict employees' outcomes (Häsänen et al., 2011). We believe that this is due, in part, to the need for a comprehensive examination of the goal setting questionnaire and the externally referenced goal difficulty measure. There is a clear need for a vigorously developed measure of goal setting to help researchers and practitioners understand how the different dimensions of goal setting can enhance efficiency and effectiveness. Schwab (1980) and Nunnally (1988) have stressed the importance of evaluating the psychometric properties, convergent validity, discriminant validity, and nomological validity of new scales prior to their widespread adoption, as have Podsakoff and MacKenzie (1994). The goal of this chapter is to re-examine the factor structure, reliability, and validity of Lee et al.'s (1991) goal setting questionnaire and Lee and Bobko's (1992) externally referenced goal difficulty measure, using two independent samples, one from the United States and one from China. We added/ revised five items to improve the psychometric properties of the goal setting question- naire. We present results on the construct validity of our measure and its relationship to goal commitment (the United States) and task performance (China).

## Our Measure

The current measure of goal setting is based on Lee et al.'s (1991) items. They identified 10 goal program dimensions: supervisor support/participation, goal stress, goal efficacy, goal rationale, use of goal setting in performance appraisal, tangible rewards, goal conflict, organizational facilitation of goal achievement, dysfunctional effects of goals, and goal clarity based on exploratory factor analysis. However, they did not examine the logical validity of this goal setting measure. According to Locke (1976), "... for a measurement to have logical validity, it must be integrated in a non-contradictory fashion with all pertinent information relevant to the phenomenon being measured" (p. 1337). In essence, to demonstrate logical validity, there should be some logical rela- tionship of the scale to the conceptual definition of the phenomenon being measured. We therefore define each of the dimensions reported by Lee et al. (1991) below. We regrouped the items according to logical validity prior to conducting a confirmatory factor analysis on the US and China data.

*Supervisor support/participation* deals with the support offered by the supervisor to facilitate goal accomplishment and the involvement allowed by the supervisor in goal setting and implementation. There were three original items in the Lee et al. measure, one of which deals with support and two of which deal with participation. The original support item was: "My boss is supportive with respect to encouraging me to reach my goals." This item appears to be a composite item. In the China sample, we broke this item down into two individual items to yield four items for this dimension. The two items were (1) "My boss is supportive of my goals" and (2) "My boss encourages me to reach my goals."

The *goal stress* dimension deals with the stress placed on an employee to attain a goal. There were three original items for this dimension. Of these three items, only two appear to map onto goal stress: "I find working toward my goals to be very stressful," and "I often fail to attain my goals." The other items captured self-referenced goal difficulty. While it can be argued that difficult goals can be expected to be stressful, difficulty and stress are distinct dimensions even though they are related. Conceptually and practically, a goal can be very difficult but not stressful. Thus, in the US sample, we retained the two items referencing goal stress. In the China sample, we followed the idea that goal stress deals with the stress placed on an employee, namely, (1) "I feel that I must accomplish my goals" and (2) "My supervisor always emphasizes that I need to accomplish my goals."

*Goal efficacy* deals with whether one feels capable of achieving the goal. There were four original items for this measure. The item "Trying for goals makes my job more fun than it would be without goals" deals with positive reactions to having a goal. It appeared to lack logical validity and thus was eliminated. We added one item in the China sample to capture the social aspect of goal efficacy: "My colleagues respect me when I reach my goals." Additionally, *goal rationale* deals with the logic underlying a goal. However, two of the items appeared to tap goal clarity: "I understand how my performance is measured on this job" and "My boss clearly explains to me what my goals are." Thus, these items were removed from the goal rationale scale. We added one item in the China sample: "My boss informs me how the goals are set."

We did not revise or add items to the remaining six goal setting dimensions. However, we removed some of the items due to lack of logical validity. *Use of goal setting in performance appraisal* refers to the degree to which goal setting has been reflected in various aspects of performance appraisals. We retained two items that explicitly address whether the supervisor conveys clearly the goals that employees have to achieve. The items include "During performance appraisal interviews, my boss comes to agreement with me on steps to be taken by each of us to solve any performance problems" and "he/she makes sure that at the end of the interview, I have a specific goal or goals in mind that I am to achieve in the future."

The sixth dimension is *tangible rewards*. It deals with whether employees can anticipate specific rewards by reaching the goal. One of the four items was deleted: "I sometimes compete with my coworkers to see who can do the best job in reaching their goals."

The seventh dimension is *goal conflict*, which assesses whether goals are consistent with each other and with one's own goals and interests. Of the eight items reported in Lee et al., only three items are directly related to goal conflict. They are "I have too many goals on this job (I am too overloaded)," "Some of my goals conflict with my personal values," and "I am given incompatible or conflicting goals by different people (or even by the same person)." We eliminated the rest of the items from this scale since they appeared to measure goal clarity and dysfunctional aspects of goal setting.

The eighth dimension is *organizational facilitation of goal achievement*. This dimension captures whether the organization provides support so that goals are achievable. The item "The goals I have on this job are challenging but reasonable (neither too hard nor too easy)" was eliminated since it represents self-referenced goal difficulty. We retained the remaining three items.

The ninth dimension is *dysfunctional effects of goals*, which refers to possible negative consequences of having goals. This scale has seven items including, for example, "My job goals serve to limit rather than raise my performance," "The goals I have on this job lead me to ignore other important aspects of my job," or "The pressure to achieve goals here leads to considerable dishonesty and cheating."

The tenth dimension is *goal clarity*, which refers to how clear and specific the goals are. We used two items from Lee et al.'s goal rationale dimension: "I understand how my performance is measured on this job" and "My boss clearly explains to me what my goals are." Additionally, one item from goal conflict was moved here: "I have unclear goals on this job." (reverse-coded). Finally, we retained three of the four goal clarity items from the Lee et al. scale by removing "The other people I work with encourage me to attain my goals," which does not appear to tap into clarity of the goal. The final dimension represents the *externally referenced goal difficulty* scale developed by Lee and Bobko (1992). Of the original six items, we removed two items that were less relevant to goal difficulty: "very high standard of performance to no standard of performance at all" and "you discover better ways of doing things to you never have to discover better ways of doing things."

To examine the psychometric properties of these goal setting measures, in addition to examining internal consistency and factor structures, we are interested in how the ten dimensions are related to goal commitment. Goal commitment is the determination to attain a goal and an unwillingness to abandon it (Hollenbeck & Klein, 1987; Locke & Latham, 1990). Goal commitment is necessary for goals to have motivational effects (Locke, Latham, & Erez, 1988). Research using college students showed that goal commitment was higher when goals were made public rather than in private, when students have higher needs for achievement, and when students have an internal locus of control (Hollenbeck, Williams, & Klein, 1989). In a meta-analytic review, Klein, Wesson, Hollenbeck, and Alge (1999) reported that two core goal attributes—specificity and difficulty—and goal processes, namely, feedback and participation or voice in the determination of the goal, are positively related to goal commitment. As a validation of the goal setting measure using US samples, we predicted that goal attributes and goal processes are positively related to goal commitment, whereas the dysfunctional effects, goal stress and goal conflict, are negatively related to goal commitment.

In sample two, we examined the relationship between the new goal setting questionnaire and task performance. The majority of goal setting studies have shown a robust positive relationship between goal setting attributes and task performance (Latham & Locke, 2007; Locke & Latham, 1990; Locke, Shaw, Saari, & Latham, 1981). In this sample, we used task performance as a criterion variable of goal setting. As in Lee et al. (1991), we expected that the goal attributes and the supportive elements of goal processes would relate positively to, while the dysfunctional aspects, goal stress and conflict, would relate negatively to task performance.

## Measures

A five-point Likert-type scale ranging from (1) "strongly disagree" to (5) "strongly agree" was used for all of the constructs except for the demographic variables. Both samples used items from the Locke and Latham's *Goal-Setting Questionnaire (GSQ)* as validated by Lee et al. (1991) and Lee and Bobko's (1992) externally referenced goal difficulty scales. Selected items were used based on logical validity. We further added five items to the goal setting measures in the China sample. In addition to examining the psychometric properties of the goal-setting questionnaire, Sample 1 also examined the relationship of the goal setting attributes and process variables to goal commitment.

We used the five-item goal commitment scale developed by Hollenbeck et al. (1989) and validated by Klein, Wesson, Hollenbeck, Wright, and DeShon (2001). The Cronbach's alpha was 0.74.

## Sample 1 (the United States)

Data were obtained from two hospitals in the United States. The data collection procedure involved administration of an online survey in which a unique survey link was sent to each employee via his or her hospital e-mail address. An independent third party company was hired to map the employee demographic data from the hospitals' Human Resources Information System (HRIS) to the survey links for each employee, and to launch and collect all survey data on behalf of the researchers. DataStar Inc., located in Waltham, Massachusetts, is a leading provider of survey management, data processing, and tabulation services for researchers. Assigning this work to an independent third party helped protect employee anonymity. The employee's identity was masked in the data and then presented to the researchers for analysis by DataStar, Inc.

The two hospitals had a combined total of 3154 employees. This total includes managers. Surveys were sent to 128 managers and 2180 employees. The total number of surveys deployed in the research study was 2308. Of those managers, 28% were male. The average age was 48.0 years and organizational tenure was 8.4 years. Of those employees, 19% were male. The average age was 42.0 years and organizational tenure was 6.7 years. The hospitals' Human Resources Information System was used to map demographic variables to unique survey links for managers and employees who reported their goal setting assessments. In total, 113 surveys from managers and 507 surveys from employees completed the online survey. The overall response rate was 26.9%.

We applied structural equation modeling with LISREL 8.54 (Jöreskog & Sörbom, 2003) to test our measurement model of the eleven goal setting constructs. With data from both managers and employees, the confirmatory factor analysis (CFA) yielded an acceptable fit to the data with $\chi^2$ (574) = 2816.36, $p < 0.001$; RMSEA = 0.083; CFI = 0.96. The results for each measure are reported in Table 35.1. All factor loadings were significant, suggesting adequate convergent validity (Table 35.1). To ensure that there was sufficient discriminant validity among all constructs, we ran a one-factor model, yielding an unacceptable fit with $\chi^2$ (629) = 7866.57, $p < 0.001$; RMSEA = 0.180; CFI = 0.88.

Table 35.2 shows the correlations among goal setting variables. The correlations ranged from 0.02 to 0.73, with an average correlation of 0.44. The goal attributes and goal processes related positively to goal commitment. In addition, dysfunctional effects, goal stress, and goal conflict related negatively to goal commitment.

## Sample 2 (China)

To examine the validity of the goal setting constructs in China, a group of data collectors distributed surveys to 400 managers and 400 frontline employees of an insurance company during work hours. Both supervisors and employees reported their goal setting assessments and demographic variables. Additionally, supervisors rated their employees' task performance. To improve the accuracy of the data, the confidentiality of the responses was affirmed with participants at the beginning stage by stating

Table 35.1 Study 1 (the United States) Confirmatory Factor Analysis of Goal Setting (113 Managers and 507 Employees)

| Items | Supervisor support/ participation ($\alpha = .89$) | Goal stress ($\alpha = .65$) | Goal efficacy ($\alpha = .63$) | Goal rationale ($\alpha = .77$) |
|---|---|---|---|---|
| 1. My boss is supportive with respect to encouraging me to reach my goals | 1.00 | | | |
| 2. My boss encourages me to reach my goals | NA | | | |
| 3. My boss lets me participate in the setting of my goals | 1.05 | | | |
| 4. My boss lets me have some say in deciding how I will go about implementing my goals | 1.07 | | | |
| 5. I find working toward my goals to be very stressful | | 1.00 | | |
| 6. I often fail to attain my goals | | 0.86 | | |
| 7. I feel that I must accomplish my goals | | NA | | |
| 8. My supervisor always emphasizes that I need to accomplish my goals | | NA | | |
| 9. My colleagues respect me when I reach my goals | | | NA | |
| 10. I usually feel that I have a suitable or effective action plan or plans for reaching my goals | | | 1.00 | |
| 11. I feel that my job training was good enough so that I am capable of reaching my job goals | | | 0.91 | |
| 12. My boss informs me how the goals are set | | | | NA |
| 13. My boss tells me the reasons for giving me the goals I have | | | | 1.00 |
| 14. I get regular feedback indicating how I am performing in relation to my goals | | | | 0.93 |

| Items | Use of goal setting in performance appraisal ($\alpha=.86$) | Tangible rewards ($\alpha=.83$) | Goal conflict ($\alpha=.78$) | Organization facilitation of goal achievement ($\alpha=.84$) |
|---|---|---|---|---|
| 15. During performance appraisal interviews, my boss comes to an agreement with me on steps to be taken by each of us to solve any performance problems | 1.00 | | | |

(Continued)

Table 35.1 (Continued)

| Items | Use of goal setting in performance appraisal ($\alpha$=.86) | Tangible rewards ($\alpha$.83) | Goal conflict ($\alpha$=.78) | Organization facilitation of goal achievement ($\alpha$.84) |
|---|---|---|---|---|
| 16. My boss makes sure that at the end of the performance appraisal interview I have a specific goal or goals to achieve in the future | 1.07 | | | |
| 17. If I reach my goals, I feel that my job security will be enhanced | | 1.00 | | |
| 18. If I reach my goals, it increases my chances for a pay raise | | 1.20 | | |
| 19. If I reach my goals, it increases my chances for a promotion | | 1.29 | | |
| 20. I have too many goals on this job (I am too overloaded) | | | 1.00 | |
| 21. Some of my goals conflict with my personal values | | | 0.86 | |
| 22. I am given incompatible or conflicting goals by different people (or even by the same person) | | | 1.03 | |
| 23. Company policies here help rather than hurt goal attainment | | | | 1.00 |
| 24. Work teams in this company work together to attain goals | | | | 1.01 |
| 25. This company provide sufficient resources (e.g., time, money, equipment, coworkers) to make goal setting work | | | | 1.12 |

| Items | Dysfunctional effects of goals ($\alpha$=.90) | Goal clarity ($\alpha$=.88) | Goal difficulty ($\alpha$=.90) |
|---|---|---|---|
| 26. My job goals lead me to take excessive risks | 1.00 | | |
| 27. My job goals serve to limit rather than raise my performance | 1.23 | | |
| 28. The goals I have on this job lead me to ignore other important aspects of my job | 1.03 | | |
| 29. The pressure to achieve goals here leads to considerable dishonesty and cheating | 0.96 | | |
| 30. Goals in this organization are used more to punish you than to help you do your job well | 1.12 | | |

Table 35.1 (Continued)

| Items | Dysfunctional effects of goals ($\alpha=.90$) | Goal clarity ($\alpha=.88$) | Goal difficulty ($\alpha=.90$) |
|---|---|---|---|
| 31. My boss wants to me to avoid mentioning negative information or problems regarding my goals or action plans | 1.05 | | |
| 32. If my boss makes a mistake that affects my ability to attain my goals, he or she refuses to admit it or discuss it | 1.02 | | |
| 33. I understand how my performance is measured on this job | | 1.00 | |
| 34. My boss clearly explains to me what my goals are | | 1.24 | |
| 35. I have unclear goals on this job (reversed) | | 0.87 | |
| 36. I understand exactly what I am supposed to do on my job | | 0.62 | |
| 37. I have specific, clear goals to aim for on my job | | 0.92 | |
| 38. If I have more than one goal to accomplish, I know which ones are most important and which are least important<br><br>For the average employee in the same level job and who has a similar level of education and experience as you, the goals that you have in relation to this employee's goals would require: | | 0.96 | |
| 39. "No challenge at all" to "extreme challenge" | | | 1.00 |
| 40. "Almost no effort" to "enormous effort" | | | 1.06 |
| 41. "No thought or skill" to "an extreme degree of thought and problem solving skill" | | | 0.88 |
| 42. "Very little persistence and tenacity" to "an enormous amount of persistence and tenacity" | | | 0.92 |

Chi-square = 2816.36, degree of freedom = 574, RMSEA = 0.083, CFI = 0.96
NA = Not in original scale, added and tested in sample 2.

Table 35.2 Study 1 (the United States) Correlations

| | 1 | 2 | 3 | 4 | 5 | 6 | 7 | 8 | 9 | 10 | 11 |
|---|---|---|---|---|---|---|---|---|---|---|---|
| 1. Supervisor support/ participation | | | | | | | | | | | |
| 2. Goal stress | -0.25 | | | | | | | | | | |
| 3. Goal efficacy | 0.64 | -0.46 | | | | | | | | | |
| 4. Goal rationale | 0.73 | -0.28 | 0.64 | | | | | | | | |
| 5. Use of goal setting in performance appraisal | 0.66 | -0.29 | 0.63 | 0.71 | | | | | | | |
| 6. Tangible rewards | 0.45 | -0.21 | 0.47 | 0.50 | 0.49 | | | | | | |
| 7. Goal conflict | -0.40 | 0.66 | -0.48 | -0.38 | -0.38 | -0.31 | | | | | |
| 8. Organization facilitation of goal achievement | 0.54 | -0.35 | 0.64 | 0.60 | 0.56 | 0.53 | -0.46 | | | | |
| 9. Dysfunctional effects of goals | -0.28 | 0.02 | -0.10 | -0.25 | -0.26 | -0.15 | 0.04 | -0.13 | | | |
| 10. Goal clarity | 0.66 | -0.25 | 0.69 | 0.69 | 0.57 | 0.41 | -0.32 | 0.51 | -0.16 | | |
| 11. Goal difficulty | 0.49 | -0.54 | 0.47 | 0.46 | 0.50 | 0.35 | -0.69 | 0.47 | -0.52 | 0.32 | |
| 12. Goal commitment | 0.44 | -0.39 | 0.59 | 0.47 | 0.44 | 0.38 | -0.44 | 0.49 | -0.15 | 0.43 | -0.48 |

N = 620. Correlations with absolute values of 0.08 or greater are significant at the $p < 0.05$ level or better (2-tailed), while those with 0.13 or greater are significant at the $p < 0.01$ level or better (2-tailed).

that the data source was only accessible to the researchers. In total, 273 surveys from managers and 283 surveys from employees were returned by mail, for an overall response rate of 69.5%.

Of the 273 managers, 165 (60.4%) were male. The average age was 31.0 years ($SD = 5.4$ years) and organizational tenure was 5.2 years ($SD = 3.1$ years). Twenty-seven (9.9%) had high school or below education, 155 (56.8%) had technical school education, 73 (26.7%) had bachelor's degrees, and 18 (6.6%) had postgraduate degrees. Of the 283 employees, 151 (57.2%) were male. The average age was 27.5 years ($SD = 5.0$ years) and organizational tenure was 3.8 years ($SD = 2.4$ years). Sixty-nine (24.4%) had high school or below education, 164 (58.0%) had technical school education, and 50 (17.7%) had bachelor's degrees.

A five-item scale originally developed by Williams and Anderson (1991) was used to measure task performance. A sample item is "S/he fulfills all formal job responsibilities." The Cronbach's alpha for this measure was 0.87.

## Results

We applied structural equation modeling with LISREL 8.54 (Jöreskog & Sörbom, 2003) to test our measurement model of the 11 goal-setting constructs. With the data from both managers and employees, the CFA yielded an acceptable fit to the data with $\chi^2$ (764) = 3,246.13, $p < 0.001$; RMSEA = 0.081; CFI = 0.95. In addition, all the factor loadings were significant, suggesting adequate convergent validity (Table 35.3).

*Table 35.3* Study 2 (China) Confirmatory Factor Analysis of Goal Setting (273 Managers and 283 Employees)

| Items | Supervisor support/ participation ($\alpha = .90$) | Goal stress ($\alpha = .86$) | Goal efficacy ($\alpha = .83$) | Goal rationale ($\alpha = .90$) |
|---|---|---|---|---|
| 1. My boss is supportive of my goals | 1.00 | | | |
| 2. My boss encourages me to reach my goals | 1.29 | | | |
| 3. My boss lets me participate in the setting of my goals | 1.27 | | | |
| 4. My boss lets me have some say in deciding how I will go about implementing my goals | 1.25 | | | |
| 5. I find working toward my goals to be very stressful | | 1.00 | | |
| 6. I often fail to attain my goals | | 0.98 | | |
| 7. I feel that I must accomplish my goals | | 1.00 | | |
| 8. My supervisor always emphasizes that I need to accomplish my goals | | 1.16 | | |
| 9. My colleagues respect me when I reach my goals | | | 1.00 | |
| 10. I usually feel that I have a suitable or effective action plan or plans for reaching my goals | | | 1.08 | |

*(Continued)*

*Table 35.3* (Continued)

| Items | Supervisor support/ participation ($\alpha = .90$) | Goal stress ($\alpha = .86$) | Goal efficacy ($\alpha = .83$) | Goal rationale ($\alpha = .90$) |
|---|---|---|---|---|
| 11. I feel that my job training was good enough so that I am capable of reaching my job goals | | | 0.70 | |
| 12. My boss informs me how the goals are set | | | | 1.00 |
| 13. My boss tells me the reasons for giving me the goals I have | | | | 1.01 |
| 14. I get regular feedback indicating how I am performing in relation to my goals | | | | 1.00 |

| Items | Use of goal setting in performance appraisal ($\alpha = .71$) | Tangible rewards ($\alpha = .74$) | Goal conflict ($\alpha = .79$) | Organization facilitation of goal achievement ($\alpha = .85$) |
|---|---|---|---|---|
| 15. During performance appraisal interviews, my boss comes to an agreement with me on steps to be taken by each of us to solve any performance problems | 1.00 | | | |
| 16. My boss makes sure that at the end of the performance appraisal interview I have a specific goal or goals to achieve in the future | 0.80 | | | |
| 17. If I reach my goals, I feel that my job security will be enhanced | | 1.00 | | |
| 18. If I reach my goals, it increases my chances for a pay raise | | 1.07 | | |
| 19. If I reach my goals, it increases my chances for a promotion | | 0.67 | | |
| 20. I have too many goals on this job (I am too overloaded) | | | 1.00 | |
| 21. Some of my goals conflict with my personal values | | | 1.32 | |
| 22. I am given incompatible or conflicting goals by different people (or even by the same person) | | | 1.27 | |
| 23. Company policies here help rather than hurt goal attainment | | | | 1.00 |
| 24. Work teams in this company work together to attain goals | | | | 1.34 |
| 25. This company provide sufficient resources (e.g., time, money, equipment, coworkers) to make goal setting work | | | | 1.38 |

| Items | Dysfunctional effects of goals ($\alpha = .84$) | Goal clarity ($\alpha = .79$) | Goal difficulty ($\alpha = .87$) |
|---|---|---|---|
| 26. My job goals lead me to take excessive risks | 1.00 | | |
| 27. My job goals serve to limit rather than raise my performance | 1.00 | | |
| 28. The goals I have on this job lead me to ignore other important aspects of my job | 1.00 | | |

*Table 35.3* (Continued)

| Items | Dysfunctional effects of goals ($\alpha = .84$) | Goal clarity ($\alpha = .79$) | Goal difficulty ($\alpha = .87$) |
|---|---|---|---|
| 29. The pressure to achieve goals her leads to considerable dishonesty and cheating | 0.78 | | |
| 30. Goals in this organization are used more to punish you than to help you do your job well | 0.81 | | |
| 31. My boss wants me to avoid mentioning negative information or problems regarding my goals or action plans | 0.84 | | |
| 32. If my boss makes a mistake that affects my ability to attain my goals, he or she refuses to admit it or discuss it | 0.72 | | |
| 33. I understand how my performance is measured on this job | | 1.00 | |
| 34. My boss clearly explains to me what my goals are | | 0.98 | |
| 35. I have unclear goals on this job (reversed) | | 0.71 | |
| 36. I understand exactly what I am supposed to do on my job | | 0.57 | |
| 37. I have specific, clear goals to aim for on my job | | 0.67 | |
| 38. If I have more than one goal to accomplish, I know which ones are most important and which are least important | | 0.57 | |
| For the average employee in the same level job and who has a similar level of education and experience as you, the goals that you have in relation to this employee's goals would require: | | | |
| 39. "No challenge at all" to "extreme challenge" | | | 1.00 |
| 40. "Almost no effort" to "enormous effort" | | | 1.15 |
| 41. "No thought or skill" to "an extreme degree of thought and problem solving skill" | | | 1.08 |
| 42. "Very little persistence and tenacity" to "an enormous amount of persistence and tenacity" | | | 1.08 |

Chi-square = 3246.13, degree of freedom = 764, RMSEA = 0.081, CFI = 0.95

To ensure that there was sufficient discriminant validity among all constructs, we ran a one-factor model, yielding an unacceptable fit with $\chi^2$ (819) = 7736.18, $p < 0.001$; RMSEA = 0.150; CFI = 0.86. Overall, the data fit the proposed measurement model well.

After matching supervisor and subordinate ratings, we obtained 264 supervisor–subordinate dyads. Table 35.4 presents the correlations among the goal setting variables and task performance for these dyads. The correlations ranged from 0.06 to 0.81, with an average correlation of 0.37. The goal attributes and goal processes related positively to task performance. In addition, dysfunctional effects, goal stress, and goal conflict related negatively to task performance.

Table 35.5 presents a comparison of the psychometric properties of the goal setting scales across studies. We were unable to obtain the psychometrics properties of the goal setting scale from Nel et al. (2004). They provided reliability estimates in their study, but

Table 35.4 Study 2 (China) Correlations

|  | 1 | 2 | 3 | 4 | 5 | 6 | 7 | 8 | 9 | 10 | 11 |
|---|---|---|---|---|---|---|---|---|---|---|---|
| 1. Supervisor support/participation |  |  |  |  |  |  |  |  |  |  |  |
| 2. Goal stress | -0.51 |  |  |  |  |  |  |  |  |  |  |
| 3. Goal efficacy | 0.49 | -0.29 |  |  |  |  |  |  |  |  |  |
| 4. Goal rationale | 0.51 | -0.40 | 0.31 |  |  |  |  |  |  |  |  |
| 5. Use of goal setting in performance appraisal | 0.16 | -0.25 | 0.08 | 0.20 |  |  |  |  |  |  |  |
| 6. Tangible rewards | 0.39 | -0.35 | 0.22 | 0.81 | 0.25 |  |  |  |  |  |  |
| 7. Goal conflict | -0.26 | 0.24 | -0.13 | -0.21 | -0.19 | -0.17 |  |  |  |  |  |
| 8. Organization facilitation of goal achievement | 0.41 | -0.30 | 0.28 | 0.65 | 0.27 | 0.61 | -0.21 |  |  |  |  |
| 9. Dysfunctional effects of goals | -0.34 | 0.31 | -0.06 | -0.39 | -0.32 | -0.39 | 0.52 | -0.42 |  |  |  |
| 10. Goal clarity | 0.49 | -0.29 | 0.27 | 0.76 | 0.29 | 0.66 | -0.28 | 0.59 | -0.49 |  |  |
| 11. Goal difficulty | 0.45 | -0.26 | 0.25 | 0.70 | 0.22 | 0.60 | -0.22 | 0.72 | -0.33 | 0.59 |  |
| 12. Task performance | 0.24 | -0.19 | 0.16 | 0.20 | 0.21 | 0.17 | -0.18 | 0.17 | -0.26 | 0.28 | 0.16 |

N = 264. Correlations with absolute values of 0.13 or greater are significant at the $p < 0.05$ level or better (2-tailed), while those with 0.16 or greater are significant at the $p < 0.01$ level or better (2-tailed).

Table 35.5 Comparison of Cronbach's Alpha Reliabilities, Means, and Standard Deviation across Studies

| Scales (5-point) |  | Current Study United States | Current Study China | Lee et al. (1991) United States | Lee & Bobko (1992) United States | Nel et al. (2004) S. Africa | Häsänen et al. (2011) Sweden |
|---|---|---|---|---|---|---|---|
| Supervisor support/participation | Mean | 3.99 | 3.21 | 3.80 |  |  | 3.73 |
|  | S.D. | 0.91 | 0.88 | 0.98 |  |  | 1.02 |
|  | Reliability | 0.89 | 0.90 | 0.82 |  | 0.88 | 0.88 |
| Goal stress | Mean | 2.52 | 2.53 | 2.30 |  |  | 2.13 |
|  | S.D. | 0.88 | 0.63 | 0.75 |  |  | 0.82 |

| Construct | Statistic | | | | | |
|---|---|---|---|---|---|---|
| Goal efficacy | Reliability | 0.65 | 0.86 | 0.68 | 0.70 | 0.74 |
| | Mean | 3.90 | 3.11 | 4.00 | | 3.83 |
| | S.D. | 0.78 | 0.67 | 0.68 | | 0.68 |
| Goal rationale | Reliability | 0.63 | 0.83 | 0.68 | 0.63 | 0.76 |
| | Mean | 3.68 | 3.43 | 3.40 | | 3.32 |
| | S.D. | 0.96 | 0.78 | 0.91 | | 1.01 |
| Use of goal setting in performance appraisal | Reliability | 0.77 | 0.90 | 0.78 | 0.81 | 0.87 |
| | Mean | 3.91 | 3.55 | 3.50 | | 3.45 |
| | S.D. | 0.82 | 0.70 | 0.83 | | 0.81 |
| Tangible rewards | Reliability | 0.86 | 0.71 | 0.88 | 0.94 | 0.87 |
| | Mean | 3.65 | 3.38 | 3.20 | | 3.14 |
| | S.D. | 0.92 | 0.73 | 0.94 | | 0.92 |
| Goal conflict | Reliability | 0.83 | 0.74 | 0.74 | 0.81 | 0.68 |
| | Mean | 2.20 | 2.87 | 2.10 | | 2.01 |
| | S.D. | 0.83 | 0.74 | 0.69 | | 0.82 |
| Organization facilitation of goal achievement | Reliability | 0.78 | 0.79 | 0.85 | 0.80 | 0.87 |
| | Mean | 3.68 | 3.51 | 3.30 | | 3.12 |
| | S.D. | 0.88 | 0.81 | 0.71 | | 0.81 |
| Dysfunctional effects of goals | Reliability | 0.84 | 0.85 | 0.63 | 0.80 | 0.75 |
| | Mean | 2.03 | 2.82 | 1.70 | | 1.70 |
| | S.D. | 0.77 | 0.61 | 0.70 | | 0.76 |
| Goal clarity | Reliability | 0.90 | 0.84 | 0.85 | 0.87 | 0.83 |
| | Mean | 3.80 | 3.34 | 4.00 | | 3.75 |
| | S.D. | 0.54 | 0.63 | 0.69 | | 0.77 |
| Goal difficulty | Reliability | 0.88 | 0.79 | 0.67 | 0.74 | 0.70 |
| | Mean | 3.99 | 3.39 | | 3.61 | |
| | S.D. | 0.78 | 0.76 | | 0.62 | |
| | Reliability | 0.86 | 0.87 | | 0.91 | |
| | | | | | 0.75 | |

did not provide the means and standard deviations of the goal setting scales used in their study conducted in South Africa. Across studies, the reliability coefficients of the goal setting scales ranged from 0.63 to 0.90. The reliability coefficients of the data from China showed further improvement ranging from 0.71 to 0.90.

## DISCUSSION

Our data from the samples of managers and employees in two hospitals in the United States and an insurance company in China show support for the revised factor structure based on logical validity. The revised goal setting measure, and Lee and Bobko's goal difficulty scale, appear to have interpretable and valid factor structure. The studies from Nel et al. (2004) and Häsänen et al. (2011) further support the psychometric soundness of the ten goal setting scales identified by Lee et al. (1991). The average correlation of the 10 goal setting scales, being part of a goal setting program, are moderately correlated (average r = 0.36 from Lee et al., 1991; average r = 0.44 from our US sample; and average r = 0.37 from our China sample). Therefore, despite higher correlations among some of the goal setting scales, these average correlations suggest that the scales are distinguishable from each other.

In the two samples, the revised goal setting scales relate predictably to goal commitment and task performance. Specifically, in the first study, as predicted, both goal clarity and the positive goal setting processes related positively, whereas the goal stress and goal conflict related negatively to goal commitment in the hospitals in the United States. However, goal difficulty was also negatively related to goal commitment. Although the moderating role of goal commitment in the goal difficulty–task performance relationship has been established (Klein et al., 1999), Klein et al. suggested that the relationship between goal difficulty level and goal commitment should be examined further. Klein et al. noted that the low correlation and the wide variance observed across studies suggest a strong possibility of moderators. Klein et al. also called for additional research to study the infrequently examined antecedents of the other goal attributes (e.g., goal conflict) and dysfunctional aspects of goal processes on goal commitment.

Similar results were obtained in Study 2 using a different occupational group in a different country, China. As predicted, both goal attributes (clarity and difficulty), as well as the positive goal setting processes, related positively, while goal stress and goal conflict related negatively to task performance. Although both goal attributes correlated significantly with task performance, goal clarity shows a stronger correlation with task performance than goal difficulty. It is possible that a strong support system (e.g., having role models, training and development opportunities) is necessary to facilitate a strong goal difficulty–task performance relationship. This may also explain the negative goal difficulty–goal commitment relationship. Having a difficult goal may lead to low goal commitment unless employees have adequate resources, and they are capable of attaining it. Despite differences in the two cultural contexts (e.g., the United States is more individualistic and values lower power distance as opposed to China, where collectivism and high power distance are valued), the factor structure of the revised goal setting questionnaire appears to generalize across these two different cultural contexts.

Future studies should attempt to replicate these results in other occupational groups and cultural contexts.

Additionally, with the current academic and practitioner's interest in creativity and innovation, it would be acknowledged that the setting of creative goals may be quite important in effecting creative performance outcomes. Over a decade ago, Shalley (1995) found that in the United States, the highest level of creativity occurred when individuals worked alone with a creativity goal under expected evaluation. (For more on goals and creativity, see Chapter 22). Will we obtain the same result if the study is conducted in collectivistic cultures such as China or India? In other words, will the presence or expectations of others (supervisors, coworkers) increase creativity in collectivistic cultures? Additionally, the present data support the validity of the goal difficulty measure. Future studies should examine whether difficult creative goals have the same effect on job performance as creative performance.

Finally, these data from two countries support the revised factor structure reported by Lee et al. (1991). The goal setting questionnaire appears to be psychometrically sound. Given the importance of goal setting in performance evaluation tools such as Management By Objectives and the balanced scorecard, practitioners and scholars can use our revised questionnaire to assess the usefulness of these programs in both the East and the West.

## References

Austin, J. T., & Vancouver, J. B. (1996). Goal constructs in psychology: Structure, process, and content. *Psychological Bulletin, 120*, 338–375.

Häsänen, L., Hellgren, J., & Hansson, M. (2011). Goal setting and plant closure: When bad things turn good. *Economic and Industrial Democracy, 32*, 135–156.

Hollenbeck, J. R., & Klein, H. J. (1987). Goal commitment and the goal setting process: Problems, prospects and proposals for future research. *Journal of Applied Psychology, 72*, 212–220.

Hollenbeck, J. R., Williams, C. R., & Klein, H. J. (1989). An empirical examination of the antecedents of commitment to difficult goals. *Journal of Applied Psychology, 74*, 18–23.

Jöreskog, K. G., & Sörbom, D. (2003). *LISREL 8: Structural equation modeling with the SIMPLIS command language*. Lincolnwood, IL: Scientific Software International.

Klein, H. J., Wesson, M. J., Hollenbeck, J. R., & Alge, B. J. (1999). Goal commitment and the goal-setting process: Conceptual clarification and empirical synthesis. *Journal of Applied Psychology, 84*, 885–896.

Klein, H. J., Wesson, M. J., Hollenbeck, J. R., Wright, P. M., & DeShon, R. P. (2001). The assessment of goal commitment: A measurement model meta-analysis. *Organizational Behavior and Human Decision Processes, 85*, 32–55.

Latham, G. P. (2009). Motivate employee performance through goal setting. In E. A. Locke (Ed.), *Handbook of principles of organizational behavior* (ch. 9, pp. 161–178). Hoboken, NJ: John Wiley & Sons.

Latham, G. P., & Locke, E. A. (2006). Enhancing the benefits and overcoming the pitfalls of goal setting. *Organizational Dynamics*, 35, 332–340.

Latham, G. P., & Locke, E. A. (2007). New developments in and directions for goal setting. *European Psychologist, 12*, 290–300.

Lee, C., & Bobko, P. (1992). Exploring the meaning and usefulness of measures of subjective goal difficulty. *Journal of Applied Social Psychology, 22*, 1417–1428.

Lee, C., Bobko, P., Earley, P. C., & Locke, E. A. (1991). An empirical analysis of a goal setting questionnaire. *Journal of Organizational Behavior, 12*, 467–482.

Lee, C., & Earley, P. C. (1992). Comparative peer evaluations of organizational behavior theories. *Organizational Development Journal, 10*, 37–42.

Locke, E. A. (1976). The nature and causes of job satisfaction. In M. D. Dunnette (Ed.), *Handbook of Industrial and Organizational Psychology* (pp. 1297–1350). Chicago: Rand McNally.

Locke, E. A., & Latham, G. P. (1984). *Goal setting: A motivational technique that works!* Englewood Cliffs, NJ: Prentice-Hall.

Locke, E. A., & Latham, G. P. (1990). *A theory of goal setting and task performance.* Englewood Cliffs, NJ: Prentice Hall.

Locke, E. A., Latham, G. P., & Erez, M. (1988). The determinants of goal commitment. *Academy of Management Review, 13*, 23–39.

Locke, E. A., Shaw, K. N., Saari, L. M., & Latham, G. P. (1981). Goal setting and task performance: 1969–1980. *Psychological Bulletin, 90*, 125–152.

Nel, D., Crafford, A., & Roodt, G. (2004). The relationship between sense of coherence and goal setting. *SA Journal of Industrial Psychology, 30*(2), 46–55.

Nunnally, J. (1988). *Psychometric theory* (2nd ed.). New York: McGraw-Hill.

Podsakoff, P. M., & MacKenzie, S. B. (1994). An examination of the psychometric properties and nomological validity of some revised and reduced substitutes for leadership scales. *Journal of Applied Psychology, 79*, 702–713.

Schwab, D. P. (1980). Construct validity in organizational behavior. In B. M. Staw & L. L. Cummings (Eds.), *Research in organizational behavior* (Vol. 2, pp. 3–43). Greenwich, CT: JAI Press.

Shalley, C. E. (1995). Effects of coaction, expected evaluation, and goal setting on creativity and productivity. *Academy of Management Journal, 38*, 483–503.

Shalley, C. E., & Kseoglu, G. (in press). Goals and creativity. In E. A. Locke and G. P. Latham (Eds.), *New developments in goal setting and task performance* (ch. 22). New York, NY: Routledge.

Williams, L. J., & Anderson, S. E. (1991). Job satisfaction and organizational commitment as predictors of organizational citizenship and in-role behaviors. *Journal of Management, 17*, 601–617.

Wright, P. M. (1990). Operationalization of goal difficulty as a moderator of the goal difficulty-performance relationship. *Journal of Applied Psychology, 75*, 227–234.

# Part XI

# Goal Setting and Self Development

# 36 Using Goal Setting Theory to Promote Personal Development[1]

*Cheryl J. Travers* School of Business and Economics, Loughborough University

## Introduction

*The reason most people never reach their goals is that they don't define them or ever seriously consider them as believable or achievable. Winners can tell you where they are going, what they plan to do along the way, and who will be sharing the adventure with them.*

*Denis Watley*

The pressures facing contemporary business managers, including management of diversity, international competition, customer satisfaction concerns, and changes in structures of organizations, require a host of interpersonal skills (Stevens & Gist, 1997). The overlap between the nature and role of management and the qualities of leadership has never been more evident, and research has revealed that manager roles and behaviors have a significant impact on the well-being and satisfaction of employees (e.g., Anderson & Ackerman Anderson, 2010). These new roles and functions of management require a high level of interactive skill and emotional control coupled with a high degree of self-management/self-regulation. As a result, an increasing number of firms offer interpersonal skills training in the United States (Filipczak, 1994), though it is not always clear how many attendees acquire these complex interpersonal skills, especially as the dynamic, complex nature of interpersonal skills are relatively hard to train in the first place (Stevens & Gist, 1997). Some researchers have argued that skill maintenance and sustainability can occur if self-management that includes goal setting is part of the process (Wexley & Nemeroff, 1975) and that the intervention increases self-efficacy (Gist, Stevens, & Baretta, 1991). Increasingly, universities, especially business schools, are expected to prepare students for industry (e.g., Pfeffer & Fong, 2004). Thus, it is important that one or more university courses teach students the interpersonal skills they will need to be effective in work settings.

As a response to this need, I developed an undergraduate module for management students designed to increase their interpersonal skills and personal development (Porter & McKibbin, 1988). Alongside diagnostic self-assessments to help individuals see the need for change (e.g., Quinn, Faerman, Thompson, & McGrath, 1996; Whetten & Cameron, 1998), a learning model that includes an initial personal assessment as the basis of further reflection, analysis, action, and learning (e.g., Bailey, Saparito, Kressel, Christensen, & Hooijberg, 1997; Cameron & Whetten, 1984; Kolb, 1984) was employed. This self-diagnostic approach provided immediate, noncritical feedback to students on their behavioral/attitudinal preferences. Feedback, a moderator variable in goal setting theory, is a necessary component for learning new behaviors.

The self-diagnostic assessment formed the basis for the exploration of the appropriate goals for the students to set.

Goal setting theory (GST) was the framework for the course that I developed. A goal reflects one's purpose; it refers to quantity, quality, rate of performance, or any desired outcome (Locke & Latham, 1990). It may also be seen as an internal representation of desired states that are accompanied by affect both as an antecedent to, and a consequence of, committing to a goal. Goals are related to affect in that people see success in terms of reaching or making progress toward their goals, especially difficult goals. Upon attaining a goal, people start to require attainment of increasingly higher goals in order to be satisfied with their performance (see Chapter 10; Locke & Latham, 1990).

The goals set by the students in my class were not quite hitting the mark. For example, extroverts, attempting to improve their listening skills, just stopped talking! So, the goals that were chosen were in many cases inappropriate. Something was needed to aid the choice of interpersonal-skills-related goals for increasing learning and performance. Consequently, I devised a reflective goal setting diary. Initial reflective activity about the self, plus recording one's thoughts and feelings, helped students choose goals matched to their identified development needs. Continuous ongoing reflection helped them to assess goal suitability throughout the goal process. Critical reflection created personal feedback throughout the goal pursuit process in order that goal adjustments could be made. This chapter presents this reflective goal setting methodology that subsequently *enabled* effective goal setting in the area of interpersonal skills development and self-management.

## Reflective Diary Keeping and Goal Setting

A critical component of this intervention was reflection (Dewey,1933; Schön, 1983, 1987) Reflection is "... *the process of internally examining and exploring an issue of concern, triggered by an experience, which creates and clarifies meaning in terms of self and which results in a changed conceptual perspective.*" (Boyd & Fales, 1983:1). Gibbs' (1988) model outlines six key stages of reflection: (1) describing what happened, followed by (2) examination of feelings and thoughts, (3) including an evaluation of the positive and negative aspects with (4) subsequent analysis where sense-making is made, (5) conclusions are drawn regarding what else can be done, followed by (6) action planning, involving actions that are to be taken in pursuing the goal.

Once the above process was used to select three goals, a diary was kept, often daily, to record personal experiences of goal attempts and subsequent outcomes in the form of their thoughts, feelings, and reflections. They also reported on others' reactions to, and feedback on, their goal-related behaviors. Keeping a diary allowed students to examine events and experiences in their natural, spontaneous context, going beyond that obtainable by more traditional research designs (Reis, 1994). Diary keeping also reduced the potential problems often caused by retrospective reporting (e.g., in interviews/questionnaires), as less time elapsed between the goal-related activity and actual reporting.

Keeping a diary also helped sustain a student emotionally through a challenging time by enabling the release of feelings about difficult experiences encountered when pursuing the goals (Travers, 2011; Fonteyn, 2001; Hancock, 1999). Redfern (1995) also suggested that by writing, thoughts can be transferred onto paper for examination and analysis. Thus, the students were able to observe all stages of their goal setting and self-regulation. This included (1) pre-goal setting and forethought, where data were gathered on developmental needs, supplemented by values and in some circumstances long-held beliefs and desires for change; this step also involved considering, and subsequently choosing, goals; (2) the actual formulation of the goals in terms of goal statements including strategies to be applied, as well as the measurement of outcomes; (3) the implementation of the plan to attain the goal and ongoing reflections on goal pursuit; and (4) a review of the goal setting process and an evaluation of the impact of goal pursuit and attainment on that individual.

## Goal Setting Theory in Academic Settings

Morisano et al. (2010) argued that for undergraduate students, who are in a transitional state with non-articulated futures, goal setting helps them specify their vision of an ideal future by reflection and elaboration on their personal goals, and that goal specificity is more powerful in this case than difficulty. This, they stated, is the most valuable contribution of a goal setting intervention.

Traditionally, GST has tended to employ objective performance-related goals with clearly defined measurement outcomes. A central theme of this chapter is that GST can be very effective when used to increase interpersonal and self-management skills (Latham & Frayne, 1989). Goal setting lies at the core of self-regulation, that is, systematic efforts to direct thoughts, feelings, and actions toward the attainment of one's goals (Zimmerman, 2000). Locke and Latham (2006) argued that goal setting can be used effectively in any domain where an individual or group has some control over an outcome.

The use of a written reflective diary to act as a tool to gain information about goal setting and to be a facilitator to goal setting is a relatively unresearched topic prior to this study. The remainder of this chapter describes this approach and presents findings related to the following research questions:

- What goal areas do these future managers set?
- What key enablers and barriers do they encounter when attempting to choose, formulate, and pursue their goals?
- What outcomes do they experience?
- What insight about GST and the process can we glean from the use of reflective diaries?
- What can we conclude about GST and its use for improving interpersonal skills?

## Research Design, Sample, and Context

This chapter presents findings that are based on a cohort of 124 final-year undergraduate students in a school of business and economics in the United Kingdom. These were attending a 4-month-long final semester course. Of these students, 51% were male, and 49% were female.

## Reflective Goal Setting Process

Initially, students were introduced to a number of diagnostic self-assessment instruments, models, and tools including the Twenty Statements Test (TST) (Kuhn & McPartland, 1951), Myers Briggs Type Indicator (MBTI) (Myers & McCauley, 1985), the Social Mirror (Covey, 1990); Johari Window (Luft & Ingham, 1955). In addition, they received coaching on goal setting theory (Locke, 2005; Locke & Latham, 1990), models of reflection (e.g., Gibbs, 1988; Scanlon & Chernomas, 1997) and keeping a reflective diary (Travers, 2011). To help them formalize and decide on the measurement of their goals, they each had a "one-to-one" coaching meeting with a tutor where they were instructed to set specific, challenging, relevant goals based on their self-awareness assessments. In terms of reflective diary keeping, they were asked to find a quiet time and place, perhaps early evening, to write regularly (daily ideally) about their goals, and not just when a goal attempt took place. They were asked to start writing straight away in order to get them used to writing and to enable them to process their goal-related thoughts and ideas almost immediately.

Once they had analyzed their own behavior, they selected three goals from the following areas: communicating with others, persuading and influencing others, managing yourself (i.e., stress, time management, well-being, resilience, health, self-organization), impression management and self-presentation, working cross-culturally, dealing with conflict, developing personal power/charisma/presence, developing positivity, self-esteem, and self confidence. They were to explain and justify to their tutor/coach their specific and challenging goal choices and form a goal statement for each. Each goal statement clearly articulated the goal target area, approach to be taken, expected outcome, and the techniques to be used to measure goal progress/attainment. The students were told that they would be assessed on the way they went about the assignment for goal setting, and not simply goal attainment. Morisano (2010) found that the number of words used to describe an ideal future when setting goals was the only predictor of academic improvement in students, suggesting that the development of a detailed specification of the desired outcome is crucial for goal commitment. In short, a well-differentiated representation of the goal is an important component of effective goal setting (see Chapter 30).

The students were asked to visualize their desired outcomes of attaining their three goals so that they could explore the discrepancy between their current behavior and their "ideal." Visualization has been found to be effective in teaching supervisors self-management skills in dealing with union shop stewards (Morin & Latham, 2000).

## The Diary Data and Analysis

Evidence for the success of this methodology can be seen in the very high number of students who were motivated to maintain their diaries throughout the entire process, moving through the stages outlined by Gibb from *descriptive,* to *reflective*, culminating in *critical reflection*. The use of the reflective diary throughout the goal setting period enabled the observation of the process over time; the fluctuations and barriers to goal success and, furthermore, the attempts to manage more than one goal at a time.

This study has an abundance of data to examine in terms of sheer volume: each person produced a 3500-word report, unlimited diaries and appendices, and a reflective-evaluation questionnaire at the end of the process. Some students wrote in brief, others wrote lengthy entries totaling a few pages per instance. Some wrote every day, sometimes twice a day; others wrote less frequently. Because of this, the data were not sufficiently uniform to enable quantitative or template analysis (King, 1998). For the purpose of this chapter, students' accounts were analyzed for mention of their goals, their attempts and progress, and their views on goal setting theory in practice. As data were in the form of ongoing diary entries with a final evaluation, students validated their own experiences, providing credibility checks, summaries, and debriefs. This suggests that the use of the diaries and the reflection by the writers themselves, coupled with myself as the reader and researcher, may come close to actual observation of the experiences recounted (Taylor, 1987; van Manen, 1990). The analysis of this data takes an interpretative approach in so far as I was trying to capture the essence of each student's account in a phenomenological sense (Berg, 2007). This approach provides a means for discovering the practical understandings of meaning and actions evident in the diaries as they unfolded.

The data are presented relevant to (1) the types of goals that were chosen and how; (2) the key issues that were encountered during goal formulation; (3) insights into the experience of goal setting over the time period by the use of the reflective diary; and (4) the students' evaluation of the use of goal setting theory.

## Results

### What Types of Goals Were Chosen and How?

Table 36.1 shows the goal areas chosen with illustrations of each. Goals were a combination of learning goals, (e.g., to learn how to be more empathetic) and performance goals (to be able to run *x* miles in *x* minutes). Some related to proximal issues of day-to-day

*Table 36.1* Goal Area Chosen (Out of 372)

| | N | % of total goals set | Example of a goal |
|---|---|---|---|
| Self-esteem/ confidence building | 59 | 16 | *On a scale of 1-10 I currently rate my self confidence at 5. I want to improve my self-confidence so that it is 8 or above by 3rd May. My longer-term goal is to increase this rating to 9 by 6th September. This is the date that I start my graduate job. I also want to feel confident enough to wear a rather expensive, tight-fitting dress that I have only ever worn once. I want to wear this on 13th May to a friend's birthday celebration.* |
| Work-related discipline/time management | 43 | 12 | *Manage my workload so that I have written all my revision notes on the lecture slides for my modules by 21st April, For each module I want to have written a summary page for all the key topics based on the compulsory reading by 2nd May. Being well prepared for my five summer exams will help me to manage my stress so that my eczema is reduced to zero patches on my arms, and the patches on my face are reduced by 80% by 13th May.* |

*(Continued)*

*Table 36.1* (Continued)

| | N | % of total goals set | Example of a goal |
|---|---|---|---|
| Assertive communication | 37 | 10 | *To improve my assertiveness by reducing the number of times I say yes to unreasonable requests by 75% so that I get what I want without denying the rights of others.* |
| Stress/ psychological well-being | 37 | 10 | *To better manage stress by specifically preventing insomnia and monitoring my ability to sleep via sleeping logs. This will follow the implementation of techniques including methods utilized by insomniacs, engaging in relaxation and stretching exercises, infusing humor into my life by watching comedy shows, etc.* |
| Health and fitness | 33 | 9 | *Start jogging on a weekly basis with an aim to build up my stamina to achieve a distance of 4 miles within a time period of 40 minutes after a 6 week period without stopping for a rest.* |
| Listening | 33 | 9 | *To improve my active listening skills around those close to me, through better concentration, so that I am able to recall what we have spoken about and ask more in-depth questions.* |
| Conflict management | 25 | 7 | *Dealing with conflict and difficult situations by learning to be more open-minded to other people's opinions and being less direct/aggressive in my approach when I disagree.* |
| Emotional awareness and regulation | 24 | 6 | *Improve my ability to communicate my emotions better—make two phone calls per week to friends to catch up, talk through the breakup of my last relationship, develop two friendships where I feel natural and open discussing my issues.* |
| Rapport/ relationship building | 24 | 6 | *Be more confident in situations where I am socially uncomfortable. Meet at least five new people every time I go out. Go to a pub quiz with three people I don't really know and then go for drinks at least three times with the quiz team.* |
| Positive thinking/ optimism | 15 | 4 | *Improve my understanding of happiness by using research to allow me to write down three things that make me happy. On top of this I will also learn and use two techniques to improve my happiness. I will achieve this by the 10th May.* |
| Impression management | 14 | 4 | *Being more reliable by responding to friends quickly and to make an effort to keep in contact with old friends. Helping people when they need help, and sticking to promises.* |
| Empathy | 10 | 3 | *Developing empathy for others by being sincere, exercising active listening, imagining myself in their position, and setting aside my own beliefs and concerns.* |
| Other: dealing with fears/ phobias, values, trust, etc. | 18 | 5 | *I will pursue my neglected ambitions of being a ghost writer, and compile a catalogue of materials ready to send to prospective artists and record companies.* |

behaviors, whereas others were linked to more distal terminal objectives and longer-term impact. As one young woman explained:

> *Having obtained my awareness of self and discovered qualities and insecurities I didn't know existed I am ready to set my goals. The goals I have chosen are the ones that are the most challenging but that will have the biggest impact on my life. And for me that is the main purpose – to push myself to achieve goals that will allow me to realize my full potential.*

Of particular interest is the number of students who chose to focus on a goal for increasing self-efficacy. Self-efficacy is fundamental to goal setting (Bandura, 1997; see Chapter 10).

A key factor for goal commitment was support and advice from trusted others, such as housemates, family, "true friends," and tutors on the course. The range of self-awareness activities helped students gain self-insight into their development needs. In many cases, old school reports, intern appraisals, and comments from family helped them choose to focus on long-standing, unresolved goals and undesirable behaviors. For example, one young woman explained:

> *The feedback that I received from school reports was that I did not contribute enough in class and I think the main reason for this was because I have always been shy. Even in lectures today I do not speak out .... This was also picked up by my manager whilst I was on placement (internship). He wanted me to speak up more in meetings, especially in brainstorming exercises, because any input may be useful. However, I know that I did not speak enough, and this was mainly because I thought people would think my answers were silly, inappropriate, and it was always frustrating when someone else had an idea that I had had but I'd been too scared to say anything. This is something I would like to correct and I think improving my overall confidence will help me achieve this ... The main reason for wanting to improve this area of my personality is because when I start my graduate job in August I will be meeting new people and I don't want my lack of confidence holding me back. I have got a job in audit which requires me to meet new clients on a daily basis.*

Aside from wanting the goal to enhance the likelihood of attaining a desired outcome, a number of students wanted to ensure their goals reflected their values. One student told how he:

> *wrote down three most important personal values before setting goals. Closely correlating goals with values should help to achieve them.*

### Key Issues That Were Encountered during Goal Choice, Formulation, and Pursuit

Ongoing diarizing in the early stages of the process enabled insights into factors affecting goal setting that are not necessarily observed in traditional goal setting research. On the whole, with guidance and support from the tutor/coaches, students were able to formulate their goals rather readily within the time frame—even though the process of creating specific goal statements was highly challenging. Many had an idea of their desired goal areas, but it was only with reflection that clarity was obtained (some called it a eureka moment) regarding the best goals to choose (i.e., not too easy and comfortable, and hence not motivating). The diaries were analyzed for comments and categorized into the following areas.

*Emotional/psychological*— Some found their goal choices daunting. They feared the openness that the process required and potential embarrassment. Though aware of the need to set these goals, they found it difficult to identify and bring into their consciousness the underlying reasons for their behavior. These often came from deeply rooted issues and, though they gained awareness of "goal need," they were quite fearful of failing, or choosing the wrong goal, in the time frame. Some saw this as a lack of courage to embark on these goals and a fear of their own limitations. Some found the process rather emotionally draining. However, it was clear in many cases that many of their goals were underpinned by some fundamental issue such as low self-esteem, or poor emotional self-insight, and they recognized the importance of a stretch goal, as one student explained:

> It's never nice to do something that is miles outside your comfort zone. But I wouldn't have wanted to have done it any other way—I'd have never opened myself up and changed as much as I did if my goals were easy.

And another exclaimed:

> How bloody hard it is to stump up the courage to set difficult goals.

*Measurement*—One of the main issues at the early goal setting stage was devising measurement procedures. Occasionally, this was a result of unrealistic expectations of what could be achieved, such as the desire for complete elimination of a particular behavior. One young woman explained:

> Unrealistic to eliminate patterns of worry and anxiety completely therefore seek incremental improvements.

The students were encouraged to create measures befitting the types of goals they set. For example, if listening was a goal, they might reflect on what they actually heard, the amount of information they obtained, how they felt after the encounter, how the other person responded, how they reacted to the listener, and any other feedback they got from any observer.

*Goal formulation*—Many students chose goals that lacked structure. They struggled with goal specificity and tangibility. For example, a male student reported:

> Goal three lacked specific activity to practice—got to April and thought the goal may not be detailed enough.

He explained that this may have been due to a lack of commitment to his goal.

For some there were so many potential goals to choose from that the problem lay in deciding on a goal. The use of self-awareness tools was helpful for most students, but some were concerned about these being too prescriptive and suggesting goals to them that were not necessarily the right ones. The benefit of ongoing reflection through the use of the diary helped counteract this issue.

*Ongoing motivation/focus and opportunities to pursue goals*—Some students reported that

> *Situations can change while you are trying to achieve goals and you need to readjust them.*

Coaching from tutors suggested ways in which students could seek opportunities for goal attainment. For example, if the ultimate goal was to perform well in employment interviews by creating an initial good impression, students were encouraged to attempt to create rapport with lots of different people in lots of different circumstances (e.g., standing at a bus stop, in a store queue). This meant that, even if an interview was not imminent, they could still learn the requisite skills to apply later.

*Handling the reflective process and diarizing*—Some students found the process of reflection difficult. Most, however, adapted to the process and talked about how they might take their diaries into the future and beyond the course (Travers, 2011).

### The Role and Impact of Measurement

A number of measurements involved the use and support of *significant others:* close friends, family, past managers, housemates, and fellow course members who knew of their goals. Some entered into *goal feedback exchange deals* with friends. Some took this further and entered into contracts with friends. For example, they handed over money as a deposit, and this was to be released only if they achieved their goal or else it was to be given to charity. This tended to be used for objectively measurable goals such as giving up smoking or doing exercise. Other options included counting spontaneous unsolicited feedback, for example, someone commenting that they had enjoyed an encounter with them. This could extend to deliberately looking for *goal achievement clues* in others' behavior, for example, someone smiling more in their company, talking more, opening up, and providing more information. This may be termed *goal-response matching*. For example, one young woman explained how her goal was to try and build rapport with others, which partly involved smiling at people she encountered. She measured how often a smile was returned or a conversation was started by the recipient of her smile. The use of the diary showed how a goal may progress in this regard. For example:

> *7th April—Although the interaction didn't last for long, I felt extremely self-conscious and uncomfortable talking in front of the rest of the group, and it was later pointed out to me that I went bright red when attempting to speak up. The experience has actually decreased my confidence levels when communicating, and as a result I am not looking forward to trying to put this goal into practice again tomorrow.*

> *8th April—Although I found it difficult to hold a conversation at length, I did manage to say "hello" or "good afternoon" to many of the walkers who passed us, and*

*surprisingly they responded. Although it was an effort to try and speak to others and at times I felt stupid, each time I got a response made me a little more confident.*

## Outcomes of Goal Setting

A vast amount of data has been gathered over the course of this research project, and much is yet to be analyzed. The data presented here is based on self-report assessments of outcomes, but feedback was acquired from others and objective measures were obtained, some which will be reported here.

Overall, highly favorable goal outcomes were reported by the students, though typically there were varying levels of success across the three goal areas chosen. Based on their ongoing reflective evaluations and end of process review, 46% of goals were deemed fully achieved, 43% partially or with a high degree of progress, and only 11% were unsuccessful. It must be noted that success is not an absolute concept here, as we can see evidence of different kinds of goal attainment. *Performance goals* can be measured when someone achieves a target weight, meets their revision schedule, or obtains specific feedback from a significant other (e.g., listening skills had improved). *Learning goals* included being able to apply assertive techniques more often, even if not every time, or knowing how to apply better coping techniques to situations to reduce stress levels, even if stress is not always managed. *Awareness goals* are those that enable goal setters to know their weaknesses and issues they face, but still continue to learn how to use techniques and models. For example, one male student explained:

> *My confidence has grown, with better awareness of situations that are stressful. I feel I have progressed in spite of missing some opportunities to be assertive, and will work on assertiveness in the future.*

Goals were found to complement rather than conflict with each other. For example, one woman did not hit her target weight, but had gained more control over her eating and exercise, which enhanced her second goal of improving self-esteem. This illustrates the power and importance of learning goals as opposed to performance outcome goals, and also shows that multiple goals are not always discrete, deriving from one central need or development area.

When little or no success was achieved with a goal, students were able to explain why with reflections in their diary. For example, it may have been due to the limited time frame, goals extending beyond the confines of the course, poorly formulated goals and inappropriate measures, or goals that were too easy.

The reflective diary was useful as an aid to goal attainment, but also as a research tool to measure success in real time. The diary of this woman shows five key "snapshots" from the beginning of the process until the end.

> Time 1: *I am not quite sure yet how I will achieve this goal, but I am going to put every effort into it because I am fed up of feeling the way I do. I would love to be able to walk into a room full of people and not feel scared or panicky, and just be able to walk with my head held high and look approachable rather than nervous.*

Time 2: *I just hope now that I really can make a difference to my self-esteem. Tomorrow I will begin to research techniques for improving this.*

Time 3: *I have been trying a couple of the steps to improve my self-confidence. I am making more effort with my appearance, and when I am out I am trying to walk better and keep a better posture. When I do stand up straight and keep my shoulders back, I instantly feel more confident, like I have a sense of purpose.*

Time 4: *I think my confidence goal is the one that I have improved the most in over the past two weeks. I don't know what it is or where it has come from, but I am starting to get this inner belief in me that I can do anything I set my mind to ... for some strange reason I actually feel jubilant; so happy and content with myself. I think this is a result of this goal, and I absolutely love what it has done for me so far.*

Time 5: *I feel like a flower that is blossoming. I don't mean that in an overly confident way, but I just mean that I have accepted who I am and am going to make the most of that. I want my appearance to reflect how I feel inside ... I have been wearing my favorite summer dresses, and I have received quite a few compliments about them and the way I look. This is the best I've felt in a long time.*

The results show that goal setting can be used successfully with interpersonal and self-management skills development. Even if the actual goal is not met, taking part in the process can lead to benefits. Goal setting, as a process, can enhance self-esteem and efficacy, coping with stress, and motivation to improve in the future, as one woman explained:

> *This piece of work has enabled me to achieve things beyond what I thought I was capable of. I have not only learnt a lot about myself and the way I handle various things in my life but now possess the motivation to keep developing these goals into the future ... it has had a huge positive effect on my life and will continue to do so in the years to come.*

More objective measures of success were obtained in this study, though this aspect of the data set has not been fully analyzed as yet. Future research should make greater use of non-self report ratings of outcomes. One way students carried out measurement was by "before and after" questionnaires on certain dependent variables, for example, "happiness":

> *Today I decided to complete the Oxford Happiness Inventory again (Argyle, 2001) seeing as we are towards the end of the course. I was curious to see if it had changed much. When I first filled it out I had a score of 4.1. Today I found that my happiness score actually increased to 4.8. I can't say I'm surprised, on the contrary. I felt that lately, and especially this week, I have been operating in a better frame of mind, being positive, motivated, and generally actively making myself feel good instead of being bogged down by coursework and the closeness of final exams.*

These kinds of objective measures, coupled with feedback from others, helped the goal setters assess their own success. For example:

> *I think the most valuable thing I have developed is my confidence. I have successfully reached my target of achieving a level of 8 on the confidence scale. My self-esteem has*

*soared and, as a result, my confidence has grown massively. I feel much more comfortable in social situations and more confident speaking up in group situations—something I never did before. My friend reflected "I am so pleased Jane's confidence is finally shining and that others have come to see how invaluable she is."*

### Facilitators of Goal Attainment and Progress

The ongoing diary methodology enabled a good grasp of which characteristics of the individual and the environment facilitated goal attainment. Most students emphasized the importance of a high level of effort and persistence on their part, and the ability to devise plans and persist with daily deadlines and goals without procrastination.

Having set specific, challenging goals was a clear enabler. An unexpected finding was the possible interconnectedness of the three goals, which lead to *"goal cross-fertilization."* For example, a person may choose to set three goals that were underpinned by low self-esteem. Working on one goal (e.g., improving their fitness), contributed to another on assertiveness as they felt more confident and attractive. The diary helped them to make *cognitive links* between behaviors and outcomes:

> *I'm really pleased with myself. It's good that I have to write this down, because it is helping me to make positive mental links between being confident and doing things like speaking to new people and positive experiences, so that in the future I am even better able to challenge negative thoughts.*

### Evaluating Goal Setting Theory

Though many found the process of choosing appropriate goals and their formulation challenging at first, the response to the process was highly favorable, and the outcomes often far in advance of what the students expected. There was a great deal of evidence of transcendence of expectations and performance akin to a state of flow (Csikszentmihalyi, 1990, 1996). The approach was something that they felt they would take away with them to use in the future. Many found that they started to apply GST to other aspects of their lives not currently under "goal scrutiny," and a few became rather evangelical regarding GST, sharing their new-found skill with friends. On occasion, some students commented that they needed a *"goal holiday"* as they found the constant focus on goals rather tiring. But many used the process as a welcome way of maintaining control of what was a very stressful time in their lives.

Part of this goal setting process involved the students evaluating the theory in practice, and the outcomes of this reflective process were highly positive overall. In terms of advantages, they found the goal moderators useful and that the process of setting goals motivated their self-regulation and provided a framework to work within. Overall, they found it an empowering experience that enabled them to have the discipline to see it through, with many saying that they had their goals at the back of their minds all of the time. They reported that having a goal drives performance, leads to logical thinking, creates the desire for change, and enables you to isolate areas of your life to focus on. Moreover, setting goals also helps in a much wider sense with life in general and can be employed in many different areas. Goals are often interconnected, and the gestalt becomes greater than the individual goals. They emphasized the role of specificity as an aid to clarity. They also found the theory easy to understand on the whole, and the benefits were clear. One of these benefits was that it ensures taking responsibility for one's reactions and responses, and hence motivates action to attain one's goals.

With regard to perceived limitations, one goal setter explained:

> *GST could possibly incorporate setbacks that people experience en route to achieving a goal and, vice versa, it could include eureka moments that the person has when experiencing a steep development.*

Also, some commented that opportunities to actually implement the goals were lacking:

> *Any changes in external environment, such as events or the inability to practice a goal as there is nowhere to use it.*

Other issues raised were around the optimal number of goals you can work on at one time and finding ways of measuring the goals. They also talked about potential goal conflict:

> *When multiple goals have been set for one individual, goal setting theory may neglect conflict that may arise between goals.*

They reported that a key challenge was to stay motivated throughout, and hence it is crucial that clear measurable benchmarks and standards are devised in order to obtain the correct balance between challenging and unobtainable goals. They believed that goal setting worked so well in this context due to initial coaching.

Many commented on the usefulness of visualization at the start of the process, specifically, visualizing what the improved behavior would look like so that a standard could be set.

Overall, the positivity expressed towards the entire process was heartening, as one young woman expressed:

> *It's been wonderful— and as hard as it is to say goodbye—I write my last words with such joy in my heart ... I did it! I learned, I implemented, and I reaped!*

## Conclusions

This study emphasizes the importance of incorporating the theoretical frameworks of goal setting, reflective learning, and the process of diary keeping for goal attainment. A reflective diary highlights the complexities in pursuing challenging goals. Thoughts and emotions experienced while striving to attain one or more goals can be monitored and reported.

Reflection allowed the students to become agents of their experiences rather than "*undergoers.*" Paying attention to how they feel and think changed how they responded to events. Diaries enabled the students to put words onto paper, and thus recruit the

"... *functional circuitries of forethought, planful proaction, aspiration, self-appraisal and self reflection*" (Bandura, 2001, p. 4).

## The Essential Skill of Goal Setting for Would-Be Managers

Goal setting is an essential skill for these future managers to have acquired for their own personal development, and also for use in their supervisory role as they will be expected to support, coach, and help others set and meet their respective goals. Having gone through this process, these students will be able to empathize with issues other goal setters may face. In many ways, what we have here is an example of teaching future managers evidence-based goal setting principles (Latham, 2009; Rousseau & McCarthy, 2007). This process has involved the key principles of GST with reflection through the maintenance of a diary. This approach has been able to teach these management students the key principles of GST, giving them ample opportunities to put these into practice, while being aware of any limitations as well as practical uses of the theory. In this study, students of management have been given opportunities to learn from evidenced-based theory that can be readily transferable to other aspects of their lives and future days as managers.

In summary, this study yielded insights into the use of GST, and showed how useful a reflective diary can be when an individual is under career and performance pressure to make personal changes. Another pertinent issue is that, due to the nature of the reflective diaries, they did not just record but also shaped the findings and the outcomes of their goal setting. As such, the diaries were not purely objective data-gathering methods, but, to some extent, each individual carried out his or her own piece of self-focused evidence-based learning and action research.

## Recommendations and Suggestions

Several recommendations made by the students had to do with the motivational aspects of the goal setting process. For example, it was crucial to make sure that the goal was important to the individual:

> "*Bear in mind that successful goals can only be developed on things which are of importance or relevance to you. It is no good writing a theoretically perfect goal if you feel no commitment or motivation to achieve it*" and "*Really think about your goals. They need to be the right ones in order to gain commitment, think about areas that you really believe you'll benefit and improve in.*"

Also, it was crucial to have vision:

> *Visualize the outcome you want to achieve with the goal you are setting. It is important to have an end state in mind as this motivates you to attain your goal.*

They suggest that it is important to decide on the kinds of rewards to employ and when to maintain interest and focus:

*Reward small accomplishments; sounds so simple, yet often nobody would think about this unless they reached their ultimate goal.*

Part of this issue with continued motivation included how you deal with setbacks:

*Also allow for setbacks. Some people may come across a setback and think about giving up. However, setbacks are part of the process on reaching the end goal: it cannot all be an upward sloping linear line.*

Aspects that keep the momentum are making sure that the goals are challenging:

*"Difficult" isn't something that stretches you a little bit. Difficult is something that you dread the thought of doing. But my word, it is rewarding when you achieve it.*

But by far the most important component was the issue of measurement:

*Knowing how to measure the goal is probably one of the most important aspects of GST. If you are not measuring, then you are only practicing what you are doing. There is no telling how much work is being achieved.*

I will end this chapter with a comment from a student that captures the impact of using a reflective goal setting diary when applying goal setting theory:

*On reflection I can see how my behavior has begun to change regarding the goals I set myself … The diary really forced me to look at key aspects of my personality and behavior and emphasized my weaknesses. My diary is very honest and not ordered to make a report but to explore my behavior, and I have found it an excellent tool in reflection and management of change.*

## Note

1  I would like to thank Ruth Hartley, Amanda Harrington, and George Hespe for their wonderful support and commitment in coaching students with their goal setting. Also, Dr Jane Glover and Tracey Preston for their invaluable help with data preparation for this chapter.

## References

Anderson, D., & Ackerman Anderson, L. (2010). *Beyond change management: How to achieve breakthrough results through conscious change leadership* (2nd ed.). San Francisco, CA: Pfeiffer.

Argyle, M. (2001). *The psychology of happiness*. East Sussex, UK: Routledge.

Bailey, J. R., Saparito, P., Kressel, K., Christensen, E., & Hooijberg, R. (1997). A model of reflective pedagogy. *Journal of Management Education*, 21(2), 155–167.

Bandura, A. (1997). *Self-efficacy: The exercise of control*. Stanford: W.H. Freeman.

Bandura, A. (2001). Social cognitive theory: An agentic perspective. *Annual Review of Psychology*, 52, 1–26.

Berg, B. L. (2007). *Qualitative research methods for the social sciences* (6th ed.). Boston: Pearson and Allyn & Bacon.

Boyd, E. M., & Fales, A. W. (1983). Reflective learning. *Journal of Humanistic Psychology*, *23*(2), 99–117.

Cameron, K. S., & Whetten, D. A. (1984). A model for teaching management skills. *Organisational Behaviour Teaching Journal*, *8*, 21–27.

Covey, S. (1990). *The seven habits of highly successful people: Powerful lessons in personal change.* New York: Free Press.

Csikszentmihalyi, M. C. (1990). *The psychology of optimal experience.* New York: Harper Row.

Csikszentmihalyi, M. C. (1996). *Finding flow: the psychology of engagement with everyday life.* New York: Basic Books.

Dewey, J. (1933). *How we think. A restatement of the relation of reflective thinking to the educative process* (revised ed.), Boston: D. C. Heath.

Filipczak, B. (1994). Looking past the numbers. *Training 31*, 67–72, 74.

Fonteyn, M. E. (2001) The use of clinical logs to improve nursing students' metacognition: A pilot study. *Journal of Advanced Nursing*, 28, 1: 149–154.

Gibbs, G. (1988). *Learning by doing: A guide to teaching and learning methods.* London: Further Education Unit.

Gist, M. E., Stevens, C. K., & Baretta, A. G. (1991). Effects of self-efficacy and post-training intervention on the acquisition and maintenance of complex interpersonal skills. *Personnel Psychology*, *44*, 837–861.

Hancock, P. (1999). Reflective practice—using a learning journal. *Nursing Standard*, *13*, 37–40.

King, N. (1998) Template analysis. In G. Symon & C. Cassell (Eds), *Qualitative methods and analysis in organisational research: A practical guide* (pp. 118–134). London: Sage.

Kolb, D. A. (1984). *Experiential learning: Experience as the source of learning and development.* Englewood Cliffs, NJ: Prentice-Hall.

Kuhn, M. H., & McPartland, T. S. (1951). An empirical investigation of self attitude. *American Sociological Review*, *19*(1), 68–76.

Latham, G. P. (2009). *Becoming the evidence-based manager: Making the science of management work.* Boston, MA: Nicholas Brealey.

Latham, G. P., & Frayne, C. A. (1989). Self management training for increasing job attendance: A follow-up and a replication. *Journal of Applied Psychology, 74,* 411–416.

Locke, E. (2005). Motivation through conscious goal setting. *Applied and Preventive Psychology*, *5*(2), 117–124.

Locke, E. A., & Latham, G. P. (1990). *A theory of goal setting and task performance.* Englewood Cliffs, NJ: Prentice Hall.

Locke, E. A., & Latham, G. P. (2006). New directions in goal setting theory. *Current Directions in Psychological Science*, *15*(5), 265–268.

Luft, J., & Ingham, H. C. (1955). *The Johari Window: A graphic model for interpersonal relations.* University of California, Western Training Laboratory.

Morisano, D., Hirsh, J. B., Peterson, J. B., Pihl, R. O., & Shore, B. M. J. (2010) Setting, elaborating, and reflecting on personal goals improves academic performance. *Applied Psychology*, Mar. 95(2), 255–264.

Morin, L., & Latham, G. (2000). The effect of mental practice and goal setting as a transfer of training intervention on supervisors' self-efficacy and communication skills: An exploratory study. *Applied Psychology*, *49*(3), 566–578.

Myers, I. B., & McCauley, M. H. (1985). *Manual: A guide to the development and use of the MBTI.* Palo Alto, CA: Consulting Psychologists Press.

Pfeffer, J., & Fong, C. T. (2004). The business school "business": Some lessons from the US experience. *Journal of Management Studies, 41*(8), 1501–1520.

Porter, L. W., & McKibbin, L. E. (1988). *Management education and development: Drift or thrust into the 21st century?* New York: McGraw-Hill.

Quinn, R. E., Faerman, S. R., Thompson, M. P., & McGrath, M. R. (1996). *Becoming a master manager*, New York: Wiley.

Redfern, E. (1995). Profiles, portfolios, and reflective practice. Part 2. *Professional Update, 3*, 10.

Reis, H. T. (1994). Domains of experience: Investigating relationship processes from three perspectives. In L. Gilmour & R. Erber (Eds), *Theoretical frameworks in personal relationships* (pp. 87–110). Hillsdale, NJ: Erlbaum.

Rousseau, D. M., & McCarthy, S. (2007). Evidence-based management: Educating managers from an evidence-based perspective. *Academy of Management Learning and Education, 6*, 94–101.

Scanlon, J. M., & Chernomas, W. M. (1997). Developing the reflective teacher. *Journal of Advanced Nursing, 25*(6), 1138–1143.

Schön, D. (1983). *The reflective practitioner*. Basic Books, New York.

Schön, D. (1987). *Educating the reflective practitioner*. San Francisco: Jossey-Bass.

Stevens, C. K., & Gist, M. E. (1997). Effects of self-efficacy and goal-orientation training on negotiation skill maintenance: What are the mechanisms? *Personnel Psychology, 50*(4), 955–978.

Taylor, M. (1987). Self-directed learning: More than meets the observers eye. In D. Boud & V. Griffin (Eds), *Appreciating adult learning: From the learner perspective*. London: Kogan Page.

Travers, C. (2011). Unveiling a reflective diary methodology for exploring the lived experiences of stress and coping. *Journal of Vocational Behavior, 79*, 204–216.

Van Manen, M. (1990). *Researching lived experience: Human science for an action sensitive pedagogy*, SUNY Series.

Wexley, K. N., & Nemeroff, W. (1975). Effectiveness of positive reinforcement and goal setting as methods of management development. *Journal of Applied Psychology, 60*, 446–450.

Whetten, D. A., & Cameron, K. S. (1998). *Developing management skills*. Reading, MA: Addison-Wesley.

Zimmerman, B. J. (2000). Attaining self-regulation: A social cognitive perspective. In M. Boekaerts, P. R. Pintrich, & M. Zeidner (Eds.), *Handbook of self-regulation* (pp. 13–39). San Diego: Academic Press.

# Part XII
# Overview and Conclusions

# 37 Goal Setting Theory

## The Current State

*Edwin A. Locke*  Robert H. Smith School of Business, University of Maryland

*Gary P. Latham*  Rotman School of Management, University of Toronto

The original version of goal setting theory was developed over a 25-year period (see Chapter 1 summary). It is an "open" theory in that in 1990 it was never considered to be the "final say." This is because science progresses in increments, by a process of discovery, using scientific methods. Our approach has been inductive (Locke, 2007; Locke & Latham, 2005); induction logically precedes deduction.

Some new findings in science are "earth-shattering." Examples include the discoveries by Newton, Darwin, and Einstein. Newton's discoveries identified causal laws representing the motions of "large" (nonatomic) objects. By showing that there were natural laws governing the universe, Newton helped bring about the Enlightenment by showing that "divine law" is not needed to "explain" nature's phenomena—rather, nature can be understood inductively: by observation, measurement, and experimentation (Harriman, 2010). Nevertheless, Newton was not omniscient. He did now know the mechanisms of gravity. He knew nothing about subatomic particles. His formulae were only accurate to a certain degree of precision; it took Einstein's theory to make the formulae more exact. Einstein's theory on the relationship between mass, energy, and the speed of light was another enormous breakthrough; his ideas might yet need revision. Darwin revolutionized thinking on the origin of the species, even though he knew nothing about DNA. In short, even great discoveries are seldom, if ever, the last word about the nature of a given phenomenon.

Goal setting theory too is inductively based; new discoveries have been and will continue to be made, leading to qualifications and additions to the theory. This inductive approach is different from the hypothetico-deductive approach that is de rigeur in behavioral science journals. (We leave it to the reader to assess the relationship between the inductive method and the longevity of goal setting theory relative to deductively based theories in the behavioral sciences). The question becomes, then, how to commence the process of theory building? The answer (Locke, 2007) includes (1) formulating clear concepts and definitions, (2) collecting data, including making systematic observations across a range of conditions, (3) taking measurements, (4) identifying causal relationships including causal mechanisms, (5) looking for limiting conditions, and (7) looking for and resolving contradictory findings. (8) Amassing evidence and integrating it into a non-contradictory whole, (9) making inductive generalizations that go beyond previous observations. This does not create timeless certainty, but it does bring contextual certainty (Peikoff, 1991). Additional discoveries widen a theory's context.

In this chapter, we summarize the discoveries relevant to goal setting theory since 1990, and show how these have enlarged the context of our theory. In doing so, we present only highlights of the preceding chapters, but readers are urged to read the complete chapters on topics that interest them for much additional information.

1.  **Goal difficulty and specificity**. Chapter after chapter in this book reveal that specific, challenging goals significantly increase performance. A question that arises is: How challenging is challenging? In laboratory experiments, difficult goals are usually set at the 90th percentile. This means that although most people work hard to increase their effort, they do not attain the goal. In field experiments, Latham and colleagues (e.g., Latham & Yukl, 1975) typically set goals that are judged to be "difficult yet attainable." Most field experiments do not report the percentage of people who attained the goal. Latham and Yukl (1976) set goals at a high level for employees, and then raised them substantially when they were initially reached. But if the goal is one that no one can reach, and no partial credit is given for goal progress, it can eventually undermine motivation, especially if the goal is tied to "all or none" monetary incentives (Lee, Locke, & Phan 1997).

    Goals should be set based on the total context (e.g., the economy, industry, competitors, available resources). As noted in Chapter 34, setting appropriate goals requires careful thinking.

    Types of Goals

    a)  *Learning goals.* Subsequent to 1990, it was discovered that if people lack the knowledge and skill to attain specific, challenging performance goals, learning goals should be set so that people acquire the requisite knowledge/ability (see Chapter 13). Specific, challenging learning goals have the same beneficial effect on performance as do challenging performance goals for those people who already have the ability to attain them.

    b)  *Stretch goals.* These goals are similar to very hard and possibly impossible goals. Nevertheless, there has been much misunderstanding about their use. Jack Welch, the former CEO of GE, used them as a supplement to "required" or minimally acceptable goals that were set based on a competitor's performance and the economic context. Stretch goals at GE did not have to be attained. Their purpose is to stimulate creative, "outside-the-box" thinking with the intent that executives will generate new ideas for improving their business (see Chapter 3).

    c)  *Goal types.* In sports (see Chapter 24) a distinction has been made between outcome goals (winning), performance goals (doing well by your own standards), and process goals (learning skills for improving performance). Process goals have been found to be very effective for training and development and are similar, if not identical, to learning goals described in Chapter 13. These three types are interrelated; process goals can help people attain performance goals, and both types of goals can help people to attain outcome goals. This triad has obvious implications for use in other domains.

    d)  *Proximal and distal goals.* Proximal goals facilitate the attainment of distal goals (Chapter 5). However, we still know relatively little about the optimum time intervals for setting these two types of goals. There are undoubtedly many context factors that need to be taken into account.

e) *Goal orientation.* Goal orientation is a trait that is nevertheless malleable. It refers to a preference for achievement goals where the focus is on either (1) performance or (2) learning (mastery). Performance and learning goals have been further subdivided into approach and avoidance. Generally, performance and learning approach goals work best (Chapters 7 and 30), and they may work even better when they are combined. Research is needed on what are called performance goals, because such goals can be of many types (e.g., winning at competition, trying to impress others, gaining rewards), which may not be equally effective. Also, research is needed on whether achievement goal effects are mediated by specific, difficult goals as would be predicted by goal setting theory.

2. **Multiple goals.** As of 1990, there had been little research on multiple goals. We simply noted some context factors that could determine how effectively they might influence task performance. As of 2012, with the exception of research on proximal and distal goals, there is still little research on this topic. However, Chapter 12 provides a useful classification of multiple goals: multiple separate goals that can be worked on simultaneously or at different times; sequentially interdependent goals in which one goal contributes to the next (e.g., proximal, distal); and reciprocally independent goals in which the causal effects work in both directions. There are several interrelated issues we believe worthy of study here such as cognitive resources, time, conflict, prioritization (importance), and planning.

3. **Goal mechanisms.** In 1990, goal setting theory specified four causal mechanisms: choice/attention, effort, persistence, and task strategies (i.e., plans or skills needed to perform a task). Subsequent to 1990, it was discovered that causal attributions for performance may influence both affect and self-efficacy (see Chapters 4 and 8.[1]) This, in turn, may affect goal choice. Positive affect may increase self-efficacy and therefore increase the goal level chosen. Progress has been made in categorizing task strategies (see Chapter 7). Specifically, four categories have been identified: (1) task-specific strategies that are already known to people and require implementation, (2) strategy development formulated through effort allocation, (3) strategies found through cognitive search, and (4) general self-regulatory strategies that include planning and self-talk. All four types affect performance. Most have been found to be affected by goal difficulty level. Task-specific and strategy development through effort have been shown to mediate goal effects. Beneficial effects of cognitive search, of course, depend on whether effective strategies are found. Task strategies may have direct effects on performance, mediate goal effects, or interact with goals (see Chapter 7). It all depends on what type of strategy knowledge is measured.

4. **Goal moderators.** The importance of goal commitment has been affirmed (see Chapter 6), especially for difficult goals. The two main sources of commitment are goal importance (desirability) and expectancy or self-efficacy. Commitment sometimes has a main effect on performance, though it is probably most important when difficult goals are assigned since self-set goals are often outcomes for which people are already committed.

Klein and colleagues developed a clear definition of commitment and validated a new four-item commitment scale (see Chapter 6). This scale should probably become the standard measure in future goal setting studies. Others (see Chapter 32) have developed two powerful methods to promote commitment. One involves "mental contrasting." This involves envisioning the goal, and the possible impediments to attaining it. Doing so likely facilitates planning. But, this only works if the goal is valued and there is high expectation of goal attainment (i.e., self-efficacy). The second method involves forming implementation intentions involving "if-then" statements that specify that one will carry out the intention through a specific action when the relevant situation arises. These two methods together are highly effective.

The importance of feedback as a moderator of goal effects has also been firmly supported (Chapter 5). Goals and feedback together work better than either one alone. People need to be able to track their progress toward goal attainment. In Chapter 5, it is suggested that feedback may work differently depending on whether (1) it is personally sought or just provided, (2) whether its source is the self (from information one can observe directly) or others, or (3) a computer. The effectiveness of each source likely depends on yet-to-be identified context factors such as trust.

We now believe that the effects of task complexity, when subjectively measured, are dependent on task knowledge rather than being an independent moderator. Ratings of complexity are typically confounded with self-efficacy (Locke & Latham, 1990). Measures of self-efficacy and actual knowledge or skill remain useful measures.

Situational factors have not been studied further to our knowledge.

5. **Goals and self-regulation.** As of 1990, self-management had received minimal attention. Today self-regulation and self-management procedures (see Chapter 11) typically consist of "treatment packages" of concepts of which goal setting is the central variable. The treatment/training intervention typically includes self-monitoring (feedback), planning, self-efficacy, self-evaluation, and self-reward. It may also involve goal revision over time. People can be successfully trained in self-management techniques (e.g., verbal self-guidance). Chapter 11 reports a meta-analysis based on 30 years of data and 90,000 participants of self-regulated learning. The strongest effects were due to goal setting, self-efficacy, effort, and persistence. In goal theory, the latter two variables mediate the beneficial effect of goal setting on performance.

6. **Goal causes.** In 1990, we identified numerous factors that affect goal choice, including factors affecting goal desirability and perceived capability. In Chapter 9, many new factors have been discovered. These include personality variables (e.g., conscientiousness, core self-evaluations, and goal orientation), implicit theories (entity versus incremental concepts of ability), and context factors.

7. **Levels of analysis.** As of 1990, most goal studies focused on individuals. Only a few studies focused on groups. Studies of Management by Objectives included individuals and organizational units. There were no firm level studies.

There is now a burgeoning literature on team goals (see Chapter 19). Many factors affect team goals, including information sharing, rewards, system design, team size, skill diversity, and team leadership. Information sharing, team reward systems, small to moderate-sized teams, homogeneity, and goal-and-process focused leadership are beneficial for performance. An individual's goals need to be congruent with team goals in order to avoid conflict. Although the macro literature on goal setting is quite limited (see Chapter 20), there have been quantitative, longitudinal studies, lasting from two to six years, of goal effects on the growth of small companies (see Chapter 28). Goal level, along with vision (a form of superordinate goal), and self-efficacy predict growth. Chapter 17 provides a qualitative report on IBM's use of goals. IBM was in need of a turnaround. The CEO, Lou Gerstner, set three superordinate goals: Win, Execute, and Team in addition to ensuring that every employee had specific goals for their respective jobs. Regular feedback was provided on goal progress. Commitment was partly ensured by voluntary turnover on the part of those who did not buy in, and the firing of those who would not commit to the goal setting process. This effective method for ensuring commitment is likely widely used in firms but has yet to be systematically investigated. The result was extraordinary financial results at IBM for the next nine years. Chapter 17 also reports on the effective use of goal setting at Boeing and the Ford Motor Company.

8. **The duration of goal effects.** Goal effects in the laboratory have been obtained in as little as one minute. Most laboratory experiments last less than an hour. But how long do goal effects last in the real world?

   Latham did a field experiment prior to 1990 where a follow-up still showed effects after seven years (see Chapter 15). In the same chapter, data collected subsequent to 1990 are presented concerning the long-term effects of an intervention system called ProMes. ProMes involves goals, measurement, and feedback for teams as well as organizational units. Significant effects have been found three years later. Also reported is a study of five years duration. The longest-duration study (see Chapter 16) on goal setting was done at AT&T, where goals were self-set for future job promotion. Goals set in year one predicted promotion rates 25 years later. The goal effect was far stronger than scores from self-report personality tests or projective tests, even after controlling for cognitive ability.

9. **Goal sources.** Locke and Latham (1990) noted that goals could be self-set, participatively set, or assigned, and that all three methods were effective for improving performance. In Chapter 26, new variations for setting goals from the field of health (e.g., dieting, exercise) are described. One is guided goal setting. An individual chooses from among a preset list of options. A written contract is typically included. Another variation is the use of a computer-managed goal setting program. Again, people choose from a set of offered options that include end goals and subgoals. Subgoals often function as plans. Computer-managed programs have also been used in education to improve students' performance (see Chapter 30). An advantage of computer-guided goal setting is that it requires no extra staffing once the program is set up and explained.

10. **Goals as mediators.** Our 1990 book included a brief discussion of goals as mediators of other factors (e.g., motivators). The main finding pertained to goals as mediators of feedback. Subsequent to 1990, this result has been replicated (see Chapter 5). Goals, often along with self-efficacy, have been found to mediate or partially mediate goal orientation, values, conflict, assigned goals (by self-set goals), participation in decision making, monetary incentives, job design, role overload, charismatic leadership, and Pygmalion leadership (see Chapters 14 and 28).

This is because goals and self-efficacy are situationally and task specific; hence, they are relatively proximal motivators. However, goals and efficacy are not necessarily full mediators of other factors. Affect, for example, may have a direct performance effect (see Chapters 4 and 8). Consciously set goals, thus far, have not been shown to mediate or partially mediate subconscious motivation. As discussed above, conscious goals have their own mediators.

11. **Subconscious priming**. In 1990, goal setting theory was based on conscious goals. There is now an enormous literature on the priming of subconscious goals. Initially this research domain was restricted to social psychology. Now it has been extended to HRM and organizational behavior (see Chapters 32 and 33). Priming, which can be accomplished in numerous ways (e.g., pictures, scrambled sentences containing key words, word matrices), affects action independently of conscious goals (see Chapters 16 and 33). Nevertheless, it is not the case that our lives are controlled by the subconscious devoid of the power to make conscious choices (see Latham & Locke, 2012, Table 1). The subconscious is primarily passive and the conscious mind (if used) is active. Of course virtually everything we know, aside from a few items held in awareness at any given time, is stored in the subconscious. Thus the subconscious is involved in some way in everything we do, including consciously made decisions. Thus far, it is not clear if priming effects are mediated by other processes, aside from functions in the brain.

12. **Self-efficacy**. Self-efficacy had a prominent role in goal setting theory in 1990 and it continues to do so today (see Chapter 10). Self-efficacy affects responses to feedback (see Chapter 5), responses to assigned goals, the choice of self-set goals (see Chapter 9), goal commitment (see Chapter 6), the quality of task strategies (see Chapter 7), self-management (see Chapter 11), learning goals (see Chapter 13), group goal setting (see Chapter 19), leadership (see Chapter 23), goal change (see Chapter 24), entrepreneurship (see Chapter 28), and education (see Chapter 30). It is an integral part of the High Performance Cycle effects on performance (see Chapter 18). There is even evidence now that self-efficacy can act as a mediator of goals (see Chapter 10). Self-efficacy is cited more often in this book than any other psychological concept aside from goals.

13. **The High Performance Cycle**. Locke and Latham (1990) argued that the high performance cycle begins with a specific, high goal, then to goal mediators and moderators, to performance, to task-related and external rewards to satisfaction to organizational commitment to the setting of subsequent goals. Chapter 18 reports the development of a questionnaire to test the model and an empirical (longitudinal, correlational) test. Partial support for the model was obtained. Demands (the equivalent of goals) affect goal mediators, which in turn affect performance. Self-efficacy and goal commitment, however, functioned as mediators rather than moderators. Organizational support affected goal commitment. Organizational commitment was not measured. Clearly, additional research is needed.

14. **The goal setting questionnaire.** A preliminary goal setting questionnaire, developed by Lee and colleagues, is in an appendix of Locke and Latham's (1990) book. Chapter 35 presents a revised goal questionnaire and the results obtained from two samples. Eleven factors were isolated. In a US sample, all the positive factors (e.g., goal clarity) correlated positively, and the negative factors (e.g., stress) correlated

negatively with goal commitment. The Chinese sample yielded similar results, with job performance as the dependent variable. Regression analyses were not done. Clearly, additional research is needed here.

15. **Goal setting in HRM.** The importance of goal setting for human resource management was stressed by Locke and Latham (1990). As noted in Chapter 21, goal setting continues to be a theoretical framework for managing an organization's human resources. This is particularly true for conducting selection interviews, performance management, training, motivating employees, and leading others. Advances since 1990 include the discovery that setting a superordinate goal is effective for gaining cooperation among organizational units, for minimizing perceptions of "we-they." Situational interviews, predicated on goal setting theory, predict team-playing behavior. Goals and goal feedback are critical determinants of training in self-management and coaching others. Goals also lie at the core of effective negotiations, including increases in employee productivity during the closing of a plant.

16. **Goal setting new domains.** In 1990, Locke and Latham focused almost exclusively on goal setting with work related tasks. The present book reports studies of goal setting in many domains, including creativity, leadership, sports, bargaining, rehabilitation and health promotion, aging, entrepreneurship, psychotherapy, and education (Chapters 22–29). Leadership (Chapter 23) was not included in our 1990 book. Yet the vast majority of definitions of leadership now emphasize the necessity of setting and clarifying goals. The relationship between transformational leadership and goal setting has been shown to be positive at high levels of goal difficulty, but not significant when goals are relatively easy to attain. In short, the effectiveness of transformational leaders depends in part on the clarity and difficulty level of the goals they set. As noted above, goal setting works in all of these areas. Each area adds incremental knowledge on the effect of setting specific difficult goals on performance. It would appear that goal setting can be applied to any activity where individuals have some control over their actions and outcomes.

17. **Goal setting and economic value.** Chapter 2 presents a utility analysis of goal setting which shows that goal setting has economic value in terms of increasing company revenue, productivity, and/or reducing labor costs. In short, goal setting, if used appropriately is an engine of wealth creation.

18. **Goal setting internationally.** Chapter 31 reports what we know about the effect of societal culture on the goal–performance relationship. A major moderating factor is individualism versus collectivism. Goal setting works in both cultures. Collectivists, however, may prefer moderate goals, whereas individualists prefer challenging goals. Both types of goals improve the performance of individualists. Reported "well-being" in individualistic cultures is tied to personal goal attainment; in collectivistic cultures, it is tied to pleasing others. Individualists do better with promotion goals and positive feedback, whereas collectivists do better with prevention goals and negative feedback. Goal specificity in teams helps overcome cultural conflicts.

19. **Problems and pitfalls.** There is nothing new on this topic since 1990. Any intervention is affected by the values of the person using it. Goal setting is no exception (see Chapter 34). This chapter identifies potential pitfalls and how to prevent or avoid them.

20. **Unexpected treat.** As this book was coming to a close, we received a fascinating post from Dr. Cheryl Travers in the United Kingdom, summarizing her years of study of the application of goal setting theory (combined with diaries) to motivate personal improvement (e.g., self-esteem, interpersonal skills) by undergraduate students. Although much data remains to be analyzed, the program appears to have been an astonishing success (see Chapter 36).

In conclusion, goal setting studies conducted after 1990, while generally supporting the original theory, have added many refinements and scores of new applications and findings. We now know more than we did then. Science has progressed. Such is the benefit of inductive theory building.

## Note

1 We do not agree with the distinction made in Chapter 8 between primary and secondary appraisal; introspection shows that emotional appraisals are primary. Nor do we agree that control theory adds anything new to goal setting theory's view of affect. Goal theory has always been dynamic.

## References

Harriman, D. (2010). *The logical leap: Induction in physics.* New York: New American Library.

Latham, G. P. & Locke, E. A. (2012). The effect of subconscious goals on organizational behavior. *International Review of Industrial Organizational Psychology.* (pp 39–63) Chichester, England: Wiley.

Latham, G. P., & Yukl, G. A. (1975). Assigned versus participative goal setting with educated and uneducated woods workers. *Journal of Applied Psychology, 60,* 299–302.

Latham, G. P., &Yukl, G. A. (1976). The effects of assigned and participative goal setting on performance and job satisfaction. *Journal of Applied Psychology, 61,* 166–171.

Lee, T. W., Locke, E. A., & Phan, S. H. (1997). Explaining the assigned goal-incentive interaction: The role of self-efficacy and personal goals. *Journal of Management, 23,* 541–559.

Locke, E. A. (2007). The case for inductive theory building. *Journal of Management, 33,* 867–890.

Locke, E. A., & Latham, G. P. (1990). *A theory of goal setting and task performance.* Englewood Cliffs, NJ: Prentice Hall.

Locke, E. A., & Latham, G. P. (2005) Goal setting theory: Theory building by induction. In K. G. Smith & M. A. Hitt (Eds.), *Great minds in management: The process of theory development.* New York: Oxford.

Peikoff, L. P. (1991). *Objectivism: The philosophy of Ayn Rand.* New York: Dutton.

# Author Index

# Subject Index